AMERICA

A NARRATIVE HISTORY

FIFTH EDITION

VOLUME II

GEORGE BROWN TINDALL
DAVID EMORY SHI

W · W · NORTON & COMPANY · NEW YORK · LONDON

FOR BRUCE AND SUSAN
AND FOR BLAIR

FOR
JASON AND JESSICA

Copyright © 1999, 1996, 1992, 1988, 1984 by W. W. Norton & Company, Inc.

The text of this book is composed in Fairfield Light,
with the display set in Torino.
Composition by Compset Inc.
Manufacturing by Courier.
Book design by Antonina Krass.
Cover art by Ralph Fasanella. *New York City* (detail). 1957.
Oil on canvas. Courtesy A.C.A. Galleries.
Cartographer: CARTO-GRAPHICS/Alice Thiede and William Thiede,
with relief maps from Mountain High Maps®, Digital Wisdom, Inc.

Acknowledgments and copyrights continue on p. A61,
which serves as a continuation of the copyright page.

The Library of Congress has cataloged the one-volume edition as follows:

Tindall, George Brown.
    America : A narrative history / George Brown Tindall,
David Emory Shi.—5th ed.
        p.   cm
    Includes bibliographical references (p.   ) and index.
    1. United States—History.   I. Shi, David Emory.   II. Title.
E178.1.T55   1997   98-41989
973—dc21

ISBN 0-393-97349-2 (pbk.)

W. W. Norton & Company, Inc., 500 Fifth Avenue, New York, N.Y. 10110
http://www.wwnorton.com

W. W. Norton & Company Ltd., 10 Coptic Street, London WC1A 1PU

2 3 4 5 6 7 8 9 0

CONTENTS

$\mathcal{P}$ART SIX / **MODERN AMERICA**

37 | CULTURAL POLITICS   1649

APPENDIX   A1

CREDITS   A61

INDEX   A65

MAPS

PREFACE

Just as history is never complete, neither is a historical textbook. We have learned much from the responses of readers and instructors to the first four editions of *America: A Narrative History.* Perhaps the most important and reassuring lesson is that our original intention has proved valid: to provide a compelling narrative history of the American experience, a narrative animated by human characters, informed by analysis and social texture, and guided by the unfolding of events. Readers have also endorsed the book's distinctive size and format. *America* is designed to be read and to carry a moderate price.

In a significant attempt to help students grasp the major themes and developments throughout the text, without compromising its intellectual integrity, *America* now contains a new pedagogical program. Part openers lay out the major ideas emphasized in upcoming chapters. Chapter organizers appear on the first page of each chapter and present key idea statements that serve as a guide through the narrative. "Making Connections" boxes appear on the final page of the text of each chapter to link significant events in the current chapter to issues in surrounding chapters. The new pedagogical program as well as the larger format and the two-color design result in an attractive, easy-to-read text that instructors and students should find inviting. The new map program also adds to the attractiveness of the book. Every map in the book has been reconsidered and redrawn, resulting in maps that are clearer and more helpful to the student.

The revisions incorporated in this new edition of *America* highlight aspects of popular culture, beginning with the culture of everyday life: how Americans spent their leisure time, what forms of recreation and entertainment they engaged in, and how the performing arts helped people to understand and deal with traumatic events such as wars and economic depressions. For example, we have incorporated new material dealing with the architecture of colonial homes, the role of taverns in eighteenth-century social life, the celebration of national holidays such as Independence Day, dueling as a manifestation of the cult of honor in the antebellum South, the emergence of professional sports and the performing arts, the popularity of minstrel shows and jazz, and the development of the radio, television, and film industries.

Taken together, these activities, as well as others like them, document the importance of popular culture in unifying a disparate nation. Such collective forms of social activity have served to democratize American life. As cultural life has become more inclusive, it has helped bridge social, racial, and ethnic differences. Such developments in popular culture in turn inform our understanding of major trends in social and political life. Thus, understanding how people of different economic and social classes gathered together at the same taverns and engaged in similar discussions and games helps explain how the diverse elements of the population were able to unite against British rule. Reading about how people of all classes went to the theater or to revival meetings both to watch and listen to what was being said and to socialize with others in the audience contributes to our knowledge of the public life. Likewise, seeing how the southern code of honor led men of all classes to take offense at the slightest perceived insult and to resort to violence to uphold their honor helps us to comprehend how people of the South were willing to resort to war to defend their land and honor. These forms of popular culture and others like them help expand and enrich our understanding of what "history" includes.

The Fifth Edition, like its predecessor, integrates social history into the narrative of American experience, detailing the folkways and contributions of those groups often underrepresented in historical treatments—women, blacks, and ethnic Americans. The Fifth Edition also continues to emphasize the importance of immigration and frontiers to the American experience. We have added a new section describing the journey on the Wilderness Trail into Kentucky, and how these hardy settlers staked out their frontier claims, built their homes, and dealt with their isolation and nurtured their sense of community. Another new section describes black migration to the West after the Civil War, including the efforts of whites to prevent African Americans from leaving the Old South and the difficulties encountered by the migrants who did reach Kansas and the Oklahoma Territory. A new section describes the origins of Sears & Roebuck as a mail-order giant, and how the Sears catalogue supplied the material and psychological needs of those in isolated areas. Also included in the Fifth Edition are new discussions of transportation in the cities and of how immigrants and native-born Americans began to participate in outdoor recreation as well as forming clubs and attending vaudeville and Wild West shows in the cities, and later going to football and baseball games.

In addition to new material dealing with popular culture, frontiers, and cities, the Fifth Edition includes new sections describing the difficulties faced by white women in the South during the Civil War, the treatment of minorities under the New Deal, developments in civil rights after World War II, how major league baseball was integrated, the problem of juvenile delinquency in the 1950s and the rise of rock 'n' roll music, new interpretations of Dwight Eisenhower and Ronald Reagan, a new section detailing the computer revolution, an expanded section on mistrust of government and the militia movement, a section on the "new economy" and Alan Greenspan's monetarist policies as supported by Bill Clinton, a section on the shift to the right of the Supreme Court and the narrowing of affirmative action programs, and a new section on the series of scandals that rocked the Clinton administration.

In preparing this Fifth Edition of *America,* we have benefited from the insights and suggestions of many people. The following scholars have provided close readings of the manuscript at various stages: Lucy Barber (University of California at Davis), Michael Barnhart (State University of New York at Stony Brook), Charles Eagles (University of Mississippi), Tera Hunter (Carnegie-Mellon University), Peter Kolchin (University of Delaware), Christopher Morris (University of Texas at Arlington), David Parker (Kennesaw State University), and Marilyn Westerkamp (University of California at Santa Cruz). Once again we thank our friends at W. W. Norton, especially Steve Forman, Jon Durbin, Sandy Lifland, and Candace Kooyoomjian, for their care and attention along the way.

—George B. Tindall
—David E. Shi

18 RECONSTRUCTION:
NORTH AND SOUTH

CHAPTER ORGANIZER

This chapter focuses on:

- the different approaches to Reconstruction.

- congressional efforts to reshape southern society.

- the role of African Americans in the early postwar years.

- national politics in the 1870s.

In the spring of 1865 the cruel war was over. At the frightful cost of 620,000 lives and the destruction of the southern economy and much of its landscape, American nationalism emerged triumphant, and some 4 million slaves emerged free. Ratification of the Thirteenth Amendment in December 1865 abolished slavery throughout the Union.

But peace had come only on the battlefields. "Cannon conquer," recognized a northern editor, "but they do not necessarily convert." Now the North faced the task of "reconstructing" a ravaged and resentful South.

THE WAR'S AFTERMATH

In the war's aftermath, important questions faced the victors in the North: Should the Confederate leaders be tried for treason? How should new governments be formed? How and at whose expense was the South's economy to be rebuilt? What was to be done with the freed slaves? Were they to be given land? social equality? education? voting rights? Such complex questions required sober reflection and careful planning, but policy makers did not have the luxury of time or the benefits of consensus.

DEVELOPMENT IN THE NORTH   To some Americans the Civil War had been more truly a social revolution than the War of Independence, for it reduced the once-dominant power of the planter elite in the national councils and elevated that of the northern "captains of industry." It is easy to exaggerate the profundity of this change, but government did become subtly more friendly to businessmen and unfriendly to those who would probe into their activities. The wartime Republican Congress had delivered on the major platform promises of 1860, which

The Grand Review of Union Troops in Victory, *Washington, D.C., May 1865.*

had cemented the allegiance of northeastern businessmen and western farmers to the party of free labor.

In the absence of southern members, Congress during the war had seized the opportunity to centralize national power. In this regard, it passed the Morrill Tariff, which doubled the average level of import duties. The National Banking Act created a uniform system of banking and bank-note currency, and helped to finance the war. Congress also passed legislation guaranteeing that the first transcontinental railroad would run along a north-central route from Omaha to Sacramento, and donated public lands and public bonds to ensure its financing. In the Homestead Act of 1862, moreover, Congress voted free homesteads of 160 acres to settlers. They had to occupy the land for five years before gaining title. The Morrill Land Grant Act of the same year conveyed to each state 30,000 acres of public land per member of Congress from the state, the proceeds from the sale of which went to create colleges of "agriculture and mechanic arts." Such measures helped stimulate the North's economy in the years after the Civil War.

DEVASTATION IN THE SOUTH   The postwar South, where most of the fighting had occurred, offered a sharp contrast to the victorious North. Along the path of General Sherman's army, one observer reported in 1866, the countryside "looked for many miles like a broad black streak of ruin and desolation." Columbia, South Carolina, said another witness, was "a wilderness of ruins," Charleston a place of "vacant houses, of widowed women, of rotting wharves, of deserted warehouses, of weed-wild gardens, of miles of grass-grown streets, of acres of pitiful and voiceless barrenness." The border states of Missouri and Kentucky had experienced a guerrilla war that lapsed into postwar anarchy perpetrated by marauding bands of bushwhackers turned outlaws, such as the notorious James boys, Frank and Jesse.

Throughout the South, property values had collapsed. Confederate bonds and money became worthless; railroads were damaged or destroyed. Cotton that had escaped destruction was seized as Confederate property or in forfeit of federal taxes. Emancipation of the slaves wiped out perhaps $4 billion invested in human flesh and left the labor system in disarray. The great age of expansion in the cotton market was over. Not until 1879 would the cotton crop again equal the record harvest of 1860; tobacco production did not regain its prewar level until

The "burned district" of Richmond, Virginia, April 1865.

1880; the sugar crop of Louisiana not until 1893; and the old rice industry of the Tidewater and the hemp industry of the Kentucky Bluegrass never regained their prewar status.

FORCED DOMESTICITY   The defeat of the Confederacy transformed much of southern society. The freeing of slaves, the destruction of property, and the free fall in land values left many among the former planter elite destitute and homeless. Amanda Worthington, a plantation mistress from Mississippi, saw her whole world destroyed. In the fall of 1865, she assessed the damage: "None of us can realize that we are no longer wealthy—yet thanks to the yankees, the cause of all unhappiness, such is the case." Genteel southerners now found themselves forced to rebuild lives and families without the help of slaves. Women accustomed to relying on slaves for their every need were unprepared for the tasks at hand. One girl could not even comb her own hair; a matron cried at night because she had no one to wash her feet. "I did the washing for six weeks," one tired woman wrote, "[and] came near ruining myself for life as I was too delicately raised for such hard work." Those who still had some money after the war often recruited former slaves to work as domestic servants. Now, however, they had to pay for their services.

BITTER IN DEFEAT   After the Civil War many former Confederates were so embittered by defeat and so resistant to the idea of living under northern rule that they abandoned their native region rather than submit to "Yankee rule." Some migrated to Canada, Europe, Mexico, South America, and Asia. Others preferred the western territories and states. Still others moved north, settling in northern and midwestern cities on the assumption that educational and economic opportunities would be better among the victors.

Most of those who remained in the South returned to find their farms and homes and communities transformed. One Confederate army captain reported that on his father's plantation "Our negroes are living in great comfort. They were delighted to see me with overflowing affection. They waited on me as before, gave me breakfast, splendid dinners, etc. But they firmly and respectfully informed me: 'We own this land now. Put it out of your head that it will ever be yours again.'"

As Union troops fanned out across the defeated South, people cursed and spat upon the troops. A Virginia woman expressed a spirited defiance common among her circle of friends: "Every day, every hour, that I live increases my hatred and detestation, and loathing of that race. They [Yankees] disgrace our common humanity. As a people I consider them vastly inferior to the better classes of our slaves." Fervent southern nationalists, both men and women, planted in their children a similar hatred of Yankees and a defiance of northern rule. One mother said that she trained her children to "fear God, love the South, and live to avenge her."

LEGALLY FREE, SOCIALLY BOUND   In the former Confederate states, the newly freed slaves suffered most of all. According to Frederick Douglass, the black abolitionist, the former slave remained dependent: "He had neither money, property, nor friends. He was free from the old plantation, but he had nothing but the dusty road under his feet. . . . He was turned loose, naked, hungry, and destitute to the open sky."

A few northerners argued that what the ex-slaves needed most was their own land. But even dedicated abolitionists shrank from endorsing measures of land reform that might have given the freed slaves more self-support and independence. Citizenship and legal rights were one thing, wholesale confiscation of property and land redistribution quite another. Instead of land or material help, the freed slaves more often got advice and moral platitudes.

According to a former Confederate general, recently freed blacks had "nothing but freedom."

In 1865 Representative George Julian of Indiana and Senator Charles Sumner of Massachusetts proposed to give freed slaves forty-acre homesteads carved out of Rebel lands taken under the Confiscation Act of 1862. But their plan for outright grants was replaced by a program of rentals since, under the law, confiscation was effective only for the lifetime of the offender. Discussions of land distribution, however, fueled rumors that freed slaves would get "forty acres and a mule," a slogan that swept the South at the end of the war. As a black man in Mississippi put it: "Gib us our own land and we take care ourselves; but widout land, de ole massas can hire us or starve us, as dey please." More lands were seized as "abandoned lands" under an act of 1864, and for default on the direct taxes that Congress had levied early in the war, than under the Confiscation Act. The most conspicuous example of confiscation was the estate of Robert E. Lee and the Custis family, which became Arlington National Cemetery, but larger amounts were taken in the South Carolina Sea Islands and elsewhere. Some of these lands were sold to freed blacks, some to Yankee speculators.

THE FREEDMEN'S BUREAU   On March 3, 1865, Congress set up within the War Department the Bureau of Refugees, Freedmen, and

Abandoned Lands, to provide "such issues of provisions, clothing, and fuel" as might be needed to relieve "destitute and suffering refugees and freedmen and their wives and children." The Freedmen's Bureau would also take over abandoned or confiscated land, but the amount of such land was limited. Agents of the Freedmen's Bureau were entrusted with negotiating labor contracts (something new for both blacks and planters), providing medical care, and setting up schools, often in cooperation with northern agencies such as the American Missionary Association and the Freedmen's Aid Society. The bureau had its own courts to deal with labor disputes and land titles, and its agents were further authorized to supervise trials involving blacks in other courts. White intransigence and the failure to grasp the intensity of racial prejudice increasingly thwarted the efforts of Freedmen's Bureau agents to protect and assist the former slaves.

Congress was not willing to strengthen the powers of the Freedmen's Bureau to reflect such problems. Beyond temporary relief measures, no program of Reconstruction ever incorporated much more than constitutional and legal rights for freedmen. These were important in themselves, of course, but the extent to which even these should go was very

The Freedmen's Bureau set up schools such as this throughout the former Confederate states.

uncertain, to be settled more by the course of events than by any clear-cut commitment to equality.

THE BATTLE OVER RECONSTRUCTION

The problem of reconstructing the South involved what governments would constitute authority in the defeated states. This problem arose first in the state of Virginia at the very beginning of the Civil War, when the thirty-five western counties of Virginia refused to go along with secession. In 1861 a loyal state government of Virginia was proclaimed at Wheeling, and this government in turn formed a new state called West Virginia, admitted to the Union in 1863. The loyal government of Virginia then carried on from Alexandria, its reach limited to that part of the state that the Union controlled. As Union forces advanced into the South, Lincoln in 1862 named military governors for Tennessee, Arkansas, and Louisiana. By the end of the following year he had formulated a plan for regular governments in those states and any others that might qualify.

LINCOLN'S PLAN AND CONGRESS'S RESPONSE   Acting under his pardon power, President Lincoln issued in late 1863 a Proclamation of Amnesty and Reconstruction, under which any rebel state could form a Union government whenever a number equal to 10 percent of those who had voted in 1860 took an oath of allegiance to the Constitution and the Union and had received a presidential pardon. Participants also had to swear support for laws and proclamations dealing with emancipation. Certain groups, however, were excluded from the pardon: civil and diplomatic officers of the Confederacy; senior officers of the Confederate army and navy; judges, congressmen, and military officers of the United States who had left their federal posts to aid the rebellion; and those accused of failure to treat captured black soldiers and their officers as prisoners of war. Under this plan, loyal governments appeared in Tennessee, Arkansas, and Louisiana, but Congress recognized them neither by representation nor in counting the electoral votes of 1864.

In the absence of any specific provisions for Reconstruction in the Constitution, politicians disagreed as to where authority properly rested. Lincoln claimed the right to direct Reconstruction under the clause that set forth the presidential pardon power, and also under the constitutional obligation of the United States to guarantee each state a republican form of government. Republican congressmen, however, argued that this obligation implied a power of Congress to act.

A few conservative and most moderate Republicans supported Lincoln's program of immediate restoration. A small but influential group known as Radical Republicans, however, favored a sweeping transformation of southern society based on granting freedmen full-fledged citizenship. The Radicals hoped to reconstruct southern society so as to mirror the North's emphasis on small-scale capitalism. This meant thwarting the efforts of the old planter class to reestablish a caste system and keep the freed blacks in a state of peonage.

The Radicals also maintained that Congress, not the president, should supervise the Reconstruction program. To this end, they helped pass in 1864 the Wade-Davis Bill, sponsored by Senator Benjamin Wade of Ohio and Representative Henry Winter Davis of Maryland. In contrast to Lincoln's 10 percent plan, the Wade-Davis Bill required that a majority of white male citizens declare their allegiance and that only those who could take an "ironclad" oath (required of federal officials since 1862) attesting to their *past* loyalty could vote or serve in the state constitutional conventions. The conventions, moreover, would have to abolish slavery, exclude from political rights high-ranking civil and military officers of the Confederacy, and repudiate debts incurred "under the sanction of the usurping power."

Passed during the closing day of the session, the Wade-Davis Bill never became law. Lincoln exercised a pocket veto. That is, he simply refused to sign it, but he issued an artful statement that he would accept any state that preferred to present itself under the congressional plan. The sponsors responded with the Wade-Davis Manifesto, which accused the president, among other sins, of usurping power and attempting to use readmitted states to ensure his reelection.

Lincoln offered his last public words on Reconstruction in his final public address, on April 11, 1865. Speaking from the White House balcony, he pronounced that the Confederate states had never left the Union. These states were simply "out of their proper practical relation with the Union," and the object was to get them "into their proper practical relation." It would be easier to do this by merely ignoring the abstract issue: "Finding themselves safely at home, it would be utterly immaterial whether they had been abroad." At a cabinet meeting, Lincoln proposed to get state governments in operation before Congress met in December. He described the Radicals as possessing feelings of hate and vindictiveness with which he did not sympathize and could not participate. He wanted "no persecution, no bloody work," no radical restructuring of southern social and economic life.

THE ASSASSINATION OF LINCOLN   That evening Lincoln went to Ford's Theater and his rendezvous with death. With his trusted bodyguard called away to Richmond and with the Metropolitan policeman assigned to his box away from his post watching the play, Lincoln was helpless as John Wilkes Booth slipped into the presidential box. Booth, a crazed actor and Confederate zealot who thought he was helping the South, blocked the door to the box and then fired his derringer pointblank at the president's head, before stabbing Lincoln's aide and jumping from the box onto the stage, crying *"Sic semper tyrannis"* (Thus always to tyrants), the motto of Virginia. The president died nine hours after he had been shot. Accomplices had also targeted Vice-President Andrew Johnson and Secretary of State William Seward. Seward and four others, including his son, were victims of severe but not fatal stab wounds. Johnson escaped injury, however, because his would-be assassin got cold feet and wound up tipsy in the barroom of Johnson's hotel.

The nation extracted a full measure of vengeance from the conspirators. Although he had escaped the night he shot Lincoln, Booth was pursued into Virginia and trapped and shot in a burning barn. His last words were: "Tell Mother I die for my country. I thought I did for the best." Three of Booth's collaborators were convicted by a military commission and hanged, along with the woman at whose boardinghouse they had plotted. Three others got life sentences, including a Maryland doctor who set the leg Booth had broken when he jumped to the stage. President Johnson eventually pardoned them all, except one who died in prison. The doctor achieved lasting fame by making common a once obscure expression. His name was Mudd. Apart from those cases, however, there was only one other execution in the aftermath of war: Henry Wirz, who commanded the infamous prison at Andersonville, Georgia, where Union prisoners were probably more the victims of war conditions than of deliberate cruelty.

City Hall in New York City, on April 24, was thronged with people anxious for a last look at Lincoln.

JOHNSON'S PLAN   Lincoln's death suddenly elevated to the White House Andrew Johnson of Tennessee, a man whose state was still in legal limbo and whose party affiliation was unclear. He was a War Democrat who had been put on the Union ticket in 1864 as a gesture of unity. Of humble origins like Lincoln, Johnson had moved as a youth from his birthplace in Raleigh, North Carolina, to Greeneville, Tennessee, where he became proprietor of a tailor shop. Self-educated with the help of his wife, he had made himself into an effective orator of the rough-and-tumble school, served as mayor, congressman, governor, and senator, then as military governor of Tennessee before he became vice-president. In the process he had become an advocate of the small farmers against the privileges of the large planters. He also shared the racial attitudes of most white yeomen. "Damn the negroes," he exclaimed to a friend during the war, "I am fighting those traitorous aristocrats, their masters."

Some of the Radicals at first thought Johnson, unlike Lincoln, to be one of them. Johnson had, for example, once asserted that treason "must be made infamous and traitors must be impoverished." Senator Benjamin Wade loved such language. "Johnson, we have faith in you,"

Andrew Johnson.

he promised. "By the gods, there will be no trouble now in running this government." But Wade would soon find him as unsympathetic as Lincoln, if for different reasons.

Johnson's very loyalty to the Union sprang from a strict adherence to the Constitution. Given to dogmatic abstractions that were alien to Lincoln's temperament, he nevertheless arrived by a different route at similar objectives. The states should be brought back into their proper relation to the Union because the states and the Union were indestructible. And like many other whites, he found it hard to accept the growing Radical movement toward suffrage for blacks. In 1865 Johnson declared that "there is no such thing as reconstruction. Those States have not gone out of the Union. Therefore reconstruction is unnecessary."

Johnson's plan to restore the Union thus closely resembled Lincoln's. A new Proclamation of Amnesty (May 1865) added to those Lincoln had excluded from pardon everybody with taxable property worth more than $20,000. These wealthy planters, bankers, and merchants were the people Johnson believed had led the South into secession. But those in the excluded groups might make special applications for pardon directly to the president, and before the year was out Johnson had issued some 13,000 such pardons. In every case Johnson ruled that pardon, whether by general amnesty or special clemency, restored one's property rights in land. Johnson's rulings nipped in the bud an experiment in land distribution that had barely begun. More than seventy years later, one freed slave, born in Orange County, North Carolina, spoke bluntly of his dashed hopes: "Lincoln got the praise for freeing us, but did he do it? He give us freedom without giving us any chance to live to ourselves and we still had to depend on the southern white man for work, food and clothing, and he held us through our necessity and want in a state of servitude but little better than slavery."

On the same day that Johnson announced his amnesty program, he issued another proclamation to his native state of North Carolina. Within six more weeks, he issued similar edicts for the other Rebel states not already organized. In each a native Unionist became provisional governor with authority to call a convention of men elected by loyal voters. Lincoln's 10 percent requirement was omitted. Johnson called upon the conventions to invalidate the secession ordinances, abolish slavery, and repudiate all debts incurred to aid the Confederacy. Each state, moreover, was to ratify the Thirteenth Amendment. Lincoln had privately advised the governor of Louisiana to consider a grant of suffrage to some blacks, "the very intelligent and those who have fought gallantly in our ranks." In his final public address he had also endorsed a limited black suffrage. Johnson repeated Lincoln's advice. He reminded the provisional governor of Mississippi, for example, that the state conventions might "with perfect safety" extend suffrage to blacks with education or with military service so as to "disarm the adversary"—the adversary being "radicals who are wild upon Negro franchise."

The state conventions for the most part met Johnson's requirements, although South Carolina and Mississippi did not repudiate their debt and the new Mississippi legislature refused to ratify the Thirteenth Amendment. Presidential agents sent to the South reported "that the mass of thinking men of the south accept the present situation of affairs in good faith." But Carl Schurz of Missouri found during his visit to the South "an *utter absence of national feeling* . . . and a desire to preserve slavery . . . as much and as long as possible." The discrepancy between the two reports is perhaps only apparent: southern whites accepted the situation because they thought so little had changed after all. Emboldened by Johnson's indulgence, they ignored his counsels of expediency. Suggestions of black suffrage were scarcely raised in the conventions and promptly squelched when they were.

SOUTHERN INTRANSIGENCE When Congress met in December 1865, for the first time since the end of the war, it faced the fact that state governments were functioning in the South, and they were remarkably like the old. Southern voters had acted with extreme disregard of northern feelings. Among the new legislative members presenting themselves were Georgia's Alexander H. Stephens, ex-vice-president of the Confederacy, now claiming a seat in the Senate, four Confederate generals, eight colonels, six cabinet members, and a host of lesser Rebels. The Congress forthwith denied seats to all members from the eleven former Confederate states. It was too much to expect, after four bloody years, that Unionists would welcome ex-Confederates like prodigal sons.

Furthermore, the new southern legislatures, in passing repressive "Black Codes" restricting the freedom of blacks, demonstrated that they intended to preserve slavery as nearly as possible. As one white southerner stressed, "the ex-slave was not a free man; he was a free Negro," and the Black Codes were intended to highlight the distinction. The codes extended to blacks certain rights they had not hitherto enjoyed, but universally set them aside as a separate caste subject to special restraints. Details varied from state to state, but some provisions were common. Existing marriages, including common-law marriages, were recognized (although interracial marriages were prohibited), and testimony of blacks was accepted in legal cases involving blacks—and in six states, in all cases. Blacks could own property. They could sue and be sued in the courts. On the other hand, blacks could not own farm lands in Mississippi or city lots in South Carolina; they were required to buy special licenses to practice certain trades in Mississippi; and in some states they could not carry firearms without a license to do so.

The codes' labor provisions confirmed suspicions that whites were seeking to preserve the slave labor system. Blacks were required to enter into annual labor contracts, with provision for punishment in case of violation. Dependent children were subject to compulsory apprenticeship and corporal punishment by masters. Vagrants were punished with severe fines and, if unable to pay, they were forced to labor in the fields for those who paid the courts for this source of cheap labor. To many people it indeed seemed that slavery was on the way back in another guise. The new Mississippi penal code virtually said so: "All penal and criminal laws now in force describing the mode of punishment of crimes and misdemeanors committed by slaves, free negroes, or mulat-

Slavery Is Dead (?) *Thomas Nast's cartoon suggests that, in 1866, slavery was only legally dead.*

toes are hereby reenacted, and decreed to be in full force against all freedmen, free negroes and mulattoes."

Faced with such evidence of southern intransigence, moderate Republicans drifted toward Radical views. Having excluded southern members, the new Congress set up a Joint Committee on Reconstruction, with nine members from the House and six from the Senate, to gather evidence and submit proposals. Initiative on the committee fell to determined Radicals who knew what they wanted: Ben Wade of Ohio, George W. Julian of Indiana—and most conspicuously of all, Thaddeus Stevens of Pennsylvania and Charles Sumner of Massachusetts.

THE RADICALS   Most Radicals had been connected with the antislavery cause. While one could be hostile to both slavery and blacks, many whites approached the question of black rights with a humanitarian impulse. Few could escape the bitterness bred by the long and bloody war, however, or remain unaware of the partisan advantage that would come to the Republican party from black suffrage. But the party of Union and freedom, after all, could best guarantee the fruits of vic-

Two leading Radicals: Senator Charles Sumner (left) *and Representative Thaddeus Stevens* (right).

tory, they reasoned, and black suffrage could best guarantee black rights.

The growing conflict of opinion over Reconstruction policy brought about an inversion in constitutional reasoning. Secessionists—and Johnson—were now arguing that their states had in fact remained in the Union, and some Radicals were contriving arguments that they had left the Union after all. Thaddeus Stevens argued that the Confederate states were now conquered provinces, subject to the absolute will of the victors. Charles Sumner maintained that the southern states, by their pretended acts of secession, had in effect committed suicide and reverted to the status of unorganized territories subject to the will of Congress. But few ever took such ideas seriously. Republicans converged instead on the "forfeited-rights theory," later embodied in the report of the Joint Committee on Reconstruction. This held that the states as entities continued to exist, but by the acts of secession and war had forfeited "all civil and political rights under the constitution." And Congress was the proper authority to determine conditions under which such rights might be restored.

JOHNSON'S BATTLE WITH CONGRESS   A long year of political battling remained, however, before this idea triumphed. By the end of 1865, Radical views had gained a majority in Congress, if one not yet large enough to override presidential vetoes. But the critical year 1866 saw the gradual waning of Johnson's power and influence; much of this was self-induced. Johnson first challenged Congress in 1866, when he vetoed a bill to extend the life of the Freedmen's Bureau. The measure, he said, assumed that wartime conditions still existed, whereas the country had returned "to a state of peace and industry." No longer valid as a war measure, the bill violated the Constitution in several ways, he declared. It made the federal government responsible for the care of indigents. It was passed by a Congress in which eleven states were denied seats. And it used vague language in defining the "civil rights and immunities" of blacks. The Congress soon moved to correct that particular defect, but for the time being Johnson's prestige remained sufficiently intact that the Senate upheld his veto.

Three days after the veto, however, Johnson undermined his already weakening prestige with a fiery assault on Radical leaders during an impromptu speech. The Joint Committee on Reconstruction, he charged, was "an irresponsible central directory" that had repudiated the principle of an indestructible Union and accepted the legality of secession by entertaining conquered-province and state-suicide theories. From that point forward, moderate Republicans backed away from a president who had opened himself to counterattack. He was "an alien enemy of a foreign state," Stevens declared. Sumner called him "an insolent drunken brute"—and Johnson was open to the charge because of an incident at his vice-presidential inauguration. Weakened by illness at the time, he had taken a belt of brandy to get him through the ceremony and, under the influence of fever and alcohol, had become incoherent.

In mid-March 1866 Congress passed the Civil Rights Act. A response to the Black Codes, this bill declared that "all persons born in the United States and not subject to any foreign power, excluding Indians not taxed," were citizens entitled to "full and equal benefit of all laws." The grant of citizenship to native-born blacks, Johnson fumed, went beyond anything formerly held to be within the scope of federal power. It would, moreover, "foment discord among the races." Johnson vetoed the bill, but this time, on April 9, 1866, Congress overrode the presidential veto. On July 16 it enacted a revised Freedmen's Bureau Bill, again overriding a veto. From that point on, Johnson steadily lost both public and political support.

THE FOURTEENTH AMENDMENT To remove all doubt about the constitutionality of the new Civil Rights Act, which was justified as implementing freedom under the Thirteenth Amendment, the Joint Committee recommended a new amendment, which passed Congress on June 16, 1866, and was ratified by the states on July 28, 1868. The Fourteenth Amendment, however, went far beyond the Civil Rights Act. It merits close scrutiny because of its broad impact on subsequent laws and litigation.

The first section asserted four principles: it reaffirmed state and federal citizenship for persons born or naturalized in the United States, and it forbade any *state* (the word "state" was important in later litigation) to abridge the "privileges and immunities" of citizens, to deprive any *person* (again an important term) of life, liberty, or property without "due process of law," or to deny any person "the equal protection of the laws."

The last three of these clauses have been the subject of lawsuits resulting in applications not widely, if at all, foreseen at the time. The "due-process clause" has come to mean that state as well as federal power is subject to the Bill of Rights, and it has been used to protect corporations, as legal "persons," from "unreasonable" regulation by the states. Other provisions of the amendment had less far-reaching effects. One section specified that the debt of the United States "shall not be questioned," but declared "illegal and void" all debts contracted in aid of the rebellion. Another section specified the power of Congress to pass laws enforcing the amendment.

Johnson's home state was among the first to ratify the Fourteenth Amendment. In Tennessee, which had harbored probably more Unionists than any other Confederate state, the government had fallen under Radical control. The state's governor, in reporting the results to the secretary of the Senate, added: "Give my respects to the dead dog of the White House." His words afford a fair sample of the growing acrimony on both sides of the Reconstruction debates. In May and July, bloody race riots in Memphis and New Orleans added fuel to the flames. Both incidents involved indiscriminate massacres of blacks by local police and white mobs. The carnage, Radicals argued, was the natural fruit of Johnson's policy. "Witness Memphis, witness New Orleans," Sumner cried. "Who can doubt that the President is the author of these tragedies?"

RECONSTRUCTING THE SOUTH

THE TRIUMPH OF CONGRESSIONAL RECONSTRUCTION As 1866 drew to an end, the congressional elections promised to be a referendum on the growing split between Johnson and the Radicals. Johnson sought to influence voters with a speaking tour of the Midwest, a "swing around the circle," which turned into an undignified shouting contest between Johnson and his critics. In Cleveland he described the Radicals as "factious, domineering, tyrannical" men, and he foolishly exchanged hot-tempered insults with a heckler. At another stop, while Johnson was speaking from an observation car, the engineer mistakenly pulled the train out of the station, making the president appear quite the fool. Such incidents tended to confirm his image as a "ludicrous boor" and "drunken imbecile," which Radical papers projected. When the returns of the congressional elections came in, the Republicans had well over a two-thirds majority in each house, a comfortable margin with which to override any presidential vetoes.

The Congress in fact enacted a new program even before new members took office. Two acts passed in 1867 extended the suffrage to African Americans in the District of Columbia and the territories. An-

This cartoon appeared at the time of the 1866 congressional elections. It shows "King Andy I" approving the execution of Radical leaders in Congress.

other law provided that the new Congress would convene on March 4 instead of the following December, depriving Johnson of a breathing spell. On March 2, 1867, two days before the old Congress expired, it passed three basic laws of congressional Reconstruction over Johnson's vetoes: the Military Reconstruction Act, the Command of the Army Act (an amendment to an army appropriation), and the Tenure of Office Act.

The first of the three acts prescribed new conditions under which the formation of southern state governments should begin all over again. The other two sought to block obstruction by the president. The Command of the Army Act required that all orders from the commander-in-chief go through the headquarters of the general of the army, then Ulysses S. Grant, who could not be reassigned outside Washington without the consent of the Senate. The Radicals had faith in Grant, who was already leaning their way. The Tenure of Office Act required the consent of the Senate for the president to remove any officeholder whose appointment the Senate had to confirm in the first place. The purpose of at least some congressmen was to retain Secretary of War Edwin M. Stanton, the one Radical sympathizer in Johnson's cabinet. But an ambiguity crept into the wording of the act. Cabinet officers, it said, should serve during the term of the president who appointed them—and Lincoln had appointed Stanton, although, to be sure, Johnson was serving out Lincoln's term.

The Military Reconstruction Act, often hailed or denounced as the triumphant victory of "Radical" Reconstruction, actually represented a compromise that fell short of a thoroughgoing radicalism. As first reported from the Reconstruction Committee by Thaddeus Stevens, it would have given military commanders in the South ultimate control over law enforcement and would have left open indefinitely the terms of future restoration. More moderate elements, however, pushed through the "Blaine Amendment." Along with programs of land confiscation and education, it scrapped the prolonged national control under which Radicals hoped to put through the far more revolutionary program of reducing the Rebel states to territories. It did require that southern states accept black suffrage and ratify the Fourteenth Amendment.

The act began with a pronouncement that "no legal state governments or adequate protection for life and property now exists in the rebel States. . . ." One state, Tennessee, which had ratified the Fourteenth Amendment, was exempted from the application of the act. The other ten were divided into five military districts, and the commanding officer of each was authorized to keep order and protect the "rights of persons and property." To that end he might use military tribunals in place of civil courts. The Johnson governments remained intact for the time being, but new constitutions were to be framed "in conformity with the Constitution of the United States," in conventions elected by male citizens twenty-one and older "of whatever race, color, or previous condition." Each state constitution had to provide the same universal male suffrage. Then, once the constitution was ratified by a majority of voters and accepted by Congress, other criteria had to be met. The state legislature had to ratify the Fourteenth Amendment, and once the amendment became part of the Constitution, any given state would be entitled to representation in Congress. Persons excluded from office-holding by the proposed amendment were also excluded from participation in the process.

Johnson reluctantly appointed military commanders under the act, but the situation remained uncertain for a time. Some people expected the Supreme Court to strike down the act, and for the time being no machinery existed for the new elections. Congress quickly remedied that on March 23, 1867, with the Second Reconstruction Act, which directed the commanders to register for voting all adult males who swore they were qualified. A Third Reconstruction Act, passed on July 19, directed registrars to go beyond the loyalty oath and determine each person's eligibility to take it, and also authorized district commanders to remove and replace officeholders of any existing "so-called state" or division thereof. Before the end of 1867 new elections had been held in all the states but Texas.

Having clipped the president's wings, the Republican Congress moved a year later to safeguard its program from possible interference by the Supreme Court, which in a series of decisions had shown a readiness to question certain actions related to Reconstruction. With the Court considering *Ex parte McCardle,* the case of a Vicksburg editor arrested for criticizing the administration of the Fourth Military District who now sought release under the Habeas Corpus Act of 1867, Congress acted. On March 27, 1868, it simply removed the power of the Supreme Court to review cases arising under the law, which Congress clearly had the right to do under its power to define the Court's appellate jurisdiction. The Court accepted this curtailment on the same day it affirmed the principle of an "indestructible union" in *Texas* v. *White* (1868). In that case it also asserted the right of Congress to reframe state governments.

THE IMPEACHMENT AND TRIAL OF JOHNSON   Congress's move to restrain the Supreme Court preceded by just a few days the opening arguments in the trial of the president in the Senate on an impeachment brought in by the House. Johnson, though hostile to the congressional program, had gone through the motions required of him. He continued, however, to pardon former Confederates and replaced several district commanders whose Radical sympathies offended him. Nevertheless a lengthy investigation by the House Judiciary Committee, extending through most of 1867, had failed to convince the House that grounds for impeachment existed.

Johnson himself provided the occasion for impeachment when he deliberately violated the Tenure of Office Act in order to test its constitutionality in the courts. Secretary of War Edwin M. Stanton had become a thorn in the president's side, refusing to resign despite his disagreements with the president's Reconstruction policy. On August 12, 1867, during a congressional recess, Johnson suspended Stanton and named General Grant in his place. Grant's political stance was ambiguous at the time, but his acceptance implied cooperation with Johnson. When the Senate refused to confirm Johnson's action, however, Grant returned the office to Stanton. The president thereupon named General Lorenzo Thomas as secretary of war after a futile effort to interest General William T. Sherman. Three days later, on February 24, 1868, the House voted to impeach the president.

Of the eleven articles of impeachment, eight focused on the charge that Johnson had unlawfully removed Stanton and had failed to give the Senate the name of a successor. Article 9 accused the president of issuing orders in violation of the Command of the Army Act. The last two articles in effect charged him with criticizing Congress by "inflammatory and scandalous harangues" and by claiming that the Congress was not legally valid without southern representatives. But Article 11 accused Johnson of "unlawfully devising and contriving" to violate the Reconstruction Acts, contrary to his obligation to execute the laws. At the least, it stated, Johnson had tried to obstruct Congress's will while observing the letter of the law.

*House of Representatives managers of the impeachment proceedings and trial of
Andrew Johnson. Among them were Benjamin Butler (R-Mass., seated left) and
Thaddeus Stevens (R-Pa., seated with cane).*

The Senate trial opened on March 5 and continued until May 26,
with Chief Justice Salmon P. Chase presiding. Seven managers from
the House, including Thaddeus Stevens and Benjamin F. Butler, directed the prosecution. The president was spared the humiliation of a
personal appearance. His defense counsel shrewdly insisted on narrowing the trial to questions that would be indictable offenses under the
law, and steered the questions away from Johnson's manifest wish to
frustrate the will of Congress. Such questions, they contended, were
purely political in nature. In the end, enough Republican senators
joined their pro-Johnson colleagues to prevent conviction. The vote,
first on May 16 and then on May 26, was 35 for guilty and 19 for not
guilty, one vote short of the two-thirds needed to convict. Thereupon
the Senate dissolved the tribunal.

In a parliamentary system Johnson probably would have been removed as leader of the government long before then. But by deciding
the case on the narrowest grounds, the Senate made it unlikely that any
future president could ever be removed except for the gravest offenses,
and almost surely not for flouting the will of Congress in executing the
laws. Impeachment of Johnson was in the end a great political mistake,
for the failure to remove the president damaged Radical morale and

support. Nevertheless, the Radical cause did gain something. To blunt the opposition, Johnson agreed not to obstruct the process of Reconstruction, named a secretary of war who was committed to enforcing the new laws, and sent to Congress the new Radical constitutions of Arkansas and South Carolina. Thereafter his obstruction ceased and Radical Reconstruction began in earnest.

REPUBLICAN RULE IN THE SOUTH   In June 1868 Congress agreed that seven states had met the conditions for readmission, all but Virginia, Mississippi, and Texas. Congress rescinded Georgia's admission, however, when the state legislature expelled twenty-eight black members and seated some former Confederate leaders. The military commander of Georgia then forced the legislature to reseat the black members and remove the Confederates, and the state was compelled to ratify the Fifteenth Amendment before being admitted in July 1870. Mississippi, Texas, and Virginia had returned earlier in 1870, under the added requirement that they too ratify the Fifteenth Amendment. This amendment, submitted to the states in 1869, ratified in 1870, forbade the states to deny any person the vote on grounds of race, color, or previous condition of servitude.

Long before the new governments were established, Republican groups began to spring up in the South, chiefly sponsored by the Union League, founded at Philadelphia in 1862 to promote support for the Union. Emissaries of the league enrolled African Americans and loyal whites, initiated them into the secrets and rituals of the order, and instructed them "in their rights and duties." Their recruiting efforts were so successful that in 1867, on the eve of South Carolina's choice of convention delegates, the league reported eighty-eight chapters, which claimed to have enrolled almost every adult black male in the state.

THE RECONSTRUCTED SOUTH

THE FREED SLAVES   To focus solely on what white Republicans did to reconstruct the defeated South creates the false impression that the freed slaves were simply pawns in the hands of others. In fact, however, southern blacks were active agents in affecting the course of Reconstruction. Although many of them found themselves liberated but destitute after the fighting ended, the mere promise of freedom raised their hopes about achieving a biracial democracy, equal justice, and economic opportunity. "Most anyone ought to know that a man is better off free than as a slave, even if he did not have anything," said the Reverend E. P. Holmes, a black Georgia preacher and former domestic servant. "I would rather be free and have my liberty."

Participation in the Union army or navy gave many freedmen a training ground in leadership. Black military veterans would form the core of the first generation of African-American political leaders in the postwar South. Military service provided many former slaves with the first opportunities to learn to read and write. Army life also alerted them to alternative social choices and to new opportunities for advancement and respectability. "No negro who has ever been a soldier," reported a northern official after visiting a black unit, "can again be imposed upon; they have learnt what it is to be free and they will infuse their feelings into others." Fighting for the Union cause also instilled a fervent sense of nationalism. A Virginia freedman explained that the United States was "now *our* country—made emphatically so by the blood of our brethren."

Former slaves established independent black churches after the war, churches that would serve as the foundation of African-American community life. In war-ravaged Charleston, South Carolina, the first new building to appear after the war was a black church on Calhoun Street; by 1866 ten more had been built. Blacks preferred Baptist churches over other denominations, in part because of their decentralized structure that allowed each congregation to worship in its own way. By 1890 there were over 1.3 million black Baptists in the South, nearly three times as many as any other black denomination. For many former slaves, churches were the first institutions they owned and controlled. In addition to forming viable new congregations, freed blacks organized thousands of fraternal, benevolent, and mutual-aid societies, clubs, lodges, and associations. Memphis, for example, had over two hundred such organizations; Richmond boasted twice that number.

The freed slaves, both women and men, also hastened to reestablish and reaffirm families. Marriages that had been prohibited were now legitimized through the assistance of the Freedmen's Bureau. By 1870 a preponderant majority of former slaves lived in two-parent households. One white editor in Georgia, lamenting the difficulty of finding black women to serve as house servants, reported that "every negro woman wants to set up house keeping" for herself and her family. To do so they often had little choice but to become tenant farmers, gaining access to land in exchange for a share of their crop. With little money or technical training, freed slaves faced the prospect of becoming wage laborers. Yet in order to retain as much autonomy as possible over their productive energies and those of their children on both a daily and seasonal basis, many husbands and wives chose sharecropping. This enabled mothers and wives to devote more of their time to domestic needs while still contributing to family income.

Black communities in the postwar South also sought to establish schools. The antebellum planter elite had denied education to blacks because they feared that literate slaves would organize uprisings. After the war the white elite worried that education programs would encourage both poor whites and blacks to leave the South in search of better social and economic opportunities. Economic leaders wanted to protect the competitive advantage afforded by the region's low-wage labor market.

The general resistance among the former slaveholding class to new education initiatives forced the freed slaves to rely on northern assistance or take their own initiative. A Mississippi Freedmen's Bureau agent noted in 1865 that when he told a gathering of some 3,000 former slaves that they "were to have the advantages of schools and education, their joy knew no bounds. They fairly jumped and shouted in gladness." Black churches and individuals helped raise the money and often built the schools and paid the teachers. Soldiers who had acquired some reading and writing skills often served as the first teachers, and the students included adults as well as children. A Florida teacher reported that a sixty-year-old former slave woman in her class was so excited by literacy that she "spells her lesson all the evening, then she dreams about it, and wakes up thinking about it."

BLACKS IN SOUTHERN POLITICS   The new role of African Americans in politics caused the most controversy, then and afterward. If largely illiterate and inexperienced in the rudiments of politics, they were little different from millions of whites enfranchised in the age of Jackson or immigrants herded to the polls by political bosses in New York and other cities after the war. Some freedmen frankly confessed their disadvantages. Beverly Nash, a black delegate in the South Carolina convention of 1868, told his colleagues: "I believe, my friends and fellow-citizens, we are not prepared for this suffrage. But we can learn.

Give a man tools and let him commence to use them, and in time he will learn a trade. So it is with voting."

Several hundred black delegates participated in the statewide political conventions. Most had been selected by local political meetings or by churches, fraternal societies, Union Leagues, and black army units from the North, although a few simply appointed themselves. "Some bring credentials," explained a North Carolina black leader, "others had as much as they could to bring themselves, having to escape from their homes stealthily at night" to avoid white assaults. The African-American delegates "ranged all colors and apparently all conditions," but free mulattoes from the cities played the most prominent roles. At Louisiana's Republican state convention, for instance, nineteen of the twenty black delegates had been born free.

By 1867, however, former slaves began to gain political influence and vote in large numbers, and this revealed emerging tensions within the black community. Some southern blacks resented the presence of

Black Suffrage. *The Fifteenth Amendment was passed in 1870 and guaranteed the right of citizens, including the right to vote, regardless of race, color or previous condition of servitude, on the federal level. But former slaves had been registering to vote and voting in large numbers in state elections since 1867, as shown here.*

northern brethren who moved south after the war, while others complained that few ex-slaves were represented in leadership positions. Northern blacks and the southern free black elite, most of whom were urban dwellers, tended to oppose efforts to confiscate and redistribute land to the rural freedmen, and many insisted that political equality did not mean social equality. As an Alabama black leader stressed, "We do not ask that the ignorant and degraded shall be put on a social equality with the refined and intelligent." In general, however, unity rather than dissension prevailed, and blacks focused on common concerns such as full equality under the law.

Brought suddenly into politics in times that tried the most skilled of statesmen, many African Americans served with distinction. Nonetheless, the derisive label "black Reconstruction" used by later critics exaggerates black political influence, which was limited mainly to voting,

A lithograph depicting five of the major black political figures of the Reconstruction period: Hiram Revels (top left) and Blanche K. Bruce (center) served in the U.S. Senate, Joseph H. Rainey (bottom left), John R. Lynch (bottom right), and James T. Rapier (top right) in the House of Representatives.

and overlooks the large numbers of white Republicans, especially in the mountain areas of the upper South. Only one of the new conventions, South Carolina's, had a black majority, 76 to 41. Louisiana's was evenly divided racially, and in only two other conventions were more than 20 percent of the members black: Florida's, with 40 percent, and Virginia's, with 24 percent. The Texas convention was only 10 percent black, and North Carolina's 11 percent—but that did not stop a white newspaper from calling it a body consisting of "baboons, monkeys, mules . . . and other jackasses."

In the new state governments, any African-American participation was a novelty. Although some 600 blacks—most of them former slaves—served as state legislators, no black man was ever elected governor. Only a few served as judges, although in Louisiana Pinckney B. S. Pinchback, a northern black and former Union soldier, won the office of lieutenant-governor and served as acting governor when the white governor was indicted for corruption. Several blacks were elected lieutenant-governors, state treasurers, or secretaries of state. There were two black senators in Congress, Hiram Revels and Blanche K. Bruce, both Mississippi natives who had been educated in the North, and fourteen black members of the House during Reconstruction. Among these were some of the ablest congressmen of the time. African Americans served in every state legislature, and in South Carolina they made up a majority in both houses for two years.

CARPETBAGGERS AND SCALAWAGS The top positions in southern state governments went for the most part to white Republicans, whom the opposition whites soon labeled "carpetbaggers" and "scalawags," depending on their place of birth. The northern opportunists who allegedly rushed South with all their belongings in carpetbags to grab the political spoils were more often than not Union veterans who had arrived as early as 1865 or 1866, drawn South by the hope of economic opportunity and by other attractions that many of them had seen in Union service. Many other so-called carpetbaggers were teachers, social workers, or preachers animated by a missionary impulse.

The "scalawags," or native white Republicans, were even more reviled and misrepresented. A jaundiced editor of a Nashville paper called them the "merest trash that could be collected in a civilized community, of no personal credit or social responsibility." Most "scalawags" had opposed secession, forming a Unionist majority in many mountain counties as far south as Georgia and Alabama, and especially in the hills of eastern Tennessee. Among the "scalawags" were several distinguished figures, including former Confederate general James A. Longstreet, who decided after Appomattox that the Old South must change its ways. He became a successful cotton broker in New Orleans, joined the Republican party, and supported the Radical Reconstruction program. Other "scalawags" were former Whigs who found the Republican party's economic program of industrial and commercial expansion in keeping with Henry Clay's earlier "American System."

THE RADICAL REPUBLICAN RECORD   The new state constitutions were objectionable to adherents of the old order primarily because of their provisions for black suffrage and civil rights. Otherwise the documents were in keeping with other state constitutions of the day, their provisions often drawn from the basic laws of northern states. Most remained in effect for some years after the end of Radical control, and later constitutions incorporated many of their features. Conspicuous among Radical innovations were such steps toward greater democracy as requiring universal manhood suffrage, reapportioning legislatures more nearly according to population, and making more state offices elective.

Given the hostile circumstances under which the Radical governments operated, their achievements are remarkable. For the first time in most of the South they established state school systems, however inadequate and ill-supported at first. The testimony is almost universal that African Americans eagerly sought education for themselves and their children. Some 600,000 black pupils were in southern schools by 1877. State governments under the Radicals also gave more attention than ever before to poor relief and to orphanages, asylums, and institutions for the deaf, dumb, and blind of both races. Public roads, bridges, and buildings were repaired or rebuilt. Blacks achieved new rights and opportunities that would never again be taken away, at least in principle: equality before the law and the rights to own property, carry on business, enter professions, attend schools, and learn to read and write.

Yet several of these Republican regimes also engaged in corrupt practices. Bids for contracts were accepted at absurd prices, and public officials took their cut. Public money and public credit were often voted to privately owned corporations, notably railroads, under conditions that invited influence peddling. But governmental subsidies—especially for transportation—were common before and after Reconstruction (and still are), and the extension of public aid had general support among all elements, including the Radicals and their enemies. Taxes and public debt rose in every state. Yet the figures of taxation and debt hardly constitute an unqualified indictment of Radical governments, since they then faced unusual and inflated costs for the physical reconstruction of public works in the South. Most states, moreover, had to float loans at outrageous discounts, sometimes at 50 to 75 percent of face value, because of uncertain conditions.

Nor, for that matter, were the breaches of public morality limited to the South or to Republicans. The Democratic Tweed Ring at the time was robbing New York City of more than $75 million, while the Republican "Gas Ring" in Philadelphia was also lining its pockets. Corruption was not invented by the Radical regimes, nor did it die with them. Louisiana's "carpetbag" governor recognized as much: "Why," he said, "down here everybody is demoralized. Corruption is the fashion." In three years Louisiana's printing bill ran to $1.5 million, about half of which went to a newspaper belonging to the young governor, who left office with a tidy nest egg and settled down to a long life as a planter. At about the same time, Mississippi's Democratic state treasurer embezzled over $315,000. During Republican rule in Mississippi, on the other hand, there was no evidence of major corruption.

WHITE TERROR   The case of Mississippi strongly suggests that whites were hostile to Republican regimes less because of their corruption than because of their inclusion of blacks. Most white southerners remained unreconstructed, so conditioned by slavery that they were unable to conceive of blacks as citizens or even free agents. In some places hostility to the new biracial regimes took on the form of white terror. In Grayson County, Texas, three whites murdered three freed slaves because they felt the need to "thin the niggers out and drive them to their holes."

The prototype of terrorist groups was the Ku Klux Klan (KKK), first organized in 1866 by some young men of Pulaski, Tennessee, as a social

This Thomas Nast cartoon chides the Ku Klux Klan and the White League for promoting conditions "worse than slavery" for southern blacks after the Civil War.

club with the costumes, secret ritual, and mumbo-jumbo common to fraternal groups. At first a group devoted to practical jokes, the founders soon turned to intimidation of blacks and white Republicans, and the KKK and imitators like Louisiana's Knights of the White Camellia spread rapidly across the South in answer to the Republican party's Union League. Klansmen rode about the countryside hiding under masks and robes, spreading horrendous rumors, issuing threats, harassing African Americans, and occasionally running amok wreaking violence and destruction.

Klansmen focused their terror on prominent Republicans, black and white. In Mississippi they killed a black Republican leader in front of his family. Three white "scalawag" Republicans were murdered in Georgia in 1870. That same year an armed mob of whites assaulted a Republican political rally in Alabama, killing four blacks and wounding fifty-four. In South Carolina the Klan was especially active. Virtually the entire white male population of York County joined the Klan, and they were responsible for eleven murders and hundreds of whippings. In 1871 some 500 masked men laid siege to the Union County jail and eventually lynched eight black prisoners. Although most Klansmen were poor farmers and tradesmen, middle-class whites—planters, merchants, bankers, lawyers, doctors, even ministers—also joined the group and participated in its brutalities.

Congress struck back with three Enforcement Acts (1870–1871) to protect black voters. The first of these measures levied penalties on persons who interfered with any citizen's right to vote. A second placed the election of congressmen under surveillance by federal election supervisors and marshals. The third (the Ku Klux Klan Act) outlawed the characteristic activities of the Klan—forming conspiracies, wearing disguises, resisting officers, and intimidating officials—and authorized the president to suspend habeas corpus where necessary to suppress "armed combinations." In 1871, the federal government singled out nine counties in upcountry South Carolina as an example, suspended habeas corpus, and pursued mass prosecutions that brought an abrupt halt to the Klan outrages. The program of federal enforcement broke the back of the Klan, whose outrages declined steadily as conservative southerners resorted to more subtle methods.

CONSERVATIVE RESURGENCE   The Klan's impact on politics varied from state to state. In the upper South it played only a modest role in facilitating a Democratic resurgence. But in the Deep South, Klan violence and intimidation had some effect. In Georgia, for instance, Republicans virtually quit campaigning and voting. In overwhelmingly black Yazoo County, Mississippi, vengeful whites used violence to reverse the political balance of power. In the 1873 elections the Republicans cast 2,449 votes and the Democrats 638; two years later the Democrats polled 4,049 votes, the Republicans 7. Throughout the South the activities of the Klan weakened black and Republican morale, and in the North they encouraged a growing weariness with the whole southern question. "The plain truth is," noted the *New York Herald,* "the North has got tired of the Negro."

The erosion of northern interest in civil rights resulted from more than weariness, however. Western expansion, Indian wars, economic opportunities, and political controversy over the tariff and the currency distracted attention from southern outrages. In addition, after a business panic that occurred in 1873 and the ensuing depression, desperate economic circumstances in the North and South created new racial tensions that helped undermine already inconsistent federal efforts to promote racial justice in the former Confederacy. Republican control in the South gradually loosened as "Conservative" parties—Democrats used that name to mollify former Whigs—mobilized the white vote.

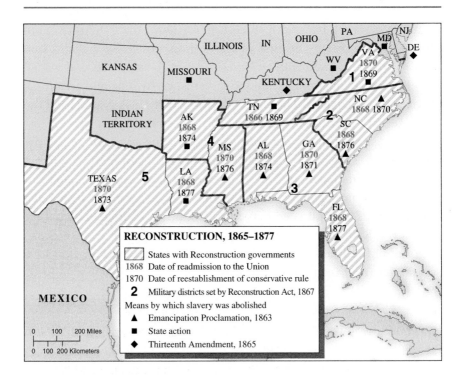

RECONSTRUCTION, 1865–1877

States with Reconstruction governments
1868 Date of readmission to the Union
1870 Date of reestablishment of conservative rule
2 Military districts set by Reconstruction Act, 1867
Means by which slavery was abolished
▲ Emancipation Proclamation, 1863
■ State action
◆ Thirteenth Amendment, 1865

Scalawags, and many carpetbaggers, drifted away from the Radical ranks under pressure from their white neighbors. Few of them had joined the Republicans out of concern for black rights in the first place. And where persuasion failed to work, Democrats were willing to use chicanery. As one enthusiastic Democrat boasted, "the white and black Republicans may outvote us, but we can outcount them."

Republican control collapsed in Virginia and Tennessee as early as 1869, in Georgia and North Carolina in 1870, although North Carolina had a Republican governor until 1876. Reconstruction lasted longest in the Deep South states with the largest black population, where whites abandoned Klan masks for barefaced intimidation in paramilitary groups such as the Mississippi Rifle Club and the South Carolina Red Shirts. By 1876 Radical regimes survived only in Louisiana, South Carolina, and Florida, and these all collapsed after the elections of that year. Later the last carpetbag governor of South Carolina explained that "the uneducated negro was too weak, no matter what his numbers, to cope with the whites."

THE GRANT YEARS

THE ELECTION OF 1868   Ulysses S. Grant, who presided over the collapse of Republican rule in the South, brought to the presidency little political experience. But in 1868 the rank-and-file voter could be expected to support "the Lion of Vicksburg" because of his record as a war leader. Both parties wooed him, but his falling-out with President Johnson pushed him toward the Republicans and built trust in him among the Radicals. They were, as Thad Stevens said, ready to "let him into the church." The Republican platform endorsed the Reconstruction policy of Congress, congratulating the country on the "assured success" of the program. One plank cautiously defended black suffrage as a necessity in the South, but a matter each northern state should settle for itself. Another urged payment of the national debt "in the utmost good faith to all creditors," which meant in gold. More important than the platform were the great expectations of a soldier-president and his slogan: "Let us have peace."

The Democrats took opposite positions on both Reconstruction and the debt. The Republican Congress, the platform charged, instead of restoring the Union had "so far as in its power, dissolved it, and subjected ten states, in the time of profound peace, to military despotism and Negro supremacy." As to the public debt, the party endorsed Representative George H. Pendleton's "Ohio idea" that, since most bonds had been bought with depreciated greenbacks, they should be paid off in greenbacks unless they specified payment in gold. With no conspicuously available candidate in sight, the convention turned to Horatio Seymour, war governor of New York and chairman of the convention. His friends had to hustle him out of the hall to prevent his withdrawal. The Democrats made a closer race of it than showed up in the electoral vote. Eight states, including New York and New Jersey, went for Seymour. While Grant swept the electoral college by 214 to 80, his popular majority was only 307,000 out of a total of over 5.7 million votes. More than 500,000 black voters accounted for Grant's margin of victory.

EARLY APPOINTMENTS   Grant had proven himself a great leader in the war, but in the White House he seemed blind to the political forces and influence peddlers around him. He was awestruck by men of

President Grant (seated at left), *with Mrs. Grant next to him, in a family portrait, 1870.*

wealth and unaccountably loyal to some who betrayed his trust. His conception of the presidency was "Whiggish." The chief executive carried out the laws; in the formulation of policy he passively followed the lead of Congress. This approach endeared him at first to party leaders, but it left him at last ineffective and left others disillusioned with his leadership.

At the outset Grant consulted nobody on his cabinet appointments. Some of his choices indulged personal whims; others simply displayed bad judgment. In some cases appointees learned of their nomination from the newspapers. As time went by Grant betrayed a fatal gift for losing men of talent and integrity from his cabinet. Secretary of State Hamilton Fish of New York turned out to be a happy exception; he guided foreign policy throughout the Grant presidency.

THE GOVERNMENT DEBT   Financial issues dominated the political agenda during Grant's presidency. After the war, the Treasury had assumed that the $432 million worth of greenbacks issued during the conflict would be retired from circulation and that the nation would revert to a "hard-money" currency—gold coins. Many agrarian and debtor groups resisted this contraction of the money supply, believing that it would mean lower prices for their crops and would make it harder for them to pay long-term debts. They were joined by a large number of Radicals who thought a combination of high tariffs and inflation would generate more rapid economic growth. In 1868 congressional supporters of such a "soft-money" policy halted the retirement of greenbacks, leaving $356 million outstanding. There matters stood when Grant took office.

The "sound" or hard-money advocates, mostly bankers and merchants, claimed that Grant's election was a mandate to save the country from the Democrats' "Ohio idea" of using greenbacks to repay government bonds. Quite influential in Republican circles, the "sound-money" advocates also had the benefit of a deeply ingrained popular assumption that hard money was morally preferable to paper currency. Grant agreed, and in his inaugural address he endorsed payment of the national debt in gold as a point of national honor. On March 18, 1869, the Public Credit Act endorsing that principle became the first act of Congress that he signed. Under the Refunding Act of 1870, the Treasury was able to replace 6 percent Civil War bonds with a new issue promising 4 to 5 percent in gold.

SCANDALS   The complexities of the "money question" exasperated Grant, but that was the least of his worries, for his administration soon fell into a cesspool of scandal. The first hint of scandal touched Grant in the summer of 1869, when the crafty Jay Gould and the flamboyant Jim Fisk connived with the president's brother-in-law to corner the gold market. Gould concocted an argument that the government should refrain from selling gold on the market because the resulting rise in gold prices would raise temporarily depressed farm prices. Grant apparently smelled a rat from the start, but he was seen in public with the speculators. As the rumor spread on Wall Street that the president had bought the argument, gold rose from $132 to $163 an ounce. When Grant finally persuaded his brother-in-law to pull out of the deal, Gould began quietly selling out. Finally, on "Black Friday," September 24, 1869, Grant ordered the Treasury to sell a large quantity of gold, and the bubble burst. Fisk got out by repudiating his agreements and hiring thugs to intimidate his creditors. "Nothing is lost save honor," he said.

The People's Handwriting on the Wall. *An 1872 engraving comments on the corruption engulfing Grant.*

The plot to corner the gold market was only the first of several scandals that rocked the Grant administration. During the campaign of 1872 the public first learned about the financial buccaneering of the Crédit Mobilier, a construction company that had milked the Union Pacific Railroad for exorbitant fees in order to line the pockets of insiders who controlled both firms. Rank-and-file Union Pacific shareholders were left holding the bag. One congressman had distributed Crédit Mobilier shares at bargain rates where, he said, "it will produce much good to us." This chicanery had transpired before Grant's election in 1868, but it now touched a number of prominent Republicans. The beneficiaries had included Speaker of the House Schuyler Colfax, later vice-president, and Representative James A. Garfield, later president. Of thirteen members of Congress involved, only two were censured by a Congress which, before it adjourned in 1873, voted itself a pay raise from $5,000 to $7,500—retroactive, it decided, for two years. A public uproar forced repeal, leaving only the raises voted the president (from $25,000 to $50,000) and Supreme Court justices.

Even more odious disclosures soon followed, and some involved the president's cabinet. The secretary of war, it turned out, had accepted bribes from merchants who traded with Indians at army posts in the West. He was impeached, but he resigned in time to elude a Senate trial. Post-office contracts, it was revealed, went to carriers who offered the highest kickbacks. The secretary of the treasury had awarded a political friend a commission of 50 percent for the collection of overdue taxes. In St. Louis a "Whiskey Ring" bribed tax collectors to bilk the government of millions in revenue. Grant's private secretary was enmeshed in that scheme, taking large sums of money and other valuables in return for inside information. There is no evidence that Grant himself was ever involved in, or that he personally profited from, any of the fraud, but his poor choice of associates earned him the public censure that was heaped upon his head.

REFORM AND THE ELECTION OF 1872   Long before Grant's first term ended, a reaction against the Reconstruction measures and against incompetence and corruption in the administration had incited mutiny within the Republican ranks. The Liberal Republicans favored free trade, gold to redeem greenbacks, a stable currency, restoring the rights of former Confederates, and civil service reform. Open revolt broke out first in Missouri where Carl Schurz, a German immigrant and war hero, led a group of Liberal Republicans that elected a governor

Horace Greeley, editor of the New York Tribune *and Liberal Republican candidate for president in 1872.*

with Democratic help in 1870 and sent Schurz to the Senate. In 1872 the Liberal Republicans held a national convention at Cincinnati that produced a compromise platform condemning the party's southern policy and favoring civil service reform, but remained silent on the protective tariff. The delegates embraced an anomalous presidential candidate: Horace Greeley, editor of the *New York Tribune,* a longtime champion of just about every reform of his time. His image as a visionary eccentric was complemented by his record of hostility to Democrats, whose support the Liberals needed. The Democrats nevertheless swallowed the pill and gave their nomination to Greeley as the only hope of beating Grant.

The result was a foregone conclusion. Republican regulars duly endorsed Radical Reconstruction and the protective tariff. Grant still had seven carpetbag states in his pocket, generous contributions from business and banking interests, and the stalwart support of the Radicals. Above all, he still evoked the imperishable glory of Appomattox. Greeley, despite an exhausting tour of the country—still unusual for a presidential candidate—carried only six southern and border states and none in the North. Grant won by 3,597,132 votes to Greeley's 2,834,125 votes, and by an electoral college vote of 286 to 66.

PANIC AND REDEMPTION Economic distress followed close upon the public scandals besetting the Grant administration. Contraction of the money supply brought about by the withdrawal of greenbacks and expansion of the railroads into sparsely settled areas had made investors cautious and helped precipitate a crisis. During 1873 the market for railroad bonds turned sour as some twenty-five railroads defaulted on their interest payments. The investment-banking firm of Jay Cooke and Company, unable to sell the bonds of the Northern Pacific Railroad, financed them with short-term deposits in hope that a European market would develop. But in 1873 the opposite happened when a financial panic in Vienna forced many financiers to unload American stocks and bonds. Caught short, Cooke and Company went bankrupt on September 18, 1873. The ensuing stampede of investors to exchange securities for cash forced the stock market to close for ten days. The Panic of 1873 set off a depression that lasted for six years, the longest and most severe that Americans had yet suffered, marked by widespread bankruptcies, unemployment, and a drastic slowdown in railroad building.

Hard times and scandals hurt Republicans in the midterm elections of 1874. The Democrats won control of the House of Representatives and gained seats in the Senate. The new Democratic House immediately launched inquiries into the scandals and unearthed further evidence of corruption in high places. The panic meanwhile focused attention once more on greenback currency.

Since greenbacks were valued less than gold, they had become the chief circulating medium. Most people spent greenbacks first and held their gold or used it to settle foreign accounts, which drained much gold out of the country. The postwar reduction of greenbacks in circulation from $432 million to $356 million had made for tight money. To relieve deflation and stimulate business, therefore, the Treasury reissued $26 million in greenbacks that had been previously withdrawn.

For a time the advocates of paper money were riding high. But in 1874 Grant vetoed a bill to issue more greenbacks. Then, in his annual message he called for the gradual resumption of specie payments—that is, the redemption of greenbacks in gold. This would make greenbacks "good as gold" and raise their value to a par with the gold dollar. Congress obliged by passing the Resumption Act of 1875. The payment in gold to people who turned in their paper money began on January 1, 1879, after the Treasury had built a gold reserve for that purpose and reduced the value of greenbacks in circulation. This act infuriated those promoting an inflationary monetary policy and provoked the formation of the National Greenback party, which elected fourteen congressmen in 1878. The much-debated "money question" was destined to remain one of the most divisive issues in American politics.

THE COMPROMISE OF 1877 Grant, despite the controversies swirling around him, was eager to run again in 1876, but the recent scandals discouraged any challenge to the two-term tradition. James G. Blaine of Maine, former Speaker of the House, emerged as the Republican front-runner, but he too bore the taint of scandal. Letters in the possession of James Mulligan of Boston linked Blaine to some dubious railroad dealings, and these "Mulligan letters" found their way into print.

A Republican campaign piece from the 1876 election: "Yankee Doodle, that's the talk—/ We've found an honest dealer;/ And o'er the course we ride or walk,/ We'll go for Hayes and Wheeler."

The Republican convention therefore eliminated Blaine and several other hopefuls in favor of Ohio's favorite son, Rutherford B. Hayes. Three times elected governor of Ohio, most recently as an advocate of hard money, Hayes had also made a name as a civil service reformer. But his chief virtue was that he offended neither Radicals nor reformers. As Henry Adams put it, he was "a third rate nonentity, whose only recommendation is that he is obnoxious to no one."

The Democratic convention in St. Louis was abnormally harmonious from the start. The nomination went on the second ballot to Samuel J. Tilden, millionaire corporation lawyer and reform governor of New York who had directed a campaign to overthrow first the notorious Tweed Ring controlling New York City politics and the Canal Ring in Albany, which had bilked the state of millions.

The campaign generated no burning issues. Both candidates favored the trend toward conservative rule in the South. During one of the most corrupt elections ever, both candidates also favored civil service reform. In the absence of strong differences, Democrats waved the Republicans' dirty linen. In response, Republicans waved the bloody shirt, which is to say that they engaged in verbal assaults on former Confederates and the spirit of rebellion, linking the Democratic party with secession and with the outrages committed against black and white Republicans in the South. As one Republican speaker insisted, "Every man that tried to destroy this nation was a Democrat. . . . The man that assassinated Abraham Lincoln was a Democrat. . . . Soldiers, every scar you have on your heroic bodies was given you by a Democrat!" The phrase "waving the bloody shirt" originated at the impeachment trial of President Johnson when Benjamin F. Butler, speaking for the prosecution, displayed the bloody shirt a Mississippi carpetbagger had been wearing when hauled out of bed and beaten by Klansmen.

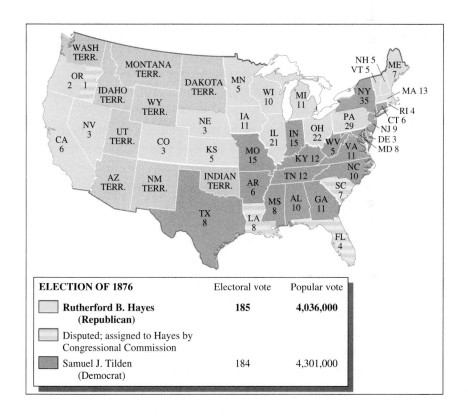

ELECTION OF 1876	Electoral vote	Popular vote
Rutherford B. Hayes (Republican)	185	4,036,000
Disputed; assigned to Hayes by Congressional Commission		
Samuel J. Tilden (Democrat)	184	4,301,000

Early election returns pointed to a Tilden victory. He enjoyed a 300,000 edge in the popular vote and had 184 electoral votes, just one short of a majority. Hayes had 165 electoral votes, but the Republicans also claimed nineteen doubtful votes from Florida, Louisiana, and South Carolina. The Democrats laid a counterclaim to one electoral vote from Oregon. But the Republicans had clearly carried Oregon. In the South the outcome was less certain, and given the fraud and intimidation perpetrated on both sides, nobody will ever know what might have happened if, to use a slogan of the day, "a free ballot and a fair count" had prevailed. As good a guess as any may be, as one writer suggested, that the Democrats stole the election first and the Republicans stole it back.

In all three of the disputed southern states, rival canvassing boards sent in different returns. In Florida, Republicans conceded the state election, but in Louisiana and South Carolina rival state governments also appeared. The Constitution offered no guidance in this unprecedented situation. Even if Congress were empowered to sort things out, the Democratic House and the Republican Senate proved unable to reach an agreement.

Finally, on January 29, 1877, the two houses decided to set up a special Electoral Commission that would investigate and report its findings. It had fifteen members, five each from the House, the Senate, and the Supreme Court. Members were so chosen as to have seven from each major party, with Justice David Davis of Illinois as the swing man. Davis, though appointed to the Court by Lincoln, was no party regular and was in fact thought to be leaning toward the Democrats. Thus, the panel appeared to be stacked in favor of Tilden.

But as it turned out, the panel got restacked the other way. Shortsighted Democrats in the Illinois legislature teamed up with minority Greenbackers to name Davis their senator. Davis accepted, no doubt with a sense of relief. From the remaining justices, all Republicans, the panel chose Joseph P. Bradley to fill the vacancy. The decision on each state went by a vote of 8 to 7, along party lines, in favor of Hayes. After much bluster and threat of filibuster by Democrats, the House voted on March 2 to accept the report and declare Hayes elected by an electoral vote of 185 to 184.

Critical to this outcome was the defection of southern Democrats who, seeing the way the wind was blowing with the composition of the

Electoral Commission, had made several informal agreements with the Republicans. On February 26, 1877, prominent Ohio Republicans (including James A. Garfield) and powerful southern Democrats struck a bargain at the Wormley House, a Washington hotel. The Republicans promised that, if elected, Hayes would withdraw the last federal troops from Louisiana and South Carolina, letting the Republican governments there collapse. In return, the Democrats promised to withdraw their opposition to Hayes, to accept in good faith the Reconstruction amendments, and to refrain from partisan reprisals against Republicans in the South.

Southern Democrats could now justify deserting Tilden because this so-called Compromise of 1877 brought a final "redemption" from the "Radicals" and a return to "home rule," which actually meant rule by white Democrats. Other, more informal promises, less noticed by the public, bolstered the Wormley House agreement. Hayes's friends pledged more support for Mississippi levees and other internal improvements, including a federal subsidy for a transcontinental railroad along a southern route. Southerners extracted a further promise that Hayes would name a white southerner as postmaster-general, the cabinet position with the most patronage jobs at hand. In return, southerners would let Republicans make Garfield Speaker of the new House.

THE END OF RECONSTRUCTION In 1877 Hayes withdrew federal troops from the state houses in Louisiana and South Carolina, and the Republican governments there collapsed—along with much of Hayes's claim to legitimacy. Hayes chose a Tennessean and former Confederate as postmaster-general. But after southern Democrats failed to permit the choice of Garfield as Speaker, Hayes expressed doubt about any further subsidy for railroad building, and none was voted. Most of the other promises were either renounced or forgotten.

As to southern promises regarding the civil rights of blacks, only a few Democratic leaders, such as the new governors of South Carolina and Louisiana, remembered them for long. Over the next three decades those rights crumbled under the pressure of white rule in the South and the force of Supreme Court decisions narrowing the application of the Reconstruction amendments. Radical Reconstruction never offered more than an uncertain commitment to equality before the law. Yet it left an enduring legacy, the Thirteenth, Fourteenth, and Fifteenth Amendments—not dead but dormant, waiting to be awakened.

MAKING CONNECTIONS

- The political, economic, and racial policies of the conservatives who overthrew the Republican governments in the southern states are described in Chapter 19.

- Several of the political scandals mentioned in this chapter were related to the railroads, a topic discussed in greater detail in Chapter 20.

- This chapter ends with the election of Rutherford B. Hayes; for a discussion of Hayes's administration, see Chapter 22.

FURTHER READING

Reconstruction has long been "a dark and bloody ground" of conflicting interpretations. The most comprehensive treatment is Eric Foner's *Reconstruction: America's Unfinished Revolution, 1863–1877* (1988). More specialized works give closer scrutiny to the aims of the principal political figures. For a study of Andrew Johnson, see Hans L. Trefousse's *Andrew Johnson: A Biography* (1989). Why Johnson was impeached is detailed in Hans L. Trefousse's *Impeachment of a President: Andrew Johnson, the Blacks, and Reconstruction* (1975).

Scholars have been fairly sympathetic to the aims and motives of the Radical Republicans. See, for instance, Herman Belz's *Reconstructing the Union* (1969) and Richard Nelson Current's *Those Terrible Carpetbaggers: A Reinterpretation* (1988). The ideology of these Radicals is explored in Michael Les Benedict's *A Compromise of Principle: Congressional Republicans and Reconstruction, 1863–1869* (1974).

The intransigence of southern white attitudes is examined in Michael Perman's *Reunion without Compromise* (1973), Dan T. Carter's *When the War Was Over: The Failure of Self-Reconstruction in the South, 1865–1867* (1985), and Richard Zuczek's *State of Rebellion: Reconstruction in South Carolina* (1996). Allen W. Trelease's *White Terror* (1971) covers the various organizations that practiced vigilante tactics, chiefly the Ku Klux Klan. The difficulties former laborers had in adjusting to the new labor system are documented in James L. Roark's *Masters without Slaves* (1977). Books on southern politics during Reconstruction include Michael Perman's *The Road to Redemption* (1984), Terry L. Seip's *The South Returns to Congress* (1983), and Mark W. Summer's *Railroads, Reconstruction, and the Gospel of Prosperity* (1984).

Numerous works have appeared on the freed blacks' experience in the South. Start with Leon F. Litwack's *Been in the Storm So Long* (1979), which covers the transition from slavery to freedom. Willie Lee Rose's *Rehearsal for Reconstruction* (1964) examines Union efforts to define the social role of former slaves during wartime emancipation. Joel Williamson's *After Slavery* (1965) argues that South Carolina blacks took an active role in pursuing their political and economic rights. For a work concerning the political activity of freed slaves in other areas of the South, see Howard N. Rabinowitz's *Southern Black Leaders of the Reconstruction Era* (1982). The role of the Freedmen's Bureau is explored in William S. McFeely's *Yankee Stepfather: General O.O. Howard and the Freedmen* (1968). The situation of freed slave women, which was often quite different than that of freed slave men, is discussed in Jacqueline Jones's *Labor of Love, Labor of Sorrow: Black Women, Work, and the Family from Slavery to Present* (1985).

The land confiscation issue is discussed in Eric Foner's *Politics and Ideology in the Age of the Civil War* (1980); Beth Bethel's *Promiseland* (1981), on a South Carolina black community; and Janet S. Hermann's *The Pursuit of a Dream* (1981), on the Davis Bend experiment in Mississippi.

The politics of corruption outside the South is depicted in William S. McFeely's *Grant: A Biography* (1981). The political maneuvers of the election of 1876 and the resultant crisis and compromise are explained in C. Vann Woodward's *Reunion and Reaction* (1951) and William Gillette's *Retreat from Reconstruction, 1869–1879* (1979).

PART FIVE

GROWING
PAINS

The northern victory in 1865 restored the Union and in the process helped to accelerate America's transformation into a modern nation-state. A distinctly national consciousness began to displace the sectional emphases of the antebellum era. During and after the Civil War, the Republican-led Congress pushed through legislation to foster industrial and commercial development and western expansion. In the process, the United States abandoned the Jeffersonian dream of a decentralized agrarian republic and began to forge a dynamic new industrial outlook generated by an increasingly national market.

After 1865, many Americans turned their attention to the unfinished business of settling a continent and completing an urban-industrial revolution begun before the war. Huge new national corporations based upon mass production and mass marketing began to dominate the economic order. As the prominent sociologist William Graham Sumner remarked, the process of industrial development "controls us all because we are all in it. It creates the conditions of our own existence, sets the limits of our social activity, and regulates the bonds of our social relations."

The industrial revolution was not only an urban phenomenon; it transformed rural life as well. Those who got in the way of the new emphasis on large-scale, highly mechanized commercial agriculture and ranching were brusquely pushed aside. Farm folk, as one New Englander stressed, "must understand farming as a business; if they do not it will go hard with them." The friction between new market forces and traditional folkways generated political revolts and social unrest during the last quarter of the nineteenth century. Fault lines appeared throughout the social order, and they unleashed tremors that exerted what one writer called "a seismic shock, a cyclonic violence" upon the body politic.

The clash between tradition and modernity came to a climax during the decade of the 1890s, one of the most strife-ridden in American history. A deep depression, agrarian unrest, and labor violence provoked fears of a class war. This turbulent situation transformed the presidential election campaign of 1896 into a clash between two rival visions of America's future. The Republican candidate, William McKinley, campaigned on behalf of modern urban-industrial values. By contrast, William Jennings Bryan, the nominee of both the Democratic and Populist parties, was an eloquent defender of America's rural past. McKinley's victory proved to be a watershed in American political and social history. By 1900 the United States would emerge as one of the world's greatest industrial powers, and it would thereafter assume a new leadership role in world affairs.

19 ∞ NEW FRONTIERS:
SOUTH AND WEST

The West and the South of the postwar period provided enticing opportunities for the distinctively American pioneering and entrepreneurial spirit to flourish. Before 1860, most people had viewed the 430 million acres between the Mississippi River and California as a barren landscape unfit for human habitation or cultivation, an uninviting land suitable only for Indians and animals. Half of the state of Texas, for instance, was still not settled at the end of the Civil War. After 1865, however, the federal government encouraged western settlement and economic exploitation. The construction of transcontinental railroads, the military conquest of the Indians, and a liberal land distribution policy combined to help lure thousands of pioneers and expectant capitalists westward. Charles Goodnight, a Texas cattleman, recalled that "we were adventurers in a great land as fresh and full of the zest of darers."

Although the first great wave of railroad building occurred in the 1850s, the most spectacular growth took place during the quarter century after the Civil War. From about 35,000 miles of track in 1865, the network grew to nearly 200,000 miles by 1897. The transcontinental rail lines led the way, and they helped populate the plains and the Far West. During the century after the Civil War, fourteen new states were created out of America's western territories.

In the postwar South, rail lines were rebuilt and supplemented with new branch lines. The defeated Confederacy, although not a frontier in the literal sense of the term, offered capitalists a fertile new ground for investment and industrial development. Proponents of a "New South" after 1865 argued that the region must abandon its single-minded preoccupation with agriculture and pursue industrial and commercial development. As a result, the South as well as the West experienced dramatic social and economic changes during the last third of the nineteenth century. By 1900, these new "frontiers" had been transformed in ways that few could have predicted.

THE NEW SOUTH

A FRESH VISION   Amid the pains of defeat and the ruins of war many southerners looked back wistfully to the plantation life that had dominated their region before the firing on Fort Sumter. A few prominent leaders, however, insisted that the postwar South must liberate itself from such nostalgia and create a modern society of small farms, thriving industries, and bustling cities. The major prophet of a New South emerged in an improbable setting—at New York's most elegant restaurant, Delmonico's—where on December 21, 1886, the New England Society of New York held its annual dinner. The main speaker was Henry W. Grady, thirty-six-year-old editor of the *Atlanta Constitution*. Grady's topic was "The New South," and his eloquent words became the most celebrated statement of what came to be called the New South Creed.

In plain yet almost poetic language, Grady set forth the vision that inspired a generation of approving southerners: "The Old South rested everything on slavery and agriculture, unconscious that these could neither give nor maintain healthy growth. The New South presents a perfect democracy, the oligarchs leading in the popular movement—a social system compact and closely knitted, less splendid on the surface, but stronger at the core—a hundred farms for every plantation, fifty homes for every palace—and a diversified industry that meets the complex need of this complex age."

Many prophets had gone before Grady, and still others stood with him as major spokesmen for the New South Creed. In the aftermath of the Civil War, these men preached with evangelical fervor the gospel of industrial development. The Confederacy, they reasoned, had lost the war because it had relied too much on King Cotton. In the future the South must follow the North's example and industrialize. From that central belief flowed certain corollaries: that a more diversified and efficient agriculture would be a foundation for economic growth, that more widespread education, especially vocational training, would promote material success, and that sectional peace and racial harmony would provide a stable environment for economic growth.

ECONOMIC GROWTH   The chief fruit of the New South ideal was an expansion of the area's textile production that began in the 1880s and overtook its older New England competitors by the 1920s. In the New South, as in New England and Old England, cotton textiles were the advance guard of industrial revolution. Already in the 1870s new cotton mills dotted the landscape of the Carolina Piedmont. From 1880 to 1900 the number of cotton mills in the South grew from 161 to 400, the number of mill workers (among whom women and children outnumbered the men) increased fivefold, and the consumption of cotton went up eightfold, from 182,000 bales to 1,479,000. Initially this development resulted mainly from southern capital and southern labor, though later the decline of the textile industry in New England contributed labor and capital to the South.

Tobacco growth also increased significantly, entering a new era with the development of two new varieties of the weed: burley, which first appeared in southern Ohio, and bright leaf, which was grown on otherwise infertile soils and cured by a charcoal process discovered by a slave in 1839. Knowledge of the bright-leaf type remained chiefly local until, in what seemed a misfortune, Union soldiers swarmed over central North Carolina in 1865.

A southern cotton press at night, 1883.

One victim of their looting was John Ruffin Green, whose bright-leaf tobacco factory was ransacked by soldiers loitering around Durham Station. Within a few weeks orders began to pour into Green's factory for the Best Flavored Spanish Smoking Tobacco "that did not bite." With this revival, Green adopted as his trademark a bull's head similar to that on Colman's mustard, made in Durham, England. It did not take long for Green and his successors to make the image of Bull Durham ubiquitous, so much so that years later Mark Twain, notorious for embellishing a good story, claimed that when he visited Egypt he never saw the pyramids because they were obscured by Bull Durham signs.

Even more important in the rise of tobacco and the city of Durham was the Duke family, who inhabited a nearby farm. At the end of the Civil War, the story goes, old Washington Duke had only fifty cents obtained from a Yankee soldier for a souvenir Confederate five-dollar bill. He took a barnful of tobacco and, with the help of his three sons, beat it out with hickory sticks, stuffed it in bags, hitched up two mules to his wagon, and set out across the state, selling tobacco as he went. By 1872 the Dukes had a factory producing 125,000 pounds of leaf annually, and Washington Duke prepared to settle down and enjoy success.

His son Buck (James Buchanan Duke), however, had the same entrepreneurial drive that animated the Carnegies and Rockefellers of that day. Buck Duke recognized early that the tobacco industry was "half smoke and half ballyhoo," and he poured large sums into advertising schemes. Duke also undersold competitors in their own markets and cornered the supply of ingredients. Eventually his competitors agreed to join forces, and in 1890 Duke brought most of them into the American Tobacco Company, which controlled nine-tenths of the nation's cigarette production and, by 1904, about three-fourths of all tobacco production. In 1911 the Supreme Court ruled that the company was in violation of the Sherman Anti-Trust Act and ordered it broken up, but by then Duke had found new worlds to conquer in hydroelectric power and aluminum.

Other natural resources helped revitalize the area along the Appalachian Mountain chain from West Virginia to Alabama. Coal production in the South (including West Virginia) grew from 5 million tons in 1875 to 49 million tons by 1900. At the southern end of the mountains, Birmingham, Alabama, sprang up during the 1870s in the shadow of Red Mountain, so named for its iron ore, and boosters soon tagged the city the "Pittsburgh of the South." Birmingham's proximity to coal, iron, and limestone gave it a strong advantage over Chattanooga, which had a meteoric career as an iron center after the war.

Rapid economic growth spawned a need for housing, and after 1870 lumbering became a thriving industry in the South. Lumber camps sprouted across the mountains and flatlands. By the turn of the century, their product, mainly southern pine, had outdistanced textiles in value. Tree cutting seemed to know no bounds, despite the resulting ecological devastation. In time the industry would be saved only by the warm climate, which fostered quick renewal, and the rise of scientific forestry, which had its beginnings on George Vanderbilt's Biltmore estate near Asheville, North Carolina. Here the nation's first school of forestry opened in 1898.

The South still had far to go to achieve the "diversified industry" that Grady envisioned in the mid-1880s, but a profusion of other products poured from southern plants: phosphate fertilizers from coastal South Carolina and Florida; oysters, vegetables, and fruits from widespread canneries; ships, including battleships, from the Newport News Shipbuilding and Drydock Company; leather products; wagons and buggies;

liquors and beverages; paper in small quantities; and clay, glass, and stone products.

At the turn of the century two great forces that would impel an even greater industrial revolution were already on the horizon: petroleum in the Southwest and hydroelectric power in the Southeast. The Corsicana oil field in Texas had been opened in 1895, and in 1901 the Spindletop gusher would bring a great bonanza. Local power plants dotted the map by the 1890s. Richmond, Virginia, boasted the nation's first electric streetcar system in 1888, and Columbia, South Carolina, opened the first electrically powered cotton mill in 1894. The greatest advance would begin in 1905 when Buck Duke's Southern Power Company set out to electrify entire river valleys in the Carolinas.

AGRICULTURE, OLD AND NEW   At the turn of the century, however, most of the South remained undeveloped, at least by northeastern standards. Despite the optimistic rhetoric of New South spokesmen, the typical southerner was less apt to be tending a loom or forge than, as the saying went, facing the eastern end of a westbound mule. King Cotton survived the Civil War and expanded into new acreage even as its export markets leveled off. The old tobacco belts of Virginia and Kentucky now reached across North Carolina and touched South Carolina. Louisiana cane sugar, probably the most war-devastated of all crops, flourished again by the 1890s.

In 1885 Seaman A. Knapp, an agriculturist from New York by way of Iowa, moved to Louisiana and developed a new rice belt on behalf of an English land company, using machinery imported from the wheatfields. In the process Knapp invented the demonstration method of agricultural education, which showed farmers the most productive practices on selected plots of land with the aim of teaching by example. Knapp later used the demonstration method to fight the boll weevil in Texas. His work led to the national system of farm and home demonstration agents.

In the old rice belt of coastal South Carolina and elsewhere, vegetable and truck farming flourished with the advent of the railroads and refrigerator cars. But the majority of southern farmers were not flourishing. A prolonged deflation in crop prices affected the entire Western world during the last third of the nineteenth century. Sagging prices made it more difficult than ever to own land. Sharecropping and tenancy grew increasingly prevalent. By 1890 most southern farms were

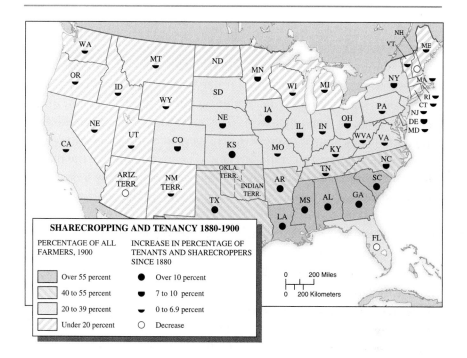

SHARECROPPING AND TENANCY 1880-1900

PERCENTAGE OF ALL FARMERS, 1900

- Over 55 percent
- 40 to 55 percent
- 20 to 39 percent
- Under 20 percent

INCREASE IN PERCENTAGE OF TENANTS AND SHARECROPPERS SINCE 1880

- Over 10 percent
- 7 to 10 percent
- 0 to 6.9 percent
- Decrease

0   200 Miles

0   200 Kilometers

worked by people who did not own the land. Tenancy rates in the Deep South belied the rosy rhetoric of New South prophets: South Carolina, 61 percent; Georgia, 60 percent; Alabama, 58 percent; Mississippi, 62 percent; and Louisiana, 58 percent.

Sharecropping and tenancy seldom produced the self-sufficiency that advocates envisioned. The sharecropper, who had nothing to offer the landowner but his labor, tilled the land in return for supplies and a share of the crop, generally about half. Tenant farmers, hardly better off, might have their own mule, plow, and line of credit with the country store, and therefore might claim a larger share, commonly three-fourths of the cash crop and two-thirds of the subsistence crop, which was mainly corn. There were, moreover, infinite variations to sharecropping that ranged from cash rental at best to outright peonage at worst. The system was generally inefficient, for the tenant lacked incentive to care for the land, and the owner had little chance to supervise the work. In addition, the system bred a morbid suspicion on both sides. The folklore of the rural South overflowed with stories of tenants who remained stubbornly shiftless and landlords who kept books with crooked pencils.

The crop lien system was equally flawed. At best, it supplied credit where cash was scarce. It worked this way: country merchants furnished supplies to small farmers in return for liens (or mortgages) on their crops. To a few tenants and farmers who seized the chance, such credit offered a way out of dependency, but to most it offered only a hopeless cycle of perennial debt. The merchant, who assumed great risks, generally charged interest that ranged, according to one publication, "from 24 percent to grand larceny." The merchant, like the planter (often the same man), required his farmer clients to grow a cash crop that could be readily sold at harvest time. So for all the wind and ink expended by promoters of a "New South" on preachments of diversification, the routines of tenancy and sharecropping geared the marketing, supply, and credit systems to a staple crop, usually cotton. The stagnation of rural life thus held millions, white and black, in bondage to privation and ignorance.

THE BOURBON REDEEMERS   In post–Civil War politics, despite the South's formal democracy, habits of deference and elitism still prevailed. "Every community," one Union officer noted in postwar South Carolina, "had its great man, or its little great man, around whom his fellow citizens gather when they want information, and to whose monologues they listen with a respect akin to humility." After Reconstruction, southern politics was dominated by small groups of such men, collectively known as Redeemers or Bourbons. The supporters of these postwar leaders referred to them as Redeemers because they supposedly "redeemed," or saved, the South from Yankee domination as well as the straitjacket of a purely rural economy. The Redeemers included a rising class of entrepreneurs who were eager to promote a more diversified economy based on industrial development and railroad expansion.

The opponents of the "Redeemers" labeled them "Bourbons" in an effort to depict them not as progressives but as reactionaries. Like the French royal family which, Napoleon said, forgot nothing and learned nothing in the ordeal of revolution, Bourbons of the postwar South were said to have forgotten nothing and learned nothing in the ordeal of the Civil War. Their Republican, Independent, and Populist adversaries fixed the label so firmly in the vocabulary of the times that Bourbon came to signify the leaders of the Democratic party, whether they were real throwbacks or, more commonly, champions of an industrial New

The Effects of Radical and Bourbon Rule in the South. *This 1880 cartoon shows the South staggering under the oppressive weight of military Reconstruction* (left) *and flourishing under the "Let 'Em Alone Policy" of Hayes and the Bourbons* (right).

South who, if they had forgotten nothing, had at least learned something. They may have worshipped at the shrine of the old order, but they embraced a new order of economic development.

These Bourbons of the New South perfected a political alliance with eastern conservatives and an economic alliance with eastern capitalists. They generally pursued a government policy of laissez-faire, except for the tax exemptions and other favors they offered to business. The Bourbons focused on cutting back the size and scope of government, including the school systems started during Reconstruction. In 1871 the southern Atlantic states were spending $10.27 per pupil; by 1880 the figure was down to $6.00, and in 1890 it stood at $7.63. Illiteracy rates in the South at the time ran at about 12 percent of the native white population and 50 percent of the black population.

Private philanthropy, however, did help to keep southern schools afloat. In 1867 George Peabody, a London banker born in Massachusetts, established the Peabody Fund for Education, which was to spend some $3.6 million on public schools by 1914. Aid from the Peabody Fund was supplemented by the $1 million in the John F. Slater Fund, established in 1882 by a donor in Connecticut and earmarked for black schools. J. L. M. Curry, onetime soldier, preacher, teacher, and politician, became the general agent of both the Peabody and the Slater Funds. Curry pursued an extensive program of speaking and building support for education. He set up teachers' associations and started some of the first summer schools for teachers, and in general tried to foster exemplary schools.

The urge to economize created in the penal system one of the darkest blots on the Bourbon record: convict leasing. Necessity gave rise to the practice immediately after the Civil War. The wartime destruction of prisons and the poverty of state treasuries combined with the demand for cheap labor on the railroads, in the mines, and in lumber and turpentine camps to make the leasing of convict labor a way for southern states to avoid expenses and generate revenues. The burden of detaining criminals grew after the war because freed slaves, who had been subject to the discipline of masters, were now subject to the criminal law. Convict leasing, in the absence of state supervision, allowed inefficiency, neglect, and disregard for human life to proliferate. White political and economic leaders often used a racial argument to rationalize the leasing of convicts, most of whom were black. An "inferior" and "shiftless" race, they claimed, required the regimen of such coercion to elevate it above its idle and undisciplined ways. In only one southern state, Texas, did blacks not constitute a majority either of the total prisoner or leased convict population.

The Bourbons scaled down not only government expenditures but also the public debt, and by a simple means—they repudiated a vast amount of debt in all the former Confederate states except Florida and Mississippi. The corruption and extravagance of Radical rule were commonly advanced as justification for the process, but repudiation did not stop with Reconstruction debts. Altogether nine states repudiated more than half of what they owed. The Bourbons, who respected the sanctity of property, were not of one mind about the process, however. In Virginia their leaders honored the state debt so zealously, and at such cost to public services, that they were temporarily ousted by an Independent rebellion, the Readjuster party.

Despite their penny-pinching ways, these frugal Bourbon regimes, so ardently devoted to laissez-faire, did respond to the demand for commissions to regulate the rates charged by railroads for commercial transport. They also established boards of agriculture and public health, agricultural experiment stations, agricultural and mechanical colleges, teacher-training schools and women's colleges, and even state colleges for African Americans.

Nor can any simplistic interpretation encompass the variety of Bourbon leaders. The Democratic party of the time was a mongrel coalition that threw Unionists, secessionists, businessmen, small farmers, hillbillies, planters, and even some Republicans together in alliance against the Reconstruction Radicals. Democrats therefore, even those who bore the Bourbon label, often marched to different drummers. And once they gained control, the conflicts inherent in any coalition began to erupt, so that Bourbon regimes never achieved complete unity in philosophy or government.

Independent movements cropped up in all the southern states, endorsing a variety of proposals including debt repudiation, inflation, usury laws, and antimonopoly laws. Locally they fought Bourbon Democrats over fencing laws (poor farmers preferred to let their scrub stock forage for itself), patronage, and issues of corruption. On occasion they joined forces with third parties such as the Greenbackers, and sometimes they elected local officials and congressmen. In Tennessee the division became so acute that the Republicans elected a governor in 1880. In Virginia, where the rebels sought reduction of the state debt, a Readjuster party captured the legislature in 1879, elected a governor in 1881, and sent their leader to the United States Senate.

For a brief time there emerged a wholesale collaboration between Republicans and Independents, which Chester A. Arthur, after he became president, promoted in the fall of 1881. The policy failed to make much headway, however, because Republicans had little in common with the Independents except their opposition to the Democrats. Moreover, the Republican machinery in the South had already been devastated by the overthrow of Reconstruction and by President Rutherford B. Hayes's policy of reconciliation with the Bourbons immediately afterward. The Republicans maintained a secure foothold only in the Blue Ridge and Smoky Mountains, "the great spine of Republicanism which runs down the back of the South," where stubborn white Unionists passed the faith on to later generations.

Perhaps the ultimate paradox of the Bourbons' rule was that these paragons of white supremacy tolerated a lingering black voice in politics and showed no haste about raising the barriers of racial separation. A number of them harbored at least some element of patrician benevolence toward blacks. The old slave owner, said a South Carolina editor, "has no desire to browbeat, maltreat, and spit upon the colored man"— clearly in part because the former slave owner saw in freedmen no threat to his status. Blacks sat in the state legislatures of South Carolina until 1900 and of Georgia until 1908; some of these black representatives were Democrats. The South sent black congressmen to Washington in every election until 1900 except one, though they always represented gerrymandered districts into which most of the state's black voters had been placed. Under the Bourbons the disenfranchisement of black voters remained inconsistent, a local matter brought about mainly by fraud and intimidation, but it occurred often enough to ensure white control of the southern states.

A like flexibility applied to other areas of race relations. The color line was drawn less strictly than it would be in the twentieth century. In some places, to be sure, racial segregation appeared before the end of Reconstruction, especially in schools, churches, hotels and rooming houses, and private social relations. In places of public accommodation such as trains, depots, theaters, and soda fountains, however, discrimination was more capricious. In 1885 a black journalist reported from his native state of South Carolina that he rode first-class cars on the railroads and in the streets, was served at saloons and soda fountains, saw blacks dining with whites at train stations, and saw a black policeman arrest a white man on the streets of Columbia. Fifteen years later such events would be rare.

DISENFRANCHISING BLACKS   During the 1890s, the attitudes that permitted such moderation eroded swiftly. One reason was that, despite signs of progress, many white racists held that blacks, freed from the restraints of slavery, were "retrogressing" toward bestiality, especially the younger blacks who had not known slavery.

Another reason was political. The rise of the Populist party in the 1890s divided the white vote to such an extent that in some places the black vote became the balance of power. Populists courted black votes and brought blacks prominently into their leadership councils. In response, the Bourbons revived the race issue, which they exploited with seasoned finesse, all the while controlling for their ticket a good part of the black vote in plantation areas. Nevertheless the Bourbons soon reversed themselves and began arguing that the black vote should be eliminated completely from southern elections. It was imperative, said the governor of Louisiana in 1894, that "the mass of ignorance, vice and venality without any proprietary interest in the State" be denied the vote. Some farm leaders hoped that disenfranchisement of blacks would make it possible for whites to divide politically without raising the specter of "Negro domination."

But since the Fifteenth Amendment made it impossible to disenfranchise blacks as such, the purpose was accomplished indirectly with devices such as poll taxes (or head taxes) and literacy tests. Some opposed such instruments of discrimination because they also trapped poor whites in the net. But this white opposition was neutralized by providing loopholes in the literacy tests through which illiterate whites could slip.

Mississippi led the way to near-total disenfranchisement of blacks. The state called a constitutional convention in 1890 to change the suffrage provisions of the old Radical constitution of 1868. The Mississippi plan set the pattern that seven more states would follow over the next twenty years. First, a residence requirement—two years in the state, one year in the election district—struck at those black tenant farmers who were in the habit of moving yearly in search of a better chance. Second, voters were disqualified if convicted of certain crimes. Third, all taxes, including a poll tax, had to be paid by February 1 of election year, which left plenty of time for white officials to lose the receipt before the fall vote. This proviso fell most heavily on the poor, most of whom were black. Fourth and finally, all voters had to be literate. The alternative, designed as a loophole for whites otherwise disqualified, was an "understanding" clause. The voter, if unable to read the Constitution, could qualify by being able to "understand" it—to the satisfaction of the registrar. Fraud was thus institutionalized rather than eliminated by "legal" disenfranchisement.

In other states, variations on the Mississippi plan added a few flourishes. In 1895 South Carolina tacked on the proviso that owning property assessed at $300 would qualify an illiterate voter. In 1898 Louisiana invented the "grandfather clause," which allowed illiterates to qualify if their fathers or grandfathers had been eligible to vote on January 1, 1867, when blacks were still excluded. Black educator Booker T.

Washington sent the convention a sarcastic telegram expressing hope that "no one clothed with state authority will be tempted to perjure and degrade himself by putting one interpretation upon it for the white man and another for the black man." By 1910 Georgia, North Carolina, Virginia, Alabama, and Oklahoma had adopted the grandfather clause. Every southern state, moreover, adopted a statewide Democratic primary between 1896 and 1915, which became the only meaningful election outside isolated areas of Republican strength. With minor exceptions, the Democratic primaries excluded black voters altogether. The effectiveness of these measures can be seen in a few sample figures. Louisiana in 1896 had 130,000 black voters registered, and in 1900 5,320. Alabama in 1900 had 121,159 literate black males over twenty-one, according to the census; only 3,742 were registered to vote.

SEGREGATION SPREADS   "Jim Crow" segregation followed hard on disenfranchisement and in some states came first. The symbolic first target was the railway train. In 1885, the novelist George Washington Cable noted that in South Carolina blacks "ride in first class cars as a right" and "their presence excites no comment." From 1875 to 1883 in

"Jim Crow," a stock character in old minstrel shows, became a synonym for racial segregation in the twentieth century. Dan Rice had developed the character in the 1830s.

fact, any racial segregation violated a federal Civil Rights Act, which forbade discrimination in places of public accommodation. But in 1883 the Supreme Court ruled on seven *Civil Rights Cases* involving discrimination against blacks by corporations or individuals. The Court held, with only one dissent, that the force of federal law could not extend to individual action because the Fourteenth Amendment, which provided that "no State" could deny citizens the equal protection of the laws, stood as a prohibition only against *state* action.

This left as an open question the validity of state laws *requiring* separate facilities under the rubric of "separate but equal," a slogan popular with the New South prophets. In 1881 Tennessee had required railroads in the state to maintain separate first-class cars for blacks and whites. In 1888 Mississippi went a step further by requiring passengers, under penalty of law, to occupy the car set aside for their race. When Louisiana followed suit in 1890, dissidents challenged the law in the case *Plessy v. Ferguson,* which the Supreme Court decided in 1896.

The test case originated in New Orleans when Homer Plessy, an octoroon (a person having one-eighth black ancestry), refused to leave a white railroad car when told to do so. He was convicted, and the case rose on appeal to the Supreme Court. The Court ruled that segregation laws "have been generally, if not universally recognized as within the competency of state legislatures in the exercise of their police power." The sole dissenter was John Marshall Harlan, a former slaveholder and Whig Unionist from Kentucky, who had written the only dissent in the *Civil Rights Cases.* The *Plessy* ruling, he predicted, would "stimulate aggressions, more or less brutal, upon the admitted rights of colored citizens."

Very soon the principle of racial segregation extended into every area of southern life, including street railways, hotels, restaurants, hospitals, recreations, sports, and employment. If an activity was overlooked by the laws, it was not overlooked in custom and practice. The editor of the *Richmond Times* expressed the prevailing view: "It is necessary that this principle be applied in every relation of Southern life. God Almighty drew the color line and it cannot be obliterated. The negro must stay on his side of the line and the white man must stay on his side, and the sooner both races recognize this fact and accept it, the better it will be for both."

As for the "aggressions, more or less brutal," that Justice Harlan foretold, they were already routine when he pronounced his dissent. From the days of slavery, race relations had operated in a context of force and violence. The period of growing discrimination at the turn of the century was one of the worst. In the decade from 1890 to 1899, lynchings in the United States averaged 188 per year, 82 percent of which occurred in the South; from 1900 to 1909 they averaged 93 per year, 92 percent in the South. Whites constituted 32 percent of the victims during the first period, only 11 percent in the latter. A young Episcopal priest in Montgomery said that extremists had proceeded "from an undiscriminating attack upon the Negro's ballot to a like attack upon his schools, his labor, his life—from the contention that no Negro shall vote to the contention that no Negro shall learn, that no Negro shall labor, and (by implication) that no Negro shall live."

WASHINGTON AND DU BOIS   A few brave souls, black and white, spoke out against the new racist measures, but by and large blacks had to accommodate to them as best they could. To be sure, the doctrine of "separate but equal" did open some doors, such as those to black schools, that had once been closed entirely. Some African Americans even began to make a virtue of necessity. The chief spokesman for this accommodationist philosophy was Booker T. Washington, the black prophet of the New South Creed. Born in Virginia of a slave mother and

Booker T. Washington.

a white father, Washington had fought extreme adversity to get an education at Hampton Institute, one of the postwar missionary schools, and then to build at Tuskegee, Alabama, a leading college for African Americans.

Washington argued that blacks should first establish an economic base for their advancement. They should focus "upon the everyday practical things of life, upon something that is needed to be done, and something which they will be permitted to do in the community in which they reside." In his famous speech at the Atlanta Cotton States and International Exposition in 1895, which propelled him to fame, Washington advised fellow blacks: "Cast down your bucket where you are—cast it down in making friends . . . of the people of all races by whom we are surrounded. Cast it down in agriculture, mechanics, in commerce, in domestic service, and in the professions." He conspicuously omitted politics and offered an oblique endorsement of segregation: "In all things that are purely social we can be as separate as the five fingers, yet one as the hand in all things essential to mutual progress."

Some people bitterly criticized Washington, then and since, for making a bad bargain: the sacrifice of broad education and of civil rights for the dubious acceptance of white conservatives and economic opportunities. W. E. B. Du Bois led blacks in this criticism of Washington. A

W. E. B. Du Bois.

native of Massachusetts, Du Bois once said defiantly that he was born "with a flood of Negro blood, a strain of French, a bit of Dutch, but thank God! no 'Anglo-Saxon.'" Du Bois first experienced southern racial practices as an undergraduate at Fisk University in Nashville. Later he earned a Ph.D. in history from Harvard and briefly attended the University of Berlin. In addition to an active career in racial protest, he left a distinguished record as a scholar and author. Trim and dapper in appearance, sporting a goatee, cane, and gloves, Du Bois possessed a combative spirit. Not long after he began his teaching career at Atlanta University in 1897, he began to assault Washington's accommodationist philosophy of black progress and put forward his own program of "ceaseless agitation."

Washington, Du Bois argued, preached "a gospel of Work and Money to such an extent as . . . to overshadow the higher aims of life." The education of blacks, he maintained, should not be merely vocational but should nurture leaders willing to challenge segregation and discrimination through political action. He believed in work, "but work is not necessarily education. Education is the development of power and ideal." He demanded that disenfranchisement and legalized segregation cease and that the laws of the land be enforced. And he provided the formula for attaining such goals: "By voting where we may vote, by persistent, unceasing agitation, by hammering at the truth, by sacrifice and work." Du Bois minced no words in criticizing Washington's philosophy: "We refuse to surrender the leadership of this race to cowards and trucklers." He called Washington's 1895 speech "the Atlanta Compromise" and argued that it had made Washington the leader of his race only in the eyes of whites.

RECONCILING TRADITION WITH INNOVATION   The ultimate achievement of the New South prophets and their allies, the Bourbons, was that they reconciled tradition with innovation. Their relative moderation in racial policy, at least before the 1890s, allowed them to embrace just enough of the new to disarm adversaries and keep control. By promoting the growth of industry, the Bourbons led the South into a new economic era, but without sacrificing a mythic reverence for the Old South. Bourbon rule left a permanent mark on the South. As the historian C. Vann Woodward has noted, "it was not the Radicals nor the Confederates but the Redeemers who laid the lasting foundations in matters of race, politics, economics and institutions for the modern South."

THE NEW WEST

For vast reaches of western America the great epics of Civil War and Reconstruction were remote events hardly touching the lives of Indians, Mexicans, Asians, trappers, miners, and Mormons scattered through the plains and mountains. There the march of Manifest Destiny continued on its inexorable course, propelled by a lust for land and a passion for profits. On one level, the settlement of the West beyond the Mississippi constitutes a colorful drama of determined pioneers overcoming all obstacles to secure their visions of freedom and opportunity amid the region's awesome vastness. But on another level, the colonization of the Far West was a tragedy of shortsighted greed and irresponsible behavior, a story of reckless exploitation that nearly exterminated the culture of Native Americans, scarred the land, and decimated its wildlife. Seen from this perspective, the history of the West is not a grand success story but a tale of hardship, frustration, and failure. Both images of the process of western settlement are accurate in some respects.

In the second tier of trans-Mississippi states—Iowa, Kansas, Nebraska—and in western Minnesota, the last frontier of farmers began spreading across the Great Plains after mid-century. From California the miners' frontier spread east through the mountains at one new strike after another. From Texas the nomadic cowboys migrated northward into the plains and across the Rockies into the Great Basin. Now there were two frontiers of settlement, east and west, and even a third to the south; in another generation there would be none.

As settlement moved west, the environment gradually altered. The Great Plains were arid, swept by dry winds that had surrendered their moisture to the Pacific coastal ranges, the Sierra Nevadas and Cascades, and the Rockies. The scarcity of water and timber rendered useless or impossible the familiar trappings of the pioneer: the axe, the log cabin, the rail fence, and the accustomed methods of tilling the soil.

For a long time the region had been called the Great American Desert, a barrier to cross on the way to the Pacific, unfit for human habitation and therefore, to white Americans, the perfect refuge for Indians. But that pattern changed in the last half of the nineteenth century as a result of new finds of gold, silver, and other minerals, completion of transcontinental railroads, destruction of the buffalo, the collapse of Indian resistance, the rise of the range-cattle industry, and the dawning realization that the arid region need not be a sterile desert. With the use of what water was available, techniques of dry farming and irrigation could make the land fruitful after all.

THE MIGRATORY STREAM   During the second half of the nineteenth century, an unrelenting stream of migrants flowed into the largely Indian and Hispanic West. Newspaper editors described western migration as a "flood tide." Millions of Anglo-Americans, African Americans, Mexicans, and European and Chinese immigrants transformed the patterns of western society and culture. Most of the settlers were relatively prosperous white, native-born farming families. Because of the expense of transportation, land, and supplies, the very poor could not afford to relocate. Three-quarters of the western migrants were men.

The largest number of foreign immigrants came from northern Europe and Canada. In the northern plains, Germans, Scandinavians, and Irish were especially numerous. Not surprisingly, these foreign settlers tended to cluster together according to ethnic and kinship ties. Norwe-

An American family on their way west.

gians and Swedes, for example, often gravitated toward others from the same home province or parish to form cohesive rural communities. In the new state of Nebraska in 1870, a quarter of the 123,000 residents were foreign-born. In North Dakota in 1890, 45 percent of the residents were immigrants. Compared to European immigrants, those from China and Mexico were much less numerous but nonetheless significant. More than 200,000 Chinese arrived in California between 1876 and 1890.

In the aftermath of the collapse of Radical Republican rule in the South, thousands of blacks began migrating west. Most of them left from Kentucky, Tennessee, Louisiana, Arkansas, Mississippi, and Texas. Some 6,000 southern blacks arrived in Kansas in 1879 alone, and as many as 20,000 may have come the following year. They came to be known as "Exodusters," making their exodus out of the South in search of a haven from racism and poverty.

The foremost promoter of black migration to the West was Benjamin "Pap" Singleton. Born a slave in Tennessee in 1809, he escaped and settled in Detroit, where he operated a boardinghouse that became a refuge for other runaway slaves. After the Civil War, he returned to Tennessee, convinced that God was calling him to rescue his black brethren. He decided that the brightest future for African Americans lay not in sharecropping or tenant farming but in farm ownership. When Sin-

Nicodemus, Kansas: a colony founded by southern blacks in the 1860s.

gleton learned that land in Kansas could be had for $1.25 an acre, he began distributing a recruiting pamphlet entitled "The Advantage of Living in a Free State" to former slaves. In 1878 Singleton led the first party of 200 colonists to Kansas, bought 7,500 acres that was formerly an Indian reservation, and established the Dunlop community.

Over the next several years, thousands of African Americans followed Singleton into Kansas, leading many southern leaders to worry about the loss of laborers from the Old South. In 1879 white Mississippians closed access to the river and threatened to sink all boats carrying black colonists to the West. An army officer reported to President Rutherford B. Hayes that "every river landing is blockaded by white enemies of the colored exodus; some of whom are mounted and armed, as if we are at war." One black migrant to Kansas who returned to Mississippi to retrieve his family was seized by whites who cut off his hands and threw them onto his wife's lap, yelling "Now go to Kansas to work!"

The exodus to Kansas and Oklahoma Territory died out by the early 1880s. Many of the settlers encountered terrible hardships. They were unprepared for the quite different living and working conditions on the Plains. Their homesteads were not large enough to be self-sufficient, and most of the black farmers were forced to supplement their income by hiring themselves out to white ranchers in the area. Drought, grasshoppers, prairie fires, and dust storms led to crop failures. The sudden influx of so many people taxed resources and patience. Although sympathizers formed the Kansas Freedmen's Relief Association and collected thousands of dollars for food and clothing, they could not keep up with the needs of the swelling tide of migrants. Many of the black pioneers soon abandoned their land and moved to the few cities in the state. Life on the frontier was not the "promised land" that people had been led to expect. Nonetheless, by 1890, some 520,000 blacks lived west of the Mississippi River. As many as 25 percent of the cowboys who participated in the Texas cattle drives were African Americans.

In 1866 Congress passed legislation establishing two "colored" cavalry units and dispatched them to the western frontier. Nicknamed "Buffalo Soldiers" by the Indians, the soldiers were mostly Civil War veterans from Louisiana and Kentucky. They built and maintained forts, mapped vast areas of the Southwest, strung hundreds of miles of telegraph lines, protected railroad construction crews, subdued hostile Indians, and captured outlaws and rustlers. For this they were paid $13 a month. Eighteen of the "Buffalo Soldiers" won Congressional Medals of Honor for their service in the West.

MINING THE WEST Miners were also diverse in ethnic background. Every race and nationality was represented in the mining communities. The miners' frontier was in fact not so much a frontier as a scattering of settlements in places unsuitable for farming, such as steep mountainsides, remote highlands, and barren deserts. The California miners of '49 set the typical pattern in which the sudden, disorderly rush of prospectors to the new find was quickly followed by the arrival of the camp followers—a motley crew of peddlers, saloonkeepers, prostitutes, card sharps, hustlers, and assorted desperadoes, out to mine the miners. If the new field panned out, the forces of respectability and more subtle forms of exploitation slowly worked their way in. An era of lawlessness gave way to vigilante rule and, finally, to a stable community.

As mining became more dependent on capital, the day of the individual prospector began to wane. The Forty-niners typically sifted the gold out of the dirt and gravel through "placer" mining or "panning," or by diverting a stream through a "sluice box" or "long tom." But once the rich diggings tailed off, efficient mining required shafts sunk into the ground or crushing mills built to extract the precious metal locked in

Hydraulic mining in the Boise basin in Idaho, circa 1875. Gold, silver, and copper prospectors invaded the West, but only a few made their fortunes.

THE NEW WEST

- Arid lands
- Grassland
- Forest
- Cattle country
- Mining

quartz. The wild rush then gave way to organized enterprise. The miners either moved on, settled down to work for the corporate mines, or took up farming in the vicinity.

The drama of the 1849 gold rush was reenacted time and again in the following three decades. Though the California fever had passed by 1851, and no big strikes were made for seven years, new finds in Colorado and Nevada revived hopes for riches. Along the South Platte River, not far from Pike's Peak in Colorado, a prospecting party found gold in 1858, and stories of success there brought perhaps 100,000 "Fifty-niners" into the country by 1859, only to find that the rumors had been greatly exaggerated.

Wagons that headed west with the legend "Pike's Peak or Bust!" on their sides were soon rumbling back with the sardonic message "Busted, by gosh." Still, a few mines proved out, some new arrivals took up farming to exploit high prices for farm products in Denver and other mining centers, and the census of 1860 showed 35,000 people still in the region. New discoveries kept occurring: near Central City in 1859, at Leadville in the 1870s, and the last important strikes in the West, again gold and silver, at Cripple Creek in 1891–1894. During these years, farming and grazing had given the economy a stable base, and Colorado had become the "Centennial State" in 1876.

While the early miners were crowding around Pike's Peak, the Comstock Lode was discovered near Gold Hill, Nevada. H. T. P. Comstock, a Canadian-born fur trapper, had drifted to the Carson River diggings opened in 1856. Possessed of a glib tongue, he talked his way into a share in a new discovery made by two other prospectors in 1859 and gave it his own name. The lode produced not only gold but a troublesome "blue earth" that turned out to contain silver. Close by, James Finney, known as "Old Virginia," located a lucrative new vein and gave his nickname to nearby Virginia City. Neither man had the foresight to develop his claim; both sold out for tiny sums what proved to be the two richest fields in the West. Within twenty years the Comstock Lode alone had yielded more than $300 million from shafts that reached hundreds of feet into the mountainside. In 1861 Nevada became a territory, and in 1864 the state of Nevada was admitted in time to give its three electoral votes to Lincoln.

The Spaniards had found silver in New Mexico, but mining in Arizona began during the Civil War, when many in a company of California volunteers, going to meet a Confederate foray into New Mexico, deserted to the promising mining country near the Colorado River. In both Arizona and Montana the most important mineral proved to be neither gold nor silver, but copper. The richest copper mines included the Anaconda Mine in Butte, Montana, and the Phelps-Dodge Mine near Bisbee, Arizona.

The last great strike before the Cripple Creek (Colorado) find of the 1890s occurred in 1874–1875 in the Black Hills of South Dakota, which belonged by treaty to the Sioux Indians. Deadwood, the site of the strike, earned brief glory as the refuge of some of the West's most notorious desperadoes: "Calamity Jane," "Wild Bill Hickok," and a host of others. But in Deadwood, as elsewhere, when the gold and silver lodes ran out there was often little to support life in an arid, infertile terrain.

The growing demand for orderly government in the West led to the hasty creation of new territories and eventually the admission of a host of new states. After Colorado was admitted in 1876, however, there was a long hiatus because of the party divisions in Congress. Democrats were reluctant to create states out of territories that were heavily Republican. After the sweeping Republican victory of 1888, however, Congress admitted the Dakotas, Montana, and Washington in 1889,

Creede, Colorado. Towns in Colorado and other Western states were established with the gold rushes of 1849 and 1859.

and Idaho and Wyoming in 1890, completing a tier of states from coast to coast. Utah entered in 1896 (after the Mormons abandoned the practice of polygamy), Oklahoma in 1907, and in 1912 Arizona and New Mexico finally rounded out the forty-eight contiguous states.

THE INDIAN WARS   As the frontier pressed in from east and west, whites pursued the Indians into what was supposed to be their last refuge. Perhaps 250,000 Indians in the Great Plains and mountain regions lived mainly off the buffalo herds, which provided food and, from their hides, clothing and shelter. In 1851 the chiefs of the principal Plains tribes had gathered at Fort Laramie in Wyoming Territory, where they had agreed to accept more or less definite tribal borders and to leave the emigrants unmolested on their trails. The treaty worked for a while, with wagon trains passing safely through Indian lands and the army building roads and forts without resistance from the Indians. Fighting resumed, however, as the emigrants began to encroach upon Indian lands on the Plains rather than merely passing through them.

From the early 1860s until the late 1870s, the frontier was ablaze with Indian wars, and intermittent outbreaks continued through the 1880s. The first serious trouble developed in Minnesota, where a volunteer militia had taken the place of army garrisons fighting in the Civil War. Fighting started in 1862 when a band of Sioux, aroused by recent land cessions, killed five whites. Some of the Sioux fled farther west, but others remained and wrought havoc on the frontier, killing or capturing some 1,000 whites until the militia in overwhelming force drove them back and inflicted a devastating revenge. Out of 400 Indians captured, 300 were sentenced to death. Eventually 38 were hanged in a mass execution.

In Colorado, where Cheyenne and Arapaho chiefs were forced to accept a treaty to abandon land that had been granted to them in treaties ten years earlier and to move westward to other lands, protesting braves began sporadic raids on the trails and mining camps. In 1864 the territorial governor persuaded most of the warring Indians to gather at Fort Lyon on Sand Creek, where they were promised protection. Despite this promise, Colonel J. M. Chivington's militia fell upon an Indian camp flying the American flag and a white flag of truce, slaughtering 450 peaceful Indians—men, women, and children. An army general called it the "foulest and most unjustifiable crime in the annals of

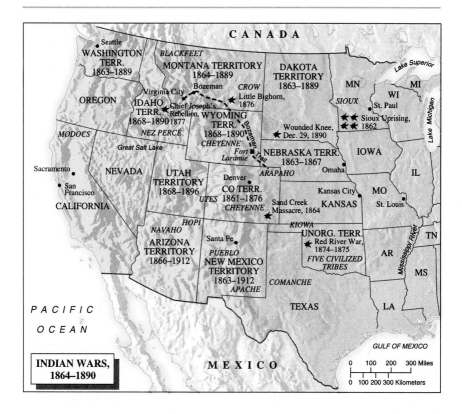

INDIAN WARS, 1864–1890

America." Chivington, a former Methodist minister, later exhibited his personal collection of 100 scalps in Denver. In 1865 the survivors surrendered unconditionally and gave up their Sand Creek reservation for lands farther west.

With other scattered battles erupting, in 1865 a congressional committee began to gather evidence on the grisly Indian wars and massacres. Its 1867 *Report on the Condition of the Indian Tribes* led to an act to establish an Indian Peace Commission charged with ending the Sioux War and removing the causes of Indian wars in general. Congress decided this was best accomplished at the expense of the Indians, by persuading them to take up life on out-of-the-way reservations. This solution continued the persistent encroachment on Indian hunting grounds.

In 1867 a conference at Medicine Creek Lodge, Kansas, ended with an agreement that the Kiowa, Comanche, Arapaho, and Cheyenne would accept lands in western Oklahoma. Smaller tribes from the southern

Plains were later resettled on reservations in the same area. In the following spring in 1868, a conference at Fort Laramie resulted in peace with the Sioux, who agreed to settle within the Black Hills reservation in Dakota Territory. But Indian resistance in the southern Plains continued until the Red River War of 1874–1875. General Philip Sheridan scattered the Indians and finally brought them to terms in the spring of 1875.

While conflict was being resolved in the south, trouble was brewing once again in the north. In 1874 Lieutenant-Colonel George A. Custer, a reckless, glory-seeking officer who graduated last in his class at West Point in 1861 and then distinguished himself as a cavalry officer during the Civil War, led an exploring expedition into the Black Hills, accompanied by gold seekers. Miners were soon filtering into the Sioux hunting grounds despite promises that the army would keep them out. The army had done little to protect the Indian lands, but when ordered to move against wandering bands of Sioux hunting on the range according to their treaty rights, the army moved vigorously.

What became the Great Sioux War was the largest military event since the end of the Civil War and one of the largest campaigns against the Indians in American history. The war lasted some fifteen months, and entailed some fifteen battles in a vast area of present-day Wyoming, Montana, South Dakota, and Nebraska. In 1876, after several indecisive encounters, Custer found the main encampment of Sioux and their Northern Cheyenne allies on the Little Bighorn River. Separated from the main body of his men, Custer and a detachment of 210, surrounded by a body of warriors numbering about 2,500, were completely annihilated.

But the Battle of the Little Bighorn was only one incident in this war. Instead of following up their victory over Custer and his forces, the Indians celebrated and renewed their hunting. When the army regained the offensive, the Indians began to melt away into the wilderness. Chief Sitting Bull escaped into Canada, only to return to the Sioux reservation several years later. Crazy Horse was captured and later murdered by his guard. The remaining Sioux were forced to give up their hunting grounds and gold fields in return for payments. Forced onto reservations situated on the least valuable lands in the region, the Indians soon found themselves struggling to subsist under harsh conditions. Many of them died of starvation or disease. When a peace commission imposed

The Battle of Little Bighorn in a pictograph by an Oglala Sioux, Amos Bad Heart Bull, 1876.

a settlement, Chief Spotted Tail said: "Tell your people that since the Great Father promised that we should never be removed, we have been moved five times. . . . I think you had better put the Indians on wheels and you can run them about wherever you wish."

In the Rockies and westward the same story of hopeless resistance was repeated. The Blackfoot and Crow had to leave their homes in Montana. In a war along the California-Oregon boundary, the Modocs held out for six months in 1871–1872 before they were overwhelmed. In 1879 the Utes were forced to give up their vast territories in western Colorado after a brief battle. In Idaho the peaceful Nez Percés finally refused to surrender lands along the Salmon River. Chief Joseph tried to avoid war, but when some unruly braves started a fight, he directed a masterful campaign against overwhelming odds, one of the most spectacular feats in the history of Indian warfare. After a retreat of 1,500 miles, through mountains and plains, across the Yellowstone region and through the Bitterroot Mountains of Montana, he was finally caught thirty miles short of the Canadian border, and exiled to Oklahoma.

The heroic Joseph maintained strict discipline among his followers, countenanced no scalpings or outrages against civilians, bought supplies that he could have confiscated, and kept his dignity to the end.

Chief Joseph of the Nez Percé tribe.

His eloquent speech of surrender was an epitaph to the warrior's last stand against the march of empire: "I am tired of fighting. Our chiefs are killed. . . . The old men are all dead. . . . I want to have time to look for my children, and see how many of them I can find. . . . Hear me, my chiefs! I am tired. My heart is sick and sad. From where the sun now stands I will fight no more forever."

A generation of Indian wars virtually ended in 1886 with the capture of Geronimo, a chief of the Chiricahua Apaches, who had fought encroachments in the Southwest for fifteen years. But there would be one tragic epilogue. Late in 1888 Wovoka (or "Jack Wilson"), a Paiute in western Nevada, fell ill and in a delirium imagined he had visited the spirit world where he learned of a deliverer coming to rescue the Indians and restore their lands. To hasten the day, he said, they had to take up a ceremonial dance at each new moon. The Ghost Dance craze fed upon old legends of a coming Messiah and spread rapidly. In 1890 the Sioux took it up with such fervor that it alarmed white authorities. An effort to arrest Chief Sitting Bull led to his death. Shortly afterward, on December 29, 1890, a bloodbath occurred at Wounded Knee, South Dakota. An accidental rifle discharge led nervous soldiers to fire into a group of Indians who had come to surrender. Nearly 200 Indians and 25 soldiers died in the "Battle of Wounded Knee." The Indian wars had ended with characteristic brutality.

Geronimo, a chief of the Chiricahua Apaches.

Over the long run the collapse of Indian resistance resulted as much from the killing off of the buffalo herds on which they subsisted as from direct suppression. White hunters felled buffaloes for sport, sometimes firing from train windows merely for the pleasure of seeing them die. In the 1870s a systematic slaughter served the fashion of buffalo robes and overcoats in the East. By the mid-1880s the herds had reached the verge of extinction.

Most frontiersmen had little tolerance for moralizing on the Indian question. Easterners who were far removed from frontier dangers took a different view. The slaughter of the Indian wars provoked widespread criticism. Politicians and religious leaders spoke out against mistreatment of Indians. In his annual message of 1877 President Hayes echoed the protest: "Many, if not most, of our Indian wars have had their origin in broken promises and acts of injustice on our part." In the 1880s Helen Hunt Jackson, a novelist and poet, focused attention on the Indian cause in *A Century of Dishonor* (1881), which struck a popular chord just as *Uncle Tom's Cabin* had done.

INDIAN POLICY   Indian policy gradually became more benevolent, but this did little to ease the plight of the Indians and actually helped to destroy the remnants of their cultures. The reservation policy inaugurated by the Peace Commission in 1867 did little more than extend a

Issue Day. *Native Americans confined to Pine Ridge Reservation in South Dakota could no longer hunt for themselves and had to wait for government-issued food rations.*

practice that dated from colonial Virginia. Partly humanitarian in motive, this policy also saved money: it cost less to house and feed Indians on reservations than it did to fight them.

Well-intentioned reformers sought to "Americanize" the Indians by dealing with them as individuals rather than as tribes. The fruition of reform efforts came in the Dawes Severalty Act of 1887. Sponsored by Senator Henry M. Dawes of Massachusetts, the act permitted the president to divide the lands of any tribe and grant 160 acres to each head of family and lesser amounts to others. To protect the Indian's property, the government held it in trust for twenty-five years, after which the owner won full title and became a citizen. Under the Burke Act of 1906, Indians who took up life apart from their tribes became citizens immediately. Members of the tribes granted land titles were subject to state and federal laws like all other persons. In 1901 citizenship was extended to the Five Civilized Tribes of Oklahoma, and in 1924 to all Indians.

But the more it changed, the more Indian policy remained the same. Despite the best of intentions, the Dawes Act created opportunities for more plundering of Indian land, and it disrupted what remained of the traditional cultures. The Dawes Act broke up reservations and often led to the loss of Indian lands to whites. Those lands not distributed to Indian families were sold, while others were lost to land sharks because of the Indians' inexperience with private ownership, or simply their weakness in the face of fraud. Between 1887 and 1934, they lost an estimated 86 million of their 130 million acres. Most of what remained was unsuited to agriculture.

CATTLE AND COWBOYS   While the West was being taken from the Indians, cattle entered the grasslands where the buffalo had roamed. The cowboy enjoyed his brief heyday, fading then into the folklore of the Wild West. From colonial times, especially in the South, cattle raising had been a common enterprise just beyond the fringe of settlement. In many cases the early slaves took care of the livestock. Later, in the West, African-American cowboys were a common sight, although they were lost from view in the novels and "horse operas" that pictured a lily-white frontier. Much of the romance of the open-range cattle industry derived from its Mexican roots. The Texas longhorns and the cowboys' horses had in large part descended from stock brought over by the Spaniards, and many of the industry's trappings had been worked out in Mexico first: the cowboy's saddle, chaps (*chaparejos*) to protect the legs, spurs, and lariat.

For many years wild cattle competed with the buffalo in the Spanish borderlands. Natural selection and contact with "Anglo" scrub cattle produced the Texas longhorns: lean and rangy, they were noted more for speed and endurance than for providing a choice steak. They had little value, moreover, because the largest markets for beef were too far away. Occasionally they were driven to market in Austin, Galveston, or New Orleans, and some even to the gold fields of California, Arizona, and Colorado. At the end of the Civil War, perhaps as many as 5 million roamed the grasslands of Texas, still neglected—but not for long. In the upper Mississippi Valley, where herds had been depleted by the war, cattle were in great demand, and the Texas cattle could be had just for the effort of rounding them up.

So the cattle drives began anew after the Civil War, but on a scale far greater than before. In 1866 a large Texas herd set out for Sedalia, Missouri, the western terminus of the Missouri-Pacific Railroad. But that route proved unsuitable because it was subject to raids by postwar bushwhackers (bandits), obstructed by woodlands, and opposed by Arkansas and Missouri farmers. New opportunities arose as railroads

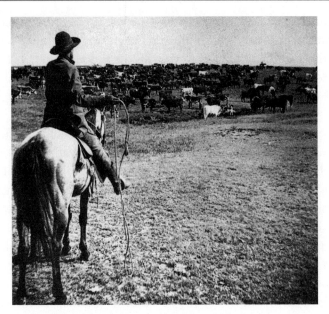

Roundup on the Sherman Ranch, Genesee, Kansas, 1902.

pushed farther west where cattle could be driven through relatively vacant lands.

Joseph G. McCoy, the youngest of three brothers already in the livestock business near Springfield, Illinois, recognized the possibilities for
moving the cattle trade west. He turned Abilene into the first successful Kansas cowtown. Located on the Kansas-Pacific Railroad at the
northern end of a trail laid out through Indian Territory by the part-
Cherokee Jesse Chisholm, Abilene was a "small, dead place, consisting
of about one dozen log huts" when McCoy arrived in early 1867.

McCoy bought up 250 acres for a stockyard, laid plans for a barn, an
office building, livestock scales, a hotel, and a bank—and sent an agent
into Indian Territory to cultivate owners of herds bound north. Over the
next few years Abilene developed into a flourishing town. But, as the
railroads moved west, so did the cowtowns and the trails: Ellsworth,
Wichita, Caldwell, and Dodge City, all in Kansas; and farther north
Ogallala, Nebraska; Cheyenne, Wyoming; and Miles City, Montana.

The cattle industry spurred rapid growth. The population of Kansas
rose from 107,000 in 1860 to 365,000 ten years later and reached almost a million by 1880. Nebraska witnessed similar increases. During

the 1860s, the cattle would be delivered to rail depots, loaded onto freight cars, and shipped east. By the time they arrived in New York or Massachusetts, some would be dead or dying and all would have lost significant weight. The secret to higher profits for the cattle industry was to devise a way to slaughter the cattle in the Midwest and ship the dressed carcasses east and west. That required refrigeration to keep the meat from spoiling. In 1869 G. H. Hammond, a Chicago meat packer, shipped the first refrigerated beef in an air-cooled car from Chicago to Boston. Eight years later, Gustavus Swift developed a more efficient system of mechanical refrigeration, an innovation that earned him a fortune and provided a major stimulus to the growth of the cattle industry.

But it was one thing to develop the processes to produce refrigerated meat; it was another to convince people to eat it. This required a major marketing campaign. Consumers balked at eating beef that had been butchered a thousand miles away. "The idea of eating meat a week or more after it had been killed," Swift's son noted, "met with a nasty-nice horror." What gradually changed public taste was the fact that dressed meat was significantly cheaper than fresh beef. In addition, Swift introduced the practice of displaying various cuts of dressed beef in butcher shops. He urged his agents in eastern cities to cut up the meat "and scatter the pieces," for "the more you cut, the more you sell." The combination of shrewd marketing and low prices soon convinced customers to prefer dressed meat.

During the twenty years after the Civil War, some 40,000 cowboys roamed the Great Plains. They were young—the average age was twenty-four—and from diverse backgrounds. Thirty percent were either Mexican or African American, and hundreds were Indians. Many others were Civil War veterans from North and South who now rode side by side, and a number had come from Europe. The life of a cowboy, for the most part, was rarely as exciting as motion pictures and television shows have depicted. Being a ranchhand involved grueling, dirty, wage labor interspersed with drudgery and boredom.

The flush times of the cowtown soon passed, and the long cattle drives played out too, because they were economically unsound. The dangers of the trail, the wear and tear on men and cattle, the charges levied on drives across Indian Territory, and the advance of farms across the trails combined to persuade cattlemen that they could best function near the railroads. As railroads spread out into Texas and the Plains, the cattle business spread with them over the High Plains as far as Montana and on into Canada.

In the absence of laws governing the range, the cattlemen at first worked out a code of action largely dictated by circumstances. As cattle often wandered onto other people's claims, cowboys would "ride the line" to keep the cattle off the next ranch as well as conducting spring roundups to separate the mixed herds. Each rancher's cattle would be distinguished by distinctive brands. But this changed in 1873 when Joseph Glidden, an Illinois farmer, invented the first effective barbed wire, which ranchers used to fence off their claims at relatively low cost. More often than not these were parts of the public domain to which they had no valid title. In that same year an eastern promoter, John W. "Bet-a-Million" Gates, one of the early agents for Glidden, gave a persuasive demonstration of the barbed wire in San Antonio. Skeptical cattlemen discovered that their meanest longhorns shied away from the fence which, as Gates put it, was light as air, stronger than whiskey, and cheaper than dirt. Orders poured in, and Gates eventually put together a virtual monopoly in the American Steel and Wire Company.

The greatest boom in the range-cattle trade came in the early 1880s, when eastern and European investors began to pour money into the "Beef Bonanza." Cattle growing, like mining, entered a season of wild speculation, and then evolved from a romantic adventure into a prosaic business, often a corporate business.

END OF THE OPEN RANGE   A combination of factors conspired to end the open range. Farmers kept crowding in and laying out homesteads on the open range, waging "barbed-wire wars" with cattlemen by either cutting the cattlemen's fences or policing their own. The boundless range was beginning to be overstocked by 1883, and expenses mounted as stock breeders formed associations to keep intruders out of overstocked ranges, to establish and protect land titles, to deal with railroads and buyers, to fight prairie fires, and to cope with rustlers and predatory beasts. The rise of sheep herding by 1880 caused still another conflict with the cattlemen. A final blow to the open-range industry came with two unusually severe winters in 1886 and 1887, followed by ten long years of drought.

For those who survived all the hazards of the range, the response to these problems was to establish legal title and fence in the lands, restrict the herds to a reasonable size, and provide shelter and hay against the rigors of winter. Moreover, as the long cattle drives ended with the advent of more rail lines and refrigerated cars, the cowboy settled into a more sedentary existence. Within merely two decades, 1866–1886, the era of the cowboy had come and gone.

RANGE WARS   The growth of the cattle industry placed a premium upon land, and conflicting claims over land and water rights ignited violent disputes between ranchers and farmers. Ranchers often tried to drive off neighboring farmers, and farmers in turn tried to sabotage the cattle barons, cutting their fences and spooking their herds. The cattle ranchers also clashed with sheepherders over access to grasslands. A strain of ethnic and religious prejudice heightened the tension between ranchers and herders. In the Southwest, shepherds were usually Mexican Americans; in Idaho and Nevada they were Basques or Mormons. Many Anglo-American cattle ranchers and cowboys viewed these ethnic and religious groups as un-American and inferior. This attitude helped them rationalize the use of violence against the sheepherders. Warfare between defenders of the bovine and ovine species gradually faded, however, as the sheep for the most part found refuge in the high pastures of the mountains, leaving the grasslands of the Plains to the cattlemen.

There also developed a perennial tension over grassland use between large and small cattle ranchers. The large ranchers fenced in huge tracts of public lands, leaving the smaller ranchers with too little pasture. To survive, the smaller ranchers cut the fences. In central Texas this practice sparked the Fence-Cutters' War of 1883–1884. Several ranchers were killed and dozens wounded before the state ended the conflict by passing legislation outlawing fence cutting. An even more violent confrontation between large and small ranchers occurred in Wyoming when members of the Wyoming Stock Association organized an assault against small ranchers, who they charged were rustling their stock. In Johnson County, Wyoming, in 1889, the cattle barons lynched James Averell, a small rancher, and Ella Watson, a prostitute embroiled in the dispute. The vigilantes were brought to trial, but the case was dismissed when the four witnesses to the hanging refused to testify.

Two years later, in 1891, the large ranchers organized a "lynching bee" to eliminate rustlers in Johnson County, and hired gunmen from

Judge Roy Bean's courthouse and saloon, Langtry, Texas, 1900.

Texas to do their bidding. On Tuesday, April 5, 1892, two dozen Texan mercenaries and an equal number of ranchers who dubbed themselves "regulators" set out to wipe out the rustlers. After killing two men, the vigilante group headed north, only to find itself surrounded by a band of small ranchers who had been alerted to their plan. The timely arrival of federal cavalry prevented a massacre. The cattle kings thereupon turned to a bounty hunter, Tom Horn, who murdered "rustlers" until he himself was caught, convicted, and hanged.

FARMERS AND THE LAND Among the legendary figures of the West, the sodbusters projected an unromantic image in contrast to the cowboys, cavalry, and Indians. Farming has always been a risky and arduous endeavor, and it was made more so on the Great Plains by the unforgiving environment. After 1865, on paper at least, the federal land laws offered favorable terms to the farmer. Under the Homestead Act of 1862 a farmer could either realize the old dream of free land simply by staking out a claim and living on it for five years, or by buying the land at $1.25 an acre after six months. But such land legislation was predicated upon an entirely different environment from that of the Plains, and the laws were never adjusted to the fact that much of the land was suited only for cattle. Cattle ranchers were forced to obtain land by gradual acquisition from homesteaders or land-grant railroads.

The unchangeable fact of aridity, rather than new land laws, shaped institutions in the New West. Where farming was impossible the cattle ranchers simply established dominance by control of the water, regardless of the laws. Belated legislative efforts to develop irrigable lands finally achieved a major success when the Newlands Reclamation Act (after the aptly named Senator Francis G. Newlands of Nevada) of 1901 set up the Bureau of Reclamation. The proceeds of public land sales in sixteen states created a fund for irrigation works, and the Reclamation Bureau set about building such major projects as Boulder (later Hoover) Dam on the Nevada-Arizona line, Roosevelt Dam in Arizona, and Elephant Butte Dam and Arrowrock Dam in New Mexico.

The lands of the New West, as on previous frontiers, passed to their ultimate owners more often from private hands than directly from the government. Many of the 274 million acres claimed under the Homestead Act passed quickly to ranchers or speculators, and thence to settlers. The land-grant railroads got some 200 million acres of the public domain in the twenty years from 1851 to 1871, and sold much of this land to build population centers and traffic along the lines. The New West of ranchers and farmers was in fact largely the product of the railroads.

The first arrivals on the sodhouse frontier faced a grim struggle against danger, adversity, and monotony. Though land was relatively cheap, horses, livestock, wagons, wells, fencing, seed, and fertilizer were not. Freight rates and interest rates on loans seemed criminally high. As in the South, declining crop prices produced indebtedness that soon became a chronic condition that led strapped western farmers to embrace virtually any plan to inflate the money supply. The virgin land itself, although fertile, resisted planting; the heavy sod broke many a plow. Since wood was almost nonexistent on the prairies, pioneer families used buffalo chips (dried dung) for fuel. Farmers and their families also fought a constant battle with the elements: tornadoes, hailstorms, droughts, prairie fires, blizzards, and pests. Swarms of locusts would cloud the horizon, occasionally covering the ground six inches deep and consuming everything in their path. A Wichita newspaper reported in 1878 that the grasshoppers devoured "everything green, stripping the foliage off the bark and from the tender twigs of the fruit trees, destroying every plant that is good for food or pleasant to the eyes, that man has planted."

As the railroads arrived bearing lumber from the wooded regions, farmers could leave their dugouts and sodhouses (homes roofed with sod) to build more familiar frame houses. New machinery helped open fresh opportunities for farmers. Back in 1838 John Deere of Illinois had developed the steel-faced plow and moldboard that conquered the clinging humus of the prairie. But its high cost encouraged further experiments, and in 1868 James Oliver of Indiana made a successful chilled-iron plow. With further improvements his "sodbuster" was soon ready for mass production, easing the task of breaking the shallow but tough grass roots of the Plains. Improvements and new inventions in threshing machines, hay mowers, planters, manure spreaders, cream separators, and other devices lightened the burden of labor but added to the capital outlay for the farmer.

In Minnesota, the Dakotas, and central California, the gigantic "bonanza farms" with machinery for mass production became the marvels of the age. On one farm in North Dakota, 13,000 acres of wheat made a single field. "You are in a sea of wheat," a bedazzled visitor wrote in 1880. "The railroad train rolls through an ocean of grain." Another bonanza farm employed over a thousand migrant workers to tend 34,000 acres.

To get a start on a family homestead required a minimum capital investment of $1,000. While the overall value of farm lands and farm products increased in the late nineteenth century, the small farmers did not keep up with the march of progress. Their numbers grew but decreased in proportion to the population at large. Wheat, like cotton in the antebellum period, provided the great export crop that evened America's balance of payments and spurred economic growth. For a variety of reasons, however, few small farmers prospered. Something was amiss, farmers began to reason, and by the decade of the 1890s they

Harvest on the Dalrymple farm, Red River Valley, Dakota Territory, 1877.

were in open revolt against the "system" of corrupt processors and avaricious bankers who they believed conspired against them.

PIONEER WOMEN   The West remained a largely male society throughout the nineteenth century. In Texas, for example, the ratio of men to women in 1890 was 110 to 1. Women continued to face traditional legal barriers and social prejudice. A wife could not sell property without her husband's approval. In Texas women could not sue except for divorce, nor could they serve on juries, act as lawyers, or witness a will.

But the fight for survival in the trans-Mississippi West made men and women more equal partners than were their eastern counterparts. Many women who lost their mates to the deadly toil of sodbusting thereafter assumed complete responsibility for their farms. In general, women on the prairie became more independent than those living domestic lives back East. One woman declared that she insisted on leaving out the phrasing about "obeying" her husband from their marriage vows. "I had served my time of tutelage to my parents as all children are supposed to. I was a woman now and capable of being the other half of the head of the family." Similar examples of independence abound. Explained one Kansas woman: "The outstanding fact is that the environ-

Woman and her family in front of their sodhouse. The difficult life on the prairie led to more egalitarian marriages.

ment was such as to bring out and develop the dominant qualities of individual character. Kansas women of that day learned at an early age to depend on themselves—to do whatever work there was to be done, and to face danger when it must be faced, as calmly as they were able."

A VIOLENT CULTURE Although often exaggerated in Hollywood films, the western frontier during the second half of the nineteenth century was indeed a violent place. Guns, rifles, and knives were everywhere evident, and people readily used them to resolve their disputes. The brutal requirements for self-preservation on the frontier or in the mining communities changed the long-standing premise of English common law that required a person to flee or retreat in the face of a violent threat. In 1876 a court ruled that a "true man" was no longer obligated "to fly" from an assailant.

The need to protect one's family or homestead in the face of threats and the frontiersman's obsessive preoccupation with masculine honor helped nourish what came to be called the Code of the West. It stressed the need for a man to stand and fight when threatened or wronged, and this spawned a reckless preoccupation with individual courage. As the famous frontier marshal James Butler ("Wild Bill") Hickok explained, "Meet anyone face to face with whom you disagree," and "if you meet him face to face and took the same risk as he did, you could get away with almost anything [including killing], as long as the bullet was in the front."

Most of the individual violence associated with the "Wild West" occurred in the cattle towns and mining communities where young single men abounded, and liquor was the most popular refreshment. This was not surprising, given that these were societies with shallow roots and populated by so many people on the lookout for the main chance. Bodie, California, in the heart of the mining region, developed a reputation as a "shooter's town." Between 1877 and 1883, there were forty-four shootings, leaving twenty-nine dead. The courts convicted only one man of murder. A few roughnecks in Bodie preferred weapons other than guns. For several months Man Eater McGowan terrorized the town. He gained his nickname from his tendency to chew on his opponents' appendages. Before being run out of town, he bit the sheriff's leg, broke a pitcher over a waiter's head, and chewed or bit off the noses or ears of a dozen others.

Perhaps the most violent region of the West between the 1860s and 1890s was central Texas, an area bounded by Houston, Fort Worth, Dallas, San Antonio, and San Angelo. This huge territory included a volatile mix of peoples—Indians, Hispanics, German immigrants, freed slaves, and former Confederate soldiers. Ethnic and racial tensions, range wars, boundary disputes, outlaw activity, and vigilantism were common. John Wesley Hardin, the West's most prolific gunman, killed over twenty men in political disputes and community feuds. Once, a drunken Hardin fired a bullet through the wall of his hotel room to silence a snoring guest. The man never snored again.

"THE FRONTIER HAS GONE"   American life reached an important juncture at the end of the nineteenth century. After the 1890 population count, the superintendent of the census noted that he could no longer locate a continuous frontier line beyond which population thinned out to fewer than two per square mile. This fact inspired the historian Frederick Jackson Turner to develop his influential frontier thesis, first outlined in his paper "The Significance of the Frontier in American History," delivered to the American Historical Association in 1893. "The existence of an area of free land," Turner wrote, "its continuous recession, and the advance of American settlement westward, explain American development." The frontier had shaped the national character in fundamental ways. It was

> to the frontier [that] the American intellect owes its striking characteristics. That coarseness and strength combined with acuteness and acquisitiveness; that practical, inventive turn of mind, quick to find expedients; that masterful grasp of material things, lacking in the artistic but powerful to effect great ends; that restless, nervous energy; that dominant individualism, working for good and for evil, and withal that buoyancy and exuberance which comes with freedom—these are traits of the frontier, or traits called out elsewhere because of the existence of the frontier.

In 1893, Turner concluded, "four centuries from the discovery of America, at the end of a hundred years under the Constitution, the frontier has gone and with its going has closed the first period of American history."

Turner's "frontier thesis" guided several generations of scholars and students in their understanding of the distinctive characteristics of

American history. His view of the frontier as the westward-moving source of America's democratic politics, open society, unfettered economy, and rugged individualism, far removed from the corruptions of urban life, gripped the popular imagination as well. But it left much out of the story. The frontier experience Turner described exaggerated the homogenizing effect of the frontier environment and virtually ignored the role of women, blacks, Indians, Mormons, Hispanics, and Asians in shaping the diverse human geography of the western United States. Turner also implied that the West would be fundamentally different after 1890 because the frontier experience was essentially over. But in many respects that region has retained the qualities associated with the rush for land, gold, timber, and water rights during the post–Civil War decades. The mining frontier, as one historian has recently written, "set a mood that has never disappeared from the West: the attitude of extractive industry—get in, get rich, get out."

MAKING CONNECTIONS

- The problems of southern and western farmers described in this chapter will set the stage for the rise of the Populists as discussed in Chapter 22.

- This is a crucial period in the evolution of race relations in the South, bridging the antebellum period and the twentieth century.

- This chapter closes with the observation that, as of 1890, according to the superintendent of the census and the historian Frederick Jackson Turner, "the frontier has gone." Where would Americans now look to fulfill their expansionist urgings?

FURTHER READING

The classic study of the emergence of the New South remains C. Vann Woodward's *Origins of the New South, 1877–1913* (1951). A more recent treatment of southern society after the end of Reconstruction is Edward L. Ayers's *Southern Crossing: A History of the American South, 1877–1906* (1995).

For Bourbon politics, see Jack P. Maddex's *The Virginia Conservatives, 1867–1879* (1970) and William J. Cooper's *The Conservative Regime: South Carolina, 1877–1890* (1968). On the development of southern politics since Reconstruction, see Dewey W. Grantham's *The Life and Death of the Solid South: A Political History* (1988).

A good survey of industralization in the South is James C. Cobb's *Industrialization and Southern Society, 1877–1984* (1984). Scholarship on the textile industry, which formed the heart of the New South's aspirations, includes Patrick J. Hearden's *Independence and Empire: The New South's Cotton Mill Campaigns, 1865–1901* (1982), David L. Carlton's *Mill and Town in South Carolina, 1880–1920* (1982), and Jacqueline D. Hall et al.'s *Like a Family: The Making of a Southern Cotton Mill World* (1987). For developments in the tobacco industry, consult Robert F. Durden's *The Dukes of Durham, 1865–1929* (1975). A fine study of convict leasing is Alex Lichtenstein's *Twice the Work of Free Labor: The Political Economy of Convict Labor in the New South* (1996).

C. Vann Woodword's *The Strange Career of Jim Crow* (3rd ed., 1974) remains the standard on southern race relations. Some of Woodward's points are challenged in Howard N. Rabinowitz's *Race Relations in the Urban South, 1865–1890* (1978), Joel Williamson's *The Crucible of Race* (1984), and John W. Cell's *The Highest Stage of White Supremacy* (1982).

Leon Litwack's *Trouble in Mind: Black Southerners in the Age of Jim Crow* (1998) treats the rise of legal segregation. David M. Oshinsky focuses on race relations and convict leasing in Mississippi in *"Worse Than Slavery": Parchman Farm and the Ordeal of Jim Crow Justice* (1996). J. Morgan Kousser's *The Shaping of Southern Politics: Suffrage Restriction and Establishment of the One-Party South, 1880–1910* (1974) handles disenfranchisement. An award-winning study of white women and the race issue is Glenda Gilmore's *Gender and Jim Crow: Women and the Politics of White Supremacy in North Carolina, 1896–1920* (1996).

Several good books discuss developments in southern agriculture. Roger L. Ransom and Richard Sutch's *One Kind of Freedom: The Economic Consequences of Emancipation* (1977) examines the origins of sharecropping. A more recent sociological analysis is Edward Royce's *The Origins of Southern Sharecropping* (1993).

Good overviews of the transformation of the West are Rodman W. Paul's *The Far West and the Great Plains in Transition, 1859–1908* (rev. ed., 1998) and Geoffrey Ward, David Duncan, and Ken Burns's *The West: An Illustrated History* (1996). The Turner thesis is best presented by Frederick Jackson Turner himself in *The Frontier in American History* (1920).

For powerful and provocative reinterpretations of the frontier and the development of the West, see William Cronon's *Nature's Metropolis: Chicago and the Great West* (1991), Patricia Nelson Limerick's *The Legacy of Conquest: The Unbroken Past of the American West* (1987), Richard White's *"It's Your Misfortune and None of My Own": A New History of the American West* (1991), Donald Worster's *Under Western Skies: Nature and History in the American West* (1992), and *Under an Open Sky: Rethinking America's Western Past* (1992), edited by William Cronon, George Miles and Jay Gitlin.

The role of blacks in western settlement is the focus of Willam L. Katz's *The Black West* (1996) and Nell Painter's *Exodusters: Black Migration to Kansas after Reconstruction* (1992). The best account of the conflicts between Indians and whites is Robert Utley's *The Indian Frontier of the American West, 1846–1890* (1984). For a presentation of the Native American side of the story, see Peter Nabokov and Vine Deloria's *Native American Testimony: A Chronicle of Indian-White Relations from Prophecy to the Present, 1492–1992* (1992).

Federal government efforts to facilitate western agriculture are detailed in William D. Rowley's *Reclaiming the Arid West: The Career of Francis G. Newlands* (1996).

20   BIG BUSINESS AND

ORGANIZED LABOR

CHAPTER ORGANIZER

This chapter focuses on:

- factors that fueled the growth of the post–Civil War economy.

- the methods and achievements of major entrepreneurs.

- the rise of large labor unions.

*A*merica's rise as an industrial and agricultural giant in the late nineteenth century is a fact of towering visibility. Between 1869 and 1899, the nation's population nearly trebled, farm production more than doubled, and the value of manufactures grew sixfold (in constant prices). Within three generations after the Civil War, the nation, which had long been a predominantly rural society dependent upon household production, governed by the requirements of the land and the rhythms of the seasons, burst forth as the world's preeminent economic power. The United States became a highly structured, increasingly centralized, urban-industrial society buffeted by the imperatives of mass production, mass consumption, and time-clock efficiency. Bigness emerged as the prevailing standard of corporate life, and social tensions worsened with the rising scale of business enterprise.

The Hand of Man, *photogravure by Alfred Stieglitz, 1902.*

The industrial revolution created huge corporations that came to dominate the economy during the late nineteenth century. An older economy dependent upon small business and craftspeople could not satisfy the rapidly growing national market. Entrepreneurs who recognized this fact focused their attention on developing systems of mass production and distribution. To do so, they took advantage of striking technological innovations. As the volume of these businesses grew, the owners sought to integrate all the processes of production and distribution into single companies, thus producing even larger firms. Others joined forces with their competitors in an effort to dominate entire industries. This process of industrial combination and concentration, whether the result of natural economic forces or human machinations, transformed the nation's economy and social order. It also provoked widespread dissent and the emergence of an organized labor movement.

THE POST–CIVIL WAR ECONOMY

ECONOMIC EFFECTS OF THE CIVIL WAR   The rise of centralized industry has led all too easily to the judgment that demands created by the Civil War powered a "takeoff" in economic growth. At the same

time, the story goes, the legislative program of the Republicans unleashed business enterprise. But the highly visible successes of wartime
profiteers in arms and supplies, of speculators in various markets, and
of tycoons such as investment banker Jay Cooke, who got rich selling
Treasury bonds, have overshadowed the actual setbacks that marked
the wartime economy. The decade of the 1860s was the only one in
which, on a per-capita basis, economic output actually *decreased,* North
and South, during the mid- to late nineteenth century.

The postwar industrial expansion, which started from a relatively high
base and moved the economy to even higher levels, may have been
fueled *indirectly* by the Civil War. Wartime inflation enhanced the position of those owning property and making profits, while entrepreneurs
forced to save by the war contributed to the immediate postwar period
of speculation. It is not clear, though, that postwar Republican policies
contributed uniquely to economic expansion. The National Banking Act
created a sounder currency, but its effects on the economy were ambiguous. Government aid in building the great transcontinental and regional
railroads simply continued the encouragement to railroads long offered
by state and federal governments. The postwar climate of favoritism to
business was but slightly strengthened by the defeat of southern agrarianism. Postwar tariffs also had ambiguous effects, hampering foreign
competitors but discouraging American exports. The emotional lift of
victory provided an important, if indirect, spur to the northern economy.
After the war Senator John Sherman of Ohio wrote to his brother
William, the famous general: "The truth is the close of the war with our
resources unimpaired gives an elevation, a scope to the ideas of leading
capitalists far higher than anything ever undertaken in this country.
They talk of millions as confidently as before of thousands."

BUILDING THE TRANSCONTINENTAL RAILROADS Railroads were
the first big business, the first magnet for the great financial markets,
and the first industry to develop a large-scale management bureaucracy.
The railroads opened the West, connected raw materials to factories
and markets, and in so doing created a national market. At the same
time, they were themselves gigantic markets for iron, steel, lumber, and
other capital goods.

The renewal of railroad building after the Civil War increased the total mileage from 30,600 in 1862 to 53,000 in 1870 and 94,000 by 1880.

During the 1880s, the greatest decade of railroad building, mileage leaped to 167,000, and then to 199,000 by 1900. Most of this construction filled out the network east of the Mississippi, but the most spectacular exploits were the monumental transcontinental lines built across the desolate plains and rugged mountains. Running through sparsely settled lands, the railroads promised little quick return, but they served the national purpose of binding the country together and so received generous government support.

Until 1850 constitutional scruples had constrained federal aid for internal improvements, although many states had subsidized railroads within their borders. But in 1850 Stephen Douglas secured from Congress a grant of public lands to subsidize two north-south railroads connecting Chicago and Mobile. Over the next twenty years, federal land grants, mainly to transcontinentals, amounted to some 129 million acres. In addition to land, the railroads received financial aid from federal, state, and local governments. Altogether the railroads received about $707 million in cash and $335 million in land.

Before the Civil War, sectional differences over the choice of routes held up the start of a transcontinental line. Secession finally permitted passage of the Pacific Railway Bill, which Lincoln signed into law in 1862. The act authorized a line along a north-central route, to be built by the Union Pacific Railroad westward from Omaha and the Central Pacific Railroad eastward from Sacramento. As amended in 1864, the act donated to these two corporations twenty sections of land per mile of track, in alternating blocs of railroad and government property, and loans of $16,000 to $48,000 per mile, depending on the difficulty of the terrain.

Both railroads began construction during the war, but most of the work was done after 1865, as the companies raced to build most of the line and thereby get most of the subsidy. The Union Pacific pushed across the plains at a rapid pace, avoiding the Rockies by going through Evans Pass in Wyoming. The work crews, with large numbers of ex-soldiers and Irish immigrants as laborers, had to cope with bad roads, water shortages, extreme weather, and Indian marauders. The movable encampments with their retinue of peddlers, gamblers, and prostitutes were aptly dubbed "Hell-on-wheels." Construction of the rail line and bridges was hasty and much of it so flimsy that it had to be redone later, but the Union Pacific pushed on to its celebrated rendezvous with the Central Pacific in 1869.

The Central Pacific crews were mainly Chinese workers lured first by the California gold rush and then by railroad jobs. Thousands of Chinese men migrated to America, raising their numbers in the United States from 7,500 in 1850 to 105,000 in 1880. Most of these "coolie" laborers were single males intent upon accumulating money and then returning to their homeland, where they could then afford to marry and buy a parcel of land. Their temporary status and dream of a good life back in China apparently made them more willing than American laborers to endure the dangerous working conditions and low pay of railroad work. Many Chinese died on the job.

The grading and hauling were very dangerous, especially in the rugged mountains. Fifty-seven miles east of Sacramento, the construction crews encountered the towering Sierras, but they were eventually able to cut through to more level country in Nevada. The Union Pacific had built 1,086 miles compared with the Central Pacific's 689 when the race ended on the salt plains of Utah at Promontory. There, on May 10, 1869, California governor Leland Stanford drove a gold spike that

The celebration after the last spike was driven at Promontory, Utah, on May 10, 1869, completing the first transcontinental railroad.

TRANSCONTINENTAL RAILROAD LINES, 1880s

symbolized the railroad's completion as the telegraph lines signaled the taps of the hammer to a celebrating nation.

The next transcontinental railroad linked the Atchison, Topeka and Santa Fe with the Southern Pacific at Needles in southern California. The Santa Fe completed its line to San Diego by 1884. Meanwhile the Southern Pacific, which had absorbed the Central Pacific, continued on by way of Yuma to El Paso in 1882, where it made connections to St. Louis and New Orleans. To the north, the Northern Pacific had connected Lake Superior with Portland by 1883, and ten years later the Great Northern, which had slowly and carefully been building westward from St. Paul, thrust its way to Tacoma—and without a land grant. Thus before the turn of the century five trunk lines existed, supplemented by connections that afforded other transcontinental routes.

FINANCING THE RAILROADS   The shady financial practices of the railroad men earned them the label of "robber barons," an epithet soon extended to other "captains of industry" as well. The building of both the Union Pacific and Central Pacific—as well as other transcontinentals—induced shameless profiteering through construction companies controlled by insiders, which overcharged the railroad companies. The Crédit Mobilier Company, according to congressional investigators, bought congressmen like sacks of potatoes and charged the Union Pacific $94 million for construction that cost at most $44 million.

In the long run, nevertheless, the federal government recovered much if not all of its investment in transcontinentals and accomplished the purpose of linking the country together. As farms, ranches, and towns sprouted around the rail lines, the value of the alternate sections of government land on either side of the tracks skyrocketed. The railroads also benefited the public by hauling government freight, military personnel and equipment, and the mails at half fare or for free. Moreover, by helping to accelerate the creation of a national market, the railroads spurred economic growth and thereby increased government revenues.

Eastern rail lines, like those in the West, were subject to financial buccaneering, which centered first on the Erie Railroad, the favorite prey of manipulators. The prince of the railroad "robber barons" was Jay Gould, a secretive trickster who mastered the fine art of buying run-

Jay Gould, prince of the railroad buccaneers.

"Commodore" Cornelius Vanderbilt consolidated control of the vast New York Central Railroad in the 1860s.

down railroads, making cosmetic improvements, paying dividends out of capital, and selling out at a profit, meanwhile using corporate funds for personal speculation and judicious bribes. Ousted by a reform group after having looted the Erie Railroad, Gould moved on to richer spoils in western railroads and a variety of other corporations, including Western Union. Nearly every enterprise he touched was either compromised or ruined, while Gould was building a fortune that amounted to $100 million upon his death at age fifty-six.

Few railroad fortunes were built in those freewheeling times by methods of pristine purity, but compared to opportunists such as Gould, most railroad owners were giants of probity. They at least took some interest in the welfare of their companies, if not always in that of the public. Cornelius Vanderbilt, called "Commodore" by virtue of his early exploits in steamboating, stands out among the railroad barons. Already rich before the Civil War, he decided to give up the hazards of wartime shipping and move his capital into land transport. Under his direction, the first of the major eastern railroad consolidations took form.

Vanderbilt engineered the merger of separate trunk lines connecting Albany and Buffalo into a single powerful rail network led by the New York Central. This accomplished, he forged connections to New York City and then tried to corner the stock of his chief competitor, the Erie

Railroad. But the directors of that line beat him there by the simple expedient of printing new Erie stock faster than he could buy it. In 1873, however, he bought the Lake Shore and Michigan Southern Railroad, which gave his lines connections into the lucrative Chicago market. After the Commodore's death in 1877, his son William Henry extended the Vanderbilt railroads to include more than 13,000 miles in the Northeast. The consolidation trend was nationwide: about two-thirds of the nation's railroad mileage fell under the control of only seven major groups by 1900.

MANUFACTURING AND INVENTIONS   The story of manufacturing after the Civil War shows much the same pattern of expansion and merger in both old and new industries. The Patent Office, which had recorded only 276 inventions during its first decade of existence, the 1790s, registered almost 235,000 in the decade of the 1890s. New processes in steel-making and refining were the foundation of the Carnegie and Rockefeller enterprises. The refrigerator car made it possible for the beef, mutton, and pork of the New West to reach a national market, giving rise to great packinghouse enterprises. Corrugated rollers that could crack the hard spicy wheat of the Great Plains provided impetus to the flour milling that centered in Minneapolis under the con-

Advertisement for a refrigerator car, 1853. The advent of refrigeration made transcontinental shipment of perishable food such as meat and seafood possible.

trol of the Pillsburys and others. In 1884 tobacco manufacturing moved into a new stage when the Duke interests employed a machine to roll cigarettes.

The list of innovations can be extended indefinitely: barbed wire, farm implements, George Westinghouse's air brake for trains (1868), steam turbines, gas distribution and electrical devices, Christopher Sholes's typewriter (1867), J. W. McGaffey's vacuum cleaner (1869), and countless others. Before the end of the century, the internal-combustion engine and the motion picture, each the work of many hands, were laying the foundations for new industries that would emerge in the twentieth century.

These technological advances altered the lives of ordinary people far more than did activities in the political and intellectual realms. In no field was this more true than in the applications of electricity to power and communications. Few if any inventions of the times could rival the importance of the telephone, which Alexander Graham Bell patented in 1876. To promote the new device the inventor and his supporters formed the National Bell Telephone Company.

Inventions such as the telephone ushered in a new age of competitive battles among companies. Almost from the first the Bell interests had to defend their patent against competitors. The most dangerous threat came from Western Union which, after turning down a chance to buy Bell's "toy," employed Thomas Edison to develop an improved version. Edison's telephone became the prototype of the modern instrument, with its separate transmitter and receiver. But Bell had a prior claim on the basic principle, and Western Union, rather than risk a legal defeat, sold its rights and properties for a tidy sum, clearing the way for the creation of a monopoly. In 1885 the Bell interests organized the American Telephone and Telegraph Company. By 1899 it was a huge holding company in control of forty-nine licensed subsidiaries and itself an operating company for long-distance lines.

In the rise of electrical industries, the name of Thomas Alva Edison stands above that of other inventors. He started his career at an early age, selling papers and candies on trains, soon learned telegraphy, and began making improvements in that and other areas. He invented the phonograph in 1877 and the first successful incandescent light bulb in 1879. Altogether he created or perfected hundreds of new devices and processes, including the storage battery, dictaphone, mimeograph, dy-

An advertisement for Edison Electric Lighting Outfits, 1890. After Thomas Edison brought basic electricity to homes, extravagances like electric Christmas tree lights became imaginable and obtainable.

namo, electric transmission, and the motion picture. In 1882, with the backing of J. P. Morgan, the Edison Electric Illuminating Company began to supply current to eighty-five customers in New York City, beginning the great electric utility industry. A number of companies making light bulbs merged into the Edison General Electric Company in 1888. Financially secure, Edison retired from business to devote himself full time once again to invention.

The use of direct current limited Edison's lighting system to a radius of about two miles. To cover more distance required an alternating current, which could be transmitted at high voltage and then stepped down by transformers. George Westinghouse, inventor of the air brake, developed the first alternating-current system in 1886 and manufactured the equipment through the Westinghouse Electric Company. Edison resisted the new method as too risky, but the Westinghouse system won the "Battle of the Currents," and the Edison companies had to switch over. After the invention of the alternating-current motor by a Croatian immigrant named Nikola Tesla, Westinghouse acquired and improved the motor and started a revolution by enabling factories to locate wherever they wished. They no longer had to cluster around waterfalls and coal supplies for their energy.

ENTREPRENEURS

Edison and Westinghouse were rare examples of inventors with the luck and foresight to get rich from the industries they created. The great captains of commerce were more often pure entrepreneurs, men skilled mainly in organizing and promoting industry. Several post–Civil War entrepreneurs stand out both for their achievements and for their special contributions: John D. Rockefeller and Andrew Carnegie, for their innovations in organization; J. Pierpont Morgan, for his development of investment banking; and Richard Sears and Alvah Roebuck, pioneers of mail-order retailing.

ROCKEFELLER AND THE OIL TRUST   Born in New York State, the son of a flamboyant, adulterous con man and a frugal, devout Baptist mother, Rockefeller moved as a youth to Cleveland. Soon thereafter, his father abandoned his family and started a new life under an assumed name with a second wife. Raised by his mother, John Rockefeller developed a passion for systematic organization and self-discipline. He was obsessed with precision, order, and tidiness. And early on, he decided to bring order and rationality to the chaotic oil industry.

Cleveland's railroad and ship connections made it a strategic location for servicing the oil fields of western Pennsylvania. The first oil well was struck in 1859 in Titusville, Pennsylvania, and led to the Pennsylvania oil rush of the 1860s. As oil could be refined into kerosene, which could be used in lighting, heating, and cooking, the economic importance of the oil rush soon came to outweigh that of the California gold rush of just ten years before. If it duplicated many of the earlier scenes of disorder, it ended by yielding more wealth. Well before the end of the Civil War, derricks checkered the area, and refineries sprang up in Pittsburgh and Cleveland.

Young Rockefeller, blessed with icy efficiency and tenacious daring, recognized the potential profits in refining oil and backed a refinery in Cleveland started by his friend Samuel Andrews. He then formed a partnership with Andrews, and in 1867 added H. M. Flagler to create the firm of Rockefeller, Andrews, and Flagler. In 1870 Rockefeller incorporated his various interests as the Standard Oil Company of Ohio, capitalized at $1 million.

Wooden derricks crowd the John Benninghoff farm on Oil Creek, Pennsylvania, 1860s.

Although Rockefeller was the largest refiner, he decided to weed out the competition, which he perceived as flooding the market with too much refined oil, which brought down prices and reduced profits. To bring order out of the chaos, in 1872 Rockefeller created the South Improvement Company, which he made the marketing agent for a large percentage of his oil shipments. By controlling this traffic, he gained clout with the railroads, which gave him large rebates (secret discounts) on the standard freight rates in order to keep his high-volume business. In some cases he forced the railroads to provide information on competitors' shipments. Rockefeller then approached his Cleveland competitors and offered to buy them out at his own price. Most of them saw the wisdom of this course. As Rockefeller put it, "the conditions were so chaotic [that is, competitive] that most of the refiners were very desirous to get out of the business." Those who resisted were forced out. As one competitor recalled, we were told that "if we did not sell out, we should be crushed out." In less than six weeks, Rockefeller took over twenty-two of his twenty-six competitors. By 1879 Standard Oil controlled 90 to 95 percent of the oil refining in the country.

Much of Rockefeller's success was based on his determination to "pay nobody a profit." Instead of depending on the products or services of other firms, known as "middlemen," Standard undertook to make its own barrels, cans, staves, and whatever else it needed. In economic

*John D. Rockefeller, whose
Standard Oil Company
dominated the oil business.*

terms this is called vertical integration. The company also kept large
amounts of cash reserves to make it independent of banks in case of a
crisis. In line with this policy, Rockefeller set out also to control his
transportation needs. With Standard owning most of the pipelines leading to railroads, plus the tank cars and the oil-storage facilities, it was
able to dissuade the railroads from servicing eastern competitors. Those
rivals who insisted on holding out then faced a giant marketing organization capable of driving them to the wall with price wars.

Eventually, in order to consolidate scattered business interests under
more efficient control, Rockefeller and his friends resorted to a new legal device: the trust. Long established in law to enable one or more people to manage property belonging to others, such as children or the
mentally incompetent, the trust now was used for another purpose—
centralized control of business. Since Standard Oil of Ohio was not
permitted to hold property out of state, it began in 1872 to place properties or companies acquired elsewhere in trust, usually with the company secretary. This was impractical, however, since the death of the
trustee would endanger the trust. To solve this problem, in 1882 he organized the Standard Oil Trust. All thirty-seven stockholders in various
Standard Oil enterprises would convey their stock to nine trustees, receiving "trust certificates" in return. The nine trustees would thus be
empowered to give central direction to all the Standard companies.

The original plan, never fully carried out, was to organize a Standard
Oil Company in each state in which the trust did business. But the

trust device, widely copied in the 1880s, proved legally vulnerable to prosecution under state laws against monopoly or restraint of trade. In 1892 the supreme court of Ohio ordered the Standard Oil Trust dissolved. For a while the company managed to unify control by the simple device of interlocking directorates, through which the board of directors of one company was made identical or nearly so to the boards of the others. Gradually, however, Rockefeller took to the idea of the holding company: a company that controlled other companies by holding all or at least a majority of their stock. He was convinced that big business was a natural result of capitalism at work. "It is too late," he declared in 1899, "to argue about the advantages of industrial combinations. They are a necessity." That same year Rockefeller brought his empire under the direction of the Standard Oil Company of New Jersey, a holding company. Though less vulnerable to prosecution under state law, some holding companies proved vulnerable to the Sherman Anti-Trust Act of 1890 (see Chapter 22). Meanwhile the term "trust" had become so fixed in the public mind that it was used to describe large combinations under holding companies as well.

CARNEGIE AND THE STEEL INDUSTRY Andrew Carnegie, like Rockefeller, experienced the untypical rise from poverty to riches that came to be known in those days as "the typical American success story." Born in Scotland, he migrated in 1848 with his family to Allegheny,

Andrew Carnegie.

Pennsylvania. Then thirteen, he started out as a bobbin boy in a textile mill at wages of $1.20 per week. At fourteen he was earning $2.50 per week as a telegraph messenger and used his spare time learning to read messages by ear. In 1853 he became personal secretary and telegrapher to Thomas Scott, then district superintendent of the Pennsylvania Railroad and later its president. When Scott moved up, Carnegie took his place as superintendent. During the Civil War, when Scott became assistant secretary of war in charge of transportation, Carnegie went with him, developed a military telegraph system, and personally helped evacuate the wounded from Bull Run.

Carnegie kept on moving—from telegraphy to railroading to bridge building and then to iron- and steel-making and investments. In 1865 Carnegie quit the railroad to devote full time to his own interests. These were mainly in iron and bridge building, but the versatile entrepreneur also made money in oil and sold railroad bonds in Europe. In 1872 he netted $150,000 on one trip, and on that trip met Sir Henry Bessemer, inventor of a new process of steel-making.

The next year Carnegie resolved to concentrate on steel, or as he put it, to put all his eggs in one basket and then watch that basket. Steel was the miracle material of the post–Civil War era, not because it was new, but because it suddenly was cheap. Until the mid–nineteenth century, the only way to make steel was from wrought iron—itself expensive—and in small quantities. Then in 1856 Bessemer invented what became known as the Bessemer converter, a process by which steel could be produced directly and quickly from pig iron. As the volume of steel rose, its price dropped, and its use soared. In 1860 the United States produced only 13,000 tons of steel. By 1880 production had reached 1.4 million tons.

Carnegie launched first the J. Edgar Thompson Steel Works, which he shrewdly named after the head of the Pennsylvania Railroad. As competitors arose, Carnegie picked them off one by one. In 1882, when the Pittsburgh Bessemer Steel Company ran into labor troubles and slackening demand, Carnegie bought out their almost-new Homestead works. When the Duquesne Bessemer Steel Company ran afoul of a smear campaign describing their rails as unsafe, Carnegie bought them out at less than cost.

Carnegie was never a technical expert on steel. He was a promoter, salesman, and organizer with a gift for finding and using men of expert

Carnegie plant at Homestead, Pennsylvania.

ability. He always insisted on up-to-date machinery and equipment, and he used times of recession to expand cheaply. Carnegie retained a large part of his annual profits during good times to tide the business over during lean years. Amid business depressions, when construction costs were low and competitors were forced to the wall, Carnegie used his surplus capital to buy them out and expand. He also preached to his employees a philosophy of constant innovation in order to reduce operating costs. In much of this Carnegie was a typical businessman of the time, if abler and luckier than most.

Carnegie stood out from other businessmen, however, as a thinker who fashioned and publicized a philosophy for big business, a conservative rationale that became deeply implanted in the conventional wisdom of some Americans. He believed that, however harsh their methods at times, he and other captains of industry were on the whole public benefactors. In his best-remembered essay, "The Gospel of Wealth," published in 1889, he argued that in the evolution of society the contrast between the millionaire and the laborer measures the distance society has come. "Not evil, but good, has come to the race from the accumulation of wealth by those who have the ability and energy that produces it." The process had been costly in many ways, but the law of competition was "best for the trade, because it insures the survival of the fittest in every department." / Soc. Darwinism

When he retired at age sixty-five, Carnegie devoted himself to dispensing his fortune for the public good, out of a sincere desire to promote social welfare and to further world peace. He called this being a "distributor" of wealth (he disliked the term "philanthropy"). He gave money to universities, libraries, hospitals, parks, halls for meetings and concerts, swimming pools, and church buildings—in that order.

Rockefeller, too, gave many gifts, mainly to education and medicine. A man of simple tastes, who opposed the use of tobacco and alcohol and believed his fortune was a public trust awarded by God, he became the world's leading philanthropist. He donated more than $500 million during his ninety-eight-year life. "I have always regarded it as a religious duty," Rockefeller said late in life, "to get all I could honorably and to give all I could."

J. P. MORGAN, THE FINANCIER J. Pierpont Morgan was born to wealth and increased it enormously. His father was a partner in a London banking house, which he later came to direct. Young Pierpont at-

J. Pierpont Morgan. *This is the famous portrait by the photographer Edward Steichen, done in 1903.*

tended boarding school in Switzerland and university in Germany. After a brief apprenticeship, he was sent in 1857 to work in a New York firm representing his father's interests, and in 1860 set himself up as its New York agent under the name of J. Pierpont Morgan and Company. This firm, under various names, channeled European capital into America and grew into a financial power in its own right.

⌐Morgan was an investment banker, which meant that he would buy corporate stocks and bonds wholesale and then sell them at a profit.⌐ The growth of large corporations put Morgan's and other investment firms in an increasingly strategic position in the economy. Since the investment business depended on the general good health of client companies, investment bankers became involved in the operation of their clients' firms, demanding places on boards of directors and helping to shape their fiscal dealings. By these means bankers could influence company policies. But this often resulted in heavy emphasis on fiscal matters to the detriment of technical innovation. Eventually people were speaking of the "money trust," the greatest trust of all, with its hand in all kinds of other enterprises.

Morgan early realized that railroads were the key to the times, and he acquired and reorganized one line after another. To Morgan, the stability brought by his operations helped the economy and the public. He believed that the railroaders and other businessmen, if unrestrained, would act like anarchists. Morgan's crowning triumph was consolidation of the steel industry, to which he was led by his interests in railroading. After a rapid series of mergers in the iron and steel industry, he bought out Carnegie's huge steel and iron holdings in 1901. Carnegie set his own price, which came to nearly $500 million, of which his personal share was nearly $300 million. In rapid succession, Morgan added other steel interests and the Rockefeller holdings in both Minnesota's Mesabi ore range and a Great Lakes ore fleet. The magnitude of such a fortune was enhanced by the absence of an income tax, a burden Americans would not face until 1914.

Altogether the new United States Steel Corporation, a holding company for these varied interests, was capitalized at $1.4 billion, a total that was heavily "watered" (valued well above the company's actual assets) but was soon made solid by large profits. The new giant was a marvel of the new century, the first billion-dollar corporation, the climactic event in that age of consolidation.

A lavish dinner celebrated the merger of the Carnegie and Morgan interests into U.S. Steel in 1901. These executives are seated at a table that is shaped like a huge rail.

SEARS AND ROEBUCK   American inventors helped manufacturers after the Civil War produce a vast number of new products, but problems of distribution remained acute. The most important challenge was how to extend the reach of modern commerce to the millions of people who lived on isolated farms and in small towns. In the aftermath of the Civil War, a traveling salesman from Chicago named Aaron Montgomery Ward decided that he could reach more people by mail than on foot and in the process could eliminate the "middlemen" whose services increased the retail price of goods. Beginning in the early 1870s, the Montgomery Ward Company began selling goods at a 40 percent discount through mail-order catalogs.

By the end of the century, a new retailer came to dominate the mail-order industry: Sears, Roebuck and Company, founded by two young midwestern entrepreneurs, Richard Sears and Alvah Roebuck, who began offering a cornucopia of goods by mail in the early 1890s. The Sears, Roebuck and Company catalog in 1897 was 786 pages long and was published in German and Swedish as well as in English. It included groceries, drugs, tools, bells, furniture, ice boxes, stoves and household utensils, musical instruments, farm implements, boots and shoes, clothes, books, and sporting goods. Sears and Roebuck claimed that they operated the "cheapest supply house on earth." One of their advertisements proclaimed: "Shop at Sears and Save." Their ability to buy goods in high volumes from wholesalers enabled them to sell items at prices below those offered in rural general stores. For example, Sears offered a sewing machine for $16 in 1897, a third as much as it cost in a retail shop. The company also specialized in fast and efficient service. "Our army of employees," the catalog claimed, "are instructed to handle every order and letter with care, in fact, to treat every customer at a distance just as they would like to be treated were they in the customer's place and the customer in theirs."

In 1895, Sears, Roebuck and Company moved from Minneapolis to Chicago, then the fastest growing city in the nation. As a rail center and busy freshwater port, Chicago was a magnet attracting manufacturers of all kinds. Alvah Roebuck thereupon decided to sell his share of the company to two Chicago businessmen, Aaron Nussenbaum and Julius Rosenwald. Nussenbaum and Rosenwald expanded the company's products to include virtually every item the public desired. By 1907, Sears, Roebuck and Company had become one of the largest business enterprises in the

Sears, Roebuck, and Company, catalog cover, 1897. Sears' extensive mail-order service and discounted prices allowed its many products to reach people in both cities and backcountry.

nation, with annual sales over $500 million. The new mail-order plant that opened in 1906 was the largest business building in the world. Soon there were regional distribution centers scattered across the country.

The Sears catalog helped create a truly national market and in the process transformed the lives of millions of people. With the advent of free rural mail delivery in 1898 and the widespread distribution of Sears catalogs, families on farms and in small towns and villages could purchase by mail the products that heretofore were either prohibitively expensive or available only to city dwellers. By the turn of the century, 6 million catalogs were distributed each year, and the catalog had become the single most widely read book in the nation except for the Bible. Rural schools that lacked readers used the catalog to teach reading and spelling. Students learned arithmetic by adding up lists of orders, and they learned geography by studying the postal zone maps included in the catalog. Some readers of the Sears catalog thought everything pictured was available for purchase. One lonely farmer wrote a letter to the company in which he proposed marriage to the "girl wearing hat number 68 on p. 153 of your catalog."

A CHANGING ENVIRONMENT FOR WORKERS

THE DISTRIBUTION OF WEALTH   Accompanying the spread of huge industrial combinations was a rising standard of living for most people. If the rich were still getting richer, a lot of other people were at least better off, and the pre–Civil War trend toward even higher concentrations of wealth slacked off. This, of course, is far from saying that disparities in the distribution of wealth had disappeared. One set of estimates reveals that in both 1860 and 1900 the richest 2 percent of American families owned more than a third of the nation's physical wealth, while the top 10 percent owned almost three-fourths. All the nation's physical assets were in the hands of half its families. Studies of social mobility in towns across the country show, however, that while the rise from rags to riches was rare, "upward mobility both from blue-collar to white-collar callings and from low-ranked to high-ranked manual jobs was quite common."

The continuing demand for unskilled or semiskilled workers, meanwhile, attracted new groups entering the workforce at the bottom: immigrants above all, but also growing numbers of women and children. Because of a long-term decline in prices and the cost of living, real wages and earnings in manufacturing went up about 50 percent between 1860 and 1890, and another 37 percent from 1890 to 1914. By modern-day standards, however, working conditions were dreary indeed. At the turn of the century, the average hourly wage in manufacturing was 21.6¢, and average annual earnings were $490. The average workweek was fifty-nine hours, or nearly six ten-hour days, but that was only an average. Most steelworkers put in a twelve-hour day, and as late as the 1920s, a great many worked a seven-day, or eighty-four-hour, week.

A NEW SOCIAL WORLD The fact that wages rose in no way discounts the high social costs of industrialization. In the crowded tenements that were built in major cities, the death rates ran substantially higher than in the countryside. Factories maintained poor health and safety conditions. In 1913, for instance, there were some 25,000 factory fatalities and 700,000 job-related injuries that required at least four weeks' disability. In this new bureaucratic world, ever-larger numbers of people were dependent on the machinery and factories of owners whom they seldom if ever saw. In the simpler world of small shops, workers and employers could enter into close personal relationships; the larger corporation, on the other hand, was likely governed by a bureaucracy in which ownership was separate from management. Much of the social history of the modern world in fact turns on the transition from a world of personal relationships to one of impersonal and contractual relationships.

UNION ORGANIZATION

DISORGANIZED PROTEST Under these circumstances it was far more difficult for workers to organize for mutual benefit than for a few captains of industry to organize for profit. Civic leaders respected property rights more than the rights of labor. Many businessmen believed that a "labor supply" was simply another commodity to be procured at the lowest possible price.

Among workers recently removed from an agrarian world, the idea of permanent unions was slow to take hold. Immigrant workers came from many cultures. They spoke different languages and harbored ethnic animosities. Many, if not most, saw their jobs as transient, the first rung on the ladder to success. They hoped to move on to a homestead, or to return with their earnings to the old farms of their European homelands. With or without unions, though, workers often staged impromptu strikes in response to wage cuts and other grievances. But such action often led to violence, and three incidents of the 1870s colored much of the public's view of labor unions thereafter.

The decade's early years saw a reign of terror in the eastern Pennsylvania coal fields, attributed to an Irish group called the Molly Maguires. Taking their name from an Irish patriot who had directed violent resistance against the British, the group was provoked by the miserable, dangerous working conditions in the mines and the owners' brutal efforts to suppress union activity. Convinced of the justness of their cause, the Molly Maguires used intimidation, beatings, and killings to right perceived wrongs against Irish workers. Later investigations have shown that agents of the mine operators themselves stirred up some of the trouble. The terrorism reached its peak in 1874–1875, and mine owners hired Pinkerton detectives to stop the movement. One of the agents who infiltrated the Mollies produced enough evidence to indict the leaders. At trials in 1876 twenty-four of the Molly Maguires were convicted; ten were hanged. The trials also resulted in a wage reduction in the mines and the final destruction of the Miners' National Association, a weak union the Mollies had dominated.

THE RAILROAD STRIKE OF 1877   Far more significant, because more widespread, was the Great Railroad Strike of 1877, the first major interstate strike. Wage cuts caused the Great Strike. After the Panic of 1873 and the ensuing depression, the major rail lines in the East had cut wages. In 1877 they made another 10 percent cut, which provoked most of the railroad workers at Martinsburg, West Virginia, to walk off the job and block the tracks. Without organized direction, however, their picketing groups degenerated into a mob that burned and plundered railroad property.

Walkouts and sympathy demonstrations spread spontaneously from Maryland to San Francisco. The strike engulfed hundreds of cities and towns, leaving in its wake over a hundred people killed and millions of dollars in property destroyed. Federal troops finally quelled the vio-

The Devastation Wrought by the Railroad Strike of 1877. *Railroad workers in Pittsburgh reacted violently to wage cuts.*

lence. The greatest outbreak began at Pittsburgh, when the Pennsylvania Railroad put on "double-headers" (long trains pulled by two locomotives) in order to reduce crews. Public sympathy for the strikers was so great at first that local militiamen, called out to suppress them, instead joined the workers. Militiamen called in from Philadelphia managed to disperse one crowd at the cost of twenty-six lives, but then found themselves besieged in the railroad's roundhouse, where they disbanded and shot their way out.

Looting, rioting, and burning went on for another day until the frenzy wore itself out. A reporter described the scene as "the most horrible ever witnessed, except in the carnage of war. There were fifty miles of hot rails, ten tracks side by side, with as many miles of ties turned into glowing coals and tons on tons of iron car skeletons and wheels almost at white heat." Public opinion, sympathetic at first, tended to blame the workers for the looting and violence. Eventually the strikers, lacking organized bargaining power, had no choice but to drift back to work. Everywhere the strikes failed.

For many people, the strike raised the specter of a worker-based social revolution like the Paris Commune of 1871, in which disgruntled mobs chanted "Bread or Blood." As a Pittsburgh newspaper warned, "This may be the beginning of a great civil war in this country between labor and capital." Equally disturbing to those in positions of corporate and political power was the presence of many women among the protesters. A Baltimore journalist noted that the "singular part of the disturbances is the very active part taken by the women, who are the wives and mothers of the [railroad] firemen." From the point of view of organized labor, however, the Great Railroad Strike demonstrated potential strength and the need for tighter organization.

THE "SAND LOT" INCIDENT   In California the railroad strike indirectly gave rise to a political movement. At San Francisco's "Sand Lot," a meeting to express sympathy for the strikers ended with attacks on some passing Chinese. Within a few days, sporadic anti-Chinese riots led to a mob attack on Chinatown. Depression had hit the West Coast especially hard, and the Chinese were handy scapegoats for frustrations.

Soon an Irish immigrant, Dennis Kearney, organized the "Workingmen's Party of California." Its platform called for the end of further Chinese immigration. A gifted agitator, himself only recently naturalized, Kearney harangued the "sand lotters" about the "foreign peril" and assaulted the rich for exploiting the poor—sometimes at gatherings beside their mansions on Nob Hill. In 1878 his new party won a hefty number of seats in a state constitutional convention, but managed to incorporate in the state's basic law little more than ineffective attempts to regulate the railroads. The workingmen's movement peaked in 1879 when it elected many members of the new legislature and the mayor of San Francisco. Kearney lacked the gift for building a durable movement, but as his party went to pieces, his anti-Chinese theme became a national issue. In 1882 Congress voted to prohibit Chinese immigration for ten years.

TOWARD PERMANENT UNIONS   Meanwhile, efforts to build a permanent union movement had begun to bear fruit. Earlier efforts, in the 1830s and 1840s, had largely been dominated by reformers with schemes that ranged from free homesteads to utopian socialism. But the 1850s had seen the beginning of "job-conscious" unions in certain skilled trades. By 1860 there were about twenty such craft unions. During the Civil War, because of the demand for labor, such unions grew in strength and numbers.

Until after the war, however, there was no overall federation of these groups. In 1866 some seventy-seven delegates organized the National Labor Union (NLU) at a convention in Baltimore and chose as their leader the head of the Iron Molders. The NLU was composed of congresses of delegates from labor and reform groups more interested in political and social reform, however, than in bargaining with employers. The groups espoused such ideas as the eight-hour workday, workers' cooperatives, greenbackism (the printing of paper money to inflate the currency and thereby relieve debtors), and equal rights for women and blacks. After the head of the union died suddenly, its support fell away quickly. The National Labor Union cannot be labeled a total failure, however. It was influential in persuading Congress to enact an eight-hour workday for federal employees and to repeal the Contract Labor Law, which had been passed during the Civil War to encourage the importation of labor. Employers had taken advantage of the Contract Labor Law to recruit foreign laborers who were willing to work for lower wages than their American counterparts. The National Labor Union, moreover, undertook to encourage the organization of black workers, but with little success.

THE KNIGHTS OF LABOR   Before the National Labor Union collapsed, another group of national standing had emerged: the Noble and Holy Order of the Knights of Labor. The name evoked the aura of medieval guilds. The founder of the Knights of Labor, Uriah S. Stephens, a Philadelphia tailor, was a habitual "joiner" involved with several secret orders, including the Masons. His early training for the Baptist ministry also affected his outlook. Secrecy, he felt, along with a semireligious ritual, would protect members against retaliation and at the same time create a sense of solidarity.

In 1869, with Stephens as leader, nine Philadelphia tailors founded the order. At first it grew slowly, but in 1873 it formed its first district assembly in the Philadelphia area. During the years of depression, as other unions collapsed, it spread more rapidly, and in 1878 its first General Assembly established a national organization. Its preamble and platform endorsed the reforms advanced by previous workingmen's groups, including producers' and consumers' cooperatives, homesteads, bureaus of labor statistics, mechanics' lien laws (to ensure payment of salaries), elimination of convict-labor competition, the eight-hour day, and greenbacks. One plank in the platform, far ahead of the times, called for equal pay for equal work by both men and women.

Throughout its existence the Knights emphasized reform measures and preferred boycotts to strikes as a way to put pressure on employers. The constitution of the order allowed as members all who had ever worked for wages except lawyers, doctors, bankers, and those who sold liquor. Theoretically it was one big union of all workers, skilled and un-skilled, regardless of race, color, creed, or sex. Each local assembly was to be formed on such a basis, but in practice some local and district assemblies were organized on a craft basis, such as the telegraphers and cigarmakers. Above these stood the General Assembly, a General Executive Board, and at the head, a Grand Master Workman.

Stephens was the first elected to this office, but in 1879 he gave way to Terence V. Powderly, the thirty-year-old mayor of Scranton, Pennsylvania. Born of Irish immigrant parents, Powderly had become a railroad switch tender at sixteen but soon moved into the machine shop. In many ways he was unsuited to his new job as head of the Knights. Also, as mayor, county health officer, and part owner and manager of a gro-

Terence V. Powderly in 1885. Powderly led the Knights of Labor at the height of the union's power.

cery store, he had too many irons in the fire. He was physically frail, sensitive to criticism, and indecisive at critical moments. He was temperamentally opposed to strikes, and when they did occur, he did not always back up the local groups involved. Yet the Knights owed their greatest growth to strikes that occurred under his leadership.

In the mid-1880s the Knights grew rapidly. In 1884 a successful strike against wage cuts in the Union Pacific shops at Denver led many railroad workers to form new assemblies. Then, in 1885, the Knights scored a startling victory over Jay Gould. Late in the previous year and early in 1885, Gould had cut workers' wages on his Missouri, Kansas, and Texas and Wabash Railroads. A spontaneous strike on these lines spread to Gould's Missouri-Pacific. As organizers from the Knights of Labor moved in, Gould restored the wage cuts. As a result of this and other successes, the Knights increased from about 100,000 members to more than 700,000 in 1886.

In 1886 the Knights peaked and then went into rapid decline. Taken by surprise in 1885, Jay Gould proceeded to set a trap for the Knights a year later. He spoke favorably of unions and expressed his wish that all railroad workers were organized, but in 1886 he provoked another strike by firing a foreman in the Texas-Pacific shops. When the Knights struck, Gould refused arbitration and hired Pinkerton agents to harass strikers and keep the trains running. The Knights had to call off the strike.

ANARCHISM The tensions between labor and management during the late nineteenth century in both the United States and Europe helped generate the doctrine of anarchism. The anarchists believed that government, any government, was in itself an abusive device used by the rich and powerful to oppress and exploit the working poor. Anarchists dreamed of the eventual disappearance of government altogether, and many of them believed that the transition to this stateless society could be hurried along by promoting revolutionary action among the masses. One favored tactic was the use of dramatic acts of violence against representatives of the government. Many European anarchists emigrated to the United States during the last quarter of the nineteenth century, and they brought with them this belief in the impact of "propaganda of the deed."

THE HAYMARKET AFFAIR   The Haymarket Affair grew indirectly out of agitation for the eight-hour workday. In 1884 union organizers set May 1, 1886, as the deadline for the institution of the eight-hour work-day in all trades. Powderly declined to join in the call for strikes on that day, but some assemblies of the Knights did. Chicago became the center of the movement, and on May 3 the International Harvester plant became the site of an unfortunate clash between strikers and policemen in which one striker was killed.

Leaders of a minuscule anarchist movement in Chicago scheduled an open meeting the following night at Haymarket Square to protest the killing. After listening under a light drizzle to long speeches promoting socialism and anarchism, the crowd was beginning to break up when a group of policemen arrived and called upon the meeting to disperse. At that point somebody threw a bomb at the police, killing one and wounding others. The police then fired into the crowd. In a trial marked by prejudice and hysteria, seven anarchist leaders were sentenced to death despite the lack of any evidence linking them to the bomb-thrower, whose identity was never established. Of these, two were reprieved and some years later pardoned, one committed suicide in prison, but four were hanged. All but one of the group were German-speaking, but that one held a membership card in the Knights of Labor.

The incident at Haymarket Square provoked widespread revulsion against the Knights and labor groups in general. Despite his best efforts, Powderly could never dissociate in the public mind the Knights from the anarchists. He clung to leadership until 1893, but after that the union evaporated. By the turn of the century it was but a memory. A number of problems accounted for the Knights' decline besides fears of their supposed radicalism: a leadership devoted more to reform than to the nuts and bolts of organization, the failure of the Knights' cooperative enterprises, and a preoccupation with politics that led the Knights to sponsor labor candidates in hundreds of local elections. They won a surprising number of races in 1886, but their political efforts proved in the end to be a flash in the pan.

The Knights nevertheless attained some lasting achievements, among them the creation of the federal Bureau of Labor Statistics in 1884 as well as several state bureaus; the Foran Act of 1885, which, though weakly enforced, penalized employers who imported contract labor (an arrangement similar to the indentured servitude of colonial times in which workers were committed to a term of labor in exchange for transportation to America); and a national law enacted in 1880 for the arbitration of labor disputes. The Knights by example also spread the idea of unionism and initiated a new type of union organization: the industrial union, an industrywide union of the skilled and unskilled, begun in special assemblies of railway and telegraph workers. Industrial unions would have the power to match that of the organized concentrations of capital, but not for some time.

The craft unions opposed such industrial unionism. Leaders of the crafts feared that joining with the unskilled would mean a loss of their separate craft identities and a loss of the bargaining power held by skilled workers. They organized workers who shared special skills, such as typographers or cigarmakers. In 1881 the Federation of Organized Trades and Labor Unions came into being as a group similar to the old National Labor Union; it was primarily an association of national craft unions but with representation of state and local assemblies as well.

GOMPERS AND THE AFL   The Knights themselves also began to organize a few special assemblies along craft lines. An effort by the Knights to organize a separate union in the New York cigar trade led the Cigarmakers International Union to call for stronger unity among the existing craft unions. In 1886 delegates from twenty craft unions met in Philadelphia and called on the Knights to cease organizing in trades for which a national union already existed. When the Knights failed to heed the suggestion, a second conference met at Columbus, Ohio, which reorganized the American Federation of Labor (AFL), originally founded in 1881. It differed in structure from the Knights in that it was a federation of national organizations, each of which retained a large degree of autonomy.

Samuel Gompers served as president of the AFL from its start until his death in 1924, with only one year's interruption. Born in London of Dutch-Jewish ancestry, Gompers came to the United States as a teenager, joined the Cigarmakers Union in 1864, and became president of his New York local in 1877. This background was significant. Cigarmakers were the intellectuals of the labor movement. To relieve the tedium of their task, they hired young men to read aloud as they worked, and debated such weighty topics as socialism and Darwinism. Nonetheless, Gompers and other leaders of the union focused on concrete economic gains, avoiding involvement with utopian ideas or politics. "At no time in my life," Gompers once said, "have I ever worked out a definitely articulated economic theory." "We have no ultimate ends," he told a Senate hearing. "We are going on from day to day. We are fighting only for immediate objects—objects that can be realized in a few years."

Such job consciousness became the policy of the AFL under Gompers, whose lifetime concern was the effectiveness of the federation. He hired organizers to spread unionism and worked as a diplomat to prevent overlapping unions and to settle jurisdictional disputes. The federation represented workers in matters of national legislation and acted as a sounding board for their cause. On occasion it exercised its power to request from members dues for the support of strikes. Gompers, it turned out, was temperamentally more fitted than Powderly for the rough-and-tumble world of unionism. He had a thick hide, liked to talk and drink with workers in the back room, and willingly used the strike to achieve favorable trade agreements, including provisos for union recognition in the form of closed shops (which could hire only union members) or union-preference shops (which could hire others only if no union members were available).

One great objective that Gompers achieved at least in principle was making the eight-hour workday standard. In 1889 the AFL voted to revive May Day demonstrations for the eight-hour workday, abandoned after the Haymarket Affair. But gradually the demonstrations under-

Samuel Gompers, head of the American Federation of Labor.

went a curious change. In 1889 the founding congress of the Socialist International in Paris voted to sponsor rallies for the eight-hour workday worldwide. Later, these evolved into demonstrations for general worker demands, labor solidarity, and socialism. Still later, Communists took up the May Day celebrations and paraded through Moscow to observe a holiday that, its origins forgotten, began with an American demand for the eight-hour workday.

The AFL at first grew slowly, but by 1890 it had surpassed the Knights of Labor in membership. By the turn of the century, it claimed 500,000 members in affiliated unions; in 1914, on the eve of World War I, it had 2 million; and in 1920, it reached a peak of 4 million. But even then it embraced less than 15 percent of the nonagricultural workers. All unions, including the unaffiliated railroad brotherhoods, accounted for little more than 18 percent of these workers. Organized labor's strongholds were in transportation and the building trades. Most of the larger manufacturing industries, including steel, textiles, tobacco, and packinghouses, remained almost untouched. Gompers never frowned on industrial unions, and several became important affiliates of the AFL: the United Mine Workers, the International Ladies' Garment Workers, and the Amalgamated Clothing Workers. But the AFL had its greatest success in organizing skilled workers.

THE HOMESTEAD STRIKE Two violent incidents in the 1890s stalled the emerging industrial union movement and set it back for the next forty years—the Homestead Steel Strike of 1892 and the Pullman Strike of 1894. The Amalgamated Association of Iron and Steel Workers, founded in 1876, had by 1891 a membership of more than 24,000 and was probably the largest craft union at that time. But it excluded the unskilled and had failed to organize the larger steel plants. The Homestead Works at Pittsburgh was an important exception. There the union had enjoyed friendly relations with the Carnegie company until H. C. Frick became its president in 1889. A showdown was delayed, however, until 1892, when the union contract came up for renewal. Andrew Carnegie, who had expressed sympathy for unions in the past, had gone to Scotland and left matters in the hands of Frick. Carnegie, however, knew what was afoot: a cost-cutting reduction in the number of workers through the use of labor-saving devices, and a deliberate attempt to smash the union.

As negotiations dragged on, the company announced it would treat workers as individuals unless an agreement was reached by June 29. A strike, or more properly a lockout of unionists, began on that date. Even before the negotiations ended, Frick had hired as plant guards 300 Pinkerton detectives whose specialty was union-busting. On the morning of July 6, 1892, when the Pinkertons floated up the Monongahela River on barges, unionists were waiting behind breastworks on shore. Who fired the first shot remains unknown, but a battle broke out in which six workers and three Pinkertons died. In the end the Pinkertons surrendered and were marched away, subjected to taunts from crowds in the street. Six days later the state militia appeared at the plant to protect the strikebreakers hired to restore production. The strike dragged on until November, but by then the union was dead at Homestead. Its cause was not helped when an anarchist shot and wounded Frick. Much of the local sympathy for the strikers evaporated.

THE PULLMAN STRIKE The Pullman Strike of 1894 was perhaps the most notable walkout in American history. It paralyzed the economies of twenty-seven states and territories making up the western half of the nation. It involved a dispute at the "model" town of Pullman, Illinois, which housed workers of the Pullman Palace Car Company. The town's idyllic appearance was deceptive. Employees were required to live there, pay rents and utility costs higher than those in nearby towns, and buy goods from company stores. During the Depression of 1893, George Pullman laid off 3,000 of 5,800 employees, and cut wages 25 to 40 percent, but not his rents and other charges. When Pullman fired three members of a grievance committee, a strike began on May 11, 1894.

During this tense period, Pullman workers had been joining the American Railway Union, founded the previous year by Eugene V. Debs. The tall, gaunt Debs was a man of towering influence and charismatic appeal. A child of working-class immigrants, he quit school in 1869 at age fourteen and began working for an Indiana railroad. There, he would later write, "I learned of the hardships of the rail in snow, sleet, and hail, of the ceaseless danger that lurks along the iron highway, the uncertainty of employment, scant wages and altogether trying lot of the workingman, so that from my very boyhood I was made to feel the wrongs of labor." He felt these wrongs so deeply that he eagerly accepted an invitation to start a local of the railroad brotherhood, a craft union of skilled workers.

Still, it was not until the Haymarket bombing that Debs saw an inevitable conflict between labor and management. By the early 1890s he had become a tireless spokesman for labor radicalism, and he launched a crusade to organize *all* railway workers—skilled or unskilled—into the American Railway Union. Soon he was in charge of a powerful new labor organization, and he quickly turned his attention to the Pullman controversy.

After Pullman refused Debs's plea for arbitration, the union workers stopped handling Pullman cars. This tied up most of the railroads in the Midwest, which also greatly affected the traffic to the West. Railroad executives then brought strikebreakers from Canada and elsewhere, instructing them to connect mail cars to Pullman cars so that interference with Pullman cars also meant interference with the mails. The U.S. attorney-general, a former railroad attorney himself, swore in 3,400 special deputies to keep the trains running. When clashes occurred between these deputies and some of the strikers, President Grover Cleveland sent federal troops into the Chicago area, where the strike was centered. The Illinois governor insisted that the state could keep order, but Cleveland claimed authority and a duty to ensure delivery of the mails.

Troops guarding the railroads during the Pullman Strike, 1894.

Meanwhile, the attorney-general won an injunction forbidding any interference with the mails or any combination to restrain interstate commerce; the principle was that a strike or boycott violated the Sherman Anti-Trust Act. On July 13 the union called off the strike and on the same day the district court cited Debs for violating the injunction and sentenced him to six months in jail. The Supreme Court upheld the decree in the case of *In re Debs* (1895) on broad grounds of national sovereignty: "The strong arm of the national government may be put forth to brush away all obstructions to the freedom of interstate commerce or the transportation of the mails." Debs served his term, during which time he read deeply in socialist literature, and he emerged to devote the rest of his life to that cause.

SOCIALISM AND THE UNIONS   The major American unions, for the most part, never allied themselves with the socialists, as many European labor movements did. But socialist ideas had been abroad in the country at least since the 1820s. Marxism, one strain of socialism, was imported mainly by German immigrants. Karl Marx's International Workingmen's Association, the First International, founded in 1864, inspired a few affiliates in the United States. In 1872, at Marx's urging, the headquarters was moved from London to New York. In 1876 the First International expired, but the next year followers of Marx in America organized the Socialist Labor party, a group so filled with immigrants that German was its official language in the first years.

The movement gained little notice before the rise of Daniel DeLeon in the 1890s. As editor of its paper, *The People,* he became the dominant figure in the party. A native of the Dutch West Indies, DeLeon had studied law and lectured for some years at Columbia University. He proposed to organize industrial unions with a socialist purpose, and to build a political party that would abolish the state once it gained power, after which the unions of the Socialist Trade and Labor Alliance would become the units of control. His ideas seem to have influenced Lenin, leader of the Bolshevik Revolution of 1917, but DeLeon preached revolution at the ballot box, not by violence.

Debs was more successful at building a socialist movement in America. To many, DeLeon seemed doctrinaire and inflexible. Debs, however, built his new party by following a method now traditional in the

Eugene V. Debs, founder of the American Railway Union and later candidate for president as head of the Socialist Party of America.

United States: he formed a coalition, one that embraced viewpoints ranging from moderate reform to doctrinaire Marxism. In 1897 Debs announced that he was a socialist and organized the Social Democratic party from the remnants of the American Railway Union. He got over 4,000 votes as its candidate for president in 1900. In 1901 his followers joined a number of secessionists from DeLeon's party, led by Morris Hillquit of New York, to set up the Socialist Party of America. In 1904 Debs polled over 400,000 votes as the party's candidate for president and more than doubled that to almost 900,000 votes in 1912, or 6 percent of the popular vote. In 1910 Milwaukee elected a socialist mayor and congressman.

By 1912 the Socialist party seemed well on the way to becoming a permanent fixture in American politics. Thirty-three cities had socialist mayors, including Berkeley, California; Butte, Montana; Flint and Jackson, Michigan; and Milwaukee, Wisconsin. The party sponsored five English daily newspapers, eight foreign-language dailies, and a number of weeklies and monthlies. Its support was not confined to urban workers and intellectuals. In the Southwest the party built a sizable grassroots following among farmers and tenants. Oklahoma, for instance, in 1910 had more paid-up party members than any other state except New York, and in 1912 gave 16.5 percent of its popular vote to Debs, a greater proportion than any other state ever gave. But the Socialist party reached its peak in 1912. During World War I, it was wracked by disagreements over America's participation in the war, and it was split thereafter by desertions to the new Communist party.

THE WOBBLIES   During the years of Socialist party growth, there emerged a parallel effort to revive industrial unionism, led by the Industrial Workers of the World (IWW). The chief base for this group was the Western Federation of Miners, organized at Butte, Montana, in 1893. Over the next decade the Western Federation was the storm center of violent confrontation with unyielding bosses who mobilized private armies against it in Colorado, Idaho, and elsewhere. In 1905 the founding convention of the IWW drew a variety of people who opposed the AFL's philosophy. Debs participated, although many of his comrades preferred to work within the AFL. DeLeon seized this chance to strike back at craft unionism. A radical manifesto issued from the meetings, arguing that the IWW "must be founded on the class struggle, and its general administration must be conducted in harmony with the recognition of the irrepressible conflict between the capitalist class and the working class."

But the IWW waged class war better than it articulated class ideology. Like the Knights of Labor, it was designed to be "One Big Union," including all workers, skilled or unskilled. Its roots were in the mining and lumber camps of the West, where unstable conditions of employment created a large number of nomadic workers, to whom neither the AFL's pragmatic approach nor the socialists' political appeal held much attraction. The revolutionary goal of the Wobblies, as they came to be called, was an idea labeled syndicalism by its French supporters: the ultimate destruction of the state and its replacement by one big union. But just how it would govern remained vague.

Like other radical groups, the IWW was split by sectarian disputes. Because of policy disagreements, all the major founders withdrew, first the Western Federation of Miners, then Debs, then DeLeon. William D. "Big Bill" Haywood of the Western Federation remained, however, and as its leader held the group together. Although since embellished in

Textile workers strike, Lawrence, Massachusetts, 1912. The IWW of this Lawrence mill engaged in a violent strike for increased wages, overtime pay, and other benefits.

myth, Haywood was in fact an imposing figure. Well over six feet tall, handsome and muscular, he commanded the attention and respect of his listeners. This hardrock miner, union organizer, and socialist from Salt Lake City despised the AFL and its conservative labor philosophy. He called Samuel Gompers "a squat specimen of humanity" who was "conceited, petulant, and vindictive." Instead of following Gompers's advice to organize only skilled workers, Haywood promoted the concept of one all-inclusive union whose credo would be the promotion of a socialism "with its working clothes on."

But Haywood and the Wobblies were reaching out to the fringe elements that had the least power and influence, chiefly the migratory workers of the West and the ethnic groups of the East. Always ambivalent about diluting their revolutionary principles, they scorned the usual labor agreements, even when they participated in them. Consequently, they engaged in spectacular battles with capital but scored few victories. The largest was a textile strike at Lawrence, Massachusetts, in 1912, that garnered wage raises, overtime pay, and other benefits. But the next year a strike of silk workers at Paterson, New Jersey, ended in disaster, and the IWW entered a rapid decline.

Branded as anarchists, bums, and criminals, the IWW was effectively destroyed during World War I, when most of its leaders were jailed for conspiracy because of their militant opposition to the war. Big Bill Haywood fled to the Soviet Union, where he married a Russian woman, died in 1928, and was honored by burial in the Kremlin wall. The Wobblies left behind a rich folklore of nomadic working men and a gallery of heroic agitators such as Elizabeth Gurley Flynn, a dark-haired Irish woman who at age eighteen chained herself to a lamppost to impede her arrest during a strike. The movement also bequeathed martyrs such as the Swedish singer and labor organizer Joe Hill, framed (so the faithful assumed) for murder and executed by a Utah firing squad. His last words were written to Haywood: "Goodbye, Bill. I die like a true blue rebel. Don't waste any time mourning. Organize." The intensity of conviction and devotion to a cause shown by Hill, Flynn, and others ensured that the IWW's ideal of a classless society did not die.

MAKING CONNECTIONS

- The Darwinian ideas implicit in the attitudes of many leading entrepreneurs, especially Andrew Carnegie, are described in greater detail in the next chapter.

- In response to the growth of the railroads, reformers in the 1880s and 1890s began to push for regulation, a trend explored in Chapter 22.

- The economic and industrial growth described in this chapter was an important factor in America's "new imperialism" in the late nineteenth century, as shown in Chapter 23.

- The socialist approach to reform was a significant influence on the Progressive movement, covered in Chapter 24.

FURTHER READING

For a masterly synthesis of post–Civil War industrial development, see Walter Licht's *Industrializing America: The Nineteenth Century* (1995). Of more specialized interest are Alfred D. Chandler's *The Visible Hand: The Managerial Revolution in American Business* (1977), and Maury Klein's *The Flowering of the Third America: The Making of an Organizational Society, 1850–1920* (1992).

On the growth of railroads see Albro Martin's *Railroads Triumphant: The Growth, Rejection, and Rebirth of a Vital American Force* (1992). Walter Licht's *Working for the Railroad: The Organization of Work in the Nineteenth Century* (1983) treats the life of the railroad workers. Gabriel Kolko's *Railroads and Regulation, 1877–1916* (1965) argues that the entrepreneurs themselves sought regulation.

On entrepreneurship in the iron and steel sector, see Thomas J. Misa's *A Nation of Steel: The Making of Modern America, 1865–1925* (1995). The best biography of the leading business tycoon is Ron Chernow's *Titan: The Life of John D. Rockefeller, Sr.* (1998).

Nathan Rosenberg's *Technology and American Economic Growth* (1972) documents the growth of invention during the period. For an absorbing biography of the foremost inventor of the era, see Neil Baldwin's *Edison: Inventing the Century* (1995).

Much of the recent scholarship on labor stresses the traditional values and the culture of work that people brought to the factory. Herbert G. Gutman's *Work, Culture, and Society in Industrializing America* (1976) best introduces these themes. The best survey remains David Montgomery's *The Fall of the House of Labor: The Workplace, the State and American Labor Activism, 1865–1925* (1987).

For the role of women in the changing workplace, see Alice Kessler-Harris's *Out to Work* (1983), Susan E. Kennedy's *If All We Did Was to Weep at Home: A History of White Working-Class Women in America* (1979), and S. J. Kleinberg's *The Shadow of the Mills: Working-Class Families in Pittsburgh, 1870–1907* (1989).

As for the labor groups, Gerald N. Grob's *Workers and Utopias* (1961) examines the difference in outlook between the Knights of Labor and the American Federation of Labor. For the Knights, see Leon Fink's *Workingmen's Democracy* (1983). Also useful is Susan Levine's *Labor's*

True Woman (1984), on the role of women in the Knights. To trace the rise of socialism among organized workers, see Nick Salvatore's *Eugene V. Debs: Citizen and Socialist* (1982) and Robert J. Constantine's *Letters of Eugene V. Debs* (1990). Strikes are discussed in Kevin Kenny's *Making Sense of the Molly Maguires* (1998), Paul Avrich's *The Haymarket Tragedy* (1984), and Paul Krause's *The Battle for Homestead, 1880–1892: Politics, Culture, and Steel* (1992).

21 ∞ THE EMERGENCE
OF URBAN AMERICA

CHAPTER ORGANIZER

This chapter focuses on:

- immigration and the growth of the modern city.

- the rise of powerful reform movements.

- the impact of Darwinian thought on the social sciences.

- literary and philosophical trends of the late nineteenth century.

*D*uring the second half of the nineteenth century, the United States experienced an urban revolution unparalleled in world history up to that point in time. As factories, mines, and mills sprouted across the landscape, cities grew up around them. The late nineteenth century, declared an economist in 1899, was "not only the age of cities, but the age of great cities." Between 1860 and 1910, the urban population grew from 6 million to 44 million. The United States was rapidly losing its rural flavor. Indeed, by 1920, more than half of the population would be living in urban areas.

The rise of big cities during the nineteenth century created a distinctive urban culture. People from different ethnic and religious back-

The elevator at Lord & Taylor store, 1873.

grounds and representing every walk of life poured into the high-rise apartment buildings and ramshackle tenements springing up in every major city. They came in search of jobs, wealth, and new opportunities. Rising wages and the availability of new consumer goods in the dazzling new downtown department stores improved the material standard of living for millions—while widening the gap between the poor and the affluent. Broadened access to public education and to public health services improved literacy and lowered infant mortality rates (although the death rate for adult black males remained quite high). Break-throughs in medical science eventually brought cures for tuberculosis, typhoid, and diphtheria—although these infectious diseases remained the century's leading killers.

The rise of metropolitan America also created an array of new social problems. Corporations became so powerful that some of their owners decided that they were above the law. When someone warned Cornelius Vanderbilt, the railroad tycoon, that he might be violating the law, he is alleged to have replied, "Law? What do I care about the law. Hain't I got the power?" Rapid urban development also produced widespread poverty and political corruption. How to feed, clothe, shelter, and educate the new arrivals taxed the imagination—and patience—of many Americans.

AMERICA'S MOVE TO TOWN

The mushrooming cities served as powerful magnets that lured workers by the millions from the countryside and overseas. This urban-industrial revolution greatly increased the national wealth and transformed the pace and tenor of American life. City people and folks who worked in factories rather than on farms, while differing significantly among themselves, also became distinctively and recognizably urban in demeanor and outlook.

EXPLOSIVE URBAN GROWTH   The frontier was a safety valve, historian Frederick Jackson Turner said in his influential thesis on American development. Its cheap lands afforded a release for the population pressures mounting in the cities. If there was such a thing as a safety valve in his own time, however, he had it exactly backward. The flow of population toward the city was greater than toward the West, and "country come to town" epitomized the American people better than the occasional city "dude" who turned up in cow country.

Much of the westward movement in fact was itself an urban movement, spawning new towns near the mining digs or at the railheads. More often than not, western towns anticipated settlement. They supplied headquarters for the land boomers and services for the hinterlands. On the Pacific coast a greater portion of the population was urbanized than anywhere else; its major concentrations were around San Francisco Bay at first, and then in Los Angeles, which became a boom town after the arrival of the Southern Pacific and Santa Fe Railroads in the 1880s. Seattle grew quickly, first as the terminus of three transcontinental railroad lines, and by the end of the century as the staging area for the Yukon gold rush. Minneapolis, St. Paul, Omaha, Kansas City, and Denver were no longer the mere villages they had been in 1860. The South, too, produced new cities: Durham, North Carolina, and Birmingham, Alabama, which were centers of tobacco and iron manufactures, and Houston, Texas, which handled cotton and cattle, and later oil.

Trade and transportation had been the city builders of the past. Eight of the nine cities that by 1860 had passed 100,000 in population were ports, and the ninth (Brooklyn) was a suburb to the largest port. By the

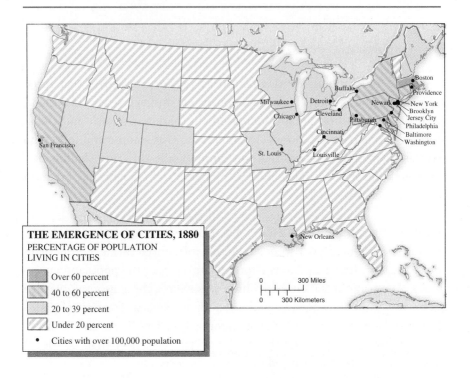

THE EMERGENCE OF CITIES, 1880
PERCENTAGE OF POPULATION
LIVING IN CITIES

Over 60 percent

40 to 60 percent

20 to 39 percent

Under 20 percent

• Cities with over 100,000 population

late nineteenth century no city could hope to thrive without at least one railroad, and most had a cluster of railroads. But it was the explosive rise of industry that powered the growth of new cities during this period. Industry brought huge concentrations of labor, and both required the proliferation of services that became synonymous with city life.

The emergence of the major cities was completed during the years from 1860 to 1910. After that, new cities sprang up only in unusual circumstances: Miami was the product of tourism brought by the coastal railroad, while Tulsa resulted from an oil boom. In those fifty years, population in incorporated towns of 2,500 or more grew from 6 million to 45 million, or from 20 to 46 percent of the nation's total population.

While the Far West had the greatest proportion of urban population, the Northeast had far greater numbers of people in its teeming cities. There the situation that Thomas Jefferson had so dreaded was coming to pass: the people "piled high up on one another in the cities," and worse, these people increasingly were landless, tool-less, and home-less—an urban proletariat with nothing but their labor to sell. By 1900

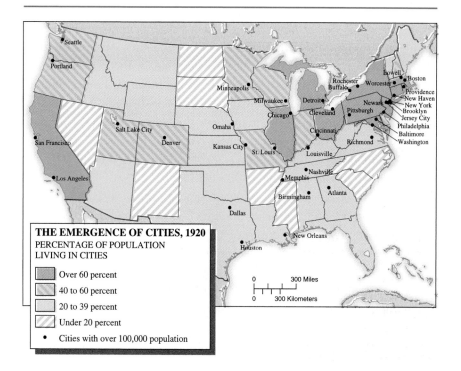

THE EMERGENCE OF CITIES, 1920
PERCENTAGE OF POPULATION
LIVING IN CITIES

- Over 60 percent
- 40 to 60 percent
- 20 to 39 percent
- Under 20 percent
- • Cities with over 100,000 population

more than 90 percent of the residents in New York's Manhattan lived in rented homes or tenements.

The cities expanded both vertically and horizontally to absorb their huge populations. In either case, transportation innovations played an important role: the elevator, the streetcar, and, before the end of the century, the first automobiles. The first safety elevator, which would not fall if the rope or cable broke, was developed in 1852 by Elisha Graves Otis. In 1889 the Otis Elevator Company installed the first electric elevator, which made possible the erection of taller buildings. Before the 1860s, few structures had gone higher than three or four stories.

Before the 1890s, the chief power sources of urban transport were either animals or steam. Horse- and mule-drawn streetcars had appeared in antebellum cities, but they were slow and cumbersome, and cleaning up after the animals added to the cost. In 1873 San Francisco became the first city to use cable cars that clamped onto a moving underground cable driven by a central power source. Some cities used steam-powered trains on elevated tracks, but by the 1890s electric trolleys were replacing these.

Such systems spread rapidly, and in some places mass-transit companies began to dig underground passages for their cars. Around the turn of the century, subway systems began operation in Boston, New York, and Philadelphia. Advances in bridge building through the use of steel and the perfection of the steel-cable suspension bridge also extended the reach of commuters. The marvels of the age were James B. Eads's cantilevered steel bridge over the Mississippi at St. Louis (1874) and John A. and Washington Roebling's cable-supported Brooklyn Bridge (1883), which linked Brooklyn to Manhattan.

The spread of mass transit allowed large numbers of people to become commuters, and a growing middle class (working folk often could not afford even the nickel fare) retreated to quieter tree-lined "streetcar suburbs" whence they could travel into the central city for business or entertainment. The pattern of urban growth often became a sprawl, since it took place usually without plan, in the interest of a fast buck, and without thought to the need for parks and public services.

The use of horse-drawn railways, cable cars, and electric trolleys helped transform the social characters of cities. Until the implementation of such new transportation systems, people of all classes lived and worked together in the central city. After the Civil War, however, the emergence of suburbs began to segregate people according to their eco-

The Brooklyn Bridge under construction, 1877.

*Central Park tunnel, 1903. The subway system helped abate the
street-level congestion that plagued cities at the turn-of-the-century.*

nomic standing. The more affluent moved outside the city, leaving the
working folk, many of whom were immigrants, behind. The poorer districts in the city became more congested and crime-ridden as the population grew, fueled by waves of newcomers from abroad.

CITY POLITICS   The sheer size of cities helped create a new form of
politics. Since individuals could hardly provide for themselves such
necessary services as transit, paving, water, sewers, street lighting and
cleaning, and fire and police protection, they came increasingly to rely
on city government. Meanwhile, many city problems were handled by
local political bosses who traded in patronage favors and graft. Big-city
political machines were not altogether sinister in their effects: they provided food and money for the poor, fixed problems at city hall, and generally helped immigrants in their adjustment to a new life. One ward
boss in Boston said: "There's got to be in every ward somebody that any
bloke can come to—no matter what he's done—and get help. Help, you
understand, none of your law and justice, but help."

   In return, the political professionals felt entitled to some reward for
having done the grubby work of the local organization. George Wash-

ington Plunkitt, for instance, a power in Tammany Hall (New York City's Democratic organization) at the turn of the century, saw nothing wrong with a little honest graft. "Well, I'm tipped off, say, that they're going to lay out a new park at a certain place. . . . I go to that place and buy up all the land I can in the neighborhood. . . . Ain't it perfectly honest to charge a good price and make a profit on my investment and foresight?" Dishonest graft would consist of "robbin' the city treasury or levyin' blackmail on disorderly houses or workin' in with the gamblers and lawbreakers." For his own epitaph Plunkitt proposed: "He Seen His Opportunities, and He Took 'Em."

MOVING FROM COUNTRY TO CITY   But whatever the problems of the cities, the wonder of their glittering new electric lights, their streetcars, telephones, amusements, newspapers and magazines, and a thousand other enticements exerted a magnetic lure on the youth of the farms. Hamlin Garland told in his autobiography, *A Son of the Middle Border,* of his mixed sense of dread and wonder at first visiting Chicago with his brother. The city first appeared from the train window enveloped in clouds of smoke, "the soaring banners of the great and gloomy inland metropolis, whose dens of vice and houses of greed had been so often reported to me." Later the two young men wandered the streets: "Everything interested us. The business section so sordid to others was grandly terrifying to us. . . . Nothing was commonplace, nothing was ugly to us."

The new cities threw into stark contrast the frustration of unending farm toil, the isolation and loneliness of country life. The exodus from the countryside was especially evident in the East, where the census documented the shift in population from country to city, and stories began to appear of entire regions where buildings were abandoned and going to ruin, where the wilderness was reclaiming farms that had been wrested from it during the previous 250 years.

THE NEW IMMIGRATION

The industrial revolution brought to American shores waves of new immigrants from every part of the globe. By the end of the century, nearly 30 percent of the residents of major cities were foreign-born.

These newcomers provided much-needed labor, but their arrival created ugly racial and ethnic tensions.

AMERICA'S PULL   European immigrants not only moved from country to city in their own lands, but increasingly they moved from the great agricultural areas of eastern and southern Europe directly to the foremost cities of America. They gathered in these cities in order to live with others of like language, customs, and religion, and also because they lacked the means to go west and take up farms. Though cities of the South and West (excepting the Far West) drew their populations mainly from the native-born of their regions, American cities as a whole drew more residents from abroad. During the peak decade of immigration, 1900–1910, 41 percent of the urban newcomers arrived from abroad, while 30 percent were American-born, 22 percent were the products of natural increase, and almost 8 percent lived in areas annexed to the cities.

Ethnic neighborhoods, sometimes populated by those from a single province or town, preserved familiar folkways and shielded newcomers from the shocks of a strange culture. In 1890 four out of five New Yorkers were foreign-born, a higher proportion than any other city in the world. New York had twice as many Irish as Dublin, as many Germans as Hamburg, and half as many Italians as Naples. "A map of the city, colored to designate nationalities," Jacob Riis (a native of Denmark) wrote in *How the Other Half Lives* (1890), "would show more stripes than . . . a zebra, and more colors than any rainbow." In 1893 Chicago claimed the largest Bohemian (Czech) community in the world, and by 1910 the size of its Polish population ranked behind only Warsaw and Lodz.

This nation of immigrants continued to draw new inhabitants for much the same reasons as always, and from much the same strata of society. Immigrants took flight from famine or the grinding lack of opportunity in their native lands. They fled racial, religious, and political persecution and compulsory military service. Yet one historian has suggested that "the desire to get cheap labor, to take in passenger fares, and to sell land have probably brought more immigrants than the hard conditions of Europe, Asia, and Africa have sent."

More immigrants probably *were* pulled by America's promise than were pushed out by conditions at home. American industries, seeking

Steerage Deck of the S.S. *Pennland, 1893. These immigrants are about to arrive at New York's Ellis Island.*

cheap labor, kept recruiting agents on watch abroad and at American ports. Railroads, eager to sell land and build up the traffic on their lines, put out tempting propaganda in a medley of languages. Many of the western and southern states set up official bureaus and agents to attract immigrants. Under the Contract Labor Law of 1864, the federal government itself encouraged immigration by helping to pay the immigrant's passage through a lien on his or her wages. The law was repealed in 1868, but not until 1885 did the government forbid companies to import contract labor, which put immigrant workers under the control of their employers. However, domestic service and some skilled occupations were exempted from the ban, and evasion was easy.

From 1820 (when by requirement of Congress official statistics on immigration began to be kept) to 1900, about 20 million immigrants entered American ports, more than half of them coming after the Civil War. The tide of immigration rose from just under 3 million in the 1870s to more than 5 million in the 1880s, then fell to a little over 3.5 million in the depression decade of the 1890s, and rose to its high-water mark of nearly 9 million in the first decade of the new century.

The numbers declined to 6 million in the 1910s and 4 million in the 1920s, after which official restrictions cut the flow of immigration down to a negligible level.

A NEW WAVE   During the 1880s, the continuing search for cheap labor combined with renewed persecutions in eastern Europe to bring a noticeable change in the source of immigration, one fraught with meaning for American social history. Before 1880 immigrants were mainly of Teutonic and Celtic origin, hailing from northern and western Europe. But by the 1870s there were signs of a change. The proportion of Latin, Slavic, and Jewish peoples from southern and eastern Europe rose sharply. After 1890 these groups made up a majority of the newcomers, and by the first decade of the new century they formed 70 percent of the immigrants to this country. Among these new immigrants were Italians, Hungarians, Czechs, Slovaks, Poles, Serbs, Croats, Slovenes, Russians, Romanians, and Greeks—all people of markedly different cultural and language stocks from those of western Europe, and most followers of different religions, including Judaism and Catholicism.

Immigrants, with identification papers, newly arrived at Ellis Island.

ELLIS ISLAND   As the number of immigrants passing through the Port of New York soared during the late nineteenth century, the state-run Castle Garden receiving center overflowed with corruption. Money-changers cheated new arrivals, railroad agents overcharged them for tickets, and baggage handlers engaged in blackmail. With reports of these abuses filling the newspapers, Congress ordered an investigation of Castle Garden, which resulted in the closure of the facility in 1890. Thereafter the federal government's new Bureau of Immigration took over the business of admitting newcomers to New York City.

To launch this effort, Congress funded the construction of a new reception center on a tiny island off the New Jersey coast, a mile south of Manhattan and some 1,300 feet from the Statue of Liberty. The statue, unveiled in 1886, was a centennial gift from the French government commemorating the Franco-American alliance during the Revolutionary War. It soon came to be viewed as a symbol of hope for immigrants passing under "Lady Liberty." In the base of the statue, workers had chiseled the poet Emma Lazarus's tribute to the promise of new life in America:

> Give me your tired, your poor,
> Your huddled masses yearning to breathe free,
> The wretched refuse of your teeming shore.
> Send these, the homeless, tempest-tossed to me,
> I lift my lamp beside the golden door!

In 1892 Ellis Island (named after its late-eighteenth-century owner, Samuel Ellis) opened its doors to the "huddled masses" of the world. Until 1954, when it closed, some 12 million people first touched American soil there. In 1907, the reception center's busiest year, more than a million new arrivals filtered through the cavernous Great Hall, an average of about 5,000 per day; in one day alone immigration officials processed some 11,750 arrivals. These were the immigrants who arrived crammed into the steerage compartments deep in the ships' hulls. Those immigrants who could afford first- and second-class cabins did not have to visit Ellis Island; they were examined on board ship, and most of them simply walked down the gangway onto the docks in lower Manhattan.

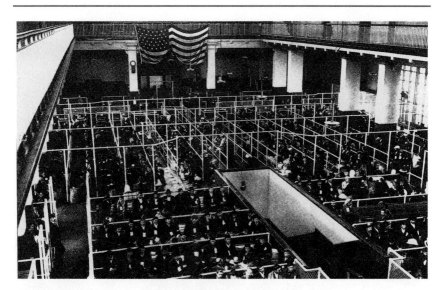

Immigrants waiting in the Registry Room for further inspections.

The prevailing atmosphere at Ellis Island was not comforting. Its bureaucratic purpose was to process immigrants, not welcome them. An army of inspectors, doctors, nurses, and public officials questioned, examined, and documented the newcomers. Inspectors asked twenty-nine probing questions, including: Have you money, relatives, or a job in the United States? Are you a polygamist? An anarchist? Doctors and nurses poked and prodded, searching for any sign of debilitating handicap or infectious disease. All the while, the immigrant worried: "Will they let me in?" Although some who were sick or lame were detained for days or weeks, the vast majority of immigrants received stamps of approval and were on their way after three or four hours. "I was jostled and dragged and shoved and shouted at," recalled one immigrant. "I took it philosophically. I had been through the performance many times before—at the Hungarian border, at Vienna, in Germany, in Holland." Only 2 percent of the newcomers were denied entry altogether, usually because they were criminals, anarchists, or carriers of some "loathsome or dangerous contagious disease," such as tuberculosis or trachoma, a contagious eye disease resulting in blindness. These luckless folk were then returned to their places of origin, with the steamship companies picking up the tab.

A health inspector checks immigrants on Ellis Island, 1909. Before being granted entry, each immigrant was examined for contagious diseases, including trachoma, an eye disease that could lead to blindness.

Between 1892 and 1954, 70 percent of all European immigrants circulated through Ellis Island (others landed at Boston, Philadelphia, Baltimore, New Orleans, and Galveston). Among the arrivals at Ellis Island were many youngsters who would distinguish themselves in their new country: songwriter Irving Berlin (Russia), football legend Knute Rockne (Norway), Supreme Court justice Felix Frankfurter (Austria), singer Al Jolson (Lithuania), and comedian Bob Hope (England). But many others found America's opportunities harder to grasp. An old Italian saying expresses the disillusionment that was felt by many: "I came to America because I heard the streets were paved with gold. When I got here, I found out three things: First, the streets weren't paved with gold; second, they weren't paved at all; and third, I was expected to pave them."

MAKING THEIR WAY   Once on American soil in Manhattan or New Jersey, the immigrants felt exhilaration, exhaustion, and usually a desperate need for work. Many were greeted by family and friends who had come over before, others by representatives of the many immigrant aid societies or by hiring agents offering jobs in mines, mills, and sweatshops. Since most knew little if any English and nothing about American employment practices, the immigrants were easy subjects for exploitation. In exchange for providing arrivals with a bit of whiskey and a job, obliging hiring agents claimed a healthy percentage of their wages. Among Italians and Greeks these agents were known as *padrones,* and they came to dominate the labor market in New York. Other contractors provided train tickets for immigrants to travel inland to jobs in cities such as Buffalo, Pittsburgh, Cleveland, Chicago, Milwaukee, Cincinnati, and St. Louis.

Eager to retain a sense of community and to use skills they brought with them, the members of ethnic groups tended to cluster in particular vocations. Poles, Hungarians, Slovaks, Bohemians, and Italians used to the pick and shovel flocked to coal mines, just as the Irish, Cornish, and Welsh had done at mid-century; Slavs and Poles comfortable with muscle work gravitated to the steel mills; Greeks preferred working in textile mills; Russian and Polish Jews peopled the sewing trades and pushcart markets of New York. A few determined peasants uprooted from their agricultural heritage made their way west and were able to find work on farms or even a parcel of land for themselves.

Most of the immigrants, however, settled in the teeming cities. Strangers in a new land, they naturally gravitated to neighborhoods populated by their own kind. These immigrant enclaves—nicknamed Little Italy, Little Hungary, Chinatown, and so on—served as crucial transitional communities between the newcomers' Old World past and their New World future. By 1920 Chicago had some seventeen separate Little Italy colonies scattered across the city representing various home provinces. In such kinship communities the immigrants could practice their religions and native customs, converse in their native tongue, and fill an aching loneliness. But they paid a price for such community solidarity. When the "new immigrants" moved into an area, older residents typically moved out, taking with them whatever social prestige and political influence they had achieved. The quality of living conditions quickly deteriorated as housing and sanitation codes went unenforced.

As the number of new arrivals mushroomed during the last quarter of the nineteenth century, cities grew so cramped and land so scarce that designers were forced to build upward. The result was the "dumbbell"

Mulberry Street, Little Italy. New York, 1906. Immigrants established their own enclaves where old-world traditions could be carried on within their new American homes.

tenement house. These structures, usually six to eight stories in height and jammed tightly against one another, lined street after street. They derived their name from the fact that housing codes required a two-foot-wide air shaft between buildings, giving each structure the appearance of a dumbbell when viewed from overhead. Twenty-four to thirty-two families would cram into each building, meaning that some city blocks housed almost 4,000 people. The tiny air shaft provided little ventilation; instead it proved to be a fire hazard, fueling and conveying flames from building to building. The early tenements were poorly heated and had toilets outside in the yard or alley for communal use. By the end of the century they would feature two toilets on each floor, available to all comers. Shoehorned into such quarters, families had no privacy, free space, or sunshine; children had few places to play except in the city streets; infectious diseases and noxious odors were rampant. Not surprisingly, the mortality rate for urban immigrants was much higher than that of the general population. In one Chicago ethnic ghetto at the end of the century, three babies of every five died before their first birthday.

THE NATIVIST RESPONSE   Not only did immigrants have to face difficult living conditions, they also confronted growing prejudice from native-born Americans. Many saw the new immigration as a threat to their way of life and their jobs. "Immigrants work for almost nothing," groused one American laborer, "and seem to be able to live on wind—something which I cannot do." Others saw in the tide of new immigrants a threat to traditional American culture and values. A Stanford University professor called them "illiterate, docile, lacking in self-reliance and initiative, and not possessing the Anglo-Teutonic conceptions of law, order, and government." The undercurrent of nativism so often present in American culture now surfaced mainly in anti-Catholic, and secondarily anti-Semitic, sentiments. The Catholic church in America, long dominated by the English-speaking Irish, became a polyglot group all the more subject to misunderstanding and persecution. Similarly, Russian and Polish Jews came from a far different tradition than the Sephardic and German Jews who preceded them. The unruly beards and long black coats of the men and the new arrivals' distinctive language, Yiddish, made them seem strange and exotic.

More than religious prejudice underlay hostility toward the latest newcomers. Cultural differences confirmed in the minds of nativists the assumption that the Nordic peoples of the old immigration were superior to the Slavic and Latin peoples of the new immigration. Many of the new immigrants were illiterate, and more appeared so because they could not speak English. Some resorted to crime in order to survive in the new land, encouraging suspicions that criminals were being quietly helped out of Europe just as they had once been transported from England to the colonies. In the early 1890s vendettas among Italian gangs in New Orleans led to the murder of the police chief and the lynching of eleven Italian suspects, an incident that convinced many that the new immigrants were criminals.

The success of the Irish in city politics was emulated by the newer groups, who also thereby offended the sensibilities of well-born natives. Political and social radicals turned up among these immigrant groups in sufficient numbers to encourage nativists to blame labor disputes on alien elements. Such charges harbored a fine irony, however, because mainline labor organizations generally favored restricting immigration to keep down the competition for jobs. Employers sometimes used immigrants as strikebreakers; those who came from peasant origins, and were unfamiliar with strikes, were apt as not to think they were merely taking jobs that others had abandoned. Employers also learned quickly that a babel of foreign tongues could confound unity of action among workers.

A resurgence of nativism in the 1880s spawned groups devoted to saving the country from imaginary papal conspiracies. The most successful of these nativist groups, the American Protective Association (APA), operated mainly in Protestant strongholds of the upper Mississippi Valley. Its organizer harbored paranoid fantasies of Catholic conspiracies, and was especially anxious to keep the public schools free from Jesuit control. The association grew slowly from its start in 1887 until 1893, when leaders took advantage of a severe depression to draw large numbers of the frustrated to its ranks. The APA soon vanished, swallowed up in the Populist and free-silver agitations, but while it lasted it promoted restricted immigration, more stringent naturalization requirements, refusal to employ aliens or Catholics, and the teaching of the "American" language in the schools.

IMMIGRATION RESTRICTION The movement to restrict immigration had mixed success beyond the exclusion of certain individuals deemed undesirable. In 1875, for instance, a new law refused entry to prostitutes and to convicts whose sentences had been remitted in other countries on condition that they leave. In 1882 a more general law added lunatics, idiots, and persons likely to become public charges, and over the years other specific undesirables joined the list. In 1891 Representative Henry Cabot Lodge of Massachusetts took up the cause of excluding illiterates—a measure that would have affected much of the new immigration even though the language did not have to be English. Bills embodying the restriction were vetoed by three presidents on the ground that they penalized people for lack of opportunity: Cleveland in 1897, Taft in 1913, and Wilson in 1915 and 1917. The last time, however, Congress overrode the veto.

Proponents of immigration restriction during the late nineteenth century did succeed in excluding the Chinese, who were victims of everything the European immigrants suffered, plus color prejudice as well. By 1880 there were some 75,000 Chinese in California, about one-ninth of the state's population. Their nemesis there was himself an immigrant (from Ireland), Dennis Kearney, leader of the Workingmen's party. Many white workers resented the Chinese for accepting lower wages, but their greatest sin, the editor of the *New York Nation* opined,

Anti-Chinese protest, California, 1880. Widespread prejudice and racism against the Chinese finally resulted in a ban on Chinese immigration with the 1882 passage of the Chinese Exclusion Act.

was perpetuating "those disgusting habits of thrift, industry, and self-denial."

Exclusion of the Chinese was initially prevented by the Burlingame Treaty, which in 1868 gave China most-favored-nation status (the same as the best conceded to any other country) with respect to travel and immigration. But by 1880 the urgent need for railway labor had ebbed, and a new treaty with China permitted the United States to "regulate, limit, and suspend" Chinese immigration. In 1882 President Chester A. Arthur vetoed a twenty-year suspension of immigration from China as actually a prohibition, but accepted a ten-year suspension, known as the Chinese Exclusion Act. The legislation closing the doors to Chinese immigrants received overwhelming support. One congressman explained that because the "industrial army of Asiatic laborers" was increasing the tension between workers and management in the American economy, "the gate must be closed." The Chinese Exclusion Act was periodically renewed before being extended indefinitely in 1902. Not until 1943 were such barriers finally removed.

The West Coast counterpart to Ellis Island was the Immigration Station on rugged Angel Island, six miles offshore from San Francisco. Opened in 1910, it served as a processing center for tens of thousands of Asian immigrants, most of them Chinese. Although the Chinese Exclusion Act had sharply reduced the flow of Chinese immigrants, it did not stop the influx completely. Those arrivals who could claim a Chinese-American parent were allowed to enter, as were certain officials, teachers, merchants, and students. The powerful prejudice the Chinese immigrants encountered helps explain why over 30 percent of the arrivals at Angel Island were denied entry. Those who appealed such denials were housed in prison-like barracks for weeks or months. One of the detainees scratched a poignant poem on a wall:

> This place is called an island of immortals,
> When, in fact, this mountainous wilderness is a prison.
> Once you see the open net, why throw yourself in?
> It is only because of empty pockets. I can do nothing else.

EDUCATION

THE SPREAD OF PUBLIC EDUCATION   The spread of public education, spurred partly by the determination to "Americanize" immigrant children, helped quicken the emergence of a new America. The growing importance of public education is evident in statistics compiled by the national commissioner of education, whose office was created in 1867. In 1870 there were 7 million pupils in public schools; by 1920 the number had risen to 22 million. The percentage of school-age children in attendance went from 57 to 78 during these years. City schools quickly became schools of several rooms and separate grades with a teacher for each. In rural areas one-room schools lingered on into the twentieth century, when good roads made it possible to bus children to "consolidated schools." Despite these signs of progress, educational leaders all too often had to struggle against a pattern of political appointments, corruption, and incompetence in the public schools.

The spread of secondary schools accounted for much of the increased enrollment in public schools. In antebellum America private academies prepared those who intended to enter college. At the beginning of the Civil War there were only about 100 public high schools in the whole country, but their number grew rapidly to about 800 in 1880 and 6,000 at the turn of the century. Their curricula at first copied the academies' emphasis on higher mathematics and classical languages, but the public schools gradually accommodated their programs to those not going on to college, devising vocational training in such arts as bookkeeping, typing, drafting, and the use of tools.

VOCATIONAL TRAINING Vocational training was most intensely promoted after the Civil War by missionary schools for African Americans such as Hampton Institute in Virginia, which trained Booker T. Washington, founder of Tuskegee Institute in Alabama. Another major prophet of the vocational training movement was Professor Calvin M. Woodward of St. Louis, who in setting up a school of engineering found his students woefully inept in the use of simple tools. He called on the public schools to teach manual skills as well as more abstract knowledge. Prodded by the National Society for the Promotion of Industrial Education, high schools installed workshops for training in carpentry, printing, drafting, bricklaying, and machine work, and for home management, or "home economics," as well.

Congress had supported vocational training at the college level for many years. The Morrill Act of 1862 granted each state 30,000 acres per representative and senator, the income from which was to be applied to teaching agriculture and the mechanic arts in what came to be known as the "land-grant colleges." Among these new institutions were Clemson University, Pennsylvania State University, and Iowa State Uni-

George Washington Carver at the Tuskegee Institute. Exclusively for African Americans, Tuskegee was one of the leading vocational schools in the country.

versity. In 1890 a Second Morrill Act provided federal grants to these colleges. Their outreach, first attempted in Farmers' Institutes, greatly expanded with the rise of the demonstration technique perfected by Seaman A. Knapp, "schoolmaster to American agriculture." In 1903, about a decade after the Mexican boll weevil crossed the Rio Grande, Knapp set up a demonstration in Texas of the best techniques then known to fight the pest. From this beginning the demonstration technique spread rapidly as a means of getting knowledge into the field.

HIGHER EDUCATION   American colleges at this time, whether church schools or state "universities," sought to instill discipline, morality, and a curriculum stressing mathematics and the classics (and in church schools, theology), along with ethics and rhetoric. History, modern languages and literature, and some science were tolerated, although laboratory work was usually limited to a professor's demonstration to the class. The college teacher was apt to be a young man seeking temporary refuge or a broken-down preacher seeking safe harbor. In 1871 a writer in *The Galaxy,* a literary monthly, called the typical professor "nondescript, a jack of all trades, equally ready to teach surveying and Latin eloquence, and thankful if his quarter's salary is not docked to whitewash the college fence."

The campus of Texas A & M College, 1895, with Ross Hall at the right.

Nevertheless, the demand for higher learning led to an increase in the college student population from 52,000 in 1870 to 157,000 in 1890 and to 600,000 in 1920. During the same years the number of institutions rose from 563 to 998 and then to 1,041, and the number of faculty from 5,553 to 15,809 to 48,615. To accommodate the diverse needs of these growing numbers, colleges moved away from rigidly prescribed courses toward an elective system. In 1866 Washington College in Virginia, under its president, Robert E. Lee, adopted electives, and after 1869 Harvard College did so under its young president Charles W. Eliot. The new approach allowed students to favor their strong points and colleges to expand their scope. But as Henry Cabot Lodge complained, it also allowed students to "escape without learning anything at all by a judicious selection of unrelated subjects taken up only because they were easy or because the burden imposed by those who taught them was light."

Women's access to higher education improved markedly in the period. Before the Civil War, a few male colleges had admitted women, and most state universities in the West were open to women from the start. But colleges in the South and East fell in line very slowly. Vassar, opened in 1865, was the first women's college to teach by the same

Students in the chemistry lab at Mount Holyoke College, 1900.

standards as the best of the men's colleges, though it had to maintain a Preparatory Department for twenty-three years to upgrade poorly prepared entrants. In the 1870s, two more excellent women's schools appeared in Massachusetts: Wellesley and Smith, the latter being the first to set the same admission requirements as men's colleges. The older women's colleges quickly moved to upgrade their standards in the same way. By the end of the century, women made up more than a third of all college students.

The dominant new trend in American higher education after the Civil War was the rise of the graduate school. The versatile professors of the antebellum era had a knowledge more broad than deep. With some notable exceptions they engaged in little research, nor were they expected to advance the frontiers of knowledge. But gradually more and more Americans experienced a different system at the German universities, where training was more systematic and focused. After the Civil War, the German system became the basis for the modern American university. Yale awarded its first Ph.D. in 1861 and Harvard its first in 1872.

The Johns Hopkins University, opened in Baltimore in 1876, set a new precedent by making graduate work its chief concern. The graduate students gathered in seminar rooms or laboratories, where under the guidance of an experienced scholar they learned a craft, much as journeymen had in the medieval guilds. The crowning achievement, signifying admission to full membership in the craft, was a masterpiece—in this case the Ph.D. dissertation, which was expected to make an original contribution to knowledge. Clark University at Worcester, Massachusetts, founded in 1887, followed the model of Johns Hopkins.

In the early 1890s two more major universities were founded to spread the gospel of Germanic education. The first, established by railroad magnate Leland Stanford (and named after his son), opened at Palo Alto, California, in 1891, and the following year the University of Chicago, endowed by oil baron John D. Rockefeller, began operation. Meanwhile other established institutions, including Columbia, Cornell, Michigan, and Wisconsin, also set up graduate schools. By 1900 American universities annually conferred hundreds of doctorates. The Ph.D. was fast becoming the ticket of admission to the guild of professors.

THE RISE OF PROFESSIONALISM

The Ph.D. revolution was but one aspect of a growing emphasis on professionalism, with its imposition of standards, licensing of practitioners, and accreditation of professional schools. The number of professional schools grew rapidly in fields such as theology, law, medicine, dentistry, pharmacy, and veterinary medicine. While these fields accounted for 60 schools in 1850, there were 146 in 1875 and 283 in 1900. Growth in numbers brought pressures for higher standards. At Harvard in 1870 one could qualify for a medical degree by attending two lecture courses for four months, proving three years of medical experience, and passing a simple examination. Harvard president Charles Eliot then insisted on requiring three years of class attendance, together with laboratory and clinical work. In 1870 the Harvard Law School developed a rough equivalent to the laboratory by introducing the "case method," which required students to dig out the rules for themselves.

Along with advanced schooling went a movement for licensing practitioners in certain fields. The first state licensing law for dentistry, for instance, came in 1868, for pharmacy in 1874, for veterinary medicine in 1886, for accounting in 1896, and for architecture in 1897. By 1894 twenty-one states held standard examinations for doctors, and fourteen others recognized only graduates from accredited medical schools. Licensing benefited the public by certifying competence in a given field, but it also benefited members of the profession by controlling the number of practitioners and thereby limiting competition.

Learned and professional associations began to proliferate after the Civil War. Earlier societies, such as the American Association for the Advancement of Science (1848), which had seemed specialized enough, made way for still more specialized groups such as the American Chemical Society (1876) and the National Statistical Association (1888). Modern-language scholars organized in 1883, American historians in 1884, economists in 1885, political scientists in 1889, folklorists in 1888, and all sponsored meetings and journals to keep members in touch with developments in the field. A host of commonplace and simple jobs entered the ranks of the "professions," including barbering, playing baseball, and planning vacations.

POPULAR CULTURE

As more people moved to large towns and cities, the new urban environment created new patterns of recreation and leisure. Whereas people in rural areas were tied into the rituals of the harvest season and intimately connected to their neighbors and extended families, most middle-class urban whites were mobile and lived in nuclear families (made up of only parents and children), and their affluence enabled them to enjoy greater leisure time and rising discretionary income.

Middle- and upper-class urban families spent much of their leisure time together at home, usually in the parlor, singing around the piano, reading novels, or playing cards, dominoes, backgammon, chess, and checkers. A new invention called the "stereopticon" was all the rage. It was a hand-held device that placed several photographs or paintings at facing angles to one another. When viewed through binocular glasses, it gave the appearance of three-dimensional views.

Where social and economic conditions remained the same as in earlier periods, popular culture remained much the same. For example, most blacks continued to live in rural areas and operated within extended family networks that included cousins, aunts, uncles, and other relatives who provided assistance and emotional support. Popular culture in rural areas included many traditional forms of entertainment, centered on the family and the planting and harvesting of crops, or the arrival of an itinerant evangelist intent upon conducting a revival or camp meeting.

In the towns and cities, however, people were not as dependent upon mobile ministers or harvest rituals and festivities, and popular culture took on new or greatly expanded dimensions that endowed life with a more cosmopolitan quality. For example, traveling circuses brought entertainment to large cities and small towns. Creative promoters such as Phineas T. Barnum and James A. Bailey made the circus the most eclectic form of entertainment. The midwestern writer Hamlin Garland recalled how the circus came to rural hamlets "trailing clouds of glorified dust and filling our minds with the color of romance. . . . It brought to our ears the latest band pieces and taught us the popular songs. It furnished us with jokes. It relieved our dullness. It gave us something to talk about."

In the congested metropolitan areas, politics became as much a form of public entertainment as it was a process of providing civic representation and public services. People flocked to hear visiting candidates give speeches in cavernous halls, outdoor plazas, or from railway cars. Huge crowds regularly attended political rallies, and membership in a political party in cities such as New York, Philadelphia, Boston, and Chicago was akin to belonging to a social club. In addition, labor unions also included activities that were more social than economic in nature, and members often visited the union hall as much to socialize as to discuss working conditions. The sheer numbers of people congregated in cities also helped generate a market for new forms of mass entertainment such as traveling wild West shows, vaudeville shows, and spectator sports.

WILD WEST SHOWS   Another touring extravaganza that enjoyed incredible popularity during the last quarter of the nineteenth century was "Buffalo Bill's Wild West" traveling show. William "Buffalo Bill" Cody was a rugged frontiersman and sharpshooter. Born in Iowa and raised in Kansas, he became a rider for the Pony Express in 1860 and later served as a Union scout during the Civil War. After the war, he operated a hotel and a freight business, but Indians captured his wagons and horses. He thereafter became a renowned buffalo hunter, providing meat for the crews building railroads. His ability earned him the nickname Buffalo Bill. From 1868 to 1872, Cody served as a scout for army troops and was awarded the Congressional Medal of Honor after a ferocious battle with Indians on the Platte River. Four years later, he participated in a skirmish with Cheyennes during which he killed and scalped a young chief, Yellow Hand.

Cody's exploits attracted the attention of writer Ned Buntline, who wrote a series of popular novels that brought international celebrity to Buffalo Bill. Always alert to financial opportunity and ever eager to exaggerate his own accomplishments, Cody took advantage of his popularity to organize a stage show. By 1883 he had broadened its scope into a traveling spectacle that included live elk and buffalo, hundreds of horses, genuine cowboys, authentic Indians, rope tricks, shooting exhibitions, cowgirl Annie Oakley, and Cody himself as the star attraction. One of his advertising promotions heralded him as "young, sturdy, a remarkable specimen of manly beauty, with the brain to conceive and the

Buffalo Bill's Wild West Show. Although the shows included geniune cowboys and authentic Indians, they romanticized the Amerian West.

nerve to execute, . . . the exemplar of the strong and unique traits that characterize a true American frontiersman."

Indians were prominently featured in the show. In 1885 Cody hired Sitting Bull, the most famous Indian chief, to ride around the arena and sign autographs. One advertisement promised "a horde of war-painted Arapahoes, Cheyenne, and Sioux Indians." Their role in the show was to stage attacks on wagon trains and stagecoaches, as well as to reenact the battle between Indians and soldiers in General George Custer's last stand at the Little Bighorn. The Indians were always portrayed as the aggressors, and the whites as the victims. These images of murderous Indians attacking helpless whites set in motion the mythic depiction of the West that later became the staple of television and movie Westerns.

For three decades, this outdoor spectacle crisscrossed the United States and the world. The Wild West shows visited metropolises such as Chicago and New York as well as smaller cities—Oakland, Memphis, and Raleigh. The shows could accommodate up to twenty thousand people for each performance and promised to present "actual scenes and genuine characters" from the West. When Buffalo Bill died in 1917, his shows died with him, but he bequeathed to Americans a new form of entertainment that his since taken deep root: the rodeo.

VAUDEVILLE   Growing family incomes and innovations in urban transportation—cable cars, subways, electric streetcars and streetlights—enabled more people to take advantage of urban cultural life. Attendance at theaters, operas, and dance halls soared. Those interested in serious music could attend concerts by symphony orchestras appearing in every major city by the end of the nineteenth century.

But by far the most popular—and diverse—form of theatrical entertainment in the late nineteenth century was known as vaudeville. The term derives from a French word meaning a play accompanied by music. It emerged in the United States in saloons whose owners wanted to attract more customers by offering free shows.

Vaudeville "variety" shows featured comedians, singers, musicians, blackface minstrels, farcical plays, animal acts, jugglers, gymnasts, dancers, mimes, and magicians. Because variety shows were held in seedy beer halls populated by drunks and prostitutes and because the entertainers often included vulgar material, they quickly developed a bad reputation. To combat such an image so as to encourage families to attend, promoters of variety shows built elegant new theaters, banned alcoholic beverages, upgraded the performers, hired policemen and bouncers to handle "rowdies," and began to use the more elegant French word "vaudeville" to describe the genre.

Vaudeville houses sprouted like mushrooms in cities across the United States in the 1870s and 1880s. They quickly became popular gathering places for all social classes and types—men, women, and children—all of whom were expected to behave according to middle-class standards of gentility and decorum when attending performances. Ushers walked the aisles and handed out cards to unruly patrons. One of them read: "Gentlemen will kindly avoid the stamping of feet and pounding of canes on the floor, and greatly oblige the Management. All applause is best shown by clapping of hands." Raucous cheering, booing, and tobacco spitting were expressly prohibited. The diverse vaudeville shows would run all day and well into the night. They included something to please every taste and, as such, reflected the heterogeneity of city life. To commemorate the opening of a palatial new Boston theater in 1894, an actress read a dedicatory poem in which she announced that "All are equals here." The vaudeville house was the people's theater; it knew "no favorites, no class." She promised the spectators that the producers would "ever seek the new" in providing entertainers who epitomized "the spice of life, Variety," with its motto, "ever to please—and never to offend."

OUTDOOR RECREATION The congestion and diseases associated with metropolitan life led many people to participate in forms of outdoor recreation intended to restore their vitality and improve their health. A movement to create city parks flourished after the construction of New York's Central Park in 1858. Its designer, Frederick Law Olmsted, viewed city parks as much more than recreational centers; he sought to create oases of culture that would promote social stability and cohesion. He was convinced that Central Park would exercise "a distinctly harmonizing and refining influence upon the most unfortunate and lawless classes of the city—an influence favorable to courtesy, self-control, and temperance." Olmsted went on to design parks for Boston, Brooklyn, Chicago, Philadelphia, and San Francisco.

Although originally intended as places where people could walk and commune with nature, the parks soon offered more vigorous forms of exercise and recreation—for men and women. During most of the nineteenth century, prevailing social attitudes scoffed at the notion of proper young women participating in even the lightest athletic endeavors. Women were deemed too delicate for such behavior. Before the Civil War, women essentially had only one exercise option: pedestrianism, the formal title for outdoor walking. After the war, however, the growing number of women enrolled in colleges began to participate in physical education, and they in turn demanded access to more vigorous sports.

Croquet and tennis courts were among the first additions to city parks because they took up little space and required little maintenance. Croquet was born in the British Isles in the mid–nineteenth century and soon migrated to most other English-speaking countries. Because croquet could be played by both sexes, it combined the virtues of sport with the opportunities of courtship. Croquet as a public sport suffered a setback in the 1890s, however, when Boston clergymen lambasted the drinking, gambling, and licentious behavior associated with it on the Boston Common, where croquet matches were held.

Lawn tennis was invented by an Englishman in 1873 and arrived in the United States a year later. By 1885 Central Park had thirty courts. Lawn tennis was originally viewed as a leisurely sport best suited for

Croquet, *1886, by Winslow Homer.*

women. The Harvard student newspaper declared in 1878 that the sport was "well enough for a lazy or *weak* man, but men who have rowed or taken part in a nobler sport should blush to be seen playing Lawn Tennis."

Even more popular than croquet or tennis was cycling or "wheeling." In the 1870s, bicycles began to be manufactured in the United States, and by the end of the century, a "bicycle craze" had swept the country. The first bicycles were called "high-wheelers" or "boneshakers" because the front wheel was huge, as much as five feet high, while the rear wheel was tiny, no more than a foot in diameter. The high-wheelers were hard to ride, uncomfortable, and dangerous, as they had no brakes. During the 1880s, an Englishman named J. K. Starley produced the first "safety bicycle." These bicycles had wheels of equal size and axles with ball bearings, which made them easier and safer to ride than high-wheelers. By 1890, bicycles had air-filled rubber tires and brakes. Millions of middle-class Americans (who could afford the new invention) discovered a new mobility and freedom through the bicycle, which had few of the drawbacks of horses. Bicycles went where pointed, did not need to be fed, and did not leave droppings in the road.

Bicycles were especially popular with women who chafed at the restricting conventions of Victorianism. The new vehicles offered exer-

Tandem tricycle. In spite of the danger and discomfort of early bicycles, wheeling became a popular form of recreation and mode of transportation.

cise, freedom, and access to the countryside. Female cyclists were able to discard their cumbersome corsets and full dresses in favor of bloomers and split skirts. Critics feared that the bicycle mania was encouraging young women to grow independent and shun conventional domestic responsibilities. Some guardians of morality believed that cycling was also sexually provocative. In 1899 the Reverend W. W. Reynolds expressed outrage because a "large number of female bicyclists wear shorter dresses than the laws of morality and decency permit, thereby inviting the improper conversations and remarks of the depraved and immoral." He deemed cycling as "detrimental to the advancement of morality."

The working poor in the cities could not afford to acquire a bicycle or join a croquet club. Nor did they have as much free time as the affluent. They toiled long hours, six days a week, and at the end of their long days they eagerly sought recreation and fellowship on street corners or on the front stoops of their apartment buildings. Organ grinders and musicians would perform on the sidewalks among the food vendors. Those with a few extra dollars to spend frequented the saloons and dance halls available in each city. New York City alone had 10,000 sa-

Steeplechase Park, Coney Island, New York. This amusement park attracted working-class patrons who could afford the inexpensive rides.

loons in 1900 featuring five-cent beer and free lunch. In the late nineteenth century, saloons often doubled as gymnasiums. Back rooms housed handball courts, pool tables, bowling alleys, and dart boards.

Many ethnic groups, especially the Germans and the Irish, formed male singing, drinking, or gymnastic clubs. Working folk also attended bare-knuckle boxing matches or baseball games, and on Sundays would gather for picnics. By the end of the century, large-scale amusement parks such as New York's Coney Island provided entertainment for the entire family. Yet many inner-city youth could not afford the trolley fare to visit a suburban amusement park, so the crowded streets and dangerous alleys became their playgrounds.

SPECTATOR SPORTS   In the last quarter of the nineteenth century, horse racing and prizefighting remained popular, but team sports also began to attract legions of fans. New spectator sports such as college football and basketball and professional baseball gained mass popularity, reflecting the growing urbanization of American life. People could gather easily for sporting events in the large cities. And news of the games could be conveyed quickly by newspapers and specialized sporting magazines relying upon telegraph reports. Saloons also posted the scores. Athletic rivalries between distant cities were made possible by the network of railroads spanning the continent and facilitating team travel. Spectator sports became urban extravaganzas, unifying the diverse ethnic groups in the large cities and attracting people with the leisure time and cash to spend (or bet) on watching others perform.

Football emerged as a modified form of soccer and rugby. The College of New Jersey (Princeton) and Rutgers played the first college football game in 1869. Some 200 students and spectators saw Rutgers win 6–4. The teams at first used twenty-five players at a time, and players literally kicked the ball along the ground. By 1880 the number of players had been reduced to eleven, and they carried the ball rather than kicking it. The players wore no protective padding or headgear, and the games often resembled organized fights. In fact, advocates of football portrayed it as a "blood sport" that provided a modern substitute for the frontier experience.

By the end of the century, scores of colleges and high schools had started football teams, and some college games attracted more than 50,000 spectators. Early games featured unregulated mayhem, however, with slugging and kicking commonplace. Scores of players died from injuries. In 1905 alone, 18 players were killed and 150 seriously injured. Gambling on college football games was also widespread, and many college coaches provided cash incentives to lure players to enroll. The president of Cornell University grew so disgusted with the evils infecting the sport that he prohibited the football team from playing the University of Michigan squad, refusing to "permit 30 men to travel 4,000 miles to agitate a bag of wind."

Football became so controversial that President Theodore Roosevelt intervened in 1905. He had long promoted strenuous exercise and "rough, manly sports" as needed antidotes for young Americans leading sedentary lives in cities. With the closing of the frontier, he feared that young boys growing up in urban centers would become effeminate and anemic. Roosevelt championed football as a means of instilling in young men the virtues of "pluck, endurance, and physical address," yet he appealed to coaches, professors, and alumni to "come to a gentlemen's agreement not to have mucker play." His appeal did little good, and the roughness and foul play continued. As a result, Columbia University and the Massachusetts Institute of Technology abolished football. Stanford and the University of California replaced it with rugby. In a further effort to curb injuries and abuses, the National Collegiate Athletics Association (NCAA) was founded in 1910.

Basketball was invented in 1891 when Dr. James Naismith, a physical education instructor, nailed two peach baskets to the walls of the YMCA training school in Springfield, Massachusetts. Naismith wanted to create an indoor winter game that could be played between the fall football and spring baseball seasons. The baskets were ten feet high because that was the height of the balcony at each end of the gym to which the baskets were attached. The first game had nine men on a side, and they used a soccer ball. Basketball quickly grew in popularity among both boys and girls. Vassar and Smith Colleges added the sport in 1892. In 1893, Vanderbilt became the first college to field a men's team.

Baseball laid claim to being America's national pastime at mid-century. Contrary to popular opinion, Abner Doubleday did not invent the game. Instead, Alexander Cartwright, a New York bank clerk and sportsman, is recognized as the father of organized baseball. In 1845 he gathered a group of merchants, stockbrokers, and physicians to form the Knickerbocker Base Ball Club of New York. They began playing a bat-and-ball game on a field at the corner of Twenty-seventh Street and Fourth Avenue in Manhattan. Soon they moved to a field in Hoboken, New Jersey. After their games they would gather at a nearby hotel bar. There they drafted a list of rules that included setting the bases 90 feet apart and allocating nine players to a side. Initially the pitcher stood 45 feet from home plate and threw the ball underhanded. Three strikes resulted in an out, but the batter had to take three swings. There were no called strikes.

The first professional baseball team was the Cincinnati Red Stockings, which made its appearance in 1869. Seven years later, seven other teams joined the Red Stockings in creating the National League. Reporters began to cover the games, and sports sections appeared in every newspaper. With professionalization came changes in the sport. Umpires were added to call balls, strikes, and outs; pitchers threw overhand rather than underhand; fielders began to use gloves; catchers donned protective equipment. Other changes in the late nineteenth century included the addition of a "walk" after four balls and fixing the distance from the pitcher to home plate at 60 feet 6 inches. In 1901 the

Professional baseball game, 1887. The excitement of rooting for the home team united all classes as they watched the athletes who graced the playing field.

American League was organized, and two years later the first World Series was held.

Baseball became the "national pastime" and the most democratic sport in America. People from all social classes (mostly men) attended the games, and ethnic immigrants were among the most faithful fans. The *St. Louis Post-Dispatch* reported in 1883 that "a glance at the audience on any fine day at the ball park will reveal . . . telegraph operators, printers who work at night, travelling men [salesmen] . . . men of leisure . . . men of capital, bank clerks who get away [from work] at 3 P.M., real estate men . . . barkeepers . . . hotel clerks, actors and employees of the theater, policemen and firemen on their day off . . . butchers and bakers." Cheering for a city baseball team gave rootless people a common loyalty and a sense of belonging.

Only white players were allowed in the major leagues. African Americans played on "minor league" teams or in all-black "Negro leagues." In 1867 the National Association of Base Ball Players excluded black clubs from membership. And the National League followed suit when it was organized nine years later. In 1887 black players were banned from minor league teams as well. That same year, the Cuban Giants, a barn-storming team made up of black players, traveled the country. A few major league white teams agreed to play them. An African-American-owned newspaper announced in early 1888 that the Cuban Giants "have defeated the New Yorks, 4 games out of 5, and are now virtually champions of the world." But it added, "the St. Louis Browns, Detroits and Chicagos, afflicted by Negrophobia and unable to bear the odium of being beaten by colored men, refused to accept their challenge."

By the end of the nineteenth century, sports of all kinds had become a major cultural phenomenon in the United States. A writer in *Harper's Weekly* announced in 1895 that "ball matches, football games, tennis tournaments, bicycle races, [and] regattas, have become part of our national life." They "are watched with eagerness and discussed with enthusiasm and understanding by all manner of people, from the day-laborer to the millionaire." One reporter in the 1890s referred to the "athletic craze" that was sweeping the American imagination. Moreover, it was in 1892 that a Frenchman, Pierre de Coubertin, called for the revival of the ancient Olympic games, and the first modern olympiad was held four years later.

THEORIES OF SOCIAL CHANGE

Every field of thought in the post–Civil War years felt the impact of Charles Darwin's *On the Origin of Species* (1859), which argued that existing species, including humanity itself, had evolved through a long process of "natural selection" from less complex forms of life. Those species that adapted to survival by reason of quickness, shrewdness, or other advantages reproduced their kind, while others fell by the wayside. The idea of species evolution shocked people of conventional religious views by contradicting a literal interpretation of the creation stories in Genesis. Heated arguments arose among scientists and clergymen. Some of the faithful rejected Darwin's doctrine, while others found their faith severely shaken not only by evolutionary theory but also by the urging of professional scholars to apply the critical standards of scholarship to the Bible itself, and by the study of comparative religion, which found parallels to biblical stories and doctrines in other faiths. Most of the faithful, however, came to reconcile science and re-

Charles Darwin.

ligion. They viewed evolution as the Divine Will, as one of the secondary causes through which God worked.

SOCIAL DARWINISM   Though Darwin's theory applied only to biological phenomena, other thinkers drew broader inferences from it. The temptation to apply evolutionary theory to the social world proved irresistible. Darwin's fellow Englishman Herbert Spencer became the first major prophet of Social Darwinism and an important influence on American thought. Spencer, whose first works anticipated Darwin, brought forth in eight weighty tomes his *System of Synthetic Philosophy* (1862–1893), an effort to embrace all fields of knowledge within an overall system of Darwinian evolution. He argued that human society and institutions, like organisms, passed through the process of natural selection, which resulted, in Spencer's chilling phrase, in the "survival of the fittest." For Spencer, social evolution implied progress, ending "only in the establishment of the greatest perfection and the most complete happiness."

If, as Spencer believed, society naturally evolved for the better, then individual freedom was inviolable, and governmental interference with the process of social evolution was a serious mistake. This view used biological laws to justify the working of the free market. Social Darwinism implied a governmental policy of hands-off; it decried the regulation of

*Herbert Spencer, the first major prophet
of Social Darwinism.*

business, the graduated income tax, sanitation and housing regulations, and even protection against medical quacks. Such interventions, Spencer charged, would help the "unfit" survive and thereby only impede progress. The only acceptable charity was voluntary, and even that was of dubious value. Spencer warned that "fostering the good-for-nothing at the expense of the good, is an extreme cruelty."

For Spencer and his many American supporters, successful businessmen and corporations were the engines of social progress. If small businesses were crowded out by trusts and monopolies, that too was part of the evolutionary process. John D. Rockefeller told his Baptist Sunday school class that the "growth of a large business is merely a survival of the fittest. . . . This is not an evil tendency in business. It is merely the working-out of a law of nature and a law of God."

The ideas of Darwin and Spencer spread quickly in America. *Popular Science Monthly,* founded in 1872, soon became the chief medium for popularizing Darwinism. That same year Darwin's chief academic disciple, William Graham Sumner, took up the new chair of political and social science at Yale. Trained for the ministry and formerly an Episcopal rector, he preached the gospel of natural selection under titles such as "What Social Classes Owe to Each Other" and "The Absurd Effort to Make the World Over."

Sumner's most lasting contribution, made in his book *Folkways* (1907), was to argue that social conditions were set by the working of tradition, or the customs of a community, and not by reason or natural laws. The implication here too was that it would be a mistake for government to interfere with established customs in the name of ideals of equality or natural rights. Democracy, according to Sumner, was a condition based not on reason but on customs arising from the availability of much free land in America. As available land diminished, customs would slowly change, showing democracy to be merely a temporary condition.

REFORM DARWINISM   The influence of Darwin and Spencer over the American mind did not go without challenge. Reform found its major philosopher in an obscure Washington civil servant, Lester Frank Ward, who had fought his way up from poverty and never lost his empathy for the underdog. Ward's book *Dynamic Sociology* (1883) singled out one product of evolution that previous pundits had neglected: the human brain. People, unlike animals, had minds that could shape social evolution. Far from being the helpless pawn of evolution, Ward argued, humanity could improve its situation by reflecting upon it and then acting. People thus had reached a stage at which they could control the process of evolution. The competition extolled by Sumner was in fact highly wasteful, as was the natural competitive process: plant or cattle

Lester Frank Ward, proponent of Reform Darwinism.

breeding, for instance, could actually improve on the results of natural selection.

Ward's Reform Darwinism challenged Sumner's conservative Social Darwinism, holding that cooperation, not competition, would better promote progress. According to Ward, Sumner's "irrational distrust of government" might have been justified in an earlier day of autocracy, but no longer under a representative system. Government could become the agency of progress by striving to reach two main goals: to ameliorate poverty, which impeded the development of the mind, and to promote the education of the masses. "Intelligence, far more than necessity," Ward wrote, "is the mother of invention," and "the influence of knowledge as a social factor, like that of wealth, is proportional to the extent of its distribution." Intellect, rightly informed by science, could plan successfully. In the benevolent "sociocracy" of the future, legislatures would function mainly to sanction decisions worked out in the sociological laboratory.

REALISM IN FACT AND FICTION

HISTORY AND THE SOCIAL SCIENCES The pervasive effect of Darwinism in late-nineteenth-century America was comparable to the effect of romanticism in the first part of the century. Like the earlier reaction against the Enlightenment's praise of reason, social thought now was turned against abstract logic and toward concrete reality.

In the milieu of Darwinism, the study of history flourished. The historian, like the biologist, studied the process of development, but in the origins and the evolution of society. Under the influence of German scholarship, and the new emphasis on science, history aspired to become "scientific." This meant examining documents and manuscripts critically, using external and internal evidence to determine validity and relevancy. The ideal of the scientific historian was to reproduce history with perfect objectivity, a noble if unreachable goal.

Lester Frank Ward's achievements in *Dynamic Sociology* (1883) qualified him as the father of American sociology, but he, like many others, thought of the book as a broad synthesis of the social studies. It fell to Albion W. Small, head of the department at the University of Chicago, to define the field specifically. In his *General Sociology* (1905), Small confined it to the scientific analysis of social phenomena with emphasis on groups in human society. As founder (1895) and editor of the *American Journal of Sociology,* Small wielded a strong influence in turning sociology from abstract speculation to the study of actual human relations. Theory, once all there was to sociology, gave way to a multitude of special interests: population, the family, ethnic groups, social class, public opinion, and social movements, to name but a few.

Economists made the same transition from abstract theory to the study of actual conditions. The American Economics Association, founded in 1885, turned its attention "not so much to speculation as to historical and statistical study of actual conditions of economic life for the satisfactory accomplishment of [economic] study" and upheld the state "as an agency whose positive assistance is one of the indispensable conditions of human progress." One economist argued that the economic problem would soon no longer be scarcity, since modern technology would make possible a surplus of goods, but distribution: how best to distribute goods and services.

PRAGMATISM   Around the turn of the century, the evolutionary idea found expression in a philosophical principle set forth in mature form by William James in his book *Pragmatism: A New Name for Some Old Ways of Thinking.* James, a professor of philosophy and psychology at

William James (left) *and John Dewey* (right).

Harvard, shared Lester Frank Ward's concern with the role of ideas in the process of evolution. Truth, to James, arose from the testing of new ideas, the value of which lay in their practical consequences. Thus, scientists could test the validity of their ideas in the laboratory and judge their import by their applications. Pragmatism reflected a quality often looked upon as genuinely American: the inventive, experimental spirit.

John Dewey, who would become the chief philosopher of pragmatism after James, preferred the term "instrumentalism," by which he meant that ideas were instruments, especially of social reform. Dewey, unlike James, threw himself into movements for the rights of labor and women, the promotion of peace, and the reform of education. He believed that education was the process through which society would gradually progress toward the goal of economic democracy.

Dewey would become the prophet of what was later labeled "progressive education." He emphasized the teaching of history, geography, and science in order to enlarge the child's personal experience. Dewey also pointed out that social conditions had so changed that schools had to find ways to inculcate values once derived from participation in family and community activities. Another important goal of the schools was to keep habits flexible to prepare children for a changing world. They needed not just knowledge but a critical intelligence to cope with a complex, modern world.

THE LOCAL COLORISTS Writers of fiction responded in different ways to the changes in American life and thought. The local color movement, which emerged after the Civil War, reflected a reunited nation engrossed with the diversity of its peoples and cultures. This movement also expressed the nostalgia of a people moving from a rural to an urban culture, and longing for those places where the old folkways survived. In California, Bret Harte, the editor of the *Overland Monthly,* burst upon the national consciousness in the late 1860s with colorful stories of the gold country such as "The Outcasts of Poker Flat" and "The Luck of Roaring Camp." Hamlin Garland, in *Main-Traveled Roads* (1891), pictured the hardscrabble existence of farmers and their wives in his native country, the upper Midwest from Wisconsin to the Dakotas.

Sarah Orne Jewett depicted the down-easters of her native Maine, most enduringly in the stories and sketches collected in *The Country of the Pointed Firs* (1896), while Mary Wilkins Freeman wrote stories of village life in Vermont and Massachusetts gathered in *A Humble Romance* (1887) and other works. Jewett's creative glance was always backward-looking and affectionate. She looked upon her parents' "generation as the one to which I really belong—I who was brought up with grandfathers and granduncles and aunts for my best playmates." She told another writer that her head was always full of old women and old houses, and when the two came together the result was a richly textured fiction marked by the essential dignity of a bygone day.

Once the passions of war and Reconstruction were spent, the South became for many northern readers an inexhaustible gallery of quaint types. George Washington Cable exploited the local color of the Louisiana Creoles and Cajuns in *Old Creole Days* (1879), *The Grandissimes* (1880), and other books. Joel Chandler Harris, a newsman and columnist, wove authentic African-American folk tales into the unforgettable stories of Uncle Remus, gathered first in *Uncle Remus: His Songs and His Sayings* (1880). Most Americans are familiar with the wonderful tar baby and the brier patch.

CLEMENS, HOWELLS, AND JAMES   The best of the local colorists could find universal truths in local life, and Samuel Langhorne Clemens (Mark Twain) transcended them all. A native of Missouri, he was forced to work at age twelve, becoming first a printer and then a Mississippi riverboat pilot. When the Civil War shut down the river traffic, he briefly joined a Confederate militia company, then left with his brother, Orion, for Nevada. He moved on to California in 1864 and first gained widespread notice with his tall tale of the gold country, "The Celebrated Jumping Frog of Calaveras County" (1865). In 1867 the San Francisco *Alta Californian* staked him to a tour of the Mediterranean, and his humorous reports on the trip, revised and collected into *Innocents Abroad* (1869), established him as a funny man much in demand on the lecture circuit. With the success of *Roughing It* (1871), an account of his western years, he moved to Hartford, Connecticut, and was able to establish himself as a full-time author and hilarious lecturer.

Clemens was the first great American writer born and raised west of the Appalachians. His early writings accentuated his western background, but for his greatest books he drew heavily upon his boyhood in a border slave state and the tall-tale tradition of southwestern humor. In *The Adventures of Tom Sawyer* (1876) he evoked in fiction the prewar

Mark Twain illustrated in the frontispiece to his novel, Tramp Abroad, *1880.*

Hannibal, Missouri, where his own boyhood was cut so short. Its story of childhood adventures is firmly etched on the American memory. *Life on the Mississippi* (1883), based on articles written eight years before, drew upon what Clemens remembered as his happiest days as a young riverboat pilot before the war.

Clemens's masterpiece, *The Adventures of Huckleberry Finn* (1884), created unforgettable characters in Huck Finn, his shiftless father, the slave Jim, the Widow Douglas, the "King," and the "Duke." The product of an erratic upbringing, Huck Finn embodied the instinct of every red-blooded American boy to "light out for the territory" whenever polite society set out to civilize him. Huck's effort to help his friend Jim escape bondage expressed well the moral dilemmas imposed by slavery on everyone. Many years later another great American writer, Ernest Hemingway, would claim that "All modern American literature comes from one book by Mark Twain, called *Huckleberry Finn.*"

But it was Twain's friend, William Dean Howells, who dominated the literary scene after the Civil War. Born in Ohio, he went to Boston in 1867 and soon became editor of the influential *Atlantic Monthly.* He left that post to devote himself to novel writing, but later served more than two decades as a columnist and critic for *Harper's Monthly.* How-

William Dean Howells (left) *and Henry James* (right).

ells proclaimed the doctrine of realism, a sort of literary version of scientific history's effort to reproduce the past as it actually happened. He wrote that realism "was nothing more or less than the truthful treatment of . . . the motives, the impulses, the principles that shape the life of actual men and women." The realist commonly wrote of the middle class in a simple and direct language, taking a pragmatic point of view of people and events.

Howells wrote novels, plays, travel books, criticism, essays, biography, and autobiography. Amid the varied output of a long and productive life, *The Rise of Silas Lapham* (1885) stands out as his most famous novel. In it Howells sympathetically portrayed a rags-to-riches paint manufacturer, one of the earliest fictional treatments of an American businessman. Soon after its publication, however, at the height of his career, Howells felt that "the bottom had dropped out" of his life. Converted to socialism by reading Tolstoy, horrified by the "civic murder" of the Haymarket anarchists, he entered a new phase. In *A Hazard of New Fortunes* (1890) he offered less sympathetic views of businessmen, included scenes of squalor and misery in New York City's Bowery district, and introduced a German-American socialist who lost his life in a police beating during a violent streetcar strike.

The third major literary figure of the times, Henry James, moved in a world far different from those of Clemens or Howells. Brother of the pragmatist philosopher William James, Henry spent most of his adult life as a voluntary expatriate in London, where he produced elegant novels that explored the society of Americans in Europe. In novels such as *Daisy Miller* (1878), *Portrait of a Lady* (1881), *The Ambassadors* (1903), and *The Golden Bowl* (1904), James explored the tensions that developed between direct, innocent, and idealistic Americans (most often young women) and sophisticated, devious Europeans. James typically wrote of the upper classes, and his stories turned less on plot than on moral dilemmas. His intense exploration of the inner selves of his characters brought him the titles of "father of the psychological novel" and "biographer of fine consciences."

LITERARY NATURALISM   During the 1890s, a younger generation of writers formed a new literary school known as naturalism. The naturalists imported scientific determinism into literature, viewing people as part of the animal world, prey to natural forces and internal drives without control or full knowledge of them.

Stephen Crane in *Maggie: A Girl of the Streets* (1893) and *The Red Badge of Courage* (1895) portrayed people caught up in environmental situations beyond their control. *Maggie* depicted a tenement girl driven to prostitution and death amid scenes so sordid that Crane had to finance publication himself. *The Red Badge of Courage,* his masterpiece, told the story of a young man going through his baptism of fire in the Civil War, and evoked nobility and courage amid the ungovernable carnage of war.

Two of the naturalists achieved a degree of popular success: Jack London and Theodore Dreiser. London was both a professed socialist and a believer in the German philosopher Friedrich Nietzsche's doctrine of the superman. In adventure stories such as *The Call of the Wild* (1903) and *The Sea Wolf* (1904), London celebrated the triumph of brute force and the will to survive. He reinforced his point about animal force in *The Call of the Wild.* The novel's protagonist is not a superman but a superdog that reverted to the wild in Alaska and ran with a wolf pack.

Theodore Dreiser shocked the genteel public probably more than the others, presenting protagonists who sinned without remorse and without punishment. *Sister Carrie* (1900), a counterpoint to Crane's *Maggie,* departed from it by having Carrie Meeber survive illicit loves and go on to success on the stage. In *The Financier* (1912) and *The Titan*

(1914), Dreiser's main character was a sexual athlete and a man of elemental force who rose to a dominant position in business and society.

SOCIAL CRITICISM   Behind their dogma of determinism, the naturalists harbored intense outrage at human misery. Other writers shared their indignation but addressed themselves more directly to protest and reform. Henry George, a California printer and journalist, was suddenly struck on a visit to New York by the contrast the city offered between wealth and poverty. "Once, in daylight, and in a city street, there came to me a thought, a vision, a call. . . . And there and then I made a vow." The vow was to seek out the cause of poverty in the midst of progress. Back in California, the spectacle of land boomers grabbing choice sites brought George a new insight. The basic social problem, he reasoned, was the "unearned increment" in wealth that came to those who owned the land. The fruit of his thought, *Progress and Poverty* (1879), a thick and difficult book, sold slowly at first, but by 1905 had sold about 2 million copies in several languages.

George held that all people had as much right to the use of the land as to the air they breathed. Nobody had a right to the value that accrued from the land, since that was created by the community, not by its owner. Labor and capital, on the other hand, did have a just claim on the wealth they produced. One justifiable solution to the problem of unearned wealth was to socialize all property in land, but that would have been too disruptive. Better simply to tax the "unearned" increment in the value of the land, or the rent. George's "single-tax" idea was intended to free capital and labor from paying tribute for the land, and to put to use lands previously held out of production by speculators. George's idea was widely propagated and actually affected tax policy here and there, but his influence on the thinking of the day came less from his "single-tax" panacea than from the paradox he posed in his title, *Progress and Poverty.*

The journalist and freelance writer Henry Demarest Lloyd addressed himself to what many found a more vital issue than Henry George's, not the monopoly in land but industrial monopoly. His best-known book, *Wealth Against Commonwealth* (1894), drew on more than a decade of studying the Standard Oil Company. Lloyd, like Lester Frank Ward, saw the key to progress in cooperation rather than competition. Economic activities in their cooperative aspects demonstrated a civilizing process; Lloyd argued that "the spectacle of the million or more employees of the railroads . . . dispatching trains, maintaining tracks, collecting fares and freights . . . is possible only where civilization has reached a high average of morals and culture." But those in charge of the machinery of industry were concerned only with wealth, not with promoting civilization. "Of gods, friends, learning, of the uncomprehended civilization they overrun, they ask but one question: How much? What is a good time to sell? What is a good time to buy?" To avoid destruction, civilization required changes. The cooperative principle should be applied "to all toils in which private sovereignty has become through monopoly a despotism over the public." Where monopoly had developed, it should be transferred to public operation in the public interest. In 1903, just before his death, Lloyd joined the Socialist party.

Thorstein Veblen brought to his social criticism a background of formal training in economics and a purpose of making economics more an evolutionary or historical science. By all accounts he taught miserably, even inaudibly, and seldom held a job for long, but he wrote brilliantly. In his best-known work, *The Theory of the Leisure Class* (1899), he examined the pecuniary values of the middle classes and introduced phrases that have since become almost clichés: "conspicuous consumption" and "conspicuous leisure." With the advent of industrial society, Veblen argued, property became the conventional basis of reputation. For the upper classes, moreover, it became necessary to consume time nonproductively as evidence of the ability to afford a life of leisure. In this and later works Veblen held that the division between industrial experts and business managers was widening to a dangerous point. The businessman's interest in profits combined with his ignorance of efficiency produced wasteful organization and a failure to realize the full potential of modern technology.

Edward Bellamy's *Looking Backward, 2000–1887* (1888) typified another genre of reform literature, the utopian novel. In Bellamy's futuristic story, a Bostonian who falls asleep in 1887 awakens in the year 2000 to find that the millennium has genuinely arrived. More than a hundred years in the future Julian West discovers a society transformed. The revolution that led to political equality has led on, by the democratic method, to a "Nationalist" society of economic equality under socialism. Everybody gets an equal share of the national product, and labor is shared by the simple method of reducing the hours for distasteful jobs until someone is willing to do the work. All this is accomplished by public control under national planning. The book enjoyed a temporary vogue, became a best-seller, and led to the founding of Nationalist Clubs. The popularity of Bellamy's book gave rise to a spate of utopian novels and some anti-utopian ones depicting model societies gone wrong.

THE SOCIAL GOSPEL

RISE OF THE INSTITUTIONAL CHURCH   The churches responded slowly to the mounting social criticism, for American Protestantism had become one of the main props of the established order. The Reverend Henry Ward Beecher, pastor of the fashionable Plymouth Congregational Church in Brooklyn, preached success, Social Darwinism, and the unworthiness of the poor. As the middle classes moved out to the streetcar suburbs, their churches followed. In the years 1868–1888, for instance, seventeen Protestant churches abandoned the areas below Fourteenth Street in Manhattan. In the center of Chicago 60,000 residents had no church, Protestant or Catholic. Where churches became prosperous they fell easily under the spell of respectability and do-nothing Social Darwinism.

A Salvation Army group in Flint, Michigan, 1894.

However, many churches responded to the human needs of the time by devoting their resources to community service and care for the unfortunate. The Young Men's Christian Association had entered the United States from England in the 1850s and grew rapidly after 1870; the Salvation Army, founded in London in 1876, came to the United States four years later. Churches in urban districts began to develop institutional features that were more social than strictly religious in function. After the Civil War, churches acquired gymnasiums, libraries, lecture rooms, and other facilities for social programs. Russell Conwell's Baptist Temple in Philadelphia included, among other features, a night school for working people that grew into Temple University.

RELIGIOUS REFORMERS   Other church leaders preached what came to be called the social gospel. One of the earliest, Washington Gladden of Columbus, Ohio, managed to preach the social gospel from the pulpit of a middle-class Congregational church. The new gospel in fact expressed the social conscience of the middle class. Gladden accepted the new ideas of evolution and textual criticism of the Bible, which he said relieved him of defending the literal truth of the story of Jonah and the whale. In his many books, Gladden argued that true Christianity lies not in rituals, dogmas, or even in the mystical experience of God, but in the principle that "Thou shalt love thy neighbor as thyself." Christian law should govern the operation of industry, with worker and employer united in serving each other's interest. He argued for labor's right to organize and complained that class distinctions split congregations as well.

The acknowledged intellectual leader of the social gospel movement, however, was the Baptist Walter Rauschenbusch, professor at the Colgate–Rochester Theological Seminary. In *Christianity and the Social Crisis* (1907) and other works, he developed a theological basis for the movement in the Kingdom of God. This kingdom existed in the churches themselves, but it embraced far more than these: "It is the Christian transfiguration of the social order. The church is one social institution alongside of the family, the industrial organization of society, and the State. The Kingdom of God is in all these, and realizes itself through them all." The church was indispensable to religion, but "the greatest future awaits religion in the public life of humanity."

THE CATHOLIC CHURCH   In the postbellum years Catholics remained inhibited from supporting the new social movements by the

Syllabus of Errors (1864), issued by Pope Pius IX, which declared erroneous such current ideas as progress, liberalism, rationalism, and socialism. The church's outlook altered drastically in 1891 when Pope Leo XIII issued his encyclical, *Rerum novarum* ("Of modern things"). This new expression of Catholic social doctrine upheld private property as a natural right but condemned capitalism for imposing poverty and degradation on workers. It upheld the right of Catholics to join labor unions and socialist movements insofar as these were not antireligious. But most American Catholics remained isolated from reform movements until the twentieth century, though many of them were among the victims of exploitation.

EARLY EFFORTS AT URBAN REFORM

THE SETTLEMENT HOUSE MOVEMENT   While preachers of the social gospel dispensed inspiration, other dedicated reformers attacked the problems of the slums from residential and community centers called settlement houses. The movement sprang from the example of Toynbee Hall, founded in a London industrial district, where an English vicar invited students to join him in "settling" in a deprived section. By 1900 perhaps a hundred settlement houses existed in the United States, some of the best known being Jane Addams's and Ellen Starr's Hull House in Chicago (1889), Robert A. Woods's South End House in Boston (1891), and Lillian Wald's Henry Street Settlement (1895) in New York.

The settlement houses mainly attracted as workers idealistic middle-class young people, a majority of them college-trained women who had few other outlets for meaningful work outside the home. Settlement workers sought to broaden the horizons and improve the lives of slum dwellers in diverse ways. At Jane Addams's Hull House, for instance, workers enrolled the neighborhood children into clubs and kindergartens, and set up a nursery to care for the infant children of working mothers. The program gradually expanded as Hull House sponsored health clinics, lectures, music and art studios, an employment bureau, men's clubs, training in skills such as bookbinding, a gymnasium, and a savings bank.

Jane Addams and other settlement house leaders realized, however, that the spreading slums made their work as effective as bailing out the

Jane Addams.

ocean with a teaspoon. They therefore organized political support for housing laws, public playgrounds, juvenile courts, mothers' pensions, workers' compensation laws, and legislation against child labor. Lillian Wald promoted the establishment of the federal Children's Bureau in 1912, and Jane Addams, for her work in the peace movement, received late in her life the Nobel Peace Prize for 1931.

The settlement house movement, however, was not immune to criticism. Critics accused settlements of subtle and not-so-subtle forms of social control and of attempts to assimilate the ethnic poor to white, middle-class Protestant standards. The cultural gap between middle-class social workers and slum dwellers could often lead to misunderstanding, and in the effort to "Americanize" immigrants, the settlement houses and agencies of education sometimes lacked sensitivity to the values of other cultures. But on balance their contributions were more positive than negative. By the end of the century both the Catholic church and Jewish agencies were taking up the settlement house movement.

WOMEN'S EMPLOYMENT AND SUFFRAGE   Settlement house workers, insofar as they were paid, made up but a fraction of all gainfully employed women. With the growth of population, the number of employed women steadily increased, as did their percentage of the labor force and of the total female population. The greatest leaps forward came in the decades of the 1880s and the 1900s, both of which were also peak decades of immigration, a correlation that can be explained by the immigrant's need for income. The number of employed women went from over 2.6 million in 1880 to 4 million in 1890, then from 5.1 million in 1900 to 7.8 million in 1910. "Between 1880 and 1900 the employment of women in most parts of the economy became an established fact," wrote one historian. "This was surely the most significant event in the modern history of women." Through all those years domestic work remained the largest category of employment for women; teaching and nursing also remained among the leading fields. The main change was that clerical work (bookkeeping, stenographic work, and the like) and sales jobs became increasingly available to women.

These changes in occupational status had little connection with the women's rights movement, which increasingly focused on the issue of suffrage. Immediately after the Civil War, Susan B. Anthony, a seasoned veteran of the movement, demanded that the Fourteenth Amendment guarantee the vote for women as well as black males. She made little impression on the defenders of masculine prerogative, however, who steadfastly insisted that women belonged in the domestic sphere. "Their mission is at home, by their blandishments and their love to assuage the passions of men as they come in from the battle of life," said a New Jersey senator.

In 1869 the unity of the women's movement was broken in a manner reminiscent of the antislavery rift three decades before. The question once again was whether the movement should concentrate on one overriding issue. Anthony and Elizabeth Cady Stanton founded the National Woman Suffrage Association to promote a women's suffrage amendment to the Constitution, but they looked upon suffrage as but one among many feminist causes to be promoted. Later that same year, Lucy Stone, Julia Ward Howe, and other leaders formed the American Woman Suffrage Association, which focused single-mindedly on the suffrage as the first and basic reform.

It would be another half century before the battle could be won, and the long struggle for referenda and state legislation on the issue focused the women's cause ever more on the primary objective of the vote. In 1890, after three years of negotiation, the rival groups united as the National American Woman Suffrage Association, with Elizabeth Cady Stanton as president for two years, to be followed by Susan B. Anthony until 1900. The work thereafter was carried on by a new generation of

*Carrie Chapman Catt, a leader in
the women's suffrage movement.*

activists, led by Anna Howard Shaw and Carrie Chapman Catt. Over
the years the movement slogged its way to some local and some partial
victories, as a few states granted women suffrage in school board or municipal elections, or bond referenda. In 1869 the Territory of Wyoming
granted full suffrage to women, and after 1890 retained women's suffrage when it became a new state. Three other western states soon followed suit: Colorado in 1893, Utah and Idaho in 1896. But women's
suffrage lost in a California referendum in 1896 by a dishearteningly
narrow margin.

The movement remained in the doldrums thereafter until the cause
easily won a Washington state referendum in 1910, and then carried
California by a close majority in 1911. The following year three more
western states—Arizona, Kansas, and Oregon—joined in to make a total of nine western states with full suffrage. In 1913 Illinois granted
women presidential and municipal suffrage. Yet not until New York
acted in 1917 did a state east of the Mississippi adopt universal suffrage. In 1878 California's Senator A. A. Sargent introduced the "Anthony Amendment," a women's suffrage provision that remained before
Congress until 1896 and then vanished until 1913, when it was finally
ratified (see Chapter 26).

Despite the focus on the vote, women did not confine their public
work to that issue. In 1866 a Young Women's Christian Association, a

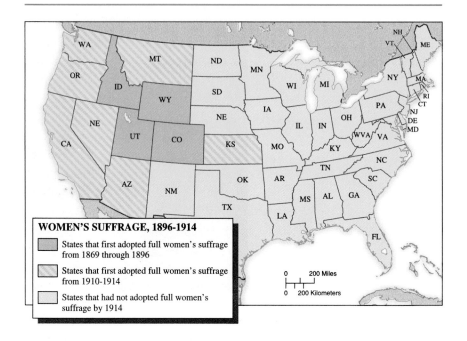

WOMEN'S SUFFRAGE, 1896-1914

- States that first adopted full women's suffrage from 1869 through 1896
- States that first adopted full women's suffrage from 1910-1914
- States that had not adopted full women's suffrage by 1914

parallel to the YMCA, appeared in Boston and spread elsewhere. The New England Women's Club, started in 1868 by Julia Ward Howe and others, was an early example of the women's clubs that then proliferated to the extent that a General Federation of Women's Clubs tied them together in 1890. Many women's clubs confined themselves to "literary" and social activities, but others became deeply involved in charities and reform. The New York Consumers League, formed in 1890, and the National Consumers League, formed nine years later, sought to make the buying public, chiefly women, aware of labor conditions. One of its devices was the "White List" of firms that met its minimum standards. The National Women's Trade Union League, founded in 1903, performed a similar function of bringing educated and middle-class women together with working women for the benefit of women unionists.

These and the many other women's groups of the time may have aroused the fear in opponents to women's suffrage that voting women would tilt toward reform. This was the fear of the brewing and liquor interests, large business interests generally, and political machine bosses. Others, mainly in the South, opposed women's suffrage on the ground that black women would be enfranchised, or because of states'-rights views.

A JUDICIAL HARBOR FOR LAISSEZ-FAIRE   Even without the support of voting women in most places, the states adopted rudimentary measures to regulate big business and labor conditions in the public interest. By the end of the century, nearly every state had provided for the regulation of railroads, if not always effectively, and had moved to supervise banks and insurance companies. Between 1887 and 1897, by one count, the states and territories passed over 1,600 laws relating to conditions of work, which limited the hours of labor, provided special protection for women, limited or forbade child labor, required regular wage payments in cash, called for factory inspections, and outlawed blacklisting or the importation of "Pinkerton men." Nearly all states had boards or commissioners of labor, and some had boards of conciliation and arbitration. Still, conservative judges limited the practical impact of such new laws.

In thwarting new regulatory efforts, the Supreme Court used a revised interpretation of the Fourteenth Amendment clauses forbidding the states to "deprive any person of life, liberty or property without due process of law" or to deny any person "the equal protection of the laws." Two significant steps of legal reasoning turned the due-process clause into a bulwark of private property. First, the judges reasoned that the word "person" in the clause included corporations, which in other connections were legally artificial persons with the right to own property, buy and sell, sue and be sued like natural persons. Second, the courts moved away from the old view that "due process" referred only to correct procedures and toward a doctrine of "substantive due process," which allowed courts to review the substance of an action. Under this line of reasoning it was possible for legislatures to pass laws so extreme (in the view of the judges) as to deprive persons of property to an unreasonable degree, and thereby violate due process.

The Supreme Court first accepted the personality of the corporation in a tax case, *Santa Clara County* v. *Southern Pacific Railroad Company* (1886). That same year the Court in *Stone* v. *Farmers Loan and Trust Company* (1886) recognized the authority of Mississippi to regulate railroad rates, but declared that there might be cases in which the Court could review the rates: "Under pretense of regulating fares and freights, the State cannot require a railroad corporation to carry persons or property without reward." In *Chicago, Milwaukee and St. Paul Railway Company* v. *Minnesota* (1890) the justices declared unconstitutional a state law that forbade judicial review of rates set by a railroad commission. "The question of the reasonableness of a rate of charge . . . is eminently a question for judicial investigation," the Court ruled, "requiring due process of law for its determination." This was a direct reversal of the ruling in *Munn* v. *Illinois* (1877) that regulation was a legislative prerogative. It remained only for the Court to overturn rates set directly by a state legislature. That it did in *Smyth* v. *Ames* (1898). The case struck down a Nebraska law for setting rates so low as to be, in the Court's view, unreasonable.

From the due-process clause the Court also derived a new doctrine of "liberty of contract," defined as being within the liberties protected by the due-process clause. Liberty, the Court ruled in 1897, involved "not only the right of the citizen to be free from the mere physical restraint of his person, . . . but the term is deemed to embrace the right of the citizen to be free in the enjoyment of all his faculties," and free "to enter into all contracts" proper to carrying out such purposes. When it came to labor laws, this translated into an employee's "liberty" to contract for work under the most oppressive conditions without interference from the state. The courts continued to apply such an interpretation well into the twentieth century.

Judges in some of the lower courts found no need to spin their theories so finely. In 1886 the Pennsylvania Supreme Court overturned an act to protect workers against payment in commodities instead of in cash, declaring it "an insulting attempt to put the laborer under a legislative tutelage, which is not only degrading to his manhood, but subversive of his rights as a citizen of the United States." The high court of West Virginia in 1889 condemned a similar law as an attempt to "foist upon the people a paternal government of the most objectionable character, because it assumes that the employer is a knave, and the laborer an imbecile." At least equally boggling in its blindness to reality was the opinion expressed by a New York judge in 1885, in which he ruled against a law forbidding cigarmaking in tenements. "It cannot be perceived," he said, "how the cigarmaker is to be improved in his health or his morals by forcing him from his home and its hallowed associations and beneficent influences, to ply his trade elsewhere."

As the turn of the century neared, opinion in the country stood poised between such conservative rigidities and a growing sense that new occasions teach new duties. "By the last two decades of the century," wrote one observer, "many thoughtful men had begun to march under various banners declaring that somewhere and somehow the promise of the American dream had been lost—they often said 'betrayed'—and that drastic changes needed to be made to recapture it."

The last two decades of the nineteenth century had already seen a slow erosion of laissez-faire values, which had found their most secure home in the courts. From the social philosophy of the reformers, Social Gospelers, and Populists there emerged a concept of the general-welfare state which, in the words of one historian, sought "to promote the general welfare not by rendering itself inconspicuous but by taking such positive action as is deemed necessary to improve the condition under which its citizens live and work." The reformers supplied no agreed-upon blueprint for a general-welfare utopia, but "simply assumed that government could promote the public interest by appropriate positive action . . . whenever the circumstances indicated that such action would further the common weal." The conflict between this notion and laissez-faire values went on into the new century, but by the mid–twentieth century, after the Progressive movement, the New Deal, and the Fair Deal, the conflict would be "resolved in theory, in practice, and in public esteem in favor of the general-welfare state."

MAKING CONNECTIONS

- As the next chapter shows, the presidential election of 1896 was in many ways a contest between the new urban values discussed in this chapter and those of a more traditional rural American society.

- The reform impulse you've read about in this chapter finds voice again in the discussion of the Progressive movement in Chapter 24.

- The nativist thinking discussed in this chapter fueled the immigration restriction laws enacted in the 1920s (Chapter 26).

FURTHER READING

The best survey of urbanization remains Charles N. Glaab and A. Theodore Brown's *A History of Urban America* (3rd ed., 1983). Gunther P. Barth discusses the emergence of a new urban culture in *City People: The Rise of Modern City Culture in Nineteenth Century America* (1980). Urban politics is surveyed in Jon C. Teaford's *The Unheralded Triumph: City Government in America, 1870–1900* (1984). Oliver E. Allen's *The Tiger: The Rise and Fall of Tammany Hall* (1994) assesses the significance of New York's famous political machine.

John Bodnar provides a synthesis of the urban immigrant experience in *The Transplanted: A History of Immigrants in Urban America* (1985). Walter Nugent's *Crossings: The Great Transatlantic Migrations, 1870–1914* (1992) provides a wealth of demographic information and insight. John Higham's *Strangers in the Land: Patterns of American Nativism, 1860–1925* (2nd ed., 1988) examines how old-stock residents reacted to the influx of newcomers.

For the growth of urban leisure and sports, see Roy Rosenzweig's *Eight Hours for What We Will: Workers and Leisure in an Industrial City, 1870–1920* (1983) and Steven A. Riess's *City Games: The Evolution of American Urban Society and the Rise of Sports* (1989). Steven A. Riess's *Touching Base: Professional Baseball and American Culture in the Progressive Era* (1980) and Dominick Cavallo's *Muscles and Morals: Organized Playgrounds and Urban Reform, 1880–1920* (1981) link athletics to new forms of organization and socialization.

Richard Hofstadter's *Social Darwinism in American Thought* (rev. ed., 1992) and Cynthia E. Russett's *Darwin in America* (1976) examine the impact of the theory of evolution. On the rise of realism in thought and the arts during the second half of the nineteenth century, see David Shi's *Facing Facts: Realism in American Thought and Culture, 1850–1920* (1995).

William L. O'Neill's *Everyone Was Brave: The Rise and Fall of Feminism in America* (1969) and Eleanor Flexner's *Century of Struggle: The Woman's Rights Movement in the United States* (rev. ed., 1975) survey the condition of women in the late nineteenth century.

22 GILDED-AGE POLITICS AND AGRARIAN REVOLT

CHAPTER ORGANIZER

This chapter focuses on:

- political developments in the Gilded Age.

- problems, both real and perceived, affecting American farmers.

- the rise of the agrarian revolt and the Populists.

- the significant election of 1896.

*I*n 1873 Mark Twain and Charles Dudley Warner created an enduring label for their times when they collaborated on a novel entitled *The Gilded Age*. The most unforgettable character in the book was an engaging rascal, Colonel Beriah Sellers, who was constantly scheming to profit from political favors. Sellers had enough counterparts in the real politics of the day to enliven that story too, and their humbuggery reinforced the novel's theme that the post–Civil War years were above all an age of corruption, profiteering, and false glitter.

Perspectives on the times would eventually change, but generations of political scientists and historians have since reinforced the two novelists' judgment. As a young college graduate in 1879, Woodrow Wilson described the state of the American political system: "No leaders, no principles; no principles, no parties." Indeed, the real movers and shakers of the Gilded Age were not the men who sat in the White House or the Congress but the captains of industry who crisscrossed the continent with railroads and decorated its cities with plumed smokestacks and gaudy mansions.

PARADOXICAL POLITICS

On the national issues of the day the major parties pursued for the most part a policy of evasion. Only on the tariff were there clear-cut divisions between protectionist Republicans and low-tariff Democrats, but there were individual exceptions even on that. On questions of the currency, regulation of big business, farm problems, civil service reform, internal improvements, and immigration, the parties differed very little.

Two factors, above all, accounted for the muddled politics of this period. Americans feared what had happened in 1860, when parties had taken clear-cut stands on a deeply felt moral issue, with bloody consequences. But the more compelling cause of political inertia was the even division between the parties. From 1869 to 1913, from the presidencies of Ulysses Grant to William Howard Taft, Republicans occupied the White House except during the two nonconsecutive terms of Grover Cleveland, but Republican domination of national politics was more apparent than real. In the years between 1872 and 1896 no president won a majority of the popular vote. In 1888 Benjamin Harrison failed to muster even a plurality over Cleveland, but carried the election anyway because his popular vote was concentrated in the states with the larger electoral votes. And while Republicans usually controlled the Senate, Democrats usually controlled the House. Only during the years 1881–1883 and 1889–1891 did a Republican president have a Republican Congress; and only between 1893 and 1895 did a Democratic president have a Democratic Congress—the only time this occurred between the Civil War and 1913, and that during a severe depression.

No chief executive between Lincoln and Theodore Roosevelt could be described as a "strong" president. None seriously challenged the prevailing view that Congress formulated policy. The function of the chief

The Bosses of the Senate. *This 1889 cartoon bitingly portrays the alliance between big business and politics in this period.*

executive, to these presidents, was simply to administer the government. At the same time, the almost equal strength of the parties in Congress worked against any vigorous new initiatives there, since most bills required bipartisan support to pass both houses, and legislators tended to vote along party lines. Congress thus was caught up in political maneuvers and could not come to grips with national issues.

Under such static conditions, the parties became vehicles for seeking office and dispensing patronage in the form of government jobs and contracts. In the choice of candidates, more than ever, "availability" outweighed ability. The ideal presidential candidate displayed an affable personality, a willingness to cooperate with the party bosses, and an ability to win votes from various factions; he resided in a pivotal state and boasted a good war record. He had no views that might alienate powerful voting blocs, and few or no political enemies. Vice-presidential candidates were chosen to balance the ticket, to placate a disappointed faction, or to improve the party's chances in a key state. This process placed a premium on candidates who were relatively obscure, or at least removed from national party battles capable of arousing opposition.

An alliance between big business and politics characterized the period. This alliance was not necessarily corrupt, since many a politician favored the interests of business out of conviction. Nor was the public as sensitive to conflicts of interest as it would be later. So James G. Blaine of Maine, and hosts of his supporters, saw nothing wrong in his accepting stock commissions from an Arkansas railroad after helping it win a land grant from Congress. It was, they thought, a reward after the event, not a bribe in advance. One Georgia senator freely accepted a retainer fee of $10,000 from the Southern Pacific Railroad, a sum larger than his salary, without losing his reputation with his constituents. Railroad passes, free entertainment, and a host of other favors were freely given to and accepted by politicians, editors, and other leaders in positions to influence public opinion.

POLITICS AND THE VOTERS   But if many observers considered this a time of political futility in which the parties refused to confront such "real issues" as the growth of an unregulated economy and its attendant social injustices, it is nonetheless clear that the voters of the time thought more was at stake. Voter turnout during the Gilded Age was commonly about 70 to 80 percent, even in the South, where the disenfranchisement of blacks was not yet complete. (By contrast, the turnout for the 1996 presidential election was barely 50 percent.) How was it then that leaders who failed to address the real issues presided over the most highly organized and politically active electorate in American history?

The answer is partly that the politicians and the voters deeply believed that they *were* dealing with crucial issues, such as the tariff, monopolies, the currency, civil service reform, and immigration. They turned out in heavy numbers for political rallies and parades. Probably more than any other generation of Americans, they had the patience to follow the intricacies of lengthy debates and heavy tomes on such matters. If the major parties then failed to resolve these issues, no later generation has resolved them either, and they remain live issues, still relevant to American life a century later.

Still another important factor in understanding the nature of Gilded-Age politics is to recognize that most of the significant political activity occurred at the state and local levels. Much more than the national Congress, state governments after the Civil War were dynamic centers of political activity and innovation. Over 60 percent of the nation's spending and taxing was exercised by state and local governments. Then, unlike today, the large cities spent far more on public services than did the federal government. And three-fourths of all public employees worked for local and state governments.

A NEW VIEW OF POLITICAL HISTORY   What most motivated party loyalties and voter turnout in these years were local economic issues and intense cultural conflicts among ethnic and religious groups. Practitioners of what has been called the "new political history" have analyzed the political effects of local, ethnic, cultural, and religious divisions. These historians approach politics less as a simple contest among economic interests, as the "progressive" historians of the earlier twentieth century saw it, than as a complex interplay of motivations, a struggle in which voters follow not simply their pocketbooks but their ethnic prejudices, cultural heritage, and religious convictions as well. According to one of the new political historians: "It has become clear to us . . . that the energies shaping public life are emotional as well as rational, cultural as well as economic."

Far from being like two empty bottles that differed only in their labels, as Woodrow Wilson said of the parties before the turn of the century, each party contained a different mixture of ingredients picked up in the course of its history. The Republican party, legitimate heir to the Whig tradition, attracted political insiders and active reformers. Party members were mainly Protestants of British descent. In their own eyes, and in the eyes of many immigrants, they were prototypical Americans. Their native seat was New England, and their other strongholds were New York and the upper Middle West, both of which they had populated with Yankee stock. Legitimate heirs to the abolitionist tradition, Republicans drew to their ranks a host of reformers and moralists, spiritual descendants of the perfectionists who populated the revivals and the reform movements of the antebellum years. The party's heritage of anti-Catholic nativism, dating from the 1850s when the Republican party had become a haven for former Know-Nothings, also made a comeback in the 1880s. The Republicans could also rely on the votes of blacks and Union veterans of the Civil War.

The Democrats, by contrast, tended to be outsiders, a heterogeneous, often unruly coalition of unlikely allies. What they had in common was that in one way or another they differed from the Republicans. The Democratic party embraced southern whites, immigrants, Catholics of any origin, Jews, freethinkers, skeptics, and all those repelled by the "party of morality." As one Chicago Democrat explained, "A Republican is a man who wants you t' go t' church every Sunday. A Democrat says if a man wants to have a glass of beer on Sunday he can have it." The Democrats were the "party of personal liberty," a combination that sometimes proved volatile. Democratic conventions tended to be more disorderly than Republican gatherings, and often the more interesting for it. There were exceptions to these broad generalizations about party affiliations: black Americans who, though outsiders, clung to the party of Lincoln, and some Protestant immigrants drawn to the Republicans by the party's image of uprightness.

The new immigration of the postbellum years, coming largely from Catholic and Jewish strongholds in eastern and southern Europe, reinforced the Democratic ranks. But the changing ethnic composition of immigrants helped revive a vicious tide of nativism that coursed through the Republican party. As mentioned in Chapter 21, a nativist group called the American Protective Association sprang up in 1887 and spread like a prairie fire through the Middle West, which became its chief stronghold. In that region especially, Republicans pressed nativist causes, calling for tighter naturalization laws, restrictions on immigration and the employment of foreigners, and greater emphasis on the teaching of the "American" language in the schools.

Prohibitionism revived along with nativism in the 1880s. Among the immigrants who crowded into the growing cities were hard-drinking Irish, beer-drinking Germans, and wine-drinking Italians. Democratic constituents in general were more fond of alcohol than Yankees, who increasingly saw saloons as the central social evil around which all others revolved, including vice, crime, political corruption, and neglect of families. Republicans across New England and the Middle West promoted prohibition and were joined after 1869 by a Prohibition party, after 1874 by the Women's Christian Temperance Union, and after 1893 by the Anti-Saloon League. Before the turn of the century, these groups attracted few Democrats to their camp.

CORRUPTION AND REFORM

While grassroots Republicans and Democrats differed over ethnic and cultural issues, their party leaders squabbled over the so-called spoils of office. Each party had its share of corrupt officials willing to buy and sell government appointments or congressional votes, yet each also witnessed the emergence of factions promoting honesty in government. This struggle for clean government soon became one of the foremost issues of the day.

CIVIL SERVICE REFORM   In the aftermath of Reconstruction, Rutherford B. Hayes admirably embodied the "party of morality." He brought to the White House in 1877 a new style of uprightness, a sharp contrast to the graft and corruption of the Grant administration. The son of an Ohio farmer, Hayes entered politics as a Whig but became one of the early Republicans, was wounded four times in the Civil War, and was promoted to major-general. As a member of the House of Representatives for one term, from 1865 to 1867, he supported the congressional Reconstruction program. Elected governor of Ohio in 1867, he served three terms. Honest and respectable, competent and dignified, he lived in a modest style with his wife, nicknamed "Lemonade Lucy" because of her refusal to serve strong drink on social occasions.

Yet Hayes's presidency suffered from the manner of his election. Snide references to him as the "*de facto* President" and "His Fraudulence" dogged his steps and denied him any chance at a second term, which he renounced from the beginning. Hayes's own party was split between so-called Stalwarts and Half-Breeds, led respectively by Senator Roscoe Conkling of New York and Senator James G. Blaine of Maine. The difference between these Republican factions was murkier than that between the parties. The Stalwarts generally supported Grant,

Rutherford B. Hayes and his wife, Lucy Ware Hayes.

a Radical southern policy, and the spoils system. The Half-Breeds took a contrary view on the first two and even vaguely supported civil service reform.

For the most part, however, the factions were loose alliances aimed at advancing the careers of Conkling and Blaine. The two men could not abide each other. Blaine once referred to Conkling as displaying a "majestic, supereminent, overpowering, turkey-gobbler strut." Conkling boasted good looks, fine clothes, and an arrogant manner. He dressed and lived flamboyantly, sporting pastel bow ties, silk scarves, moon-colored vests, and patent-leather shoes. Yet underneath his glamorous facade he was a ruthless power broker. Conkling viewed politics as a brute struggle for control. "Parties," he once declared, "are not built by deportment or by ladies' magazines, or gush." Politics "is a rotten business," he added. "Nothing counts except to win."

Hayes thought otherwise, and he aligned himself with the growing public discontent over the corruption that had prevailed under Grant. American leaders were just learning about the merit system for public employees long established in the bureaucracies of France and Germany, and the new British practice in which civil service jobs were filled by competitive examination. Prominent leaders such as James A. Garfield in the House and Carl Schurz in the Senate embraced civil service reform, and both Hayes and vice-presidential candidate Samuel J. Tilden raised the issue during the campaign of 1876. Hayes repeated his support for reform in his inaugural address.

Although Hayes failed to get legislation on the subject, he did mandate his own rules for merit appointments: those already in office would be dismissed only for the good of the government and not for political reasons; party members would have no more influence in appointments than other respectable citizens; no assessments of government employees for political contributions would be permitted; and no officeholder could manage election campaigns for political organizations, although all could vote and express opinions.

The issue of honest and effective government culminated in a dispute over the federal customs houses. They were notorious centers of corrupt politics, filled with political appointees with little or nothing to do but draw salaries and run political machines. Importers sometimes found that they might gain favor by cooperating with corrupt customs officials, and might be punished for making trouble. An inquiry into operations at the New York Customs House revealed that both collector Chester A. Arthur and naval officer Alonzo Cornell were guilty of "laxity" and of using the customs house for political management on behalf of Senator Roscoe Conkling's organization. When Hayes hinted that resignations would be welcomed, Conkling responded with an attack on reformers in a speech to the state Republican convention: "Their vocation . . . is to lament the sins of other people. Their stock in trade is rancid, canting self-righteousness."

On October 15, 1877, after removing Arthur and Cornell, Hayes named replacements, only to have the nominees rejected when Conkling appealed to the "courtesy of the Senate," an old custom whereby senators might control appointments in their own states. During a recess in the summer of 1878, however, Hayes appointed new replacements. When Congress reassembled, the administration put pressure on senators and, with Democratic support, the nominations were appropriate. Even this, however, did not end the New York Customs House episode; it would flare up again under the next president.

For all his efforts to clean house, Hayes's vision of government's role remained limited. On the economic issues of the day he held to a conservative line that would guide his successors for the rest of the century. His solution to labor troubles, demonstrated in the Great Railroad Strike of 1877, was to send in troops and break the strike. His answer to demands for an expansion of the currency was to veto the Bland-Allison Act, which required only a limited expansion of silver currency through the government's purchase for coinage of $2 million to $4 million worth of silver per month. (The act passed anyway when Congress overrode Hayes's veto.)

GARFIELD AND ARTHUR   With Hayes unavailable for a second term, the Republicans were forced to look elsewhere in 1880. The Stalwarts, led by Conkling, brought Grant forward for a third time, still a strong contender despite the tarnish of his administration's scandals. For two days the Republican convention in Chicago was deadlocked, with Grant holding a slight lead over Blaine. On the thirty-fifth ballot Wisconsin suddenly switched sixteen votes to Senator-elect James A. Garfield, and on the thirty-sixth ballot the convention stampeded to the dark-horse candidate, carrying him to the nomination. As a sop to the Stalwarts, the convention named Chester A. Arthur, the deposed collector of the New York Customs House for vice-president.

The Democrats selected Winfield Scott Hancock, a Union commander at Gettysburg, to counterbalance the Republicans' Major-General Garfield and thus ward off "bloody-shirt" attacks on their party as the vehicle of Rebellion. Former rebels, nevertheless, advised their constituents to "vote as you shot"—that is, against Republicans. In an election characterized by widespread bribery, Garfield eked out a plurality of only 39,000 votes with 48.5 percent of the vote, but with a comfortable margin of 214 to 155 in the electoral college.

A native of Ohio, Garfield graduated from Williams College, became president of Hiram College in Ohio, was admitted to the bar, and won election to the Ohio Senate as a Republican in 1859. During the Civil War, he distinguished himself at Shiloh and Chickamauga and was mustered out as a major-general when he went to Congress in 1863. Noted for his oratory and parliamentary skills, he became one of the outstanding leaders in the House and eventually its Speaker.

On July 2, 1881, President Garfield started on a vacation in New England to get away from the siege of office seekers. As he passed through the Baltimore rail station, a deranged office seeker named Charles Guiteau shot him in the back. "I am a Stalwart," Guiteau explained to the arresting officers. "Arthur is now President of the United States," an announcement that would prove crippling to the Stalwarts. Garfield lingered near death for two long, hot months, his suffering eased by a contrived air conditioner—a blower rigged up by navy engineers to pass air over a vault of ice into the president's sickroom. Finally, on September 19, Garfield died of complications resulting from the shooting, having been president for a little over six months.

One of the chief henchmen of Stalwart leader Roscoe Conkling was now president. "Chet Arthur, President of the United States?" one of his friends exclaimed, "Good God!" Little in Arthur's past, except for his record as an abolitionist lawyer who had helped secure the freedom of a fugitive slave, raised hopes that he would rise above customs-house politics. A native of Vermont, he had attended Union College, become a lawyer, and made a political career in appointive offices, most notably as New York quartermaster-general during the Civil War and collector of customs from 1871 to 1878.

Chester A. Arthur.

But Arthur demonstrated rare qualities as president. He distanced himself from Conkling and the Stalwarts and established a genuine independence, almost a necessity after Guiteau's announcement. As president, Arthur vigorously prosecuted the Star Route Frauds, a kickback scheme on contracts for postal routes that involved his old political cronies. The president further surprised Washington in 1882 with the veto of an $18 million river and harbors bill, a "pork-barrel" measure that included something for most congressional districts. He also vetoed the Chinese Exclusion Act (1882), which in his view violated the Burlingame Treaty of 1868. Congress proceeded to override both vetoes.

Most startling of all was Arthur's emergence as something of a civil service and tariff reformer. Stalwarts had every reason to expect him to oppose the merit system, but instead he allied himself with the reformers. While the assassin Guiteau had unwittingly added a certain urgency to the public support of reform, the defeat of a reform bill in 1882 sponsored by "Gentleman George" Pendleton, Democratic senator from Ohio, aroused public opinion further.

The Pendleton Civil Service Act finally passed in 1883, setting up a three-member Civil Service Commission independent from the regular cabinet departments, the first such federal agency established on a permanent basis. About 14 percent of all government jobs would now be filled on the basis of competitive examinations rather than political favoritism. What was more, the president could enlarge the class of affected jobs at his discretion. This had important consequences over the years, because after each of the next four presidential elections the "outs" emerged as victors. Each new president thus had a motive to enlarge this category of government jobs, because it would shield his own appointees from political removal.

The high protective tariff, a heritage of the Civil War, had by the early 1880s raised revenues to the point that the government actually enjoyed an embarrassment of riches, a surplus that drew money into the Treasury and out of circulation. Some argued that lower tariff rates would reduce prices and the cost of living, and at the same time leave more money in circulation to fuel economic growth. In 1882 Arthur named a special commission to study the problem. The Tariff Commission recommended a 20 to 25 percent rate reduction, which gained Arthur's support, but Congress's effort to enact the proposal was marred by logrolling (the trading of votes to benefit different legislators' local interests), resulting in the "Mongrel Tariff" of 1883, so called because of its diverse rates for different commodities. The tariff provided for a slight rate reduction, perhaps by 5 percent, but it actually raised the duty on some articles.

SCURRILOUS CAMPAIGN   When the 1884 election campaign began, Arthur's record might have commended him to the voters, but it did not please leaders of his party. So the Republicans dumped Arthur and turned to the glamorous Senator James G. Blaine of Maine, longtime

Senator James G. Blaine of Maine.

leader of the Half-Breeds. Blaine was the consummate politician. He never forgot a name or a face, he inspired the party faithful with his oratory, and at the same time he knew how to wheel and deal in the back rooms. He managed eloquence even when spouting the platitudes of party loyalty, waving the bloody shirt, and twisting the British lion's tail—the last of which held special appeal for the Irish, a group not normally drawn to Republicans. Blaine did have his enemies, however. Democratic newspapers, for example, turned up evidence of his corruption. Based on references in the "Mulligan letters," they claimed that Blaine was in the pocket of the railroad barons, and that he had sold his votes on measures favorable to their interests.

During the campaign, more letters surfaced with disclosures embarrassing to Blaine. For the reform element of the Republican party, this was too much, and one after another, prominent leaders and supporters of the party bolted the ticket. Party regulars scorned them as "googoos"—the "good-government" crowd who ignored partisan realities—and the editor of the *New York Sun* jokingly called them Mugwumps, after an Algonquian word meaning a great chieftain. To party regulars, in what soon became a stale joke, Mugwumps were unreliable Republicans who had their "mugs" on one side of the fence and their "wumps" on the other.

The rise of the Mugwumps, however, influenced the Democrats to nominate Stephen Grover Cleveland as a reform candidate. Cleveland rose rapidly from obscurity to the White House. One of many children in the family of a small-town Presbyterian minister, he had been forced by his father's death to go to work at an early age. He won a job as clerk in a law office, read law, passed the bar examination, and became an assistant state attorney-general in New York in 1863 and later sheriff of Erie County. He first attracted national attention as mayor of Buffalo, where he was elected in 1881, for battling graft and corruption. In 1882 he was elected as governor, and he continued to build a reform record by fighting New York's corrupt Tammany Hall organization. As mayor and as governor, he repeatedly vetoed what he considered special-privilege bills serving selfish interests.

A stocky 250-pound man, Cleveland seemed the stolid opposite of Blaine. He possessed little charisma, but impressed the public with his stubborn integrity. One supporter said that "We love him for the enemies he has made."

Then a scandal erupted when the *Buffalo Evening Telegraph* revealed that as a bachelor Cleveland had had an affair with an attractive Buffalo widow, who had named him as the father of a child born to her in 1874, though there was no proof of paternity. Cleveland, it seemed, was only one of several likely fathers, but he took responsibility and provided for the child. When supporters asked Cleveland what to say, he answered "Tell the truth." The respective escapades of Blaine and Cleveland provided some of the most colorful battle cries in American political history. "Blaine, Blaine, James G. Blaine, the continental liar from the state of Maine," Democrats chanted. Republicans countered with "Ma, ma, where's my pa? Gone to the White House, ha, ha, ha!"

Near the end of the campaign, Blaine and his supporters committed two fateful blunders. The first occurred at New York's fashionable Delmonico's restaurant, where Blaine went to a private dinner with several millionaire bigwigs, including John Astor and Jay Gould, to discuss campaign finances. Cartoons and accounts of "Belshazzar's Feast" festooned the opposition press for days. The second fiasco cost Blaine much of the Irish vote when a delegation of Protestant ministers visited

Another Voice for Cleveland. *This 1884 cartoon attacks "Grover the Good" for fathering an illegitimate child.*

Republican headquarters in New York, and one of them referred to the Democrats as the party of "rum, Romanism, and rebellion." The judgment had a certain validity, but the tone was insolent. Blaine, who was present, let pass and perhaps failed to catch the implied insult to Catholics—a fatal oversight, since he had always cultivated Irish-American support with his anti-British talk and public reminders that his mother was Catholic. Democrats spread word that he had let the insult pass, even that he had made it himself.

The incident may have tipped the election. The electoral vote in Cleveland's favor stood at 219 to 182, but the popular vote ran far closer: Cleveland's plurality was fewer than 30,000 votes.

CLEVELAND AND THE SPECIAL INTERESTS   For all of Cleveland's hostility to the spoils system and politics as usual, he represented no sharp break with the conservative policies of his predecessors, except in opposing governmental favors to business. "A public office is a public trust" was one of his favorite mottoes. He held to a strictly limited view of government's role in both economic and social matters, a rigid philosophy illustrated by his 1887 veto of the Texas Seed Bill, an effort to appropriate funds to meet the urgent need of drought victims for seed grain. Back to Congress it went with a lecture on the need to limit the powers and functions of government—"though the people support the government the government should not support the people," Cleveland asserted.

Despite his strong philosophical convictions, Cleveland had a mixed record on the civil service. He had good intentions, but he also had a party hungry for partisan appointments, with the first Democratic president since the election of James Buchanan in 1856. Before his inauguration Cleveland repeated his support for the Pendleton Act; he would not remove able government workers on partisan grounds. But he inserted one significant exception: those who had used federal jobs to forward the interests of the opposition party. In many cases, especially in the post offices, he thus had ample excuse to remove people who had practically made their offices into Republican headquarters.

Party pressures gradually forced Cleveland's hand. To a friend he remarked: "The damned everlasting clatter for office continues . . . and makes me feel like resigning." When he left office about two-thirds of the federal officeholders were Democrats, including all internal revenue

Grover Cleveland made the issue of tariff reform central to the politics of the late 1880s.

collectors and nearly all the heads of customs houses. At the same time, however, Cleveland had extended the number of federal jobs subject to civil service regulation to about 27,000 employees, almost double the number that had been covered when he came in. Yet he satisfied neither Mugwumps nor spoilsmen; indeed, he managed to antagonize both.

On other matters Cleveland's stubborn courage and concern for protecting the public Treasury led him into conflicts with predatory interests, conflicts that eventually cost him the White House. One such dispute arose over misuse of the public domain in the West. Cleveland's secretary of the interior and the commissioner of the General Land Office uncovered one case after another of fraud and mismanagement: bogus surveys by government surveyors, public lands used fraudulently by lumber companies, mine operators, and cattle ranchers with the collusion of government officials, and at least 30 million acres of railroad land grants subject to forfeiture because the required lines were not built.

The administration sued railroads to recover such lands. It nullified exploitive leases of Indian lands, such as that of one cattle company that had leased 6 million acres from the Cherokees for $100,000 and subleased the land for about five times as much. Cattle barons were ordered to remove fences enclosing water holes and grasslands on the open range. In all, during Cleveland's first term about 81 million acres of public lands were restored to the federal government.

Cleveland incurred the wrath of Union military veterans by his firm stand against their pension raids on the Treasury. Congress had passed the first Civil War pension law in 1862 to provide for Union veterans disabled in service and for the widows, orphans, and dependents of veterans. By 1882 the Grand Army of the Republic, an organization of Union veterans and a powerful pressure group, was trying to get pensions paid for any disability, no matter how it was incurred. Meanwhile many veterans succeeded in pushing private pension bills through an obliging Congress. In Washington, lawyers built careers on filing claims and pressing for special laws to benefit veterans.

Insofar as time permitted, Cleveland examined such bills critically and vetoed the dubious ones. Although he signed more than any of his predecessors, running pension costs up from $56 million to $80 million, he also vetoed more. A climax came in 1887 when Congress passed the Dependent Pension Bill, which provided funds for veterans dependent upon manual labor and unable to work for any reason, whether or not the reason was service connected. Cleveland sent it back with a ringing veto, declaring that the pension list would become a refuge for frauds rather than a "roll of honor."

About the middle of his term Cleveland assaulted new special interests, leading to the adoption of an important new policy, railroad regulation. Since the late 1860s, states had adopted railroad regulatory laws, and from the early 1870s, Congress had debated federal legislation. In 1886 a Supreme Court decision finally spurred action. In the case of *Wabash Railroad* v. *Illinois*, the Court denied the state's power to regulate rates on interstate traffic. Cleveland thereupon urged that since this "important field of control and regulation [has] thus been left entirely unoccupied," Congress should act.

It did, and in 1887 Cleveland signed into law an act creating the Interstate Commerce Commission (ICC), the first such independent regulatory commission. The law empowered its five members to investigate carriers and prosecute violators. All rates had to be "reasonable and just." Railroads were forbidden to grant secret rebates to preferred shippers, discriminate against persons, places, and commodities, or enter into pools (secret agreements among competing railroads to fix rates). The commission's actual powers, however, proved to be weak when first tested in the courts. Though creating the ICC seemed to conflict with Cleveland's fear of big government, it accorded with his fear of big business. The Interstate Commerce Act, to his mind, was a legitimate exercise of sovereign power.

THE TARIFF ISSUE   Cleveland's most dramatic challenge to special interests focused on tariff reform. Why was the tariff such an important and controversial issue? By the late nineteenth century, many observers had concluded that the formation of huge corporate "trusts" was not a natural development of a maturing capitalist system. Instead, they charged that government policies had fostered big business at the expense of small producers and retailers. Among those policies was an excessively high protective tariff. "The mother of all trusts is the tariff bill," proclaimed one leading business executive. By shielding American manufacturers from foreign competition, the tariff, critics argued, made it easier for them to combine into ever-larger entities. The high tariff also enabled large corporations to restrict production and fix prices. "The heart of the trust problem is in our tariff system of plunder," declared the head of the New England Free Trade League. "The quickest and most certain way of reaching the evils of trusts is not by direct legislation against them, or by constitutional amendment, but by the abolition of tariff duties."

Cleveland agreed. He had entered office as the leader of the traditional low-tariff party, but Democrats were far from unified on the issue, and Cleveland himself confessed at first to limited understanding of the tariff question. Like most politicians of the time, he hesitated to plunge into that tangled thicket. But with greater exposure to the question and further study, he concluded that the rates were too high and included many inequities. Near the end of 1887 Cleveland devoted his entire annual message to the subject. He did so in the full knowledge that he was focusing attention on a political minefield on the eve of an election year, against the warnings of his advisers. "What is the use of being elected if you don't stand for something?" he asked.

Cleveland's message offered a classic summary of the tariff arguments against protection. He noted that tariff revenues had bolstered the surplus, making the Treasury "a hoarding place for money needlessly withdrawn from trade and the people's use." The tariff pushed up prices for everybody, and while it was supposed to protect American workers against the competition of cheap foreign labor, the most recent census showed that of 17.4 million Americans gainfully employed, only 2.6 million were in "such manufacturing industries as are claimed to be benefitted by a high tariff."

It was evident, moreover, that competition produced better prices for buyers. Business combinations could push prices up to the artificial level set by the prices of dutied foreign goods, but prices often fell below that level when domestic producers were in competition, "proof that someone is willing to accept lower prices for such commodity and that such prices are remunerative." Congress, Cleveland argued, should study the more than 4,000 articles subject to tariff duties with an eye to cutting the cost of necessities and of the raw materials used in manufacturing. "Our progress toward a wise conclusion will not be improved by dwelling upon the theories of protection and free trade. . . . It is a condition which confronts us, not a theory." The final sentence became an epigram so infectious that for the next few years public speakers worked it nearly to death.

That did not stop Blaine and other Republicans from denouncing the message as pure "free trade," a doctrine all the more suspect because it was also British policy. The House Ways and Means Committee soon reported a bill calling for modest tariff reductions from an average level of about 47 percent of the value of imported goods to about 40 percent. House Democrats rallied to its support, some of them under assurances that it could not become law. Passed by the House, the bill stalled in the Republican Senate and finally died a lingering death in committee. If Cleveland's talk accomplished his purpose of drawing party lines more firmly, it also confirmed the fears of his advisers. The election of 1888 for the first time in years highlighted a difference between the major parties on an issue of substance.

Cleveland was the obvious nominee of his party. The platform endorsed "the views expressed by the President in his last message to Congress." The Republicans passed up old warhorses such as Blaine and Sherman and turned to the obscure Benjamin Harrison, who had all the attributes of availability. The grandson of President William Henry Harrison, and a flourishing lawyer in Indiana, the diminutive Harrison resided in a pivotal state and also had a good war record. There was little in his political record to offend any voter. He had lost a race for governor and served one term in the Senate (1881–1887). The Republican platform accepted Cleveland's challenge to make the protective tariff the chief issue, and promised generous pensions to veterans.

As insurance against tariff reduction, manufacturers gave generously to the Republican campaign fund, which was used to denounce Cleveland's un-American "free trade" and his pension vetoes. Personal attacks too were leveled against Cleveland. The old charges of immorality had played out. After Cleveland entered the White House he had married young Frances Folsom, who later presented him with a daughter whose name would be immortalized one day by the "Baby Ruth" candy bar. During the campaign, though, the rumor went abroad that a drunken Cleveland had taken to wife-beating. On the eve of the election Cleveland suffered a more devastating blow from the phony "Murchison letter." A California Republican had written British minister Sir Lionel Sackville-West using the false name "Charles F. Murchison." Posing as an English immigrant, he asked advice on how to vote. Sackville-West, engaged at the time in sensitive negotiations over British and American access to Canadian fisheries, hinted that he should vote for Cleveland. The letter aroused a storm of protest against foreign intervention and further linked Cleveland to British free-traders. Democratic explanations never caught up with the public's original sense of outrage.

Still, the outcome was close. Cleveland won the popular vote by 5,538,000 to 5,447,000, but that was poor comfort. The distribution of votes was such that Harrison, with the key states of Indiana and New York on his side by virtue of the sordid, but common practice of paying voters, carried the electoral college by 233 to 168.

REPUBLICAN REFORM UNDER HARRISON As president, Harrison became a competent and earnest figurehead, overshadowed by his secretary of state, James G. Blaine. He proved something of a cold fish in personal relations. "Harrison can make a speech to ten thousand men and every man of them will go away his friend," said one observer. "Let him meet the same ten thousand in private and every one will go away his enemy." When his campaign manager reported the election returns, Harrison exclaimed fervently: "Providence has given us the victory." The cynical adviser later remarked that Harrison "ought to know that Providence hadn't a damn thing to do with it" and opined that the president "would never know how close a number of men were compelled to approach a penitentiary to make him president."

BILLION- DOLLARISM ? HOLE

In an attack on Benjamin Harrison's spending policies, this cartoon shows Harrison pouring Cleveland's huge surplus down a hole.

Harrison had aroused the hopes of civil service reformers when he declared that "fitness and not party service should be the essential and discriminating test" for government employment. Nevertheless he appointed a wealthy Philadelphia merchant as his postmaster-general, allegedly as a reward for a generous contribution. The first assistant postmaster-general announced less than a year later: "I have changed 31,000 out of 55,000 fourth-class postmasters and I expect to change 10,000 more before I finally quit." Harrison made a few feckless efforts to resist partisan pressures, but the party leaders had their way. His most significant gesture at reform was to name young Theodore Roosevelt to the Civil Service Commission.

Harrison owed a heavy debt to the old-soldier vote, which he discharged by naming an officer of the Grand Army of the Republic to the position of pension commissioner. "God help the surplus," the new commissioner reportedly exclaimed. He proceeded to approve pensions with such abandon that the secretary of the interior removed him six months and several million dollars later. In 1890 Congress passed, and Harrison signed, the Dependent Pension Act, substantially the same measure that Cleveland had vetoed. The pension rolls shot up from 490,000 in 1889 to 966,000 in 1893.

During the first two years of Harrison's term, the Republicans controlled the presidency and both houses for only the second time in the twenty years between 1875 and 1895. They were positioned to have pretty much their own way, and they made the year 1890 memorable for some of the most significant legislation enacted in the entire period. In addition to the Dependent Pension Act, Congress and the president approved the Sherman Anti-Trust Act, the Sherman Silver Purchase Act, the McKinley Tariff, and the admission of Idaho and Wyoming as new states, which followed the admission of the Dakotas, Montana, and Washington in 1889.

Both parties had pledged themselves to do something about the growing power of trusts and monopolies. The Sherman Anti-Trust Act, named for Senator John Sherman, chairman of the Senate Judiciary Committee that drafted it, sought to incorporate into federal law a long-standing principle against "restraint of trade." It forbade contracts, combinations, or conspiracies in restraint of trade or in the effort to establish monopolies in interstate or foreign commerce. A broad consensus put the law through, but its passage turned out to be largely symbolic. During the next decade successive administrations expended little effort on enforcement. From 1890 to 1901 only eighteen lawsuits were instituted, and four of those were against labor unions.

Congress meanwhile debated currency legislation against the backdrop of growing distress in the farm regions of the West and South. Hard-pressed farmers were agitating for an increased coinage of silver to inflate the currency, which would raise commodity prices, making it easier for farmers to earn the money with which to pay their debts.

The silverite forces were also strengthened, especially in the Senate, by members from the new western states that had silver-mining interests. Congress passed the new Sherman Silver Purchase Act in 1890, replacing the Bland-Allison Act of 1878. It required the Treasury to purchase 4.5 million ounces of silver each month and to issue in payment Treasury notes redeemable in either gold or silver. But the act failed to satisfy the demands of the silverites. Although the amount of silver purchased doubled, it was still too little to have an inflationary impact on the economy. Eastern business and financial groups, on the other hand, saw a threat to the gold reserve in the growth of paper currency that holders could redeem in gold at the Treasury. The stage was set for the currency issue to eclipse all others in a panic that would sweep the country three years later.

Republicans took their victory over Cleveland as a mandate not just to maintain the protective tariff but to raise it. Piloted through by William McKinley, House Ways and Means chairman, and Senator

Nelson W. Aldrich, the McKinley Tariff of 1890 raised duties on manufactured goods to an average of about 50 percent, the highest to that time. And it included three new departures. First, the protectionists reached out for farmers' votes with high duties on agricultural products. Second, they sought to lessen the tariff's impact on consumers by putting sugar, a universal necessity, on the free list—thus reducing its cost—and then compensating Louisiana and Kansas sugar growers with a bounty of 2¢ a pound out of the federal Treasury. And third, they included a reciprocity section, which empowered the president to hike duties on sugar, molasses, tea, coffee, and hides to pressure countries exporting those items into reducing unreasonably high duties on American goods.

The absence of a public consensus for higher tariffs became clearly visible in the 1890 midterm elections. By the time the November congressional election returns were in, it seemed apparent, at least to Democrats, that the voters had repudiated the McKinley Tariff with a landslide of Democratic votes. In the new House, Democrats outnumbered Republicans by almost three to one; in the Senate, the Republican majority was reduced to eight.

One of the election casualties was McKinley himself, the victim of tricks the Democrats used to reinforce the widespread revulsion against the increased duties. But there was more to the election than the tariff. Voters also reacted against the baldly partisan measures of the Harrison administration and its extravagant expenditures on pensions and other programs. Democrats raised a ruckus about the Republicans' "billion-dollar Congress," to which the Speaker of the House responded with the question: "Isn't this a billion dollar country?" But with expenditures rising and revenues dropping, largely because the tariff was so high as to discourage imports, the nation's Treasury surplus was rapidly shrinking.

The large Democratic vote in 1890 may have also been a reaction to Republican efforts to legislate against alcohol and eliminate funding for state-supported Catholic schools. Between 1880 and 1890, sixteen out of twenty-one states outside the South held referenda on constitutional prohibition of alcoholic beverages. Only six states voted for prohibition, however. With the politics of righteousness, then, Republicans were playing a losing game, arousing wets (anti-Prohibitionists) on the Democratic side. In 1889 Wisconsin Republicans compounded their party's problems by pushing through a law that struck at parochial schools. The law held that a school could be accredited only if it taught the basic subjects in English. That was the last straw: it turned large numbers of outraged immigrants into Democratic activists. In 1889 and 1890 the Democrats swept state after state.

THE PROBLEMS OF FARMERS

Frustrated by the unwillingness of Congress to meet their demands and ease their plight, disgruntled farmers began to organize after the Civil War. Like so many of their counterparts laboring in urban factories, they realized that social change could be provoked only by demonstrations of power, and power lay in numbers. But unlike labor unions, farm organizations faced a more complex array of economic variables affecting their livelihood. They had to deal with more than just management; bankers, processors, railroad and grain elevator operators, and the world market all played a role in affecting the agricultural sector. So too did the unpredictable forces of nature: droughts, blizzards, insects, erosion. Other important obstacles to collective action by farmers included the deeply ingrained tradition of rugged individualism and physical isolation. American farmers had long prided themselves on their self-reliant hardihood, and many balked at sacrificing their independence. Consequently, farm activists discovered that it was often difficult to develop and maintain a cohesive organization. Yet, for all the difficulties, they persevered, and the results were dramatic, if not completely successful. Thus, for example, the deep-seated unrest in the farming communities of the South and West began to find voice in the Granger movement, the Alliance movement, and in the new People's party, agrarian movements of considerable political and social significance.

THE DIVERSITY OF FARM INTERESTS   Agricultural interests after the Civil War diverged and in some cases conflicted with one another. In the Great Plains, the railroads were the largest landowners. In addition, there were large absentee landowners, some foreign, who leased out vast tracts of lands. There were also huge "bonanza" farms that employed hundreds of seasonal workers. The majority of rural folk in the

South and West, however, were moderate-size landowners, small land speculators, small landowners, tenant farmers, and hourly wage workers. In 1870, for example, 32 percent of farm laborers in the Great Plains owned no land or implements.

Those farm folk most involved with organized political protest were not the tenants or farm laborers but the middle-size landholding class and the bankers and small merchants in surrounding towns who depended upon the agricultural economy for their livelihoods. The middle-size farmers were the ones who experienced rapidly rising land values and rising indebtedness. They were therefore most concerned about railroad regulation and monetary policy. These farmers, rather than landless workers, were in a position to produce a crop surplus for sale and therefore to benefit from any inflation in commodity prices. Such farmers were thus concerned with land values and crop prices rather than with land redistribution schemes that would have given tenants or croppers or farm hands access to their own land.

ECONOMIC CONDITIONS   For some time, farmers in the South and Midwest had been subject to worsening economic and social conditions. The source of their problems was a long-term decline in commodity prices from 1870 to 1898, the product of domestic overproduction and growing international competition for world markets. The vast new lands brought under cultivation poured an ever-increasing supply of farm products into the market, driving down prices. This effect was reinforced as innovations in transportation and communications brought American farmers ever more into international competition, further increasing the supply of farm commodities. Considerations of abstract economic forces, however, puzzled many farmers. They would never quite understand how want could be caused by plenty. How could one speak of overproduction when so many remained in need? Instead, they reasoned, there must be a screw loose somewhere in the system.

The railroads and the processors who handled the farmers' products were seen as the prime villains. Farmers resented the high railroad rates that prevailed in farm regions with no alternative forms of transportation. Individual farmers could not get the rebates the Rockefellers could extract from railroads, and they could not exert the political influence wielded by the railroad lobbies. In other ways farmers found them-

"I Feed You All," a poster showing the farmer at the center of society, first published in Prairie Farmer *in 1869.*

selves with little bargaining power as either buyers or sellers. When they tried to sell wheat or cotton, the buyer set the price; when they went to buy a plow point, the seller set the price.

High tariffs operated to farmers' disadvantage because they protected manufacturers against foreign competition, allowing them to raise the prices of factory goods on which farmers depended. Farmers, however, had to sell their wheat, cotton, and other staples in foreign markets, where competition lowered prices. Tariffs inflicted a double blow on farmers because insofar as they hampered imports, they indirectly hampered exports by making it harder for foreign buyers to get the necessary American currency or exchange to purchase American crops.

Debt, too, had been a perennial problem of agriculture. After the Civil War, farmers became ever more enmeshed in debt—western farmers incurred mortgages to cover the costs of land and machinery, while southern farmers used crop liens. As commodity prices dropped, the burden of debt grew because farmers had to cultivate more wheat or cotton to raise the same amount of money; and by growing more they furthered the vicious cycle of surpluses and price declines.

AN INADEQUATE CURRENCY   Ultimately, farm discontent focused on the currency issue, magnifying this grievance out of proportion to all others. The basic problem with the nation's currency in the late nineteenth century was that it lacked the flexibility to grow along with America's expanding economy. From 1865 to 1890 the amount of currency in circulation actually decreased from about $30 to $27 per capita. Three types of currency existed then: greenbacks, national bank notes, and hard money (gold and silver coins or certificates). The amount of greenback money in circulation had been set at $346 million in 1878, and had remained fixed at that amount, despite agitation for more paper money by debtors (largely farmers) and expansion-minded business leaders. National bank notes, based on government bonds, actually contracted in volume as the government paid off its bonds, which it was able to do rapidly with revenues from tariffs and land sales.

Metallic currency dated from the Mint Act of 1792, which authorized free and unlimited coinage of silver and gold at a ratio of 15 to 1.* The phrase "free and unlimited" simply meant that owners of precious metals could have any quantity of their gold or silver coined free, except for a nominal fee to cover costs. A fixed ratio of values, however, could not reflect fluctuations in the relative market value of the metals. When gold rose to a market value higher than that reflected in the official ratio, owners ceased to present it for coinage. The country was actually on a silver standard until 1837, when Congress changed the ratio to 16 to 1, which soon reversed the situation. Silver became more valuable in the market than in coinage, and the country drifted to a gold standard.

This state of affairs prevailed until 1873, when Congress passed a general revision of the coinage laws and dropped the then-unused provision for the coinage of silver. The action came, however, just when silver production began to increase, reducing its market value through the growth in supply. Under the old laws this would have induced owners of silver to present it at the mint for coinage. Soon advocates of currency inflation began to denounce the "crime of '73," which they had scarcely noticed at the time. Gradually a suspicion, and in some cases a belief, grew that creditor interests had conspired in 1873 to ensure a scarcity of money. But the silverites had little more legislative success than the advocates of greenback inflation. The Bland-Allison Act of 1878 and

---

*The ratio meant that the amount of precious metal in a silver dollar weighed fifteen times as much as that in a gold dollar. This reflected the relative values of silver and gold at the time.

the Sherman Silver Purchase Act of 1890 provided for some silver coinage, but too little in each case to offset the overall contraction of the currency.

THE GRANGER MOVEMENT   When the Department of Agriculture sent Oliver H. Kelley on a tour of the postbellum South in 1866, it was the isolation of farm folk that most impressed him. Resolving to do something about it, Kelley and some government clerks in 1867 founded the Patrons of Husbandry, better known as the Grange (an old word for granary), as each chapter was called. In the next few years the Grange mushroomed, reaching a membership as high as 1.5 million by 1874. The Grange started as a social and educational response to the farmers' isolation, but as it grew it began to promote farmer-owned co-operatives for buying and selling. Their ideal was to free themselves from the conventional marketplace.

The Grange soon became indirectly involved in politics through independent third parties, especially in the Midwest during the early 1870s. The Grangers' chief political goal was to regulate the rates charged by railroads and warehouses. In five states they brought about the passage of "Granger Laws," which at first proved relatively ineffective, but laid a foundation for stronger legislation to follow. Owners subject to their regulation challenged these laws in cases that soon advanced to the

Members of the Crescent Grange, Anoka County, Minnesota, 1880.

Supreme Court, where the plaintiffs in the "Granger Cases" claimed to have been deprived of property without due process of law. In a key case involving warehouse regulation, *Munn* v. *Illinois* (1877), the high court ruled that the state under its "police powers" had the right to regulate property in the interest of the public good where that property was clothed with a public interest. If regulatory power were abused, the ruling said, "the people must resort to the polls, not the courts." Later, however, the courts would severely restrict state regulatory powers.

The Granger movement gradually declined (but never vanished) as members' energies were drawn off into cooperatives, many of which failed, and into political action. Out of the independent political movements of the time there grew in 1875 a party calling itself the Independent National party, more commonly known as the Greenback party because of its emphasis on that issue. In the 1878 midterm elections it polled over 1 million votes and elected fifteen congressmen. But in 1880 the party's fortunes declined, and it disintegrated after 1884.

FARMERS' ALLIANCES   As the Grange lost energy, other farm organizations grew in size and significance: the Farmers' Alliances. Like the Grange, the Farmers' Alliances offered social and recreational opportunities, but they also emphasized political action. Farmers throughout the South and Midwest, where tenancy rates were highest, rushed to join the Alliance movement. They saw in collective action a way to seek relief from the hardships created by chronic indebtedness, declining prices, and devastating droughts. Unlike the Grange, which was a national organization that tended to attract larger and more prosperous farmers, the Alliance was a grassroots local organization representing marginal farmers.

The Alliance movement absorbed existing farm groups and organized new locals. It swept the cotton belt and established strong positions in Kansas and the Dakotas. In 1886, a white minister in Texas, which had one of the largest and most influential Alliance movements, responded to the appeals of black farmers and organized the Colored Alliance. The white leadership of the Alliance movement in Texas endorsed this development because the Colored Alliance stressed that its objective was economic justice, not social equality. By 1890, the Alliance movement had members from New York to California numbering about 1.5 million, and the Colored Farmers' Alliance claimed over 1 million members.

Members of the Texas Alliance, 1870s. Alliance groups united local farmers, fostered a sense of community, and influenced political policies.

A powerful attraction for many isolated, struggling farmers and their families was the sense of community provided by the Alliance. An Alliance gathering resembled what one observer described as "a religious revival . . . a pentecost . . . in which the tongue of flame sat upon every man, and each spake as the spirit gave him utterance."

The Alliance movement welcomed rural women and men over sixteen years old who displayed a "good moral character," believed in God, and demonstrated "industrious habits." One North Carolina woman expressed her appreciation for the "grand opportunities" the Alliance provided women to emerge from traditional domesticity. "Drudgery, fashion, and gossip," she declared, "are no longer the bounds of woman's sphere." One of the Alliance publications made the point explicitly: "The Alliance has come to redeem woman from her enslaved condition, and place her in her proper sphere." The number of women in the Alliance movement grew rapidly, and many assumed key leadership roles.

The Alliance movement sponsored an ambitious social and educational program, and about 1,000 affiliated newspapers. But unlike the Grange, the Alliance also proposed from the start an elaborate economic program. In 1890 Alliance agencies and exchanges in some eighteen states claimed a business of $10 million, but they soon went the way of the Granger cooperatives, victims of discrimination by wholesalers, manufacturers, railroads, and bankers, and also of their own inexperienced management and overextended credit.

The Alliance movement also was ready to enter the political fray to help farmers. In Texas, for example, in 1886 a devastating drought brought matters to a head. When President Grover Cleveland vetoed a bill to aid Texas farmers, Alliance leaders resolved to challenge the Democratic party at the polls. Although conservative members whose primary allegiance was to the Democratic party left the movement, many members remained who were ready to carry out the fight both locally and nationally.

In 1887 Charles W. Macune, the new Alliance president, announced his intention to exert pressure on Congress to assist southern farmers. In addition, he proposed that Texas farmers create their own Alliance Exchange in an effort to free themselves from their dependence on processors and banks. Members of the Exchange would sign joint notes, borrow money from banks, and purchase their goods and supplies from a new corporation created by the Alliance in Dallas. The Exchange would also build its own warehouses to store and market the crops of members. While their crops were being stored, member farmers could obtain credit from the warehouse cooperative so they could buy goods and supplies.

This grand "cooperative" scheme collapsed when the Texas banks refused to accept the joint notes from Alliance members. This led Macune and others to focus their energies on what Macune called a "subtreasury plan." Under this plan, farmers would be able to store their crops in new government warehouses and obtain government loans for up to 80 percent of their crops' value at 1 percent interest. Besides providing immediate credit, the plan would allow the farmer the leeway to hold a crop for a better price later, since he would not have to sell it at harvest time to pay off debts. The plan would also promote inflation because these loans to farmers would be made in new legal-tender notes.

The subtreasury plan went before Congress in 1890 but was never adopted. Its defeat as well as setbacks to other proposals convinced many farm leaders that they needed political power to secure railroad regulation, currency inflation, state departments of agriculture, antitrust laws, and farm credit.

FARM POLITICS   In the West, where hard times had descended after the blizzards of 1887, farmers were ready for third-party action. In the South, however, white Alliance members hesitated to bolt the Democratic party, seeking instead to influence or control it. Both approaches gained startling success. Independent parties under various names upset the political balance in western states, almost electing a governor under the banner of the People's party (also known as the Populist party) in Kansas (a Populist was elected governor in 1892) and taking control of one house of the legislature there and both houses in Nebraska. In South Dakota and Minnesota, Populists gained a balance of power in the legislatures, while Kansas sent a Populist to the Senate.

The farm movement produced colorful leaders, especially in Kansas, where Mary Elizabeth Lease advised farmers "to raise less corn and more hell." Born in Pennsylvania to parents who were political exiles from Ireland, she grew up within a family traumatized by the Civil War. Her two brothers were killed in battle, and her father died in Georgia's notorious Andersonville Prison. Afterward Lease migrated to Kansas, taught school, raised a family, and finally failed at farming in the mid-1880s. She then studied law for a time, "pinning sheets of notes above her wash tub," and through strenuous effort became one of the state's first female lawyers. At the same time, she took up public speaking on behalf of various causes ranging from Irish nationalism to temperance to women's suffrage. By the end of the 1880s Lease had joined the Al-

Mary Elizabeth Lease, 1890.

liance as well as the Knights of Labor, and she soon applied her gifts as a fiery speaker to the cause of free silver. A tall, proud, and imposing woman, Lease drew attentive audiences. "The people are at bay," she warned in 1894, "let the bloodhounds of money beware."

"Sockless Jerry" Simpson was an equally charismatic agrarian radical. Born in Canada, he had served as a seaman on Great Lakes steamships before buying a farm in northern Kansas. He, his wife, and young daughter made a go of the farm, but when he saw his child crushed to death in a sawmill accident, he and his wife relocated to the southern part of the state. There he raised cattle for several years before losing his herd in a blizzard.

Simpson embraced the Alliance movement, and in 1890 he campaigned for Congress. A shrewd man with huge, callused hands and pale blue eyes, he simplified the complex economic and political issues of the day. "Man must have access to the land," he maintained, "or he is a slave." He warned Republicans: "You can't put this movement down by sneers or by ridicule, for its foundation was laid as far back as the foundation of the world. It is a struggle between the robbers and the robbed." Simpson dismissed his Republican opponent, a wealthy railroad lawyer, as an indulgent pawn of the corporations whose "soft white hands" and "silk hosiery" betrayed his true priorities. His outraged opponent thereupon shouted that it was better to have silk socks than none at all, providing Simpson with his folksy nickname. "Sockless Jerry" won a seat in Congress, and so too did many other friends of "the people" in the Midwest.

In the South, the Alliance won equal if not greater success by forcing the Democrats to nominate candidates pledged to their program. The southern states elected four pro-Alliance governors, seven pro-Alliance legislatures, forty-four pro-Alliance congressmen, and several senators. Among the most respected of the southern Alliance leaders was Tom Watson of Georgia. The son of prosperous slaveholders who lost everything after the Civil War, he became a successful lawyer and orator on behalf of the Alliance cause. Watson took the lead in appealing to black tenant farmers and sharecroppers to join with their white counterparts in ousting the Bourbon white political elite. "You are kept apart," he told black and white farmers, "that you may be separately fleeced of your earnings."

Tom Watson.

THE POPULIST PARTY AND THE ELECTION OF 1892   The success of the Alliances led many to consider the formation of a third political party on the national level. In 1891 a conference in Cincinnati brought together delegates from farm, labor, and reform organizations to discuss strategy. The meeting endorsed a national third party and formed a national executive committee of the People's party. Few southerners were at Cincinnati, but many approved the third-party idea after their failure to move the Democratic party toward the subtreasury plan. In 1892 a larger meeting at St. Louis called for a national convention of the People's party at Omaha to adopt a platform and choose candidates.

The platform focused on issues of finance, transportation, and land. Its financial program demanded implementation of the subtreasury plan, free and unlimited coinage of silver at the 16 to 1 ratio, an increase in the amount of money in circulation to $50 per capita, a graduated income tax, and postal savings banks to protect depositors who otherwise risked disastrous losses in small-town banks vulnerable to farm depression. As to transportation, the time had come "when the railroad corporations will either own the people or the people must own the railroads." Let government therefore nationalize the railroads, and the telephone and telegraph systems as well. The Populists called for the government to reclaim from railroads and other corporations lands "in excess of their actual needs," and to forbid land ownership by aliens. Finally, the platform endorsed the eight-hour workday and restriction of immigration. The party took these last positions to win sup-

A Populist gathering in Callaway, Nebraska, 1892.

port from the urban workers, whom Populists looked upon as fellow "producers."

The party's platform turned out to be more exciting than its candidate. Iowa's James B. Weaver, an able, prudent man, carried the stigma of his defeat on the Greenback ticket twelve years before. To balance Weaver, who had been a Union general, the party named a former Confederate general for vice-president.

The Populist party was the startling new feature of the 1892 campaign. The major parties renominated the candidates of 1888, Democrat Grover Cleveland and Republican Benjamin Harrison. The tariff issue monopolized their attention. Both major candidates polled over 5 million votes, but Cleveland carried a plurality of the popular votes and a majority of the electoral college. Weaver polled over 1 million votes, and carried Colorado, Kansas, Nevada, and Idaho, for a total of twenty-two electoral votes. Alabama was the banner Populist state of the South, with 37 percent of its vote for Weaver.

ECONOMIC DEPRESSION AND THE SILVER SOLUTION

THE DEPRESSION OF 1893 Cleveland's second administration stumbled early. Before it ended, Cleveland had antagonized every major segment of the public: the farmers and silverites opposed his efforts to maintain the gold standard, business groups disliked his attempt to lower the tariff, and a large segment of labor resented his efforts to suppress the Pullman Strike. Worst of all, his second term coincided with one of the most devastating business panics in history, set off just before he took office by the failure of the Philadelphia and Reading Railroad and a panic on Wall Street.

By 1894 many had reached bottom. That year some 750,000 people went out on strike, including the Pullman workers; millions found themselves unemployed; railroad construction workers, laid off in the West, began tramping east and talked of marching on Washington. Few of them made it to the capital.

One group that did was the Army of the Commonweal of Christ, led by Jacob S. Coxey, a wealthy Ohio quarry owner turned Populist who demanded that the federal government provide unemployed people with jobs. Coxey, his wife, and their son, Legal Tender Coxey, rode in a carriage ahead of some 400 hardy protesters as they straggled into Washington. Police arrested Coxey for walking on the grass, but his army as well as the growing political strength of populism struck fear into many Americans. Critics portrayed Populist candidates as "hayseed socialists" whose election would endanger property rights.

The 1894 midterm elections took place amid this climate of anxiety. The outcome disappointed the Populists, who had expected to profit from the discontent. North Carolina's was the only southern legislature lost by the Democrats, and that for only four years. Nationally, the elections amounted to a severe setback for Democrats, and the Republicans were the chief beneficiaries. The Populists emerged with six senators and seven representatives. They had polled 1.5 million votes for their congressional candidates and still expected the festering discontent to carry them to power in 1896.

SILVERITES VS. GOLDBUGS   In the mid-1890s events conspired to focus all concerns on the currency issue. One of the causes of the 1893 depression had been the failure of a British banking house, which led many British investors to unload their American holdings in return for gold. To plug this drain on the Treasury, the president sought repeal of the Sherman Silver Purchase Act to stop the issuance of silver notes redeemable in gold. Cleveland won the act's repeal in 1893, but at the cost of irreparable division in his own party. To further build the gold reserve, the administration struck a deal with banking titan J. P. Morgan in 1895. He and other financiers promised to supply half the gold needed to buy up a series of government bond issues, and to use their influence to stop demands on the Treasury. The deal worked, but it created the unfavorable image of Cleveland and the financial oligarchy working hand in glove.

Meanwhile the American Bimetallic League, heavily financed by silver miners, raised the agitation for silver coinage to a crescendo. The growing importance of the currency issue presented a dilemma for Populists: Should the party promote the whole spectrum of reform it advocated, or should it try to ride the silver issue into power? The latter was the practical choice. So the Populist leaders decided, over the protest of more radical members, to hold their 1896 convention last, confident that the major parties would at best straddle the silver issue and that they would then reap a harvest of bolting silverite Republicans and Democrats.

THE ELECTION OF 1896   Contrary to these expectations, the major parties took opposite positions on the currency issues. The Republicans, as expected, chose William McKinley on a gold-standard platform. McKinley, a former congressman and governor of Ohio, benefited from the political steamroller organized by his campaign manager.

On the Democratic side, the pro-silver forces captured the convention for their platform. William Jennings Bryan arranged to give the closing speech for the silver plank. The son of a judge who was a fervent

William Jennings Bryan, whose "Cross of Gold" speech at the 1896 Democratic convention roused the delegates and secured him the party's presidential nomination.

Baptist moralist, Bryan was a two-term congressman from Nebraska who had been swept out in the Democratic losses of 1894; he had distinguished himself mainly with an exhausting three-hour speech against repeal of the Sherman Silver Purchase Act. In the months before the convention he had traveled the South and West, speaking for free silver. His rehearsed phrases swept the convention into a frenzy:

> I come to speak to you in defense of a cause as holy as the cause of liberty—the cause of humanity. . . . We have petitioned, and our petitions have been scorned. We have entreated, and our entreaties have been disregarded. We have begged, and they have mocked when our calamity came. We beg no longer; we entreat no more; we petition no more. We defy them!

By the time Bryan reached his conclusion, there was little doubt that he would get the nomination: "You shall not press down upon the brow of labor this crown of thorns. You shall not crucify mankind upon a cross of gold!"

The next day Bryan won the nomination on the fifth ballot, and in the process the Democratic party was fractured beyond repair. Disappointed pro-gold Democrats walked out of the convention and nominated their own candidate, Senator John M. Palmer of Illinois. "Fellow Democrats," he announced, "I will not consider it any great fault if you decide to cast your vote for William McKinley."

When the Populists met in St. Louis two weeks later, they faced an impossible choice. They could name their own candidate and divide the silver vote, or they could endorse Bryan and probably lose their identity. In the end they backed Bryan, but chose their own vice-presidential candidate, former representative Thomas E. Watson of Georgia, and invited the Democrats to drop their vice-presidential nominee—an action that Bryan refused to countenance.

The thirty-six-year-old Bryan launched a whirlwind campaign. He crisscrossed the country, exploiting his spellbinding eloquence. McKinley, meanwhile, conducted a "front-porch campaign," receiving selected delegations of supporters at his home in Canton, Ohio, and giving only prepared responses. McKinley's campaign manager, Mark Hanna, shrewdly portrayed Bryan as a radical whose "communistic spirit" would ruin the capitalist system. Many observers agreed with the

"BLOWING HIMSELF AROUND THE COUNTRY." An anti-Populist cartoon of 1896 depicting Bryan blowing hot air at his supporters.

portrait. The *New York Tribune* denounced Bryan as a "wretched rattle-pated boy, posing in vapid vanity and mouthing resounding rottenness." Theodore Roosevelt had equally strong opinions. "The silver craze surpasses belief," he wrote a friend. "Bryan's election would be a great calamity."

By preying upon such fears, Hanna raised a huge campaign chest to finance an army of Republican speakers who traveled the country in support of McKinley. In the end the Democratic-Populist-Silverite candidates were overwhelmed by the well-organized and well-financed Republican campaign. McKinley won the popular vote by 7.1 million to 6.5 million and the electoral college vote by 271 to 176.

Bryan carried most of the West and the South below the border states, but found little support in the metropolitan centers east of the Mississippi and north of the Ohio and Potomac Rivers. In the critical midwestern battleground, from Minnesota and Iowa eastward to Ohio, Bryan carried not a single state. Many Catholic voters, normally drawn to the Democrats, were no doubt repelled by Bryan's Baptist evangelical style. Farmers in the Northeast, moreover, were less attracted to agrarian radicalism than were farmers in the wheat and cotton belts, where there were higher rates of tenancy and a narrower range of crops. Among factory workers in the cities, Bryan found even less support.

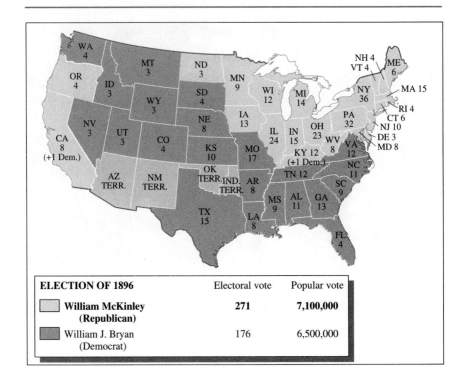

ELECTION OF 1896	Electoral vote	Popular vote
William McKinley (Republican)	**271**	**7,100,000**
William J. Bryan (Democrat)	176	6,500,000

They found it easier to identify with McKinley's "full dinner pail" than with Bryan's free silver. Some workers may have been intimidated by business owners' threats to close shop if the "Demopop" heresies triumphed.

A NEW ERA   The election of 1896 had been a climactic political struggle. Urban-industrial values had indeed taken firm hold of the political system. The first important act of the McKinley administration was to call a special session of Congress to raise the tariff again. The Dingley Tariff of 1897 became the highest to that time.

By 1897 economic prosperity was returning, helped along by inflation of the currency, which bore out the arguments of greenbackers and silverites. But the inflation came, in one of history's many ironies, from neither greenbacks nor silver, but from a new flood of gold into the market and into the mints. During the 1880s and 1890s, new discoveries of gold in South Africa, in the Canadian Yukon, and in Alaska led to spectacular new gold rushes. In 1900, Congress passed a Gold Standard Act, which marked an end to the silver movement.

The old issues of tariffs and currency gave way to concerns over the Spanish-American War, which ushered in a new era. "The Spanish War finished us," said Populist Tom Watson. "The blare of the bugle drowned the voice of the Reformer." And yet to compound this irony, most of the Populists' 1892 Omaha platform, which had seemed so radical and controversial at the time, would be in effect within two decades.

MAKING CONNECTIONS

- This chapter concludes with the suggestion that the Spanish-American War, a major event on the horizon, marked the end of the reform spirit of the Populists.

- The laissez-faire policies of the Gilded Age were challenged by Progressive reform activists, discussed in Chapter 24.

- William Jennings Bryan was one of the most prominent figures in American politics and political culture over some thirty years.

FURTHER READING

For overviews of the Gilded Age see Robert H. Wiebe's *The Search for Order, 1877–1920* (1967), John A. Garraty's *The New Commonwealth, 1877–1890* (1968), and Vincent P. DeSantis's *The Shaping of Modern America, 1877–1920* (2nd ed., 1989). Nell Painter's *Standing at Armageddon: The United States, 1877–1919* (1987) focuses on the experience of the working classes.

Party politics is the emphasis of H. Wayne Morgan's *From Hayes to McKinley: National Party Politics, 1877–1896* (1969) and Richard J. Jensen's *The Winning of the Midwest: Social and Political Conflict,*

1888–1896 (1971). Public participation in politics is explained in Paul Kleppner's *Who Voted? The Dynamics of Electoral Turnout, 1870–1980* (1982).

On the Gilded-Age presidents, see William S. McFeely's *Grant: A Biography* (1981), Allan Peskin's *Garfield: A Biography* (1978), Thomas C. Reeves's *Gentleman Boss: The Life of Chester Alan Arthur* (rev. ed., 1991), and Lewis L. Gould's *The Presidency of William McKinley* (1980).

Scholars have also examined various Gilded-Age issues and interest groups. John G. Sproat's *The Best Men: Liberal Reformers in the Gilded Age* (1968) and Gerald W. McFarland's *Mugwumps, Morals, and Politics, 1884–1920* (1975) examine the issue of reforming government service. Tom E. Terrill's *The Tariff, Politics, and American Foreign Policy, 1874–1901* (1973) lends clarity to that complex issue. The finances of the Gilded Age are covered in Irwin Unger's *The Greenback Era: A Social and Political History of American Finance, 1865–1879* (1964) and Walter T. K. Nugent's *Money and American Society, 1865–1880* (1968).

One of the most controversial works on populism is Lawrence Goodwyn's *The Populist Movement: A Short History of the Agrarian Revolt in America* (1978). Goodwyn's emphasis on the cooperative nature of agrarian protest and his criticism of the western branch as a sham movement contradicted the prevailing interpretations. A more judicious account is Robert C. McMath, Jr.'s *American Populism: A Social History, 1877–1898* (1993). Jeffrey Ostler's *Prairie Populism: The Fate of Agrarian Radicalism in Kansas, Nebraska, and Iowa, 1880–1892* (1993) minimizes the role of the financial panic in stimulating the grassroots movement.

PART SIX

MODERN AMERICA

The United States entered the twentieth century in a state of flux. Since the election of Thomas Jefferson in 1800, the country had seen itself relentlessly transformed. A rural, agrarian society largely detached from the concerns of international affairs turned into a highly industrialized, urban culture with a growing involvement in world politics and commerce. In other words, the United States in 1900 was on the threshold of modernity.

The prospect of modernity both excited and scared Americans. Old truths and beliefs clashed with unsettling new scientific discoveries and social practices. People debated the legitimacy of Darwinism, the existence of God, the dangers of jazz, and the federal effort to prohibit alcoholic beverages. The automobile, airplane, and radio helped shrink the distances of time and space and accelerate a national consciousness. In the process, the United States began to emerge from its isolationist shell. Throughout most of the nineteenth century, policy makers had sought to isolate America from the intrigues and conflicts of the great European powers. As early as 1780, John Adams had warned Congress against involving the United States in the affairs of Europe. "Our business with them, and theirs with us," he wrote, "is commerce, not politics, much less war." George Washington echoed this sentiment in his farewell address upon leaving the presidency, warning Americans to avoid "entangling alliances" with foreign governments.

With only a few exceptions, American statesmen during the nineteenth century had followed such advice. Noninvolvement in foreign wars and nonintervention in the internal affairs of foreign governments formed the pillars of American foreign policy until the end of the century. During the 1890s, however, expanding commercial interests around the world led Americans to expand the horizons of their concerns. Imperialism was the order of the day among the great European powers, and a growing number of American expansionists demanded that the United States also adopt a global ambition and join in the hunt for new territories and markets. Such motives helped spark the Spanish-American War of 1898 and helped to justify the resulting acquisition of American colonies outside the continental United States. Entangling alliances with European powers soon followed.

The outbreak of the Great War in Europe in 1914 posed an even greater challenge to the American tradition of isolation and noninterven-

The New Deal helped revive public confidence and put people back to work, but it did not end the Great Depression. It took a world war to restore full employment. The necessity of mobilizing the nation in support of the Second World War also served to accelerate the growth of the federal government. And the unparalleled scope of the war helped catapult the United States into a leadership role in world politics. The creation of a nuclear bomb to help end the war ushered in a new era of atomic diplomacy that held the fate of the world in the balance. For all of the new creature comforts associated with modern life, Americans in 1945 found themselves living amid an array of new anxieties.

tion. The prospect of a German victory over the French and Britis
threatened the European balance of power, which had long ensure
security of the United States. By 1917 it appeared that Germany
emerge triumphant and begin to menace the Western Hemisphere
Woodrow Wilson's crusade to use American intervention in World
to transform the world order in accordance with his idealistic prin
dislodged American foreign policy from its isolationist moorings. I
spawned a prolonged debate about the role of the United States in
affairs, a debate that World War II would resolve for a time on the
internationalism.

At the same time that the United States was entering the world
a great military power it was also becoming a great industrial pow
Cities and factories sprouted across the landscape. An abundance
jobs served as a magnet attracting millions of immigrants from eve
ner of the globe. They were not always welcomed nor were they re
similated. Ethnic and racial strife, as well as labor agitation, incre
the turn of the century. In the midst of such social turmoil and un
leled economic development, American reformers made their first
tained attempt to adapt their political and social institutions to th
ties of the industrial age. The worst excesses and injustices of
urban-industrial development—corporate monopolies, child labo
cal corruption, hazardous working conditions, urban ghettos—we
nally addressed in a comprehensive way. During the Progressive E
(1900–1917), local, state, and federal governments sought to rei
excesses of industrial capitalism and develop a more rational and
public policy.

A conservative Republican resurgence challenged the notion o
regulatory state during the 1920s. Free enterprise and corporate c
ism witnessed a dramatic revival. But the stock market crash of 1
helped propel the United States and many other nations into the
economic downturn in history. The unprecedented severity of the
Depression renewed public demands for federal government prog
protect the general welfare. "This nation asks for action," declare
dent Franklin D. Roosevelt in his 1933 inaugural address. The n
New Deal initiatives and agencies instituted by Roosevelt and his
cratic administration created the framework for a welfare state th
since served as the basis for American public policy.

23 ⟨⟩ AN AMERICAN EMPIRE

CHAPTER ORGANIZER

This chapter focuses on:

- the circumstances that led to America's "new imperialism."

- the causes of the Spanish-American War.

- Theodore Roosevelt's foreign policy in Asia and Latin America.

Throughout most of the late nineteenth century, Americans displayed what one senator called "only a languid interest" in foreign affairs. With the major diplomatic issues stemming from the Civil War having been quickly settled, an isolationist mood swept across the United States, which continued to enjoy what one historian has called "free security": wide oceans as buffers on either side, the British navy situated between America and the powers of Europe, and militarily weak neighbors in the Western Hemisphere.

Yet the notion of America having a "Manifest Destiny" ordained by God to expand its territory and influence remained alive in the decades after the end of the Civil War. Several prominent political and business leaders argued that the rapid industrial development of the United States meant that the nation needed to acquire foreign territories to gain easier access to vital raw materials. In addition, as their exports grew, American companies and farmers would become increasingly intertwined in the world economy. This, in turn, would require an expanded American naval presence to protect the shipping lanes. And a modern steam-powered navy needed bases to replenish the coal and water required for its ships. For these reasons and others, the United States during the last quarter of the nineteenth century began to expand its presence beyond the Western Hemisphere.

TOWARD THE NEW IMPERIALISM

During the last quarter of the nineteenth century, European powers unleashed a new surge of imperialism in Africa and Asia, where they seized colonies, protectorates, and economic privileges. All of Africa except Liberia and Ethiopia fell under outside dominion. Above all, the new imperialism was economic, a quest for markets and raw materials.

Most Americans were concerned about world markets as developments in transportation and communication quickened the pace of commerce and diplomacy. From the first, exports of farm products had been the basis of American economic growth. Now the conviction grew that American manufacturers had matured to the point where they could outsell foreign goods in the world market. But should the expansion of markets lead to territorial expansion as well? Or to intervention in the internal affairs of other countries? On this point Americans disagreed, but a small, yet vocal group of public officials advocated overseas possessions, regardless of the implications. They included Senator Albert J. Beveridge of Indiana and Senator Henry Cabot Lodge of Massachusetts, Theodore Roosevelt, and not least of all, Captain Alfred Thayer Mahan.

NAVAL POWER   During the 1880s, Captain Mahan became the leading proponent of sea power. A graduate of the Naval Academy, he served for years as president of the Naval War College at Newport, Rhode Island. A series of his lectures on naval history grew into a volume published in 1890, *The Influence of Sea Power upon History, 1660–1783,* in which he argued that national greatness and prosperity flowed from sea power, which had a fundamentally economic importance. To Mahan, modern economic development called for a powerful navy, a strong merchant marine, foreign commerce, colonies, and naval bases. The age of steam made a network of coaling stations a new matter of strategic concern. Mahan expounded on his version of America's destiny—to control the Caribbean, build an isthmian canal, and spread Western civilization in the Pacific. He publicized his ideas in popular journals and began to shape public opinion.

Even before Mahan's writings became influential a gradual expansion of the navy had begun. In 1880 the nation had fewer than a hundred seagoing vessels, many of them rusting or rotting at the docks. By the time Cleveland entered office, four new steel vessels had been authorized, and Cleveland's navy secretary got funds for twenty more.

IMPERIALIST THEORY   Certain intellectual currents of the day worked to bolster the new spirit of Manifest Destiny. The Darwinian idea of natural selection afforded a handy argument for imperialism. If natural selection worked in the biological realm, would it not apply also in human society? Among nations, as among individuals, the fittest survive and prevail. "There is apparently much truth in the belief that the wonderful progress of the United States, as well as the character of the people, are the results of natural selection," Darwin wrote in *The Descent of Man* (1871).

John Fiske, the historian and popular lecturer on Darwinism, developed racial corollaries from Darwin's idea. In *American Political Ideas* (1885), he stressed the superior character of "Anglo-Saxon" institutions and peoples. The English "race," he argued, was destined to dominate the globe in the institutions, traditions, language, even in the blood of the world's peoples. Josiah Strong, a Congregational minister, added the sanction of religion to theories of racial superiority. In his book *Our Country: Its Possible Future and Its Present Crisis* (1885), Strong argued that "Anglo-Saxons" embodied two great ideas: civil liberty and "a pure spiritual Christianity." The Anglo-Saxon was "divinely commissioned to be, in a peculiar sense, his brother's keeper."

EXPANSION IN THE PACIFIC

For expansionists, Asia offered an especially alluring temptation. President Andrew Johnson's secretary of state, William H. Seward, believed that the United States must inevitably exercise commercial domination "on the Pacific Ocean, and its islands and continents." Eager for American manufacturers to exploit Asian markets, Seward believed the

In a sardonic comment on Seward's purchase of Alaska in 1866, this cartoon shows Seward and President Andrew Johnson carting a huge iceberg of "Russian America . . . to cool down the Congressional majority."

United States first had to remove all foreign interests from the northern Pacific coast and gain access to that region's valuable ports. To that end, he cast covetous eyes on the crown colony of British Columbia, sandwiched between Russian America (Alaska) and Washington Territory.

Late in 1866, while encouraging annexation sentiment among the British Columbians, Seward learned of Russia's desire to sell Alaska, which had become unprofitable. He leaped at the opportunity, and in 1867 the United States bought Alaska for $7.2 million, thus removing Russia, the most recent colonial power, from the New World. Critics scoffed at "Seward's folly" of buying the Alaskan "icebox," but it proved in time to be the biggest bargain for the United States since the Louisiana Purchase.

Seward's successors at the State Department sustained his expansionist vision, and key ports in the Pacific Ocean remained the major focus of overseas activity through the rest of the nineteenth century. Two island groups occupied especially strategic positions about twenty degrees from either side of the equator: Samoa on the south and Hawaii (the Sandwich Islands) on the north. Both had major harbors, Pago Pago and Pearl Harbor, respectively. In the years after the Civil War American interest in these islands gradually deepened.

SAMOA   In 1878, the Samoans signed a treaty with the United States that granted a naval base at Pago Pago and extraterritoriality for Americans (meaning that in Samoa they remained subject only to American law), exchanged trade concessions, and called for the United States to extend its good offices in case of a dispute with another nation. The Senate ratified this accord, and in the following year the German and British governments worked out similar arrangements with other islands of the Samoan group. There matters rested until civil war broke out in 1887. The Germans backed a pretender against the native Samoan king and finally installed him under a German protectorate. The sequel to this incident was a conference in Berlin (1889) that established a tripartite protectorate, with Germany, Great Britain, and the United States in an uneasy partnership.

HAWAII   In Hawaii, the Americans had a clearer field. The islands, a united kingdom since 1795, had a sizable settlement of American missionaries and planters and were strategically more important to the United States than Samoa. Occupation by another major power might have posed a threat to American commercial interests and even to American defense.

In 1875 the kingdom entered a reciprocal trade agreement under which Hawaiian sugar would enter the United States duty free and under which Hawaii promised that none of its territory would be leased or granted to a third power. This agreement resulted in a boom in sugar production, and American settlers in Hawaii soon formed an economic elite. The trade agreement was renewed in 1887, when it was amended to grant the United States exclusive right to a fortified naval base at Pearl Harbor near Honolulu.

White planters in Hawaii built their fortunes on cheap immigrant labor, mainly Chinese, Japanese, and Portuguese. By the 1890s, the native population had been reduced to a minority by smallpox and other foreign diseases, and Asians quickly became the most numerous group in Hawaii.

Queen Liliuokalani.

In 1887, the Americans on the islands forced the king to accept a new constitution that created a constitutional government, which they dominated. In 1890, however, the McKinley Tariff destroyed Hawaii's favored position in the sugar trade by putting the sugar of all countries on the free list and granting growers in the continental United States a 2¢ subsidy per pound of sugar. This led to an economic crisis in Hawaii and affected the political situation as well.

In 1891, when the king's sister, Liliuokalani, ascended the throne, she began efforts to reclaim a measure of power and to eliminate white control of the government. Hawaii's white population then staged a revolt against Queen Liliuokalani early in 1893 and seized power. The American minister brought in marines to support the coup. As he cheerfully reported to Washington, "The Hawaiian pear is now fully ripe, and this is the golden hour for the United States to pluck it." Within a month, a committee of the new government turned up in Washington with a treaty of annexation.

The treaty, however, appeared just weeks before President Benjamin Harrison left office, and Democratic senators blocked ratification. President Cleveland withdrew the treaty and sent a special commissioner to investigate. He removed the American marines and reported that the Americans in Hawaii had acted improperly. Most Hawaiians opposed annexation, the commissioner found. He concluded that the revolution had been engineered mainly by the American sugar planters hoping to get the subsidy for sugar grown in the United States. Cleveland proposed to restore the queen to power in return for amnesty to the revolutionists. The provisional government refused to give up power, however, and on July 4, 1894, they proclaimed the Republic of Hawaii, which had in its constitution a standing provision for American annexation. When McKinley became president in 1897, he was looking for an excuse to annex the islands. This excuse was found when the Japanese, also hoping to take over the islands, sent warships to Hawaii. McKinley responded by sending American warships and asked the Senate to approve a treaty to annex Hawaii. When the Senate could not muster the two-thirds majority needed to approve the treaty, McKinley used a joint resolution of the House and Senate to achieve his aims. This resolution passed by simple majorities in both houses, and Hawaii was annexed in the summer of 1898.

DIPLOMATIC INCIDENTS IN THE 1880S AND 1890S

In the 1880s and 1890s, incidents in the Bering Sea and in Venezuela drew Americans into foreign affairs. At issue in the Bering Sea was the practice of pelagic (oceanic) sealing by foreign nationals, mostly Canadians, in offshore waters where the difficulty of distinguishing males and females resulted in the loss of many pups when their mothers were killed.

In 1886 American revenue cutters began seizing Canadian ships engaged in the practice, and three years later Congress declared the Bering a closed sea under United States dominion. In an exchange of notes in 1890, however, the British foreign minister refused to accept the legitimacy of Congress's claim. There was a flurry of bluster in the American press, but never much chance that the two countries would come to blows over what one newspaper called "a few greasy, ill-smelling sealskins." Eventually, an arbitration treaty of 1892 declared that, while the Bering was an open sea, pelagic sealing was forbidden within sixty miles of the Pribilof Islands. Later, in 1911, a treaty with Britain, Russia, and Japan prohibited pelagic sealing throughout the North Pacific and Bering Sea.

Far more serious was the Venezuelan boundary dispute with British Guiana, which had simmered since colonial days but took on new urgency when gold was found in the disputed area. When Venezuela suspended diplomatic relations with Britain in 1887, the American State Department suggested arbitration, but the matter remained unsettled in 1892 when Cleveland was reelected to the White House.

In 1895 Congress passed a Republican-sponsored resolution for arbitration of the dispute, and Cleveland was forced to get tough with the British or see his political opponents do it. He may even have found the occasion a welcome diversion from his domestic problems. His secretary of state, Richard L. Olney, drafted a note in which he invoked the Monroe Doctrine against British interference in the affairs of the New World. Cleveland claimed to have softened the "verbiage" a bit, but still dubbed it a "20 inch gun" note. Olney hoped that the note would provoke a quick reply, but the British minister let it lie for a maddening four months. The British assumed the note was largely for domestic American consumption anyway.

Britain finally rejected the demand for arbitration and noted that the Monroe Doctrine was not recognized international law, and in any case was irrelevant to a boundary dispute. Cleveland pronounced himself "mad clear through" at such a rebuff to the "friendly" suggestion of the United States. Congress, at Cleveland's request, unanimously voted for a commission to run a boundary line in spite of the British. Enthusiasm for war swept the country. Theodore Roosevelt vented his opinion that "this country needs a war." But diplomats on both sides recognized that it was in everyone's interest to negotiate rather than risk the outbreak of war. The British faced more urgent problems in South Africa, and through the good offices of the United States finally came around to an arbitration treaty with Venezuela, signed in 1897. By the time an international commission handed in its findings in 1899, the focus of public attention was elsewhere. The settlement turned out to be almost what the British had offered in the first place.

THE SPANISH-AMERICAN WAR

Until the 1890s, a certain ambivalence about overseas possessions had checked America's drive to expand. Suddenly, in 1898 and 1899,

José Martí, leader of the Cuban revolt against Spanish rule.

the inhibitions collapsed, and American power thrust its way to the far reaches of the Pacific. The occasion for this explosion of imperialism lay neither in the Pacific nor in the quest for bases and trade, but to the south in Cuba. The chief motive was a sense of outrage at another country's imperialism.

"CUBA LIBRE"   Throughout the second half of the nineteenth century, Cubans had repeatedly revolted against Spanish rule, only to be ruthlessly suppressed. All the while, American investments in Cuba, mainly in sugar and mining, were steadily rising. The United States in fact traded more with Cuba than Spain did.

On February 24, 1895, insurrection broke out again. Simmering discontent with Spanish rule had been aggravated by the Wilson-Gorman Tariff of 1894, which took sugar off the free list in the midst of a depression already damaging to the market for Cuban sugar. Raw sugar prices collapsed, putting Cubans out of work and thereby rekindling their desire for rebellion. Public feeling in the United States supported the rebels. Many Americans extended help to the Cuban Revolutionary party, which organized the revolt from headquarters in New York. Its leader, José Martí, returned to the island soon after the new outbreak and died in a skirmish with Spanish troops.

The insurrectionists waged guerrilla warfare and sought to damage the economic life of the island, which in turn would excite the concern of American investors. The strategy dictated hit-and-run attacks on trains, railways, and plantations. Americans often compared the insurrection to their own War of Independence. In 1896 Spanish general Valeriano Weyler adopted a policy of gathering Cubans behind Spanish lines, often in detention (*reconcentrado*) centers so that no one could join the insurrections by night and appear peaceful by day. In some of the centers, a combination of tropical climate, poor food, and unsanitary conditions quickly brought a heavy toll of disease and death. The American press promptly christened the Spanish commander "Butcher" Weyler.

Events in Cuba supplied exciting copy for the popular press. William Randolph Hearst's *New York Journal* and Joseph Pulitzer's *New York World* were at the time locked in a monumental struggle for circulation. "It was a battle of gigantic proportions," one journalist later wrote, "in which the sufferings of Cuba merely chanced to furnish some of the most convenient ammunition." Another device of the circulation war was the newfangled comic strip, and one of the most popular was "The Yellow Kid." By association, the sensationalism at which the papers vied came to be called "yellow journalism." Hearst emerged as the undisputed champion, with his *Journal* excelling at invective against "Weyler the brute, the devastator of haciendas, the destroyer of men."

At the outset, the Cleveland administration tried to protect American rights in Cuba but avoided involvement beyond an offer of mediation. Mounting public sympathy for the cause, however, prompted concern in Congress. By concurrent resolution on April 6, 1896, the two houses endorsed official recognition of the Cuban belligerents and urged the president to seek a peace on the basis of Cuban independence. Cleveland, however, denied any designs against Spanish rule and offered to cooperate with Spain in bringing peace on the basis of allowing Cubans a measure of self-governance. The Spanish politely refused.

PRESSURE FOR WAR   America's posture of neutrality changed sharply when McKinley entered office. He had been elected on a platform that endorsed independence for Cuba as well as American control of Hawaii and the construction of an isthmian canal. In 1897 Spain's queen regent offered Cuba autonomy (self-government without formal independence) in return for peace. What the Cubans might once have welcomed, however, they now rejected, insurrectionists and Spanish loyalists alike.

The battleship Maine, *funded in 1886, shown here entering Havana Harbor in 1898.*

Spain was impaled on the horns of a dilemma, unable to end the war and unready to give up Cuba.

Early in 1898 events moved rapidly to arouse opinion against Spain. On January 25, the American battleship *Maine* docked in Havana Harbor, ostensibly on a courtesy call. On February 9 Hearst's *New York Journal* released the text of a letter from Spanish minister Depuy de Lôme to a friend in Havana, stolen from the post office by a Cuban spy. In the letter de Lôme called President McKinley "weak and a bidder for the admiration of the crowd, besides being a would-be politician who tries to leave a door open behind himself while keeping on good terms with the jingoes of his party." This was hardly more extreme than what McKinley's assistant secretary of the navy, Theodore Roosevelt, had said about him: that the "white-livered" president had "no more backbone than a chocolate eclair." But that comment had remained private. De Lôme resigned to prevent further embarrassment to his government.

Six days later, during the night of February 15, 1898, the *Maine* exploded in Havana Harbor and sank with a loss of 266 men, most of whom died in their hammocks. The ship's captain, one of only 84 survivors, scribbled a telegram to Washington: "*Maine* blown up in Havana Harbor at nine forty tonight and destroyed. Many wounded and doubtless more killed or drowned. . . . Public opinion should be suspended until further report."

But those eager for a war with Spain saw no need to withhold judgment; they demanded an immediate declaration. Roosevelt called the

An American cartoon depicts the sinking of the Maine *in Havana Harbor.*
The uproar created by the incident and its coverage in the "yellow press"
edged McKinley toward war.

sinking "an act of dirty treachery on the part of the Spaniards." A naval
court of inquiry reported that an external mine had set off an explosion
in the ship's magazine. Lacking hard evidence, the court made no effort
to fix the blame, but the yellow press had no need of evidence. The outcry against Spain reached a crescendo in the words "Remember the
Maine!" Never mind that Spain could have derived little benefit from
such an act. A comprehensive study in 1976 concluded that the sinking
of the *Maine* was an accident, the result of an internal explosion triggered by a fire in its coal bunker.

Under the mounting pressure of public excitement, McKinley tried
to maintain a steady course. But the weight of outraged public opinion
and militants in his own party such as Theodore Roosevelt and Henry
Cabot Lodge eroded his neutrality. As one congressman remarked,
McKinley "keeps his ear to the ground so close that he gets it full of
grasshoppers much of the time." On March 9, however, the president
coaxed from Congress a $50 million appropriation for defense. Still,
McKinley sought to avoid war, as did most business spokesmen. Such

caution infuriated Roosevelt. "We will have this war for the freedom of Cuba," he fumed on March 26, "in spite of the timidity of the commercial interests."

The Spanish government, sensing the growing militancy in the United States, announced a unilateral cease-fire in early April 1898. On April 10 the Spanish minister gave the State Department a message that amounted to a surrender: the United States should indicate the nature and duration of the armistice; Cuba would have an autonomous government; and the two countries would submit the question of the sinking of the *Maine* to arbitration. The United States minister to Spain then cabled from Madrid: "I hope nothing will now be done to humiliate Spain, as I am satisfied that the present government is going, and is loyally ready to go, as fast and as far as it can." McKinley, he predicted, could win a settlement by August 1 on any terms: autonomy, independence, or cession of Cuba to the United States.

But the message came too late. The following day McKinley sent Congress what amounted to a war message. He asked for power to use armed forces in Cuba to protect American property and trade. The Cuban situation, McKinley said, was a constant menace to the peace. On April 20 a joint resolution of Congress went beyond endorsing the use of the armed forces: it declared Cuba independent and demanded withdrawal of Spanish forces. The Teller Amendment, added on the Senate floor, disclaimed any American designs on Cuban territory. McKinley signed the resolution, and a copy went off to the Spanish government, with notice that McKinley would execute it unless Spain gave a complete and satisfactory response by noon, April 23. Meanwhile, on April 22 the president announced a blockade of Cuba's northern coast and the port of Santiago. Under international law this was an act of war. Rather than give in to an ultimatum, the Spanish government declared war on April 24. Congress then, determined to be first, declared war on April 25, retroactive to April 21, 1898.

Why such a rush into war after the American minister had predicted that Spain would cave in before the summer was out? Chiefly because too much momentum and popular pressure had already built up for a confidential message to change the course of events. Also, leaders of the business community, which tolerates uncertainty poorly, were now demanding a quick resolution of the problem. Many lacked faith in the willingness or ability of the Spanish government to carry out a moderate policy in the face of a hostile public opinion. Still, it is fair to ask why McKinley did not take a stand for peace, knowing what he did. He might have defied Congress and public opinion, but in the end he decided that the political risk was too high. The ultimate blame for war, if blame must be levied, belongs to the American people for letting themselves be whipped up into such a hostile frenzy.

DEWEY TAKES MANILA   The war itself was short, lasting four months. John Hay, soon to be secretary of state, called it "a splendid little war." The war's end was also the end of Spain's once great New World empire, which had begun with Columbus. It marked as well the emergence of the United States as a world power. If American participation saved many lives by ending the insurrection in Cuba, it also led to American involvement in another insurrection, in the Philippines, and created a host of problems that persisted into the twentieth century.

The war was barely under way before the navy produced a spectacular victory in an unexpected quarter—Manila Bay. While public attention focused on Cuba, young Theodore Roosevelt was thinking of the Philippines. As assistant secretary of the navy, he had Commodore George Dewey appointed commander of the small American squadron in Asia, and had ordered it to engage Spain in the Philippines in case of war. President McKinley had approved those orders.

Arriving late on April 30 with four cruisers and two gunboats, Dewey destroyed or captured all the Spanish warships in Manila Bay. The Spanish force lost 381 men, while Dewey's squadron suffered only 8 wounded. Dewey, without an occupation force, was now in awkward possession of Manila Bay. Promised reinforcements, he stayed while foreign warships hung about the scene like watchful vultures, ready to take over the Philippines if the United States did not do so. Land reinforcements finally arrived, and with the help of Filipino insurrectionists under Emilio Aguinaldo, Dewey's forces entered Manila on August 13.

THE CUBAN CAMPAIGN   While these events transpired halfway around the world, the war reached a surprisingly quick climax closer to home. The U.S. navy blockaded the Spanish navy at Santiago. Although the navy was fit, the army could muster only an ill-assorted guard of 28,000 regulars and about 100,000 militiamen. Altogether during the war about 200,000 more militiamen were recruited, chiefly as state volunteers. The armed forces suffered badly from both inexperience and

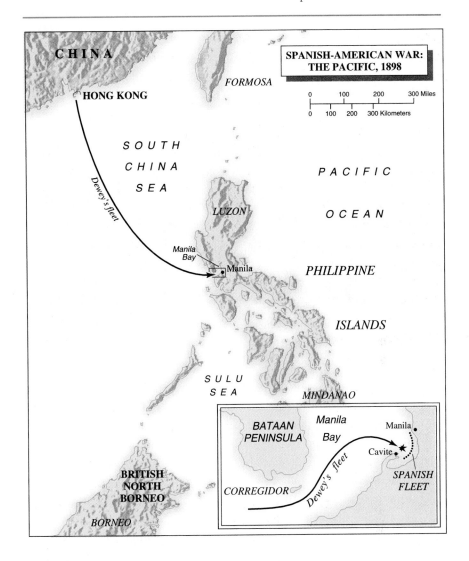

maladministration, with the result that more died from disease than from enemy action. The United States's salvation was that Spanish forces were even worse off.

A force of some 17,000 American troops hastily assembled at Tampa. One significant element of that force was the First Volunteer Cavalry, better known as the "Rough Riders" and best remembered because Lieutenant-Colonel Theodore Roosevelt was second in command. Eager to get "in on the fun," and "to act up to my preachings," Roosevelt had quit the Navy Department soon after war was declared. He ordered

Lieutenant-Colonel Theodore Roosevelt posing with his "Rough Riders" after the battle of San Juan, 1898.

a custom-fitted, fawn-colored uniform with yellow trim from Brooks Brothers, grabbed a dozen pairs of spectacles, and rushed to help organize a volunteer regiment of Ivy League athletes, leathery ex-convicts, Indians, and southwestern sharpshooters. Their landing at the southeastern tip of Cuba was a mad scramble, as the horses were mistakenly sent elsewhere, leaving the "Rough Riders" to become the "Weary Walkers."

Land and sea battles around Santiago broke Spanish resistance. On July 1, about 7,000 Americans took the fortified village of El Caney from about 600 of the enemy garrison. While a much larger force attacked San Juan Hill, a smaller unit, including the dismounted Rough Riders, together with black soldiers from two cavalry units, seized the enemy position atop nearby Kettle Hill. In the midst of the fray, Roosevelt satisfied his bloodlust by seeing a Spaniard he shot double up "neatly as a jackrabbit." He later claimed that he "would rather have led that charge than served three terms in the U.S. Senate." A friend wrote to Roosevelt's wife that her husband was "revelling in victory and gore."

The two battles put American forces atop heights from which to the west and south they could bring Santiago and the Spanish fleet under siege. On July 3 the Spanish navy made a gallant run for it, but its decrepit ships were little more than sitting ducks for the newer American fleet, which included five battleships and two cruisers. The casualties were as one-sided as at Manila: 474 Spanish were killed and wounded and 1,750 were taken prisoner, while only one American was killed and one wounded. Santiago surrendered with a garrison of 24,000 on July 17. On July 25 an American force moved into Spanish-held Puerto Rico against minor resistance.

The next day the Spanish government sued for peace. After discussions lasting two weeks, an armistice was signed on August 12, less than four months after the war's start and the day before Americans entered Manila. The peace protocol specified that Spain should give up Cuba, and that the United States should annex Puerto Rico and occupy Manila pending disposition of the Philippines. Among more than 274,000 Americans who served during the war and the ensuing demobilization, 5,462 died, but only 379 in battle. Most succumbed to malaria, typhoid, dysentery, or yellow fever.

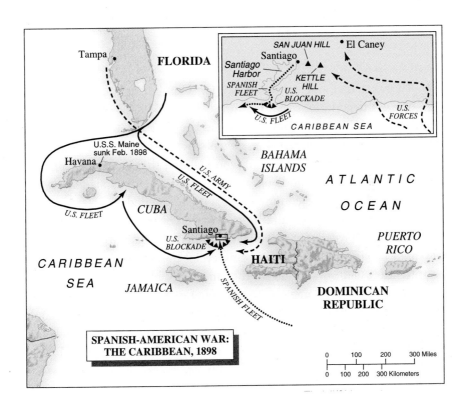

**SPANISH-AMERICAN WAR:
THE CARIBBEAN, 1898**

"Well, I Hardly Know Which to Take First." *At the end of the nineteenth century, it seemed that Uncle Sam had developed a considerable appetite for foreign territory.*

THE DEBATE OVER ANNEXATION   On October 1, a peace commission opened negotiations that led to the Treaty of Paris, signed on December 10. Most of the major points had been settled in the peace protocol, but the fundamental question of the status of the Philippines remained unanswered. McKinley, who claimed that at first he himself could not locate the islands on a map, gave ambiguous signals to the peace commission. The commission itself was divided.

There had been no demand for annexation of the Philippines before the war, but Dewey's victory quickly kindled expansionist fever. Businessmen began thinking of the commercial possibilities in the nearby continent of Asia, such as oil for the lamps of China and textiles for its millions. Missionary societies saw the chance to save the "little brown brother." The Philippines promised to provide a useful base for all such activities. It was neither the first nor the last time that Americans would get caught up in fantasies of "saving" Asia or getting rich there. McKinley pondered the alternatives and later explained his reasoning to a group of Methodists:

And one night late it came to me this way—I don't know how it was, but it came: (1) that we could not give them back to Spain—that would be cowardly and dishonorable; (2) that we could not turn them over to France or Germany—our commercial rivals in the Orient—that would be bad business and discreditable; (3) that we could not leave them to themselves—they were unfit for self-government—and they would soon have anarchy and misrule over there worse than Spain's was; and (4) that there was nothing left for us to do but to take them all, and to educate the Filipinos, and uplift and civilize and Christianize them, and by God's grace do the very best we could by them, as our fellowmen for whom Christ also died. And then I went to bed, and went to sleep and slept soundly.

In one brief statement he had summarized the motivating ideas of imperialism: (1) national honor, (2) commerce, (3) racial superiority, and (4) altruism. Spanish negotiators raised the delicate point that American forces had no claim by right of conquest, and had even taken Manila after the armistice. American negotiators finally offered the Spanish compensation of $20 million. The treaty thus added to American territory Puerto Rico, Guam (a Spanish island in the Pacific), and the Philippines.

Meanwhile Americans had taken other giant steps in the Pacific. Hawaii had been annexed in the midst of the war. Within a year of the peace treaty, in 1899, after another outbreak of fighting over the royal succession in Samoa, Germany and the United States agreed to partition the Samoa Islands. The United States annexed the easternmost islands; Germany took the rest, including the largest island. Britain ceded its claims in Samoa in return for German concessions in the Pacific and in Africa. Meanwhile, in 1898 the United States had laid claim to Wake Island, located between Guam and the Hawaiian islands, which would become a vital link in a future trans-Pacific cable line.

The Treaty of Paris had yet to be ratified in the Senate, where most Democrats and Populists, and some Republicans, opposed it. Anti-imperialists argued that acquisition of the Philippines would undermine democracy. They appealed to traditional isolationism, American principles of self-government, the inconsistency of liberating Cuba and annexing the Philippines, the involvement in foreign entanglements that would undermine the logic of the Monroe Doctrine, and the danger that the Philippines would become an Achilles heel, expensive if not

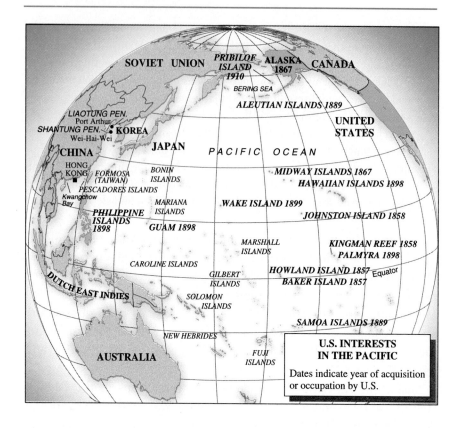

impossible to defend. The prospect of incorporating so many alien peoples into American life was not the least of some people's worries. "Bananas and self-government cannot grow on the same piece of land," one senator claimed.

The opposition might have been strong enough to kill the treaty had not the populist Democrat William Jennings Bryan influenced the vote for approval. Ending the war, he argued, would open the way for the future independence of Cuba and the Philippines. Finally, ratification came on February 6, 1899, by a margin of more than two to one. A week later, the deciding vote of the vice-president defeated a resolution for Philippine independence. That same month in *McClure's* magazine the British poet Rudyard Kipling published "The White Man's Burden," in which he called the American people to a new duty:

> Take up the White Man's burden—
> Send forth the best ye breed—

Go, bind your sons to exile
To serve your captive's need;
To wait in heavy harness
On fluttered folk and wild—
Your new-caught sullen peoples,
Half devil and half child.

By this time Americans had already clashed with Filipino insurrectionists near Manila. The Filipino leader, Emilio Aguinaldo, had been in exile until Commodore Dewey brought him back to Luzon to make trouble for the Spanish. Since Aguinaldo's forces were more or less in control of the islands outside of Manila, what followed was largely an American war of conquest that lasted more than two years. Organized Filipino resistance collapsed by the end of 1899, but even after the capture of Aguinaldo in 1901, sporadic guerrilla action lasted until mid-1902. It was a sordid little war, with massacres and torture on both sides.

Against the backdrop of this nasty guerrilla war the great debate over imperialism continued. The treaty debates inspired a number of anti-imperialist groups, which united in 1899 as the American Anti-Imperialist League. The league attracted members representing many shades

Emilio Aguinaldo (seated third from right) *and other leaders of the Filipino insurgents.*

of opinion; the main thing they had in common was that most belonged to an older generation. Andrew Carnegie footed the bills, but on imperialism at least union leader Samuel Gompers agreed with him. Presidents Charles Eliot of Harvard and David Starr Jordan of Stanford supported the group, along with social reformer Jane Addams. The drive for power, said the philosopher William James, had caused the nation to "puke up its ancient soul."

ORGANIZING THE NEW ACQUISITIONS   Such criticism, however, did not faze the expansionists. Senator Beveridge boasted in 1900: "The Philippines are ours forever. And just beyond the Philippines are China's illimitable markets. We will not retreat from either. . . . The power that rules the Pacific is the power that rules the world. That power will forever be the American Republic."

In the Philippines McKinley had already moved toward setting up a civil government. In 1900 he dispatched a commission under Judge William Howard Taft with instructions to set up a system of government. Unlike some of the Americans on the scene, Taft seemed to like the Filipinos, encouraged them to participate, and eventually convinced Filipino representatives to sit on the commission itself.

On July 4, 1901, military government ended. Under an act of Congress, Taft became the civil governor with appointed provincial governors under his authority. The Philippine Government Act, passed by Congress in 1902, declared the Philippine Islands an "unorganized territory" and made the inhabitants citizens of the Philippines. In 1916 the Jones Act affirmed America's intention to grant the Philippines independence at an indefinite date. Finally, the Tydings-McDuffie Act of 1934 offered independence after a tutelary period of ten more years. A constitution was drafted and ratified, and on September 17, 1934, Manuel Quezon was elected the first president of the Philippines. Independence finally took effect on July 4, 1946.

Puerto Rico had been acquired in part to serve as an American outpost on the approaches to the Caribbean and any future isthmian canal. On April 12, 1900, the Foraker Act established a civil government on the island. The act that was passed two years later for the Philippines would resemble this one. The president appointed a governor and eleven members of an executive council, and an elected House of Delegates made up the lower house of the legislature. Residents of the island were citizens of Puerto Rico but not of the United States until

1917, when the Jones Act granted United States citizenship and made both houses of the legislature elective. In 1947 the governor also became elective, and in 1952 Puerto Rico became a commonwealth with its own constitution and elected officials, a unique status. Like a state, Puerto Rico is free to change its constitution insofar as it does not conflict with the United States Constitution.

The Foraker Act of 1900 also levied a temporary duty on imports from Puerto Rico. The tariff was challenged in the federal courts on the grounds that the island had become part of the United States, but the Supreme Court upheld the tariff. In this and other "Insular Cases" federal judges faced a question that went to the fundamental nature of the American Union and to the civil and political rights of the people in America's new possessions: Does the Constitution follow the flag? The Court ruled in effect that it did not unless Congress extended it.

Having liberated the Cubans from Spanish rule, the Americans found themselves propping up a shaky new Cuban government whose economy was in a state of collapse. Bad relations between American soldiers and Cubans set in almost immediately. When McKinley set up a military government for the island late in 1898, it was at odds with rebel leaders from the start.

Many Europeans expected annexation, and General Leonard Wood, who became Cuba's military governor in 1899, thought this the best solution. But the United States finally did fulfill the promise of independence for Cuba after the military regime had restored order, gotten schools under way, and improved sanitary conditions. The problem of disease in Cuba provided a focus for the work of Dr. Walter Reed, who made an outstanding contribution to the health of people in tropical climates around the world. Named head of the Army Yellow Fever Commission in 1900, he directed experiments with volunteers that proved the theory of a Cuban physician that yellow fever was carried by stegomyia mosquitoes. These experiments led the way to effective control of the disease.

In 1900, at President McKinley's order, General Wood called an election for a Cuban constitutional convention, which drafted a basic law modeled on that of the United States. The Platt Amendment to the Army Appropriations Bill passed by Congress in 1901, however, sharply restricted the independence of the new government. The amendment required Cuba never to impair its independence by treaty with a third power, to maintain its debt within the government's power to repay out of ordinary revenues, and to acknowledge the right of the United States to intervene for the preservation of Cuban independence and the maintenance of "a government adequate for the protection of life, property, and individual liberty." Finally, Cuba was called upon to sell or lease to the United States lands to be used for coaling or naval stations—a proviso that led to an American naval base at Guantanamo Bay, a base still in operation.

Under pressure, the Cuban delegates added the Platt Amendment as an appendix to their own constitution. As early as 1906 an insurrection arose against the new government, and President Theodore Roosevelt responded by sending Secretary of War William Howard Taft to "sit on the lid"—weighing in at more than 300 pounds, he was not a bad choice for the job. Backed up by American armed forces, Taft assumed full governmental authority, as he had in the Philippines, and the American army stayed until 1909, when a new Cuban president was peacefully elected. Further interventions would follow for more than two decades.

IMPERIAL RIVALRIES IN EAST ASIA

During the 1890s, not only the United States but also Japan emerged as a world power. Commodore Matthew Perry's voyage of 1853–1854 had opened Japan to Western ways, and the country began modernization in earnest after the 1860s. Flexing its new muscles, Japan defeated China's stagnant empire in the Sino-Japanese War (1894–1895) and as a result picked up the Pescadores Islands and the island of Taiwan (renamed Formosa). China's weakness, demonstrated in the war, brought the great powers into a scramble for "spheres of influence" on that remaining frontier of imperialist expansion. Russia secured the privilege of building a railroad across Manchuria and established itself in Port Arthur and the Liaotung Peninsula. The Germans moved into Shantung, the French into Kwangchow Bay, the British into Wei-Hai-Wei.

The bright prospect of American trade with China dimmed with the possibility that the great powers would throw up tariff barriers in their own spheres of influence. The British, ensconced at Hong Kong since 1840, had more to lose though, for they already had the largest foreign trade with China. Just before the Spanish-American War, in 1898, the

British suggested joint action with the United States to preserve the integrity of China, and renewed the proposal early in 1899. Both times the Senate rejected the request because it risked an entangling alliance.

CHINA AND THE "OPEN DOOR"   In its origins and content, what soon came to be known as the Open Door Policy resembled the Monroe Doctrine. In both cases the United States proclaimed unilaterally a hands-off policy, which the British had earlier proposed as a joint statement. The policy outlined in Secretary of State John Hay's Open Door Note, dispatched in 1899 to London, Berlin, and St. Petersburg, and a little later to Tokyo, Rome, and Paris, proposed to keep China open to trade with all countries on an equal basis. More specifically it called upon foreign powers, within their spheres of influence: (1) not to interfere with any treaty port (a port open to all by treaty) or any vested interest, (2) to permit Chinese authorities to collect tariffs on an equal basis, and (3) to show no favors to their own nationals in the matter of harbor dues or railroad charges. Hay's request that each of the powers accept these principles was, one diplomat later wrote, like asking everyone who believes in truth to stand: the liars would be the first on their feet. As it turned out, none except Britain accepted Hay's principles, but none rejected them, either. The rest gave equivocal answers, usually conditioned on the action of the others. So Hay blandly announced that all powers had accepted the policy. None stood to deny it.

The Open Door Policy, if rooted in the self-interest of American businessmen eager to exploit the markets of China, also tapped the deep-seated sympathies of those who opposed imperialism, especially as it endorsed China's territorial integrity. But it had little more legal standing than a pious affirmation. When the Japanese, concerned about Russian pressure in Manchuria, asked how the United States intended to enforce the policy, Hay replied that America was "not prepared . . . to enforce these views on the east by any demonstration which could present a character of hostility to any other power." So it would remain for forty years, until continued Japanese expansion would bring America to war in 1941.

THE BOXER REBELLION   A new crisis arose in 1900, when a group of Chinese nationalists known to the Western world as Boxers ("Fists of Righteous Harmony") rebelled against foreign encroachments on China

The forces of the Western powers and Japan occupying the Forbidden City in Peking after putting down the Boxer Rebellion.

and laid siege to foreign embassies in Peking. An international expedition of British, German, Russian, Japanese, and American forces mobilized to relieve the embassy compound. Hay, fearful that the intervention might become an excuse to dismember China, took the opportunity to further refine the Open Door Policy. The United States, he said in a circular letter of July 3, 1900, sought a solution that would "preserve Chinese territorial and administrative integrity" as well as "equal and impartial trade with all parts of the Chinese Empire."

Six weeks later, the expedition reached Peking and quelled the Boxer Rebellion. The occupying powers then agreed to settle for an indemnity from China of approximately $333 million. Of this total the United States received $25 million, of which nearly $11 million was refunded to China once all claims were paid. Most of this the Chinese government put into a fund to support Chinese students in American colleges.

ROOSEVELT'S BIG STICK DIPLOMACY

More than any other American of his time, Theodore Roosevelt helped transform the role of the United States in world affairs. The country had emerged from the Spanish-American War a world power, and he insisted that this entailed major new responsibilities. To ensure that his country accepted such international obligations, Roosevelt stretched both the Constitution and executive power to the limit. In the process he pushed a reluctant nation onto the center stage of world affairs.

ROOSEVELT'S RISE   Born in 1858, the son of a wealthy New York merchant and a Georgia belle, Roosevelt grew up in Manhattan in cultured comfort, visited Europe as a child, spoke German fluently, and was graduated Phi Beta Kappa from Harvard in 1880. A sickly, scrawny boy with poor eyesight, he built himself up by sheer force of will into a physical and intellectual athlete who became a lifelong practitioner of the "strenuous life." Boxer, wrestler, mountain climber, hunter, and outdoorsman, he was also a dedicated bird watcher, renowned historian and essayist, and outspoken moralist. His energy and fierce competitive spirit were both inexhaustible and infectious, and he was ever willing to express opinions on any and all subjects.

Within two years of graduating from Harvard, Roosevelt won election to the New York legislature and published *The Naval War of 1812,* the first of a number of historical, biographical, and other writings to flow from his pen. But with the world seemingly at his feet, disaster struck. In 1884 his beloved mother, only forty-eight years old, died. Eleven hours later, in the same house, his twenty-two-year-old wife died in his arms, soon after giving birth to their first child. That night Roosevelt drew a large cross over the entry in his diary: "The light has gone out of my life." The double funeral was so wrenching that the officiating minister wept throughout his prayer.

In an attempt to recover from this "strange and terrible fate," Roosevelt sold the family house and moved west to take up the cattle business on the Dakota frontier. There he played the part of a patrician cowboy, adorned in a buckskin shirt, silver spurs, and alligator boots. He told a relative he was "having a glorious time here." The blue-blooded New Yorker relished hunting, leading roundups, capturing outlaws, fighting Indians—and reading Tolstoy by the campfire. When a drunken cowboy, a gun in each hand, tried to bully the tinhorn Roosevelt, teasing him about his glasses, the feisty Harvard dude laid him out with one punch. Although his western career was brief, he never quite got over being a cowboy.

Back in New York City, Roosevelt ran for mayor in 1886 and lost, and later served six years as civil service commissioner and two years as

New York City's police commissioner. In the latter capacity he loved to don a black cloak and broad-brimmed hat and patrol the streets at midnight. When he came upon a sleeping policeman, Roosevelt would rap the man with his nightstick. In 1897, McKinley appointed the conscientious Roosevelt assistant secretary of the navy. After serving in Cuba and hastening into print his own account of the Rough Riders, Roosevelt easily won the governorship of New York, arousing audiences with his impassioned speeches and powerful personality.

In the 1900 presidential contest, the Democrats turned once again to William Jennings Bryan, who sought to make imperialism the "paramount issue" of the campaign. The Democratic platform condemned the Philippine conflict as "an unnecessary war" that had "placed the United States, previously known and applauded throughout the world as the champion of freedom, in the false and un-American position of crushing with military force the efforts of our former allies to achieve liberty and self-government."

The Republicans welcomed the issue. They renominated McKinley and named Roosevelt his running mate. After his role in both the Philippine and Cuban action, Roosevelt had virtually become "Mr. Imperialism." McKinley outpolled Bryan by 7.2 million to 6.4 million in the popular vote and by 292 to 155 in the electoral vote. But less than a year later, on September 6, 1901, while McKinley attended a reception

This 1900 cartoon shows the Republican vice-presidential candidate, Theodore Roosevelt, overshadowing his running mate, President McKinley.

at the Pan American Exposition in Buffalo, a fanatical anarchist named Leon Czolgosz approached him with a gun concealed in a bandaged hand and fired at point-blank range. McKinley died six days later, and Theodore Roosevelt was suddenly elevated to the White House. "Now look," Mark Hanna, the Ohio businessman and politico, erupted, "that damned cowboy is President of the United States!"

Six weeks short of his forty-third birthday, Roosevelt was the youngest man ever to reach the White House, but he brought to it more experience in public affairs than most and perhaps more vitality than any. One observer compared him to Niagara Falls, "both great wonders of nature." Roosevelt's glittering spectacles, glistening teeth, and over-flowing gusto were a godsend to the cartoonists, who added another trademark when he pronounced the adage: "Speak softly, and carry a big stick."

Along with Roosevelt's boundless energy went an unshakable right-eousness and a tendency to cast every issue in moral and patriotic terms. He considered the presidency his "bully pulpit," and he deliv-ered fist-smacking speeches on the virtues of righteousness, honesty, civic duty, and strenuosity. Yet his boundless energy left a false impres-sion of impulsiveness, and his talk of morality cloaked a cautious prag-matism. Roosevelt could get carried away on occasion, but as he said of his foreign policy steps, this was likely to happen only when "I am as-sured that I shall be able eventually to carry out my will by force." In-deed, nowhere was President Roosevelt's forceful will more evident than in his conduct of foreign affairs.

BUILDING THE PANAMA CANAL   After the Spanish-American War, the United States became more deeply involved in the Caribbean area. One issue overshadowed every other in the region: the Panama Canal. The narrow isthmus of Panama had excited dreams of an interoceanic canal ever since Balboa's crossing in 1513. Admiral Mahan regarded a canal as important to American commerce and naval power, a point dra-matized in 1898 by the long voyage of the battleship *Oregon* around South America's Cape Horn to join the American fleet off Cuba.

Transit across the isthmus had first become a strong concern of the United States in the 1840s, when it became an important route to the California gold fields. Two treaties dating from that period loomed years later as obstacles to construction of a canal. The Bidlack Treaty (1848) with Colombia (then New Granada) guaranteed both Colombia's sovereignty over Panama and the neutrality of the isthmus, so that "free transit . . . not be embarrassed in any future time." In the Clayton-Bulwer Treaty (1850) the British agreed to acquire no more Central American territory, and the United States joined them in agreeing to build or fortify a canal only by mutual consent.

After the Spanish-American War, Secretary of State Hay commenced talks with the British ambassador to establish such consent. The outcome was the Hay-Pauncefote Treaty of 1900, but the Senate rejected it on the grounds that it forbade fortification of the canal and required that the canal be neutral even in time of war. By then a bill was already pending in Congress for a Nicaraguan canal, and the British apparently decided to accept the inevitable. In 1901 the Senate ratified a second Hay-Pauncefote Treaty, which simply omitted reference to the former limitations.

Other obstacles remained, however. From 1881 to 1887 a French company under Ferdinand de Lesseps, who had engineered the Suez

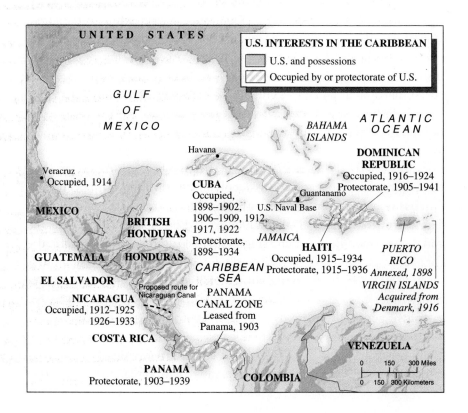

Canal in 1877, had spent nearly $300 million and some 20,000 lives to dig less than a third of the canal through Panama, then under the control of Colombia. The company now wanted $109 million for its holdings. An Isthmian Canal Commission, appointed by McKinley, reported in 1901 that a Nicaraguan route would be cheaper. When the House of Representatives quickly passed an act for construction there, the French company lowered its price to $40 million, and the Canal Commission switched to Panama.

Meanwhile Secretary Hay had opened negotiations with Ambassador Thomas Herrán of Colombia. In return for a Canal Zone six miles wide, the United States agreed to pay $10 million in cash and a rental fee of $250,000 a year. The United States Senate ratified the Hay-Herrán Treaty in 1903, but the Colombian Senate held out for $25 million in cash. At this action of those "foolish and homicidal corruptionists in Bogotá," Theodore Roosevelt, by then president, flew into a rage punctuated by references to "dagoes" and "contemptible little creatures." Meanwhile in Panama, an isolated province long at odds with the remote Colombian authorities in Bogotá, feeling was heightened by Colombia's rejection of the treaty. One Manuel Amador, an employee of the French canal company, then hatched a plot in close collusion with the company's representative, Philippe Bunau-Varilla. He visited Roosevelt and Hay and, apparently with inside information, informed the conspirators that the U.S.S. *Nashville* would call at Colón in Panama on November 2.

With an army of some 500, Amador staged a revolt the next day. Colombian troops, who could not penetrate the overland jungle, found American ships blocking the sea lanes. On November 13 the Roosevelt administration received its first ambassador from Panama, whose name happened to be Philippe Bunau-Varilla, and he signed a treaty that extended the Canal Zone from six to ten miles in width. For $10 million down and $250,000 a year, the United States received "in perpetuity the use, occupation and control" of the zone. The U.S. attorney-general, asked to supply a legal opinion upholding Roosevelt's actions, responded wryly: "No, Mr. President, if I were you I would not have any taint of legality about it."

In 1904 Congress created a new Isthmian Canal Commission to direct construction. Despite sanitary problems, the biggest obstacle at first, Roosevelt instructed the commission to make the "dirt fly." He later explained: "I took the Canal Zone and let Congress debate; and while the debate goes on the Canal does also."

Panama Canal Construction. *The Panama Canal linked the Atlantic and Pacific, making interoceanic crossings possible.*

And so did a rankling resentment in Colombia. By needlessly offending Latin American sensibilities, Roosevelt had committed one of the greatest blunders in American foreign policy. Colombia eventually got its $25 million from the Harding administration in 1921, but only once America's interest in Colombian oil had lubricated the wheels of diplomacy. There was no apology, but the payment was made to remove "all misunderstandings growing out of the political events in Panama, November, 1903." The canal opened on August 15, 1914, less than two weeks after the outbreak of World War I in Europe.

THE ROOSEVELT COROLLARY   Even without the canal, the United States would have been concerned about the stability of the Caribbean area, and particularly with the activities of any hostile power there. A prime excuse for intervention in those days was to force the collection of debts owed to foreign nationals. In 1904 a crisis over the debts of the Dominican Republic gave Roosevelt an opportunity to formulate American policy in the Caribbean. In his annual address to Congress in 1904, he set forth what came to be known as the Roosevelt Corollary to the Monroe Doctrine: the principle, in short, was that since the Monroe Doctrine prohibited intervention in the region by Europeans, the

The World's Constable. *Theodore Roosevelt, shown here as the world's police-man, wields the "big stick" symbolizing his approach to diplomacy.*

United States was justified in intervening first to forestall the actions of outsiders.

In the president's words, the Roosevelt Corollary held that: "Chronic wrongdoing . . . may in America, as elsewhere, ultimately require intervention by some civilized nation, and in the Western Hemisphere the adherence of the United States to the Monroe Doctrine may force the United States, however reluctantly, in flagrant cases of such wrongdoing or impotence, to the exercise of an international police power." As put into practice by mutual agreement with the Dominican Republic in 1905, the Roosevelt Corollary called for the United States to install and protect a collector of customs who would apply 55 percent of the revenues to debt payments.

THE RUSSO-JAPANESE WAR   In East Asia, meanwhile, the Open Door Policy received a serious challenge when rivalry between Russia and Japan flared into a fight. By 1904 the Japanese had grown convinced that the Russians threatened their own ambitions in China and Korea. On February 8, Japan launched a surprise attack that devastated the Russian fleet. The Japanese then occupied Korea and drove the Russians back into Manchuria. But neither side could score a knockout blow, and neither relished a prolonged war. Roosevelt sought to maintain a balance between the two powers and offered to mediate their conflict. When the Japanese signaled that they would welcome a negotiated settlement, Roosevelt agreed to sponsor a peace conference in Portsmouth, New Hampshire. In the Treaty of Portsmouth, signed on September 5, 1905, the concessions all went to the Japanese. Russia acknowledged Japan's "predominant political, military, and economic interests in Korea" (Japan would annex the kingdom in 1910), and both powers agreed to evacuate Manchuria.

AMERICA'S RELATIONS WITH JAPAN Japan's show of strength against Russia raised doubts among American leaders about the security of the Philippines. During the Portsmouth talks, Roosevelt sent William Howard Taft to meet with the Japanese foreign minister in Tokyo. The two men negotiated the Taft-Katsura Agreement of July 29, 1905, in which the United States accepted Japanese control of Korea and Japan disavowed any designs on the Philippines. Three years later, the Root-Takahira Agreement, negotiated by Secretary of State Elihu Root and the Japanese ambassador, endorsed the status quo and reinforced the Open Door Policy by supporting "the independence and integrity of China" and "the principle of equal opportunity for commerce and industry in China."

Behind the diplomatic facade of goodwill, however, lay mutual distrust. For many Americans the Russian threat in East Asia now gave way to the "yellow peril" of Japan.* Racial animosities on the West Coast helped sour relations with Japan. In 1906 the San Francisco school board ordered students of Chinese, Japanese, and Korean descent to attend a separate public school. The Japanese government sharply protested such prejudice, and President Roosevelt managed to talk the school board into changing its mind after making sure that Japanese authorities would not issue passports to "laborers" except former residents of the United States, the parents, wives, or children of residents, or those who already possessed an interest in an American farming enterprise. This "Gentlemen's Agreement" of 1907, the precise terms of

*The term "yellow peril" was apparently coined by Kaiser Wilhelm II of Germany.

which have never been revealed, halted the influx of Japanese immigrants and brought some respite to racial agitations in California.

THE UNITED STATES AND EUROPE   During the years of expansionism, the United States cast its gaze westward and southward. But events in Europe also required attention. While Roosevelt was moving toward mediation of the Russo-Japanese War in 1905, another dangerous crisis began brewing in Morocco. There, on March 31, 1905, German kaiser Wilhelm II stepped ashore at Tangier and gave a saber-rattling speech criticizing French and British interests in North Africa. The kaiser's speech aroused a diplomatic storm of dangerous proportions. Roosevelt felt that the United States had something at stake in preventing the outbreak of a major war. At the kaiser's behest, he talked the French and British into attending an international conference at Algeciras, Spain, with American delegates present. Roosevelt then maneuvered the Germans into accepting his lead.

The Act of Algeciras, signed in 1906, affirmed the independence of Morocco and guaranteed an open door for trade there, but provided for the training and control of Moroccan police by France and Spain. The United States Senate ratified the agreement, but only with the proviso that it was not to be construed as a departure from America's traditional policy of noninvolvement in European affairs. It was a departure, of course, and one that may well have prevented a general war, or at least postponed it until 1914. Roosevelt received the Nobel Peace Prize in 1906 for his work at Portsmouth and Algeciras. For all his bellicosity on other occasions, he had earned it.

Before Roosevelt left the White House, he celebrated America's rise to world power with one great flourish. In 1907 he sent the entire fleet of the United States navy, by then second in strength only to the British, on a grand tour around the world, their commander announcing he was ready for "a feast, a frolic, or a fight." He got mostly the first two, and none of the last. At every port of call the "Great White Fleet" set off rousing celebrations, down the Atlantic coast of South America, up the West Coast, out to Hawaii, and down to New Zealand and Australia. It was the first such show of American naval might in the Pacific, and many feared the reaction of the Japanese, for whose benefit Roosevelt had in fact staged the show. They need not have worried, for in Japan the flotilla got the greatest welcome of all. Thousands of schoolchildren turned out waving tiny American flags and singing "The Star-Spangled Banner" in English. The triumphal procession continued home by way of the Mediterranean and steamed back into American waters in 1909, just in time to close out Roosevelt's presidency on a note of success.

But it was a success that would have mixed consequences. As one insightful student of Roosevelt's role in America's rise to world power wrote: "One comes away from the study with admiration for Roosevelt's ability, his energy, and his devotion to his country's interests as he saw them but with a sense of tragedy that his abilities were turned toward imperialism and an urge for power, which were to have consequences so serious for the future." Roosevelt had influenced the United States "in a direction that . . . was to bring her face to face with grave dangers" before the mid–twentieth century.

MAKING CONNECTIONS

- The Spanish-American War marked a turning point in American foreign policy. America's emergence as a global power is a central theme in the twentieth century.

- Theodore Roosevelt's foreign policy displayed an activist approach to the presidency. In the next chapter, we see the connections between his foreign policies and his approach to domestic affairs.

FURTHER READING

An excellent survey of the diplomacy of the era is Charles Campbell's *The Transformation of American Foreign Relations, 1865–1900* (1976). For background to the events of the 1890s, see Walter LeFeber's *The American Search for Opportunity, 1865–1913* (1993) and David Healy's *U. S. Expansionism: The Imperialist Urge in the 1890s* (1970). The dispute over American policy concerning Hawaii is covered in

Thomas J. Osborne's *"Empire Can Wait": American Opposition to Hawaiian Annexation, 1893–1898* (1981).

Ivan Musicant's *Empire by Default: The Spanish-American War and the Dawn of the American Century* (1998) is the most comprehensive volume on the conflict. Frank Freidel's *The Splendid Little War* (1958) shows what the war was like for those who fought it. Gerald F. Linderman's *The Mirror of War: American Society and the Spanish-American War* (1974) discusses the war at home. For the war's aftermath in the Philippines, see Stuart C. Miller's *"Benevolent Assimilation": American Conquest of the Philippines, 1899–1903* (1982). Robert L. Beisner's *Twelve Against Empire: The Anti-Imperialists, 1898– 1900* (1985) handles the debate over annexation.

A good introduction to American interest in China is Michael H. Hunt's *The Making of a Special Relationship: The United States and China to 1914* (1983). Also useful is Marilyn B. Young's *The Rhetoric of Empire: America's China Policy, 1893–1901* (1968). Kenton J. Clymer's *John Hay: The Gentleman as Diplomat* (1975) examines the role of this key secretary of state in forming policy.

For American policy in the Caribbean and Central America, see Walter LeFeber's *Inevitable Revolutions: The United States in Central America* (1983) and Bruce J. Calder's *The Impact of Intervention: The Dominican Republic During the U.S. Occupation of 1916–1924* (1984). David McCullough's *The Path between the Seas: The Creation of the Panama Canal, 1870–1914* (1977) presents the fullest account of how the United States secured the Panama Canal.

24 THE PROGRESSIVE ERA

CHAPTER ORGANIZER

This chapter focuses on:

- the social bases of progressivism.

- the basic elements of progressive reform.

- the presidencies of Theodore Roosevelt, William H. Taft, and Woodrow Wilson.

- the significance of the election of 1912.

Theodore Roosevelt's emergence as a national leader coincided with the onset of what historians have labeled the Progressive Era (1900–1917). The rise of the so-called Progressive movement had many causes, the most powerful of which was the devastating depression of the 1890s and its attendant social unrest. The depression brought hard times to the cities and provoked both the fears and consciences of the rapidly growing middle and upper-middle classes. By the turn of the century, so many activists were at work seeking to improve social conditions that people began to speak of a "Progressive Era," a time of fermenting idealism and constructive social, economic, and political change.

ELEMENTS OF REFORM

Progressivism was a reform movement so varied and comprehensive it almost defies definition. The progressives saw themselves as engaged in a crusade against the abuses of urban political bosses and corporate robber barons. Their goals were greater democracy and social justice, honest government, more effective regulation of business, and a revived commitment to public service. They believed that the scope of local, state, and federal government authority should be expanded to accomplish these goals. Doing so, they hoped, would ensure the "progress" of American society. The "real heart of the movement," declared one self-described progressive reformer, was "to use the government as an agency of human welfare."

But the Kansas editor William Allen White hinted at a paradox in the movement when he called progressivism just populism that had "shaved its whiskers, washed its shirt, put on a derby, and moved up into the middle class." As White suggested, urban business and professional leaders brought to progressivism a certain respectability and political savvy that the Populists had lacked. They also brought a more businesslike, efficient approach to reform. While one strand in the varied fabric of progressivism retained the resonant appeal of agrarian democracy and its antitrust traditions, a new emphasis on efficiency soon gained ascendancy.

Another paradox in the movement was that it contained an element of conservatism. In some cases, the regulation of business turned out actually to be regulation proposed *by* business leaders who preferred regulated stability to the chaos and uncertainty of unrestrained competition. Much like the reform spirit of the 1830s and 1840s, once called Jacksonian Democracy, progressivism was diverse in both origins and tendencies. Few people adhered to all of the varied progressive causes.

What reformers shared was a common assumption that the complex social ills and tensions generated by the urban-industrial revolution required new responses. Governments were now called upon to extend a broad range of direct services: schools, good roads (a movement propelled first by cyclists and then by automobilists), conservation, public health and welfare, care of the handicapped, farm loans and demonstration agents, among other things. Such initiatives represented the first tentative steps toward what would become known during the 1930s and after as the welfare state.

ANTECEDENTS TO PROGRESSIVISM Populism was indisputably one of the catalysts of progressivism. The Populist platform of 1892 outlined many reforms that would be accomplished in the Progressive Era. Many Populists, in addition, believed that their movement achieved vindication in the Progressive Era. Editor William Allen White wrote that populism "was the beginning of a movement that in another decade was to change the politics of the nation: indeed it was a symptom of a worldwide drift to liberalism, which reached its peak . . . twenty-five years later."

After the collapse of the farmers' movement and the revival of the agricultural sector at the turn of the century, the focus of the reform spirit shifted to cities, where middle-class activists had for years attacked the problems of political bossism and urban development. The Mugwumps, those gentlemen reformers who had fought the spoils system and promoted a civil service based on merit, supplied the Progressive movement with an important element of its thinking, the honest-government ideal. Over the years, their ranks had been supplemented and the honest-government outlook broadened by leaders who confronted such new urban problems as crime, vice, and the efficient provision of gas, electricity, water, sewers, mass transit, and garbage collection.

Finally, another significant force in fostering the spirit of progressivism was the growing familiarity with socialist doctrines and their critiques of living and working conditions. The Socialist party of the time served as the left wing of progressivism. Still, most progressives found socialist remedies unacceptable, and the progressive reform impulse grew in part from a desire to counter the growing influence of socialist doctrines. More important in spurring progressive reform were social critics who dramatized the need for reform.

THE MUCKRAKERS The writers who thrived on exposing scandal got their name when Theodore Roosevelt compared them to a character in John Bunyan's *Pilgrim's Progress:* "A man that could look no way but downwards with a muckrake in his hands." The "muckrakers are often

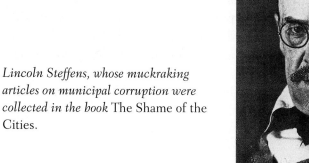

Lincoln Steffens, whose muckraking articles on municipal corruption were collected in the book The Shame of the Cities.

indispensable to . . . society," Roosevelt said, "but only if they know when to stop raking the muck."

Henry Demarest Lloyd is sometimes cited as the first of the muckrakers for his critical examination of the Standard Oil Company and other monopolies, *Wealth against Commonwealth* (1894). Lloyd exposed the growth of corporate giants responsible to none but themselves, able to corrupt if not control governments. Another early muckraker was Jacob Riis, a Danish immigrant who, as an influential New York journalist, exposed slum conditions in *How the Other Half Lives* (1890). The chief outlets for these social critics were the inexpensive popular magazines that began to flourish in the 1890s, such as the *Arena* and *McClure's* magazine, founded in 1893 by Samuel S. McClure, an Irish immigrant who had begun the first newspaper syndicate in the country.

The golden age of muckraking is sometimes dated from 1902 when *McClure's* began to run articles by the reporter Lincoln Steffens on municipal corruption, later collected into a book: *The Shame of the Cities* (1904). *McClure's* also ran Ida M. Tarbell's *History of the Standard Oil Company* (1904). Tarbell provided a more detailed treatment than the earlier book by Lloyd, but it was all the more damaging in its detail. Other outstanding books that began as magazine articles exposed corruption in the stock market, the meat industry, the life insurance business, and the political world.

Without the muckrakers, progressivism surely would never have achieved the popular support it had. In feeding the public's appetite for facts about their new urban-industrial society, the muckrakers demonstrated one of the salient features of the Progressive movement, and one of its central failures. The progressives were stronger on diagnosis than on remedy. They professed a naive faith in the power of democracy. Let the people know, expose corruption, and bring government close to the people, went the rationale, and the correction of evils would follow automatically. The cure for the ills of democracy, it seemed, was more democracy.

THE FEATURES OF PROGRESSIVISM

DEMOCRACY The most important reform with which the progressives tried to democratize government was the direct primary, or the nomination of candidates by the vote of party members. Under the existing convention system, only a small proportion of the voters attended the local caucuses or precinct meetings that sent delegates to county, and in turn to state and national, conventions. While the system allowed seasoned leaders to sift the candidates, it also lent itself to domination by political professionals who were able to come early and stay late. Direct primaries at the local level had been held sporadically since the 1870s, but after South Carolina adopted the first statewide primary in 1896, the movement spread within two decades to nearly every state.

The primary was but one expression of a broad movement for direct democracy. In 1898 South Dakota became the first state to adopt the initiative and referendum, procedures that allowed voters to enact laws directly. If a designated number of voters petitioned to have a measure put on the ballot (the initiative), the electorate could then vote it up or down (the referendum). Oregon adopted a whole spectrum of reform measures, including a voter registration law (1899); the initiative and referendum (1902); the direct primary (1904); a sweeping corrupt-practices act (1908); and the recall (1910), whereby public officials could be removed by petition and vote. Within a decade nearly twenty states had adopted the initiative and referendum and nearly a dozen the recall.

Most states adopted the party primary even in the choice of United States senators. Nevada was first, in 1899, to let voters express a choice that state legislators of their party were expected to follow in choosing senators. The popular election of senators required a constitutional amendment, and the House of Representatives, beginning in 1894, four times adopted such an amendment, only to see it defeated in the Senate, which came under increasing attack as a "millionaire's club." By 1912 thirty states had provided preferential primaries. The Senate in that year finally accepted the inevitable and agreed to the Seventeenth Amendment, authorizing popular election of senators. The amendment was ratified in 1913.

EFFICIENCY A second major theme of progressivism was the "gospel of efficiency." In the business world during those years, Frederick W. Taylor, the original "efficiency expert," was developing the techniques he summed up in his book *The Principles of Scientific Management* (1911): efficient management of time and costs, the proper routing and scheduling of work, standardization of tools and equipment, and the like. "Taylorism," as scientific management came to be known, promised to reduce waste through the careful analysis of labor processes. By breaking down the production process into separate steps and by metic-

Poster to encourage on-the-job productivity, 1920s. With a series of posters, the Mather Poster Company aimed to keep workers focused, productive, and loyal.

WHY ROB YOURSELF?

Taking two hours to do an hour's task robs you of an hour's results

Results Win Progress for You

ulously studying the time it took each worker to perform a task, Taylor sought to discover the optimum technique for the average worker and establish performance standards for each job classification. The promise of higher wages, he believed, would motivate workers to exceed the "average" expectations.

As they incorporated Taylor's theories and "time-motion studies" into their operations, American manufacturers highlighted the quest for efficiency and order that characterized the Progressive Era. But many workers resented Taylor's innovations. They saw in scientific management a tool for employers to make them work faster than was healthy or fair. Yet Taylor's system brought concrete improvements in productivity—especially among those industries whose production processes were highly standardized and where jobs were rigidly defined. "In the future," Taylor predicted in 1911, "the system [rather than the individual workers] will be first."

In government, the efficiency movement demanded the reorganization of agencies to prevent overlapping, to establish clear lines of authority, and to fix responsibility. One long-held theory had it that the greater the number of offices chosen by popular vote, the greater the degree of democracy, but progressives considered this inefficient. They believed that voters could make wiser choices if they had a shorter ballot and chose fewer officials in whom power and responsibility were clearly lodged.

Two new ideas for making municipal government more efficient gained headway in the first decade of the new century. The commission system, first adopted by Galveston, Texas, in 1901, when local government there collapsed in the aftermath of a devastating hurricane and tidal wave, placed ultimate authority in a board composed of elected administrative heads of city departments—commissioners of sanitation, police, utilities, and so on. The more durable idea, however, was the city-manager plan, under which a professional administrator ran the government in accordance with policies set by the elected council and mayor. Staunton, Virginia, first adopted the plan in 1908. By 1914 the National Association of City Managers heralded the arrival of a new profession.

When America was a pre-industrial society, Andrew Jackson's notion that any reasonably intelligent citizen could perform the duties of any public office may have been true. In the more complex age of the early

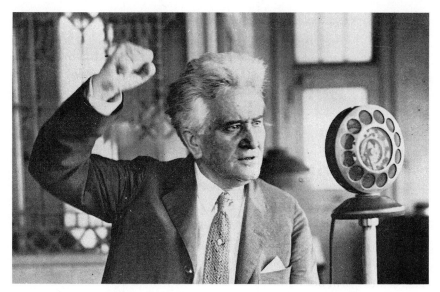

Robert M. La Follette.

twentieth century it was apparent that many functions of government and business had come to require expert specialists. This principle was promoted by Governor Robert M. La Follette of Wisconsin, who advocated progressivism and established a Legislative Reference Bureau to provide research, advice, and help in the drafting of legislation. The "Wisconsin Idea" of efficient government was widely publicized and copied. La Follette also worked for such reforms as the primary, stronger railroad regulation, the conservation of natural resources, and workmen's compensation.

Born in a log cabin and educated at the University of Wisconsin, the short, muscular La Follette possessed an abiding faith in grassroots democracy, in the power and judgment of the people. He was more enlightened about modern trends than William Jennings Bryan, and equally intense, sincere, and determined. He was also Bryan's equal as an orator; La Follette could talk for hours without taxing himself or his listeners.

Progressive counterparts to La Follette also appeared in other states. As counsel to a legislative committee in New York, Charles Evans Hughes became a national figure by uncovering spectacular insurance frauds and won the New York governorship in 1906. Voters in Georgia and Alabama that year elected governors who promised to regulate the railroads. Hiram Johnson, after getting a conviction of the grafting boss of San Francisco in 1908, won the California governorship in 1910 on the promise of reining in the Southern Pacific Railroad.

REGULATION   Of all the problems facing American society at the turn of the century, one engaged a greater diversity of reformers, and elicited more—and more controversial—solutions than any other: the regulation of giant corporations, which became a third major theme of progressivism. Concern over the concentration of economic power had brought bipartisan support to the passage of the Sherman Anti-Trust Act in 1890, but the act had turned out to be more symbolic than effective.

The problem of economic power and its abuse offered a dilemma for progressives. Four broad solutions were available, but of these, two were extremes that had limited support: letting business work out its own destiny under a policy of laissez-faire, or adopting a socialist program of public ownership. At the municipal level, however, the socialist alternative was rather widely adopted in public utilities and transportation—so-called gas and water socialism—but otherwise was not seriously considered as a general policy. The other choices were either to adopt a policy of trust-busting in the belief that restoring old-fashioned competition would best prevent economic abuses, or to accept big business in the belief that it brought economies of scale, but to regulate it to prevent abuses.

Efforts to restore the competition of small firms proved unworkable, partly because breaking up large combinations was complex and difficult. The trend over the years was toward regulation rather than dissolution of big business. To some extent regulation and "stabilization" won acceptance among businessmen who, whatever respect they paid to competition in the abstract, preferred not to face it in practice. As time passed, however, regulatory agencies often came under the influence or control of those they were supposed to regulate. Railroad men, for instance, generally had more intimate knowledge of the intricate details involved in their business, giving them the advantage over the outsiders who might be appointed to the Interstate Commerce Commission.

SOCIAL JUSTICE   A fourth important feature of the progressive spirit was the impulse toward social justice, which motivated diverse ac-

Kohinore Mine, Pennsylvania, 1891. Child labor was rampant until the progressive National Child Labor Committee spearheaded a movement to prohibit employing young children.

tions—from private charities to campaigns against child labor and liquor. The settlement house movement of the late nineteenth century had spawned a corps of social workers and genteel reformers devoted to the uplift of slum dwellers. But with time it became apparent that social evils extended beyond the reach of private charities and demanded the power of the state.

Labor legislation was perhaps the most significant reform to emerge from the drive for social justice. The National Child Labor Committee, organized in 1904, led a movement for laws banning the still widespread employment of young children. Through publicity, the organization of state and local committees, and a telling documentation of the evils of child labor by the photographer Lewis W. Hine, the committee within ten years brought about legislation in most states banning the labor of underage children (the minimum age varied from twelve to sixteen) and limiting the working hours of older children.

Closely linked with the child-labor reform movement was a concerted effort to regulate the hours of work for women. Spearheaded by Florence Kelley, the head of the National Consumers League, this pro-

Triangle Shirtwaist Company Fire, New York City, 1911.

gressive crusade prompted the passage of state laws to ameliorate the distinctive hardships that long working hours imposed on women who were wives and mothers. Many states also outlawed night work and labor in dangerous occupations for both women and children. But numerous exemptions and inadequate enforcement often virtually nullified the laws.

The Supreme Court pursued a curiously erratic course in ruling on state labor laws. It upheld a Utah law limiting the working day in mining and smelting to eight hours as a proper exercise of the state police power to protect the health and safety of workers. In *Lochner v. New York* (1905), however, the Court voided a ten-hour day because it violated workers' "liberty of contract" to accept any terms they chose. But in *Muller v. Oregon* (1908), the high court upheld a ten-hour law for women largely on the basis of sociological data regarding the effects of long hours on the health and morals of women. In *Bunting v. Oregon* (1917), the Court accepted a ten-hour day for both men and women, but held out for twenty more years against state minimum-wage laws.

Legislation to protect workers against avoidable accidents gained impetus from disasters such as the 1911 fire at the Triangle Shirtwaist

Company in New York in which 146 people, mostly women, died for want of adequate exits. They either were trapped on the three upper floors of a ten-story building, or they plunged to the street below. Stricter building codes and factory inspection acts followed. One of the most important advances along these lines was the series of workers' compensation laws enacted after Maryland led the way in 1902. Accident insurance systems replaced the old common-law principle that an injured worker was entitled to compensation only if he could prove employer negligence, a costly and capricious procedure from which the worker was likely to win nothing or, as often happened, excessive awards from overly sympathetic juries.

PROHIBITION   For many progressive activists the cause of liquor prohibition was a fifth area for action. Opposition to strong drink was an ideal cause in which to merge the older private ethics with the new social ethics. Given the moral disrepute of saloons, prohibitionists could equate the "liquor traffic" with progressive suspicion of bossism and "special interests." When reform pressures mounted, prohibition offered an easy outlet, bypassing the complexities of corporate regulation.

A temperance meeting in Kansas, late nineteenth century.

The battle against booze dated far back into the nineteenth century. The Women's Christian Temperance Union had promoted the cause since 1874, and a Prohibition political party had entered the elections in 1876. But the most successful political action followed the formation in 1893 of the Anti-Saloon League, an organization that pioneered the strategy of the single-issue pressure group. Through its singleness of purpose, it forced the prohibition issue into the forefront of state and local elections. At its "Jubilee Convention" in 1913 the Anti-Saloon League endorsed a prohibition amendment to the Constitution, adopted by Congress that year. By the time it was ratified six years later, state and local action already had dried up areas occupied by nearly three-fourths of the nation's population.

ROOSEVELT'S PROGRESSIVISM

Theodore Roosevelt adopted a cautious version of progressive reform. He cultivated party leaders in Congress, and he steered away from such political thickets as the tariff and banking issues. When he did approach the explosive issue of the trusts, he always took care to reassure the business community. For him, politics was the art of the possible. Unlike the more advanced progressives and the doctrinaire "lunatic fringe," as he called them, he would take half a loaf rather than none at all. Roosevelt acted in large part out of the conviction that reform was needed to keep things on an even keel. He believed that control should rest in the hands of sensible Republicans, and not with irresponsible Democrats or, worse, the growing socialist movement.

EXECUTIVE ACTION   At the outset of his presidency in 1901, Roosevelt took up McKinley's policies and promised to sustain them. He worked with Republican leaders in Congress, against whom the minority of new progressives was as yet powerless. Yet Roosevelt would accomplish more by vigorous executive action than by passing legislation, and in the exercise of executive power he would not be inhibited by points of legal detail. He argued that, as president, he might do anything not expressly forbidden by the Constitution.

Caution suffused Roosevelt's first annual message, delivered in 1901, but he felt impelled to take up the trust problem in the belief that it might be more risky to ignore it. His message carefully balanced argu-

No Lack of Big Game.
*A 1905 cartoon shows
Roosevelt going after the
trusts.*

ments on both sides of the question. He endorsed the "sincere conviction that combination and concentration should be, not prohibited, but supervised and within reasonable limits controlled." The first essential was "knowledge of the facts—publicity . . . the only sure remedy we can now invoke." Later would follow regulatory legislation, perhaps based on the experience of the Interstate Commerce Commission (ICC).

In 1902 Roosevelt carried the trust issue to the people on a tour of New England and the Midwest. He endorsed a "square deal" for all, calling for enforcement of existing antitrust laws and stricter controls on big business. From the outset, however, Roosevelt believed that wholesale trust-busting was wrongheaded. Effective regulation was better than a futile effort to restore small business, which might be achieved only at a cost to the efficiencies of scale gained in larger operations.

Because Congress boggled at regulatory legislation, Roosevelt sought to force the issue by a more vigorous prosecution of the Sherman AntiTrust Act. He chose his target carefully. In the case against the sugar trust (*United States* v. *E. C. Knight and Company*, 1895), the Supreme Court had declared manufacturing a strictly intrastate activity. Railroads, however, were beyond question engaged in interstate commerce and thus subject to federal authority.

In 1902 Roosevelt ordered his attorney-general to move against the Northern Securities Company, a firm vulnerable to both the law and public opinion. That company, formed the previous year, had taken shape during a gigantic battle between E. H. Harriman of the Union Pacific and James J. Hill and J. P. Morgan of the Great Northern and Northern Pacific for the stock of the Northern Pacific, which was crucial to shipping in the Northwest. The stock battle raised the threat of a panic on the New York Stock Exchange and led to a settlement in which the chief contenders made peace. They formed Northern Securities as a holding company to control the Great Northern and Northern Pacific. In 1904 the Supreme Court ordered the railroad combination dissolved.

THE COAL STRIKE   Support for Roosevelt's use of the "big stick" against corporations was strengthened by the stubbornness of mine owners in the anthracite coal strike of 1902. On May 12 the United Mine Workers (UMW) walked off the job in Pennsylvania and West Virginia, demanding a 20 percent wage increase, a reduction in daily hours from ten to nine, and official union recognition. The mine operators, having granted a 10 percent raise two years before, dug in their heels against further concessions, and shut down in preparation for a long struggle to starve out the miners. Their spokesman, George F. Baer, the president of the Reading Railroad, helped the union cause more than his own with an arrogant pronouncement: "The rights and interests of the laboring man will be protected and cared for," he said, "not by the labor agitators, but by the Christian men to whom God in his infinite wisdom has given control of the property interests of the country."

Facing the prospect of a nationwide coal shortage, Roosevelt called a conference at the White House. The mine owners, led by Baer, attended but refused even to speak to the UMW leaders. The "extraordinary stupidity and temper" of the "wooden-headed" owners outraged Roosevelt. The president wanted to grab Baer "by the seat of his breeches" and "chuck him out" a White House window. After the conference ended in an impasse, Roosevelt threatened to take over the mines and run them with the army. When a congressman questioned the constitutionality of such a move, an exasperated Roosevelt roared: "To hell with the Constitution when the people want coal!" Militarizing the mines would have been an act of dubious legality, but the owners feared that Roosevelt might actually do it and that public opinion would support him.

The coal strike ended in October 1902 with an agreement to submit the issues to an arbitration commission named by the president. The agreement enhanced Roosevelt's prestige, although it produced only a partial victory for the miners. By the arbitrators' decision in 1903, the miners won a nine-hour day but only a 10 percent wage increase, and no union recognition.

TOWARD A SECOND TERM   Roosevelt continued to use his execu-tive powers to enforce the Sherman Anti-Trust Act, but he drew back from further antitrust legislation. Altogether his administration initiated about twenty-five antitrust suits; the most notable victory came in *Swift and Company* v. *United States* (1905), a decision against the "beef trust" through which most of the meat packers had avoided competitive bid-ding in the purchase of livestock. In this decision, the Supreme Court put forth the "stream-of-commerce" doctrine, which overturned its pre-vious holding that manufacturing was strictly intrastate. Since both livestock and the meat products of the packers moved in the stream of interstate commerce, the Court reasoned, they were subject to federal regulation. This interpretation of the interstate commerce power would be broadened in later years until few enterprises would remain beyond the reach of federal regulation.

In 1903 Congress passed the Elkins Act, which made it illegal to take as well as to give rebates. In that same year, Congress created a new Bu-reau of Corporations to study and report on the activities of interstate corporations. Its findings could lead to antitrust suits, but its purpose was rather to help corporations correct malpractices and avoid the need for lawsuits. Many companies, among them United States Steel and In-ternational Harvester, worked closely with the bureau, but others held back. When Standard Oil refused to turn over its records, the govern-ment brought an antitrust suit that resulted in its breakup in 1911. The Supreme Court broke up the American Tobacco Company at the same time. This approach fell short of the direct regulation that Roosevelt preferred, but without a congressional will to pass such laws, little more was possible. Trusts that cooperated were left alone; others had to run the gauntlet of antitrust suits.

Theodore Roosevelt as an apostle of prosperity (top) and as a Roman tyrant (bottom). Roosevelt's energy, spirit, righteousness, and impulsiveness led people to have distinct reactions to his personality.

Roosevelt's policies built a coalition of progressive- and conservative-minded voters that assured his election in his own right in 1904. The convention chose him by acclamation. The Democrats, having lost with Bryan twice, turned to Alton B. Parker who, as chief justice of New York, had upheld labor's right to the closed shop (requiring that all employees be union members) and the state's right to limit hours of work. Despite his liberal record, party leaders presented him as a safe conservative, and his acceptance of the gold standard as "firmly and irrevocably established" bolstered such a view. The effort to present a candidate more conservative than Roosevelt proved a futile gesture for the party that had twice nominated Bryan. Despite Roosevelt's trust-busting proclivities, most businessmen, according to the *New York Sun,* preferred the "impulsive candidate of the party of conservatism to the conservative candidate of the party which the business interests regard as permanently and dangerously impulsive." Even J. P. Morgan and E. H. Harriman contributed handsomely to Roosevelt's campaign chest.

An invincible popularity plus the sheer force of his personality swept Roosevelt to an impressive victory by a popular vote of 7.6 million to 5.1 million. Parker carried only the Solid South of the former Confederacy and two border states, Kentucky and Maryland (with an electoral vote of 336 for Roosevelt and 140 for Parker). On election night, Roosevelt announced that he would not run again, a statement he later would regret.

LEGISLATIVE LEADERSHIP   Elected in his own right, Roosevelt approached his second term with heightened confidence and a stronger commitment to progressive reform. In 1905 he devoted most of his annual message to the regulation and control of business. This understandably irked many of his corporate contributors. Said steel baron Henry Frick, "We bought the son of a bitch and then he did not stay put." The independent-minded Roosevelt took aim at the railroads first. The Elkins Act of 1903, finally outlawing rebates, had been a minor step. Railroad executives themselves welcomed it as an escape from shippers clamoring for special favors. But a new proposal for railroad regulation endorsed by Roosevelt was something else again. It sought to extend the authority of the ICC and give it effective control over rates.

Enacted in 1906, the Hepburn Act for the first time gave the ICC power to set maximum freight rates. The commission no longer had to go to court to enforce its decisions. While the carriers could challenge the rates in court, the burden of proof now rested on them rather than on the Interstate Commerce Commission. In other ways, too, the Hepburn Act enlarged the mandate of the ICC. Its reach now extended beyond railroads to pipelines, express companies, sleeping-car companies, bridges, and ferries, and it could prescribe a uniform system of bookkeeping to provide uniform statistics.

Railroads took priority, but a growing movement for the regulation of meat packers, food processors, and makers of drugs and patent medicines reached fruition, as it happened, on the very day after passage of the Hepburn Act. Discontent with abuses in these fields had grown rapidly as a result of the muckrakers' revelations. They supplied evidence of harmful preservatives and adulterants in the preparation of "embalmed meat" and other food products. The *Ladies' Home Journal* and *Collier's* published evidence of false claims and dangerous ingredients in patent medicines. One of the more notorious "medicines," Lydia Pinkham's Vegetable Compound, was advertised to work wonders in the relief of "female complaints"; it was no wonder, for the compound was 18 percent alcohol.

But perhaps the most telling blow against such abuses was struck by

Muckraking reports on fraudulent drugs and patent medicines, such as Lydia Pinkham's Vegetable Compound, prompted a growing movement for government regulation.

Upton Sinclair's novel *The Jungle* (1906). Sinclair meant the book to be a tract for socialism, but its main impact came from its portrayal of filthy conditions in Chicago's meat-packing industry: "It was too dark in these storage places to see well, but a man could run his hand over these piles of meat and sweep off handfuls of the dried dung of rats. These rats were nuisances, and the packers would put poisoned bread out for them, they would die, and then rats, bread, and meat would go into the hoppers together." Roosevelt read *The Jungle*—and reacted quickly. He sent two agents to Chicago, and their report confirmed all that Sinclair had said: "We saw meat shovelled from filthy wooden floors, piled on tables rarely washed, pushed from room to room in rotten box carts, in all of which processes it was in the way of gathering dirt, splinters, floor filth, and the expectoration of tuberculous and other diseased workers."

The Meat Inspection Act of 1906 required federal inspection of meats destined for interstate commerce and empowered officials in the Agriculture Department to impose sanitation standards. The Pure Food and Drug Act, enacted the same day, placed restrictions on the makers of prepared foods and patent medicines, and forbade the manufacture, sale, or transportation of adulterated, misbranded, or harmful foods, drugs, and liquors.

CONSERVATION   One of the most enduring legacies of the Roosevelt years was his energetic support for the conservation movement. Concern for protecting the environment grew with the rising awareness that exploitation of natural resources was despoiling the frontier. As early as 1872, Yellowstone National Park had been set aside as a public reserve (the National Park Service would be created in 1916 after other parks had been added). In 1881 Congress had created a Division of Forestry in the Department of Agriculture, and Roosevelt's appointment of Gifford Pinchot, one of the country's first scientific foresters, as chief brought vigorous administration of forests on public lands. The president strove to halt the unchecked destruction of the nation's natural resources and wonders by providing a barrier of federal regulation and protection. To do so, Roosevelt added fifty federal wildlife refuges, approved five new national parks, and initiated the system of designating national monuments such as the Grand Canyon. He also used the Forest Reserve Act (1891) to exclude from settlement or harvest some 172

Gifford Pinchot, chief of the Forestry Service under Roosevelt.

million acres of timberland. Lumber barons were irate, but Roosevelt held firm. As he bristled, "I hate a man who would skin the land."

Forestry chief Pinchot worked vigorously, with the president's support, to develop programs and public interest in conservation. Congressional resistance to their proposals led Pinchot and Roosevelt to publicize the cause through a White House Conference on Conservation in 1908, and later that year by setting up a National Conservation Commission, which proposed a thorough survey of resources in minerals, water, forests, and soil. Within eighteen months, some forty-one state conservation commissions had sprung up, and a number of private groups took up the cause. The movement remained divided, however, between those who wanted to conserve resources for continuous human use and those who wanted to set aside wilderness areas. Pinchot, for instance, won the enmity of naturalist John Muir in 1906 when he endorsed a water reservoir in the wild Hetch Hetchy Valley of Yosemite National Park to supply the needs of San Francisco.

FROM ROOSEVELT TO TAFT

In 1908 Roosevelt declared "I have had a great time as president" and prepared to turn over the mantle. Unlike most presidents, he was strong enough to handpick a successor to carry out "the policies." He decided that the heir to the White House should be Secretary of War William Howard Taft, and the Republican convention ratified the choice on its first ballot in 1908. The Democrats, whose conservative strategy had backfired in 1904, decided to give William Jennings Bryan one more chance at the highest office. Still vigorous at forty-eight, Bryan retained a faithful following, but once again it was not enough. Roosevelt advised Taft: "Do not answer Bryan; *attack* him. Don't let him make the issues." Taft followed Roosevelt's advice, declaring that Bryan's election would result in a "paralysis of business."

The Republican platform declared its support of Roosevelt's policies, including conservation and further strengthening of the ICC. On the tariff and the use of labor injunctions, the platform made vague references to revision but without any specifics. The Democratic platform hardly differed on regulation, but it endorsed a lower tariff and an AFL-supported plank opposing court injunctions against labor actions. In the end, the voters opted for Roosevelt's chosen successor: Taft swept the electoral college by 321 to 162. The real surprise of the election, however, was the strong showing of the Socialist party candidate, labor hero Eugene V. Debs. His 421,000 votes revealed the depth of working-class resentment in the United States.

Once out of office, still only fifty, Roosevelt went on a big-game hunt in Africa, prompting his old foe J. P. Morgan to mutter, "Let every lion do his duty." The new president he left behind was an entirely different kind of political animal, in fact hardly a political animal at all. Offspring of a family long prominent in Cincinnati—his father had been Grant's attorney-general—Taft had progressed through appointive offices, from judge in Ohio to solicitor in the Justice Department, federal judge, commissioner and governor-general in the Philippines, and secretary of war. The presidency was the only elective office he ever held. Later he would be chief justice (1921–1930), a job more suited to his temperament.

Weighing over 300 pounds, Taft had the dubious distinction of being the heaviest president in history. When he cabled a friend that he had just returned from a long horseback ride, the friend asked, "How is the horse?" Taft loved eating and playing golf or poker, but he detested politics. Taft never felt comfortable in the White House. He once observed that whenever someone said "Mr. President," he looked around for Roosevelt. The political dynamo in the family was his wife, Nellie, who had

William Howard Taft.

wanted the White House more than he. One of the major tragedies of Taft's presidency was that Helen "Nellie" Taft suffered a debilitating stroke soon after they entered the White House, and for most of his term she remained unable to serve as his political adviser.

DOLLAR DIPLOMACY   In foreign affairs Taft practiced what critics labeled "dollar diplomacy." The policy had its origin in China in 1909, when President Taft personally cabled the Chinese government on behalf of American financiers interested in an international consortium to finance railroad lines in the Yangtze Valley. The American government regarded such cooperation "as best calculated to maintain the Open Door and the integrity of China." In 1911 the Americans were let in on the deal with British, French, and German capitalists, and in 1912 entered an even larger scheme to make a gigantic loan to the new Chinese Republic. Both schemes were repudiated, however, when Woodrow Wilson became president in 1913, and the American investors, lacking support from the government, withdrew.

In Latin America "dollar diplomacy" worked differently and with somewhat more success. The idea was to encourage American bankers to help prop up the finances of shaky governments in the Caribbean region. In 1910 the administration got several lenders to invest in the national bank of Haiti. In 1911 it signed treaties with Nicaragua and Honduras providing them with private loans to bolster their treasuries and ensuring payment by installing American collectors of customs. The Senate refused to go along with the treaties, but the administration continued its private appeals for American bankers to assume debts in the region.

In 1912, however, when the Nicaraguan president asked for help in putting down disorders, American marines entered the country. An American collector of customs was then installed and the government was placed on a monthly allowance doled out by a commission of two Americans and one Nicaraguan. American forces stayed until 1925, then returned in 1926 to stay until 1933. Similar forcible interventions occurred in Haiti in 1915 and the Dominican Republic in 1916.

TARIFF REFORM   Taft's domestic policies generated a storm of controversy within his own party. Contrary to Republican tradition, he preferred a lower tariff, and he made this the first important issue of his presidency. But if in pressing an issue that Roosevelt had skirted Taft seemed the bolder of the two, he proved the less adroit.

A tariff bill passed the House with surprising ease. It lowered rates less than Taft would have preferred but made some important reductions and enlarged the free list. But the chairman of the Senate Finance Committee, Nelson W. Aldrich, guided through a bill drastically revised by more than 800 changes. What came out of a conference committee was a measure close to the final Senate version, although Taft did get some reductions on important items: hides, iron ore, coal, oil, cottons, boots, and shoes.

In response to the higher rates in Aldrich's bill, a group of midwestern Republicans took the Senate floor to fight what they considered a corrupt throwback to the days when the Republican party had served big business unquestioningly. In all, ten progressive Republicans joined the Democrats in an unsuccessful effort to defeat the bill. Taft at first agreed with them; then, fearful of a party split, he backed the majority and agreed to an imperfect bill. He lacked Roosevelt's love of a grand battle as well as his gift for working both sides of the street. Temperamentally conservative, inhibited by scruples about interfering too much with the legislative process, he drifted into the orbit of the Republican Old Guard and quickly alienated the progressive wing of his party, whom he tagged "assistant Democrats." He made things worse by labeling the new bill the best tariff the Republican party had ever passed.

BALLINGER AND PINCHOT   In 1910 Taft's policies drove the wedge deeper between the Republican factions. What came to be called the Ballinger-Pinchot controversy made Taft appear to be a less reliable custodian of Roosevelt's conservation policies than he actually was. Taft's secretary of the interior, Richard A. Ballinger of Seattle, was well aware that many westerners opposed conservation programs on the ground that they held back full development of the region. The strongest conservation leaders were often easterners such as Roosevelt and Gifford Pinchot of Pennsylvania. Ballinger threw open to commercial use more than a million acres of waterpower sites that Roosevelt had withdrawn in the guise of ranger stations. Ballinger's reasoning was that the withdrawal had "gone far beyond legal limitations," and Taft agreed. At about the same time, Ballinger turned over certain coal lands in Alaska to a group of Seattle men, some of whom he had represented as a lawyer. Apparently without Ballinger's knowledge, this group had already agreed to sell part of the lands to a banking syndicate.

This was too much for one investigator with the General Land Office, who went to Chief of Forestry Pinchot with evidence of the collusion. Pinchot in turn called it to the attention of Taft, who then fired the investigator for his pains. When Pinchot went public with the controversy, he in turn was fired for insubordination early in 1910. A joint congressional investigation exonerated Ballinger from all charges of fraud or corruption, but progressive suspicions created such pressure that he resigned in 1911.

In firing Pinchot, Taft acted on the strictly legal view that his training had taught him to value, but circumstances tarnished his image in the public mind. "In the end," one historian has written, "the Ballinger-Pinchot affair had more impact on politics than it did on conservation." Taft had been elected to carry out the Roosevelt policies, his opponents said, and he was carrying them out—"on a stretcher."

Meanwhile, in the House of Representatives rebellion had broken out among the more progressive Republicans. When the regular session opened in 1910, the insurgents joined Democrats in voting to investigate Ballinger. Flushed with that victory, they resolved to clip the wings of Speaker Joseph G. Cannon (R-Ill.), a conservative who held almost a stranglehold on procedures by his power to appoint all committees and their chairmen, and especially by his control of the Rules Committee, of which he was a member. A coalition of Democrats and progressive Republicans overrode a ruling from the Speaker and proceeded to adopt new rules offered by George W. Norris (R-Neb.) that enlarged the Rules Committee from five to fifteen members, made them elective by the House, and excluded the Speaker as a member. About forty Republicans joined the Democratic minority in the move. In the next Congress the rules would be further changed to make all committees elective.

Events had conspired to cast Taft in a conservative role at a time when progressive sentiment was riding high in the country. The result was a severe rebuke to the president in the congressional elections of 1910, first by the widespread defeat of pro-Taft candidates in the Republican primaries, then by the election of a Democratic majority in the House and of enough Democrats in the Senate that progressive Republicans could wield the balance of power.

TAFT AND ROOSEVELT   In 1910 Roosevelt had returned from his travel abroad. He had been reading news accounts and letters about the Taft "betrayal," but unlike some of his supporters, he refused to break with his successor. With rather severe politeness, however, Roosevelt refused an invitation to visit the White House. But, he wrote Taft: "I shall keep my mind open as I keep my mouth shut." Neither was easy for Roosevelt, whose followers urged him to action. Soon he was rallying support for the Republican gubernatorial candidate in New York, and then he was off on a speaking tour of the West in advance of the congressional elections. In Kansas, he gave a catchy name to his latest principles, the "New Nationalism." Roosevelt issued a stirring call for an array of new federal regulatory laws, a social-welfare program, and new measures of direct democracy, including the old Populist demands for the initiative, recall, and referendum. His purpose was not to revolutionize American life but to save it from the threat of revolution. "What I have advocated," he explained a few days later, "is not wild radicalism. It is the highest and wisest kind of conservatism."

Relations between Roosevelt and Taft remained tense, but it was another year before they came to an open break. It happened in the fall of 1911, when the Taft administration announced an antitrust suit against

United States Steel, citing specifically as cause the company's acquisition of the Tennessee Coal and Iron Company in 1907, a move to which Roosevelt had given tacit approval in the belief that it would avert a panic. In mid-November Roosevelt published a sharp attack on Taft's "archaic" attempt to restore competition. The only sensible response to the problem, he argued, was to accept business combinations under modern circumstances but to enlarge the government's power to regulate them. Roosevelt's entry into the next presidential campaign was now only a matter of time.

Not all progressive Republicans wanted Roosevelt back in the White House. A sizable number proposed to back Senator Robert La Follette in 1912, but some of La Follette's supporters were ready to switch if Roosevelt entered the race. An opening came on February 2, 1912, when La Follette betrayed signs of nervous exhaustion in a rambling speech in Philadelphia. As his following began to drop away, a group of seven Republican governors met in Chicago and called on Roosevelt to become a candidate. On February 24 Roosevelt decided to enter the race. "I hope that so far as possible the people may be given the chance, through direct primaries," Roosevelt wrote the governors, "to express their preference." He had decided that Taft had "sold the Square Deal down the river." He now dismissed Taft as a "hopeless fathead."

The rebuke implicit in Roosevelt's decision to run against Taft, his chosen successor, was in many ways undeserved. During Taft's first year in office one political tempest after another left his image irreparably damaged. The three years of solid achievement that followed came too late to restore its luster or to reunite his divided party. Taft had at least attempted tariff reform, which Roosevelt had never dared. He replaced Ballinger and Pinchot with men of impeccable credentials in conservation matters. He won from Congress the power to protect public lands for any reason, and was the first president to withdraw oil lands from use. Under the Appalachian Forest Reserve Act (1911), he enlarged the national forest by purchase of lands in the East. In the end his administration withdrew more public lands in four years than Roosevelt's had in nearly eight, and brought more antitrust suits, by a score of eighty to twenty-five.

In 1910, with Taft's support, Congress passed the Mann-Elkins Act, which empowered the ICC for the first time to initiate rate changes, extended regulation to telephone and telegraph companies, and set up a

Commerce Court to expedite appeals from the ICC rulings. Taft also established the Bureau of Mines and the Federal Children's Bureau (1912), and he called for statehood for Arizona and New Mexico and territorial government for Alaska (1912). The Sixteenth Amendment (1913), authorizing a federal income tax, was ratified with Taft's support before he left office, and the Seventeenth Amendment (1913), providing for the popular election of senators, was ratified soon after he left office.

Despite this record, Roosevelt now hastened Taft's demise. In all but two of the thirteen states that held presidential primaries, Roosevelt won, even in Taft's Ohio. But the groundswell of popular support was no match for Taft's decisive position as president and party leader. In state conventions the party regulars held the line, so that Roosevelt entered the Republican national convention about 100 votes short of victory. The Taft forces proceeded to nominate their man by the same "steamroller" tactics that had nominated Roosevelt in 1904.

Outraged at such "naked theft," the Roosevelt delegates assembled in a rump convention. "If you wish me to make the fight I will make it," Roosevelt told the delegates, who then issued a call for a Progressive party convention, which assembled in Chicago on August 5. Roosevelt appeared, feeling "fit as a bull moose." He was "stripped to the buff and

A skeptical view of Roosevelt, the Bull Moose candidate in 1912.

ready for the fight," he said. "We stand at Armageddon and we battle for the Lord." But few professional politicians turned up. Progressive Republicans decided to preserve their party credentials and fight another day. For the time being, with the disruption of the Republican party, the progressive torch was about to be passed on to the Democrats.

WILSON'S PROGRESSIVISM

WILSON'S RISE   The emergence of Thomas Woodrow Wilson as the Democratic nominee climaxed a political rise even more rapid than that of Grover Cleveland. In 1910, before his nomination and election as governor of New Jersey, Wilson had been president of Princeton University, but he had never run for public office. Born in Staunton, Virginia, in 1856, the son of a "noble-saintly mother" and a stern Presbyterian minister, he had grown up in Georgia and the Carolinas during the Civil War and Reconstruction.

Young Wilson, tall, slender, with a lean, long, sharply chiseled face, inherited his father's unquestioning piety, once declaring that "so far as religion is concerned, argument is adjourned." Wilson also developed a consuming ambition to "serve" humankind. Driven by a sense of destiny and duty, as well as by a certain moral fastidiousness, he once confessed: "I am too intense." Wilson nurtured a righteous commitment to principle that would prove to be his Achilles' heel.

Wilson graduated from Princeton in 1879, and after law school at the University of Virginia tried a brief, unfulfilling, and profitless legal practice in Atlanta. From there he went to the new Johns Hopkins University in Baltimore, where he found his calling in the study of history and political science.

Wilson's dissertation, *Congressional Government*, published in 1885, argued that the president, like the British prime minister, should be the leader of party government, as active in directing legislation as in the administration and enforcement of laws. In calling for a strong presidency he expressed views closer to those of Roosevelt than those of Taft. He also shared Roosevelt's concern that politicians should promote the general welfare rather than narrowly serve special interests. And, like Roosevelt, he was critical of big business, organized labor, socialists, and agrarian radicalism.

After Johns Hopkins, Wilson taught at Bryn Mawr and then Wesleyan College before moving to Princeton in 1890. There he quickly earned renown for his scintillating lectures, vigorous mind, and sharp debating skills. In 1902 he was unanimously elected president of the university. In that position he showed the first evidence of reform views. "We are not put into this world to sit still and know," he stressed in his inaugural address. "We are put into it to act." And act he did.

At Princeton Wilson modernized the curriculum, expanded and improved the faculty, introduced the tutorial system, and raised admissions standards. But he failed in his attempts to restructure the social life of Princeton undergraduates and to integrate the new graduate school with the university. He believed that the deeply entrenched system of campus eating clubs (similar to fraternities) was undemocratic, anti-intellectual, and divisive. Wilson proposed to replace the exclusive clubs with residential colleges, or quadrangles, where students would live under the supervision of unmarried faculty members. Unaware of the volatility of this issue, he failed to consult alumni, faculty, and trustees before announcing his intentions. The result was a firestorm of criticism that forced Wilson to withdraw his proposal. In a similar fashion, he failed to marshal a consensus for his proposals regarding the location of the new graduate school. He wanted it integrated with the undergraduate college; others wanted it completely separate. The dean opposed him and won the battle by gaining strong alumni backing. Thereafter Wilson faced a choice of giving up or leaving.

At this juncture, the Democratic boss of New Jersey offered Wilson his support for the 1910 gubernatorial nomination, and Wilson accepted. The party leaders sought a respectable candidate to ward off progressive challengers, but they discovered too late that the supposedly innocent schoolmaster actually had an iron will of his own. Like Roosevelt, Wilson had come to shed some of his original conservatism and to view progressive reform as a necessary expedient in order to stave off more radical social change. Elected as a reform candidate, Governor Wilson promoted progressive measures and pushed them through the legislature. He pressured lawmakers to enact a workers' compensation law, a corrupt-practices law, measures to regulate public utilities, and ballot reforms. Such strong leadership in a state known as the "home of the trusts" for its lenient corporation laws brought Wilson to national attention.

Wilson campaigning from a train platform.

In the spring of 1911 a group of southern Democrats in New York opened a Wilson presidential campaign headquarters, and Wilson set forth on strenuous tours into all regions of the country, denouncing special privilege and political bossism. But by convention time, despite a fast start, the Wilson campaign seemed headed for defeat by Speaker Bennett Champ Clark of Missouri, who garnered supporters among Bryanites, the Hearst newspapers, and party hacks. Clark had enough for a majority in the early ballots, but the Wilson forces combined with supporters of Oscar Underwood of Alabama to prevent a two-thirds majority. On the fourteenth ballot Bryan came over to Wilson. When the Democratic boss of Illinois deserted Clark on the forty-second ballot and the Underwood delegates went over to Wilson on the forty-sixth, he clinched the nomination.

THE ELECTION OF 1912   The 1912 campaign involved four candidates: Wilson and Taft represented the two major parties while Eugene Debs ran as a Socialist and Roosevelt headed the Progressive party ticket. No sooner did the formal campaign open than Roosevelt's candidacy almost ended. While entering a car on his way to deliver a speech in Milwaukee, he was shot by a fanatic. The bullet went through Roosevelt's overcoat, spectacles case, and folded speech, then fractured a rib before lodging just below his right lung. "Stand back, don't hurt the man," he yelled at the crowd as they mobbed the attacker. Roosevelt then demanded that he be driven to the auditorium to deliver his speech. His dramatic sense unhampered, he showed the audience his bloodstained shirt and punctured text and vowed: "It takes more than this to kill a bull moose." He apologized for his halting delivery, but completed his speech before letting doctors remove the bullet.

As the campaign developed, Taft quickly lost ground. "There are so many people in the country who don't like me," he lamented. The campaign settled down to a running debate over the competing ideologies of the two front-runners: Roosevelt's "New Nationalism" and Wilson's "New Freedom." The inchoate ideas that Roosevelt fashioned into his New Nationalism had first been presented systematically in *The Promise of American Life* (1909) by Herbert Croly, a then-obscure New York journalist. Its central point was often summarized in a useful catchphrase: Hamiltonian means to achieve Jeffersonian ends, meaning that Alexander Hamilton's program of governmental intervention, once identified with the business interests, should be used to achieve democratic and egalitarian Jeffersonian goals. The times required people to give up Jeffersonian prejudices against big government and use a strong central government to achieve democratic ends in the interest of the people.

The old nationalism had been used "by the sinister . . . special interests," Roosevelt said. His New Nationalism would enable government to achieve social justice, and more specifically to effect such reforms as graduated income and inheritance taxes, workers' compensation, regulation of the labor of women and children, and a stronger Bureau of Corporations. These and more went into the platform of the Progressive party, which called for a federal trade commission with sweeping authority over business and a tariff commission to set rates on a "scientific basis."

Before the end of his administration, Wilson would be swept into the current of New Nationalism too. But initially he adhered to the decentralizing antitrust traditions of his party. Before the start of the campaign Wilson conferred with Louis D. Brandeis, a progressive lawyer from Boston who focused Wilson's thought much as Croly had focused Roosevelt's. Brandeis's design for the New Freedom differed from Roosevelt's New Nationalism in its belief that the federal government should restore the competition among small economic units rather than regulate huge monopolies. This required a vigorous antitrust policy,

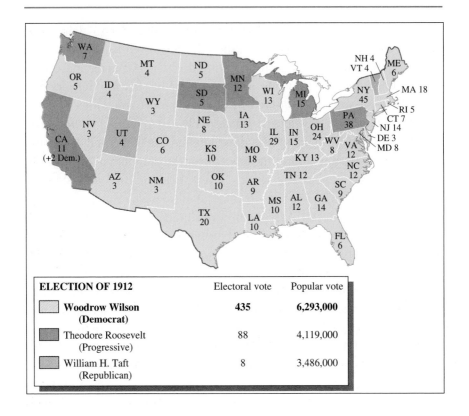

ELECTION OF 1912	Electoral vote	Popular vote
Woodrow Wilson (Democrat)	**435**	**6,293,000**
Theodore Roosevelt (Progressive)	88	4,119,000
William H. Taft (Republican)	8	3,486,000

lowering tariffs to allow competition with foreign goods, and breaking up the concentration of financial power in Wall Street. But Brandeis and Wilson saw the vigorous expansion of federal power as only a temporary necessity, not a permanent condition. Roosevelt, who was convinced that both corporate concentration and an expanding federal government were permanent developments, dismissed the New Freedom as mere fantasy.

The Republican schism between Taft and Roosevelt opened the way for Woodrow Wilson to win by 435 electoral votes to 88 for Roosevelt and 8 for Taft. But in popular votes, Wilson had only 42 percent of the total. Roosevelt received 27 percent, Taft 23 percent, and Debs 6 percent. It was the victory of a minority over a divided opposition. Taft took his loss with grace. When Yale University offered him the Kent Chair of Constitutional Law, the rotund ex-president accepted, noting, however, that a "Sofa of Law" might be more appropriate. In 1921 President

Harding appointed Taft to the Supreme Court, and he served with distinction as chief justice until his death in 1930.

The election of 1912 was significant in several ways. First, it was a high-water mark for progressivism. The election was the first to feature presidential primaries. The two leading candidates debated the basic issues of progressivism in a campaign unique for its focus on vital alternatives and for its high philosophical tone. Taft, too, despite his temperament and associations, showed his own progressive instincts. And the Socialist party, the left wing of progressivism, polled over 900,000 votes for Eugene V. Debs, its highest proportion ever.

Second, the election gave Democrats effective national power for the first time since the Civil War. For two years during the second Cleveland administration, 1893–1895, they had held the White House and majorities in both houses of Congress, but they had fallen quickly out of power during the most severe depression in American history to that time. Now, under Wilson, they again held the presidency and were the majority in both the House of Representatives and the Senate.

Third, the election of Wilson brought southerners back into the orbit of national and international affairs in a significant way for the first time since the Civil War. In Washington, one reporter said, "you feel it in the air . . . you listen to evidence of it in the mellow accent with which the South makes our English a musical tongue." Wilson himself once reported that "the only place in the world where nothing has to be explained to me is the South." Five of his ten cabinet members were born in the South, three still resided there, and William Jennings Bryan, the secretary of state, was an idol of the southern masses. At the president's right hand, and one of the most influential members of the Wilson circle, at least until 1919, was Colonel Edward M. House of Texas. On Capitol Hill southerners, by virtue of their seniority, held the lion's share of committee chairmanships. As a result, much of the progressive legislation of the Wilson era would bear the names of the southerners who guided it through Congress.

Fourth and finally, the election of 1912 had begun to alter the character of the Republican party. Even though most party professionals remained, the defection of the Bull Moose Progressives had weakened the party's progressive wing. The leader of the Republican party that would return to power in the 1920s would be more conservative in tone and temperament.

WILSONIAN REFORM   Wilson's inaugural address voiced in eloquent tones the ideals of social justice that animated many progressives. "We have been proud of our industrial achievements," he said, "but we have not hitherto stopped thoughtfully enough to count the human cost . . . the fearful physical and spiritual cost to the men and women and children upon whom the dead weight and burden of it all has fallen pitilessly the years through." He promised specifically a lower tariff and a new banking system. "This is not a day of triumph; it is a day of dedication. Here muster, not the forces of party, but the forces of humanity."

If Roosevelt had been a strong president by force of personality, Wilson became a strong president by force of conviction. The president, he wrote in *Congressional Government,* "is . . . the political leader of the nation, or has it in his choice to be. The nation as a whole has chosen him, and is conscious that it has no other political spokesman. His is the only national voice in affairs."

Wilson courted popular support, but he also courted members of Congress through personal contacts, invitations to the White House, and visits to the Capitol. He used patronage power to reward friends and punish enemies. He might have acted through a progressive coalition, but chose instead to rely on party loyalty. "I'd rather trust a machine Senator when he is committed to your program," he told his navy secretary, "than a talking Liberal who can never quite go along with others because of his admiration of his own patented plan of reform." Wilson therefore made use of the party caucus, in which disagreements among Democrats were settled.

THE TARIFF   Wilson's leadership faced its first big test on the issue of tariff reform. He summoned Congress into special session and addressed it in person—the first president to do so since John Adams. (Roosevelt was said to have asked, "Why didn't I think of that?") Congress acted vigorously on tariff reductions. Only four Democrats bolted the party line as the new bill passed the House easily.

The crunch came in the Senate, the traditional graveyard of tariff reform. Swarms of lobbyists got so thick in Washington, Wilson said, that "a brick couldn't be thrown without hitting one of them." The president turned the tables with a public statement that focused the spotlight on the "industrious and insidious" tariff lobby. "It is of serious interest to the country," he said, "that the people at large should have no lobby and

"A Near-Futurist Painting." The sponsors of the Underwood-Simmons Tariff look on as Wilson takes the lead on the tariff issue, Chicago Tribune, *April 1913.*

be voiceless in these matters, while great bodies of astute men seek to create an artificial opinion and to overcome the interests of the public for their private profit."

The Underwood-Simmons Tariff became law in 1913. It reduced import duties on 958 items, raised them on only 86, and left 307 the same. It lowered the overall average duty from about 37 percent to about 29 percent. A free list of some 300 items, about 100 of them new to the list, included important consumer goods and raw materials: sugar, wool, iron ore, steel rails, agricultural implements, cement, coal, wood and wood pulp, and many farm products. The act lowered tariffs but raised internal revenues with the first income tax levied under the newly ratified Sixteenth Amendment: 1 percent on incomes over $3,000 ($4,000 for married couples) and a surtax graduated from 1 percent on incomes of about $20,000 to 6 percent on incomes above $500,000. The highest total tax rate thus would be 7 percent.

THE FEDERAL RESERVE   Before the new tariff had cleared the Senate, the administration proposed the first major banking and currency reform since the Civil War. The Glass-Owen Federal Reserve Act of 1913 created a new banking system, with regional reserve banks supervised by a central board of directors. There would be twelve Federal Reserve Banks, each owned by member banks in its district. All national banks became members; state banks and trust companies could join if

Reading the Death Warrant.
*Wilson's plan for banking and
currency reform spells the death
of the "Money Trust," according to
this cartoon.*

they wished. Each member bank had to subscribe 6 percent of its capital to the Federal Reserve Bank and deposit a portion of its reserves there, the amount depending on the size of the community.

These "bankers' banks" dealt chiefly with their members and not at all with individuals. Along with other banking functions, the chief service to member banks was to rediscount their loans, that is, to take them over in exchange for Federal Reserve Notes, which member banks might then use to make further loans. The Federal Reserve Notes in turn were based 40 percent on government gold and 60 percent on commercial and agricultural paper (the promissory notes signed by borrowers). This arrangement made it possible to expand both the money supply and bank credit in times of high business activity, or as the level of borrowing increased. A Federal Reserve Board named three of the nine members on each Reserve Bank's board (member banks chose the remaining six) and carried out general supervision, including review of the rediscount rates. These rates might be raised to fight inflation by tightening credit, or lowered to stimulate business by making credit more easily available.

This new system corrected three great defects in the previous arrangements. Now bank reserves could be pooled, affording greater security; both the currency and bank credit became more elastic; and the concentration of reserves in New York was lessened. The system represented a new departure in active governmental intervention and control in one of the most sensitive segments of the economy.

ANTITRUST LAWS   In his campaign Wilson had made trust-busting the central focus of the New Freedom. The concentration of economic power had continued to grow despite the Sherman Anti-Trust Act and the watchdog agency, the Bureau of Corporations. Wilson's solution to the problem was revision of the Sherman Act to define more explicitly what counted as "restraint of trade." He decided to make a strong Federal Trade Commission (FTC) the cornerstone of his antitrust program. Created in 1914, the five-member commission replaced Roosevelt's Bureau of Corporations and assumed new powers to define "unfair trade practices" and to issue "cease-and-desist" orders when it found evidence of unfair competition.

Having now embraced the principle of "controlled competition," Wilson seemed to lose interest in the antitrust bill drafted by Henry D. Clayton (D-Ala.) of the House Judiciary Committee, which followed the president's original idea of defining specific acts in restraint of trade. The Clayton Antitrust Act, passed in 1914, outlawed such practices as price discrimination (charging different customers different prices for the same goods), "tying" agreements that limited the right of dealers to handle the products of competing manufacturers, interlock-

Mr. Wilson Taking Charge of the School. *A cartoon depicting the professorial president taking on big business.*

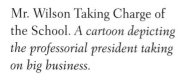

ing directorates connecting corporations with a capital of more than $1 million (or banks with more than $5 million), and corporations' acquisition of stock in competing corporations. In every case, however, conservative forces in the Senate qualified these provisions by tacking on the weakening phrase "where the effect may be to substantially lessen competition" or words of similar effect. And conservative southern Democrats and northern Republicans amended the act to allow for broad judicial review of the Federal Trade Commission's decisions, thus further weakening its freedom of action. In accordance with the president's recommendation, however, corporate officials were made individually responsible for any violations. Victims of price discrimination and tying agreements could sue for compensation equaling three times the amount of damages suffered.

Agrarian radicals, in alliance with organized labor, won a stipulation that supposedly exempted farm labor organizations from the antitrust laws, but actually only declared them not to be, per se, unlawful combinations in restraint of trade. Injunctions in labor disputes, moreover, were not to be handed down by federal courts unless "necessary to prevent irreparable injury to property." Though hailed by Samuel Gompers as labor's "Magna Carta," these provisions were actually little more than pious affirmations, as later court decisions would demonstrate. Wilson himself remarked that the act did little more than affirm the right of unions to exist by forbidding their dissolution for being in restraint of trade.

Administration of the antitrust laws generally proved disappointing to the more vehement progressives under Wilson. The president reassured business that his purposes were friendly. As his secretary of commerce put it later, Wilson hoped to "create in the Federal Trade Commission a counsellor and friend to the business world." But its first chairman lacked forcefulness, and under its next head, a Chicago industrialist, the FTC practically abandoned its function of watchdog. The Justice Department meanwhile offered help and advice to businessmen interested in arranging matters so as to avoid antitrust prosecutions. The appointment of conservative men to the Interstate Commerce Commission and the Federal Reserve won plaudits from the business world and profoundly disappointed progressives.

SOCIAL JUSTICE   Wilson had never been a strong progressive of the social-justice persuasion. He had carried out promises to lower the tariff, reorganize the banking system, and strengthen the antitrust laws. Swept along by the course of events and the pressures of more far-reaching progressives, he was pushed further than he intended to go on some points. The New Freedom was now complete, he wrote late in 1914; the future would be "a time of healing because a time of just dealing." Although Wilson endorsed state action for women's suffrage, he declined to support a suffrage amendment because his party platform had not. He withheld support from federal child-labor legislation because he regarded it as a state matter. He opposed a bill for federal support of rural credits (low-interest loans to farmers) on the ground that it was "unwise and unjustifiable to extend the credit of the government to a single class of the community."

Not until the second anniversary of his inauguration (March 4, 1915) did Wilson sign an important piece of social-justice legislation, the La Follette Seamen's Act. The product of stubborn agitation by the eloquent president of the Seamen's Union, the act strengthened safety requirements, reduced the power of captains, set minimum food standards, and required regular wage payments. Seamen who jumped ship before their contracts expired, moreover, were relieved of the charge of desertion.

PROGRESSIVISM FOR WHITES ONLY   Like many other progressives, Woodrow Wilson showed little interest in the plight of African Americans. In fact, he shared many of the racist attitudes prevalent at the time. Although Wilson denounced the Ku Klux Klan's "reign of terror," he sympathized with its motives to restore white rule in the postwar South and to relieve whites of the "ignorant and hostile" power of the black vote. As a student at Princeton, Wilson had declared that "universal suffrage is the foundation of every evil in this country." He opposed giving the vote to uneducated whites, but he detested the enfranchisement of blacks, arguing that Americans of Anglo-Saxon origin would always resist domination by "an ignorant and inferior race." He believed that white resistance to black rule was "unalterable."

Later, as a politician, Wilson courted black voters, but he rarely consulted African-American leaders and repeatedly avoided opportunities to associate with them in public. Many of the southerners he appointed to his cabinet were uncompromising racists who systematically began segregating the employees in their agencies, even though the agencies had been integrated for over fifty years. Workplaces were segregated by race, as were toilets, drinking fountains, and areas for work breaks. When black leaders protested these actions, Wilson replied that such racial segregation was intended to eliminate "the possibility of friction" in the federal workplace.

PROGRESSIVE RESURGENCE   The need to weld a winning coalition in 1916 pushed Wilson back onto the road of reform. Progressive Democrats were restless, and after war broke out in Europe in August 1914, further divisions arose over defense and foreign policy. At the same time, the Republicans were repairing their own rift, as the Progressive party showed little staying power in the midterm elections and Roosevelt showed little will to preserve it. It was plain to most observers that Wilson could shape a majority only by courting progressives of all parties. In 1916 Wilson scored points with them when he nominated Louis D. Brandeis to the Supreme Court. Conservatives waged a vigorous battle against Brandeis, but Senate progressives rallied to win confirmation of the social-justice champion, the first Jewish member of the Supreme Court.

Meanwhile Wilson began to embrace a broad program of farm and labor reforms. On farm credit, after having first opposed it he reversed himself abruptly, now supporting a proposal to set up land banks to sponsor long-term farm loans. The Federal Farm Loan Act became law in 1916. Under the control of a Federal Farm Loan Board, twelve Fed-

Louis D. Brandeis.

eral Land Banks paralleled the Federal Reserve Banks and offered farmers loans of five to forty years' duration at low interest rates.

Thus the dream of cheap rural credits, sponsored by a generation of Alliance members and Populists, came to fruition. Democrats never embraced the Populist subtreasury plan, but made a small step in that direction with the Warehouse Act of 1916. This measure authorized federal licensing of private warehouses, and federal backing made their receipts for stored produce more acceptable as collateral for short-term bank loans to farmers. Other concessions to farm demands came in the Smith-Lever Act of 1914 and the Smith-Hughes Act of 1917, both of which passed with little controversy. The first provided federal grants-in-aid for farm demonstration agents under the supervision of land-grant colleges. The measure made permanent a program that had started a decade before in Texas and that had already spread to many localities. The second measure extended agricultural and mechanical education to high schools through grants-in-aid.

Farmers with automobiles had more than a passing interest as well in the Federal Highways Act of 1916, which provided dollar-matching contributions to states with highway departments that met certain federal standards. The measure authorized distribution of $75 million over five years, and marked a sharp departure from Jacksonian opposition to internal improvements at federal expense, just as the Federal Reserve System departed from Jacksonian banking principles. Although the argument that highways were one of the nation's defense needs weakened constitutional scruples against the act, it still restricted support to "post roads" used for the delivery of mail. A renewal act in 1921 would mark the beginning of a systematic network of numbered U.S. highways.

The progressive resurgence of 1916 broke the logjam on labor reforms as well. Advocates of child-labor legislation persuaded Wilson that social-justice progressives would regard his stand on the issue as an important test of his humanitarian concerns, and Wilson overcame doubts of its constitutionality to support and sign the Keating-Owen Child Labor Act, which excluded from interstate commerce goods manufactured by children under fourteen. Both the Keating-Owen Act and a later act of 1919 to achieve the same purpose with a prohibitory tax were ruled unconstitutional by the Supreme Court on the ground that regulation of interstate commerce could not extend to the conditions of labor. Effective action against the social evil of child labor had to await the New Deal of the 1930s, although it seems likely that discussion of the issue contributed to the sharp reduction in the number of underage workers during the next few years.

Another important accomplishment was the eight-hour workday for railroad workers, a measure that the Supreme Court upheld. The Adamson Act of 1916 was brought about by a threatened strike of railroad brotherhoods demanding the eight-hour workday and other concessions. Wilson, who objected to some of the union demands, nevertheless went before Congress to request action on the hours limitation. The resulting Adamson Act required an eight-hour workday, with time and a half for overtime, and appointed a commission to study the problem of railroad labor.

In Wilson's first term progressivism reached its zenith. A creative time, the age of progressivism established at the beginning of the twentieth century a framework within which American politics and society would still function, by and large, near the end of the century. Progressivism had conquered the old dictum that the government is best which governs least, whatever political rhetoric might be heard to the contrary. Progressivism, an amalgam of agrarian, business, governmental, and social reform, amounted in the end to a movement for positive government. From two decades of ferment (three, if the Populist years are counted) the great fundamental contribution of progressive politics was the firm establishment and general acceptance of the public-service concept of the state.

THE LIMITS OF PROGRESSIVISM

The Progressive Era was an optimistic age in which reformers of various hues assumed that no problem lay beyond solution. But like all great historic movements, progressivism displayed elements of paradox and irony. Despite its talk of democracy, it was the age of disenfranchisement for southern blacks—an action seen by many whites as progressive. The initiative and referendum, supposedly democratic reforms, proved subject to manipulation by well-financed publicity campaigns. And much of the public policy of the time came to be formulated by experts and members of appointed boards, not by broad segments of the population. There is a fine irony in the fact that the drive to increase the political role of ordinary people moved parallel with efforts to strengthen executive leadership and exalt expertise. This age of efficiency and bureaucracy, in business as well as government, brought into being a society in which more and more of the decisions affecting people's lives were made by unknown policy makers.

Progressivism was largely a middle-class movement in which the poor and unorganized had little influence. The supreme irony was that a movement so dedicated to the rhetoric of democracy should experience so steady a decline in voter participation. In 1912, the year of the Bull Moose campaign, voting dropped off by between 6 and 7 percent. The new politics of issues and charismatic leaders proved to be less effective in turning out voters than party organizations and bosses had been. And by 1916 the optimism of an age that looked to infinite progress was already confronted by a vast slaughter. Europe had already stumbled into war, and America would soon be drawn in. The twentieth century, which dawned with such bright hopes, held in store episodes of unparalleled horror.

MAKING CONNECTIONS

- Many of the progressive reforms described in this chapter—particularly business regulation and the growth of the welfare state—provided the seeds for the New Deal reforms of the 1930s (Chapter 28).

- The progressive impulse carried on after World War I, but was transformed by the new political and social conditions of postwar America. Progressive reforms such as Prohibition and women's suffrage were enacted after the war, but the moralistic strain in progressivism took an ugly turn in the Red Scare and immigration restriction.

- The next chapter shows how Wilson's foreign policy in Latin America and Europe reflected the same moralism that guided his domestic policy.

FURTHER READING

A splendid introduction to the topic of progressivism can be found in Arthur S. Link and Richard L. McCormick's *Progressivism* (1983). Progressivism has been interpreted in many ways. Robert H. Wiebe's *The Search for Order, 1877–1920* (1967) presents the organizational model for reform. Richard Hofstadter's *The Age of Reform: From Bryan to F.D.R.* (1955) examines an emerging middle-class consensus as the basis of reform. Gabriel Kolko sees reform as a means of social control in *The Triumph of Conservatism* (1963). Dewey W. Grantham's *Southern Progressivism: The Reconciliation of Progress and Tradition* (1983) shows the distinctiveness of reform in that region. See also Alan Dawley's *Struggles for Justice: Social Responsibility and the Liberal State* (1991).

Biographers of the three progressive presidents elaborate on the complexity of reform. Edmund Morris's *The Rise of Theodore Roosevelt* (1979) and H. W. Brands's *T.R.: The Last Romantic* (1997) offer compelling portraits. For the Taft years, see Paolo E. Coletta's *The Presidency of William Howard Taft* (1973). Arthur S. Link's multivolume biography *Wilson* (1947–1965)—particularly *The New Freedom* (1956)—is the place to start on that president. John Milton Cooper, Jr., compares Roosevelt and Wilson in *The Warrior and the Priest* (1983).

The evolution of government policy toward business is examined in Martin J. Sklar's *The Corporate Reconstruction of American Capitalism, 1890–1916:The Market, the Law, and Politics* (1988). Roy Lubove's *The Progressives and the Slums* (1962), Mina Carson's *Settlement Folk: Social Thought and the American Settlement Movement, 1885–1930* (1990), and Jack M. Holl's *Juvenile Reform in the Progressive Era* (1971) examine the problem of urban decay.

Robert Kanigel's *The One Best Way: Frederick Winslow Taylor and the Enigma of Efficiency* (1997) highlights the role of efficiency in the Progressive Era. Samuel P. Hays's *Conservation and the Gospel of Efficiency: The Progressive Conservation Movement, 1890–1920* (rev. ed., 1969) and Harold T. Pinkett's *Gifford Pinchot: Private and Public Forester* (1970) cover conservation and the Ballinger-Pinchot controversy.

An excellent study of the role of women in progressivism's emphasis on social justice is Kathryn Kish Sklar's *Florence Kelley and the Nation's Work: The Rise of Women's Political Culture, 1830–1900* (1995).

25 ✐ AMERICA AND THE GREAT WAR

hroughout the nineteenth century, the United States reaped the benefits of its geographic distance from the wars that plagued Britain and Europe. The Atlantic Ocean provided a welcome buffer. During the early twentieth century, however, events combined to end the nation's comfortable isolation. Spectacular industrial development and ever-expanding world trade entwined American national interests with the fate of Europe. In addition, the development of steam-powered ships and submarines meant that foreign navies could threaten American security. At the same time, the election of Woodrow Wilson brought to the White House a stern moralist determined to impose his standards for right conduct on renegade nations. This combination of circumstances led the outbreak of war in Europe in 1914 to become a profound crisis for Americans, a crisis that in the end would transform the nation's role in international affairs.

WILSON AND FOREIGN AFFAIRS

Woodrow Wilson brought to the presidency little background in the study of diplomacy and none at all in its practice. The former college professor admitted as much when he remarked just before taking office, "It would be an irony of fate if my administration had to deal chiefly with foreign affairs." But events in Latin America and Europe were to make the irony all too real. From the summer of 1914, when the guns of August heralded a catastrophic world war, foreign relations increasingly overshadowed all else, including Wilson's domestic program.

AN IDEALIST'S DIPLOMACY Although lacking in international experience, Wilson did not lack ideas or convictions in this area. He saw himself as a man of destiny who would help create a new world order governed by morality and idealism rather than by crass national interests. The product of a Calvinist past, he brought to diplomacy a version of progressivism animated by righteousness. His election had put him on a course charted "by no plan of our conceiving, but by the hand of God who led us into this way." Both Wilson and his secretary of state, William Jennings Bryan, believed that America had been called to advance democracy and moral progress in the world. If they did not always follow principle at the expense of national self-interest, they did in many respects try to develop a diplomatic policy based on idealism.

During 1913–1914, Bryan negotiated some thirty "cooling-off" treaties under which participating nations pledged not to go to war over any disagreement for a period of twelve months pending discussion by an international arbitration panel. The treaties, however, were of little consequence, soon forgotten in the revolutionary sweep of world events that would make the twentieth century the bloodiest in recorded history.

One of the first applications of Wilsonian idealism to foreign policy came when the president renounced "dollar diplomacy." The government, he said, was not supporting any "special groups or interest." As good as his word, he withdrew U.S. support of the Six-Power Consortium then preparing to float a large loan to China. Such a monopolistic grant, he said, would compromise China's integrity and possibly involve the United States in a future intervention. Without governmental backing, American bankers withdrew from the project.

INTERVENTION IN MEXICO   Closer to home, Wilson found it harder to take such high ground. Nor did the logic of his "missionary diplomacy" always imply nonintervention. Mexico, which had been in the throes of revolution for nearly three years, presented a thorny problem. For most of the thirty-five years from 1876 to 1911, President Porfirio Díaz had dominated Mexico. As military dictator he had suppressed opposition and showered favors on his followers and on foreign investors, who piled up holdings in Mexican mines, petroleum, railroads, and agriculture. But eventually the dictator's hold slipped, and in 1910 popular resentment boiled over into revolt. A year later, revolutionary armies occupied Mexico City, and Díaz fled.

The leader of the rebellion, Francisco I. Madero, proved unable to manage the tough adversaries attracted by the scramble for power. In 1913 General Victoriano Huerta assumed power, and Madero was murdered soon afterward. Confronted with a military dictator ruling Mexico, Wilson enunciated a new doctrine of nonrecognition: "We hold . . . that just government rests upon the consent of the governed." Recognition, formerly extended routinely to governments that exercised *de facto* power, now might depend on judgments of their legality; an immoral government presumably would not pass muster.

General Victoriano Huerta, whose seizure of power in Mexico in 1913 aroused Wilson's opposition.

Huerta's hold on power remained unsure, and for a while Wilson resisted the impulse to intervene. In 1913 he sought to quiet fears of intervention by declaring that the United States "will never again seek one additional foot of territory by conquest." Nevertheless he obliquely expressed sympathy with the revolutionary movement and began to put diplomatic pressure on Huerta. Early in 1914 he removed an embargo on arms to Mexico in order to help the resurgent revolutionaries under Venustiano Carranza of the Constitutionalist party, and stationed warships off Veracruz to halt arms shipments to Huerta.

On April 9, 1914, several American sailors gathering supplies in Tampico strayed into a restricted area and were arrested. The local commander, a Huertista, quickly released them and sent an apology to the American naval commander. There the incident might have ended, but the naval commander demanded that the Mexicans salute the American flag. Wilson backed him up and got from Congress authority to use force to bring Huerta to terms. Before the Tampico incident could be resolved, Wilson authorized a naval force to enter Veracruz and stop the imminent landing of an arms shipment. American marines and sailors went ashore on April 21, 1914, and occupied the town at a cost of 19 killed. The Mexicans lost at least 200 killed.

In Mexico the American occupation aroused the opposition of all factions, and Huerta tried to rally support against foreign invasion. At this juncture Wilson accepted an offer of mediation by the ABC powers (Argentina, Brazil, and Chile), which proposed withdrawal of United States forces, the removal of Huerta, and installation of a provisional government sympathetic to reform. Huerta refused, but the moral effect of the proposal, his isolation abroad, and the growing strength of his foes forced him to leave office. The Carranzistas entered Mexico City, and the Americans left Veracruz in late 1914. A year later, the United States and several Latin American governments recognized Carranza as president of Mexico.

Still, the troubles south of the border continued. The prolonged disorders had spawned independent bands of bandits, Pancho Villa's among the wildest. All through 1915, fighting between the forces of Villa and Carranza continued sporadically. In 1916 Villa seized a train and murdered sixteen American mining engineers in a deliberate attempt to provoke American intervention, discredit Carranza, and build himself up as an opponent of the "Gringos." That failing, he crossed the border

Pancho Villa (center) *and his followers rebelled against the president of Mexico and antagonized the United States with violent attacks against "gringos."*

on raids into Texas and New Mexico. On March 9 he entered Columbus, New Mexico, burned the town, and killed seventeen Americans.

Wilson then had to abandon his policy of "watchful waiting." With the reluctant consent of Carranza, he sent General John J. Pershing across the border with a force of 11,000 men and mobilized 150,000 National Guardsmen along the frontier. For nearly a year Pershing went on a fruitless chase after Villa through northern Mexico and, missing his quarry, was ordered home in 1917. Carranza then pressed his own war against the bandits and put through a new liberal constitution in 1917. Mexico was by then well on the way to a more orderly government.

PROBLEMS IN THE CARIBBEAN   In the Caribbean, Wilson found it as hard to act on his ideals as in Mexico. The "dollar diplomacy" practiced by the Taft administration encouraged bankers in the United States to aid debt-plagued governments in Haiti, Guatemala, Honduras, and Nicaragua. Despite Wilson's public stand against using military force to back up American investments, he kept the marines in

Nicaragua, where they had been sent by Taft in 1912, to prevent re-newed civil war. Then in 1915 he dispatched more marines to Haiti af-ter two successive revolutions and subsequent disorders. "I suppose," Wilson told Secretary of State Bryan, "there is nothing to do but to take the bull by the horns and restore order." The American forces stayed in Haiti until 1934. Disorders in the Dominican Republic brought Ameri-can marines to that country in 1916; they remained until 1924. The presence of these additional U.S. military forces in the region only ex-acerbated the Yankee phobia among many Latin Americans. And as the *New York Times* charged, Wilson's frequent interventions made Taft's dollar diplomacy look like "ten cent diplomacy."

AN UNEASY NEUTRALITY

Problems in Latin America and the Caribbean loomed larger in Wilson's thinking than the gathering storm in Europe. When the thun-derbolt of war struck Europe in the summer of 1914, it struck most Americans, one North Carolinian wrote, "as lightning out of a clear sky." Whatever the troubles in Mexico, whatever disorders and inter-ventions agitated other countries, it seemed unreal that civilized Eu-rope could descend into such an orgy of destruction. Since the fall of Napoleon in 1815, Europe had known local wars but only as interrup-tions of a general peace that contributed to a century of unprecedented material progress.

But peace ended with the assassination in Sarajevo of Austrian arch-duke Franz Ferdinand by a Serbian nationalist. Austria-Hungary's deter-mination to punish Serbia provoked Russia to mobilize in sympathy with its Slavic friends in Serbia. This is turn triggered a European sys-tem of alliances: the Triple Alliance or Central Powers (Germany, Aus-tria-Hungary, and Italy) and the Triple Entente or Allied Powers (France, Great Britain, and Russia). When Russia refused to stop its mobilization, Germany, which backed Austria-Hungary, declared war on Russia on August 1, 1914, and on Russia's ally France two days later. Germany then invaded Belgium to get at France, which brought Great Britain into the war on August 4. Japan, eager to seize German holdings in the Pacific, declared war on August 23, and Turkey entered on the side of the Central Powers in October. Although allied with the Central

EUROPE AT WAR, 1914
- Central Powers (Triple Alliance)
- Allied Powers (Triple Entente)
- Neutral countries

Powers, Italy initially stayed out of the war, and then struck a bargain under which it joined the Allied Powers in 1915.

AMERICA'S INITIAL REACTIONS   Shock in the United States gave way to gratitude that an ocean stood between America and the battle-fields. "Our isolated position and freedom from entangling alliances," said the *Literary Digest,* "inspire our press with cheering assurance that we are in no peril of being drawn into the European quarrel." President Wilson repeatedly issued routine declarations of neutrality. He urged the American people to be "impartial in thought as well as action."

That was more easily said than done. In the 1910 population of 92 million, more than 32 million were "hyphenated Americans," first- or second-generation immigrants who retained ties to their old countries.

Among the more than 13 million from the countries at war, by far the largest group was German-American, numbering 8 million. And 4 million Irish-Americans harbored a deep-rooted enmity to England. These groups instinctively leaned toward the Central Powers.

But old-line Americans, largely of British origin, supported the Allied Powers. If, as has been said, Britain and the United States were divided by a common language, they were united by ties of culture and tradition. Americans identified also with France, which had contributed to American culture and ideas, and to independence itself. Britain and France, if not their ally Russia, seemed the custodians of democracy, while Germany more and more seemed the embodiment of autocracy and militarism. If not a direct threat to the United States, Germany would pose at least a potential threat if it destroyed the balance of power in Europe. High officers of the United States government were pro-British in thought from the outset. Robert Lansing, first counselor of the State Department, Walter Hines Page, ambassador to London, and Colonel Edward House, Wilson's close adviser, saw in German militarism a potential danger to America.

Just what effects the propaganda of the warring powers had is unclear. The Germans and the British were most active, but German propaganda, which played on American dislike of Russian autocracy and

Most Americans leaned toward the Allied Powers, but all were shocked at the outbreak of the Great War. In this cartoon, the Samson-like War pulls down the temple of Civilization.

anti-Semitism, fell mainly upon barren ground. Only German-Americans and Irish-Americans responded to a "hate England" theme. From the outset, the British had one supreme advantage in this area. Once they had cut the direct cable from Germany early in the war, nearly all news from the battlefronts had to clear through London. Highly exaggerated reports of German atrocities were convincing to Americans, and there were real atrocities enough in the German occupation of Belgium to affront American feelings.

A STRAINED NEUTRALITY   At first the war brought a slump in American exports and the threat of a depression, but by the spring of 1915 the Allies' demand for supplies generated a wartime boom. The Allies at first financed their purchases by disposing of American securities, but ultimately they needed loans. Early in the war, Secretary Bryan informed banker J. P. Morgan that loans to any warring nation were "inconsistent with the true spirit of neutrality." Money, he warned, "is the worst of all contrabands because it commands everything else." Yet Wilson quietly began approving short-term credits to sustain trade with the Allies. When in the fall of 1915 it became apparent that the Allies could no longer carry on without long-term credit, the administration removed all restrictions, and J. P. Morgan soon extended a loan of $500 million to England and France. American investors would advance over $2 billion to the Allies before the United States entered the war, and only $27 million to Germany.

The administration nevertheless clung to the fond hope of neutrality through two and a half years of warfare in Europe and tried to uphold the traditions of "freedom of the seas," which had guided American policy since the Napoleonic Wars. As the German drive through Belgium and toward Paris finally ground down into the stalemate of trench warfare, trade on the high seas assumed a new importance. In a war of attrition, survival depended on access to supplies, and in such a war British naval power counted for a great deal. With the German fleet outnumbered and bottled up almost from the outset, the war in many ways assumed the pattern that had once led America into war with Britain in 1812.

On August 6, 1914, Secretary Bryan called upon the belligerents to accept the Declaration of London, drafted and signed in 1909 by leading powers but never ratified by the British. That document, the culmination of nineteenth-century liberal thought on the rules of warfare, reduced the list of contraband items and specified that a blockade was legal only when effective just outside enemy ports. The Central Powers promptly accepted. The British almost as promptly refused, lest they lose some of their advantage in sea power. Beginning with an Order in Council of August 20, 1914, Britain gradually extended the list of contraband goods to include all sorts of things formerly excluded, such as food, cotton, wood, and certain ores. Wilson protested, but U.S. ambassador Page, personally pro-British, assured British foreign secretary Sir Edward Grey that the two could find ways of getting around the problem. The British consequently gave little serious heed to further protests.

In November 1914 the British declared the whole North Sea a war zone, sowed it with mines, and ordered neutral ships to enter only by the Strait of Dover, where they could be easily searched. In March 1915 they further announced that they would seize ships carrying goods with a presumed enemy destination, ownership, or origin. Previous policies had required search on the high seas and this, combined with Britain's new policy, caused extended delays, sometimes running into months. The same Order in Council also directed British ships to stop vessels carrying German goods via neutral ports. When the State Department protested, Grey reminded the Americans that this was the same doctrine of continuous voyage on which the United States had acted in the 1860s to keep British goods out of the Confederacy.

NEUTRAL RIGHTS AND SUBMARINES   British actions, including blacklisting of American companies that traded with the enemy and censorship of the mails, raised some old issues of neutral rights, but the German reaction introduced an entirely new question. With the German fleet bottled up by the British blockade, few surface vessels could venture out to harass the enemy. On February 4, 1915, in response to the "illegal" British blockade, the German government proclaimed a war zone around the British Isles. Enemy merchant ships in those waters were liable to sinking by submarines, the Germans declared, "although it may not always be possible to save crews and passengers." As the chief advantage of U-boat (*Unterseeboot*) warfare was in surprise, it violated the established procedure of stopping enemy vessels on the high seas and providing for the safety of passengers and crews before

Americans were outraged when a German torpedo sank the Lusitania *on May 7, 1915.*

sinking the vessel. Since the British sometimes flew neutral flags as a ruse, neutral ships in the zone would also be in danger.

The United States pronounced the German policy "an indefensible violation of neutral rights" and warned that Germany would be held to "strict accountability" for any destruction of American lives and property. If the meaning of the phrase was unclear, the stern tone of the note was unmistakable. On March 28, 1915, one American drowned when the Germans sank the British steamer *Falaba* in the Irish Sea. On May 1 the American tanker *Gulflight* went down with a loss of two lives. The administration was divided on the proper course of action. Bryan wanted to say that American citizens entered the war zone at their own risk; his counselor, Robert Lansing, and Colonel House wanted a possible break in diplomatic relations with Germany. Then, as Wilson pondered the alternatives, the sinking of the British Cunard liner *Lusitania* provoked a crisis.

On May 7, 1915, the captain of the German submarine U-20 sighted a four-stack liner moving slowly through the Irish Sea and fired a torpedo. It hit the mark, and the ship exploded and sank within a few minutes. Only as it tipped into the waves was he able to make out the name *Lusitania* on the stern. Before the ship left New York bound for Liverpool, the German embassy had published warnings in the American press against travel to the war zone, but among the 1,198 persons lost were 128 Americans.

The public was outraged. It was an act of piracy, Theodore Roosevelt declared. Wilson, however, urged patience: "There is such a thing as a man being too proud to fight. There is such a thing as a nation being so right that it does not need to convince others by force that it is right." Bit his previous demand for "strict accountability" forced him to make a strong response. On May 13 Bryan reluctantly signed a note demanding that the Germans abandon unrestricted submarine warfare, disavow the sinking, and pay reparations. The Germans responded that the ship had been armed (which it was not) and carried a cargo of small arms and ammunition (which it did). A second note on June 9 repeated American demands in stronger terms. The United States, Wilson asserted, was "contending for nothing less high and sacred than the rights of humanity." Bryan, unwilling to risk war over the issue, resigned in protest and joined the peace movement as a private citizen. His successor, Robert Lansing, signed the note.

In response to the uproar over the *Lusitania,* the German government had secretly ordered U-boat captains to avoid sinking large passenger vessels. When, despite the order, two American lives were lost in the sinking of the British liner *Arabic,* bound for New York, the Germans paid an indemnity and offered a public assurance on September 1, 1915: "Liners will not be sunk by our submarines without warning and without safety of the lives of non-combatants, provided that the liners do not try to escape or offer resistance." With this *Arabic* pledge, Wilson's resolute stand seemed to have resulted in a victory for his policy.

During the fall of 1915, Wilson's trusted adviser Edward M. House proposed to renew a mediation effort he had explored on a visit to London, Paris, and Berlin the previous spring—before the *Lusitania* sinking. In early 1916 House visited those capitals again, but found neither side ready to begin serious negotiations. The French and British would soon be engaged in destructive battles at Verdun and the Somme, and both were determined to fight until they could bargain from strength.

Peace advocates in Congress now challenged the administration's policy on neutral rights. In 1916 resolutions were introduced in the

House and Senate warning Americans against traveling on armed belligerent vessels. Such surrender to the German threat, Wilson asserted, would be a "deliberate abdication of our hitherto proud position as spokesmen, even amidst the turmoil of war, for the law and the right." He warned that if the United States accepted a single abatement of right, then "the whole fine fabric of international law might crumble under our hands piece by piece." The administration managed to defeat both resolutions by a solid margin. On March 24, 1916, a U-boat torpedoed the French steamer *Sussex,* injuring two Americans. When Wilson threatened to break off relations, Germany renewed its pledge that U-boats would not torpedo merchant and passenger ships. This *Sussex* pledge implied the virtual abandonment of submarine warfare.

THE DEBATE OVER PREPAREDNESS   The *Lusitania* incident, and more generally the quarrels over neutral commerce, contributed to a growing demand for a stronger American army and navy. On December 1, 1914, the champions of preparedness organized the National Security League to promote their cause. After the *Lusitania* sinking, Wilson asked the War and Navy Departments to draft proposals for expansion.

Progressives and pacifists and many from the rural South and West were opposed to military expansion. Their antiwar sentiments tapped into the traditional American suspicion of military establishments, es-

Helping the President. *In this 1915 cartoon, Wilson holds to the middle course between the pacifism of Bryan (shown on left with sign "Let us avoid unnecessary risks") and the belligerence of Roosevelt (shown on right with a sign "Let us act without unnecessary delay").*

pecially of standing armies, which dated back to the colonial period. The new Democratic leader in the House opposed "the big Navy and big Army program of the jingoes and war traffickers." In the East, leaders of the peace movement organized a League to Limit Armament. Jane Addams and suffragist Carrie Chapman Catt organized a Women's Peace party.

The administration's plan to enlarge the regular army and create a national reserve force of 400,000 ran into stubborn opposition in the House Military Affairs Committee. Wilson was forced to accept a compromise between advocates of an expanded force under federal control and advocates of a traditional citizen army. The National Defense Act of 1916 expanded the regular army from 90,000 to 175,000 and permitted gradual enlargement to 223,000. It also expanded the National Guard to 440,000, made provision for their training, and gave federal funds for summer training camps for civilians.

The bill for an increased navy had less trouble because of the general feeling expressed by the navy secretary that there was "no danger of militarism from a relatively strong navy such as would come from a big standing army." The Naval Construction Act of 1916 authorized between $500 million and $600 million for a three-year program of enlargement.

Forced to relent on preparedness, progressives who opposed the action determined that the financial burden should rest on the wealthy people they held responsible for the effort. The income tax became their weapon. Supported by a groundswell of popular support, they wrote into the Revenue Act of 1916 changes that doubled the basic income tax rate from 1 to 2 percent, lifted the surtax to a maximum of 13 percent (for a total of 15 percent) on incomes over $2 million, added an estate tax graduated up to a maximum of 10 percent, levied a 12½ percent tax on gross receipts of munitions makers, and added a new tax on corporation capital, surplus, and excess profits. The new taxes on wealth amounted to the most clear-cut victory of radical progressives in the entire Wilson period, a victory further consolidated and advanced after America entered the war. It was the capstone to the edifice of progressive legislation that Wilson supported in preparation for the election of 1916.

THE ELECTION OF 1916   As the 1916 election approached, Republicans hoped to regain their normal majority, and Roosevelt hoped to be their leader again. But he had committed the deadly sin of bolting his party in 1912 and, what was more, expressed a bellicosity on war issues that would scare off voters. Needing somebody who would draw Bull Moose Progressives back into the fold, the regulars turned to Justice Charles Evans Hughes, who had a progressive record as governor of New York from 1907 to 1910. On the Supreme Court since then, he had neither taken a stand in 1912 nor spoken out on foreign policy. The remnants of the Progressive party gathered in Chicago at the same time as the Republicans. Roosevelt had held out the vain hope of getting both nominations, but he now declined to lead a moribund party. Two weeks later the Progressive National Committee disbanded the party and endorsed Hughes; a minority, including their vice-presidential nominee, came out for Wilson.

The Democrats, as expected, chose Wilson once again, and in their platform endorsed a program of social legislation, neutrality, and reasonable preparedness. The party further commended women's suffrage to the states, denounced groups that placed the interests of other countries above those of the United States, and pledged support for a postwar League of Nations to enforce peace with collective security mea-

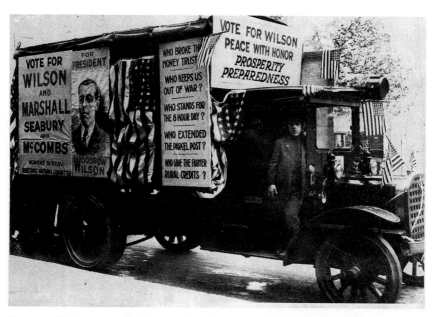

Peace with Honor. *Wilson's neutral policies proved popular in the 1916 campaign.*

sures against aggressors. The Democrats found their most popular issue, however, when the keynote speaker, a former New York governor, got an unexpected response to his recital of historic cases in which the United States had refused under provocation to go to war. As he mentioned successive examples, the crowd chanted "What did we do? What did we do?" and the speaker responded: "We didn't go to war! We didn't go to war!" The peace theme, refined into the slogan "He kept us out of war," became the rallying cry of the campaign, one that had the merit of taking credit without making any promises for the future.

Rooseveltians found themselves drawn in large numbers to Wilson. The impression of Democratic purpose and effectiveness was heightened by Republican feuding and ineptitude. On foreign policy, Hughes worked both sides of the street. While trying to keep the votes of German-Americans and other "hyphenates," Hughes refused to disavow Roosevelt, who was going around the country denouncing the kaiser. On social-reform issues Wilson was far ahead of Hughes, and Hughes found himself often the captive of old-line Republican bosses more eager to punish Bull Moose Progressives than to win the election for Hughes.

In the end, Wilson's twin rallying cries of peace and progressivism, a unique combination of issues forged in the legislative and diplomatic crucibles of 1916, brought victory. Early returns showed a Republican sweep in the East and Midwest, signaling a victory for Hughes, but the outcome remained in doubt until word came that Wilson had carried California by 3,772 votes. The final vote showed a Democratic sweep of the Far West and South, enough for victory in the electoral college by 277 to 254, and in the popular vote by 9 million to 8.5 million.

LAST EFFORTS FOR PEACE   Immediately after the election, Wilson began to plan another peace move, whereupon the German government announced on December 12 its readiness to begin discussion of peace terms. Six days later Wilson sent identical notes to the belligerent powers, asking each to state its war aims. The Germans responded promptly that they would state theirs only to a conference of the belligerents at a neutral site (although it soon became clear that they intended to seize new territory along the Baltic Sea, in the Congo of Africa, and in France, Belgium, and Luxembourg). In January 1917 the Allies made it plain that they intended to require reparations, break up the Austro-Hungarian and Ottoman Empires, and destroy German power.

Wilson then decided to make one more appeal, in the hope that public opinion would force the hands of the warring governments. Speaking before the Senate on January 22, 1917, he asserted the right of the United States to a share in laying the foundations for a lasting peace, which would have to be a "peace without victory," for only a "peace among equals" could endure. The peace must be based on the principles of government by the consent of the governed, freedom of the seas, and disarmament, and must be enforced by an international league for peace established to make another such catastrophe impossible. "I would fain believe," the president ended, "that I am speaking for the silent mass of mankind everywhere who have as yet had no place or opportunity to speak their real hearts out concerning the death and ruin they see to have come already upon the persons and homes they hold most dear."

Although Wilson did not know it, he was already too late. Exactly two weeks before he spoke, impatient German military leaders had decided to wage unrestricted submarine warfare. They took the calculated risk of provoking American anger in the hope of scoring a quick knockout. On January 31 the new policy was announced, effective the next day. All vessels in the war zone, belligerent or neutral, would be sunk without warning. "Freedom of the seas," said the *Brooklyn Eagle,* "will now be enjoyed by icebergs and fish."

On February 3, 1917, Wilson told a joint session of Congress that the United States had broken diplomatic relations with the German government. Three weeks later he asked for authority to arm American merchant ships and "to employ any other instrumentalities or methods that may be necessary and adequate to protect our ships and our people." There was little quarrel with arming merchant ships, but bitter opposition to Wilson's vague reference to "any other instrumentalities or methods." A group of eleven or twelve die-hard noninterventionists filibustered the measure until the regular session expired on March 4. Thus, in Wilson's words: "A little group of willful men, representing no opinion but their own, have rendered the great Government of the United States helpless and contemptible." On March 12 the State Department announced that a forgotten law of 1792 allowed the arming of merchant ships regardless of congressional inaction.

Word had reached Wilson on February 25 that the British had intercepted and decoded an important message from German foreign secretary Arthur Zimmermann to his minister in Mexico. The note instructed the envoy to offer an alliance and financial aid to Mexico in case of war between the United States and Germany. In return for diversionary action against the United States, Mexico would recover "the lost territory in Texas, New Mexico, and Arizona."

On March 1, news of the Zimmermann Telegram broke in the American press and outraged the public. Wilson felt it betrayed a trust he had shown in permitting the Germans to use American wireless facilities to transmit the message. Then, later in March, a revolution overthrew Russia's czarist government and established the provisional government of a Russian Republic. The fall of the czarist autocracy allowed Americans the illusion that all the major Allied Powers were now fighting for constitutional democracy. Not until November 1917 was this illusion shattered, when the Bolsheviks seized power in Russia.

AMERICA'S ENTRY INTO THE WAR

In March 1917 German submarines sank five American merchant vessels in the North Atlantic. On March 20 Wilson's cabinet unanimously endorsed a declaration of war, and the following day the president called a special session of Congress. When it met on April 2, Wilson asked Congress to recognize the war that Imperial Germany was already waging against the United States, then turned to a discussion of the issues. The German government had revealed itself as a natural foe of liberty, and therefore "The world must be made safe for democracy. Its peace must be planted upon the tested foundations of political liberty." The war resolution passed the Senate by a vote of 82 to 6 on April 4. The House concurred, 373 to 50, and Wilson signed the measure on April 6, 1917. It was Good Friday.

How had it come to this, less than three years after Wilson's proclamation of neutrality? Prominent among the various explanations of America's entrance into the war were the effects of British propaganda and America's deep involvement in trade with the Allies, which some observers then and later credited to the intrigues of war profiteers and munitions makers. Some Americans thought German domination of Europe would be a threat to American security, especially if it meant the destruction or capture of the British navy. But whatever the influence of such factors, they likely would not have been decisive without the issue of submarine warfare. Once Wilson had taken a stand for the traditional rights of neutrals and noncombatants, he was to some extent at the mercy of decisions by the German high command and was led step by step into a war over what to a later generation would seem a rather quaint, if noble, set of principles.

AMERICA'S EARLY ROLE   The scope of America's role in the European war remained unclear. Few on either side of the Atlantic expected more from the United States than a token military effort. Despite Congress's preparedness measures, the army remained small and rudimentary. The navy also was largely undeveloped. This began to change, however, when Rear Admiral William S. Sims assumed command of American ships in European waters. He then systematically built up the United States Navy, bringing the first contingent of six American destroyers to Queenstown, Ireland, in May 1917, and more later. The Americans, in addition, made two important contributions to Allied naval strategy. Previously, merchant ships had survived through speed and evasive action. Sims persuaded the Allies to adopt a convoy system of escorting merchant ships in groups. The result was a decrease in Allied shipping losses from 881,000 tons in April 1917 to 289,000 in

A Liberty Loan poster with an "honor roll" of ethnic Americans.

November of the same year. Later the United States Navy conceived and laid a gigantic minefield across the North Sea that threatened the U-boats' access to the North Atlantic.

Within a month of the declaration of war, British and French missions arrived in the United States. First they requested money with which to buy supplies, a request Congress had already anticipated in the Liberty Loan Act, which added $5 billion to the national debt in "Liberty Bonds." Of this amount, $3 billion could be loaned to the Allied Powers. The United States was also willing to furnish naval support, credits, supplies, and munitions, but to raise and train a large army, equip it, and send it across a submarine-infested ocean seemed out of the question. Marshal Joseph Joffre, who came with the French mission, nevertheless insisted that the United States send a token force to bolster morale, and on June 26, 1917, the first contingent of Americans, about 14,500 men commanded by General John J. Pershing, began to disembark on the French coast. Pershing and his troops were able to reach Paris by July 4. Pershing soon decided that the war-weary Allies would be unable to mount an offensive by themselves. He advised the War Department that plans should be made to send a million American troops by the following spring. It was done—through strenuous efforts.

When the United States entered the war, the combined strength of the regular army and National Guard was only 379,000; at the end it would be 3.7 million. The need for such large numbers of troops converted Wilson to the idea of conscription. Under the Selective Service Act of 1917, all men aged twenty-one to thirty (later, from eighteen to forty-five) had to register for service. Registrants went into five classes, the first being able-bodied unmarried men without dependents. From this group alone came all the 2.8 million ultimately drafted. All told, about 2 million Americans crossed the Atlantic and about 1.4 million saw some action. Training of the soldiers went on in thirty-two camps, half of them located in the South for climatic reasons. The example of the Spanish-American War was well learned: the camps were for the most part sanitary and equipped with modern plumbing, hospitals, and recreation centers.

Wilson and his secretary of war, Newton D. Baker, as well as many others, saw the mobilization of hundreds of thousands of young men as an opportunity for social engineering. To improve the recruits' character and outlook while preparing them for war, Wilson and Baker created the Commission on Training Camp Activities (CTCA). The idea was to inculcate middle-class "progressive" virtues and values into recruits while they were undergoing their military training. The CTCA produced sex education programs to prevent the spread of venereal diseases, worked with local authorities to police "red-light" districts near the military bases and to arrest prostitutes, and sponsored sporting events and entertainment programs, dances and religious services, all designed to minister to the physical and moral well-being of the trainees.

MOBILIZING A NATION   Complete economic mobilization on the home front was also necessary to conduct the war efficiently. Still, a lingering lack of coordination made wartime mobilization in the United States difficult. It was not the Wilson administration's finest hour. The Army Appropriation Act of 1916 had created a Council of National Defense, which in turn led to the creation of other wartime agencies. The Lever Food and Fuel Control Act of 1917 created a Food Administration, headed by Herbert Hoover, a future president. Hoover, a mining engineer and former head of the Commission for Relief in Belgium, sought to raise production while reducing civilian use of foodstuffs.

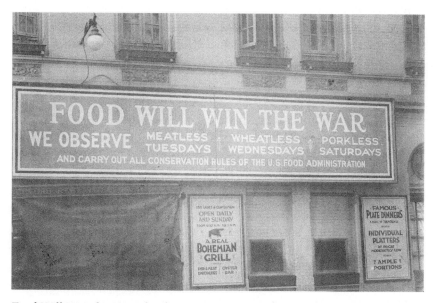

Food Will Win the War, *the slogan of the Food Administration, appears over the entrance of this "real Bohemian Grill."*

"Food will win the war" was the slogan. Hoover directed a propaganda campaign promoting "Meatless Tuesdays," "Wheatless Wednesdays," "Porkless Saturdays," the planting of victory gardens, and the use of left-overs.

The War Industries Board (WIB), established in 1917, soon became the most important of all the mobilization agencies. It was headed by Bernard Baruch, a brilliant Wall Street speculator, who exercised a virtual dictatorship over the economy. Under Baruch the purchasing bureaus of the United States and Allied governments submitted their needs to the board, which set priorities and planned production. The board could allocate raw materials, tell manufacturers what to produce, order construction of new plants, and, with the approval of the president, fix prices. For the sake of greater efficiency the WIB standardized product styles and designs.

A NEW LABOR FORCE   The closing off of foreign immigration, and the movement of 4 million men from the workforce into the armed services created a labor shortage. To meet it, women, blacks, and other ethnic minorities were encouraged to enter industries and agricultural activities heretofore dominated by white males. Northern businesses sent recruiting agents into the Deep South to find workers for their factories and mills, and over 400,000 southern blacks began the "Great Migration" northward during the war years, a mass movement that continued unabated through the 1920s. Mexican-Americans followed the same migratory pattern. Recruiting agents and newspaper editors portrayed the North as the "land of promise" for southern blacks suffering from their region's depressed agricultural economy and rising racial intimidation and violence. The African-American newspaper *Chicago Defender* exclaimed: "To die from the bite of frost is far more glorious than at the hands of a mob." By 1930 the number of African Americans living in the North had tripled from 1910 levels.

But the newcomers were not always welcomed above the Mason-Dixon line. Many native white workers resented the new arrivals, and racial tensions sparked riots in cities across the country. In 1917 over forty African Americans and nine whites were killed during a riot over employment in a defense plant in East St. Louis. Two years later the toll of a Chicago race riot was nearly as high, with twenty-three black and fifteen white deaths. In these and other incidents of racial violence the pattern was the same. Whites angered by the influx of blacks into

Women taking the place of male work-ers on the Great Northern Railway, Great Falls, Montana, 1918.

their communities would seize upon an incident to rampage through black neighborhoods, killing, burning, and looting, while white police-men looked the other way or encouraged the hooliganism.

American intervention in World War I also had a significant impact on women. Initially, women supported the war effort in traditional ways. They helped organize war-bond and war-relief drives, conserved foodstuffs and war-related materials, supported the Red Cross, and joined the Army nurse corps. But as the scope of the war widened, both government and industry sought to mobilize women workers for service on farms, loading docks, and railway crews, as well as in armaments in-dustries, machine shops, steel and lumber mills, and chemical plants. Many women leaders saw such opportunities as a real breakthrough. "At last, after centuries of disabilities and discrimination," said a speaker at a Women's Trade Union League meeting in 1917, "women are com-ing into the labor and festival of life on equal terms with men." A black woman who exchanged her job as a live-in servant for work in a factory declared: "I'll never work in nobody's kitchen but my own any more. No indeed, that's the one thing that makes me stick to this job."

In fact, however, war-generated changes in female employment were limited and brief. About a million women participated in "war work," but most of them were young and single and already working outside the home. Most returned to their previous jobs once the war ended. In fact, male-dominated unions encouraged women to revert to their stereotypical domestic roles after the war ended. The Central Federated Union of New York baldly insisted that "the same patriotism which induced women to enter industry during the war should induce them to vacate their positions after the war." The anticipated gains of women in the workforce failed to materialize. In fact, by 1920 the 8.5 million working women made up a smaller percentage of the labor force than they had in 1910. Still, one lasting result of women's contributions to the war effort was Woodrow Wilson's decision to endorse female suffrage. In the fall of 1918 he told the Senate that giving women the vote was "vital to the winning of the war."

The wartime emergency placed organized labor in a position to make solid advances in employment and wages, despite the rise in consumer prices. A newly created United States Employment Service placed some 4 million workers in war-related jobs. Labor unions benefited from expanded employment, the increased demand for labor, and government policies favorable to collective bargaining. From 1913 to 1918 AFL membership increased by 37 percent.

WAR PROPAGANDA   The exigencies of winning the war led the government to mobilize more than economic life: the progressive gospel of efficiency suggested mobilizing public opinion as well. On April 14, 1917, eight days after the declaration of war, an executive order established the Committee on Public Information, composed of the secretaries of state, war, and the navy. Its executive head, George Creel, a Denver newsman, sold Wilson on the idea that the best approach to influencing public opinion was "expression, not repression"—propaganda instead of censorship. Creel organized a propaganda machine to convey the Allies' war aims to the people, and above all to the enemy, where it might encourage the forces of moderation. To sell the war, Creel gathered a remarkable group of journalists, photographers, artists, entertainers, and others useful to his purpose. A film division produced such pictures as *The Beast of Berlin*. Hardly any public group escaped a harangue by one of the 75,000 Four-Minute Men, organized to give short speeches on Liberty Bonds, the need to conserve food and fuel, and other timely topics.

CIVIL LIBERTIES   By arousing public opinion to such a frenzy, however, the war effort channeled the zeal of progressivism into grotesque campaigns of "Americanism" and witch-hunting. Wilson had foreseen such consequences. "Once lead this people into war," he said, "and they'll forget there even was such a thing as tolerance." Popular prejudice equated anything German with disloyalty. Symphonies refused to perform Bach and Beethoven, schools dropped courses in the German language, and patriots translated "sauerkraut" into "liberty cabbage," "German measles" into "liberty measles," and "dachshunds" into "liberty pups."

While mobs hunted spies and chased rumors, the federal government stalked bigger game, with results often as absurd. Under the Espionage and Sedition Acts, criticism of government leaders and war policies was in effect outlawed. The Espionage Act of 1917 set penalties of up to $10,000 and twenty years in prison for those who gave aid to the enemy, who tried to incite insubordination, disloyalty, or refusal of duty in the armed services, or who circulated false reports and statements with intent to interfere with the war effort. The postmaster-general could bar from the mails anything that violated the act or advocated treason, insurrection, or forcible resistance to any United States law. The Sedition Act of 1918 extended the penalties to those who did or said anything to obstruct the sale of Liberty Bonds or to advocate cutbacks in production, and—just in case something had been overlooked—for saying, writing, or printing anything "disloyal, profane, scurrilous, or abusive" about the American form of government, the Constitution, or the army and navy.

The Espionage and Sedition Acts generated more than 1,000 convictions. The impact of the acts fell with most severity upon Socialists and other radicals. In Chicago over 100 members of the Industrial Workers of the World went on trial for opposing the war effort. All were found guilty, and the IWW never fully recovered from the blow. Victor Berger, Socialist congressman from Milwaukee, received a twenty-year sentence for editorials in the *Milwaukee Leader* that called the war a capitalist conspiracy. Eugene V. Debs, who had polled over 900,000 votes for president in 1912, ardently opposed American intervention, declaring that "I am opposed to every war but one; I am for that war heart and soul, and that is the world-wide revolution." He repeatedly urged American men to refuse to serve in the military, even though he knew he could be prosecuted for such remarks under the Espionage Act. "I would a thousand times rather be a free soul in jail than a sycophant and a coward in the streets," he told a Socialist gathering in 1918. He received his wish. Two weeks later Debs was arrested and eventually given a twenty-year prison sentence for encouraging draft resistance. In 1920, still in jail, he polled nearly 1 million votes for president.

In two important decisions just after the war, the Supreme Court upheld the Espionage and Sedition Acts. *Schenck v. United States* (1919) upheld the conviction of a man for circulating antidraft leaflets among members of the armed forces. In this case Justice Oliver Wendell Holmes said: "Free speech would not protect a man in falsely shouting fire in a theater, and causing a panic." The act applied where there was "a clear and present danger" that speech in wartime might create evils Congress had a right to prevent. In *Abrams v. United States* (1919) the Court upheld the conviction of a man who circulated pamphlets opposing intervention in Russia. Here Holmes and Louis Brandeis dissented from the majority view. The "surreptitious publishing of a silly leaflet by an unknown man," they argued, posed no danger to government policy.

"THE DECISIVE POWER"

American troops played little more than a token role in the European fighting until early 1918. Before that they were parceled out in quiet sectors mainly for training purposes. All through 1917 the Allies remained on the defensive, and late in the year their situation turned desperate. In October the Italian lines collapsed and were overrun by Austrian forces. With the help of Allied troops from France, the Italians finally held their ground. In November the Bolshevik Revolution overthrew the infant Russian Republic, and the new Soviet government dropped out of the war. With the Central Powers now free to concentrate their forces on the Western Front, the American war effort became a "race for France" to restore the balance of strength. French premier Georges Clemenceau appealed to the Americans to accelerate their mobilization: "A terrible blow is imminent," he predicted to an American journalist. "Tell your Americans to come quickly."

THE WESTERN FRONT   On March 21, 1918, Clemenceau's prediction came true when the Germans began the first of several offensives to try to end the war before the Americans arrived in force. On the Somme River they broke through at the juncture of British and French sectors and penetrated thirty-five miles, nearly to Amiens. Farther

Fresh troops moving to an advanced position near the front, France.

north, the Germans struck in Flanders, where the Allies still held a corner of Belgium. At this critical point, on April 14 the Allies made French general Ferdinand Foch the supreme commander of all Allied forces.

On May 27 the Germans began their next drive along the Aisne River, took Soissons, and pushed on to the Marne River along a forty-mile front. By May 1918 there were 1 million fresh American troops in Europe, and for the first time they made a difference. In a counterattack American forces retook Cantigny on May 28 and held it. A week later, on June 2–3, a marine brigade blocked the Germans at Belleau Wood. American army troops took Vaux and opposed the Germans at Château-Thierry. Though these actions had limited military significance, their effect on Allied morale was immense. Each was a solid American success, and together they reinforced Pershing's demand for a separate American army.

Before that could come to pass, the turning point in the western campaign came on July 15, 1918, in the Second Battle of the Marne. On both sides of Reims, the eastern end of a great bulge toward Paris, the Germans commenced their push against the French lines. Within three days, however, they had stalled, and the Allies, mainly with American troops, went on the offensive.

THE WESTERN FRONT, 1918

- - - The Western Front, March 1918

······· German offensive, spring 1918

→ Allied counteroffensive

—— The Western Front, November 1918

Soon the British, French, and Americans began to roll the German front back toward and into Belgium. Then on August 10 the first U.S. Army was organized and assigned the task of liquidating the Germans at St. Mihiel, southeast of Verdun. There, on September 12, an army of more than 500,000 staged the first strictly American offensive of the war. Within three days the Germans had pulled back. The great Meuse-Argonne offensive, begun on September 26, then employed American divisions in a drive toward Sédan and its railroad, which supplied the entire German front. The largest American action of the war, it involved 1.2 million American troops and cost 117,000 American casualties, including 26,000 dead. But along the front from Sédan to Flanders the Germans were in retreat. "America," wrote German general Erich Ludendorff, "thus became the decisive power in the war."

A gun crew firing on entrenched German positions, 1918.

THE BOLSHEVIKS AND THE WAR When the war broke out in 1914, Russia was one of the Allied Powers. Over the next three years, the Russians suffered some 5.5 million casualties. By 1917, there were shortages of ammunition for Russian troops and food for the Russian people. The czarist government was in disarray, and after the czar's abdication, it first gave way to a provisional republican government, which in turn succumbed in November 1917 to a revolution led by Vladimir Lenin and his Bolshevik party, who promised war-weary Russians "Peace, Land, and Bread."

Once in control of the government, the Bolsheviks unilaterally stopped fighting. With German troops deep in Russian territory, and with armies of "White" Russians (anti-Bolsheviks) organizing resistance to their power, on March 3, 1918, the Bolsheviks concluded a separate peace with Germany in the Treaty of Brest-Litovsk. In an effort to protect Allied supplies and to encourage anti-Bolshevik forces in the developing Russian civil war, Wilson sent American forces into Russia's Arctic ports to prevent military supplies from falling into German hands. On August 2, 1918, some 8,000 American troops landed there and two weeks later in eastern Siberia, where they remained until April 1920 in an effort to curb the growing Japanese ambitions there.

The Allied intervention in Russia failed because the Bolsheviks were able to consolidate their power. Russia took no further part in World War I and did not participate in the peace settlement. The intervention also generated among Soviets long-lasting suspicion of the West.

THE FOURTEEN POINTS   As the war was ending, the question of war aims arose again. Neither the Allies nor the Central Powers, despite Wilson's prodding, had stated openly what they hoped to gain. Wilson repeated that the Americans had no selfish ends. "We desire no conquest, no dominion," he stressed in his war message of 1917. "We seek no indemnities for ourselves, no material compensation for the sacrifices we shall freely make. We are but one of the champions of the rights of mankind." Unfortunately for his purpose, after the Bolsheviks seized power in November 1917, they published copies of secret treaties in which the Allies had promised territorial gains in order to win Italy, Romania, and Greece to their side. When an Interallied Conference in Paris late in 1917 failed to agree on a statement of aims, Colonel House advised Wilson to formulate his own.

During 1917 House had been drawing together an informal panel of American experts called "the Inquiry" to formulate plans for peace. With advice from these experts, Wilson himself drew up a statement that would become the famous Fourteen Points. These he delivered to a joint session of Congress on January 8, 1918, "as the only possible program" for peace. The first five points in general terms called for open diplomacy, freedom of the seas, removal of trade barriers, reduction of armaments, and an impartial adjustment of colonial claims based on the interests of the populations involved. Most of the remainder called on the Central Powers to evacuate occupied lands and to allow self-determination for various nationalities, a crucial principle for Wilson. Point 13 proposed an independent Poland with access to the sea. Point 14, the capstone in Wilson's thinking, championed a general association of nations to secure guarantees of independence and territorial integrity to all countries, great and small.

The Fourteen Points set forth a commitment in which Wilson persisted, but they also served the purposes of psychological warfare. One of their aims was to keep Russia in the war by a more liberal statement of purposes—a vain hope, as it turned out. Another was to reassure the Allied peoples that they were involved in a noble cause. A third was to

*Salvation Army worker writing a letter
home for a wounded soldier.*

drive a wedge between the governments of the Central Powers and
their peoples by the offer of a reasonable peace. Wilson's promise of
"autonomous development" for the subject nationalities of Austria-
Hungary (Point 10) might have weakened the polyglot Hapsburg Empire, though he did not intend to break up the empire. But the chaos
into which central Europe descended in 1918, and the national aspirations of the empire's peoples, took matters out of his hands.

On September 29, 1918, German general Ludendorff advised his
government to seek the best peace terms possible. On October 3, a new
chancellor made the first German overtures for peace on the basis of
the Fourteen Points. A month of diplomatic fencing followed between
Colonel House and Allied representatives. Finally, when he threatened
to pursue separate negotiations, the Allies accepted the Fourteen Points
as a basis of peace, but with two significant reservations: they reserved
the right to discuss freedom of the seas, and they demanded reparations
for war damages.

Meanwhile the German home front was being torn apart by a loss of
morale, culminating in a naval mutiny at Kiel. Germany's allies dropped
out of the war: Bulgaria on September 29, 1918, Turkey on October 30,
and Austria-Hungary on November 3. On November 9, 1918, the kaiser
abdicated, and a German Republic was proclaimed. On November 11,
at 5 A.M., an armistice was signed. Six hours later, at the eleventh hour

Celebration of the Armistice ending World War I, New York City, November 1918.

of the eleventh day of the eleventh month, the guns fell silent. Under the Armistice the Germans had to evacuate occupied territories, pull back behind the Rhine, and surrender their naval fleet, railroad equipment, and other materials. The Germans were assured that the Fourteen Points would be the basis for the peace conference.

THE FIGHT FOR THE PEACE AT HOME AND ABROAD

DOMESTIC UNREST   Wilson made a fateful decision to attend in person the peace conference that convened in Paris on January 18, 1919. It shattered precedent for a president to leave the country for so long, but it dramatized all the more Wilson's messianic vision and his desire to ensure his goal of a lasting peace. From one viewpoint it was a shrewd move, for his prestige and determination made a difference in Paris. But he lost touch with developments at home. His progressive coalition was already unraveling under the pressures of wartime discontent (a state of war officially existed until 1921). Western farmers complained about the government's control of wheat prices while southern cotton producers rode the wartime inflation. Eastern businessmen chafed at revenue policies designed, according to the *New York Sun,* "to pay for the war out of taxes raised north of the Mason and Dixon Line." Organized labor, despite manifest gains, was unhappy with inflation and the problems of reconversion to a peacetime economy.

In the midterm elections of 1918, Wilson made matters worse with a partisan appeal for a Democratic Congress to ensure support of his foreign policies. Republicans, who for the most part had supported war measures, took affront. In elections held on November 5, a week before the Armistice, the Democrats lost control of both houses of Congress. With an opposition majority in the new Congress, Wilson further weakened his standing by failing to involve a single prominent Republican in the peace negotiations. Humorist Will Rogers joked that Wilson was telling the Republicans, "I tell you what, we will split 50-50. I will go and you fellows can stay." Former president Taft groused that Wilson's real intention in going to Paris was "to hog the whole show."

When Wilson reached Europe in December 1918, enthusiastic demonstrations greeted him in Paris. The cheering millions saw in the American idealist a prophet of peace and a spokesman for humanity. Their heartfelt support no doubt strengthened his hand at the conference, but Wilson had to deal with some tough-minded statesmen.

On his way to the Paris Peace Conference, Wilson was welcomed as a hero in Europe. Here he reviews a line of troops at Calais.

The Paris conference comprised a body of delegates from all countries that had declared war or broken diplomatic relations with Germany. It was controlled by the Big Four: the prime ministers of Britain, France, and Italy, and the president of the United States. Japan restricted its interests to Asia and the Pacific. French premier Georges Clemenceau was a stern realist who had little patience with Wilson's utopianism. "God gave us the Ten Commandments and we broke them," Clemenceau sneered. "Wilson gave us the Fourteen Points—we shall see." Clemenceau insisted on harsh measures to weaken Germany and ensure French security. David Lloyd George of England was a gifted politician fresh from electoral victory on the slogan "Hang the Kaiser." Vittorio Orlando of Italy was there to pick up the spoils promised in the secret Treaty of London (1915).

THE LEAGUE OF NATIONS   Wilson carried the point that his cherished League of Nations must come first, in the conference and in the treaty. Whatever compromises he might have to make, whatever mistakes might result, Wilson believed that a permanent agency of collective security would assure international stability. Wilson presided over the commission set up to work out a charter for the League.

Article X of the covenant, which Wilson called "the heart of the League," pledged members to consult on military and economic sanctions against aggressors. The use of arms would be a last (and an improbable) resort. The League, it was assumed, would exercise enormous moral influence that would make military action unnecessary. The League structure allowed each member an equal voice in the Assembly; the Big Five (Britain, France, Italy, Japan, and the United States) and four other nations would make up the Council; the administrative staff in Geneva would make up the Secretariat; and finally, a Permanent Court of International Justice (set up in 1921 and usually called the World Court) could "hear and determine any dispute of an international character."

On February 14, 1919, Wilson reported the finished draft of the League covenant to the plenary session of the conference and departed the next day for a month-long visit home to conduct routine business. Already he faced rumblings of opposition, and shortly before his return to Paris, Henry Cabot Lodge, the chairman of the Senate Foreign Relations Committee, announced that the covenant was unacceptable "in the form now proposed." His statement bore the signatures of thirty-nine Republican senators or senators-elect, more than enough to block ratification. That evening Wilson confidently retorted: "When the treaty comes back, gentlemen on this side will find the covenant not only in it, but so many threads of the treaty tied to the covenant that you cannot dissect the covenant from the treaty without destroying the whole vital structure."

TERRITORY AND REPARATIONS   Back in Paris, Wilson grudgingly conceded to French demands for territorial concessions and reparations from Germany that would keep it weak for years to come. Wilson clashed sharply with Clemenceau, and after the president threatened to leave the conference, they settled on a demilitarized Rhineland (up to 50 kilometers [31 miles] beyond the Rhine River), Allied occupation of this zone for fifteen years, and League administration of the Saar Basin. France could use Saar coal mines for fifteen years, after which a plebiscite would determine the region's status.

In other territorial matters Wilson had to compromise his principle of national self-determination. There was in fact no way to make boundaries correspond to ethnic divisions. The folk wanderings of centuries had left mixed populations scattered throughout central Europe. In some areas, moreover, national self-determination yielded to other interests: the Polish Corridor, for instance, gave Poland its much-needed outlet to the sea through German territory, and the South Tyrol, home for some 200,000 German-speaking Austrians, gave Italy a more defensible frontier at the Brenner Pass. One part of the Austro-Hungarian Empire became Czechoslovakia, which included the German-speaking Sudetenland, an area favored with good defenses. Another part of the empire united with Serbia to create the kingdom of Yugoslavia. Still other substantial parts passed to Poland (Galicia), Romania (Transylvania), and Italy (Trentino and Trieste). All in all, despite aberrations, the new boundaries more nearly followed the ethnic divisions of Europe than the prewar lines.

The discussion of reparations (payments by the vanquished to the victors) was among the longest and most bitter at the conference. Despite a pre-Armistice agreement that Germany would be liable only for civilian damages, Clemenceau and Lloyd George proposed reparations for the entire cost of the war, including veterans' pensions. On this

EUROPE AFTER VERSAILLES
·········· 1914 boundaries
New nations
Plebiscite areas
Occupied area

point Wilson made perhaps his most fateful concessions. He accepted in the treaty a clause by which Germany confessed responsibility for the war and thus for its entire costs. The "war guilt" clause offended Germans and caused persistent bitterness.

On May 7, 1919, the victorious powers presented the treaty to the German delegates, who returned three weeks later with 443 pages of criticism protesting that the terms violated the Fourteen Points. A few changes were made, but when the Germans still refused to sign, Marshal Foch prepared to move his army across the Rhine. Finally, on June 28, 1919, the Germans signed the treaty in the Hall of Mirrors at Versailles.

WILSON'S LOSS AT HOME   Wilson returned home with the Versailles Treaty on July 8, 1919. Two days later he called on the Senate to accept "this great duty." The force of Wilson's idealism struck deep, and he returned amid a great clamor of popular support. A third of the state legislatures had endorsed the League, as had thirty-three of forty-eight governors.

Yet, Senator Henry Cabot Lodge, chairman of the Senate Foreign Relations Committee, harbored doubts. He did not want the United States to withdraw from world affairs, but he felt that the outcome at Versailles exhibited the weakness in "the beautiful scheme of making mankind virtuous by a statute or a written constitution." Americans, thought Lodge, were too prone to promise more than they could deliver when great principles entailed great sacrifices. Foreign policy would have to be built up from what the public would sustain rather than be imposed from above. A staunch Republican with an intense dislike for Wilson, Lodge sharpened his partisan knives. He knew the undercurrents already stirring up opposition to the treaty: the resentment of German, Italian, and Irish groups in the United States, the disappointment of liberals at Wilson's compromises on reparations and territories, the distractions of demobilization and the resulting domestic problems, and the revival of isolationism. Lodge's close friend, Theodore Roosevelt, still a popular figure, lambasted the League, noting that he keenly distrusted a "man who cares for other nations as much as his own."

Others agreed. In the Senate a group of "irreconcilables," fourteen Republicans and two Democrats, were unwilling to allow America to enter the League on any terms. They were mainly western or midwestern progressives who feared that foreign commitments threatened domestic reforms. The irreconcilables would be useful to Lodge's purpose, but he belonged to a larger group of "reservationists" who insisted on limiting American participation in the League and its actions. Wilson pointed out to them that the agreement already stipulated that with a veto in the League Council the United States could not be obligated to do anything against its will.

Lodge, who set more store by the old balance of power than by the new idea of collective security, brought forward a set of amendments or reservations. Wilson responded by agreeing to interpretive reservations, but to nothing that would reopen the negotiations. He especially opposed weakening Article X, which provided for collective action against aggression.

By September, with momentum for the treaty slackening, Wilson decided to go to the people and, as he put it, "purify the wells of public

The League of Nations Argument in a Nutshell. *J. N. "Ding" Darling's summation of the League controversy.*

opinion." Against the advice of doctors and friends he set forth on a tour through the Midwest to the West Coast, pounding out speeches on his typewriter between stops. In all he traveled 8,000 miles in twenty-two days, gave thirty-two major addresses and eight informal ones, refuted his opponents, and voiced warnings.

For a while Wilson seemed to be regaining the initiative, but then his body rebelled. On October 2, 1919, Wilson suffered a severe stroke and paralysis on his left side, leaving him an invalid for the rest of his life. For more than seven months he did not meet the cabinet. His protective wife kept him isolated from all but the most essential business. Wilson's disability intensified his stubbornness. He might have done better to stay in the White House and secure the best compromise possible, but now he refused to yield anything. As he scoffed to an aide, "Let Lodge compromise." Wilson ended up committing what one historian called the supreme infanticide, the destruction of his own brainchild.

Lodge was determined to amend the treaty before it was ratified. The Senate adopted fourteen of his reservations, most having to do with the League. Wilson especially opposed the reservation to Article X, which he said, "does not provide for ratification but, rather, for the nullification of the treaty." As a result, the Wilsonians found themselves thrown into an unlikely combination with irreconcilables, who opposed the treaty under any circumstances. The Senate vote was 39 for and 55 against. On the question of taking the treaty without reservations, irreconcilables and reservationists combined to defeat ratification again, with 38 for and 53 against.

In the face of public reaction, however, the Senate voted to reconsider. But the stricken Wilson remained adamant: "Either we should enter the League fearlessly, accepting with responsibility and not fearing the role of leadership which we now enjoy, contributing our efforts toward establishing a just and permanent peace, or we should retire as gracefully as possible from the great concert of powers by which the world was saved." On March 19, 1920, twenty-one Democrats deserted Wilson and joined the reservationists, but the treaty once again fell short of a two-thirds majority by a vote of 49 yeas and 35 nays. The real winner was the smallest of the three groups in the Senate, neither the Wilsonians nor the reservationists but the irreconcilables.

When Congress declared the war at an end by joint resolution on May 20, 1920, Wilson vetoed the action; it was not until July 2, 1921, after he left office, that a joint resolution ended the state of war with Germany and Austria-Hungary. Peace treaties with Germany, Austria, and Hungary were ratified on October 18, 1921, but by then Warren Gamaliel Harding was president of the United States.

Three Senators Refuse the Lady a Seat. *Americans reacted against the Senate's defeat of the Versailles peace treaty.*

LURCHING FROM WAR TO PEACE

The Versailles Treaty, for all the time it took in the Senate, was but one issue clamoring for public attention in the turbulent period after the war. Demobilization proceeded without plan, indeed without much sense that a plan was needed once the war was over. The sudden cancellation of war contracts left workers and business leaders to cope with reconversion on their own. Wilson's leadership was missing. He had been preoccupied by the war and the League, and once broken by his illness, he became strangely grim and peevish. His administration floundered through its last two years.

THE SPANISH FLU Amid the confusion of postwar life many Americans confronted a virulent menace that produced far more casualties than the war itself. It became known as the Spanish flu, and its contagion spread around the globe. Erupting in the spring of 1918 and lasting a year, the pandemic killed more than 22 million people throughout the world, twice as many as the number who died in World War I. In the United States alone the flu accounted for more than 500,000 deaths, five times the number of combat deaths in France.

American servicemen returning from France brought the flu with them, and it raced through the congested army camps and naval bases. Still, no one seemed alarmed, for the flu remained a common if severe ailment. But then the hospitalized men started dying by the dozens, and it became obvious that this was no ordinary flu virus. In addition to the usual symptoms—coughing, chills, fever, body aches—the afflicted suffered from vomiting, dizziness, labored breathing, nosebleeds, and profuse sweating. Many contracted pneumonia as well, and a startling number of patients died. Some 43,000 American servicemen died of influenza in 1918.

By September 1918 the epidemic had spread to the civilian population. In that month alone 10,000 Americans died from the disease. It was a baffling development. "Nobody seemed to know what the disease was, where it came from or how to stop it," observed the editors of *Science* magazine in 1919. Evangelist Billy Sunday blamed the plague on the Germans, charging that they had brought it across the Atlantic on submarines: "There's nothing short of hell they haven't stooped to do

Office workers with gauze masks during the Spanish flu epidemic, 1918.

since the war began. Darn their hides!" Millions of people began wearing surgical masks to work. Phone booths were locked up, as were other public facilities such as dance halls, poolrooms, and theaters. Even churches and saloons in many communities were declared off limits. Still the death toll rose. In Philadelphia 528 people were buried in a single day. From September 1918 to June 1919 some 675,000 Americans died of flu and pneumonia, and fully one-quarter of the population had contracted the illness. Life insurance companies nearly went bankrupt, hospitals were besieged, and cemeteries soon ran out of burial space.

Yet by the spring of 1919 the pandemic had run its course. It ended as suddenly—and as inexplicably—as it had begun. Although another outbreak occurred in the winter of 1920, the population had grown more resistant to its assaults. No disease, plague, war, famine, or natural catastrophe in world history killed so many people in such a short time. The most remarkable aspect of the flu pandemic was that people for the most part took it in stride. People seemed resigned to biological forces beyond their control while issues of war and peace in Europe and the home-front economy continued to dominate the headlines.

THE ECONOMIC TRANSITION   The problems of postwar readjustment were worsened by general labor unrest. Prices continued to rise after the war, and discontented workers, released from wartime constraints, were more willing to strike for their demands. In 1919, more than 4 million workers went out in thousands of disputes. Some workers in the East won their demands early in the year, but after a general strike in Seattle, public opinion began to turn hostile. The Seattle mayor denounced the walkout of 60,000 workers as evidence of Bolshevik influence. The strike lasted only five days, but public alarm over the affair damaged the cause of unions across the country.

An AFL campaign to organize steelworkers suffered from charges of radicalism against its leader, William Z. Foster, who had joined the Socialists in 1900 and later emerged as a Communist. Attention to Foster's radicalism obscured the squalid conditions that had marked the steel industry since the Homestead Strike of 1892. The twelve-hour day, often combined with a seven-day week, was common for steelworkers. On September 22, 1919, after U.S. Steel refused to talk, about 340,000 workers walked out. But the union succumbed to a back-to-work movement and gave up the strike four months later. When information about conditions became widely known, public opinion turned in favor of the steelworkers, but too late: the strike was over. Steelworkers remained unorganized until the 1930s.

The most celebrated postwar labor dispute was the Boston Police Strike. Though less significant than the steel strike in the numbers involved, it inadvertently launched a presidential career. On September 9, 1919, most of Boston's police force went out on strike. Governor Calvin Coolidge mobilized the National Guard to keep order, and after four days the strikers were ready to return, but the police commissioner refused to take them back. When labor leader Samuel Gompers appealed for their reinstatement, Coolidge responded in words that suddenly turned him into a national figure: "There is no right to strike against the public safety by anybody, anywhere, any time."

RACIAL FRICTION   The summer of 1919 also brought a season of race riots, both in the North and South. What black leader James Weldon Johnson called "the Red Summer" ("Red" here signified blood) began in July, when whites invaded the black section of Longview, Texas, in search of a teacher who had allegedly accused a white woman of a li-

A victim of racial rioting in Chicago, July 1919.

aison with a black man. They burned shops and houses and ran several African Americans out of town. A week later in Washington, D.C., reports of attacks on white women aroused white mobs, and for four days gangs of white and black rioters waged race war in the streets until soldiers and driving rains ended the fighting. These were but preliminaries to the Chicago riot of late July in which 38 people were killed and 537 injured. The climactic disorders of the summer occurred in the rural area around Elaine, Arkansas, where black tenant farmers tried to organize a union. According to official reports, 5 whites and 25 blacks died, but whites told one reporter in the area that in reality more than 100 blacks died. Altogether twenty-five race riots took place in 1919, and more threatened.

THE RED SCARE   Public reaction to the wave of labor strikes and race riots was influenced by the impact of the Bolshevik Revolution. A minority of radicals thought America's domestic turbulence, like that in Russia, was the first scene in a drama of world revolution. A much larger public was persuaded that they might be right. After all, a tiny faction in Russia had exploited confusion to impose its will. In 1919 the Socialist party, already depleted by wartime persecution, suffered the further defection of radicals inspired by the Russian example. Left-wing members formed the Communist and the short-lived Communist Labor parties. Wartime hysteria against all things German was readily transformed into a postwar Red Scare.

Fears of revolution might have remained latent except for the actions of a lunatic fringe. In April 1919 the post office intercepted nearly forty bombs addressed to various prominent citizens. One slipped through and blew off the hands of a Georgia senator's maid. In June another destroyed the front of Attorney-General A. Mitchell Palmer's house in Washington. The random violence of these criminals formed no part of Bolshevik tactics, but many Americans saw Red on all sides and condoned attacks on all kinds of minorities in retaliation.

Soon the government itself was promoting witch-hunts. Attorney-General Palmer harbored an entrenched distrust of aliens and a strong desire for the presidency. In 1919 the Justice Department decided to deport radical aliens, and Palmer set up as the head of the new General Intelligence Division the young J. Edgar Hoover, who began to collect an index file on radicals. Raids began on November 7, 1919, when agents swooped down on the Union of Russian Workers in twelve cities. On December 22 the transport ship *Buford,* dubbed the "Soviet Ark," left New York for Finland with 249 people, including assorted anarchists, criminals, and public charges. All were deported to Russia without benefit of a court hearing. On January 2, 1920, a series of police raids in dozens of cities swept up some 5,000 suspects, many taken from their houses without arrest warrants, of whom more than half were kept in custody. That same month the New York legislature expelled five duly elected Socialist members.

Basking in popular approval, Palmer continued to warn of the Red menace, but like other fads and alarms, the mood passed. By the summer of 1920 the Red Scare had begun to evaporate. Communist revolutions in Europe died out, leaving Bolshevism isolated in Russia; bombings tapered off; the wave of strikes and race riots receded. The attorney-general began to seem more threatening to civil liberties than a handful of radicals. By September 1920, when a bomb explosion at the corner of Broad and Wall Streets in New York killed thirty-eight people, Americans were ready to take it for what it was, the work of a crazed mind and not the start of a revolution. The Red Scare nevertheless left a lasting mark on American life. Part of its legacy was the continuing crusade for "100 percent Americanism" and restrictions on immigration. It left a stigma on labor unions and contributed to the anti-union open-shop campaign—the "American Plan," its sponsors called it. But for many Americans the chief residue of the Great War and its disordered aftermath was a profound disillusionment that pervaded American thought in the postwar decades.

MAKING CONNECTIONS

- The Red Scare at the end of World War I led to a wave of nativism and immigration restriction, outlined in the next chapter.

- This chapter ends by noting the "profound disillusionment" Americans felt with efforts to reform the world. The political aspect of that disillusionment—the turn to "normalcy" of the 1920s—is discussed in Chapter 27.

- The treaty ending World War I was designed to cripple Germany's military strength. But as Chapter 29 shows, within two decades Adolf Hitler was leading a rebuilt German military force into World War II.

FURTHER READING

Frederick S. Calhoun's *Power and Principle: Armed Intervention in Wilsonian Foreign Policy* (1986) surveys one aspect of Wilsonian diplomacy. For the Mexican intervention, consult John S. D. Eisenhower's *Intervention!: The United States and the Mexican Revolution, 1913–1917* (1993). A lucid and thoughtful overview of events covered in this chapter is Daniel M. Smith's *The Great Departure: The United States and World War I, 1914–1920* (1965).

A number of scholars have concentrated on the neutrality issue. Arthur S. Link, Wilson's greatest biographer, is sympathetic to the ideals of the president in *Woodrow Wilson: Revolution, War, and Peace* (1979). For a more critical review, see Ross Gregory's *The Origins of American Intervention in the First World War* (1971). A notable recent biography is August Heckscher's *Woodrow Wilson: A Biography* (1991).

Edward M. Coffman's *The War to End All Wars: The American Military Experience in World War I* (1968) is a detailed presentation of America's military involvement. David M. Kennedy's *Over Here: The First World War and American Society* (1980) surveys the impact of the war on the home front. Maurine Weiner Greenwald's *Women, War, and Work: The Impact of World War I on Women Workers in the United States* (1980) discusses the role of women. Ronald Schaffer's *America in the Great War: The Rise of the War Welfare State* (1991) shows the effect of war mobilization on business organization. Richard Polenberg's *Fighting Faiths: The Abrams Case, the Supreme Court, and Free Speech* (1987) examines the prosecution of a case under the 1918 Sedition Act.

How American diplomacy fared in the making of peace has received considerable attention. In addition to the Link book on Wilson, the role of the president is treated in Robert H. Ferrell's *Woodrow Wilson and World War I, 1917–1921* (1985), Arno J. Mayer's *Politics and Diplomacy in Peacemaking: Containment and Counterrevolution at Versailles, 1918– 1919* (1967) and N. Gordon Levin, Jr.'s *Woodrow Wilson and World Politics: America's Response to War and Revolution* (1968). Thomas J. Knock interrelates domestic affairs and foreign relations in his explanation of Wilson's peacemaking in *To End All Wars: Woodrow Wilson and the Quest for a New World Order* (1992).

The problems of the immediate postwar years are chronicled by a number of historians. On the Spanish flu, see Alfred W. Crosby's *America's Forgotten Pandemic: The Influenza of 1918* (1990). Labor tensions are examined in David E. Brody's *Labor in Crisis: The Steel Strike of 1919* (1965) and Francis Russell's *A City in Terror: 1919, the Boston Police Strike* (1975). On racial strife, see William Tuttle, Jr.'s *Race Riot: Chicago in the Red Summer of 1919* (1970). The fear of Communists is analyzed in Robert K. Murray's *Red Scare: A Study in National Hysteria, 1919–1920* (rev. ed., 1980).

26 ⮑ THE MODERN TEMPER

CHAPTER ORGANIZER

This chapter focuses on:

- the reactionary strains of the 1920s.

- the social ferment of the 1920s.

- the influence of modernism in American culture.

The horrors of World War I dealt a shattering blow to the widespread belief that civilization was progressing, a myth that had dominated the public consciousness for a century and that had been so powerful a stimulant to progressivism. The war's unimaginable carnage produced a postwar disillusionment among young intellectuals that challenged old values.

A new "modernist" sensibility emerged among artists, writers, and intellectuals. At once a mood and a movement, modernism emerged first in Europe at the end of the nineteenth century and became a pervasive international force by 1920. It arose out of a widespread recognition that Western civilization had entered an era of bewildering change. New technologies, new modes of transportation and communication, and new scientific discoveries such as quantum mechanics and relativity theory combined to rupture perceptions of reality and generate new forms of artistic expression. "One must never forget," declared Gertrude Stein, the experimentalist poet, "that the reality of the twentieth century is not the reality of the nineteenth century, not at all." Modernism introduced a whole series of intellectual and artistic movements: impressionism, futurism, dadaism, surrealism, Freudianism. As the French painter Paul Gauguin acknowledged, the upheavals of modernism produced "an epoch of confusion."

At the same time that the war and its turbulent aftermath provided an accelerant for modernism, it also stimulated political and social radicalism. The postwar wave of strikes, bombings, Red Scares, and race riots convinced many that America had entered a frightening new era of diversity and change. Defenders of tradition located the germs of radicalism in the polyglot cities teeming with immigrants and foreign ideas. The defensive mood of the 1920s fed on a growing tendency to connect American nationalism with nativism, Anglo-Saxon racism, and militant Protestantism.

REACTION IN THE TWENTIES

NATIVISM   The foreign connections of so many radicals strengthened the sense that the seeds of sedition were foreign borne. The most cele-

Sacco and Vanzetti. *From a series of paintings by Ben Shahn, 1931–1932.*

brated criminal case of the times seemed to prove the connection. It involved two Italian-born anarchists, Nicola Sacco and Bartolomeo Vanzetti. Arrested on May 5, 1920, for a payroll robbery and murder in South Braintree, Massachusetts, they were brought for trial before a judge who privately referred to the defendants as "those anarchist bastards." The question of the two men's guilt remains disputed, and the belief persists in some quarters that they were sentenced for their political ideas and their ethnic origins rather than for any crime they had committed. The case became a great radical and liberal cause célèbre of the 1920s, but despite pleas for mercy and public demonstrations around the world on behalf of the two men, they went to the electric chair on August 23, 1927, their last appeals denied.

The surging postwar nativism generated new efforts to restrict immigration. A pseudo-scientific racism bolstered anti-immigration groups. It found expression in a widely read book, Madison Grant's *The Passing of the Great Race* (1916)—the great race being the Nordics of northern Europe, threatened by the Slavic and Latin people of eastern and southern Europe. The flow of immigrants, slowed by the war, rose again at its end. From June 1920 to June 1921, more than 800,000 persons entered the country, 65 percent of them from southern and eastern Europe; and more were on the way.

An alarmed Congress passed the Emergency Immigration Act of 1921, which restricted new arrivals each year to 3 percent of the foreign-born of any nationality as shown in the 1910 census. A new quota law in 1924 reduced the number to 2 percent based on the 1890 census, which included fewer of the "new" immigrants. This law set a permanent limitation, which became effective in 1929, of slightly over 150,000 per year based on the "national origins" of the American people as of 1920. Since national origins could not be determined with precision, officials were called upon to use available statistics on migration, natural increase, and "such other data as may be found reliable." However inexact the quotas, their purpose was clear: to tilt the balance in favor of immigrants from northern and western Europe, who were assigned about 85 percent of the total. The law completely excluded people from East Asia—a gratuitous insult to the Japanese, who were already kept out of the United States by their "Gentlemen's Agreement" with Theodore Roosevelt.

On the other hand, the law left the gate open to new arrivals from Western Hemisphere countries, so that an ironic consequence was a great increase in the Hispanic Catholic population of the United States. The legal arrivals from Mexico peaked at 89,000 in 1924. Lower figures after that date merely reflect policies of the Mexican government to clamp down on the outflow of labor and stronger American enforcement of old regulations such as the 1882 exclusion of those immigrants likely to become public charges. Waves of illegal immigrants continued to come, however, in response to southwestern agriculture's demand for "stoop" labor. People of Latin American descent (chiefly Mexicans, Puerto Ricans, and Cubans) became the fastest-growing ethnic minority in the country.

THE KLAN   During the postwar years, the nativist tradition took on a new form, a revived Ku Klux Klan modeled on the group founded during Reconstruction. But, in a striking departure from its predecessor, the new Klan was devoted to "100 percent Americanism" and restricted its membership to native-born white Protestants. The new Klan was determined to protect its warped notion of the American way of life not only from African Americans, but also from Roman Catholics, Jews, and immigrants. America was no melting pot, the Klan's founder William J. Simmons warned: "It is a garbage can! . . . When the hordes of aliens walk to the ballot box and their votes outnumber yours, then that alien horde has got you by the throat." A habitual joiner and promoter of fraternal orders, Simmons had gathered a hooded group near Atlanta on Thanksgiving night, 1915. There, "bathed in the sacred glow of the fiery cross, the invisible empire was called from its slumber of half a century to take up a new task."

In going nativist, the Klan had gone national and was no longer restricted to the South. Its appeal reached areas as widely scattered as Oregon and Maine. It thrived in small towns and cities in the North, and especially in the Midwest. It flourished outside the South among the urban social mainstream, attracting clergymen, engineers, accountants, managers and superintendents, small businessmen, and store owners. And it was preoccupied with the defense of white ("native") women and Christian morals. The robes, the flaming crosses, the eerie processionals, the kneeling recruits, the occult liturgies—all tapped a deep urge toward mystery and brought drama into the dreary routine of a thousand communities.

The Klan was a reflex against shifting moral standards, the declining influence of churches, and the broadmindedness of city dwellers and

In 1925 the Ku Klux Klan staged a 40,000-man parade down Pennsylvania Avenue in Washington, D.C.

college students. In the Southwest, it became more than anything else a moral crusade. "It is going to drive the bootleggers forever out of this land," declared a Texan. "It is going to bring clean moving pictures . . . clean literature . . . break up roadside parking . . . enforce the laws . . . protect homes." To achieve such moral goals, the Klan employed night riding intimidation and floggings.

Simmons, always something of a dreamer, betrayed a fatal inability to control the tough customers attracted to the Klan. In 1922 a revolt toppled Simmons who, threatened with violence, abdicated to a new Imperial Wizard, Hiram Wesley Evans, a dentist from Dallas. The hooded order thereafter tried to become a political power. Officeholders either cultivated the Klan or were struck dumb on the subject. But the Klan never achieved much politically. The order had neither a political program nor a dynamic leadership. Unlike kindred movements in postwar Europe, it conjured up no Mussolini, no Hitler.

Estimates of its peak membership, probably inflated, range from 3 million to 8 million, but the Klan's influence evaporated as quickly as its numbers grew. For one thing, the Klan suffered from a decline in nativist excitement after passage of the 1924 immigration law. For another, it suffered recurrent factional quarrels and schisms. And its willing use of violence tarnished its moral pretensions. The "best people" of many towns had joined what they thought was an agency of reform, but they drifted away as the Klan became a cloak for immorality and corruption.

FUNDAMENTALISM   While the Klan saw a threat mainly in the alien menace, many adherents of the old-time religion saw threats from modernism in the churches: new ideas that the Bible should be studied in the light of modern scholarship (the "higher criticism") or that it could be reconciled with biological theories of evolution. Fearing that such notions had infected schools and even pulpits, orthodox Christians took on a militant new fundamentalism. The movement had acquired a name and definition from a series of pamphlets, *The Fundamentals* (1910). The fundamentalists were distinguished less by their belief in a faith that many others shared than by their posture of hostility toward any other belief.

Among rural fundamentalist leaders only William Jennings Bryan had the following, prestige, and eloquence to make the movement a popular crusade. Although advancing age had cost Bryan his commanding physical presence, he remained as optimistic, pious, and silver-tongued as ever. In 1921 Bryan sparked a drive for laws to prohibit the teaching of evolution in the public schools. He denounced Darwin with the same zeal he had once directed against William McKinley. "Evolution," he said, "by denying the need or possibility of spiritual regeneration, discourages all reforms, for reform is always based upon the regeneration of the individual." Anti-evolution bills began to turn up in legislatures, but the only victories came in the South—and there were few of those. Some officials took direct action without legislation. Governor Miriam "Ma" Ferguson of Texas outlawed textbooks upholding Darwinism. "I am a Christian mother," she declared, "and I am not going to let that kind of rot go into Texas schoolbooks."

The climax came in Tennessee, where in 1925 the legislature passed a bill outlawing the teaching of evolution in public schools and colleges. The governor, unwilling to endanger a pending school program, signed the bill with the hope that it would probably never be applied. He was

Courtroom Scene during the Scopes Trial. *The media, food vendors, and other assorted characters flocked to Dayton to hear the case against John Scopes, the teacher who taught evolution.*

wrong. In Dayton, Tennessee, citizens convinced a young high school teacher, John T. Scopes, to accept an offer from the American Civil Liberties Union to defend a test case—chiefly to put their town on the map. They succeeded beyond their wildest hopes: the publicity was worldwide, and enduring. Before the opening day of the "monkey trial" on July 13, 1925, the streets of Dayton swarmed with publicity hounds, curiosity seekers, evangelists and atheists, a blind mountaineer who proclaimed himself the world's greatest authority on the Bible, hot-dog and soda-pop hucksters, and a miscellany of reporters.

The two stars of the show—Bryan, who had offered his services to the prosecution, and Clarence Darrow, renowned trial lawyer of Chicago and confessed agnostic—united at least in their determination to make the trial an exercise in public education. When the judge ruled out scientific testimony, however, the defense called Bryan as an expert witness on biblical interpretation. In his dialogue with Darrow, he repeatedly entrapped himself in literal-minded interpretations and indeed his ignorance of biblical history and scholarship. He insisted that a "great fish" actually swallowed Jonah, that Joshua literally made the sun stand still, that the world was created in 4004 B.C.—all, according to Darrow, "fool ideas that no intelligent Christian on earth believes." It was a bitter scene. At one point the two men, their patience exhausted in the broiling summer heat, lunged at each other, shaking their fists, prompting the judge to adjourn court.

The next day testimony ended. The only issue before the court, the judge ruled, was whether Scopes had taught evolution, and no one denied that he had. He was found guilty, but the Tennessee supreme court, while upholding the act, overruled the $100 fine on a legal technicality. The chief prosecutor accepted the higher court's advice against "prolonging the life of this bizarre case" and dropped the issue. With more prescience than he knew, Bryan had described the trial as a "duel to the death." A few days after it closed, he died suddenly of a heart condition aggravated by heat and fatigue.

After the Dayton trial, the fundamentalists had spent their fury. Their very victories were self-defeating, for they served to publicize evolution, the doctrine they opposed as heresy. The states that went through the fiercest controversies became prime markets for books on evolution, and the movement roused a liberal defense of academic freedom.

PROHIBITION   Prohibition offered another example of reforming zeal channeled into a drive for moral righteousness and social conformity. Around the turn of the century the leading temperance organizations, the Women's Christian Temperance Union and the Anti-Saloon League, had converted from efforts to change individuals to a campaign for legal Prohibition. Building upon the general moral disrepute of saloons, they were able to equate the "liquor traffic" with the trusts and "special interests." At the same time, contrary to certain old-time folk beliefs that alcohol was beneficial, medical and scientific opinion now showed that it did more harm than good. By the 1910s, the Anti-Saloon League had become one of the most effective pressure groups in American history, mobilizing Protestant churches behind its single-minded battle to elect "dry" candidates.

At its "Jubilee Convention" in 1913, the league endorsed a national Prohibition Amendment to the Constitution. The 1916 elections finally produced two-thirds majorities for Prohibition in both houses of Congress. Soon the wartime spirit of sacrifice, the need to use grain for food, and wartime hostility to German-American brewers transformed the cause virtually into a test of patriotism. On December 18, 1917, Congress sent to the states the Eighteenth Amendment which, one year after ratification on January 16, 1919, banned the manufacture, sale, or transport of intoxicating liquors.

By then, however, about three-fourths of the American people already lived in states and counties that were legally dry. In 1919 the Volstead Act defined as "intoxicating" all beverages containing more than 0.5 percent alcohol, which became illegal once the Eighteenth Amendment went into effect in 1920.

But a new law did not convince people to stop drinking. Instead it provoked them to use ingenious—and illegal—ways to satisfy their thirst for alcohol. The Eighteenth Amendment had been in effect fewer than eight months when authorities found a still with a daily capacity of 130 gallons near Austin, Texas, on a farm belonging to Morris Shepard, the "Father of National Prohibition." Congress never supplied adequate enforcement, if such was indeed possible given the public thirst, the spotty support of local officials, and the profits to be made in bootlegging. In Detroit, across the river from Ontario, where liquor was still legal, the liquor industry during the Prohibition Era was second in size only to the auto industry. Speakeasies, hip flasks, and cocktail parties were among the social innovations of the Prohibition Era, along with increased drinking by women.

It would be too much to say that Prohibition gave rise to organized crime, for organized vice, gambling, and extortion had long been prac-

Speakeasy by Ben Shahn, 1933–1934. After passage of the Eighteenth Amendment, Americans would gather in hidden "speakeasies" to enjoy liquor while avoiding the laws of Prohibition.

ticed, and often tied in with the saloons. But Prohibition supplied criminals with a new source of enormous income, while the automobile and the submachine gun provided greater mobility and firepower. Gangland leaders showed remarkable gifts for exploiting loopholes in the law, when they did not simply bribe policemen and politicians. One crime boss who operated in the Midwest bought a chain of drugstores so he could order medicinal liquors and then hijack his own trucks as they transported the goods.

The most celebrated gangster and racketeer (a word coined in the 1920s) was "Scarface" Al Capone, who moved from New York to Chicago in 1920 and within a few years became the city's leading bootlegger and gambling and vice lord. In 1927 his bootlegging, prostitution, and gambling empire brought him an income of $60 million, which he flaunted in expensive suits and silk pajamas, a custom-upholstered and bulletproof Cadillac, an entourage of bodyguards, and lavish support for city charities. Capone always insisted that he was merely providing the public with goods and services it demanded: "They say I violate the prohibition law. Who doesn't?" He neglected to say that he himself had also bludgeoned to death several conspiring police lieutenants and ordered the execution of dozens of his rival criminals. Law-enforcement

Al Capone (center) *in 1929.*

officials led by FBI agent Eliot Ness began to smash his bootlegging operations in 1929, but they were unable to pin anything on Capone until a Treasury agent infiltrated his gang and uncovered evidence that nailed him for tax evasion. Tried in 1931, Capone was sentenced to eleven years in prison.

In light of the illegal activities of Capone and other organized-crime members, it came as no great surprise in 1931 when a commission under former attorney-general George W. Wickersham reported evidence that enforcement of Prohibition had broken down. Of the commission's eleven members, only five approved continued efforts to enforce Prohibition without change, four favored modifications, and two personally favored repeal. Still, the commission as a whole voted for further efforts to make Prohibition work, and President Hoover chose to stand by what he called the "experiment, noble in motive and far-reaching in purpose."

THE ROARING TWENTIES

In many ways the defensive temper of the 1920s and the repressive movements it spawned seemed the dominant trends of the times, but they arose in part as reactions to a social and intellectual revolution that seemed about to rip America away from its old moorings. In various labels given to the times, it was an era of excess, the Jazz Age, the Roaring Twenties, the ballyhoo years, the aspirin age. During those years, a new cosmopolitan, urban America confronted an old insular, rural America, and cultural conflict reached new levels of tension.

The smart set of the sophisticated metropolis developed an active disdain for the old-fashioned rural/small-town values of the hinterlands. Sinclair Lewis's novel *Main Street* (1920) portrayed the stifling, mean, cramped life of the prairie town, depicting a "savorless people, gulping tasteless food, and sitting afterward, coatless and thoughtless, in rocking chairs prickly with inane decorations, listening to mechanical music, saying mechanical things about the excellence of Ford automobiles, and viewing themselves as the greatest race in the world."

The banality of small-town life became a pervasive theme in much of the literature of the time. In *Look Homeward, Angel* (1929), Thomas Wolfe scandalized his native Asheville, North Carolina, with his unrelenting drive to escape the encircling hills and flee to the "billion-footed city." Writing for the *Smart Set* and *American Mercury,* the Baltimore journalist H. L. Mencken was the most merciless in his attacks on the American "booboisie." The daily panorama of America, he wrote, had become "so inordinately gross and preposterous . . . that only a man who was born with a petrified diaphragm can fail to laugh himself to sleep every night, and to awake every morning with all the eager, unflagging expectation of a Sunday-school superintendent touring the Paris peep-shows." The hinterlands responded with counterimages of cities infested with vice, crime, corruption, and foreigners.

THE JAZZ AGE   Writer F. Scott Fitzgerald dubbed the postwar era the "Jazz Age" because young people were willing to experiment with new forms of recreation and sexuality. The new jazz music bubbling up in New Orleans, Kansas City, Memphis, New York City, and Chicago blended African and European musical traditions into a distinctive sound characterized by improvisation, "blue notes," and polyrhythms. Its leading performers included King Oliver, Jelly Roll Morton, Louis Armstrong, and Bessie Smith. The syncopated rhythms of jazz were im-

Frankie "Half Pint" Jackson and His Band at the Sunset Cafe, Chicago, 1920s. *Jazz emerged during this period as an especially American expression of the modernist spirit. Black artists bent musical conventions to give fuller rein to improvisation.*

mensely popular among rebellious young adults and helped spawn care-free new dance steps such as the Charleston and Black Bottom, gyra-tions that shocked guardians of morality.

If people were not listening to "ragtime" or "jazz" music or to the fam-ily radio shows that became the rage in the 1920s, they were frequent-ing movie theaters. By 1930 there were more than 23,000 of them around the country, and they drew more than 95 million customers each week. In Muncie, Indiana, a small city of 35,000 people, there were nine movie theaters operating seven days a week. Movies were by far the most popular form of mass culture in the twenties, and films be-came even more favored after the introduction of sound in 1927. *The Jazz Singer,* starring Al Jolson, was the first feature-length "talkie."

THE NEW MORALITY Much of the shock to old-timers during the Jazz Age came from the revolution in manners and morals, evidenced first among young people, and especially on the college campuses. In *This Side of Paradise* (1920), a novel of student life at Princeton, F. Scott Fitzgerald wrote of "the great current American phenomenon, the 'petting party.'" None of the Victorian mothers, he said, "had any idea how casually their daughters were accustomed to be kissed." From such novels and from magazine pieces, the heartland learned about the

The cartoonist John Held's depiction of the modern coed, June 1926.

wild parties, bathtub gin, promiscuity, speakeasies, roadhouses, "shimmy dancers," and the new uses to which automobiles were put on secluded lovers' lanes.

Writers also informed the nation about the "new woman" eager to exercise new freedoms. These independent females discarded corsets, sported bobbed hair, heavy makeup, and skirts above the ankles; they smoked cigarettes and drank beer, drove automobiles, and in general, defied old Victorian expectations for womanly behavior.

Sex came to be discussed with a new frankness during the 1920s. One father said his daughter "would talk about anything; in fact, she hardly ever talked about anything else." Much of the talk derived from a spreading awareness of Dr. Sigmund Freud, the Viennese father of psychoanalysis. When in 1909 Freud visited Clark University in Massachusetts, he was surprised to find himself so well known "even in prudish America." The following year the first English translation of his *Three Contributions to a Theory of Sex* appeared. By the 1920s and 1930s, his ideas had begun to percolate into the popular awareness, and the talk spread in society and literature about libido, inhibitions, Oedipus complexes, transference, sublimation, and repression.

An obsession with sex permeated much of the literature and popular media of the day. Radio singers during the 1920s belted out songs with titles such as "Hot Lips," "I Need Lovin'," and "Burning Kisses." James Branch Cabell, who became famous when his novel *Jurgen* (1919) was banned in Boston, exploited his "phallic candor" in a string of novels, while Eugene O'Neill used Freudian themes onstage in *Desire under the Elms* (1924), *Mourning Becomes Electra* (1931), and other plays. Sex became the stock-in-trade of a prosperous tabloid press, and a new form of literature, the confession magazine, featured lurid stories about women who had gone wrong. In motion pictures "America's Sweetheart," the maidenly Mary Pickford, yielded stardom to the "vamp," Theda Bara. A rising protest over such movie fare as *Up in Mabel's Room, Sinners in Silk,* and *Her Purchase Price* impelled the movie industry to adopt stringent regulations about the content and language in films.

Fashion also reflected the rebellion against prudishness and a loosening of inhibitions. In 1919 women's skirts were typically six inches above the ground; by 1927 they were at the knees, and the "flapper"— with her bobbed hair, rolled stockings, cigarettes, lipstick, and sensuous dancing—was providing a shocking model of the new feminism. The

Women of the 1920s emulated the style of Cotton Club dancers: bobbed hair, short skirts, and lipstick.

name derived from the way fashionable women allowed their galoshes to "flap" about their ankles. Conservative moralists saw the flappers as just another sign of a degenerating society. Others saw in the "new women" an expression of American individualism. "By sheer force of violence," explained the *New York Times* in 1929, the flapper has "established the feminine right to equal representation in such hitherto masculine fields of endeavor as smoking and drinking, swearing, petting, and upsetting the community peace."

By 1930, however, the thrill of rebellion was waning; the revolution against Victorian codes had run its course. Its extreme expressions aroused doubts that the indulgence of lust equaled liberation. Still, some new folkways had come to stay. In *Middletown* (Muncie, Indiana), the subject of Robert and Helen Lynd's classic community study in the mid-1920s, a young man told them on their return in 1935 that young people had "been getting more and more knowing and bold. The fellows regard necking as a taken-for-granted part of a date." In the late 1930s, a survey disclosed that among college women almost half (47 percent) had yielded their virginity before marriage, but of these three-quarters had had sexual relations only with their future spouses.

The most pervasive change brought by the new moral code was in its views of marriage. The old code had made the husband head and mas-

Margaret Sanger (in coat with fur collar) *founded the American Birth Control League and opened the first public clinic for counseling on contraception.*

ter of the family, responsible for its support, while limiting the wife's "sphere" to the care of the home and children and the nurturing of the husband. By the 1930s, a code exalting romantic love and companionship as the basis for marriage had gained ascendancy. One sociologist announced that the "breaking of the former taboo on sex has made possible for younger men and women a healthier attitude toward marital relationship" and a greater chance for mutual happiness. More important than breaking taboos may have been the social and economic evolution of a century that had taken away functions the family once had and delivered them to the factory, the school, and other institutions. People expressed alarm in the 1920s at the rising divorce rate. The rate declined briefly with the onset of the Great Depression in 1929, but picked up again during the later 1930s and 1940s. The divorce rate reflected perhaps less an increase in unsatisfactory marriages than a greater willingness and ability to abandon an intolerable situation.

THE WOMEN'S MOVEMENT Voting rights for women arrived in 1920. It had been an unconscionably long time in coming. The suffrage movement, which had been in the doldrums since 1896, sprang back to life in the second decade of the new century. In 1912 Alice Paul, a

Quaker social worker, returned from an apprenticeship with the militant suffragists of England, and became head of the National American Woman Suffrage Association's Congressional Committee. Paul told female activists to picket state legislatures, target and "punish" politicians who failed to endorse suffrage, chain themselves to public buildings, provoke police into arresting them, undertake hunger strikes, and even adopt what the British militants called the "argument of the broken windowpane."

Paul's militant tactics and single-minded focus on the federal amendment increasingly drove a wedge between her and the larger national group. The Congressional Union, formed by her committee in 1913, became a separate organization in 1915 and changed its name to the Woman's party in 1916. This group copied the British suffragists in holding the party in power responsible for failure to act, a reasonable stance under a parliamentary system but one that led them to oppose every Democrat, which the mainline suffragists found self-defeating in America. Alice Paul nevertheless knew how to get publicity for the cause. By 1917 she and her followers were picketing the White House and deliberately provoking arrests, after which they went on hunger strikes in prison. The authorities obligingly cooperated in making martyrs. They arrested them by the hundreds.

A march for women's suffrage, 1915.

Meanwhile, Carrie Chapman Catt became head of the National Suffrage Association once again in 1915 and revived it through her gift for organization. She brought with her a legacy of about $1 million from Mrs. Frank Leslie, publisher of *Leslie's Weekly,* dedicated "to the furtherance of the cause of woman suffrage." The money became available in 1917 and contributed to organizing the final campaigns for voting rights. For several years, President Wilson evaded the issue of an amendment, but he voted for suffrage in a New Jersey referendum and supported a plank in the 1916 Democratic platform endorsing state action for women's suffrage. He also addressed the National Suffrage Organization that year, and thereafter worked closely with its leaders.

Finally, in 1918, after the House had passed the "Anthony Amendment," Wilson went before the Senate to plead for its passage there. The Senate fell short of the needed two-thirds majority by two votes, but the attention centered on the issue helped defeat two antisuffrage senators. On June 4, 1919, the Senate finally adopted the amendment by a bare two-thirds majority. Ratification of the Nineteenth Amendment took another agonizing fourteen months. The Tennessee legislature had the distinction of completing the ratification, on August 21, 1920. It was one of the climactic achievements of the Progressive Era.

Even before ratification, the suffrage organization began transforming itself into the League of Women Voters, founded in 1919, and women thereafter entered politics in growing numbers. But, it was often noted, this did not usher in a sudden release of women from all the trammels of custom and law. What was more, the suffrage victory left the broader feminist movement prey to a letdown that lasted for a generation. A few years after the triumph, Carrie Chapman Catt wrote that suffragists were disappointed "because they miss the exaltation, the thrill of expectancy, the vision which stimulated them in the suffrage campaign. They find none of these appeals to their aspiration in the party of their choice."

One group, however, wanted to take matters further. Alice Paul and the Woman's party set a new feminist goal, first introduced in Congress in 1923: an Equal Rights Amendment that would eliminate any remaining legal distinctions between the sexes—including the special legislation for the protection of working women put on the books in the previous fifty or so years. It would be another fifty years before Alice Paul would see Congress adopt her amendment in 1972; she did not live, however, to see it fall short of ratification.

The sharp increase in the number of women in the workforce during World War I proved short-lived, but in the longer view a steady increase in the numbers of employed women occurred in the 1920s and, surprisingly, continued through the depression decade of the 1930s. Still, this phenomenon represented more evolution than revolution. The greatest breakthroughs had come in the nineteenth century, and by 1900 women had at least a token foothold in most occupations. By 1910 they made up almost a quarter of all nonagricultural workers, and in 1920 they were found in all but 35 of the 572 job categories listed by the census. The continued entry of women into the workforce brought their numbers up from 8 million in the 1920 census to 10 million in 1930, and 13 million in 1940. Still, these women remained concentrated in traditional occupations: domestics, office workers, teachers, clerks, salespeople, dressmakers, milliners, and seamstresses. On the eve of World War II, women's work was little more diversified than it had been at the turn of the century, but by 1940 it was on the verge of a great transformation.

THE "NEW NEGRO" The discriminations that have befallen African Americans and women have many parallels, and the loosening of restraints for both have often coincided. The most significant development in black life during these years was the Great Migration northward. The movement of blacks to the North began in 1915–1916, when rapidly expanding war industries were experiencing a labor shortage at a time when the war prevented replacement by foreign immigrants; legal restrictions on immigration continued the movement in the 1920s. Altogether, between 1910 and 1920, the Southeast lost some 323,000 blacks, or 5 percent of the native black population, and by 1930 it had lost another 615,000, or 8 percent of the native black population in 1920. With the migration, a slow but steady growth in black political influence set in. Blacks were freer to speak and act in a northern setting; they also gained political leverage by concentrating in large cities located in states with many electoral votes.

Along with political activity came a bristling spirit of protest among blacks, a spirit that received cultural expression in a literary and artistic movement known as the "Harlem Renaissance." Claude McKay, a Jamaican immigrant, was the first significant writer of the movement, which was a rediscovery of black folk culture and an emancipation from the genteel tradition. Poems collected in McKay's *Harlem Shadows* (1922)

A Negro Family Just Arrived in Chicago from the Rural South, 1922. *Between 1910 and 1930 almost 1 million blacks left the South in the Great Migration north.*

expressed defiance in such titles as "If We Must Die" and "To the White Fiends." Other emergent writers included the versatile and prolific Langston Hughes, poet, novelist, and columnist; Zora Neale Hurston, folklorist and novelist; Countée Cullen, poet and novelist; and James Weldon Johnson, who portrayed the black mecca in *Black Manhattan.* Perhaps the greatest single creation of the time was Jean Toomer's novel *Cane,* which pictured the lives of simple folk in Georgia's black belt and the sophisticated inhabitants of Washington's brown belt. White writers such as Eugene O'Neill and Sherwood Anderson also took up the theme of what one observer in 1925 called the "New Negro," but more often than not they merely abandoned the old stereotype of the "darkie" for a new stereotype of the exotic primitive, a caricature the more fully alive for its want of inhibitions.

In its extreme expression the spirit of the New Negro found an outlet in what came to be called "Negro nationalism," which exalted black-

Marcus Garvey, founder of the United Negro Improvement Association and a leading spokesman for "Negro nationalism" in the 1920s.

ness, black cultural expression, and black exclusiveness. The leading spokesman for such views was the flamboyant Marcus Garvey. In 1916 he brought to New York the United Negro Improvement Association (UNIA), which he had started in his native Jamaica two years before. His organization grew rapidly under the strains of the postwar years. Racial bias, he said, was so ingrained in whites that it was futile to appeal to their sense of justice. Garvey told American blacks to liberate themselves from the surrounding white culture. "We have outgrown slavery," he declared, "but our minds are still enslaved to the thinking of the Master Race." He saw every white person as a "potential Klansman" and therefore endorsed the "social and political separation of all peoples to the extent that they promote their own ideals and civilization." Such a separatist message appalled other black leaders. W. E. B. Du Bois, for example, labeled Garvey "the most dangerous enemy of the Negro race." Garvey and his aides created their own black version of Christianity, organized their own fraternal lodges and community cultural centers, started their own businesses, and published their own newspaper. Garvey's message of racial pride and self-reliance appealed to many blacks who had arrived in the northern cities during the Great

Migration and grown frustrated and embittered with the hypocrisy of American democracy during the postwar economic slump.

Delivering the keynote address at the first convention of the UNIA in 1920, Garvey declared that the only lasting hope for blacks was to flee America and build their own republic in Africa. Garvey quickly enlisted half a million members and claimed as many as 6 million by 1923. At that point he was charged with fraudulent use of the mails in fund-raising. Found guilty, he went to the Atlanta penitentiary in 1925, where he remained until President Calvin Coolidge pardoned and deported him to Jamaica in 1927. Garvey died in obscurity in London in 1940, but the memory of his movement kept alive an undercurrent of racial nationalism that would reemerge later under the slogan of "black power."

A more lasting and influential force for racial equality was the National Association for the Advancement of Colored People (NAACP), started with one writer's call for a revival of the abolitionist spirit in response to a 1908 race riot in Springfield, Illinois. Plans laid at a meeting in 1909 led to a formal organization in 1910. Black participants came mainly from a group associated with Du Bois and called the Niagara Movement, which had met each year since 1905 at a place associated with antislavery (Niagara Falls, Oberlin, Boston, Harper's Ferry) and issued a defiant statement against discrimination.

Although most white progressives did not embrace the NAACP, the new group took seriously the progressive idea that the solution to social problems began with informing the people, and it planned an active press bureau to accomplish this. Du Bois became its director of publicity and research, and editor of its journal, *The Crisis*. The NAACP's main strategy was to focus on legal action designed to bring the Fourteenth and Fifteenth Amendments back to life. One early victory came with *Guinn* v. *United States* (1915). The Supreme Court struck down Oklahoma's grandfather clause, used in the state to deprive blacks of the vote. In *Buchanan* v. *Worley* (1917) the Court invalidated a residential segregation ordinance in Louisville, Kentucky.

In 1919 the NAACP launched a campaign against lynching, a still common form of vicious racism. An anti-lynching bill to make mob murder a federal offense passed the House in 1922, but it lost to a filibuster by southern senators. The bill stayed before the House until 1925, and NAACP field secretary James Weldon Johnson believed the continued agitation of the issue did more than the bill's passage would have to reduce lynchings, which decreased to a third of what they had been in the previous decade.

The emergent black political renaissance found its most important expression in two events: Oscar DePriest's election from a Chicago district in 1928 as the first black congressman since 1901, the first ever from the North; and the fight against the confirmation of Judge John J. Parker for the Supreme Court in 1930. When President Hoover submitted Parker's name, the NAACP found that, as the 1920 Republican candidate for governor of North Carolina, Parker had pronounced Negro suffrage "a source of evil and danger." The NAACP conducted its campaign, Du Bois said, "with a snap, determination, and intelligence never surpassed in colored America." Parker lost by the close vote of 41 to 39; his defeat represented the first instance of a significant black impact on Congress since Reconstruction.

THE CULTURE OF MODERNISM

SCIENCE AND SOCIAL THOUGHT As the twentieth century advanced, the easy faith in progress and reform expressed by Social Gospelers and other liberals fell victim to a series of frustrations and disasters: the Great War, the failure of the League of Nations, the failure of Prohibition, the Great Depression, the rise of Communist and fascist dictators, and continuing world crises. New currents in science and social thought also challenged the belief in a rational or melioristic universe. Darwin's biology portrayed humans as more akin to apes than to angels. And Darwin's contemporary, Karl Marx, portrayed people as creatures of economic self-interest. In capitalist society, Marx argued, freedom was an illusion: people were actually driven by impersonal economic forces. In Freud's psychology people were also driven, but by needs arising from the depths of the unconscious. Thus Darwin, Marx, and Freud suggested that rational humans did not control their fate.

Startling new findings in physics further shook the verities underlying American life and thought in the progressive period. The conventional wisdom since Sir Isaac Newton had held the universe to be governed by laws that the scientific method could ultimately uncover. A world of such certain order bolstered hopes of infinite progress in human knowledge. But this world of order and certainty disintegrated

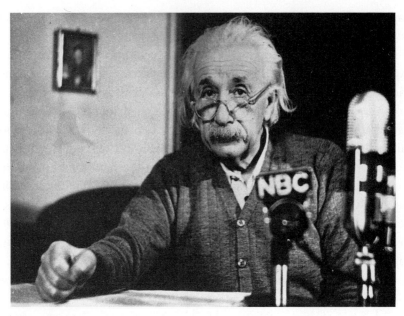

Albert Einstein.

when Albert Einstein, a young German physicist working in the Swiss patent office, announced his theory of relativity, which maintained that space, time, and mass were not absolutes but relative to the location and motion of the observer. Newton's mechanics, according to Einstein, worked well enough at relatively slow speeds, but the more nearly one approached the velocity of light (about 186,000 miles per second) the more all measuring devices would change accordingly, so that yard-sticks would become shorter, clocks and heartbeats would slow down. An observer on another planet moving at a different speed would see a quite different universe from the one we see. Even more incredibly, people traveling on a spaceship at incredible velocity, and unaware that for them time had slowed relative to earth time, might return to find that centuries had passed in their absence.

Certainty dissolved the farther one reached out into the universe. The same thing happened the farther one reached down into the minute world of the atom. The discovery of radioactivity in the 1890s showed that atoms were not irreducible units of matter but that some of them emitted particles of energy. What this meant, Einstein noted, was that mass and energy were not separate phenomena but interchangeable. In 1907 Einstein quantified this relationship in the famous and deceptively simple formula $E = mc^2$, energy equals mass times the speed of light squared.

Meanwhile the German physicist Max Planck found that electromagnetic emissions of energy, whether as electricity or light, came in little bundles, which he called quanta. The development of the quantum theory suggested that atoms were far more complex than once believed and, as the German physicist Werner Heisenberg stated in his principle of uncertainty in 1927, ultimately indescribable. One could never know both the position and the velocity of an electron, Heisenberg concluded, because the very process of observation would affect the behavior of the particle, altering its position and velocity.

Heisenberg's thesis meant that beyond a certain point things could not possibly be measured, so human knowledge had limits. "The physicist thus finds himself in a world from which the bottom has dropped clean out," a Harvard mathematician wrote in 1929. He had to "give up his most cherished convictions and faith. The world is not a world of reason, understandable by the intellect of man, but as we penetrate ever deeper, the very law of cause and effect, which we had thought to be a formula to which we could force God Himself to subscribe, ceases to have any meaning." Hard for the public to grasp, such findings proved too much even for Einstein, who spent much of the rest of his life in quest of an explanation that would combine electromagnetism and gravitation in one system and unify the relativity and quantum theories. "I shall never believe that God plays dice with the world," Einstein said.

Though few people understood it, Einstein's theory of relativity captured the imagination of a public whose common experience told them that observers differently placed got a different view of things. The ideas of relativity and uncertainty led people to deny absolute values in any sphere of society, and thus undermined the concepts of personal responsibility and absolute standards. Anthropologists aided the process by transforming the word *culture,* which had before meant refinement, into a term for the whole system of ideas, folkways, and institutions within which any group lived. Even the most primitive groups had cultures and, all things being relative, one culture should not impose its value judgments on another. Two students of Columbia University anthropology professor Franz Boas, Ruth Benedict and Margaret Mead, were especially effective in spreading this viewpoint. Benedict's *Patterns of Culture* (1934), a steady seller, introduced millions to the different values of unusual cultures, from the North American Indians to Pacific islanders, and Mead's *Coming of Age in Samoa* (1928) celebrated the healthfulness of the uninhibited sex she observed there.

MODERNIST LITERATURE   The cluster of scientific ideas associated with Darwin and Einstein inspired a revolution in the minds of intellectuals and creative artists, which they expressed in a new "modernism." The modernist world was one in which, as Karl Marx said, "All that is solid melts into air." Where nineteenth-century writers and artists took for granted an accessible world that could be readily observed and accurately represented, self-willed modernists viewed the "real" as something to be created rather than copied, expressed rather than reproduced. They thus concluded that the subconscious regions of the psyche were more interesting and potent than reason, common sense, and logic.

In the various arts, related technical features appeared: abstract painting that represented an inner mood rather than a recognizable image of an object, atonal music, free verse in poetry, stream-of-consciousness narrative, and interior monologues in stories and novels. Writers showed an intense concern with new forms in language in an effort to avoid outmoded forms and structures and to violate expectations and shock their audiences.

The search for the new centered in America's first major artistic bohemias in Chicago and New York, especially the area in lower Manhattan known as Greenwich Village. In 1913 the Armory Show in New York, which went then to Chicago, Philadelphia, and Boston, shocked traditionalists with its display of the latest works by experimental and nonrepresentational artists: post-impressionists, expressionists, primitives, and cubists. Pablo Picasso's work made its American debut there. The show aroused shocked indignation and not a little good-natured ridicule, but it was a huge success. Audiences flocked to the show, and buyers afterward snapped up the pieces for sale.

The chief American prophets of modernism were in neither Chicago nor New York, but were American expatriates in Europe: Ezra Pound and T. S. Eliot in London and Gertrude Stein in Paris, all deeply concerned with creating new and often difficult styles of modernist expression. Pound, as foreign editor for *Poetry,* became the conduit through which many American poets achieved publication in America and Britain. At the same time, he became the leader of the imagist movement, a revolt against the ornamental verbosity of Victorian poetry in favor of the concrete image.

Pound's most important protégé was T. S. Eliot, who in 1915 contributed to *Poetry* his first major poem, "The Love Song of J. Alfred Prufrock," the musings of an ineffectual man who "after tea and cakes and ices" could never find "the strength to force the moment to its crisis." Eliot's *The Waste Land* (1922) made few concessions to readers in its arcane allusions, its juxtaposition of unexpected metaphors, its deep sense of postwar disillusionment and melancholy, and its suggestion of a burned-out civilization; but it became for a generation almost the touchstone of the modern temper, along with the Irishman James Joyce's stream-of-consciousness novel *Ulysses,* published the same year. As poet and critic in the *Criterion,* which he founded in 1922, Eliot became the arbiter of modernist taste in Anglo-American literature.

Gertrude Stein, in voluntary exile since 1903, was with her brother, Leo, an early champion of modern art and a collector of early Cézannes, Matisses, and Picassos. Long regarded as no more than the literary eccentric who wrote "A rose is a rose is a rose is a rose," she came later to

Pablo Picasso's portrait of Gertrude Stein, 1906.

be recognized as one of the chief originators and propagators of modernist prose style, beginning with *Three Lives* (1906). Stein sought to capture interior moods in her writing, developing in words the equivalent of nonrepresentational painting.

But Stein was long known chiefly through her influence on such other expatriates as Ernest Hemingway, whom she told: "All of you young people who served in the war, you are the lost generation." The earliest chronicler of that generation, F. Scott Fitzgerald, blazed up brilliantly and then quickly flickered out, like all the tinseled, sad young people of his novels. Successful and famous at age twenty-four with *This Side of Paradise* (1920), along with his wife, Zelda, he lived in and wrote about the "greatest, gaudiest spree in history," and then both had their crack-up in the Great Depression. What gave depth to the best of his work was what a character in *The Great Gatsby* (1925), his finest novel, called "a sense of the fundamental decencies" amid all the surface gaiety—and almost always a sense of impending doom.

Ernest Hemingway's first novel, *The Sun Also Rises* (1926), pictures an even more desperate search for life. It focuses on a group of Ameri-

The Fitzgeralds Celebrate Christmas. *F. Scott Fitzgerald and his wife, Zelda, lived in and wrote about the "greatest, gaudiest spree in history."*

cans in Europe who career about frantically from the bistros of Paris to the bullrings of Spain. Young Jake Barnes, emasculated by a war wound, cannot marry his love, Lady Brett Ashley. "Oh, Jake," she says in the poignant ending, "we could have had such a damned good time together." "Yes," he replied. "Isn't it pretty to think so?" Hemingway's second novel, *A Farewell to Arms* (1929), is another tale of lost love. Based on Hemingway's war experience in the ambulance corps in northern Italy, it describes the love affair of a driver and a nurse who abandon the war for Switzerland, where the young woman dies in childbirth.

These novels contain the lively, even frenetic action and the cult of athletic masculinity (epitomized by the bullfighter), which became the stuff of the public image Hemingway cultivated for himself and the hallmark of such novels as *Death in the Afternoon* (1932), *To Have and Have Not* (1937), *For Whom the Bell Tolls* (1940), and *The Old Man and the Sea* (1952). Hundreds of writers tried to imitate Hemingway's terse style, but few had his gift, which lay less in what he had to say than in the way he said it.

THE SOUTHERN RENAISSANCE   As modernist literature arose as a response to the changes taking place in Western civilization, so did southern literature of the twenties reflect a world in the midst of rebirth. A southern renaissance in writing emerged from the conflict between the dying world of tradition and the modern, commercial world struggling to be born in the aftermath of the Great War. While in the South the conflict of values aroused the Ku Klux Klan and fundamentalist furies that tried desperately to bring back the world of tradition, it also inspired the vitality and creativity of the South's young writers. Allen Tate, a talented young poet, novelist, and critic, saw in the South the "curious burst of intelligence that you get at a crossing of the ways, not unlike, on an infinitesimal scale, the outburst of poetic genius at the end of the sixteenth century when commercial England began to crush feudal England."

In Nashville, *The Fugitive: A Journal of Poetry* (1922–1925) announced the arrival of the most influential group in American letters since the New England transcendentalists. The Fugitive poets began as a group of student intellectuals at Vanderbilt University who first gathered for discussions in 1915, then regrouped after the war with young Professor John Crowe Ransom as their dean and mentor. Four of the group eventually stood out in their commitment to literature as a profession: Ransom, Donald Davidson, Allen Tate, and Robert Penn Warren. The Fugitives admired T. S. Eliot and were committed to the new doctrines of modernism in literature. They revolted against the twin images of southern sentimentalists and commercial boosters. *"The Fugitive,"* Ransom wrote, "flees from nothing faster than from the high-caste Brahmins of the Old South."

It dawned on them that they had protested too much, however, when reporters drawn to the Scopes trial mocked the Bible Belt and the Benighted South. In reaction, the Fugitives began to seek a usable past in the southern agrarian tradition. They brought others into the project, and their manifesto, *I'll Take My Stand* (1930), by twelve southerners, appeared just when industrial capitalism seemed on the verge of collapse. The Vanderbilt agrarians championed, in Donald Davidson's words, a "traditional society . . . that is stable, religious, more rural than urban, and politically conservative," a society in which human needs were supplied by "Family, bloodkinship, clanship, folkways, custom, community. . . ." In the end, their agrarianism proved less important as a social-economic force than as a context for creative literature. Yet their image of the agrarian South, as one critic later wrote, provided "a rich, complex metaphor through which they presented a critique of the modern world."

"One may reasonably argue," wrote a critic in 1930, "that the South is the literary land of promise today." Just the previous year two vital figures had emerged: Thomas Wolfe, with *Look Homeward, Angel,* and William Faulkner, with *Sartoris* and *The Sound and the Fury.* Fame rushed in first on Wolfe and his native Asheville, North Carolina, which became in the 1920s a classic example of the scandalized community. "Against the Victorian morality and the Bourbon aristocracy of the South," Wolfe had "turned in all his fury," newspaper editor Jonathan Daniels, a former classmate, wrote. The reaction was not an uncommon response to the works of the southern renaissance, created by authors who had outgrown their "provincial" hometowns and looked back from new perspectives acquired through travel and education.

For all his gargantuan lust for experience and knowledge, his demonic drive to escape the encircling hills for the "fabled" world outside, his agonized search for some "lost lane-end into heaven," Wolfe never completely severed his roots in the South. *Look Homeward, Angel,* his first novel, remained his most successful; it was the lyrical and search-

William Faulkner.

ing biography of Eugene Gant's (actually Wolfe's) youth in Altamont (Asheville) and his college days in Pulpit Hill (Chapel Hill). It established him as "the giant among American writers of sensitive youth fiction."

William Faulkner's achievement, more than Wolfe's, was rooted in the coarsely textured social world that produced him. Born near Oxford, Mississippi, he grew up there and transmuted his hometown into the fictional Jefferson, Yoknapatawpha County. After a brief stint with the Royal Canadian Air Force he passed the postwar decade in what seemed to fellow townspeople an aimless drifting. He briefly attended classes at the University of Mississippi, worked at odd jobs, and went to New Orleans where he wrote *Soldiers' Pay* (1926), a novel of postwar disillusionment, and *Mosquitoes* (1927), a caricature of the New Orleans bohemians yachting on Lake Pontchartrain. Between books he shipped out briefly for Europe, and after knocking around the Gulf coast, returned to Oxford.

There, in writing *Sartoris* (1929), he began to discover that his "own little postage stamp of native soil was worth writing about" and that he "would never live long enough to exhaust it." With *Sartoris* and the creation of his mythical land of Yoknapatawpha, Faulkner kindled a blaze of creative energy. Next, as he put it, he wrote his gut into *The Sound and the Fury* (1929). It was one of the triumphs of the modernist style, but most early readers, taking their cue from the title instead of the critics, found it signified nothing.

Modernism and the southern literary renaissance, both of which emerged from the crucible of the Great War and its aftermath, were products of the twenties. But the studied alienation of the artists of the 1920s did not survive the decade. The onset of the Great Depression in 1929 seemed to spark a renewed sense of commitment and affirmation in the arts, as if people could no longer afford the art-for-art's-sake affectations of the 1920s. Alienation would give way to social purpose in the decade to come.

MAKING CONNECTIONS

- The next chapter discusses the growing consumer culture of the 1920s, an economic aspect of the "Roaring Twenties" described here.

- Chapter 28 describes changes in American literary culture wrought by the Great Depression—from the modernism discussed in this chapter to a return of social significance and the cultural "rediscovery of America" in the 1930s.

- The status of women in the workforce remained stable in the 1920s, despite the successes of the women's movement. That status changed, at least temporarily, during World War II. Chapter 30 traces the increase in women in the workforce.

FURTHER READING

For a standard survey of the interwar period, start with William E. Leuchtenburg's *The Perils of Prosperity, 1914–1932* (rev. ed., 1993). The best introduction to the culture of the 1920s remains Loren Baritz's *The Culture of the Twenties* (1970). See also Lynn Dumenil's *The Modern Temper: American Culture and Society in the 1920s* (1995). Paula S.

Fass's *The Damned and the Beautiful: American Youth in the 1920s* (1977) describes the social attitudes of youth.

John Higham's *Strangers in the Land: Patterns of American Nativism, 1860–1925* (rev. ed., 1988) details the story of immigration restriction. Paul Avrich's *Sacco and Vanzetti: The Anarchist Background* (1991) treats the famous case. For analysis of the revival of Klan activity, see Nancy MacLean's *Behind the Mask of Chivalry: The Making of the Second Ku Klux Klan* (1994). Two contrasting views of prohibition are Andrew Sinclair's *Prohibition: The Era of Excess* (1962) and Norman H. Clark's *Deliver Us from Evil: An Interpretation of American Prohibition* (1976).

Women's suffrage is treated extensively in Eleanor Flexner's *Century of Struggle: The Women's Rights Movement in the United States* (rev. ed., 1975). See Charles F. Kellogg's *NAACP: A History of the National Association for the Advancement of Colored People* (1967) for his analysis of the pioneering court cases against racial discrimination. Nathan I. Huggins's *Harlem Renaissance* (1971) assesses the cultural impact of the Great Migration in New York. On the migration to Chicago, see James R. Grossman's *Land of Hope: Chicago, Black Southerners, and the Great Migration* (1989). Nicholas Lemann's *The Promised Land* (1991) is a fine exposition of the changes brought about by the Great Migration in both the South and North.

Much of our treatment of "modernism" comes from Daniel J. Singal's *The War Within: From Victorian to Modernist Thought in the South, 1919–1945* (1982). Stanley Coben's *Rebellion Against Victorianism: The Impetus for Cultural Change in 1920s America* (1991) surveys the appeal of "modernism" among writers, artists, and intellectuals. On developments in physics, see Stanley Goldberg's *Understanding Relativity: Origin and Impact of a Scientific Revolution* (1984). Nathan G. Hale, Jr.'s *Freud and the Americans* (1971) examines the impact of psychoanalysis.

27 ∞ REPUBLICAN RESURGENCE AND DECLINE

> ### CHAPTER ORGANIZER
>
> This chapter focuses on:
>
> - the conservatism in the presidencies of Harding, Coolidge, and Hoover.
>
> - growth in the American economy in the 1920s.
>
> - the causes of the Great Depression.

The progressive coalition that reelected Woodrow Wilson in 1916 proved to be quite fragile, and by 1920 it had fragmented. It unraveled for several reasons. Radicals and other opponents of the war grew disaffected with America's entrance into the conflict and the war's aftermath. Organized labor resented the administration's unsympathetic attitude toward the strikes of 1919–1920. Farmers of the Great Plains and West thought that wartime price controls had discriminated against them. Intellectuals also drifted away from their former support of progressivism. They became disillusioned with the emphases on grassroots democracy because of popular support for Prohibition and the anti-evolution movements. The larger middle class became preoccupied with building a new business civilization "based not upon monopoly and restriction," in the words of one historian, "but upon a whole new set of business values—mass production and consumption, short hours and high wages, full employment, welfare capitalism." Progressivism's final triumphs at the national level were already pretty much foregone conclusions before the war's end: the Eighteenth Amendment, ratified in 1919, which imposed national Prohibition, and the Nineteenth Amendment, ratified in 1920, which extended women's suffrage to the entire country.

Progressivism, however, did not disappear in the 1920s. Progressives dominated Congress during much of the decade even while the White House was in conservative Republican hands. The progressive impulse for "good government" and public services remained strong, especially at the state and local levels, where movements for good roads, education, public health, and social welfare all gained momentum during the decade. Much of the progressive impulse for reform, however, was transformed into the drive for moral righteousness and conformity animating the Ku Klux Klan and the fundamentalist movement. Prohibition, at first a direct outgrowth of the reform spirit, came to be increasingly associated with the narrow intolerance of the times.

"NORMALCY"

HARDING'S ELECTION   Wilson's physical collapse during 1919 symbolized his political deterioration as well. Most Americans had grown weary of idealistic crusades and were suspicious of leaders sounding the trumpet of reform. Wilson himself recognized this fact. "It is only once in a generation," he remarked, "that a people can be lifted above material things. That is why conservative government is in the saddle two-thirds of the time."

When the Republicans met in Chicago in 1920, the Old Guard party regulars found their man in Ohio senator Warren Gamaliel Harding, who had set the tone of his campaign when he told a Boston audience: "America's present need is not heroics, but healing; not nostrums, but normalcy; not revolution, but restoration; not agitation, but adjustment; not surgery, but serenity; not the dramatic, but the dispassionate; not experiment, but equipoise; not submergence in internationality, but sustainment in triumphant nationality." His speeches, said one Democrat, were "an army of pompous phrases moving over the landscape in search of an idea."

Despite his clumsy rhetoric, Harding caught the mood of the times, a longing for "normalcy" rather than government activism and experimentalism. Harding fit the bill for presidential candidate because, though he might not set the pulses pounding, he had few enemies and had all the classic attributes of availability. The vice-presidential choice fell on Calvin Coolidge, who had caught the public fancy with his opposition to the Boston Police Strike.

The Democrats chose James Cox, former newsman and former governor of Ohio, on the forty-fourth ballot. For vice-president the convention named Franklin D. Roosevelt, who as assistant secretary of the navy occupied the same position his Republican cousin Theodore had held before him. The Democratic platform, while broadly endorsing the New Freedom, did not fully endorse the League of Nations. Cox waged an active campaign while the Republicans kept Harding home to conduct a front-porch campaign in the McKinley style—they even redid Harding's porch to look like McKinley's. The Republican platform was a masterpiece of evasion on the League of Nations. It pledged the party to "agreement among the nations to preserve the peace of the world" but "without the compromise of national independence." The phrasing satisfied both reservationists and irreconcilables.

The breakup of the Wilsonian coalition doomed the Democrats. In the words of progressive editor William Allen White, Americans in 1920 were "tired of issues, sick at heart of ideals, and weary of being noble." Wilson therefore became the Republicans' target rather than Cox, who remained a nonentity, and the country voted overwhelmingly for a "return to normalcy." Harding got 16 million votes, about 60 percent of the total, to 9 million for Cox. Harding's electoral vote margin was 404 to 127. Cox carried no state outside the Solid South, even there losing Tennessee.

EARLY APPOINTMENTS AND POLICY   Harding in office had much in common with Ulysses Grant. His cabinet, like Grant's, mixed some of the "best minds" in the party, whom he had promised to seek out, with some of the worst, cronies who sought him out. Charles Evans Hughes, like Grant's Hamilton Fish, became a distinguished secretary of state. Herbert Hoover in the Commerce Department, Andrew W.

Warren Harding "bloviating" on the stump.

Mellon in Treasury, and Henry C. Wallace in Agriculture functioned efficiently and made policy on their own. Among the others, the secretary of the interior landed in prison and the attorney-general narrowly escaped serving time. Many lesser offices went to members of the "Ohio Gang," a group with which Harding met in a "Little House on K Street" to get away from the pressures of the White House.

Until he became president, Harding had loved politics. He was the party hack par excellence, "bloviating" (a verb of his own making, which meant speaking with gaseous eloquence) on the stump, jollying it up in the clubhouse and cloakroom, hobnobbing with the great and near-great in Washington. As president, however, Harding was simply in over his head, and self-doubt overwhelmed him. "I don't think I'm big enough for the Presidency," he confided to a friend. Harding much preferred to get away with the "Ohio Gang," who shared his taste for whiskey, poker, and women. Alice Roosevelt Longworth, Theodore Roosevelt's oldest daughter, witnessed one poker session in the president's study. "Harding wasn't a bad man," she said later. "He was just a slob."

Harding and his friends set about dismantling or neutralizing as many of the social and economic components of progressivism as they could. To that end, Harding took advantage of four Supreme Court vacancies by appointing conservatives, including Chief Justice William Howard Taft, who announced that he had been "appointed to reverse a few decisions." During the 1920s, the Taft Court struck down a federal child-labor law and a minimum-wage law for women, issued numerous injunctions against striking unions, and passed rulings limiting the powers of federal regulatory agencies.

Moreover, Harding established a pro-business tone reminiscent of the McKinley White House. To sustain economic growth, Secretary of the Treasury Mellon instituted a Republican policy of reduced government spending and lower taxes. To get a better handle on expenditures, he persuaded a lukewarm Congress to pass the Budget and Accounting Act of 1921, which created a new Bureau of the Budget, headed by a Chicago banker, to prepare a unified budget, and a General Accounting Office to audit the accounts. This act realized a long-held progressive desire to bring greater efficiency and nonpartisanship to the budget preparation process. General tax reductions from the wartime level were warranted, but Mellon insisted that they should go mainly to the rich, on the Hamiltonian principle that wealth in the hands of the few would augment the general welfare through increased capital investment. Mellon's admirers tagged him "the greatest Secretary of the Treasury since Alexander Hamilton."

In Congress a group of western Republicans and southern Democrats fought a dogged battle to preserve the graduated scale built into wartime taxes, but Mellon, in office through the 1920s, eventually won out. At his behest, Congress in 1921 repealed the wartime excess-profits tax and lowered the maximum rate on personal income from 65 to 50 percent. Subsequent revenue acts lowered the maximum rate to 40 percent in 1924 and 20 percent in 1926. The Revenue Act of 1926 extended further benefits to high-income groups by lowering estate taxes and repealing the gift tax. Unfortunately, much of the tax money released to wealthy people seems to have fueled the speculative excess of the late 1920s as much as it fostered gainful enterprise. Mellon, however, did balance the federal budget for a time. Governmental expenditures fell from $6.4 billion in 1920 to $3.4 billion in 1922, and to a low of $3 billion in 1927. The national debt went down from $25.5 billion in 1919 to $16.9 billion in 1929.

In addition to tax cuts, Mellon favored the time-honored Republican policy of high tariffs, and innovations in the chemical and metal industries revived the argument for protection of infant industries from foreign competition. The Fordney-McCumber Tariff of 1922 increased rates on chemical and metal products as a safeguard against the revival of German industries that had previously commanded the field. To please the farmers, who historically benefited little from tariffs, the new act further extended the duties on farm products.

Higher tariffs, however, had ramifications that had never prevailed before and that were not quickly perceived. During the war, the United States had been transformed from a debtor to a creditor nation. In former years foreign capital had flowed into the United States, playing an important role in the economic expansion of the nineteenth century. But the private and public credits given the Allies during the war had reversed the pattern. Mellon insisted that the European powers must repay all that they had borrowed. But the tariff walls erected around the country made it all the harder for other nations to sell in the United States and thus acquire the dollars or credits with which to repay their war debts. For nearly a decade, further extensions of American loans and investments sent more dollars abroad, postponing the reckoning.

Rounding out the Republican economic program during the 1920s was a more lenient attitude toward government oversight of corporations. Neither Harding nor his successor, Coolidge, could dissolve the regulatory agencies, but they named commissioners who sought to make them more effective for a business constituency that now saw advantages in friendly regulation. Harding named conservative advocates of big business to the Interstate Commerce Commission, the Federal Reserve Board, and the Federal Trade Commission. In 1925 Coolidge's appointee as chairman of the FTC said the commission would not be used "as a publicity bureau to spread socialistic propaganda." He and his colleagues decided to withhold publicity on all cases until they were settled. Senator George Norris characterized the new appointments as "the nullification of federal law by a process of boring from within." Senator Henry Cabot Lodge agreed, boasting that "we have torn up Wilsonism by the roots."

A CORRUPT ADMINISTRATION Republican conservatives such as Lodge and Mellon were at least operating out of conviction. Members of the "Ohio Gang," however, used White House connections to line their own pockets. In 1923 Harding learned that an official of the Veterans Bureau was systematically looting medical and hospital supplies. The official fled to Europe and resigned. Harding's general counsel then committed suicide in Harding's old house in Washington. Not long afterward, a close buddy of the attorney-general also shot himself. The corrupt crony held no appointment, but had set up an office in the Justice Department from which he peddled influence for a fee. The attorney-general himself was implicated in the fraudulent handling of German assets seized after the war. When discovered, he refused to testify on the ground that he might incriminate himself. Twice brought to court, he was never indicted, for want of evidence, possibly because he had destroyed pertinent records. These were but the most visible among many scandals that touched the Justice Department, the Prohibition Bureau, and other agencies under Harding.

But one major scandal rose above all these petty peculations. Teapot Dome, like Watergate fifty years later, became the catchword for an epoch of corruption. An oil deposit under the sandstone Teapot Rock in Wyoming, Teapot Dome had been set aside as a naval oil reserve administered by the Interior Department under Albert B. Fall. At the time the move seemed a sensible attempt to unify control over public reserves.

Juggernaut. *This 1924 cartoon shows the dimensions of the Teapot Dome scandal.*

But once Fall had control, he signed contracts letting private interests exploit the oil deposits: Harry Sinclair's Mammoth Oil Company at Teapot Dome, Wyoming, and Edward L. Doheny's Pan-American Petroleum and Transport Company at Elk Hills, California. Fall argued that these contracts were in the government's interest. Yet why did Fall act in secret, without allowing competitive bids?

Suspicion grew when Fall's standard of living suddenly rose. It turned out that he had taken loans of about $400,000 (which came in "a little black bag") from Sinclair and Doheny. As the scandal unraveled, Fall emerged as a figure of tragic weakness. Once wealthy, he had lost extensive mine holdings in the Mexican Revolution, which left him with little more than an expensive dream ranch in New Mexico. Desperate for money, he took loans extended by two old friends—he and Doheny and Sinclair had once worked together in the mines. For the rest of his life, Fall insisted that the loans were unrelated to the oil leases, and that he had contrived a good deal for the government, but at best the circumstances revealed a fatal blindness to his impropriety.

The question of bribery aside, Fall's actions outraged conservationists. A senatorial investigation laid out the whole mess during 1924 to the accompaniment of public outrage. Harding himself avoided the humiliation of public disgrace. How much he knew is unclear, but he knew enough to become visibly troubled. "My God, this is a hell of a job!" he confided to the editor William Allen White. "I have no trouble with my enemies, I can take care of my enemies all right. But my damn friends, my God-damn friends, White, they're the ones that keep me walking the floor nights!" In 1923 Harding left on what would be his last journey, a western speaking tour and a trip to the Alaska Territory. Back in Seattle, he suffered an attack of food poisoning. He recovered briefly, then died in a San Francisco hotel of either coronary or cerebral thrombosis.

Not since the death of Lincoln had there been such an outpouring of grief for a "beloved President," for the kindly, ordinary man with the face of a Roman senator, the man who found it in his heart (as Wilson had not) to pardon Eugene Debs, the Socialist who had been jailed for opposing U.S. entry into World War I. Harding not only received Debs at the White House, but also pressured the steel magnates into giving up their barbarous seven-day workweek. As the black-streamered funeral train moved toward Washington, then back to Ohio, millions stood by the tracks to honor their lost leader. Eventually, however, grief yielded to scorn and contempt. For nearly a decade, the revelations of scandal were paraded before committees and then courts. Harding's long extramarital affair with Nan Britton came to light, first the birth of their illegitimate child, and later their pathetic couplings in a White House closet. Harding's love letters to another man's wife also surfaced. As a result of his amorous detours and corrupt associates, Harding's foreshortened administration came to be widely viewed as one of the worst in American history.

Recent assessments of Harding's presidency, however, suggest that the scandals obscured some real accomplishments. Some historians credit Harding for leading the nation out of the turmoil of the postwar years and creating the foundation for the decade's remarkable economic boom. Revisionists also stress that he was a hardworking president who played a far more forceful role than previously assumed in shaping his administration's economic and foreign policies and in shepherding legislation through Congress. But even Harding's foremost scholarly defender admits that he lacked good judgment and "probably should never have been president."

"SILENT CAL"   Some kind of charmed existence seemed to put Calvin Coolidge in the right place at the right time. The news of Harding's death came when he was visiting his father in the mountain village of Plymouth, Vermont, his birthplace. There at 2:47 on the morning of August 3, 1923, by the light of a kerosene lamp, Colonel John Coolidge administered the oath of office to his son. The rustic simplicity of Plymouth, the very name itself, evoked just the image of roots and solid integrity that the country would long for amid the coming disclosures of corruption. The new first lady, Grace Coolidge, was as unpretentious as her husband, and Alice Roosevelt Longworth found the new atmosphere of the White House "as different as a New England front parlor is from the back room in a speakeasy."

Coolidge brought to the White House a clear conviction that the presidency should revert to its Gilded-Age stance of passive deference to Congress. "Four-fifths of our troubles," Coolidge predicted, "would disappear if we would sit down and keep still." He abided by this rule, insisting on twelve hours of sleep and an afternoon nap. H. L. Mencken asserted that Coolidge "slept more than any other president, whether by day or by night. Nero fiddled, but Coolidge only snored."

Warren Harding (left) *and Calvin Coolidge* (right).

Americans took to their hearts the unflappability of "Silent Cal," his inactivity, and the pictures of him fishing, pitching hay, and wearing Indian bonnets while primly clad in business suit and necktie. His taciturn nature became the subject of affectionate humor, often no doubt apocryphal, as in the story of a dinner guest who bet Coolidge that she could make him say three words. "You lose," he replied.

The image of "Silent Cal," however, distorts as much as it illuminates his character. Although a man of few words, he was not as bland or as dry as critics claimed. Yet he was conservative. Herbert Hoover, the secretary of commerce, once stressed that Coolidge was a "real conservative, probably the equal of Benjamin Harrison. He was a fundamentalist in religion, in the economic and social order, and in fishing, too." (He used live worms for bait.) Even more than Harding, Coolidge embraced the orthodox creed of business. "The chief business of the American people is business," he intoned. "The man who builds a factory builds a temple. The man who works there worships there." Where Harding had sought to balance the interests of labor, agriculture, and industry, Coolidge focused on industrial development at the expense of the other two areas. He sought to unleash the free-enterprise system and, even more than Harding, he strove to end government regulation of business and industry. His pro-business stance led the *Wall Street Journal* to exult: "Never before, here or anywhere else, has a government been so completely fused with business."

THE 1924 ELECTION   Coolidge was also married to politics, and he proved better at it than Harding. He distanced himself from the Harding scandals, and put in charge of the prosecutions two lawyers of undoubted integrity. Coolidge quietly took control of the Republican party machinery and seized the initiative in the campaign for nomination, which he won with only token opposition.

The Coolidge luck held as the Democrats fell victim to internal dissensions. The source of the party's trouble was its uneasy alliance of incongruous elements, which lent much truth to humorist Will Rogers's classic statement: "I am a member of no organized political party. I am a Democrat." The party's divisions illustrated the deep alienation growing up between the metropolis of the Roaring Twenties and the more traditional hinterland, a gap that the Democrats could not bridge. After much factional fighting, it took the Democrats 103 ballots to bestow the tarnished nomination on John W. Davis, a Wall Street lawyer from West Virginia who could hardly outdo Coolidge in conservatism.

Meanwhile a growing farmer-labor coalition was mobilizing a third-party effort. In Minnesota during 1922 and 1923, a new Farmer-Labor party elected two United States senators, a congressman, and some lesser officeholders. In 1922 the railroad unions, smarting from administration opposition, sponsored a Conference for Progressive Political Action that got the support of many farmers who were suffering from price declines at the time. Meeting in Cleveland on July 4, 1924, the conference reorganized as the Progressive party and nominated Robert M. La Follette for president. The Wisconsin reformer also won the support of Minnesota's Farmer-Labor party, the Socialist party, and the American Federation of Labor.

In the campaign Coolidge chose to focus on La Follette, whom he called a dangerous radical who would turn America into a "communistic and socialistic state." The country preferred to "keep cool with Coolidge," who swept both the popular and electoral votes by decisive majorities. Davis took only the Solid South, and La Follette carried only his native Wisconsin. The popular vote went 15.7 million for Coolidge, 8.4 million for Davis, and 4.8 million for La Follette—the largest popular vote ever polled by a third-party candidate. The electoral voting result was 382 to 136 to 13, respectively.

THE NEW ERA

Business executives interpreted the Republican victory as a vindication of their leadership, and Coolidge saw in the surging prosperity of the time a confirmation of his philosophy. In fact, the prosperity and technological achievements of the time known as the New Era had much to do with Coolidge's victory over the Democrats and Progressives. Those in the large middle class who before had formed an important part of the Progressive party coalition were now absorbed instead in the new world created by advances in communications, transportation, and business organization.

More people than ever before had the money and leisure to taste of the affluent society, and a growing advertising industry fueled its appetites. By the mid-1920s advertising had become both a huge enterprise and a major institution of social control. Old-time values of thrift and saving gave way to a new economic ethic that made spending a virtue. The innovation of installment buying made increased consumption feasible for many. A newspaper editorial insisted that the American's "first importance to his country is no longer that of citizen but that of consumer. Consumption is a new necessity."

MOVIES, RADIO, AND THE ECONOMY Consumer-goods industries fueled much of the boom from 1922 to 1929. Moderately priced creature comforts, including items such as hand cameras, wristwatches, cigarette lighters, vacuum cleaners, washing machines, and linoleum, became increasingly available. Inventions in communications and transportation, such as motion pictures, radio, telephones, and automobiles, not only fueled the boom but also brought transformations in society.

In the 1890s a quick sequence of inventions had made it possible for a New York audience to see the first moving picture show in 1896. By 1905 the first movie house opened in Philadelphia, and within three years there were nearly 10,000 scattered across the nation. By 1915 Hollywood had become the center of movie production, grinding out

Charlie Chaplin in a scene from his classic film, The Kid.

Westerns and the timeless comedies of Mack Sennett's Keystone Studios, where a raft of slapstick comedians, most notably Charlie Chaplin, perfected their art into a form of social criticism.

Birth of a Nation, directed in 1915 by D. W. Griffith, became a triumph of cinematic art that marked the arrival of the modern motion picture and at the same time perpetuated a grossly distorted image of Reconstruction. Based on Thomas Dixon's novel *The Clansman,* the movie featured stereotypes of villainous carpetbaggers, sinister mulattoes, blameless white southerners, and faithful "darkies." The film grossed $18 million and revealed the industry's enormous potential. By the mid-1930s, every large American city and most small towns had theaters, and movies replaced oratory as the chief mass entertainment of Americans. A further advancement in technology came with the "talkies." The first movie with sound accompaniment appeared in 1926, but the success of talking pictures was established by *The Jazz Singer* (1927), starring Al Jolson.

Radio broadcasting had an even more spectacular growth. Except for experimental broadcasts, radio served only for basic communication until 1920. In that year station WWJ in Detroit began transmitting news bulletins from the *Detroit Daily News,* and KDKA in Pittsburgh, owned by the Westinghouse Company, began regular programs. The

Radio Broadcast, *mid-1920s. Radios gained such popularity that within a decade millions would tune into newscasts, soap operas, sporting events, and church services.*

first radio commercial aired in New York in 1922. By the end of that year, there were 508 stations and some 3 million receivers in use. In 1926 the National Broadcasting Company, a subsidiary of RCA, began linking stations into a network; the Columbia Broadcasting System entered the field the next year. In 1927 a Federal Radio Commission was established to regulate the industry; in 1934 it became the Federal Communications Commission, with authority over other forms of communication as well.

AIRPLANES, AUTOMOBILES, AND THE ECONOMY   Advances in transportation were equally startling. Wilbur and Orville Wright of Dayton, Ohio, built and flew the first airplane at Kitty Hawk, North Carolina, in 1903. But the use of planes advanced slowly until the outbreak of war in 1914, after which the Europeans rapidly developed the plane as a military weapon. When the United States entered the war, it still had no combat planes—American pilots did battle in British or French aircrafts. An American aircraft industry developed during the war but foundered in the postwar demobilization. Under the Kelly Act of 1925,

Orville Wright pilots the first flight of a power-driven airplane, while his brother, Wilbur, runs alongside.

however, the government began to subsidize the industry through air-mail contracts. The Air Commerce Act of 1926 started a program of federal aid to air transport and navigation, including aid in establishing airports.

A psychological boost to aviation came in 1927 with the solo flight of Charles A. Lindbergh, Jr., from New York to Paris in thirty-three hours and thirty minutes. The deed, which won him a prize of $25,000, was dramatic. He flew through a dense fog for part of the way and at times

Charles Lindbergh in front of the airplane he piloted across the Atlantic, The Spirit of St. Louis.

dropped to within ten feet of the water before sighting the Irish coast and regaining his bearings. The parade down Broadway in his honor surpassed even the celebration of the Armistice.

By 1930 the industry had forty-three airlines, which carried 385,000 passengers over routes totaling 30,000 miles. Another great impetus came after 1936 when the slow Ford trimotor plane gave way to the more efficient twin-engine Douglas DC-3 as the chief passenger plane. In 1940, nineteen airlines carried 2.8 million passengers over routes of 43,000 miles.

By far the most significant economic and social development of the time was the automobile. The first motor car had been manufactured for sale in 1895, but the founding of the Ford Motor Company in 1903 revolutionized the industry. Ford's reliable Model T (the celebrated "tin lizzie") came out in 1908 at a price of $850 (in 1924 it would sell for $290). Ford vowed "to democratize the automobile. When I'm through everybody will be able to afford one, and about everyone will have one."

He was right. In 1916 the total number of cars manufactured passed 1 million; by 1920 more than 8 million were registered, and in 1929 more than 23 million. The production of automobiles consumed large amounts of the nation's steel, rubber, glass, and textile output, among other materials. It gave rise to a gigantic market for oil products just as the Spindletop gusher (1901) in Texas heralded the opening of vast southwestern oil fields. It quickened the movement for good roads, fi-

Ford Motor Company's Highland Park Plant, 1913. *Gravity slides and chain conveyors aided the mass production of automobiles.*

nanced in large part from a gasoline tax, speeded transportation, encouraged the sprawl of suburbs, and sparked real-estate booms in California and Florida.

By virtue of its size and importance, the automobile industry became the salient example of mass production. When Ford brought out the Model T in 1908, demand ran far ahead of production. Ford then hired a factory expert who, by rearranging the plant and installing new equipment, met his production goal of 10,000 cars in twelve months. The next year Ford's new Highland Park plant was planned with job analysis in mind. In 1910 gravity slides were installed to move parts from one workbench to the next, and by the end of 1913 the system was complete, with endless chain conveyors pulling the parts along feeder lines and the chassis down the final assembly line.

STABILIZING THE ECONOMY   The drive for efficiency, which had been a prominent feature of the progressive impulse, was now powering the wheels of mass production and consumption, and had become a cardinal belief of Republican leaders. Herbert Hoover, who served as secretary of commerce through the Harding-Coolidge years, was himself an engineer who had made a fortune in far-flung mining operations in Australia, China, Russia, and elsewhere. Out of his experiences in business and his management of Belgian relief, the Food Administration, and other wartime activities, Hoover had developed a philosophy that he set forth in his book *American Individualism* (1922). The idea might best be called "cooperative individualism," or in one of his favorite terms, "associationalism." The principle also owed something to his Quaker upbringing, which taught him the virtue of the work ethic and mutual help. When he applied it to the relations of government and business, Hoover prescribed a kind of middle way between the regulatory and trust-busting traditions, a way of voluntary cooperation.

As secretary of commerce, Hoover was a human dynamo who made the trifling Commerce Department into the government's most dynamic agency. During a period of governmental retrenchment, he was engaged in expansion. Through an enlarged Bureau of Foreign and Domestic Commerce he sought out new opportunities and markets for business. A Division of Simplified Practice in the Bureau of Standards sponsored more than a thousand conferences on design, production, and distribution, carried forward the wartime move toward standardization of everything from automobile tires and paving bricks to bedsprings and toilet paper, and reduced in number the different kinds of bolts, nuts, and screws. "When I go to ride in an automobile," Hoover told the author Sherwood Anderson, "it does not matter to me that there are a million automobiles on the road just like mine. I am going somewhere and I want to get there in what comfort I can and at the lowest cost." In 1926 Hoover created a Bureau of Aviation and the next year set out to bring order into the new field of radio with the Federal Radio Commission.

Hoover's priority was the burgeoning trade-association movement. Through trade associations, business leaders in a given field would gather and disseminate information on everything: sales, purchases, shipments, productions, and prices. This information allowed them to make plans with more confidence, the advantages of which included predictable costs, prices, and markets, as well as more stable employment and wages. Sometimes abuses crept in as trade associations engaged in price-fixing and other monopolistic practices, but the Supreme Court in 1925 held the practice of sharing information as such to be within the law.

THE BUSINESS OF FARMING   During the 1920s, agriculture remained a weak sector in the economy, in many ways as weak as its position in the 1890s, when cities flourished and agriculture languished. Briefly after the war, the farmers' hopes soared on wings of prosperity. The wartime boom lasted into 1920, and then prices collapsed. Wheat went in eighteen months from $2.50 a bushel to less than $1; cotton from 35¢ per pound to 13¢. Low prices persisted into 1923, especially in the wheat and corn belts, and after that improvement was spotty. A bumper cotton crop in 1926 resulted only in a price collapse and an early taste of depression in much of the South, where foreclosures and bankruptcies spread.

Yet in many ways farmers shared the entrepreneurial outlook of the New Era. Farms, like corporations, were getting larger, more efficient, and more mechanized. By 1930 about 13 percent of all farmers had tractors, and the proportion was even higher on the western plains. Better plows, drills, cultivators, planters, and other machines were part of the mechanization process that accompanied improved crop yields, fertilizers, and animal breeding.

Farm organizations of the mid- to late 1920s moved away from the alliance with urban labor that marked the Populist Era and toward a new view of farmers as businessmen. During the postwar farm depression, the idea of marketing cooperatives became the farmer's equivalent of the businessman's trade-association movement. Farm groups formed regional commodity-marketing associations that pushed for ironclad contracts with producers to deliver their crops over a period of years. They also promoted "orderly marketing," which required standards and grades, efficient handling of commodities and advertising, and a businesslike setup with professional technicians and executives.

One farm group carried into the twentieth century the old-time gospel of populism. The Farmers' Union, founded in Texas in 1902, emerged in the 1920s mainly as a western wheat-belt group. It was soon overshadowed by the American Farm Bureau Federation, a new group representing the emerging "businesslike" attitude of commercial agriculture in the New Era. Founded in 1920 at a meeting in Chicago, the Farm Bureau was an unexpected outgrowth of the farm demonstration movement. Its philosophy stemmed in part from business leaders who supported the county farm bureaus, but more directly from the larger commercial farmers in its membership. Farm Bureau strength in the Midwest and South represented what by the 1920s was being called a "marriage of cotton and corn."

But if concern with marketing co-ops and other businesslike approaches drew farmers farther away from populism, it was still inevitable that farm problems should invite political solutions. The most effective political response to the falling crop prices of the early 1920s was the formation of the farm bloc, a coalition of western Republicans and southern Democrats that put through an impressive, if fairly moderate, program of legislation from 1921 to 1923. The farm bloc pushed legislation to prevent collusion designed to keep farm prices down. It won an act to exempt farm cooperatives from antitrust laws, and another that set up twelve intermediate credit banks on the model of the Federal Land Banks. The new banks filled the gap of six months to three years between the provisions of short-term loans under the Federal Reserve System and long-term loans by the Federal Land Banks, and could lend to cooperative producing and marketing associations.

Meanwhile a new panacea appeared on the horizon. In 1924 Senator Charles L. McNary of Oregon and Representative Gilbert N. Haugen of Iowa introduced the first McNary-Haugen Bill. It sought to secure "equality for agriculture in the benefits of the protective tariff." Complex as it would have been in operation, it was simple in conception: in short, a plan to dump American farm surpluses on the world market in order to raise prices in the home market. The goal was to achieve "parity"—that is, to raise domestic farm prices to a point where they would have the same purchasing power relative to other prices they had had between 1909 and 1914, a time viewed in retrospect as a golden age of American agriculture.

A McNary-Haugen Bill passed both houses of Congress in 1927, only to be vetoed by President Coolidge. The process was repeated in 1928. Coolidge pronounced the measure an unsound effort at price-fixing, and un-American and unconstitutional to boot. In a broader sense, however, McNary-Haugenism did not fail. The debates made the farm problem into an issue of national policy and defined it as a problem of surpluses. The evolution of the McNary-Haugen plan, moreover, revived the idea of an alliance between the South and West, a coalition that in the next decade became a dominant influence on national farm policy. That policy would follow a different procedure, but its chief focus would be on surpluses and its goal would be "parity."

SETBACKS FOR UNIONS   Urban workers shared more than farmers in the affluence of the times. "A workman is far better paid in America than anywhere else in the world," a French visitor wrote in 1927, "and his standard of living is enormously higher." Non-farm workers gained about 20 percent in real wages between 1921 and 1928, while farm income rose only 10 percent. The benefits of this rise, however, were distributed unevenly. Miners and textile workers suffered a decline in real wages. In these and other trades, technological unemployment followed the introduction of new methods and machines, because technology destroyed as well as created jobs.

Organized labor, however, did no better than organized agriculture in the 1920s. In fact, unions suffered a setback after the growth years of the war. The Red Scare and strikes of 1919 left the uneasy impression that unions practiced subversion, an idea that the enemies of unions promoted. The brief postwar depression of 1921 further weakened the unions, and they felt the severe impact of open-shop associations that proliferated across the country after the war, led by chambers of commerce and other business groups. In 1921 business groups in Chicago designated the open shop the "American Plan" of employment. While the open shop in theory implied only the employer's right to hire anyone, in practice it meant discrimination against unionists and refusal to recognize unions even in shops where most of the workers belonged to one.

Nor were employers always above the use of strong-arm methods, such as requiring "yellow-dog" contracts that forced workers to agree to stay out of unions, using labor spies, exchanging blacklists, and resorting to intimidation and coercion. Some employers tried to kill the unions with kindness. They introduced programs of "industrial democracy" guided by company unions or various schemes of "welfare capitalism" such as profit-sharing, bonuses, pensions, health programs, recreational activities, and the like. The benefits of such programs were often considerable.

Prosperity, propaganda, welfare capitalism, and active hostility combined to cause union membership to drop from about 5 million in 1920 to 3.5 million in 1929. In 1924 Samuel Gompers, founder and longtime president of the AFL, died; William Green of the mine workers, who took his place, embodied the conservative, even timid, attitude of unions during the period. The outstanding exception to the anti-union policies of the decade was passage of the Railway Labor Act in 1926, which abolished the Railway Labor Board and substituted a new Board of Mediation. The act also provided for the formation of railway unions "without interference, influence, or coercion," a statement of policy not extended to other workers until the 1930s.

The Cash Register Chorus
*sings of its ties to Coolidge in
this 1924 cartoon.*

PRESIDENT HOOVER, THE ENGINEER

HOOVER VS. SMITH   On August 2, 1927, while on vacation in the Black Hills of South Dakota, President Coolidge passed out slips of paper to reporters with the statement: "I do not choose to run for President in 1928." Exactly what he meant puzzled observers then and since. Apparently he at least half hoped for a convention draft, but his statement cleared the way for Herbert Hoover to mount an active campaign. Well before the 1928 Republican convention in Kansas City, Hoover was too far in the lead to be stopped. The platform took credit for prosperity, cost-cutting ("raised to a principle of government"), debt and tax reduction, and the protective tariff ("as vital to American agriculture as it is to manufacturing"). It rejected the McNary-Haugen program, but promised a farm board to promote orderly marketing as a way to manage surpluses.

The Democratic nomination went to Governor Alfred E. Smith of New York. The party's farm plank, while not endorsing McNary-Haugen, did pledge "economic equality of agriculture with other industries." Like the Republicans, the Democrats promised to enforce the Volstead Prohibition Act and, aside from calling for stricter regulation of waterpower resources, promised nothing that departed from the conservative position of the Republicans.

The Democratic party had had its fill of factionalism in 1924, and all remained fairly harmonious until Smith made two controversial decisions. In his acceptance speech he expressed a personal desire to liberalize the Volstead Act, and then he selected for national party chairman a man who was Catholic, "wet," a General Motors executive, and at least until recently a Republican. Hoover by contrast had pronounced Prohibition "a great social and economic experiment, noble in motive and far-reaching in purpose," and called for better enforcement.

The two candidates projected sharply different images that obscured the essential likeness of their programs. Hoover was the Quaker son of middle America, the successful engineer and businessman, the architect of Republican prosperity, while Smith was the prototype of those things rural/small-town America distrusted: the son of Irish immigrants, Catholic, and anti-Prohibition. Outside the large cities all those attributes were handicaps he could scarcely surmount, for all his affability and wit.

In the election Hoover won in the third consecutive Republican landslide, with 21 million popular votes to Smith's 15 million, and an even more top-heavy electoral vote majority of 444 to 87. Hoover even cracked the Solid South, leaving Smith only a hard core of six Deep South states plus Massachusetts and Rhode Island. The election was above all a vindication of Republican prosperity. But the shattering defeat of the Democrats concealed a portentous realignment in the making. Smith had nearly doubled the vote for Davis, the Democratic candidate of four years before. Smith's image, though a handicap in the hinterlands, swung big cities back into the Democratic column. In the farm states of the West there were signs that some disgruntled farmers had switched over to the Democrats. A coalition of urban workers and unhappy farmers was in the making.

HOOVER IN CONTROL   The milestone year 1929 dawned with high hopes. Business seemed good, incomes were rising, and the chief architect of Republican prosperity was about to enter the White House. "I have no fears for the future of our country," Hoover told the audience at his inauguration. "It is bright with hope." For Hoover the presidency crowned a career of steady ascent, first in mining, then in public service. Hoover's image combined the benevolence fitting a director of wartime relief and the efficiency of a businessman and administrator.

Forgotten in the rush of later events would be Hoover's credentials as progressive and humanitarian. Over the objection of Treasury Secretary Mellon, he announced a plan for tax reductions in the low-income brackets. He took action against corrupt patronage practices, and refused to countenance "Red hunts" or interference with peaceful picketing of the White House. He defended his wife's right to entertain the wife of Oscar DePriest, the first black congressman since 1901 and the first ever from the North; sought more federal money for all-black Howard University; and proposed that the membership of the new federal parole board reflect the number of blacks and women in prison.

Hoover's program to stabilize business carried over into his program for agriculture, the most visibly weak sector of the economy. To treat the malady of glutted markets he offered two main remedies: federal help for cooperative marketing and higher tariffs on farm products. In 1929 he pushed through a special session of Congress the Agricultural Marketing Act, which set up a Federal Farm Board with a revolving loan

"I have no fears for the future of our country," Herbert Hoover told his audience at his inauguration in 1929.

fund of $500 million to help farm cooperatives market the major commodities. The act also provided a program in which the Farm Board could set up "stabilization corporations" empowered to buy surpluses off the market. Unluckily for any chance of success the plan might have had, it got under way almost simultaneously with the onset of the depression that fall.

Farmers gained even less from tariff revision. What Hoover won after fourteen months of struggle with competing local interests was in fact a general upward revision of duties on manufactures as well as farm goods. The Hawley-Smoot Tariff of 1930 carried duties to an all-time high. Rates went up on some 70 farm products and more than 900 manufactured items. More than 1,000 economists petitioned Hoover to veto the bill because, they said, it would raise prices to consumers, damage the export trade and thus hurt farmers, promote inefficiency, and provoke foreign reprisals. Events proved them right, but Hoover felt that he had to go along with his party in an election year.

THE ECONOMY OUT OF CONTROL   The tariff did nothing to check a deepening crisis of confidence in the economy. After the slump of 1921, the idea grew that with recovery business had entered a New Era

Miami Beach, 1925. *A real-estate boom transformed southern Florida in the early 1920s, but the bubble burst in mid-1926.*

of permanent growth. But real growth propelled an expansive ballyhoo, and a growing contagion of get-rich-quick schemes. Speculative mania fueled the Florida real-estate boom that began when the combination of Coolidge prosperity and Ford's "tin lizzies" gave people extra money and made Florida an accessible playground. By 1925 Miami had become a scene of frantic excitement. In the funfair of fast turnover the reckless speculator was, if anything, more likely to gain than the prudent investor, and the "binder boys" perfected to a fine art the practice of making money at little or no risk. The principle was to pay a small "binder" fee for an option to buy on promise of a later down payment, then reap a profit by selling such binders that might pass through a dozen hands and might or might not convey title. By mid-1926, when there were no more "bigger fools" left to whom one could "pass the baby," the Florida bubble burst.

For the losers it was a sobering lesson, but it proved to be but an audition for the Great Bull Market in stocks. Until 1927 stock values had gone up with profits, but then they began to soar on wings of pure speculation. Mellon's tax reductions had released money that, with the help of aggressive brokerage houses, found its way to Wall Street. Instead of trading binders on real estate, one could buy stock on margin—that is, make a small down payment (the "margin") and borrow the rest from a broker who held the stock as security against a down market. If the stock declined and the buyer failed to meet a margin call for more money, the broker could sell the stock to cover his loan. Brokers' loans more than doubled from 1927 to 1929.

Gamblers in the market ignored warning signs. By 1927 residential construction and automobile sales were catching up to demand, business inventories rose, and the rate of consumer spending slowed. By mid-1929 production, employment, and other measures of economic activity were declining. Still the stock market rose.

By 1929 the market had entered a fantasy world. Conservative financiers and brokers who counseled caution were ignored. Hoover was worried, and he urged stock exchange and Federal Reserve officers to discourage speculation. In August the Federal Reserve Board raised the rate on loans to member banks (the rediscount rate) to 6 percent, but with no effect. On September 4 stock prices wavered, and the day after that they dropped, opening a season of fluctuations. The Great Bull Market staggered on into October, trending downward but with enough good days to keep hope alive. On October 22 a leading bank president told reporters: "I know of nothing fundamentally wrong with the stock market or with the underlying business and credit structure."

THE CRASH AND ITS CAUSES   The next day prices crumbled, and the day after that a wild scramble to unload stocks lasted until word arrived that leading bankers had formed a pool to stabilize prices. Prices steadied for the rest of the week, but after a weekend to think the situation over, stockholders began to unload on Monday. On Tuesday, October 29, the most devastating single day in the market's history, brokers reported sales of 16.4 million shares (at the time 3 million shares traded was a busy day). The plunge in prices fed on itself as brokers sold the shares they held for buyers who failed to meet their margin calls. During October, stocks on the New York Exchange fell in value by 37 percent.

Business and government leaders initially expressed hope. According to President Hoover, "the fundamental business of the country" was sound. Some speculators who got out of the market went back in for

Apprehensive crowds gathered on the steps of the Subtreasury Building, across from the New York Stock Exchange, as news of a stock collapse spread, October 29, 1929.

bargains but found themselves caught in a slow, tedious erosion of values. By March 1933, the value of stocks on the New York Exchange was less than a fifth of the value at the market's peak. The *New York Times* stock average, which stood at 452 in September 1929, bottomed at 52 in July 1932.

Caution became the watchword for consumers and businesspeople. Buyers held out for lower prices, orders fell off, wages fell or ceased altogether, and the decline in purchasing power brought further cutbacks in business. From 1929 to 1932 Americans' personal incomes declined by more than half. Unemployment continued to rise. Farmers, already in trouble, faced catastrophe. More than 9,000 banks closed during the period, hundreds of factories and mines shut down, and thousands of farms were foreclosed for debt and sold at auction.

The crash had revealed the fundamental business of the country to be unsound. Too many businesses had maintained prices and taken profits while holding down wages with the result that about one-third of the personal income went to only 5 percent of the population. By plowing most profits back into expansion rather than wage increases, business brought on a growing imbalance between rising productivity and declining purchasing power. As the demand for goods declined, the rate of investment in the new plants began to decline. For a time the softness of purchasing power was concealed by greater use of installment buying, and the deflationary effects of high tariffs were concealed by the volume of loans and investments abroad that supported foreign demand for American goods. But the flow of American capital abroad began to dry up when the stock market began to look more attractive. Swollen profits and dividends, together with the Mellon tax policies, enticed the rich into market speculation. When trouble came, the bloated corporate structure collapsed.

Governmental policies also contributed to the debacle. Mellon's tax reductions brought oversaving, which helped diminish demand for consumer goods. The growing money supply fed the fever of speculation. Hostility toward labor unions discouraged collective bargaining and may have worsened the prevalent imbalances in income. High tariffs discouraged foreign trade. Lax enforcement of antitrust laws encouraged concentration, monopoly, and high prices.

Another culprit was the gold standard. The world monetary system remained fragile throughout the 1920s. When economic output, prices, and savings began dropping in 1929, policy makers—certain that they

Secretary of the Treasury Andrew Mellon, described by one reporter as "a tired double-entry bookkeeper who is afraid of losing his job."

had to keep their currencies tied to gold at all costs—either did nothing or tightened money supplies, thus exacerbating the downward spiral. The only way to restore economic stability within the constraints of the gold standard was to let prices and wages continue to fall, allowing the downturn, in Andrew Mellon's words, to "purge the rottenness out of the system." What happened instead was that such passivity turned a recession into the world's worst depression.

THE HUMAN TOLL OF DEPRESSION   The devastating collapse of the economy caused immense social hardships. By 1933 there were over 13 million people out of work. As factories shut down, banks closed, farms went bankrupt, and millions of people found themselves not only jobless, but also homeless and penniless. Hungry people lined up at churches and soup kitchens; others rummaged through trash cans behind restaurants. Many slept on park benches or in back alleys. Others congregated in makeshift shelters in vacant lots. Thousands of men in search of jobs "rode the rails." These "hobos" or "tramps," as they were derisively called, sneaked onto empty railway cars and rode from town to town looking for work. During the winter, homeless people wrapped themselves in newspapers to keep warm, referring to them sarcastically as "Hoover blankets." Some grew weary of their grim fate and ended their lives. Suicide rates soared during the 1930s.

HOOVER'S EFFORTS AT RECOVERY   Not only did the policies of public officials help bring on economic collapse, but few public leaders acknowledged the crisis: all that was needed, they thought, was a slight correction of the market. Those who held to the dogma of laissez-faire thought the economy would cure itself. The best policy, Secretary Mellon advised, would be to "liquidate labor, liquidate stocks, liquidate the farmers, liquidate real estate." Hoover himself had little patience with speculators, but he was unwilling now to sit by and let events take their course. Hoover in fact did more than any president had ever done before in such dire economic circumstances. Still, his own philosophy, now hardened into dogma, set limits to governmental action, and he was unready to set it aside even to meet an emergency.

Hoover believed that the nation's fundamental business structure was sound and that the country's main need was confidence. In speech after speech, he exhorted the public to keep up hope, and he asked business owners to keep the mills and shops open, maintain wage rates, and spread the work to avoid layoffs—in short to let the first shock fall on corporate profits rather than on purchasing power. In return, union leaders, who had little choice, agreed to refrain from wage demands and strikes. As it happened, however, words were not enough, and the prediction that good times were just around the corner (actually made by the vice-president, though attributed to Hoover) eventually became a sardonic joke.

Hoover did more than try to reassure the American public. He hurried the building of public works in order to provide jobs, but state and local cutbacks more than offset new federal spending. At Hoover's demand the Federal Reserve returned to an easier credit policy, and Congress passed a modest tax reduction to put more purchasing power in people's pockets. The Federal Farm Board stepped up its loans and its purchases of farm surpluses, only to face bumper crops in 1930 despite droughts in the Midwest and Southwest. The high Hawley-Smoot Tariff, proposed at first to help farmers, brought reprisals abroad, devastating foreign trade.

As always, depression hurt the party in power. Democrats exploited Hoover's predicament for all it was worth, and more. But their role in building the depression image of Hoover has been overblown. In 1930 the floundering president was easy game. During the war, "to Hooverize" had signified patriotic sacrifice; now the president's name signified distress. Near the city dumps, along the railroad tracks, the dispossessed huddled in shacks of tarpaper and galvanized iron, old packing boxes, and abandoned cars. These squalid settlements became known as "Hoovervilles"; a "Hoover flag," was an empty pocket turned inside out. In November 1930 the Democrats gained their first national victory since 1916, winning a majority in the House and enough gains in the Senate to control it in coalition with western agrarians.

One irony of the time was that the great humanitarian of wartime relief was recast as the stubborn opponent of depression relief. But Hoover was still doing business at the same old stand: his answer remained voluntarism. When the head of the Emergency Committee for Employment strongly recommended a governmental spending program for road building and other public works, the president turned it down. His annual message to Congress in December 1930 demanded that each community and state undertake the relief of distress "with that sturdiness and independence which built a great Nation."

In the first half of 1931 economic indicators rose, renewing hope for

Hoovervilles in New York's Central Park, 1931.

an upswing. Then, as recovery beckoned, another shock occurred. In May 1931 the failure of Austria's largest bank triggered panic in central Europe. To halt the domino effect of spreading defaults, President Hoover proposed a one-year moratorium on both reparations and war-debt payments. The moratorium, as it happened, became permanent simply by process of default. The major European nations accepted the moratorium and later also a temporary "standstill" on settlement of private obligations between banks. The general shortage of monetary exchange drove Europeans to withdraw their gold from American banks and dump their American securities. One European country after another abandoned the gold standard and devalued its currency. Even the Bank of England went off the gold standard. The United States meanwhile slid into the third bitter winter of depression.

CONGRESSIONAL INITIATIVES   With a new Congress in session, demands for federal action impelled Hoover to stretch his individualistic philosophy to its limits. He was ready now to use governmental resources at least to shore up the financial institutions of the country. In 1932 the new Congress set up the Reconstruction Finance Corporation

(RFC) with $500 million (and authority to borrow $2 billion more) for emergency loans to banks, life insurance companies, building and loan societies, farm mortgage associations, and railroads. Under former vice-president Charles G. Dawes, it authorized $1.2 billion in loans within six months. The RFC staved off bankruptcies, but Hoover's critics found in it favoritism to business, the most damaging instance of which was a $90 million loan to Dawes's own Chicago bank, made soon after he left the RFC in 1932. The RFC nevertheless remained a key agency through the New Deal and World War II.

Further help to the financial structure came with the Glass-Steagall Act of 1932, which broadened the definition of commercial loans that the Federal Reserve would support. The new arrangement also released about $750 million in gold formerly used to back Federal Reserve Notes, countering the effect of foreign withdrawals and domestic hoarding of gold at the same time that it enlarged the supply of credit. For homeowners the Federal Home Loan Bank Act of 1932 created with Hoover's blessing a series of discount banks for home mortgages. They provided for savings and loan and other mortgage agencies a service much like that the Federal Reserve System provided to commercial banks.

Hoover's critics said all these measures reflected a dubious "trickle-down" theory. If government could help banks and railroads, asked New York senator Robert G. Wagner, "is there any reason why we should not likewise extend a helping hand to that forlorn American, in every village and every city of the United States, who has been without wages since 1929?" The contraction of credit devastated debtors such as farmers and those who made purchases on the "installment plan" or who held "balloon-style" mortgages whose monthly payments increased over time. By 1932 members of Congress were filling the hoppers with bills for federal measures to provide relief to individuals. At that point Hoover might have pleaded "dire necessity" and taken the leadership of the relief movement and salvaged his political fortunes.

Instead he held back and only grudgingly edged toward federal relief. On July 21, 1932, Hoover signed the Emergency Relief and Construction Act, which avoided a direct federal dole to individuals but gave the RFC $300 million for relief loans to the states, authorized loans of up to $1.5 billion for state and local public works, and appropriated $322 million for federal public works.

Relief for farmers had long since been abandoned. In mid-1931 the government quit buying surpluses and helplessly watched prices slide. In 1919 wheat had fetched $2.16 a bushel; by 1932 it had sunk to 38¢. Cotton brought 17¢ a pound in 1929; before the 1932 harvest it went to 5¢. Other farm prices declined comparably. Net cash income for farmers dropped more than 55 percent from 1929 to 1932. Between 1930 and 1934, ownership of nearly a million farms passed from the farmers to the mortgage holders.

FARMERS AND VETERANS IN PROTEST   Faced with the loss of everything, some desperate farmers began to defy the law. Angry mobs stopped foreclosures and threatened to lynch the judges sanctioning them. In Nebraska farmers burned corn to keep warm. Iowans formed the militant Farmers' Holiday Association, which called a farmers' strike and forcibly blocked deliveries of produce.

In the midst of the crisis, there was desperate if nebulous talk of revolution. "Folks are restless," Mississippi governor Theodore Bilbo told reporters in 1931. "Communism is gaining a foothold. . . . In fact, I'm getting a little pink myself." Bilbo was doing his usual put-on, but across the country the once-obscure Communist party began to draw crowds to its rallies and willing collaborators into its "hunger marches." In Alabama it formed a Share Croppers Union and reaped a propaganda windfall when the party went to the defense of the Scottsboro Boys, nine black itinerants accused on flimsy evidence of raping two white girls on a freight train in northern Alabama. Around Harlan, Kentucky, desperate coal miners embraced the Communist-run National Mine Workers' Union, which eventually fell victim to guns and whips and ultimately to the rock-ribbed faith of miners who heard leaders "denounce our government and our flag and our religion." Yet, for all the sound and fury, few Americans were converted to the Communist view during the 1930s. Party membership in America never rose much above 100,000.

Fears of mass disorder arose when unemployed veterans converged on Washington in the spring of 1932. The "Bonus Expeditionary Force" grew quickly to more than 15,000. Their purpose was to get immediate payment of the bonus to world-war veterans that Congress had voted in 1924. The House approved a bonus bill, but when the Senate voted it down, most of the veterans went home. The rest, having no place to go,

Unemployed veterans, members of the "Bonus Expeditionary Force," clash with Washington, D.C., police at Anacostia Flats, July 1932.

camped in vacant government buildings and in a shantytown at Anacostia Flats, within sight of the Capitol.

The chief of the Washington police gave the squatters a friendly welcome and won their trust. But a fearful White House fretted. Eager to disperse them, Hoover convinced Congress to pay for their tickets home. More left, but others stayed even after Congress adjourned, hoping at least to meet with the president. Late in July the administration ordered the government buildings cleared. In the ensuing melee, one policeman panicked, fired into the crowd, and killed two veterans. The president then acceded to a request from his secretary of war to move in about 700 soldiers under General Douglas MacArthur, aided by junior officers Dwight D. Eisenhower and George S. Patton, Jr. The soldiers drove out the unarmed veterans and their families, injuring dozens. The one fatality—from tear gas—was an eleven-week-old boy born at Anacostia.

General MacArthur claimed that the "mob," animated by "the essence of revolution," was about to seize control of the government. The administration insisted that the Bonus Army consisted mainly of Communists and criminals, but neither a grand jury nor the Veterans Administration could find evidence to support the charge. One observer wrote before the incident: "There is about the lot of them an atmosphere of hopelessness, of utter despair, though not of desperation. . . . They have no enthusiasm whatever and no stomach for fighting."

Their mood, and the mood of the country, echoed that of Hoover himself. He worked hard, but took no joy from his labors. "I am so tired," he sometimes said, "that every bone in my body aches." News conferences became more strained and less frequent. When friends urged him to seize the reins of leadership he said, "I can't be a Theodore Roosevelt," or "I have no Wilsonian qualities." The gloom, the sense of futility, communicated itself to the country. In a mood more despairing than rebellious, people waited to see what another presidential campaign would produce.

MAKING CONNECTIONS

- This chapter discusses setbacks for labor unions during the Republican administrations of the 1920s. In the next chapter, unions win new protections under Franklin Roosevelt's New Deal.

- An element of the "normalcy" discussed in this chapter was American isolationism from global affairs. Chapter 29 discusses that isolationism in the context of the coming of World War II.

- Compare the characteristics of 1920s American society with the postwar society and culture of the 1950s, discussed in Chapter 32.

FURTHER READING

A fine synthesis of events immediately following the First World War is Ellis W. Hawley's *The Great War and the Search for a Modern Or-*

der: A History of the American People and Their Institutions, 1917–1933 (1979).

For an introduction to Harding, see Francis Russell's *The Shadow of Blooming Grove: Warren G. Harding in His Times* (1968). Robert K. Murray's *The Harding Era: Warren G. Harding and His Administration* (1969) is more favorable to Harding. On Coolidge, see Donald R. McCoy's *Calvin Coolidge: The Silent President* (1967). Studies on Hoover include Joan Hoff Wilson's *Herbert Hoover: Forgotten Progressive* (1975) and George Nash's multivolume work, *The Life of Herbert Hoover* (1983–1987). Other works on politics include Burl Noggle's *Teapot Dome: Oil and Politics in the 1920s* (1962) and David Burner's *The Politics of Provincialism: The Democratic Party in Transition, 1918–1932* (1968).

The impact of transportation is gauged in Reynold M. Wik's *Henry Ford and Grassroots America* (1972). Roland Marchand's *Advertising the American Dream: Making Way for Modernity, 1920–1940* (1985) covers the development of national advertising in the 1920s. Susan J. Douglas's *Inventing American Broadcasting, 1899–1922* (1989) is a cultural history of the formative years of radio. Motion pictures are the subject of Robert Sklar's *Movie-Made America: A Cultural History of American Movies* (1975) and Lary May's *Screening out the Past: The Birth of Mass Culture and the Motion Picture Industry* (1980).

Overviews of the depressed economy are found in Charles P. Kindleberger's *The World in Depression, 1929–1939* (rev. ed., 1986) and Peter Fearon's *War, Prosperity and Depression: The U.S. Economy, 1917–1945* (1987). John Kenneth Galbraith details the fall of the stock market in *The Great Crash, 1929* (1955). A different interpretation is given in Peter Temin's *Did Monetary Forces Cause the Great Depression?* (1976).

John A. Garraty's *The Great Depression: An Inquiry into the Causes, Course, and Consequences of the Worldwide Depression of the Nineteen-Thirties* (1986) describes how people survived the depression. First-hand accounts of the Great Depression can be found in Tom E. Terrill and Jerrold Hirsch's *Such As Us: Southern Voices of the Thirties* (1978), Studs Terkel's *Hard Times* (1970), Robert S. McElvaine's *Down and Out in the Great Depression: Letters from the Forgotten Man* (1983), and *"Slaves of the Depression": Workers' Letters about Life on the Job* (1989), edited by Gerald Markowitz and David Rosner.

28 ✺ NEW DEAL AMERICA

CHAPTER ORGANIZER

This chapter focuses on:

- the social effects of the Great Depression and Roosevelt's efforts at relief, recovery, and reform.

- criticism of the New Deal, from both the right and the left.

- how the New Deal greatly expanded the federal government's authority and responsibilities.

- the change in cultural direction in the 1930s.

*U*pon arriving in the White House Franklin Roosevelt inherited a nation mired in an unprecedented economic depression. He and a supportive Congress immediately adopted bold measures to relieve the human suffering and promote economic recovery. Such initiatives provided the foundation for what came to be called welfare capitalism. A three-pronged strategy guided the New Dealers. They first sought to remedy the financial crisis and provide short-term emergency relief for the jobless. They then tried to promote industrial recovery through increased federal spending and co-operative agreements between management and organized labor. The third prong of the New Deal strategy involved efforts to raise commodity prices (and thereby farm income) by paying farmers to reduce crops and herds, thereby shrinking supply and raising prices. None of these initiatives worked perfectly, but they combined to restore hope and energy to a nation mired in depression and uncertainty.

FROM HOOVERISM TO THE NEW DEAL

FDR'S ELECTION   On June 14, 1932, while the Bonus Army was still encamped in Washington, Republicans gathered in Chicago to renominate Hoover. The delegates went through the motions in a mood of defeat. By contrast, the Democrats converged on Chicago confident that they would nominate the next president. New York governor Franklin D. Roosevelt was already the front-runner with most of the delegates lined up, and he went over the top on the fourth ballot.

In a bold gesture, Roosevelt flew to Chicago and appeared before the convention in person to accept the nomination instead of awaiting formal notification. "Let it . . . be symbolic that . . . I broke traditions," he told the delegates. "Republican leaders not only have failed in material things, they have failed in national vision, because in disaster they have held out no hope. . . . I pledge you, I pledge myself to a new deal for the American people." What the New Deal would be Roosevelt himself had little idea as yet, but unlike Hoover, he was flexible and willing to experiment. What was more, his upbeat personality communicated joy and hope. His campaign song was "Happy Days Are Here Again."

Born in 1882 into a wealthy family, educated by governesses and tutors at Springwood, his father's rambling Hudson River Valley estate, young Franklin led the cosmopolitan life of a young patrician. After attending Groton, an elite Connecticut boarding school, he earned degrees from Harvard and Columbia University Law School. While a law student, he married his distant cousin, Anna Eleanor Roosevelt, the niece of President Theodore Roosevelt.

Franklin Roosevelt began work with a prominent Wall Street law firm, but soon lost interest in legal affairs and decided to enter politics. In 1910 he won a Democratic seat in the New York State Senate. As a freshman legislator he displayed the contradictory qualities that would always characterize his political career: an aristocrat with a sincere affinity for common folk; a traditionalist with a penchant for experiment; an affable charmer with a luminous smile and upturned chin who also harbored profound convictions; and a skilled political tactician with a shrewd sense of timing and a distinctive willingness to listen to and learn from others.

In 1912 Roosevelt backed Wilson, and for both of Wilson's terms he served as assistant secretary of the navy. Then, in 1920, largely on the strength of his name, he became Democrat James Cox's running mate. The following year, at age thirty-nine, his career seemed cut short by an attack of poliomyelitis that left him permanently crippled, unable to stand or walk without braces. But the struggle for recovery transformed the once supercilious young aristocrat into one of the most outgoing political figures of the century. A friend recalled that he emerged from his struggle with polio "completely warm-hearted, with a new humility of spirit" that led him to identify with the poor and suffering. Justice Oliver Wendell Holmes, Jr., later summed up his qualities this way: "A second-class intellect—but a first-class temperament."

For seven years, aided by his talented wife Eleanor, Roosevelt fought his way back to health and in 1928 emerged again on the national scene to nominate Al Smith for the presidency. At Smith's urging, he ran for governor of New York to strengthen the ticket, and he won while Smith was losing the state to Hoover in the race for president. Reelected governor by a whopping majority of 700,000 in 1930, Roosevelt became the favorite for president in 1932.

Partly to dispel doubts about his health, Roosevelt set forth on a grueling campaign tour. He blamed the depression on Hoover and the Republicans, and he began to define what he meant by the "New Deal." Like Hoover, Roosevelt promised to balance the budget, but he was willing to incur short-term deficits to prevent starvation and dire want. On the tariff, he was evasive. On farm policy, he offered several options pleasing to farmers and ambiguous enough not to alarm city dwellers. He did call for strict regulation of utilities and for at least some development of public power, and he consistently stood by his party's pledge to repeal the Prohibition Amendment. Perhaps most important, he recognized that a mature economy would require national planning. "The country needs, and, unless I mistake its temper, the country demands bold, persistent experimentation. . . . Above all, try something."

What came across to voters, however, was less the content of Roosevelt's speeches than the confidence of the man. By contrast, Hoover

Governor Franklin D. Roosevelt, the Democratic nominee, campaigning in Topeka, Kansas. Roosevelt's confidence inspired voters.

lacked assurance. He could turn a neat phrase, but many elegant passages suffered from his pedestrian delivery. Democrats, he argued, ignored the international causes of the depression. They were taking a reckless course. Roosevelt's policies, he warned, "would destroy the very foundations of our American system." Pursue them, and "grass will grow in the streets of a hundred cities, a thousand towns." But few were listening. Amid the persistent depression, the country wanted a new course, a new leadership, a new deal.

Many concerned observers took a dim view of both candidates. Those who believed that only a radical departure would suffice went over to Socialist Norman Thomas, who polled 882,000 votes, and a few preferred the Communist party candidate, who got 103,000. The wonder is that a desperate people did not turn in greater numbers to radical candidates. Instead they swept Roosevelt into office with 22.8 million votes to Hoover's 15.8 million. Hoover carried only four states in New England plus Pennsylvania and Delaware, and lost in the electoral college by 472 to 59.

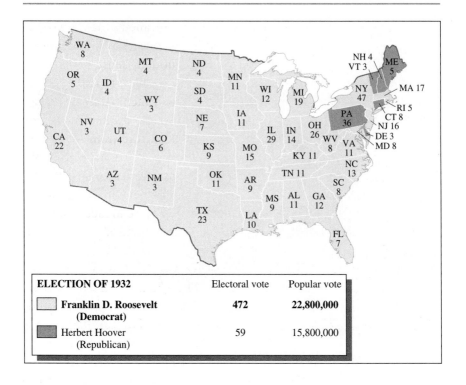

ELECTION OF 1932	Electoral vote	Popular vote
Franklin D. Roosevelt (Democrat)	472	22,800,000
Herbert Hoover (Republican)	59	15,800,000

THE INAUGURATION For the last time the country waited four months, until March 4, for a new president and Congress to take office. The Twentieth Amendment, ratified on February 6, 1933, provided that presidents would thereafter take office on January 20 and the newly elected Congress on January 3.

The bleak winter of 1932–1933 became what one historian called "the interregnum of despair." Amid spreading destitution and misery, unemployment continued to rise, and panic struck the banking system. As bank after bank announced they were closing and did not have adequate cash to repay depositors, people rushed to their own bank to remove their deposits. Many discovered that they, too, were caught short. The "run" on the banks exacerbated the crisis. In Michigan, where automobile production stalled, the threat of runs on the banks impelled the governor to extend the Lincoln's Birthday closing indefinitely. As the panic spread, governors of other states also found excuses for imposing banking holidays. When the Hoover administration ended, four-fifths of the nation's banks were closed, and the country teetered on the brink of economic paralysis.

The profound crisis of confidence that prevailed when Roosevelt took the oath of office on March 4, 1933, gave way to a mood of expectancy. The new president conveyed a confident sense of vigor and action. First, he asserted "that the only thing we have to fear is fear itself—nameless, unreasoning, unjustified terror which paralyzes needed efforts to convert retreat into advance." Roosevelt warned that emergency measures might call for a temporary departure from the normal balance of executive and legislative authority. If need be, he said, "I shall ask the Congress for the remaining instrument to meet the crisis—broad executive power to wage a war against the emergency as great as the power that would be given me if we were in fact invaded by a foreign foe." It was a measure of the country's mood that this call received the loudest applause.

Many people used the nation's mobilization for World War I as a model for dealing with the economic crisis. Many of Roosevelt's appointees had been involved in the wartime mobilization. Other cabinet officers drew upon backgrounds in social work. Frances Perkins, the secretary of labor, was the first female cabinet member. A graduate of Mount Holyoke, she worked with Jane Addams at Chicago's Hull House at the turn of the century. Later she was appointed executive secretary of the Consumers League in New York and became an enormously effective advocate for labor reform.

Franklin Delano Roosevelt (right) *and a glum Herbert Hoover ride to the Capitol on inauguration day.*

COMPETING SOLUTIONS   Roosevelt's "brain trust" of advisers developed conflicting opinions about how best to rescue the economy from depression. Some promoted vigorous enforcement of the antitrust laws as a means of restoring competition; others argued just the opposite, saying that antitrust laws should be suspended so as to enable large corporations to collaborate with the federal government and thereby better manage the overall economy. Still others called for a massive expansion of welfare programs and a prolonged infusion of increased government spending to address the profound human crisis and revive the economy.

For his part, Roosevelt vacillated among these three schools of thought. He was willing to try some elements of each without ever embracing one approach completely. When asked by a reporter to label his philosophy, Roosevelt replied: "Philosophy? I am a Christian and a Democrat—that's all." His willingness to act decisively and to experiment with new programs and policies set his presidency apart. He was a pragmatist rather than an ideologue. As he once explained, "Take a method and try it. If it fails admit it frankly and try another." He liked to say, "I have no expectation of making a hit every time I come to bat. What I seek is the highest possible batting average." Roosevelt's "New Deal," therefore, would take the form of a series of trial-and-error actions.

STRENGTHENING THE MONETARY SYSTEM   The first order of business for the new administration was to free up the channels of finance. On his second day in office, Roosevelt called Congress to meet in special session on March 9, and then declared a four-day banking holiday. It took Congress only seven hours to pass the Emergency Banking Relief Act, which permitted sound banks to reopen and provided managers for those that remained in trouble. On March 12, in the first of his radio "fireside chats," the president insisted that it was safer to "keep your money in a reopened bank than under the mattress." The following day, deposits in reopened banks exceeded withdrawals, and by March 15 banks controlling nine-tenths of the nation's banking resources were once again open. The crisis had ended, and the new administration was ready to get on with its broader program.

In rapid order Roosevelt undertook to meet two specific pledges in the Democratic platform. At his behest, Congress passed an Economy Act granting the executive branch the power to cut salaries, reduce pay-

The Galloping Snail. *A vigorous Roosevelt drives the Congress to action in this* Detroit News *cartoon, March 1933.*

ments to veterans for non-service-connected disabilities, and reorganize federal agencies in the interest of economy. The Beer-Wine Revenue Act amended the Volstead Act to permit sale of beverages with an alcoholic content of 3.2 percent. The Twenty-first Amendment, already submitted by Congress to the states, would be declared ratified on December 5, thus ending the "noble experiment" of Prohibition.

The measures of March were but the beginning. During the session from March 9 to June 16, the so-called Hundred Days, Congress received and enacted fifteen major proposals from the president with a dizzying speed unlike anything seen before in American history:

March 9	The Emergency Banking Relief Act
March 20	The Economy Act
March 31	Establishment of the Civilian Conservation Corps
April 19	Abandonment of the gold standard
May 12	The Federal Emergency Relief Act
May 12	The Agricultural Adjustment Act, including the Thomas Amendment, which gave the president powers to expand the money supply
May 12	The Emergency Farm Mortgage Act, providing for the refinancing of farm mortgages
May 18	The Tennessee Valley Authority Act, providing for the unified hydroelectric development of the Tennessee Valley

May 27	The Federal Securities Act, requiring full disclosure in the issue of new securities
June 5	The Gold Repeal Joint Resolution, which abrogated the gold clause in public and private contracts
June 13	The Home Owners' Loan Act, setting up the Home Owners' Loan Corporation to refinance home mortgages
June 16	The National Industrial Recovery Act, providing for a system of industrial self-regulation under federal supervision and for a $3.3 billion public-works program
June 16	The Glass-Steagall Banking Act, separating commercial and investment banking and establishing the Federal Deposit Insurance Corporation
June 16	The Farm Credit Act, which reorganized the agricultural credit system

With the banking crisis over, there remained an acute debt problem for farmers and homeowners, and a lingering distrust of the banks, which might yet be aroused again. By executive decree, Roosevelt reorganized all farm credit agencies into the Farm Credit Administration (FCA). By the Emergency Farm Mortgage Act and the Farm Credit Act, Congress authorized extensive refinancing of farm mortgages at lower interest rates. Within seven months, the FCA loaned distressed farmers more than $100 million, nearly four times as much as all the land-bank loans made the previous year.

The Home Owners' Loan Act provided a similar service to city dwellers through the new Home Owners' Loan Corporation (HOLC). The HOLC refinanced mortgage loans at lower monthly payments for strapped homeowners. This helped slow the rate of foreclosures. The Glass-Steagall Banking Act further shored up confidence in the banking system. It created the Federal Deposit Insurance Corporation (FDIC) to guarantee bank deposits up to $5,000. To prevent speculative abuses, it separated investment and commercial banking corporations and extended the Federal Reserve's regulatory power over credit. The Federal Securities Act required the full disclosure of information about new stock and bond issues, at first by registration with the Federal Trade Commission, later with the Securities and Exchange Commission (SEC), which was created to regulate the stock and bond markets.

Throughout 1933 Roosevelt tinkered with devaluation of the currency as a way to raise prices and thus ease the debt burden. Having already put an embargo on the withdrawal of gold deposits at the outset of his administration, on April 5 he used powers granted by the Emergency Banking Act to order all gold turned in to the Federal Reserve Banks. On April 19 the government officially abandoned the gold standard: the consequent decline in the value of the dollar increased the prices of commodities and stocks at home. The Gold Repeal Joint Resolution canceled the gold clause in federal and private obligations, made all contracts payable in legal tender, and thus completed the abandonment of the gold standard. The experiment ended when Congress passed the Gold Reserve Act of January 30, 1934, which authorized the president to impound all gold in the Federal Reserve Banks and reduce the theoretical gold value of the dollar. By executive order he set the price of an ounce of gold at $35, which in effect reduced the dollar's gold content. It was done, Roosevelt said, "to make possible the payment of . . . debts at more nearly the price level at which they had been incurred." Prices did rise, and the high price set on gold drew most of the world's supply to the United States, where it was buried in the vaults at Fort Knox, Kentucky.

RELIEF MEASURES   In 1933 relieving the widespread personal distress caused by the Great Depression was an urgent priority, as it would remain until World War II. As Roosevelt once remarked, the "test of our progress is not whether we add to the abundance of those who have much. It is whether we provide enough for those who have too little." As a first step toward such relief Congress created the Civilian Conservation Corps (CCC), which was designed to give work to unemployed and unmarried young men aged eighteen to twenty-five.

Nearly 3 million young men took to the woods to work at a variety of CCC jobs in forests, parks, recreational areas, and soil conservation projects. As part of the CCC, they built roads, bridges, camping facilities, and fish hatcheries, planted trees, taught farmers how to control soil erosion, and fought fires. They were paid a nominal sum of $30 a month, of which $25 went home to their families. The enrollees could also take education courses and earn high school diplomas. Directed by army officers and foresters, they worked under a semimilitary discipline

A CCC camp in the Berkshire Mountains of New England, 1933.

and provided perhaps the most direct analogue of war in the whole New Deal. Like the military at the time, the CCC camps were racially segregated. In Texas, African Americans were initially told that the camps were for whites only, and this falsehood helps explain the low number of blacks enrolled. Only 400 black Texans, less than 5 percent of the total number of men enrolled, participated in the CCC.

The Federal Emergency Relief Administration (FERA), created with an authorization of $500 million, addressed the broader problems of human distress. Harry L. Hopkins, an indefatigable social worker who had directed Roosevelt's state relief efforts in New York, pushed the program with a boundless energy. The FERA expanded the assistance that had begun under Hoover's RFC, but with a difference. Federal monies flowed to the states in grants rather than "loans." While FERA continued to channel aid through state agencies to relief clients mainly in the form of direct cash payments, Hopkins enlarged its scope by gradually developing work programs for education, student aid, rural rehabilitation, and for the many jobless wanderers across the country. He pushed an "immediate work instead of dole" approach on local officials, but they preferred the dole as an easier and quicker way to reach the needy.

The first large-scale experiment with work relief was the Civil Works Administration (CWA), created during the winter of 1933–1934, when it had become apparent that even the largesse of the FERA would not prevent widespread privation. The CWA provided jobs and wages to those able to work. It was implemented hastily, and many of its projects were "make-work" jobs such as leaf-raking and ditch-digging; but it spent over $900 million (mostly in wages) for a variety of useful projects, from highway repairs to teaching jobs that helped keep the schools open. The CWA, unlike the FERA, was a federal operation from top to bottom. The CWA was abandoned in the spring of 1934, having served its purpose of helping people weather the winter; but Roosevelt and Hopkins continued to favor work relief over the dole, which they believed to have a debilitating psychological effect on the unemployed.

RECOVERY THROUGH REGULATION

Beyond rescuing the banks and providing relief to the unemployed lay the long-term goals of recovery for agriculture and business. Members of Franklin Roosevelt's "brain trust" were largely heirs to Theodore Roosevelt's New Nationalism. Like the earlier progressives, they insisted that the trend toward economic concentration was inevitable. They also believed that the mistakes of the 1920s showed that the only way to operate an integrated economy at capacity and in the public interest was through efficient regulation and organized central planning, not through trust-busting. The success of centralized planning during World War I reinforced such ideas. New farm and recovery programs sprang from their beliefs.

AGRICULTURAL RECOVERY: THE AAA The sharp decline in commodity prices after 1929 meant that many farmers could not afford to plant or harvest their crops. The Agricultural Adjustment Act of 1933 contained nearly every major plan applicable to farm relief, but only some of its provisions were implemented. The act sought to control farm production through compensating farmers for voluntary cutbacks in production in an effort to restore farm prices to "parity," or the same level they had reached relative to other prices during the farmers' golden age of 1909–1914 (1919–1929 for tobacco). The act covered seven "basic commodities," a number later enlarged, and the money for benefit payments came from a processing tax levied on each—at the cotton gin, for example, or the flour mill.

But by the time Congress acted, the growing season was already advanced. The prospect of another bumper cotton crop forced the AAA to sponsor a plow-under program. To destroy a growing crop was a "shocking commentary on our civilization," Agriculture Secretary Henry A. Wallace lamented. "I could tolerate it only as a cleaning up of the wreckage from the old days of unbalanced production." Moreover, given the oversupply of hogs, some 6 million little pink pigs were slaughtered "before they could reach the full hogness of their hogdom." It could be justified, Wallace said, only as a means of helping farmers to do with pigs what steelmakers did with pig iron—cut production to fit the market and therefore raise prices.

It worked temporarily. Cotton farmers received about $112 million in benefit payments, and the crop was reduced by about 4 million bales below the preprogram estimate. Cotton prices rose from 5¢ a pound in May to above 11¢ per pound in July (parity was 12.7¢), but sagged again as the crop came in. In an effort to take up the slack, the president set up the Commodity Credit Corporation (another CCC!), which extended loans first on cotton and later on other crops kept in storage and off the market. In principle, if not in form, it was a revival of the old Farmers' Alliance–Populist subtreasury plan. Loans averaged 10¢ per pound on the 1933 crop and 12¢ per pound in 1934, pegged at those levels because no farmer had to sell for less. But the carryover surplus from the crops of previous years still weighed the market—and prices—down.

Another drastic step was taken in 1934 with passage of the Bankhead Cotton Control Act, which specified that all farmers had to accept cotton production quotas if two-thirds of a county's voters authorized them; farmers who tried to sell more than their share of the quota would be stopped by a prohibitive tax. Almost all of the counties in Texas complied with the Bankhead Act. By 1936 Texans had signed almost 900,000 cotton reduction contracts, more than twice that of any other state. The Kerr-Smith Tobacco Control Act of 1934 applied similar quotas to tobacco.

For a while these farm measures worked. By the end of 1934, Secretary of Agriculture Wallace could report significant declines in wheat,

<u>Dust Storm Approaching, 1930s.</u> *When a dust storm blew in, it would bring complete darkness as well as sand and grit that would soon cover every surface, both inside and out.*

cotton, and corn production and a simultaneous increase in commodity prices. Farm income increased by 58 percent between 1932 and 1935. The AAA, however, was only partially responsible for such gains. The devastating drought that settled over the Plains states between 1932 and 1935 played a major role in reducing production and creating the epic "dust bowl" migrations so poignantly evoked in John Steinbeck's *Grapes of Wrath.* Many of these migrant families had actually been driven off the land by AAA benefit programs that encouraged large farmers to take the lands worked by tenants and sharecroppers out of cultivation first.

Although it created unexpected problems, the AAA achieved real successes in boosting the overall farm economy. Then on January 6, 1936, in *United States* v. *Butler,* the Supreme Court, by a vote of six to three, declared the AAA's processing tax unconstitutional because farm production was intrastate and thus beyond the reach of the power of Congress to regulate interstate commerce. The administration hastily devised a new plan in the Soil Conservation and Domestic Allotment Act, which it pushed through Congress in six weeks. The new act omitted processing taxes and acreage quotas, but provided benefit payments for soil conservation practices that took land out of soil-depleting staple crops, thus indirectly achieving crop reduction. Since the money came out of general funds and not from taxes, this approach was not vulnerable to lawsuits. The act boosted a developing conservation movement directed by the Soil Conservation Service, which had been created in 1935.

The act was an almost unqualified success as an engineering and educational project because it went far to heal the scars of erosion and the plague of dust storms. But soil conservation nevertheless failed as a device for limiting production. With their worst lands taken out of production, farmers cultivated their fertile acres more intensively. In response, Congress passed the Second Agricultural Adjustment Act in 1938, which reestablished the earlier programs but left out the processing taxes. Benefit payments would come from general funds. By the time the second AAA reached a test in the Supreme Court, changes in the Court's personnel had changed its outlook. This time the law was upheld as a legitimate exercise of the interstate commerce power. Agriculture, like manufacturing, was now held to be in the stream of commerce.

INDUSTRIAL RECOVERY: THE NRA   The industrial counterpart to the AAA was the National Industrial Recovery Act (NIRA), passed on June 16, 1933, the two major parts of which dealt with economic recovery and public-works projects designed to put people to work. The latter part, Title II, created the Public Works Administration (PWA) with $3.3 billion for public buildings, highway programs, flood control, and other improvements. Under the direction of Interior Secretary Harold L. Ickes, the PWA indirectly served the purpose of work relief. Ickes directed it toward well-planned permanent improvements rather than the provision of hasty make-work, and he used private contractors rather than placing workers directly on the government payroll. PWA workers built Virginia's Skyline Drive, New York's Triborough Bridge, the Overseas Highway from Miami to Key West, and Chicago's subway system.

The more controversial and ambitious part of the NIRA created the National Recovery Administration (NRA), headed by General Hugh S. Johnson. Its purposes were twofold: first, to stabilize business by reducing competition through the implementation of codes that set wages

In this cartoon employer and employee agree to cooperate in the spirit of unity that inspired the National Recovery Administration.

and prices, and second, to generate more purchasing power by providing jobs, defining labor standards, and raising wages. In each major industry, committees representing management, labor, and government drew up the codes of fair practice. Code Number 1, which dealt with the textile industry, imposed restraints on plant expansion, limited operations to eighty hours a week, and required reports on operations every four weeks. The labor standards featured in every code set a forty-hour workweek and minimum weekly wages of $13 ($12 in the South, where living costs were lower), which more than doubled earnings in some cases. Announcement of a proviso against child labor under the age of sixteen did "in a few minutes what neither law nor constitutional amendment had been able to do in forty years," Johnson said.

As the drafting of other codes began to drag, Johnson proposed a "blanket code" pledging employers generally to observe the same labor standards as applied to cotton textiles. He launched a crusade to whip up popular support for the NRA and its symbol of compliance, the "Blue Eagle," which had been modeled on an Indian thunderbird and embellished with the motto "We do our part." The eagle decal was displayed in shop windows and stamped on products. It was a gamble, but the public responded. Some 2 million employers signed the pledge, and the impact of the campaign broke the logjam in code making.

Labor unions, already hard pressed by the economic downturn and the loss of members, however, were understandably concerned about the NRA's efforts to reduce competition by allowing businesses to cooperate in fixing wages and prices. To gain their support, the NRA included a provision (Section 7a) that guaranteed the right of workers to organize unions. But while prohibiting employers from interfering with labor organizing efforts, the NRA did not create adequate enforcement measures, nor did it require employers to bargain in good faith with labor representatives.

For a time the NRA worked, perhaps because a new air of confidence had overcome the depression blues and the downward spiral of wages and prices had subsided. But as soon as economic recovery began, the honeymoon ended. The daily annoyances of code enforcement inspired growing hostility among business owners. Charges mounted that the larger companies dominated the code authorities and that price-fixing robbed small producers of the chance to compete. In 1934 an investigating committee substantiated at least some of the charges. Limiting production, moreover, had discouraged investment. And because the NRA wage codes excluded agricultural workers and domestic workers, three out of every four employed blacks derived no direct benefit from the program. By 1935 the NRA had developed more critics than friends. When it died in May 1935, struck down by the Supreme Court as unconstitutional, few paused to mourn.

The NRA experiment was generally a failure, but it left an enduring mark. With dramatic suddenness the codes had set new standards, such as the forty-hour workweek and the end of child labor, from which it was hard to retreat. The NRA's endorsement of collective bargaining spurred the growth of unions. The codes, moreover, advanced trends toward stabilization and rationalization that were becoming the standard practice of business at large and that, despite misgivings about the concentration of power, would be further promoted by trade associations.

REGIONAL PLANNING: THE TVA   The philosophy of the New Deal embraced more than the restrictive approaches of the NRA. The cre-

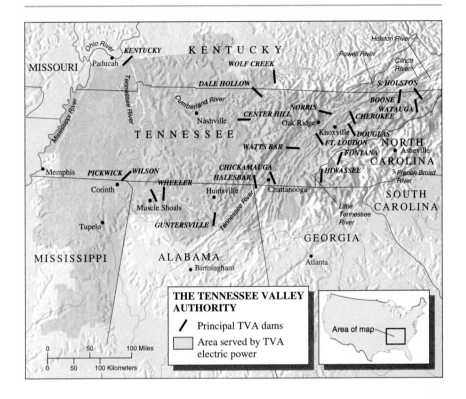

THE TENNESSEE VALLEY
AUTHORITY

/ Principal TVA dams

☐ Area served by TVA
electric power

Area of map

ation of the Tennessee Valley Authority (TVA) was a truly bold venture. Among the measures of Roosevelt's first Hundred Days, most of which were efforts to redress the ills of depression, the TVA refuted the idea that the economy had reached its full measure of mature development. It was the product neither of a single imagination nor of a single concept, but of an unfolding progression of purposes. In 1916, when the government started electric power plants and facilities to produce nitrates for fertilizers and explosives at Muscle Shoals, Alabama, strengthening national defense was the aim. New objectives unfolded in succession: production of nitrate fertilizers as well as nitrate explosives, general industrial development, and cheap public power, to be used as a "yardstick" for private utility rates. Water-power development pointed in turn to navigation, the control of stream flow for both power and flood control, and to conservation of soil and forests to prevent silting. The chain of connections led ultimately to the concept of overall planning for an entire regional watershed, which included a total drainage area of 41,000 square miles overlapping seven states, four-fifths the size of England.

Through the 1920s Nebraska senator George W. Norris had fought off efforts to sell the Alabama project to private companies, but had never won enough support for his goal of public control of the entire electrical power industry. In 1932, however, he backed Roosevelt, and then gained the new president's support for a vast enlargement of the Muscle Shoals project.

Muscle Shoals, Roosevelt said, "gives us the opportunity . . . of setting an example of planning, not just for ourselves but for generations to come, tying in industry and agriculture and forestry and flood prevention . . . over a distance of a thousand miles." The region needed help. The Tennessee River Valley was one of the most underdeveloped and poverty-stricken regions of the country, and illiteracy and disease were rampant. On May 18, 1933, Congress created the TVA as a multipurpose public corporation. Mobilizing local support under Director David E. Lilienthal's slogan of "grassroots democracy," the TVA won almost universal loyalty among the people of the region. By 1936 it had six dams completed or underway, and a master plan to build nine high dams on the main river, which would create the "Great Lakes of the South," and other dams on the tributaries. The agency, moreover, opened the rivers for navigation, fostered soil conservation and forestry, experimented with fertilizers, drew new industry to the region, encouraged the formation of labor unions, improved schools and libraries, and sent cheap power pulsating through the valley.

Cheap public power, Lilienthal's main passion, became more and more the TVA's reason for being—a purpose that would become all the more important during World War II. The TVA's success at generating greater power consumption and lower rates awakened private utilities to the mass consumer markets. Cheap power transported farmers of the valley from the age of kerosene to the age of electricity. "The women went around turning the switches on and off," said a Farm Bureau man who witnessed the transition. "The light and wonder in their eyes was brighter than that from the lamps." The TVA's first rural cooperative, set up at Corinth, Mississippi, in 1934, pointed the way to the electrification of the nation's farms in the decade that followed. The Rural Electrification Administration (REA), formed as a relief agency by presidential order in 1935, achieved a permanent statutory basis in 1936. By

Constructing the Fontana Dam, under the aegis of Roosevelt's TVA.

1940 it had extended loans of more than $321 million to rural electrical cooperatives.

THE SECOND NEW DEAL

During Roosevelt's first year in office his programs and his personal charms aroused massive support. The president's travels and speeches, his twice-weekly press conferences, and his "fireside chats" over the radio generated vitality from a once-remote White House. In the congressional elections of 1934 the Democrats actually increased their strength in both the House and the Senate, an almost unprecedented midterm victory for the party in power. When it was over, only seven Republican governors remained in office throughout the country.

Criticism of the New Deal was muted or reduced to helpless carping. But as the sense of crisis passed, the spirit of unity relaxed. In 1934 a group of conservative businessmen and politicians, including Al Smith and John W. Davis, two previous Democratic presidential candidates, formed the American Liberty League to oppose New Deal measures and to "teach the necessity of respect for the rights of person and property."

THUNDER ON THE LEFT   But the real threat to Roosevelt in those years came from the hucksters of social nostrums, old and new. The most flamboyant of the group, by far, was Louisiana's "Kingfish," Senator Huey P. Long, Jr. A short, strutting man with a round, rosy face and pug nose, Long sported pink suits and pastel shirts, red ties, and two-toned shoes. He loved to make people think he was a country bumpkin, though underneath the carefully calculated image was a shrewd lawyer and consummate demagogue. First as governor of Louisiana, then as political boss of the state, he delivered to its citizens tax favors, roads, schools, free textbooks, charity hospitals, and generally better public services, all at the cost of corruption and personal dictatorship.

Louisiana, however, became only the base from which Long ventured out to conquer other worlds. The vehicle was his Share Our Wealth program, first unveiled in 1932 and refined over the next three years. In one version Long proposed to liquidate large personal fortunes, guarantee every family an allowance of $5,000 and every worker an annual income of $2,500, grant pensions to the aged, reduce the hours of labor, pay veterans' bonuses, and assure a college education for every qualified

The "Kingfish," Huey Long, governor of Louisiana.

student. Whether he had a workable plan or not, his scheme dramatized a fundamental issue in a society that had solved the problem of production but not that of distribution, an issue few politicians were so imprudent as to tackle directly. By early 1935 Huey Long was claiming 27,431 Share Our Wealth Clubs and a file of 7.5 million names.

Still another popular scheme appealed to the elderly. A California doctor, Francis E. Townsend, outraged by the sight of three haggard old women raking through garbage cans, proposed pensions for the aged. In 1934 he announced the Townsend Plan. It called for payments of $200 a month to every citizen over sixty who retired from employment and who promised to spend the money within the month. The plan had the lure of providing both financial security for the aged and job openings for the young. As the Townsend Club grew, critics noted that the cost would be more than half the national income. "I'm not in the least interested in the cost of the plan," Townsend blandly told a House committee.

A third huckster of panaceas, Father Charles E. Coughlin, the "radio priest" of Michigan, founded the National Union for Social Justice in 1934. In broadcasts over the CBS radio network, he promoted schemes for the coinage of silver and attacks on bankers that carried growing overtones of anti-Semitism.

Coughlin, Townsend, and Long drew support largely from a desperate lower middle class. Of the three, Long had the widest following. A survey showed that he could draw 5 million to 6 million votes as a third-party candidate for president, perhaps enough to undermine Roosevelt's chances of reelection. Beset by pressures from both ends of the political spectrum, Roosevelt drifted through months of hesitation in 1934 before deciding to "steal the thunder" from the left with new programs of reform and social security. Political pressures impelled Roosevelt, but so did the growing influence of Justices Louis Brandeis and Felix Frankfurter. These men urged Roosevelt to be less cozy with big business and to push for restored competition and heavy taxes on large corporations.

LIGHTNING FROM THE COURT What finally galvanized the president into action was the behavior of the Supreme Court. In *Schechter Poultry Corporation v. United States* (1935), quickly tagged the "sick chicken" case, the defendants, who provided poultry to kosher retailers, had been convicted of selling an "unfit chicken" and violating other code provisions as well. The high court ruled unanimously that Congress had delegated too much power to the executive branch when it granted the code-making authority under the NRA and had exceeded its power under the commerce clause. Chief Justice Charles Evans Hughes held that the poultry in question had "come to permanent rest within the state," although it had been moved across state lines. The Court's decision outraged Roosevelt. In a press conference soon afterward, he said: "We have been relegated to the horse-and-buggy definition of interstate commerce." The same line of reasoning, he warned, might endanger many other New Deal programs. The Court seemed to be denying the government the authority to deal with the greatest economic calamity in American history.

LEGISLATIVE ACHIEVEMENTS   In an effort to salvage his legislative program, Roosevelt launched the so-called Second New Deal in 1935. The initiative broke the stalemate in Congress, which passed what Roosevelt called "must" legislation:

July 5	The Wagner National Labor Relations Act, guaranteeing the right of labor to organize and bargain collectively
August 14	The Social Security Act, providing unemployment and old-age insurance and public-welfare programs
August 23	The Banking Act of 1935, strengthening the Federal Reserve System
August 28	The Wheeler-Rayburn Public Utility Holding Company Act, preventing the pyramiding of holding companies
August 30	The Revenue Act of 1935, which increased taxes on the wealthy

The National Labor Relations Act, often called the Wagner Act, gave workers the right to bargain through unions of their own choice and prohibited employers from interfering with union activities. A National Labor Relations Board of five members could supervise plant elections and certify unions as bargaining agents where a majority of the workers approved. The board could also investigate the actions of employers and issue "cease-and-desist" orders against specified unfair practices. Under the protection of the law, union activities quickly intensified.

"Yes, You Remembered Me."
The social legislation of the
Second New Deal prompted this
depiction of FDR as the friend
of "The Forgotten Man."

The Social Security Act of 1935, Roosevelt announced, was the New Deal's "cornerstone" and "supreme achievement." Indeed, it has proven to be the most far-reaching of all the New Deal initiatives. The concept had its roots in the proposal of progressives early in the 1900s for a federal system of social security for the aged, indigent, disabled, and unemployed. Other nations had already enacted such programs, but the United States remained steadfast to its deeply rooted tradition of individual self-reliance. The Great Depression, however, revived the idea, and Roosevelt masterfully guided the legislation through Congress.

The Social Security Act included three major provisions. Its centerpiece was a pension fund for retired people over the age of sixty-five. In 1937, workers and employers began contributing payroll taxes to establish the fund, which three years later started to yield retirees average payments of $22 per month, a modest sum even for those depressed times. Roosevelt stressed that the pension program was not intended to guarantee a comfortable retirement; it was designed to supplement other sources of income and protect the elderly from some of the "hazards and vicissitudes of life." Only later did American voters and politicians come to perceive Social Security as the *primary* source of retirement income for most of the aged. By 1998 the average monthly payment was about $1,000.

The Social Security Act also set up a shared federal-state unemployment insurance program, financed by a payroll tax on employers. In addition, the new legislation committed the national government to a broad range of social-welfare activities based on the assumption that "unemployables"—people who were unable to work—would remain a state responsibility while the national government would provide work relief for the able-bodied. To that end the law inaugurated federal grants-in-aid for three state-administered public assistance programs—old-age assistance, aid for dependent children, aid for the blind—and further aid for maternal, child welfare, and public health services.

Conservative critics charged that the Social Security system warred against traditions of American individualism. One New Jersey senator lamented that the new law would "take all the romance out of life. We might as well take the child from the nursery, give him a nurse, and protect him from every experience that life affords." But the new federal program was relatively conservative. It was the only government pension program in the world financed by taxes on the earnings of current workers. Most countries funded such programs out of general tax revenues. Moreover, the Social Security payroll tax was regressive: based on a single fixed rate for all, regardless of income level, the tax hurt the poor more than the rich. It also weakened Roosevelt's efforts to revive the economy. The new Social Security tax took money out of workers' pockets and placed it into a trust fund, thus exacerbating the deflation of the money supply that was one of the main causes of the depression. By taking discretionary income away from workers, the government blunted the sharp increase in public consumption needed to restore the health of the economy. Another limit to the Social Security system was its initial exclusion of those classes of workers who needed financial security the most: farm workers, domestics, and the self-employed (these groups have since gained access to the program).

Roosevelt regretted these limitations, but he considered them compromises that would ensure congressional passage of the Social Security Act and enable it to withstand court challenges. As he replied to an aide who criticized funding the pension program through employee contributions, "I guess you're right on the economics, but those taxes were never a problem of economics. They are politics all the way through. We put those payroll contributions there so as to give the contributors a moral, legal, and political right to collect their pensions and their unemployment benefits. With those taxes in there, no damn politician can ever scrap my Social Security program."

In addition to the Social Security Act, the "Second New Deal" included a bill providing work relief for jobless workers. To manage these programs, the Works Progress Administration (WPA), headed by Harry L. Hopkins, replaced the Federal Emergency Relief Administration. The act did not provide a dole, which, Roosevelt told Congress, had been "a narcotic, a subtle destroyer of the human spirit." Rather, the WPA paid people to work, building permanent monuments on the landscape in the form of buildings, bridges, hard-surfaced roads, airports, and schools. The WPA also employed a wide range of talents in the Federal Theater Project, the Federal Art Project, and the Federal Writers' Project. The National Youth Administration, under the WPA, gave part-time employment to students, set up technical training programs,

Artists on WPA *by Moses Soyer, 1935–1936. By sponsoring unemployed artists, the Federal Art Project under the WPA brought original American art to the popular forefront and left a powerful political and cultural legacy.*

and provided aid to jobless youth. Although the WPA took care of only about 3 million out of some 10 million jobless at any one time, in all it helped some 9 million clients before it expired in 1943.

The Banking Act of 1935 strengthened the Federal Reserve Board's ability to regulate member banks and diminished the power of private bankers in the money market. It concentrated in the board's hands all open-market operations—that is, the buying or selling of government securities to increase (by buying) or decrease (by selling) the money supply. The act greatly strengthened the board's control of the whole monetary system.

The Public Utility Holding Company Act struck at financial corruption in the public utility industry. Like railroads in the 1800s, utilities in their early stages of growth had spawned buccaneers interested more in manipulation than in good business. The act passed despite the high-pressure lobbying tactics of the utilities. It limited the sphere of utility holding companies and forbade the pyramiding (separate companies using the same directors on their boards) of such companies.

The last of the major laws passed during this period was the Revenue Act of 1935, sometimes called the Wealth Tax Act, but popularly known as the "Soak the Rich Tax." In asking for the law, Roosevelt told Congress: "Our revenue laws have operated in many ways to the unfair advantage of the few, and they have done little to prevent an unjust concentration of wealth and economic power." The Revenue Act raised surtax rates on incomes above $50,000, and steeply graduated taxes to a maximum of 75 percent on incomes above $5 million. Estate and gift taxes went up, as did the corporate tax on all but small corporations—those with less than $50,000 income. Congress even added to Roosevelt's recommendations an "excess-profits" levy on corporate earnings above 10 percent.

Business owners fumed over Roosevelt's tax and spending policies. The wealthy resented their loss of status and the growing power of government and labor. They vented an intemperate rage against Roosevelt, whom they called "a traitor to his own class," and against all the works of the New Deal. Many landmarks of a once stable and secure world now seemed threatened, from the gold standard itself to one's right to run a business as one saw fit. Hoover called the New Deal an attack on "the whole philosophy of individual liberty." Visitors to the home of

J. P. Morgan, Jr., were cautioned not to mention Roosevelt's name lest it raise his blood pressure.

By "soaking" the rich and enacting Social Security programs, Roosevelt stole much of the thunder from the political left, although the results fell short of the promise. The new tax law failed to increase revenue significantly, nor did it result in a redistribution of income. At the same time, the hoopla over "soaking the rich" obscured the more significant impact of both the Social Security payroll tax—which fell more heavily on lower incomes—and the policy of returning indigents to the care of the states. Most states, insofar as they assumed this burden, raised the needed revenue with sales taxes, which were also regressive. Such taxes impeded economic recovery by reducing total purchasing power.

Roosevelt seemed to have moved in a radical direction, but the extent of the new departure taken by the Second New Deal is easy to exaggerate. Such measures as work relief, Social Security, utility regulation, and progressive income taxes had long been in the works in Congress. The president himself had little use for theoretical speculation. He was still pursuing the bold experiments he had promised before the election. "Roosevelt's program," one historian has written, "rested on the assumption that a just society could be secured by imposing a welfare state on a capitalist foundation."

CONTINUING HARDSHIPS   Although the flurry of New Deal programs helped ease the devastation wrought by the depression, it did not restore prosperity. Nor did it end widespread human suffering. As late as 1939, some 9.5 million workers (17 percent of the labor force) remained unemployed. Prolonged economic hardship continued to create personal tragedies and tremendous social strains. Poverty led desperate people to do desperate things. Petty theft soared during the thirties, as did street-corner begging and prostitution. In Pittsburgh an unemployed father, desperate to feed his starving children, stole a loaf of bread from a neighbor, was arrested, and hanged himself in shame. Although the divorce rate dropped during the thirties, in part because couples could not afford to live separately or pay the legal fees to obtain divorces, all too often husbands down on their luck simply deserted their wives. In 1940 a survey revealed that 1.5 million husbands had

A commodity relief line in San Antonio, Texas, 1939.

left home. A California woman reported to a friend that her husband "went north about three months ago to try his luck. The first month he wrote pretty regularly. . . . For five weeks now we have had no word from him. . . . Don't know where he is or what he is up to."

Many couples decided to postpone marriage because of hard times. Some 800,000 marriages were delayed during the 1930s, and the total number of marriages declined by one-fourth compared to the previous decade. With their own future uncertain, married couples often decided not to have children; the birthrate plummeted during the depression. Those with children sometimes could not support them. In 1933 the Children's Bureau reported that one out of every five children was not getting enough to eat. Often, struggling parents sent their children to live with relatives or friends. Some 900,000 other children simply left home and joined the army of homeless "tramps."

DUST BOWL MIGRANTS   Uprooted farmers and their families joined a migratory stream rushing from the South and Midwest toward California, buoyed by currents of hope and desperation. One couple claimed they had heard "how much money a man could make out there and we wanted to go."

Although frequently lumped together as "Okies," the dust bowl refugees were actually from cotton-belt communities in Arkansas, Texas, and Missouri as well as Oklahoma. During the 1930s and 1940s, some 800,000 people left those four states and headed toward the West. Not all were farmers; many were professionals, white-collar workers, retailers, and farm implement salesmen whose jobs had been tied to the health of the agricultural sector. Ninety-five percent of the dust bowl migrants were white, and most were young adults in their twenties and thirties who relocated with spouses and children. Some traveled on trains or buses, others hopped a freight or hitched a ride; most rode in their own cars, the trip taking four to five days on average.

Many of the dust bowl migrants who had come from cities gravitated to urban areas—Los Angeles, San Diego, or San Francisco. Half the newcomers, however, moved into the San Joaquin Valley, the agricultural heartland of the state. There they discovered that California was no paradise. Only a few of the migrants could afford to buy land. Most men and women found themselves competing with local Hispanics and Asians for seasonal work as pickers in the cotton fields or orchards of large corporate farms. As one local health department report observed, the migrant workers "harvest cotton in the fall, go on relief until May, harvest the potatoes in the spring, work the vegetables and fruits in the summer and rest on relief until cotton harvest again." Living in tents or crude cabins and frequently on the move, they suffered from exposure and from poor sanitation. They also felt the sting of social prejudice. Native Californians scared by the influx of poor newcomers treated them with hostility and called them demeaning names. Steinbeck explained that "Okie us'ta mean you was from Oklahoma. Now it means you're a dirty son-of-a-bitch. Okie means you're scum. Don't mean nothing in itself, it's the way they say it."

Such hostility led a third of the "Okies" to return to their native states. Most of the farm workers who stayed tended to fall back upon their old folkways rather than assimilate themselves into their new surroundings. These gritty "plain folk" brought with them their own prejudices against blacks and ethnic minorities as well as a potent tradition of evangelical Protestantism and a distinctive style of music variously labeled "country," "hillbilly," or "cowboy." This "Okie" subculture remains a vivid part of California society today.

MINORITIES AND THE NEW DEAL   The depression was especially traumatic for those minorities who historically were the most disadvantaged groups in American society. However progressive Roosevelt was on social issues, he refused to assault long-standing patterns of racism and segregation for fear of alienating powerful southern Democrats in Congress. As a result, many of the New Deal programs were for whites only. The Federal Housing Administration (FHA), for example, refused to guarantee mortgages on houses purchased by blacks in white neighborhoods. The Civilian Conservation Corps and the Tennessee Valley Authority both practiced racial segregation. The Social Security Act excluded domestic and migrant workers from its coverage, and the National Labor Relations Act excluded farm workers from its provisions. Moreover, minorities who applied for governmental assistance often were the victims of discrimination. In Houston, Texas, relief payments to blacks and Chicanos averaged 25 percent less than payments to whites. Of 10,344 WPA supervisors hired in the southern states, only 11 were African Americans.

The efforts of the Roosevelt administration to raise crop prices by reducing production proved especially devastating for blacks and Chicanos. To earn the federal payments for reducing crop production as provided by the AAA and other New Deal agricultural programs, many farm owners would first take out of cultivation the marginal lands worked by tenants and sharecroppers. This would drive tenants off farms and cost the jobs of many migrant workers. In Texas, for example, farmers eagerly took advantage of AAA subsidies to destroy 40 percent of the cotton crop. From 1930 to 1940, the number of African-American tenant farmers in Texas decreased from 65,000 to 32,000, while the number of landless black agricultural laborers increased by 25,000; some 20,000 other blacks left the state in search of better opportunities. Over 200,000 black tenant farmers nationwide were displaced by the AAA.

Mexican Americans suffered even more. Thousands of Mexicans had migrated to the United States during the 1920s, most of them settling in California, New Mexico, Arizona, Colorado, Texas, and the midwestern states. But because many Mexican Americans were unable to prove their citizenship, either out of ignorance of the regulations or because their migratory work hampered their ability to meet residency requirements, they were denied access to the many new federal relief programs under the New Deal. As economic conditions worsened, government officials called for the deportation of Mexican-born Americans to avoid the costs of providing them public services and relief. Local governments were even more vigorous in promoting repatriation. By 1935, over 500,000 Mexican Americans and their American-born children had returned to Mexico. The state of Texas alone returned over 250,000 people.

Deportation became such a popular solution in part because of the rising level of involvement among Mexican-American workers in union activities. In 1933 Mexican-American women in El Paso, Texas, formed the Society of Female Manufacturing Workers to protest wages as low as 75 cents a day. The same year some 18,000 cotton pickers went on strike in California's San Joaquin Valley. Police crushed the strike by burning the workers' camps.

Native Americans were encouraged by Roosevelt's appointment of John Collier as the commissioner of the Bureau of Indian Affairs (BIA). As commissioner, Collier steadily increased the number of Native Americans employed by the BIA and lobbied strenuously with the heads of New Deal agencies to ensure that Indians gained access to the various relief programs. In response, the CCC created an Indian Division, and the AAA and other programs employed Indians on projects intended to improve the quality of living on the reservations. Collier also reversed an earlier BIA decision denying the right of Indians to practice their own religions.

Collier's primary objective was passage of the Indian Reorganization Act. He intended the new legislation to revoke the provisions of the Dawes General Allotment Act (1887), which had sought to "Americanize" the Indians by breaking up their tribal lands and allocating them to individuals. Collier insisted that this was a misguided failure. The Dawes Act had produced only widespread poverty and demoralization among the Indians. It had failed because it was based on the faulty assumption that all Americans should conform to a universal cultural norm. Collier hoped to reinvigorate traditional Indian cultural traditions by restoring land to tribes, granting Indians the right to charter business enterprises and establish self-governing constitutions, and providing federal funds for vocational training and economic development.

Because of stiff opposition, both from assimilated Indians who had prospered under the Dawes Plan, and from western congressmen who criticized Collier for restoring Native American cultural traditions and religious practices, the six-page Indian Reorganization Act (also known as the Wheeler-Howard Act) that Congress passed and Roosevelt signed in 1934 was a much diluted version of Collier's original fifty-page proposal. The result was that the "Indian New Deal" brought only a partial improvement in the lives of Native Americans.

COURT DECISIONS AND BLACK VOTERS   During the 1930s, the NAACP's legal campaign gathered momentum. A major setback occurred in *Grovey v. Townsend* (1935), which upheld the Texas Democrats' white primary as the practice of a voluntary association and thus not subject to state action. But the *Grovey* decision held up for only nine years and marked the end of major decisions that for half a century had narrowed application of the Reconstruction Amendments. A trend in the other direction had already set in. Two important precedents rose from the celebrated Scottsboro case in 1931, in which nine black youths were convicted of raping two white women while riding a freight train in Alabama. The first verdict failed, the high court ruled in *Powell v. Alabama* (1932), for want of due process because the judge's appointing "all of the members of the bar" to defend the accused imposed "no substantial or definite obligation upon anyone." Another verdict fell to a judgment in *Norris v. Alabama* (1935) that the systematic exclusion of blacks from Alabama juries had denied the defendants equal protection of the law—a principle that had significant and widespread impact on state courts.

Like Woodrow Wilson, Franklin Roosevelt did not give a high priority to racial issues. As a consequence, many of his New Deal programs failed to help minorities, and in a few instances the new initiatives unintentionally discriminated against those least able to help themselves. Nonetheless, Roosevelt included people in his administration who did care deeply about racial issues. As his first term drew to a close in 1936, Roosevelt found that there was a de facto "Black Cabinet" of some thirty to forty advisers in government departments and agencies, people who were wrestling with racial issues and the plight of African Americans. Moreover, by 1936, many black voters were fast transferring their political loyalty from Republicans to Democrats and would vote accordingly in the coming presidential election.

ROOSEVELT'S SECOND TERM

THE 1936 CAMPAIGN   The popularity of Roosevelt and the New Deal impelled the Republican convention in 1936 to avoid candidates too closely identified with the "hate-Roosevelt" contingent. The party chose Governor Alfred M. Landon of Kansas, a former Bull Moose Progressive, who had fought the Ku Klux Klan and favored regulation of business. While conservative in matters of finance, Landon had endorsed many New Deal programs. The most progressive Republican candidate in years, he was probably more liberal than most of his backers, and clearly more so than the party's platform, which accused the New Deal of usurping power.

The chief hope of the Republicans was that the followers of Coughlin, Townsend, and other dissidents would combine to draw enough votes away from Roosevelt to throw the election to them. But that possibility faded when an assassin gunned down Huey Long. Coughlin, Townsend, and a remnant of the Long movement did support Representative William Lemke of North Dakota on a Union party ticket, but it was a forlorn and foredoomed effort that polled only 882,000 votes.

In 1936 Roosevelt forged a new electoral coalition that would affect national politics for years to come. While holding the support of most traditional Democrats North and South, FDR made strong gains among beneficiaries of the farm program in the West. In the northern cities he held on to the support of ethnic groups pleased by New Deal welfare measures and by greater recognition in federal government appointments. Middle-class voters, whose property had been saved by New Deal measures, flocked to Roosevelt's support, along with intellectuals stirred by the ferment of new ideas in government. The revived labor movement threw its support to Roosevelt, and Socialist voters deserted Norman Thomas for the New Deal coalition.

In perhaps the most seismic and enduring change in the political landscape during the 1930s, a majority of politically active blacks moved away from their traditional adherence to the Republican party.

African-American voters for the first time cast the majority of their ballots for a Democratic president. "My friends, go home and turn Lincoln's picture to the wall," a journalist told black Republicans. "That debt has been paid in full."

On election day Roosevelt carried every state except Maine and Vermont with a popular vote of 28 million to Landon's 17 million, and won what was the closest to a unanimous electoral vote since Monroe's victory in 1820, by 523 to 8. Democrats would dominate Republicans in the new Congress, by 77 to 19 in the Senate and 328 to 107 in the House. Roosevelt said he felt as if he had experienced "baptism by total immersion."

ELEANOR ROOSEVELT   One of the keys to Roosevelt's unprecedented popularity was his wife, Anna Eleanor Roosevelt, an enormous political asset and one of the most influential women of her time. Theodore Roosevelt's favorite niece, she had lost both parents by age ten and was a shy, withdrawn, ungainly youth. But Eleanor grew into a tall, willowy, outgoing woman. After spending three years at a private boarding school in England, she returned to New York and began dating her fifth cousin Franklin. They were very different. Eleanor had grown up in a dysfunctional family. Her father was an alcoholic who had impregnated a servant girl, and her mother was a cold, self-absorbed socialite who viewed

An intelligent, principled, and candid woman, First Lady Eleanor Roosevelt became a political figure in her own right. Here she is waving to delegates at the Democratic convention in 1940.

her daughter as an embarrassment. By contrast, Franklin had been smothered with family affection and attention. As an only child of wealthy and privileged parents, he grew up assuming that he should be the center of attention. Supremely confident of his own power and abilities, he conveyed an air of untroubled ebullience that inspired and delighted people. Perhaps what attracted him to Eleanor was her contrasting qualities. She was intelligent, bookish, and prematurely serious, a person of high ideals and principles.

Yet after their marriage in 1905, the very qualities that attracted Franklin to Eleanor began to irritate and alienate him. Her deeply embedded insecurities and fear of failure kept her from participating in activities that he enjoyed—golf, swimming, driving. She also hated the social requirements of politics. Where he could invoke his natural charm and gregariousness in any setting, she found casual conversation with strangers a painful exercise. She once admitted that "I must have spoiled a good deal of the fun for Franklin because of this inability to feel at ease" in social situations. Still another wedge that served to separate Franklin and Eleanor was the meddling of Roosevelt's indomitable mother, Sara. She refused to relinquish her son to her daughter-in-law. She repeatedly intruded upon Eleanor's efforts to raise her six children, and Franklin steadfastly stayed out of the fray.

Biographers suggest that it was such tensions between Eleanor and Franklin that led him during his thirties to engage in an affair with Lucy Mercer, Eleanor's secretary. When Eleanor discovered a cache of love letters from Mercer to her husband in 1918, "the bottom dropped out of my own particular world & I faced myself, my surroundings, my world honestly for the first time." She told Franklin that he must either renounce Lucy or seek a divorce. He chose to end the affair in order to save his political future and his inheritance (his mother said she would disown him if he ever divorced). Thereafter, Eleanor demanded a separate bedroom. Three years later, in 1921, Franklin contracted polio and was paralyzed from the waist down. Eleanor stepped in to deliver his speeches and attend political gatherings. Her daughter Anna recalled that the onset of polio "was very instrumental in bringing them [her parents] much closer into a very real partnership. They were finding mutual interests on a totally different level."

Now free to pursue new avenues of self-fulfillment, Eleanor Roosevelt in the White House became more of a public figure than any pre-

vious First Lady. She had her own staff, held her own press conferences, enjoyed access to Democratic party leaders, and spoke candidly
to the president about appointing women to government posts and
about his plans for various New Deal programs. As one journalist wrote
in 1940, "She never lets the President or his administrators think that
all is well, that there is time to rest from advancing their liberal objectives." Eleanor once asked Franklin if he objected to her candor and her
activism. "No, certainly not," he replied. "You can say anything you
want. I can always say, 'Well, that is my wife; I can't do anything about
her.'"

Eleanor's passion was social service. As a teen she had volunteered to
work in a New York settlement house, and she remained ardently concerned about issues of human welfare and rights for women and blacks.
She convinced Congress to improve housing conditions for the poor in
the District of Columbia, and she repeatedly reminded the president of
pockets of injustice hidden from public scrutiny. As her secretary recalled, Eleanor Roosevelt "lived to be kind." She came to relish traveling around the country, representing FDR and the New Deal, defying
local segregation ordinances by eating with blacks in segregated facilities, supporting women's causes, highlighting the plight of unemployed
youth, and imploring Americans to live up to their egalitarian and humanitarian ideals.

Eleanor Roosevelt became her husband's most visible and effective
liaison with many liberal groups, brought labor leaders, women activists, and black spokesmen into the White House after hours, and deflected criticism of the president by taking progressive stands and running political risks he himself dared not. He was the politician, she
once remarked, she the agitator. A Maine fisherman described her
uniquely endearing qualities: "She ain't stuck up, she ain't dressed up,
and she ain't afraid to talk."

THE COURT-PACKING PLAN   As Thomas Jefferson and Andrew
Jackson had found (and Lyndon Johnson, Richard Nixon, and Ronald
Reagan later discovered), some malevolent fate seems to dog presidents
who win smashing victories. Roosevelt found himself deluged in a sea
of troubles soon after his reelection. His second inaugural address,
given on January 20, 1937, suggested that he was ready to move toward
even further reform. The challenge of American democracy, he said,
was that millions of citizens "at this very moment are denied the greater

part of what the very lowest standards of today call the necessities of life. . . . I see one-third of a nation ill-housed, ill-clad, ill-nourished." The election of 1936 had been a mandate for more extensive reforms, he argued; and the overwhelming Democratic majorities in Congress ensured their passage. But one major roadblock stood in the way: the Supreme Court.

By the end of the 1936 term, the Court had ruled against New Deal laws in seven of the nine major cases it reviewed. Having struck down both major accomplishments of the First New Deal, the AAA and the NRA, the Court in 1936 denied that states had the power to fix minimum wages. Since it had already ruled, in 1923, that the federal government had no such power, it had left, as Roosevelt protested, a " 'no-man's land,' where no Government—State or Federal" could act. Suits against the Social Security and Wagner Labor Relations Acts now pended. Given the established trend of rulings, often by margins of five to four or six to three, the Second New Deal seemed in danger of being nullified like the first.

For that reason, Roosevelt and his attorney-general decided to change the Court by enlarging it, a move for which there was ample precedent and power. Congress, not the Constitution, determined the

An editorial cartoon commenting on Roosevelt's grandiose plan to enlarge the Supreme Court.

size of the Court, which at different times had numbered six, seven, nine, and ten justices, and in 1937 numbered nine. Roosevelt sent his plan to Congress without having consulted congressional leaders or more than a few within his administration. He wanted to create up to fifty new federal judges, including six new Supreme Court justices, and to diminish the power of judges who had served ten or more years or had reached the age of seventy.

The "court-packing" maneuver, as opponents quickly tagged it, backfired on Roosevelt. The plan was a shade too contrived. In implying that older judges were impaired by senility, it affronted the elder statesmen of Congress and the Court, especially eighty-year-old Louis D. Brandeis, who was both the oldest and the most liberal of the justices. It also ran headlong into a deep-rooted veneration of the courts and aroused fears that another president might use the precedent for quite different purposes. One Virginia senator feared "the reversal of those decisions of the Court that saved the civilization of the South," by which he meant decisions upholding white supremacy. In the Senate the Republicans shrewdly stood aside while the Democrats plunged into a family squabble.

As it turned out, no direct vote ever tested senatorial convictions on the matter. Unforeseen events blunted Roosevelt's drive to change the Court. A sequence of Court decisions in the spring of 1937 reversed previous judgments in order to uphold a Washington State minimum-wage law, the Wagner Act, and the Social Security Act. What prompted the reversal was the shift of a single vote. Justice Owen Roberts had previously sided with a quartet of conservative justices known as the "Four Horsemen." In 1937 Roberts inexplicably joined the four other members who had been sympathetic to the New Deal. This "switch in time that saved nine" made Roosevelt's court-packing plan irrelevant. Never again did the Supreme Court strike down a New Deal program.

Roosevelt later claimed he had lost the battle but won the war. The Court had reversed itself on important New Deal legislation, and Roosevelt was able to appoint new justices in harmony with the New Deal because of several retirements. But the episode created dissension in his party and blighted Roosevelt's own prestige. For the first time Democrats in large numbers deserted the "champ," and the opposition found an issue on which it could openly take the field. During the first eight months of 1937, the momentum of Roosevelt's great 1936 victory was lost.

A NEW DIRECTION FOR LABOR   Rebellions erupted on other fronts even while the Court bill pended. Under the impetus of the New Deal, the dormant labor movement stirred anew. When Section 7a of the National Industrial Recovery Act demanded in every industry code a statement of the workers' right to organize, alert unionists quickly translated it to mean "The President wants you to join the union."

John L. Lewis of the United Mine Workers was among the first to exploit the spirit of the NIRA. Leading a union decimated by depression, he rebuilt it from 150,000 members to 500,000 within a year. Spurred by the mine workers' example, Sidney Hillman of the Amalgamated Clothing Workers and David Dubinsky of the International Ladies' Garment Workers joined Lewis in promoting a campaign to organize workers in the mass-production industries. As leaders of some of the few *industrial* unions (made up of all workers) in the AFL, they found the more restrictive *craft* unions (made up of skilled male workers) to be obstacles to organizing the basic industries.

In 1934 they persuaded the AFL and its president, William Green, to charter industrial unions in the unorganized industries. But Green and other craft unionists saw these "federal" unions as temporary pools from which to draw members into the crafts. Lewis and the industrial unionists saw them as a chance to organize on a massive scale. In 1935, with passage of the Wagner Act, action began in earnest. The industrial unionists formed a Committee for Industrial Organization (CIO), and craft unionists began to fear submergence by the mass unions. Jurisdictional disputes divided them, and in 1936 the AFL expelled the CIO unions, which then formed a permanent structure called after 1938 the Congress of Industrial Organizations. The rivalry spurred both groups to greater efforts.

The CIO's major organizing drives in the automobile and steel industries began in 1936, but until the Supreme Court upheld the Wagner Act in 1937 there was little compliance with unions on the part of industry. Companies used blacklisting, private detectives, labor spies, vigilante groups, and intimidation. Early in 1937 automobile workers spontaneously adopted a new technique, the "sit-down strike," in which workers refused to leave the workplace until the employers granted collective-bargaining rights.

Led by the fiery young autoworker and union organizer Walter Reuther, thousands of employees at General Motors' assembly plants in Flint, Michigan, occupied the factories and stopped all production. Women workers supported their male counterparts by picketing at the plant entrances. The wives, daughters, and mothers of the strikers formed a Women's Auxiliary to feed the workers who slept at the plants. Management refused to recognize the union efforts. Company officials called in police to harass the strikers, sent spies to union meetings, and threatened to fire the workers. They also pleaded with Roosevelt to dispatch federal troops. He refused, while at the same time expressing his displeasure with the sit-down strike. The standoff lasted over a month. Then, on February 11, the company relented and signed a contract recognizing the United Auto Workers (UAW). Other automotive companies soon followed suit. And the following month, United States Steel capitulated to the Steel Workers Organizing Committee (later the United Steelworkers of America), granting it recognition, a 10 percent wage hike, and a forty-hour workweek.

Having captured two giants of heavy industry, the CIO went on in the next few years to organize much of industrial America: rubber, oil, electronics, and a part of the textile industry, in which unionists had to fight protracted struggles to organize scattered plants. The slow pace of labor organizing in textiles denied the CIO a major victory in the South comparable to its swift conquest of autos and steel, but even there a labor movement appeared that was at last something more than a vehicle for sporadic revolt. Violence punctuated these struggles, most vividly at the Republic Steel plant in Chicago, where police killed ten strikers in 1937. Company guards brutally beat up Walter Reuther and other labor organizers at Henry Ford's River Rouge plant in Detroit. In Harlan County, Kentucky, deputized company hoodlums conducted a reign of terror until the National Labor Relations Board forced operators to bargain with the United Mine Workers late in 1938.

The Wagner Act put the power of the federal government behind the principle of unionization. In the Congress, a Senate subcommittee under Robert M. La Follette, Jr., exposed violent practices against unions. President Roosevelt refused to use force against sit-down strikers, though he was opposed to the tactic. The unions, he said, would soon

CIO pickets jeering at nonstriking workers entering a mill, 1941.

learn that they could not continue to use a "damned unpopular" tactic. Roosevelt himself had come late to the support of unions and sometimes took exception to their behavior. In the fall of 1937 he became so irritated with the warfare between Lewis and Republic Steel that he pronounced "a plague on both your houses." The grandiloquent Lewis, who for a year had been trying to organize a union for steelworkers, responded: "It ill behooves one who has supped at labor's table and who has been sheltered in labor's house to curse with equal fervor and fine impartiality both labor and its adversaries when they become locked in a deadly embrace." In 1940 an angry Lewis would back the Republican presidential candidate, but he would be unable to carry the labor vote with him. As workers became more organized, they more closely identified with the Democratic party.

A SLUMPING ECONOMY The years 1935 and 1936 had seen steady economic improvement. By the spring of 1937 output had moved above the 1929 level. The prosperity of early 1937 was achieved largely through governmental spending. On top of relief and public-works outlays, Congress in 1936 provided for cash payments of veterans' bonuses upon demand. But in 1937 Roosevelt, worried about deficits and inflation, ordered sharp cuts in spending. At the same time the Treasury began to diminish disposable income by collecting $2 billion in Social Security taxes. Private spending could not fill the gap left by reductions in government spending, and business still lacked the faith to risk large investments. The result was that the economy suddenly stalled, and then slid into a deep business slump sharper than that in 1929. The Dow Jones stock average fell some 40 percent between August and October. By the end of the year 2 million people had been thrown out of work; scenes of the earlier depression reappeared.

The recession provoked a fierce debate within the administration. One group, led by Treasury Secretary Henry Morgenthau, Jr., favored less spending and a balanced budget. The slow pace of recovery, Morgenthau thought, resulted from the reluctance of business to invest, and that resulted in turn from fear that federal spending would bring inflation and heavy taxes. The other group, which included Harry Hopkins and Harold Ickes, argued for renewed government spending. The recession, they noted, had come just when the budget was brought into balance. This view echoed that of the English economist John Maynard Keynes, who had given extended development to the idea in his book *The General Theory of Employment, Interest and Money* (1936). Keynesian economics offered a convenient theoretical justification for what New Dealers had already done in pragmatic response to existing conditions.

ECONOMIC POLICY AND LATE REFORMS   Roosevelt waited as the rival theorists sought his approval. When the spring of 1938 failed to bring recovery, he endorsed the ideas of the spenders. On April 14, 1938, he asked Congress to adopt a large-scale spending program, and Congress voted $33 billion, mainly for public works by the PWA and the WPA, with lesser amounts for other programs. In a short time the increase in spending reversed the economy's decline, but the recession and Roosevelt's reluctance to adopt the truly massive, sustained government spending called for in Keynesian theory forestalled the achievement of full recovery. Only during World War II would employment reach pre-1929 levels.

The Court fight, the sit-down strikes, and the recession in 1937 all undercut Roosevelt's prestige and dissipated the mandate of the 1936 elections. When the 1937 congressional session ended, the only major new reforms enacted for the benefit of the "ill-housed, ill-clad, [and] ill-nourished" were the Wagner-Steagall National Housing Act and the Bankhead-Jones Farm Tenant Act. In 1938 the Democratic Congress enacted three more major reforms, the last of the New Deal era: the Second Agricultural Adjustment Act; the Food, Drug and Cosmetic Act; and the Fair Labor Standards Act.

The Housing Act set up the United States Housing Authority (USHA) in the Department of the Interior, which extended long-term loans to local agencies willing to assume part of the cost for slum clearance and public housing. The agency also subsidized low rents. Later, during World War II, it financed housing in connection with defense projects.

The Farm Tenant Act addressed the problem of rural poverty. In some ways the New Deal's larger farm program, the AAA, had aggravated the problem; although tenants were supposed to be kept on in spite of government-sponsored cutbacks in production, landlords often made the most of cutbacks by evicting workers and withholding their shares of benefit payments. The Tenant Act was administered by a new agency, the Farm Security Administration (FSA). The program made available rehabilitation loans to shore up marginal farmers and prevent their sinking into tenancy. It also made loans to tenants for purchase of their own farms. In the end, however, the FSA proved to be little more than another relief operation that tided a few farmers over difficult times. A more effective answer to the problem, sadly, awaited mobilization for war, which took many tenants off into the military services or defense industries, broadened their horizons, and taught them new skills.

The Agricultural Adjustment Act of 1938 was a response to renewed crop surpluses and price declines during the recession. It reenacted the basic devices of the earlier AAA with some new twists. Before the government could apply marketing quotas to a given crop, for instance, it had to hold a plebiscite among the growers and win a two-thirds majority. The new Food, Drug and Cosmetic Act broadened the coverage of the 1906 Pure Food and Drug Act and forbade the use of false or misleading advertising. Enforcement of the advertising provision became the responsibility of the Federal Trade Commission. The Fair Labor Standards Act applied to enterprises that operated in or affected interstate commerce. It set a minimum wage of 40¢ an hour and a maximum workweek of forty hours, to be put into effect over several years. The act also prohibited child labor under the age of sixteen, and prohibited it under eighteen in hazardous occupations.

THE LEGACY OF THE NEW DEAL

SETBACKS FOR THE PRESIDENT   As the New Deal turned its focus from recovery to reform, an effective opposition emerged within the president's party, especially in the southern wing. Local power elites in the South felt that the New Deal jeopardized their position. They felt threatened, too, when in 1936 the Democratic convention eliminated the two-thirds rule for nominations, thereby removing the South's veto power, and seated African-American delegates. Southern Democrats were at best uneasy bedfellows with organized labor and northern blacks. Senator "Cotton" Ed Smith of South Carolina and several other southern delegates walked out of the convention, with Smith declaring that he would not support any party that views "the Negro as a political and social equal." Some disgruntled southern Democrats drifted toward coalition with conservative Republicans. By the end of 1937, a bipartisan conservative bloc had coalesced.

In 1938 the conservative opposition stymied an executive reorganization bill amid cries that it would lead to dictatorship. They also secured drastic cuts in the undistributed-profits and capital gains taxes to help restore business "confidence." The House also set up a Committee on Un-American Activities chaired by Martin Dies of Texas, who took to the warpath against Communists. Soon he began to brand New Dealers as Red dupes. "Stalin baited his hook with a 'progressive' worm," Dies wrote in 1940, "and New Deal suckers swallowed bait, hook, line, and sinker."

As the political season of 1938 advanced, Roosevelt unfolded a new idea as momentous as the Court plan—a proposal to reshape the Democratic party in the image of the New Deal. He announced his purpose to intervene in Democratic primaries as the party leader, "charged with the responsibility of carrying out the definitely liberal declaration of principles set forth in the 1936 Democratic platform." He wanted his own supporters nominated. Instead of succeeding, however, the effort backfired and broke the spell of presidential invincibility, or what was left of it. As in the Court fight, Roosevelt had risked his prestige while handing his adversaries persuasive issues. His opponents tagged his intervention in the primaries an attempted "purge"; the word evoked visions of Adolf Hitler and Joseph Stalin, tyrants who had purged their Nazi and Communist parties in blood.

The elections of November 1938 handed the administration another setback, a result partly of the friction among Democrats. Their majority in the House fell from 229 to 93, in the Senate from 56 to 42. The margins remained large, but the president headed a restive and divided party. In his State of the Union message in 1939, Roosevelt for the first time proposed no new reforms, but spoke of the need "to invigorate the process of recovery, in order to *preserve* our reforms." In the same year, the administration won an extension of Social Security and finally put through its reorganization plan. Under the Administrative Reorganization Act, the president could "reduce, coordinate, consolidate, and reorganize" the agencies of government. With that, Roosevelt's domestic initiatives feebly ended. The conservative coalition and the administration had reached a standoff.

EMERGENCE OF THE BROKER STATE The New Deal had lost momentum, but it had wrought some enduring changes. By the end of the 1930s, the power of the national government was vastly enlarged over what it had been in 1932. Government had taken on the duty of ensuring the economic and social stability of the country. It had established minimum standards for labor conditions and public welfare. It had helped middle-class Americans hold on to their savings, their homes, and their farms. The protection afforded by deposit insurance, unemployment pay, and Social Security pensions would come to be universally accepted as safeguards against such disasters as the depression.

Roosevelt had steered a course between the extremes of laissez-faire and socialism. The First New Deal had experimented for a time with a managed economy under the NRA, but had abandoned that experiment for a turn toward enforcing competition and priming the economy with government spending. The effect of heavy governmental expenditures, which finally lifted the economy out of the depression during World War II, seemed to confirm the arguments of Keynesians.

Roosevelt himself, impatient with theory, was a pragmatist in developing policy: he kept what worked and discarded what did not. The result was, paradoxically, both profoundly revolutionary and profoundly conservative. The New Deal left America greatly changed in many ways, its economy more managed than before. At the same time, it left the basic capitalistic structure of the economic system in place. "For a permanent correction of grave weaknesses in our economic system," Roosevelt said, "we have relied on new applications of old democratic processes."

CULTURE IN THE THIRTIES

Pragmatism made a comeback not only in government policy during the 1930s, but in artistic expression as well. Artists of all kinds seemed to abandon the alienation of the 1920s in favor of renewed social purpose.

In the early 1930s, a renewed sense of social commitment sometimes took the form of allegiance to revolution. For a time, leftist politics and rhetoric made significant inroads in literary circles. By the summer of 1932, even the "golden boy" of the lost generation, F. Scott Fitzgerald, could declare that "to bring on the revolution, it may be necessary to work within the Communist party." In 1932 fifty-three artists and intellectuals signed an open letter endorsing the Communist party candidate for president. But few writers remained Communists for long. Writers being a notoriously independent lot, they rebelled at demands to hew to a shifting line.

LITERATURE AND THE DEPRESSION Among the writers who sang songs with social significance, at least two novelists deserve special notice: John Steinbeck and Richard Wright. The single piece of fiction that best captured the ordeal of the depression, John Steinbeck's *The Grapes of Wrath* (1939), was also the most memorable "proletarian" novel of the times because it treated workers as genuine people rather than as cardboard stereotypes. Steinbeck had taken the trouble to travel with displaced "Okies" driven from the Oklahoma dust bowl by foreclosures and farm combines to pursue the illusion of jobs in the fields of California's Central Valley. The story focused on the Joad family as they made their painful journey from Oklahoma west along U.S. 66, enticed by job ads that were actually aimed at producing a labor surplus and depressing wages. Met chiefly with contempt and rejection, caught up in labor agitations, Ma Joad strove to keep hope alive. At the end, even as

Richard Wright, author of Native Son *and* Black Boy.

the family was breaking up under the pressure, she grasped at a broader loyalty: "Use'ta be the fambly was fust. It ain't so now. It's anybody. Worse off we get, the more we got to do."

Among black novelists the supreme genius was Richard Wright. Born on a plantation near Natchez, Mississippi, the son of a matriarch whose husband deserted the family, Wright grew up in the course of moving from town to town, ended his formal schooling with the ninth grade (as valedictorian of his class), worked in Memphis, and greedily devoured books he borrowed on a white friend's library card, all the while saving up to go North and escape the racism of the segregated South. He arrived in Chicago on the eve of the depression, and his period as a Communist from 1934 to 1944 gave him an intellectual framework that did not, however, overpower his fierce independence. His first book, *Uncle Tom's Children* (1938), a collection of four novellas, and his autobiographical *Black Boy* (1945) revealed in their very rebellion against racial injustice his ties to the South, for, he wrote, "there had been slowly instilled into my personality and consciousness, black though I was, the culture of the South."

Native Son (1940), Wright's masterpiece, is set in the Chicago he had come to know before moving on to New York. It tells the story of Bigger Thomas, a product of the black ghetto, a man hemmed in and finally impelled to murder by forces beyond his control. "They wouldn't let me live and I killed," he said unrepentantly at the end. Somehow Wright managed to sublimate into literary power his own bitterness and rage at what he called "The Ethics of Living Jim Crow," an art he never quite mastered. In the black experience, he wrote, America had "a past tragic enough to appease the spiritual hunger of even a James; and . . . in the oppression of the Negro a shadow athwart our national life dense and heavy enough to satisfy even the gloomy broodings of a Hawthorne."

POPULAR ART AND SOCIAL DOCUMENTARY   In the 1930s, America experienced what *Fortune* magazine called "a sort of cultural revolution," largely through the Works Progress Administration (WPA) projects in writing, arts, music, theater, and historical research. Americans learned that, like it or not, they had a culture and had had one all along—it had simply been overlooked. Now Americans tried to make up for lost time by tracking the culture down, recording, restoring, and celebrating it. They became intrigued with American art of all kinds, and particularly that least influenced by Europe: primitive, folk, or, as it was called most often, "popular" art. American "regionalist" artists, such as Grant Wood and Thomas Hart Benton, turned their attention to their homeland.

The human tragedy of the Great Depression also helped stimulate a new genre: social documentary. The New Deal, through the WPA's Federal Writers' Project, pioneered in the oral history of the "inarticulate." In *These Are Our Lives* (1939), the Writers' Project gathered case histories of workers, sharecroppers, and blacks in North Carolina, Tennessee, and Georgia in a form that the historian Charles A. Beard called "literature more powerful than anything I have read in fiction." *Lay My Burden Down* (1944) presented the life stories of former slaves as recorded by Writers' Project interviewers.

During the 1930s, talented social reporters teamed with photographers: Erskine Caldwell and Margaret Bourke-White, *You Have Seen Their Faces* (1937) and *Say, Is This the USA?* (1941); Paul S. Taylor and Dorothea Lange, *An American Exodus* (1939); and James Agee and Walker Evans, *Let Us Now Praise Famous Men* (1941). The last of these, a sensitive, effective portrait of tenant life in Alabama, got little notice at the time but gradually came to be recognized as a unique masterpiece of documentation and art. The Farm Security Administration built up an enormous photographic documentation of everyday life in America, making familiar in the credits such names as Dorothea Lange and Ben Shahn.

POPULAR CULTURE DURING THE DEPRESSION While many of America's most talented writers and artists dealt directly with the human suffering and social tensions provoked by the Great Depression, the more popular cultural outlets such as radio programs and movies provided patrons with a welcome "escape" from the decade's grim realities.

By the 1930s, radio had become a major source of family entertainment. More than 10 million families owned a radio, and by the end of the decade the number had tripled. "There is radio music in the air, every night, everywhere," reported a San Francisco newspaper. "Anybody can hear it at home on a receiving set which any boy can put up in an hour."

Millions of housewives listened to formulaic radio "soap operas" during the day. The shows lasted fifteen minutes and derived their name from their sponsors, soap manufacturers. The recipe for a successful soap opera, noted one writer, was to provide "twelve minutes of dialogue, add predicament, villainy, and female suffering in equal measure, throw in a dash of nobility, sprinkle with tears, season with organ music, cover with a rich announcer sauce, and serve five times a week." The soap operas provided struggling people with distractions as well as a sense of comparative well-being. As one female listener explained, "I can get through the day better when I hear they have sorrows, too."

Late afternoon radio programs were directed at children home from school. In the evening after supper, families would gather around the radio to listen to newscasts, comedies such as *Amos 'n Andy* and the husband-and-wife team of George Burns and Gracie Allen, adventure dramas such as *Superman, Jack Armstrong, The Lone Ranger, Dick Tracy,* and *The Green Hornet,* and "big band" musical programs, all interspersed with commercials. On Sundays, most radio stations broadcast church services. Fans could also listen to baseball and football games or boxing matches. Franklin Roosevelt was the first president to take full advantage of the popularity of radio broadcasting. He hosted sixteen "fireside chats" to generate public support for his New Deal initiatives.

In the late 1920s, what had been "silent" films were transformed by the introduction of sound. The "talkies" made the movie industry by far the most popular form of entertainment during the 1930s—much more popular than today. The introduction of double features in 1931 and the construction of outdoor drive-in theaters in 1933 also boosted inter-

Frankenstein. *Popular 1930s movies included the gangster, horror, and animation genres that provided the viewer with pure entertainment and often relieved them from the burdens of the Depression.*

est and attendance. More than 60 percent of the population—70 million people—saw at least one movie each week. Adults paid a quarter and children a dime for their tickets. "The immense influence of Hollywood in our national life," declared a writer in 1936, ". . . seems to be accepted as a matter of fact. Manners, clothes, speech, tastes, all are affected by the actors and actresses of the motion picture screen as they never were by the popular figures of the stage or by any of our popular idols."

Films of the 1930s rarely dealt directly with the hard times of the depression or with racial and ethnic tensions. An exception was the film version of *The Grapes of Wrath* (1940) and classic documentaries by Pare Lorenz entitled *The River* (1937) and *The Plow That Broke the Plains* (1936). Much more common were movies intended for pure entertainment that transported viewers into the realm of adventure, spectacle, and fantasy. People relished "shoot 'em up" gangster films, Walt Disney's animated cartoons, spectacular musicals, "screwball" comedies, and classic horror films such as *Dracula* (1931), *Frankenstein* (1931), *The Werewolf* (1932), and *The Mummy* (1932).

The appeal of gangster films perhaps reflected public sympathy with gritty characters determined to succeed whatever the consequences. *Little Caesar* (1930), *Public Enemy Number One* (1931), and *Scarface* (1932) portrayed the rise and fall of brutal mobsters and in the process made stars of "tough guys" Edward G. Robinson, James Cagney, and Paul Muni. Dozens of similar films followed.

By the time Roosevelt was inaugurated in 1933, theatrical dance musicals choreographed and directed by Busby Berkeley had also captured the popular imagination. Flamboyant, if inane, musicals such as *42nd Street* (1933), *The Gold Diggers* (1933), and *Dames* (1934) reinforced Roosevelt's upbeat assurance that "happy days are here again!" Berkeley used elaborate sets, multiple cameras, flocks of chorus girls, and huge orchestras to produce entertainment extravaganzas.

But the best way to escape the daily troubles of the depression was to watch one of the zany comedies perfected by the Marx Brothers, former vaudeville performers. As one Hollywood official explained, the movies during the 1930s were intended to "laugh the big bad wolf of the depression out of the public mind." *Cocoanuts* (1929), *Animal Crackers* (1930), and *Monkey Business* (1931) introduced Americans to the anarchic antics of Chico, Groucho, Harpo, and Zeppo Marx. These madcap

The Marx Brothers performing one of their many madcap routines.

comedians combined slapstick humor with verbal wit to create plotless masterpieces filled with irreverent satire.

In 1939 the movie version of Margaret Mitchell's historical novel *Gone with the Wind* appeared in Technicolor, then still a novelty. It starred Clark Gable and Vivien Leigh and at 220 minutes was the longest feature film up to that time. It was also the most popular. The Civil War drama captured the romantic imagination of a nation just as a horrific world war was breaking out in Europe and Asia.

MAKING CONNECTIONS

- In the mid-1930s, just as Roosevelt was getting the New Deal into place, the growing conflict in Europe began to assume more and more of his (and America's) attention: Chapter 29 shows how Roosevelt went from combating the depression to leading the United States into World War II.

- Harry Truman, Roosevelt's successor in the White House, tried unsuccessfully to expand the idea of the New Deal into new areas (national health insurance and federal aid to education, for example), a topic covered in Chapter 31.

FURTHER READING

An engaging introduction to the decade of the New Deal is Anthony J. Badger's *The New Deal: The Depression Years, 1933–1940* (1989). Van L. Perkins's *Crisis in Agriculture* (1969) and Sidney Baldwin's *Poverty and Politics: The Rise and Decline of the Farm Security Administration* (1969) look at agricultural reforms. Michael E. Parrish's *Securities Regulation and the New Deal* (1970) and Ellis W. Hawley's *The New Deal and the Problem of Monopoly: A Study in Economic Ambivalence* (1966) analyze government attempts to forestall another market crash.

Alan Brinkley's *The End of Reform: New Deal Liberalism in Recession and War* (1995) suggests that the New Deal reformers did not go far enough in their efforts to curb big business. Bernard Bellush's *The Failure of the NRA* (1977) studies government relations with business. William R. Brock's *Welfare, Democracy, and the New Deal* (1988) describes the development of welfare policy.

For scholarship about the various groups involved in the New Deal, consult Lois Scharf's *To Work and to Wed: Female Employment, Feminism, and the Great Depression* (1980), on women; Nancy J. Weiss's *Farewell to the Party of Lincoln: Black Politics in the Age of FDR* (1983) and Harvard Sitkoff's *A New Deal for Blacks* (1978), on blacks; and John M. Allswang's *A House of All Peoples: Ethnic Politics in Chicago, 1890–1936* (1971), on immigrants.

Works on the critics of the New Deal include T. Harry Williams's *Huey Long* (1969) and Alan Brinkley's *Voices of Protest: Huey Long, Father Coughlin, and the Great Depression* (1982). For leftist reactions to reform, see Harvey Klehr's *The Heyday of American Communism: The Depression Decade* (1984) and David Shannon's *The Socialist Party of America* (1955).

One interest group that both supported and criticized New Deal policies was organized labor. See Sidney Fine's *Sit-down: The General Motors Strike of 1936–1937* (1969) and Jerold S. Auerbach's *Labor and Liberty: The La Follette Committee and the New Deal* (1966).

The fullest introduction to the New Deal in the South remains the relevant chapters in George B. Tindall's *The Emergence of the New South, 1913–1945* (1967). How southern farmers fared is examined in David E. Conrad's *The Forgotten Farmers: The Story of the Sharecroppers in the New Deal* (1965). Dan T. Carter provides an insightful analysis of the influence of reform on race relations in the 1930s in his *Scottsboro: A Tragedy of the American South* (1969).

James M. Gregory's *American Exodus: The Dust Bowl Migration and Okie Culture in California* (1989) describes the migratory movement's effect on American culture. For the cultural impact of the New Deal, consult Richard H. Pells's *Radical Visions and American Dreams: Cultural and Social Thought in the Depression Years* (1973) and Richard D. McKinzie's *The New Deal for Artists* (1973).

29   FROM ISOLATION
TO GLOBAL WAR

CHAPTER ORGANIZER

This chapter focuses on:

- isolationism and peace movements between the two World Wars.

- America's response to German aggression in Europe.

- how events in Asia led to Japan's attack on Pearl Harbor and America's entry into the global war.

*I*n the late 1930s, as the winds of war swept across Asia and Europe, the focus of American politics moved abruptly from domestic to foreign affairs. Another Democratic president had to shift attention from social reform to military preparedness and war. And the public again had to wrestle with the painful choice between involving the country in volatile world affairs and remaining aloof and officially neutral.

POSTWAR ISOLATIONISM

THE LEAGUE AND THE UNITED STATES   Between Woodrow Wilson and Franklin Roosevelt lay two decades of isolation from foreign entanglements. The postwar mood expressed in the election of 1920 set the pattern. The voters yearned for a restored isolationism, and President-elect Harding lost little time in disposing of the League of Nations. "You just didn't want a surrender of the United States," he told the people in his victory speech. "That's why you didn't care for the League, which is now deceased." The spirit of isolation found other expressions as well: the higher tariff walls, the Red Scare, the rage for "100 percent Americanism," and restrictive immigration laws by which a nation of immigrants all but shut the door to any more newcomers.

The United States may have felt the urge to leave a wicked world to its own devices, but it could hardly stop the world and get off. American business, despite the tariff walls, now had worldwide connections. American investments and loans abroad put in circulation the dollars that purchased American exports. Overseas possessions, moreover, directly involved the country in world affairs, especially in the Pacific. Even the League of Nations was too great a fact to ignore, although messages from the League at first went unanswered by American diplomats. By the end of 1922, however, the United States had "unofficial observers" at the League's headquarters in Geneva, and after 1924 American diplomats gradually entered into joint efforts on such matters as the international trade in drugs and arms, the criminal traffic in women and children, and a variety of economic, cultural, and technical conferences.

Americans had mixed feelings about adherence to the World Court. The Permanent Court of International Justice (the World Court), established by the League of Nations at The Hague in the Netherlands in 1922, was open to any country, whether a member of the League or not. The idea of bringing foreign disputes before a panel of jurists appealed to legal-minded Americans; the United States had in fact urged the idea in previous years. Still, it smacked too much of extranational authority for isolationists, even though its jurisdiction was always optional. Repeated efforts to join the World Court therefore met with rebuff from the Senate. Franklin D. Roosevelt pressed the issue in 1935, and the Senate voted 52 to 36 in favor, falling short of a two-thirds majority. American judges served on the Court panel, but the United States stayed out.

WAR DEBTS AND REPARATIONS   Probably nothing did more to heighten American isolationism—or anti-American feeling in Europe—than the war-debt tangle. When in 1917 the Allies had begun to exhaust their ability to pay for American military supplies, the United States government had advanced them funds first for the war effort and then for postwar reconstruction. A World War Foreign Debt Commission, created by Congress in 1922, renegotiated the Allied debt to America to a total of about $11.5 billion. Adding the interest payable over sixty-two years to this principal, the Allied debt totaled over $22 billion.

To most Americans it all seemed a simple matter of obligation, but Europeans commonly had a different perception. In the first place, Americans who thought their loan money had flowed to Europe were wrong: most of it went toward purchases of military supplies in the United States, which fueled the wartime boom. Then, too, the Allies held off the enemy at great cost of blood and treasure while the United States was raising an army. American states, the British noted, had repudiated debts to British investors after the Revolution; and the French pointed out that they had never been repaid for help in the American Revolution. But most difficult were the practical problems of repayment. To get dollar exchange, European debtors had to sell their goods to the United States, but American tariff walls went higher in 1921 and 1922, and again in 1930, making debt payment harder. Payment in gold would have undermined the European currencies.

The French and British insisted that they could pay America only as they themselves collected reparations from defeated Germany. Twice during the 1920s the resulting strain on Germany brought the structure of international payments to the verge of collapse, and both times the Reparations Commission called in private American bankers to work out rescue plans.

The whole structure finally did collapse during the Great Depression. In 1931 President Hoover negotiated a moratorium on both German reparations and Allied payment of war debts, thereby indirectly accepting the connection between the two. The purpose, among other things, was to shore up American private loans of several billion dollars in Germany, which for the time had kept the international credit structure intact. Once the United States had accepted the connection between reparations and war debt, the Allies virtually canceled German reparations. At the end of 1932, after Hoover's debt moratorium ended, most of the European countries defaulted on their war debts to the United States; by 1934 all but Finland had defaulted. In retaliation, Congress passed the Johnson Debt Default Act of 1934, which prohibited even private loans to any defaulting government.

ATTEMPTS AT DISARMAMENT   Yet, for all the isolationist sentiment of the time, Wilsonian idealism had struck a responsive chord in many Americans. A lingering doubt, tinged with guilt, haunted many Americans about their rejection of membership in the League. Before long Harding's advisers hit upon a happy substitute—disarmament. The conviction had grown after World War I that excessive armaments had been the war's cause, and that arms limitation would bring lasting peace. The United States had no intention of maintaining a large army, but under the building program begun in 1916, it constructed a navy second only to that of Britain. Neither the British nor the Americans had much stomach for the cost of a naval armaments race with each other, but both shared a common concern with the alarming growth of Japanese power.

During and after the war, Japanese-American relations grew increasingly strained. The United States objected to continued Japanese encroachments in Asia. In 1902 Japan had made a defensive alliance with Great Britain, directed then at Russia but invoked in 1914 against Germany in order to pick up German concessions and territories in East Asia. The Japanese quickly took the Shantung Peninsula and the islands of Micronesia, which Germany had purchased not long before from Spain. The Paris Peace Conference reluctantly confirmed Japanese seizure of the Shantung Peninsula, to the outrage of the Chinese, and the League of Nations authorized a Japanese mandate of Micronesia north of the equator. Occupation of Micronesia put the Japanese squarely athwart eastern approaches to the Philippines.

During the war the Japanese had grabbed the chance for further moves against China. In 1915 the cabinet in Tokyo issued what came to be known as the Twenty-one Demands, which would have brought China virtually under Japanese control. The United States protested, and fortunately the Japanese decided not to force their most rigorous demands. In 1917, after the United States entered the war, Viscount Kikujiro Ishii visited Washington to secure American recognition of Japan's expanding claims in Asia as had France, Britain, and Russia. Secretary of State Lansing entered an ambiguous agreement that recognized Japan's "special interests [translated by the Japanese as 'paramount interests'] in China." Americans were unhappy with the Lansing-Ishii Agreement, but it seemed the only way to preserve the appearance of friendship.

To deal with the growing strains, President Harding invited eight principal foreign powers to the Washington Armaments Conference in 1921. The American secretary of state Charles Evans Hughes, in what was expected to be a perfunctory greeting, announced that "the way to disarm is to disarm." The only way out of an armaments race, he said, "is to end it now." It was one of the most dramatic moments in American diplomatic history. In less than fifteen minutes, one electrified reporter said, Hughes had destroyed more tonnage "than all the admirals of the world have sunk in a cycle of centuries."

The Washington Armaments Conference, 1921. *The Big Five at the conference were* (from left): *Prince Tekugawa (Japan), Arthur Balfour (Great Britain), Charles Evans Hughes (United States), M. Briand (France), and H. E. Carlo Sanchez (Italy).*

Delegates from the United States, Britain, Japan, France, and Italy then reached agreement on a Five-Power Naval Treaty (1922) incorporating Hughes's plan for tonnage limits and a naval hiatus of ten years during which no battleships would be built. These powers also agreed to refrain from further fortification of their Pacific possessions. The agreement in effect partitioned the world: U.S. naval power became supreme in the Western Hemisphere, Japanese power in the western Pacific, British power from the North Sea to Singapore.

Two other major agreements emerged from the Washington Conference. With the Four-Power Treaty, the United States, Britain, Japan, and France agreed to respect each other's possessions in the Pacific, and to refer any disputes or any outside threat to consultation. The Nine-Power Treaty for the first time formally pledged the signers to support the principle of the Open Door enunciated by Secretary of State John Hay at the turn of the century. The Open Door enabled all nations to compete for trade and investment opportunities in China on an equal footing rather than allow individual nations to create economic monopolies in particular regions of the country. The signers of the Nine-Power Treaty also promised to respect the territorial integrity of China. The nations involved, in addition to those signing the Five-Power Treaty, were China, Belgium, Portugal, and the Netherlands.

With these agreements in hand, Harding could boast of a brilliant diplomatic stroke that relieved taxpayers of the need to pay for an enlarged navy, and warded off potential conflicts in the Pacific. A grateful Senate approved the naval treaty with only one dissenting vote. The Four-Power Treaty aroused real opposition, but finally passed with the support of Democrats after the Senate tacked on a reservation that "there is no commitment to armed force, no alliance, no obligation to join in any defense."

There was the rub. Though the agreements tapped a deep urge toward peacemaking, they were uniformly without obligation and without teeth. The signers of the Four-Power Treaty agreed only to consult, not to help each other militarily, a point that was clear even before the Senate tacked on its reservation. The formal endorsement of the Open Door in the Nine-Power Treaty was just as ineffective, and the American people remained unwilling to uphold the principle with anything but pious affirmation. The naval disarmament treaty set limits only on capital ships (battleships and aircraft carriers); the race to build cruisers, destroyers, submarines, and other smaller craft continued. Expansionist Japan withdrew from the agreement in 1934. Thus, twelve years after the Washington Conference, the dream of naval disarmament died.

THE KELLOGG-BRIAND PACT   During and after World War I, the ideal of abolishing war caught the American imagination. Peace societies thrived and spawned innumerable programs. In 1921 a wealthy Chicagoan founded the American Committee for the Outlawry of War. "We can outlaw this war system just as we outlawed slavery and the saloon," said one of the more enthusiastic converts.

The glorious vision of abolishing war at the stroke of a pen culminated in the signing of the Kellogg-Briand Pact in 1928. This unique treaty started with an initiative from French foreign minister Aristide Briand, who had busied himself winning allies against a possible resurgence of German power. In 1927 Briand proposed to Secretary of State Frank B. Kellogg an agreement that the two countries would never go to war against each other. This innocent-seeming proposal was actually a clever ploy to draw the United States into the French security system by the back door. In any future war, for instance, such a pact would inhibit the United States from reprisals against any French intrusions on neutral rights. Kellogg gave the idea a cool reception, and was outraged to discover that Briand had urged leaders of the American peace movements to put pressure on the government to sign.

Finally Kellogg turned the tables on Briand. He countered with a scheme to have all nations sign the pact, an idea all the more acceptable to the peace organizations. Caught in a trap of his own making, the French foreign minister finally relented. The Pact of Paris (its official name), signed on August 27, 1928, solemnly declared that the signatories "condemn recourse to war . . . and renounce it as an instrument of national policy." Eventually sixty-two powers adhered to the pact, but all explicitly or tacitly reserved "self-defense" as an escape hatch. The United States Senate included a reservation declaring the preserving of the Monroe Doctrine necessary to self-defense, and then ratified the agreement by a vote of 85 to 1. One senator who voted for "this worthless, but perfectly harmless peace treaty" wrote a friend later that he feared it would "confuse the minds of many good people who think that peace may be secured by polite professions of neighborly and brotherly love."

*Plans for international disarmament, popular in the 1920s, proved imprac-
tical.*

THE "GOOD NEIGHBOR" POLICY   In Latin America the spirit of
peace and noninvolvement helped allay resentments against "Yankee
imperialism," which had been freely practiced in the Caribbean during
the first two decades of the century. The Harding administration agreed
in 1921 to pay the republic of Colombia the $25 million it had once de-
manded for America's use of Panama Canal rights. In 1924 American
troops left the Dominican Republic, occupied since 1916, although
United States officials continued to collect customs duties there for another twenty-five years.

The marines left Nicaragua in 1925, but returned a year later at the
outbreak of disorders and civil war. There in 1927, the Coolidge administration brought both parties into an agreement for American-super-
vised elections, but one rebel leader, César Augusto Sandino, held out,
and the marines stayed until 1933. The unhappy legacies of this intervention were enmity toward the United States and a ruthless, corrupt
Nicaraguan National Guard, created to keep order after the marines
left, but used in 1936 to set up the dictatorship of Anastasio Somoza.
These legacies continue to have their effects down to the present day.

The troubles in Nicaragua increased strains with Mexico. Relations were already soured by repeated Mexican threats to expropriate American oil properties. In 1928, however, the American ambassador was able to get an agreement protecting American rights acquired before 1917. Expropriation did in fact occur in 1938, but the Mexican government then agreed to reimburse American owners.

In 1928, with problems apparently clearing in Mexico and Nicaragua, President Coolidge traveled to Havana to open the Pan-American Conference. It was an unusual gesture of friendship, and so was the choice of Charles Evans Hughes, the former secretary of state, to head the American delegation. Hughes announced the United States' intention to withdraw its marines from Nicaragua and Haiti as soon as possible, although he did block a resolution declaring that "no state has the right to intervene in the affairs of another."

At the end of 1928 President-elect Hoover began a tour of ten Latin American nations. Once in office he reversed Wilson's policy of refusing to recognize "bad" regimes and reverted to the older policy of recognizing governments in power, regardless of their behavior. In 1930 he generated more goodwill by permitting publication of a memorandum drawn up in 1928 by Undersecretary of State J. Ruben Clark. The Clark Memorandum denied that the Monroe Doctrine justified American intervention in Latin America. It stopped short of repudiating intervention on any grounds, but that fine point hardly blunted the celebration in Latin America. Although Hoover never endorsed the Clark Memorandum, he never intervened in the region. Before he left office, steps had already been taken to withdraw American forces from Nicaragua and Haiti.

Franklin D. Roosevelt likewise embraced "the policy of the good neighbor" and soon advanced it in practice. In 1933, at the Seventh Pan-American Conference, the United States supported a resolution saying "No state has the right to intervene in the internal or external affairs of another." Under Roosevelt the marines completed their withdrawals from Nicaragua and Haiti, and in 1934 the president negotiated with Cuba a treaty that abrogated the Platt Amendment and thus ended the last formal claim to a right of intervention in Latin America. Roosevelt reinforced hemispheric goodwill in 1936, when he opened the Eighth Pan-American Conference with a speech declaring that outside aggressors "will find a Hemisphere wholly prepared to consult together for our mutual safety and our mutual good."

WAR CLOUDS

JAPANESE INCURSIONS IN CHINA   The lessening of irritants in the Western Hemisphere during the 1930s proved an exception in an otherwise dismal world scene, as war clouds thickened over Europe and Asia. Actual conflict erupted first in Asia, where unsettled conditions in China had invited foreign encroachments since before the turn of the century. In 1929 Chinese nationalist aspirations and China's subsequent clashes with Russia convinced the Japanese that their own extensive rights in Manchuria, including the South Manchurian Railway, were in danger.

The Japanese army at the time had a nationalist movement of its own, led by a strong cadre of young officers devoted to ousting corrupt politicians and bringing about a moral regeneration for Japan. Economic pressures strengthened this nationalist movement, for Japan was suffering from the Great Depression and Chinese boycotts of Japanese goods. Manchuria offered both a tempting target and a promising market. Japanese occupation of Manchuria began with the Mukden Incident of 1931, when an explosion destroyed a section of railway track

Japan's seizure of Manchuria in 1931 prompted this American condemnation.

near that city. The Japanese "Kwantung Army," based in Manchuria to guard the railway, blamed the incident on the Chinese and used it as a pretext to begin its occupation, which it extended during the winter of 1931–1932 to all of Manchuria. In 1932 the Japanese converted Manchuria into the puppet empire of "Manchukuo."

The Manchuria Incident, as the Japanese called their undeclared war, was a flagrant breach of the Nine-Power Treaty, the Kellogg-Briand Pact, and Japan's pledges as a member of the League of Nations. But when China asked the League and the United States for help, neither responded. President Hoover was unwilling to invoke either military or economic sanctions. Secretary of State Henry Stimson, who would have preferred to do more, warned in 1932 that the United States refused to recognize any treaty, agreement, or situation that violated American treaty rights, the Open Door, or the territorial integrity of China, or any situation brought about by violation of the Kellogg-Briand Pact. This statement, later known as the Stimson Doctrine, had no effect on Japanese action, for later in the same month the Japanese navy attacked and briefly occupied Shanghai, China's great port city.

Indiscriminate bombing of Shanghai's civilian population aroused indignation but no further Western action. When the League of Nations condemned Japanese aggression in 1933, Japan withdrew from the League. During the spring of 1933, hostilities in Manchuria gradually subsided and ended with a truce. Then an uneasy peace settled upon East Asia for four years, during which time the leaders of Japan's military further extended their political sway.

ITALY AND GERMANY The rise of the Japanese militarists paralleled the rise of dictators in Italy and Germany. In 1922 Benito Mussolini had seized power in Italy. After returning from World War I as a wounded veteran, he had organized the fascist movement, a hybrid of nationalism and socialism. The movement's name came from the ancient Roman *fasces,* a symbol of authority. The program, and above all Mussolini's promise to restore order and pride in a country fragmented by dissension, enjoyed a wide appeal. Once in power, Mussolini largely abandoned the socialist part of his platform and gradually suppressed all political opposition. By 1925 he wielded dictatorial power as Il Duce (the leader) in a one-party state.

To most Americans there was always something ludicrous about the strutting Mussolini, since Italy afforded but a limited power base in the

Mussolini and Hitler in Munich, Germany, June 1940.

total European picture. But Germany was another matter, and Americans were not amused, even at the beginning, by Il Duce's counterpart, Adolf Hitler. Hitler's National Socialist (Nazi) party duplicated the major features of Italian fascism, including the ancient Roman salute. The impotence of Germany's democratic Weimar Republic in the face of world depression offered Hitler his opening. Made chancellor on January 30, 1933, he swiftly intimidated the opposition, won dictatorial powers from a subservient Reichstag (parliament), and in 1934 assumed the title of Reichsführer (national leader) with absolute powers. The Nazi police state cranked up the engines of tyranny, persecuting socialists and Jews, whom Hitler blamed for all Germany's troubles, and rearming in defiance of the Versailles Treaty. Hitler flouted international agreements, pulled Germany out of the League of Nations in 1933, and frankly proclaimed that he meant to extend control over all German-speaking peoples. Despite one provocation after another, the European democracies lacked the will to resist his bold grab for power.

THE MOOD IN AMERICA   Most Americans, absorbed by the problems of the depression, chose to retreat all the more into isolationism during the early 1930s. During the presidential the campaign of 1932, Roosevelt renounced his Wilsonian past and stated that he now opposed joining the League of Nations. Once in office, he rejected an early chance to deal with economic problems on an international basis.

This dealt a severe blow to international cooperation. The epilogue was Europe's final default on the war debts, and further American drift toward isolation.

The chief exception to the administration's isolationism was Secretary of State Cordell Hull's grand scheme of reciprocal trade agreements. Hull, a former Tennessee judge and congressman, believed that free trade among all nations would advance understanding and peace. In 1934 the administration threw its support behind Hull's pet project, and over the objections of business interests and Republicans, Congress adopted the Trade Agreements Act, which authorized the president to lower tariff rates as much as 50 percent for countries that made similar concessions on American products. Agreements were made with fourteen countries by the end of 1935, reaching a total of twenty-nine by 1945. The economic results are hard to measure, since the intervening years were so troubled.

Another scheme for building foreign markets, diplomatic recognition of Soviet Russia, won more support in business quarters than had the reciprocity plan. The vast expanse of Russia stirred fantasies of a trade boom, much as China had at the turn of the century. By 1933 the reasons for American refusal to recognize the Bolshevik regime had grown stale. Japanese expansionism in Asia, moreover, gave Russia and the United States a common concern. Given an opening by the shift of opinion, Roosevelt invited Maxim Litvinov, Soviet commissar for foreign affairs, to visit Washington. After nine days of talks, a formal exchange of notes on November 16, 1933, signaled the renewal of diplomatic relations. Litvinov promised that his country would abstain from propaganda in the United States, extend religious freedom to Americans in the U.S.S.R., and reopen the question of czarist debts to America.

THE EXPANDING AXIS   But a catastrophic chain of events in Asia and Europe sent the world hurtling toward disaster. In 1934 Japan renounced the Five-Power Naval Treaty. In 1935 Mussolini commenced an Italian conquest of Ethiopia. The same year a referendum in the Saar Basin, held in accordance with the Versailles Treaty, delivered that coal-rich region into the hands of Hitler. In 1936 Hitler reoccupied the Rhineland with armed forces, in violation of the Versailles Treaty but without any forceful response from the French. The year 1936 also brought the Spanish Civil War, which began with an uprising of the

Spanish armed forces in Morocco, led by General Francisco Franco. In three years Franco had established a fascist dictatorship with help from Hitler and Mussolini while the democracies stood by and left the Spanish Republic to its fate. On July 7, 1937, Japanese and Chinese troops clashed at the Marco Polo Bridge near Peking. The incident quickly developed into a full-scale war that the Japanese persisted in calling the "China Incident." It was the beginning of World War II in Asia, two years before war came to Europe. That same year Japan joined Germany and Italy in the "Anti-Comintern Pact," allegedly directed at the Communist threat, thus establishing the Rome-Berlin-Tokyo "Axis."

By 1938 the peace of Europe trembled in the balance. Having rebuilt German military force, Hitler forced the *Anschluss* (union) of Austria with Germany in March 1938, and six months later took the Sudeten territory from Czechoslovakia after signing an agreement at Munich under which Britain and France abandoned a country that had probably the second-best army in central Europe. The mountainous Sudetenland, largely German in population, was vital to the defense of Czechoslovakia. Having promised that this was his last territorial demand, Hitler in March 1939 brazenly violated his pledge and occupied the remainder of Czechoslovakia and seized formerly German territory from

German troops entering Prague, the capital of Czechoslovakia, April 1939.

AGGRESSION IN EUROPE, 1935–1939

← Aggressive moves

Axis Powers

Lithuania. In quick succession the Spanish Republic finally collapsed, and Mussolini seized the kingdom of Albania. Finally, during the summer, Hitler heated up a "war of nerves" over control of the free city of Danzig and the Polish Corridor, and on September 1 launched his conquest of Poland. A few days before, he had signed a nonaggression pact with Soviet Russia. Having deserted Czechoslovakia, Britain and France now honored their commitment to go to war if Poland were invaded.

DEGREES OF NEUTRALITY   During these years of deepening crisis, the Western democracies seemed paralyzed, hoping in vain that each concession would appease the appetites of fascist dictators. The Americans retreated more deeply into isolation. The prevailing mood was reinforced by a Senate inquiry into the role of bankers and munitions makers in World War I. Under Senator Gerald P. Nye of North Dakota, a progressive Republican, the committee sat from 1934 to 1937, and concluded that bankers and munitions makers had made scandalous profits from the war. Although Nye never showed that greed for profit had actually impelled Woodrow Wilson into war, millions of Americans became convinced that Uncle Sam had been duped by the "merchants of death."

Like generals who are said to be always preparing for the last war, Congress occupied itself with keeping out of the last war. Neutrality laws of the 1930s moved the United States toward complete isolation from the quarrels of Europe. Americans wanted to keep out of war, but their sympathies were more strongly than ever with the Western democracies, and the triumph of fascist aggression aroused growing fears for national security.

In 1935 President Roosevelt signed the first in a series of neutrality acts, one that anticipated Italy's invasion of Ethiopia. The Neutrality Act of 1935 forbade the sale of arms and munitions to all belligerents whenever the president proclaimed that a state of war existed. Ameri-

A 1938 cartoon showing U.S. foreign policy entangled by the serpent of isolationism.

cans who traveled on belligerent ships thereafter did so at their own risk. Roosevelt would have preferred discretionary authority to levy an embargo only against aggressors, but reluctantly accepted the act because it would be effective only for six months, and for the time being "meets the need of the existing situation." That is, it would actually be enforced against Italy in its war with Ethiopia. When he signed the act on August 31, Roosevelt nevertheless urged reconsideration of the arms embargo on all belligerents: "History is filled with situations that call for some flexibility of action. It is conceivable that situations may arise in which the wholly inflexible provisions . . . of this act . . . might drag us into war instead of keeping us out."

On October 3, 1935, Italy invaded Ethiopia and the president invoked the Neutrality Act. One shortcoming in its provisions became apparent right away: the key problem was neither arms traffic nor passenger travel, but trade in contraband not covered by the Neutrality Act. While Italy did not need to buy arms, since it had its own arms industry, it did need to buy raw materials, such as oil, which were not covered by the Neutrality Act. Secretary of State Hull warned that citizens trading with the belligerents, meaning in effect Italy since there was little trade with Ethiopia, did so at their own risk. He asked, moreover, for a "moral embargo" on oil and other products. Nonetheless, sanctions imposed under the Neutrality Act had no deterrent effect on Mussolini or his suppliers. In the summer of 1936, Il Duce completed his conquest of Ethiopia.

When Congress reconvened in 1936, it extended the arms embargo and added a provision forbidding loans to belligerents. Then in July 1936, while Italian troops mopped up the last resistance in Ethiopia, the Spanish army led by Franco revolted in Morocco. Ironically, Roosevelt now became more isolationist than some of the isolationists. Although the Spanish Civil War involved a fascist uprising against a recognized, democratic government, Roosevelt accepted the French and British position that only nonintervention would localize the fight. There existed, moreover, a strong bloc of pro-Franco Catholics in America who worried that the Spanish Republic was a threat to the church. They feared an atheistic Communist influence in the Spanish government; intrigues by Spanish Communists did prove divisive and the Soviet Union in fact did supply aid to the Republic, but nothing like the quantity of German and Italian assistance to Franco.

Roosevelt sought another "moral embargo" on the arms trade, and asked Congress to extend the neutrality laws to cover civil wars. Congress did so in 1937 with only one dissenting vote. The Western democracies then stood witness while German and Italian soldiers, planes, and armaments supported Franco's overthrow of Spanish democracy, which was completed in 1939.

In the spring of 1937 isolationist sentiment reached a peak. A Gallup poll found that 94 percent of its respondents preferred efforts to keep out of war over efforts to prevent war. That same spring Congress passed yet another neutrality law. It continued restraints on arms sales and loans, forbade Americans to travel on belligerent ships, and prohibited the arming of American merchant ships trading with belligerents. The president also won discretionary authority to require that goods other than arms or munitions exported to belligerents be placed on a cash-and-carry basis (that is, the purchaser of the goods would have to pay in cash and then carry them away in its own ships). This was an ingenious scheme to preserve a profitable trade without running the risk of war.

The new law faced its first test in July 1937, when Japanese and Chinese forces clashed at the Marco Polo Bridge west of Peking. Since nei-

Japanese troops enter Peking after the clash at the Marco Polo Bridge, July 1937.

ther side declared war, Roosevelt was able to use his discretion about invoking the neutrality law. He decided to wait, and in fact never invoked it. This was because its net effect would have favored the Japanese, since China had greater need of arms but few means to get supplies past the Japanese navy. A flourishing trade in munitions to China flowed around the world as ships carried arms across the Atlantic to England, where they were reloaded onto British ships bound for Hong Kong. Roosevelt, by inaction, had challenged strict isolationism.

Roosevelt soon ventured a step further. On October 5, 1937, he denounced the "reign of terror and international lawlessness" in which 10 percent of the world's population threatened the peace of the other 90 percent. "When an epidemic of physical disease starts to spread, the community approves and joins in a quarantine of the patients in order to protect the health of the community. . . ." There should also be a quarantine against nations "creating a state of international anarchy and instability from which there is no escape through mere isolation or neutrality." On the whole, public reaction to the speech was mixed. The president quickly backed off from its implications and refused to spell out any specific program.

Then, on December 12, 1937, Japanese planes bombed and sank the American gunboat *Panay*, which had been lying at anchor in the Yangtze River and prominently flying the American flag, and then Japan attacked three Standard Oil tankers. Two members of the *Panay* crew and an Italian journalist died; thirty more were injured. Though the Japanese government apologized and paid the reparations demanded—nearly $2.25 million—the incident reinforced American animosity toward Japan. The private boycott of Japanese goods spread, but isolationist sentiment continued strong, as was vividly demonstrated by support for the Ludlow Amendment in Congress. The proposed constitutional amendment would have required a public referendum for a declaration of war except in case of attack on American territory. Only by the most severe pressure from the White House, and a vote of 209 to 188, was consideration of the measure tabled in 1938.

After the German occupation of Czechoslovakia in 1939, Roosevelt no longer pretended impartiality in the impending European struggle. He urged Congress to repeal the embargo and permit the United States to sell arms on a cash-and-carry basis to Britain and France, but to no avail. When the Germans attacked Poland on September 1, 1939, Roosevelt proclaimed neutrality, but in a radio talk said that he did not, like

Wilson, ask Americans to remain neutral in thought because "even a neutral has a right to take account of the facts."

Roosevelt summoned Congress into special session, and asked it once again to amend the Neutrality Act. "I regret the Congress passed the Act," the president said. "I regret equally that I signed the Act." This time he got what he wanted. Under the Neutrality Act of 1939 the Allies could send their own freighters to the United States, buy supplies with cash, and take away arms or anything else they wanted. American ships, on the other hand, were excluded from belligerent ports and from specified war zones. Roosevelt then designated as a war zone the Baltic Sea and the waters around Great Britain and Ireland from Norway south to the coast of Spain. One effect of this move was to relieve Hitler of any inhibitions against using unrestricted submarine warfare to blockade Britain.

American attitudes continued to vacillate. As the war crisis developed, an isolationist policy of "hands off" prevailed. Once the great democracies of western Europe faced war, American public opinion, appalled at Hitler's tyranny, supported measures short of war to help their cause. "What the majority of the American people want," an editor wrote in the *Nation,* "is to be as un-neutral as possible without getting into war." On October 3, while Congress debated repeal of the arms embargo, the foreign ministers of the American republics adopted the Declaration of Panama, which created a "chastity belt" around the Americas, south of Canada, a zone 300 to 1,000 miles wide in which belligerents were warned not to pursue naval action. This unneutral action prohibited German naval activity near North and South American coasts. For a time it seemed that the Western Hemisphere could remain insulated from the war. After Hitler overran Poland in less than a month, the war in Europe settled into an unreal stalemate that began to be called the "phony war." What lay ahead, it seemed, was a long war of attrition in which Britain and France would have the resources to outlast Hitler. The illusion lasted through the winter.

THE STORM IN EUROPE

BLITZKRIEG   In the spring of 1940 the winter's long *Sitzkrieg* suddenly erupted into *Blitzkrieg*—lightning war. At dawn on April 9, without warning, Nazi troops entered Denmark and disembarked along the

French refugees fleeing German troops, June 1940.

Norwegian coast. Denmark fell in a day, Norway within a few weeks. On May 10 Hitler unleashed his dive bombers and panzer tank divisions on neutral Belgium and the Netherlands. On May 21 German troops reached the English Channel, cutting off a British force sent to help the Belgians and French. A desperate evacuation from the beaches at Dunkirk enlisted every available British boat from warship to tug. Some 338,000 men, about a third of them French, escaped to England.

Having outflanked the forts on France's eastern defense perimeter, the Maginot Line, the German forces rushed ahead, cutting the French armies to pieces and spreading panic by strafing refugees in a deliberate policy of terror. On June 10 Italy entered the war as Germany's ally. "I need only a few thousand dead to enable me to take my seat . . . at the peace table," Il Duce said. On June 14 the swastika flew over Paris. On June 22 French delegates, in the presence of Hitler, submitted to his terms in the same railroad car in which German delegates had been forced to sign the Armistice of 1918.

AMERICA'S GROWING INVOLVEMENT   Britain now stood alone, but in Parliament the new prime minister, Winston Churchill, breathed defiance. "We shall go on to the end," he said; "we shall never surrender." Despite the grim resolution of the British, America seemed suddenly vulnerable as Hitler turned his air force against Britain. President Roosevelt, who in his annual budget had requested $1.9 billion for defense, now asked for more, and called for the production of 50,000 combat planes a year. By October 1940, Congress had voted more than $17 billion for defense. In response to Churchill's appeal for military supplies, the War and Navy Departments began releasing stocks of arms, planes, and munitions to the British.

In June 1940 the president set up the National Defense Research Committee to coordinate military research, including a secret look into the possibility of developing an atomic bomb, suggested the previous fall by Albert Einstein and other scientists. To bolster national unity, Roosevelt named two Republicans to the defense posts in his cabinet: Henry L. Stimson as secretary of war and Frank Knox as secretary of the navy.

The summer of 1940 brought the desperate Battle of Britain, in which the Royal Air Force, with the benefit of the new technology of radar, outfought the numerically superior German Luftwaffe and finally forced the Germans to postpone plans to invade England. Submarine warfare meanwhile strained the resources of the battered Royal Navy. To relieve the pressure, Churchill urgently requested the transfer of

St. Paul's Cathedral looms above the destruction wrought by German bombs during the Blitz. Churchill's response: "We shall never surrender."

American destroyers. Secret negotiations led to an executive agreement under which fifty "overaged" American destroyers went to the British in return for ninety-nine-year American leases on naval and air bases in Newfoundland, Bermuda, the Bahamas, Jamaica, St. Lucia, Trinidad, Antigua, and British Guiana. Roosevelt disguised the action as being necessary for hemisphere defense. It was, he declared, "the most important action in the reinforcement of our national defense that has been taken since the Louisiana Purchase." Two weeks later, Congress adopted the first peacetime conscription in American history, requiring the registration of all men aged twenty-one to thirty-five for a year's military service within the United States.

The new state of affairs prompted vigorous debate between "internationalists," who believed national security demanded aid to Britain, and isolationists, who charged that Roosevelt was drawing the United States into a needless war. In 1940 the nonpartisan Committee to Defend America by Aiding the Allies was organized. It drew its strongest support from the East and West Coasts and the South. On the other hand, isolationists formed the America First Committee, which included among its members Herbert Hoover and Charles A. Lindbergh, Jr. Before the end of 1941, the committee had about 450 chapters around the country, but probably two-thirds of its members lived within a 300-mile radius of Chicago. The isolationists argued that the war involved, in Senator William E. Borah's words, "nothing more than another chapter in the bloody volume of European power politics," and that a Nazi victory, while distasteful, would pose no threat to national security.

A THIRD TERM FOR FDR In the midst of this turbulence, the quadrennial presidential campaign came due. Isolationist sentiment was strongest in the Republican party and both the leading Republican candidates were noninterventionists, but neither loomed as a man of sufficient stature to challenge the "champ," assuming Roosevelt decided to run again. Senator Robert A. Taft of Ohio, son of the former president, lacked popular appeal, and New York district attorney Thomas E. Dewey, who had won fame as a "racket buster," at thirty-eight seemed young and unseasoned. This left an opening for an inspired group of political amateurs to promote the dark-horse candidacy of Wendell L. Willkie of Indiana.

Willkie seemed at first an unlikely choice: a former Democrat who had voted for Roosevelt in 1932, a utilities president who had fought the TVA, but in origins a Hoosier farm boy whose disheveled charm inspired strong loyalty. Unlike the front-runners, he openly supported aid to the Allies, and the Nazi *Blitzkrieg* had brought many other Republicans to the same viewpoint. When the Republicans met at Philadelphia on June 28, six days after the French surrender, the convention was stampeded by the cry of "We Want Willkie" from the galleries.

The Nazi victory in France also ensured another nomination for Roosevelt. The president cultivated party unity behind his foreign policy and kept a sphinx-like silence about his intentions regarding the war. The world crisis reconciled southern conservatives to the man whose foreign policy, at least, they supported. At the July convention in Chicago Roosevelt won nomination for a third term with only token opposition.

Through the summer Roosevelt assumed the role of a man above the political fray, busy rather with urgent matters of defense and diplomacy: Pan-American agreements for mutual defense, the destroyer-bases deal, and visits to defense facilities that took the place of campaign trips. Willkie was reduced to attacks on New Deal red tape and promises to run the programs better. In the end, however, he switched to an attack on Roosevelt's conduct of foreign policy. In October he warned: "If you re-elect him you may expect war in April, 1941." To this Roosevelt responded, "I have said this before, but I shall say it again and again and again: Your boys are not going to be sent into any foreign wars." Neither man distinguished himself with such hollow statements, since both knew the risks of all-out aid to Britain, which both supported.

Roosevelt won the election by a comfortable margin of 27 million votes to Willkie's 22 million, and a wider margin of 449 to 82 in the electoral college. Even so, the popular vote was closer than any presidential vote since 1916. But given the dangerous world situation, a majority of the voters agreed with the Democrats' slogan: "Don't switch horses in the middle of the stream."

THE ARSENAL OF DEMOCRACY Bolstered by the mandate for an unprecedented third term, Roosevelt moved quickly for greater measures to aid Britain. Since the outbreak of war Roosevelt had corre-

Women picketing the White House to urge defeat of the lend-lease program. Like Senator Burton Wheeler they feared that lend-lease would "plow under every fourth American boy."

sponded with Winston Churchill, who soon after the election informed Roosevelt that British cash was fast running out. Since direct American loans would arouse memories of earlier war-debt defaults—the Johnson Act of 1934 forbade such loans anyway—the president created an ingenious device to bypass that issue and yet supply British needs, the "lend-lease" program.

In a fireside chat, Roosevelt told the nation that it must become "the great arsenal of democracy" because of the threat of Britain's fall. In his annual message to Congress on January 6, 1941, he warned that only the British navy stood between America and the peril of attack. Greater efforts to bolster British defenses were therefore imperative: "They do not need manpower. They do need billions of dollars worth of the weapons of defense." At the end of the speech he enunciated the Four Freedoms for which the democracies fought: freedom of speech, freedom of worship, freedom from want, and freedom from fear. The Lend-Lease Bill, introduced in Congress on January 10, authorized the president to sell, transfer, exchange, lend, lease, or otherwise dispose of arms and other equipment and supplies to "any country whose defense the President deems vital to the defense of the United States."

For two months a bitter debate over the bill raged in Congress and the country. Isolationists saw it as the point of no return. "The lend-lease-give program," said Senator Burton K. Wheeler, "is the New Deal's triple A foreign policy; it will plow under every fourth American boy." Roosevelt pronounced this "the rottenest thing that has been said in public life in my generation." Administration supporters denied that lend-lease would lead to war, but it did manifestly increase the risk. Lend-lease became law in March.

While the nation debated, the war was spreading. In October 1940 when the presidential campaign approached its climax, Mussolini launched attacks on Greece and, from Italian Libya, on the British in Egypt. But he miscalculated, and his forces had to fall back in both cases. In the spring of 1941, German forces under General Erwin Rommel joined the Italians in Libya, forcing the British, whose resources had been drained to help Greece, to withdraw into Egypt. In April 1941 Nazi armored divisions overwhelmed Yugoslavia and Greece, and by the end of May airborne forces subdued the Greek island of Crete, putting Hitler in a position to menace the entire Middle East. With Hungary, Romania, and Bulgaria forced into the Axis fold, Hitler controlled nearly all of Europe.

On June 22, 1941, German armies suddenly fell upon Russia. Frustrated in the purpose of subduing Britain, Hitler sought to eliminate the potential threat on his rear with another lightning stroke. The Russian plains offered an ideal theater for *Blitzkrieg*, or so it seemed. With Romanian and Finnish allies, the Nazis moved on a 2,000-mile front from the Arctic to the Black Sea with seeming invincibility. Then, after four months, the Russian soldiers rallied in front of Leningrad, Moscow, and Sevastopol. During the winter of 1941–1942, Hitler's legions began to learn the bitter lesson the Russians had taught Napoleon and the French in 1812.

Winston Churchill had already decided to offer British support to the Soviet Union in case of such an attack. "If Hitler invaded Hell," he said, "I would make at least a favorable reference to the Devil in the House of Commons." Roosevelt adopted the same policy, offering American aid two days after the attack. Stalinist Russia, so long as it held out, ensured the survival of Britain. American aid was now indispensable to

Europe's defense, and the logic of lend-lease led on to deeper American involvement. To deliver aid to Britain, goods had to be maneuvered through the German U-boat "wolf packs" in the North Atlantic. So in April 1941, Roosevelt informed Churchill that the United States Navy would extend its patrol areas in the North Atlantic nearly all the way to Iceland.

In August 1941 Roosevelt and Churchill held a secret naval rendezvous off Newfoundland, where they drew up a statement of principles that came to be known as the Atlantic Charter. In effect the "common principles" upon which the parties based "their hopes for a better future for the world" amounted to a joint statement of war aims, its eight points a mixture of the idealistic goals of the New Deal and Wilson's Fourteen Points. It called for the self-determination of all peoples, equal access to raw materials, economic cooperation, freedom of the seas, and a new system of general security. In September it was announced that fifteen anti-Axis nations, including the Soviet Union, had endorsed the statement.

Thus Roosevelt had led the United States into a joint statement of war aims with the anti-Axis powers. It was not long before shooting incidents involved Americans in the North Atlantic. The first attack on an American warship occurred on September 4 when a German submarine fired two torpedoes at the destroyer *Greer*. The president announced a week later orders to "shoot on sight" any German or Italian raiders ("rattlesnakes of the Atlantic") that ventured into American defensive waters. Five days later, the United States Navy began convoying merchant vessels all the way to Iceland. Then on October 17, while the destroyer *Kearny* was attacking German submarines, it sustained severe damage and loss of eleven lives from a German torpedo. Two weeks later, a submarine torpedoed and sank the destroyer *Reuben James*, with a loss of ninety-six officers and men, while it was on convoy duty west of Iceland. This action hastened Congress into making the changes in the Neutrality Act already requested by the president. On November 17 the legislation was in effect repealed when the bans on arming merchant vessels and allowing them to enter combat zones and belligerent ports were removed. Step by step the United States had given up neutrality and embarked on naval warfare against Germany. Still, the American people hoped to avoid taking the final step into all-out war. The decision for war came in an unexpected quarter—the Pacific.

THE STORM IN THE PACIFIC

JAPANESE AGGRESSION   After the Nazi victories in the spring of 1940, relations with Japan also took a turn for the worse. Japanese militarists, bogged down in the vastness of China, now eyed new temptations in South Asia: French Indochina, the Dutch East Indies, British Malaya, and Burma. Here they could cut off one of China's last links to the West, the Burma Road. What was more, they could incorporate into their "Greater East Asia Co-Prosperity Sphere" the oil, rubber, and other strategic materials that the crowded homeland lacked. As it was, Japan depended on the United States for important supplies, including 80 percent of its oil. During the summer of 1940, Japan forced the helpless French government at Vichy to permit the construction of Japanese airfields in French-controlled northern Indochina and to cut off the railroad into South China. The United States responded with a loan to China and the Export Control Act of July 2, 1940, which authorized the president to restrict the export of arms and other strategic materials to Japan. Gradually Roosevelt extended embargoes on aviation gas, scrap iron, and other supplies.

On September 27, 1940, the Tokyo government signed a Tripartite Pact with Germany and Italy, by which each pledged to declare war on any nation that attacked any of them. The pact could have been directed against either the United States or the Soviet Union. The Germans hoped to persuade Japan to enter Siberia when Nazi forces entered the Soviet Union from the west. The Soviet presence in Siberia did inhibit the Japanese impulse to move southward, but on April 13, 1941, while the Nazis were sweeping through the Balkans, Japan signed a nonaggression pact with the Soviet Union and, once the Nazis invaded Russia in June, the Japanese were freed of any threat from the north.

In July 1941 Japan announced that it was assuming a protectorate over all of French Indochina. Roosevelt took three steps in response: he froze all Japanese assets in the United States; he restricted exports of oil to Japan; and he merged the armed forces of the Philippines with the Army of the United States and put their commander, General Douglas MacArthur, in charge of all United States forces in East Asia. By September the oil restrictions had tightened into an embargo. The Japanese estimated that their oil reserves would last two years at most, eighteen months in case of an expanded war. Forced by the embargo to secure other oil supplies, the Japanese army and navy began to perfect plans for attacks on the Dutch and British colonies to the south.

Actions by both sides put the United States and Japan on the way to a war that neither wanted. In his regular talks with the Japanese ambassador, Secretary of State Cordell Hull demanded that Japan withdraw from Indochina and China as the price of renewed trade. A more flexible position might have strengthened the moderates in Japan. The Japanese were not then pursuing a concerted plan of aggression comparable to Hitler's. The Japanese military had stumbled crazily from one act of aggression to another without approval from the government in Tokyo. Premier Fumimaro Konoye, however, while known as a man of liberal principles who preferred peace, caved in to pressures from the militants. Perhaps he had no choice.

The Japanese warlords, for their part, seriously misjudged the United States. The desperate wish of Americans to stay out of war might still have enabled the Japanese to conquer the British and Dutch colonies before an American decision to act. But the warlords decided that they dared not leave the American navy intact and the Philippines untouched on the flank of their new lifeline to the south.

TRAGEDY AT PEARL HARBOR   Thus a tragedy began to unfold with a fatal certainty—mostly out of sight of the American people, whose attention was focused on the war in the Atlantic. Late in August 1941 Premier Konoye proposed a personal meeting with President Roosevelt. Hull advised Roosevelt not to meet unless agreement on fundamentals could be reached in advance. Soon afterward, on September 6, an imperial conference approved preparations for a surprise attack on Hawaii and gave Premier Konoye six more weeks to reach a settlement. The Japanese emperor's clear displeasure with the risks of an attack afforded the premier one last chance to pursue a compromise, but the stumbling block was still the presence of Japanese troops in China. In October Konoye urged War Minister Hideki Tojo to consider withdrawal while saving face by keeping some troops in North China. Tojo countered with his "maximum concession" that Japanese troops would stay no longer than twenty-five years if the United States stopped aiding China. Faced with this rebuff and with Tojo's threat to resign and bring down the cabinet, Konoye himself resigned on October 15; Tojo became premier the next day. The war party now assumed complete control of the government.

On the very day that Tojo became premier, a special Japanese envoy conferred with Hull and Roosevelt in Washington. His arrival was largely a cover for Japan's war plans, although neither he nor the Japanese ambassador knew that. On November 20 they presented Tojo's final proposal. Japan would occupy no more territory if the United States would cut off aid to China, restore trade, and help Japan get supplies from the Dutch Indies. In that case Japan would pull out of southern Indochina immediately and abandon the remainder once peace had been established with China—presumably on Japanese terms. Tojo expected the United States to refuse such demands. On November 26 Hull repeated the demand that Japan withdraw altogether from China.

The Attack on Pearl Harbor. *The view from a Japanese fighter plane shows American battleships in vulnerable positions.*

That same day a Japanese naval force began heading secretly across the North Pacific toward Pearl Harbor.

Washington already knew that war was imminent. Reports of Japanese troop transports moving south from Formosa prompted Washington to send warnings to American commanders in the Pacific, and to the British government. The massive movements southward clearly signaled attacks on the British and the Dutch possessions. American leaders had every reason to expect war in the southwest Pacific, but none expected that Japan would commit most of its carriers to another attack 5,000 miles away at Pearl Harbor.

In the early morning of December 7, 1941, Americans decoded the last part of a fourteen-part Japanese message breaking off the negotiations. Japan's ambassador was instructed to deliver the message at 1 P.M. (7:30 A.M. in Honolulu), about a half hour before the Japanese attack, but delays held up delivery until more than an hour later than scheduled. The War Department sent out an alert at noon that something was about to happen, but the message, which went by commercial telegraph because radio contacts were broken, arrived in Hawaii eight and a half hours later. Even so, the decoded Japanese message had not mentioned Pearl Harbor, and everyone still assumed that any Japanese move would be in Southeast Asia.

It was still a sleepy Sunday morning when the first Japanese planes roared down the west coast and the central valley of Oahu to begin their assault. At 7:53 A.M. the flight commander, Mitsuo Fuchida, sounded the cry "Tora! Tora! Tora!" ("Tiger! Tiger! Tiger!"), the signal that the attackers had taken the American navy by surprise. For nearly two hours the Japanese planes kept up their attack on an unsuspecting Pacific Fleet. Of the eight battleships in Pearl Harbor, three were sunk, one grounded, one capsized, and the others badly battered. Altogether nine-

The Attack on Pearl Harbor. *The view from an American airfield shows the destruction and confusion brought on by the surprise attack.*

teen ships were sunk or disabled. At the adjoining Hickam Field and other airfields on the island the Japanese found planes parked wing to wing, and destroyed in all about 150 of them. Few were able to get airborne, and Japanese losses numbered fewer than thirty planes. Before it was over the raid had killed more than 2,400 American servicemen and civilians, and wounded 1,178 more.

The surprise attack fulfilled the dreams of its planners, but it fell short of total success in two ways. The Japanese ignored the onshore facilities and oil tanks that supported the fleet, without which the surviving ships might have been forced back to the West Coast, and they missed the American aircraft carriers that had fortuitously left a few days earlier. In the naval war to come, these carriers would prove decisive.

Later the same day (December 8 in the western Pacific) Japanese forces began assaults on the Philippines, Guam, and Midway, and on the British forces in Hong Kong and the Malay Peninsula. With one stroke the Japanese had silenced America's debate on neutrality, and a suddenly unified and vengeful nation prepared for the struggle. The next day President Roosevelt delivered his war message to Congress in a speech long remembered by most Americans:

> Yesterday, December 7, 1941—a date which will live in infamy—the United States of America was suddenly and deliberately attacked by naval and air forces of the Empire of Japan. . . .
>
> The facts of yesterday speak for themselves. The people of the United States have already formed their opinions and well understand the implications to the very life and safety of our Nation. . . .

Congress voted for the war resolution unanimously, with the sole exception of Representative Jeanette Rankin, a pacifist who was unable in good conscience to vote for war in 1917 or 1941. For several days it was uncertain whether war with the other Axis Powers would follow. The Tripartite Pact was ostensibly for defense only, and it carried no obligation for them to enter, but Hitler, impatient with continuing American aid to Britain, willingly joined his Asian allies. On December 11, Germany and Italy declared war on the United States. The separate wars that were being waged by armies in Asia and Europe had become one global conflict.

MAKING CONNECTIONS

- The United States tried to stake out a neutral position in the growing world conflict. Compare this to earlier American attempts at neutrality, from the Napoleonic Wars era of Jefferson's administration onward.

- The American alliance with the Soviet Union described in this chapter proved to be temporary: after the war, the Americans and the Soviets would be adversaries in a great cold war, the beginnings of which are outlined in Chapter 31.

- The Japanese conquest of French Indochina (Vietnam) would play an important role in the events leading to American involvement in the region, a topic discussed in Chapter 33.

FURTHER READING

The best overview of interwar diplomacy remains Selig Adler's *The Uncertain Giant: American Foreign Policy between the Wars* (1965). Joan Hoff Wilson's *American Business and Foreign Policy, 1920–1933* (1971) highlights the efforts of Republican administrations during the 1920s to promote international commerce. Robert Dallek's *Franklin D. Roosevelt and American Foreign Policy, 1932–1945* (1979) provides a judicious assessment of Roosevelt's foreign policies during the 1930s.

Other scholars have concentrated on particular diplomatic issues of the 1920s. Thomas H. Buckley's *The United States and the Washington Conference, 1921–1922* (1970) examines disarmament. For a study of the Kellogg-Briand Pact, see Robert H. Ferrell's *Peace in Their Time: The Origins of the Kellogg-Briand Pact* (1968). Relations between the United States and Europe are covered in Frank Costigliola's *Awkward Dominion: American Political, Economic, and Cultural Relations with*

Europe, 1919–1933 (1984). A comprehensive analysis of American responses to Nazi aggression is Arnold Offner's *American Appeasement: United States Foreign Policy and Germany, 1933–1938* (1969).

For American relations in East Asia during the period, see Akira Iriye's *After Imperialism: The Search for a New Order in the Far East, 1921–1931* (1965) and the relevant chapters in Walter LaFeber's *The Clash: A History of U.S.-Japan Relations* (1997). More specific studies are Warren I. Cohen's *America's Response to China: An Interpretive History of Sino-American Relations* (2nd ed., 1981) and Jonathan G. Utley's *Going to War with Japan, 1937–1941* (1985). For relations with Latin America, see Irwin F. Gellman's *Good Neighbor Diplomacy: United States Policies in Latin America, 1933–1945* (1979). The best general account of the onset of World War II is Donald Watt's *How War Came: The Immediate Origins of the Second World War, 1938–1939* (1990).

A noteworthy study of America's entry into World War II is Waldo Heinrichs's *Threshold of War: Franklin D. Roosevelt and American Entry into World War II* (1988). Bruce M. Russett's *No Clear and Present Danger* (1972) provides a critical account of American actions. Other interpretations of Roosevelt's diplomacy include Robert A. Divine's *The Reluctant Belligerent* (2nd ed., 1979) and Patrick Hearden's *Roosevelt Confronts Hitler: America's Entry into World War II* (1986). American relations with Great Britain are detailed in David Reynolds's *The Creation of the Anglo-American Alliance, 1937–1941* (1981).

On Pearl Harbor, see Gordon W. Prange's *Pearl Harbor: The Verdict of History* (1986). The Japanese perspective is given in Robert J. C. Butow's *Tojo and the Coming of War* (1961).

30 ❧ THE SECOND WORLD WAR

CHAPTER ORGANIZER

This chapter focuses on:

- the social and economic effects of World War II, especially in the West.

- how the Allied forces won the war.

- the efforts of the Allies to shape the postwar world.

The Japanese attack on Pearl Harbor ended a period of tense neutrality for the United States, and launched America into an epochal event that would transform the nation's social and economic life as well as its position in international affairs. The Second World War would become the most destructive and far-reaching war in history. It was a conflict so terrible and capricious, so surreal in its intensity and obscene in its cruelties, that it altered the image of war itself. Devilish new instruments of destruction were invented— plastic explosives, flame throwers, proximity fuses, rockets, jet airplanes, and atomic weapons—and systematic genocide emerged as an explicit war aim of the Nazis. Racist propaganda flourished on both sides, and excited hatred of the enemy caused many military and civilian prisoners to be executed. Over 50 million deaths were attributed to the war, and the physical destruction was incalculable. Whole cities were leveled, nations dismembered, and societies transformed. Latin America was the only region to escape the war's fury. The world is still struggling to cope with its consequences.

AMERICA'S EARLY BATTLES

SETBACKS IN THE PACIFIC   In early December 1941, all attention was focused on halting the Japanese advance and mobilizing the whole nation for war. For months after the attack on Pearl Harbor the news from the Pacific was "all bad," as President Roosevelt frankly confessed. In quick sequence these Allied outposts fell to the enemy before the end of December 1941: Guam, Wake Island, the Gilbert Islands, and Hong Kong. The fall of Rangoon in Burma cut off the Burma Road, the main supply route to Nationalist China. In the Philippines, where General Douglas MacArthur abandoned Manila on December 27, the main American forces, outmanned and outgunned, held out on Bataan Peninsula until April 9, and then on "The Rock," the fortified island of Corregidor. MacArthur slipped away in March, when he was ordered to

American prisoners of war, captured by the Japanese in the Philippines, 1942.

Australia to take command of Allied forces in the southwest Pacific. By May 6, 1942, when American forces surrendered Corregidor, Japan controlled a new empire that stretched from Burma eastward through the Dutch Indies and extending to Wake Island and the Gilberts.

The Japanese might have consolidated an almost impregnable empire with the resources they had seized. But the Japanese navy succumbed to what one of its admirals later called "victory disease." Its leaders resolved to push on into the South Pacific, isolate Australia, and strike again at Hawaii. Japanese planners hoped to draw out and destroy the American navy before the productive power of the United States could be brought to bear on the war effort.

A Japanese mistake and a stroke of American luck, however, enabled the United States Navy to frustrate the plan. Japan's failure to destroy the shore facilities at Pearl Harbor left the base relatively intact, and most of the ships damaged on December 7 lived to fight another day. The aircraft carriers at sea during the attack spent several months harassing Japanese outposts. Their most spectacular exploit, an air raid on Tokyo itself, was launched on April 18, 1942. B-25 bombers took off from the carrier *Hornet* and, unable to land on its deck, proceeded to China. The raid caused only token damage but did much to lift American morale amid a series of defeats elsewhere.

CORAL SEA AND MIDWAY   American forces finally halted the Japanese advances in two decisive naval battles. The Battle of the Coral Sea (May 7–8, 1942) stopped a fleet convoying Japanese troop transports toward New Guinea. Planes from the *Lexington* and *Yorktown* sank one Japanese carrier, damaged another, and destroyed smaller ships. American losses were greater, and included the carrier *Lexington,* but the Japanese advance on Australia was repulsed.

Less than a month after the Coral Sea engagement, Admiral Isoruku Yamamoto, the Japanese naval commander, decided to force a showdown in the central Pacific. With nearly every ship under his personal command, he headed for Midway Island, from which he hoped to render Pearl Harbor helpless. This time it was the Japanese who were the victims of surprise. American cryptanalysts had by then broken the Japanese naval code, and Admiral Chester Nimitz, commander of the central Pacific, knew what was up. He reinforced Midway with planes and carriers.

The first Japanese foray against Midway, on June 4, severely damaged the island, but at the cost of about a third of the Japanese planes. Before another attack could be mounted, American torpedo planes and dive bombers had caught three of the four Japanese carriers in the process of servicing their planes. Most of the first wave of slow American torpedo bombers were shot down, but dive bombers disabled three Japanese carriers and left them to sink. The Japanese lost an additional carrier; the Americans, a carrier and a destroyer. The Japanese navy, having lost its four best aircraft carriers, all veterans of Pearl Harbor, was forced into retreat less than six months after the attack on Hawaii. The Japanese defeat at Midway was the turning point of the Pacific war.

SETBACKS IN THE ATLANTIC   Early American setbacks in the Pacific were matched by setbacks in the Atlantic. Since the *Blitzkrieg* of 1940, German submarine "wolf packs" had wreaked havoc in the North Atlantic. In 1942, after an ominous lull, German submarines suddenly appeared off American shores and began to sink coastal shipping. Nearly 400 ships were lost in American waters before effective countermeasures brought the problem under control. The naval command accelerated the building of small escort vessels, meanwhile pressing into patrol service all kinds of surface craft and planes, some of them civilian. During the second half of 1942, the losses diminished to a negligible number.

MOBILIZATION AT HOME

The Pearl Harbor attack ended not only the long debate between isolation and intervention but also the long depression that had ravaged the country in the 1930s. The war effort would require all of America's huge productive capacity and full employment of the workforce. Soon after Pearl Harbor, Winston Churchill recalled that, thirty years before, one observer had compared the United States to a gigantic boiler: "Once the fire is lighted under it, there is no limit to the power it can generate." Mobilization was in fact already further along than preparedness had been in 1916–1917. The Selective Service had been in effect for more than a year, and the army had grown to more than 1.4 million men by July 1941. With America's entry into the war, men between eighteen and forty-five now became subject to the draft. Altogether more than 15 million men and women would serve in the armed forces over the course of the conflict.

ECONOMIC CONVERSION   The economy, too, was already partially mobilized by lend-lease and defense efforts. The War Powers Act of 1941 had given the president a mandate to reshuffle government agencies, and a Second War Powers Act empowered the government to allot materials and facilities as needed for defense, with penalties for those who failed to comply.

The War Production Board (WPB), created in 1942 on the model of its counterpart during the First World War, directed industrial conversion to war production. Auto makers switched to producing tanks, shirt factories began to make mosquito netting, and the manufacturers of refrigerators, stoves, and cash registers began to produce munitions. The Reconstruction Finance Corporation, a New Deal agency, now financed war plants.

The war effort required conservation as well as production. "Use it up, wear it out, make do or do without," became the prevailing slogan.

Mobilization for war deflected many New Deal programs.

People collected scrap metal and grew their own food in backyard "victory gardens." The government named special administrators, or "czars," to promote production of rubber and oil. The president of Union Pacific Railroad, now the rubber "czar," pushed construction of synthetic rubber plants, which by 1944 produced 800,000 tons, or 87 percent of the country's requirements. Tire and gasoline rationing began in earnest. Through the Office of Scientific Research and Development, Dr. Vannevar Bush mobilized thousands of "scientists against time" to create and modify radar, sonar, the proximity fuse, the bazooka, means to isolate blood plasma, and numerous other innovations.

The pressure of wartime needs and the stimulus of government spending sent the gross national product soaring from $100 billion in 1940 to $214 billion in 1945, a rise of 114 percent. The figure for total government expenditures was twice as great as the total of all previous federal spending in the history of the republic, about 10 times what America spent in World War I, and 100 times the expenditures during the Civil War.

FINANCING THE WAR   To cover the war's huge cost the president preferred taxes to borrowing. "I would rather pay one hundred percent of taxes now than push the burden of this war onto the shoulders of my grandchildren," he said. Taxes also relieved upward pressures on prices. The wartime Congress, however, dominated by conservatives, feared taxes more than deficits and refused to go more than halfway with Roosevelt's fiscal prudence. The Revenue Act of 1942 provided for only about $7 billion in increased revenue, less than half that recommended by the Treasury. It also greatly broadened the tax structure. Whereas in 1939 only about 4 million people filed returns, the new act, in the words of a tax historian, "made the Federal income tax a genuine mass tax."

The federal government paid for about 45 percent of its 1939–1946 costs with tax revenues. Roosevelt would have preferred to cover more, but the figure compared favorably with 30 percent for World War I and 23 percent for the Civil War. To cover the rest of its costs, the government borrowed from the public. War-bond drives, including a Victory Drive in 1945, induced citizens to put aside more than $150 billion in bonds. Financial institutions picked up most of the rest of the government's debt. In all, by the end of the war the national debt had grown to about $260 billion, about six times its size at the time of Pearl Harbor.

As the economy finally recovered from the throes of the depression, many became converts to the Keynesian argument that only massive government spending had finally been able to end the depression.

The basic economic problem was no longer finding jobs but finding workers for the booming shipyards, aircraft factories, and gunpowder mills. Millions of people, especially women, who had lived on the margin of the economic system were now brought fully into the economy. Stubborn poverty did not disappear, but for most of those who stayed home the war spelled neither hardship nor suffering but a better life than ever before, despite shortages and rationing.

ECONOMIC CONTROLS Increased incomes and spending during the war conjured up the specter of inflation. Some of the available money went into taxes and war bonds, but even so, more was sent chasing after civilian goods just as production was converting to war needs. Consumer durables such as cars, washing machines, and nondefense housing in fact ceased to be made at all. It was apparent that only strict restraints would keep prices of scarce commodities from soaring out of sight. The administration, having tried in 1933 to raise prices, now reversed its ground and set out to hold them down. In 1942, Congress authorized the Office of Price Administration (OPA) for the first time to set price ceilings. With prices frozen, goods had to be allocated through rationing, with coupons doled out for sugar, coffee, gasoline, automobile tires, and meats.

Wages and farm prices, however, were not controlled, and this complicated things. War prosperity offered farmers a chance to recover from two decades of distress, and farm-state congressmen fought successfully to raise both floors and ceilings on farm prices. Higher food prices reinforced worker demands for higher wages, but the War Labor Board tried to hold the line. Finally, under the Stabilization Act of 1942, the president won new authority to control wages and farm prices. At the same time, he set up the Office of Economic Stabilization under James F. Byrnes, who left his seat on the Supreme Court to coordinate the effort. Stabilization proved to be one of the most complex jobs of the war effort, subject to constant sniping by special interests.

Both business and workers chafed at the wage and price controls. On occasion the government seized industries threatened by strike. The coal mines and railroads both came under government operation for a short time in 1943, and in 1944 the government briefly took over the Montgomery-Ward Company. Soldiers had to carry its chairman bodily out of his office when he stubbornly defied orders of the War Labor Board. Despite these problems, the government effort to stabilize wages and prices was on the whole a success story. By the end of the war, consumer prices had risen about 31 percent, a record far better than the World War I rise of 62 percent.

DOMESTIC CONSERVATISM   In domestic politics the wartime period witnessed a growing conservatism. Discontent with price controls, labor shortages, rationing, and a hundred other petty vexations spread. In 1942 the congressional elections registered a national swing against the New Deal. Republicans gained forty-six seats in the House and nine in the Senate, chiefly in the farm areas of the midwestern states. Democratic losses outside the South strengthened the southern delegation's position within the party, and the delegation itself reflected conservative victories in southern primaries. A coalition of conservatives proceeded to eviscerate "nonessential" New Deal agencies. In 1943 Congress abolished the Works Progress Administration, the National Youth Administration, and the Civilian Conservation Corps, began to dismantle the Farm Security Administration, and liquidated the National Resources Planning Board.

Organized labor, despite substantial gains during the war, felt the impact of the conservative trend. In the spring of 1943, when John L. Lewis led the coal miners out on strike, widespread resentment led Congress to pass the Smith-Connally War Labor Disputes Act, which authorized the government to seize plants useful to the war. In 1943 a dozen states adopted laws variously restricting picketing and other union activities, and in 1944 Arkansas and Florida set in motion a wave of "right-to-work" legislation that outlawed the closed shop (requiring that all employees be union members).

SOCIAL EFFECTS OF THE WAR

MOBILIZATION AND THE DEVELOPMENT OF THE WEST   The dramatic expansion of defense production after 1940 and the mobilization of millions of men into the armed forces accelerated economic development and the population boom in the western states. Nearly 8 million people moved into the states west of the Mississippi River between 1940 and 1950. The states witnessing the largest population growth during the war were California, Oregon, Washington, Nevada, Utah, Texas, and Arizona. Most of this expansion occurred in metropolitan centers. Indeed, the Far West experienced the fastest rate of urban growth in the country. Small cities such as Phoenix and Albuquerque mushroomed, while Seattle, San Francisco, Los Angeles, and San Diego witnessed dizzying growth. San Diego's population, for example, increased by 147 percent between 1941 and 1945.

Abundant jobs at high wages enticed people to the western states. California alone garnered 10 percent of all the defense contracts during the war years. In Texas, manufacturing employment almost doubled between 1940 and 1945. Los Angeles, which in 1939 was the seventh largest manufacturing center in the nation, had by 1943 become second only to Detroit in industrial activity. City services could not keep up with the influx of workers and military personnel. Employees at Seattle's shipyards and the Boeing airplane plant lived in tents because of a housing shortage. To address the problem, Congress passed the Lanham Act, which authorized the federal government to finance over a million new temporary housing units across the country. Yet this federal housing program did not meet the demand. Some women workers at a San Diego defense plant lived eight to a room in a company dormitory.

The migration of workers to new defense jobs in the West had significant demographic effects. Communities that earlier had few African Americans witnessed an influx of blacks. Lured by news of job openings and higher wages, African Americans from Texas, Oklahoma, Arkansas, and Louisiana headed west. During the war years Seattle's black population jumped from 4,000 to 40,000, Portland's from 2,000 to 15,000.

WOMEN   The war marked an important watershed in the changing status of women. The proportion of women working had barely altered from 1910 to 1940, but with millions of men going into military service, the demand for labor shook up old prejudices about sex roles in the workplace—and in the military. Nearly 200,000 women served in the Women's Army Corps (WAC) and the navy's equivalent, Women Accepted for Volunteer Emergency Service (WAVES). Lesser numbers joined the Marine Corps, the Coast Guard, and the Army Air Force.

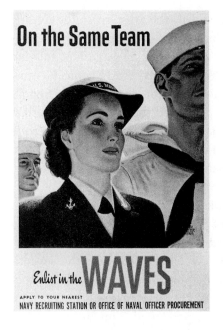

Women in the Military. *This navy recruiting poster urged women to join the WAVES (Women Accepted for Voluntary Services).*

Even more significant were the over 6 million women who entered the workforce during the war, an increase of over 50 percent and in manufacturing alone of some 110 percent. Old barriers fell overnight as women became toolmakers, machinists, crane operators, lumberjacks, stevedores, blacksmiths, and railroad track workers.

By 1944 women made up 14 percent of all workers in shipbuilding and 40 percent in aircraft plants. The government, desperate for laborers in defense industries, launched an intense publicity campaign to draw women into traditional male jobs. "Do your part, free a man for service," one ad pleaded. "Rosie the Riveter," a beautiful model dressed in overalls, became the cover girl for the recruiting campaign. One striking feature of the new labor scene was the larger proportion of older, married women in the workforce. In 1940 about 15 percent of married women went into gainful employment; by 1945 it was 24 percent. In the workforce as a whole, married women for the first time outnumbered single women. Attitudes sharply changed from those of the depression days, when over 80 percent of Americans opposed work by married women; by 1942 a poll showed 60 percent in favor of hiring married women in war industries. Defense jobs, however, were the ones most vulnerable to postwar cuts.

Women Workers. *These women took the place of men in constructing airplanes for use in the war.*

Still, there were many vocal opponents to this new trend. One disgruntled male legislator asked what would happen to traditional domestic tasks if women were in factories: "Who will do the cooking, the washing, the mending, the humble homey tasks to which every woman has devoted herself; who will rear and nurture the children?" Many women, however, were eager to get away from the grinding routine of domestic life. One female welder remembered that her wartime job "was the first time I had a chance to get out of the kitchen and work in industry and make a few bucks. This was something I had never dreamed would happen." And it was something that many women did not want to relinquish after the war.

BLACKS   The most volatile issue ignited by the war was probably that of African-American participation in the defense effort. From the start black leaders demanded full recognition in the armed forces and defense industries. Eventually about a million African Americans served in the armed forces, in every branch and every theater. But they served usually in segregated units. Every army camp had its separate facilities

Tuskegee Airmen, 1942. *One of the last segregated military training schools, the flight school at Tuskegee trained African-American men for combat during World War II.*

and its periodic racial "incidents." The most important departure was a 1940 decision to give up segregation in officer candidate schools, except those for air force cadets. A separate flight school at Tuskegee, Alabama, trained about 600 black pilots, many of whom distinguished themselves in combat.

War industries were even less accessible to black influence and pressure, although government policy theoretically opposed discrimination. In 1941 A. Philip Randolph, the tall, gentlemanly head of the Brotherhood of Sleeping Car Porters, organized a March on Washington Movement to demand an end to discrimination in defense industries. The administration, alarmed at the prospect of a mass descent on Washington, struck a bargain. The Randolph group called off its march in return for an executive order that forbade discrimination in defense work and training programs by requiring a nondiscrimination clause in defense contracts, and set up the Fair Employment Practices Commission (FEPC). The FEPC's authority was chiefly moral, since it had no power to enforce directives. It nevertheless offered willing employers the chance to say they were following government policy in giving jobs to black citizens, and no doubt persuaded others to go along.

Blacks quickly broadened their drive for wartime participation into a more inclusive social and political front. Early in 1942 the *Pittsburgh*

Courier endorsed the "Double V," which stood for victory at home and abroad. The slogan became immensely popular in black communities, and reflected a growing urge to rid the world not just of Hitler but of Hitlerism, as one editor put it. Blacks began to challenge more openly all kinds of discrimination, including racial segregation itself. "It was as if some universal message had come through to the great mass of Negroes," a sociologist wrote in 1943, "urging them to dream new dreams and to protest against the old order." A foundation was being laid for a great expansion of civil rights efforts after the war. Membership in the NAACP grew during the war from 50,000 to 450,000. Blacks could look forward to greater political participation after the Supreme Court, in *Smith* v. *Allwright* (1944), struck down Texas's white primary on the ground that Democratic primaries were part of the election process and thus subject to the Fifteenth Amendment.

The growing militancy of blacks aroused antagonism from some whites. Racial violence during this period did not approach the level of that in World War I, but growing tensions on a hot summer afternoon in Detroit sparked incidents at a park. Fighting raged through June 20–21, 1943, until federal troops arrived on the second evening. Twenty-five blacks and nine whites had been killed.

HISPANICS   As rural folk moved to the western cities, the farm counties experienced a labor shortage. In an ironic about-face, local and federal government authorities who before the war strove to force Mexican alien laborers back across the border now recruited them to harvest crops. The Mexican government, however, first insisted that the United States ensure certain minimum work and living conditions before it would assist in providing the needed workers. The result was the creation of the *bracero* program in 1942. Mexico agreed to provide seasonal farm workers in exchange for a promise by the American government not to draft them into military service. The workers were hired on year-long contracts that offered wages at the prevailing rate, and American officials provided transportation from the border to their job sites. Under this *bracero* program, some 200,000 Mexican farm workers entered the western United States. At least that many more crossed the border as illegal aliens.

The influx of peoples created new tensions. The rising tide of Mexican Americans in Los Angeles provoked a growing stream of anti-Hispanic editorials and incidents. Even though Mexican Americans fought in the war with great valor, earning seventeen Congressional Medals of Honor, there was constant conflict between servicemen and Mexican-American gang members and teenage "zoot-suiters" in southern California. "Zoot suits" were the flamboyant clothes worn by some young Chicano men. In 1943, several thousand off-duty sailors and soldiers, joined by hundreds of local white civilians, rampaged through downtown Los Angeles streets, assaulting Hispanics, blacks, and Filipinos. The violence lasted a week and came to be labeled the "zoot suit" riots.

NATIVE AMERICANS   Indians may have supported the war effort more fully than any other group in American society. Almost a third of eligible Native American men, over 25,000 people, served in the armed forces. Another one-fourth worked in defense-related industries. Thousands of Indian women volunteered as nurses or joined the Women's Voluntary Service. As was the case with African Americans, Indians benefited from the broadening experiences afforded by the war. Those who left reservations to work in defense plants or to join the military gained new vocational skills as well as a greater awareness of American society and how to succeed within it.

Why did Native Americans fight for a nation that had stripped them of their lands and decimated their heritage? Some felt that they had no choice. Mobilization for the war effort ended many New Deal programs that had provided Indians with jobs. Reservation Indians thus faced the necessity of finding new jobs elsewhere. Many viewed the Nazis and Japanese warlords as threats to their own homeland. Others saw in the war an opportunity to revitalize the warrior tradition. Joseph Medicine Crow remembered that, while fighting in Europe, he "never thought" about the traditional requirements for a young Crow male to earn his status as a warrior, but "afterwards, when I came back and went through this telling of the war deeds ceremony, why, I told my war deeds, and lo and behold I completed the four requirements to become a chief." The most common sentiment, however, seems to have been a genuine sense of patriotism.

Whatever the reasons, Indians distinguished themselves in the military during the war. Unlike their African-American counterparts, Indian servicemen were integrated within the regular units. Perhaps the most distinctive activity performed by Indians was their service as "code talkers." Every military branch used Indians—Oneidas, Chippewas, Sauks,

Foxes, Comanches, and Navajos—to encode and decipher messages so as to prevent enemy discovery. The Dineh (Navajo) developed their own specialized dictionary to convey idiomatic military terms. For example, a submarine became an "iron fish" and a machine gun was a "fast shooter."

JAPANESE AMERICANS   The record on civil liberties during World War II was on the whole better than that during World War I, if only because there was virtually no opposition to the war effort after the attack on Pearl Harbor. Neither German Americans nor Italian Americans faced the harassments meted out to their counterparts in the previous war; few had much sympathy for Hitler or Mussolini. The shameful exception to an otherwise improved record was the treatment given to more than 100,000 Americans of Japanese descent (Nisei), who were forcibly removed from homes and businesses on the West Coast to "War Relocation Camps" in the interior. Caught up in the war hysteria and racial prejudice provoked by the attack on Pearl Harbor, President Roosevelt initiated the removal of Japanese Americans when he issued

Japanese Americans boarding a bus that would take them to War Relocation Camps, 1942.

Executive Order 9066 on February 19, 1942. More than 60 percent of the internees were U.S. citizens; a third were under the age of nineteen. Forced to sell their farms and businesses at great losses, the internees lost not only their liberty but also their property. Few, if any, were disloyal, but all were victims of fear and racial prejudice.

This was especially the case in the months following the attack on Pearl Harbor. A California barbershop offered "free shaves for Japs" but noted that it was "not responsible for accidents." Others were even blunter. Idaho's governor declared: "A good solution to the Jap problem would be to send them all back to Japan, then sink the island." As one Japanese American poignantly complained, "What really hurts most is the constant reference to us evacuees as 'Japs.' 'Japs' are the guys we are fighting. We're on this side and we want to help. Why won't America let us?" Many did support the effort. Japanese-American Hawaiians and mainlanders made up two of the most celebrated infantry units in the war, fighting with distinction on the Italian front. Other thousands of Nisei served as interpreters and translators, the "eyes and ears" of the American armed forces in the Pacific. Not until 1983 did the government finally recognize the injustice of the internment policy. That year it authorized granting those Nisei still living $20,000 each in compensation.

THE ALLIED DRIVE TOWARD BERLIN

By mid-1942, the "home front" began to get news from the war fronts that some of the lines were holding at last. Japanese naval losses at the Coral Sea and Midway had secured Australia and Hawaii. By mid-year a motley fleet of American air and sea sub-chasers was ending six months of happy hunting for German U-boats off the Atlantic coast. This was all the more important because war plans called for the defeat of Germany first.

WAR AIMS AND STRATEGY   There were many reasons for giving top priority to defeating Hitler. Nazi forces in western Europe and the Atlantic posed a more direct threat to the Western Hemisphere; German war potential was greater and German science was more likely to come up with some devastating new weapon. Lose in the Atlantic, General

George Marshall grimly predicted, and you lose everywhere. Despite such assumptions, Japanese attacks involved Americans directly in the Pacific war from the start, and as a consequence, during the first year of fighting more Americans went to the Pacific than across the Atlantic.

The Pearl Harbor attack brought British prime minister Winston Churchill quickly to Washington for lengthy talks about a common war plan. Thus began a wartime alliance between the United States and Great Britain, a partnership marked almost as much by disagreement and suspicion as it was by common purposes. As Churchill later re-marked, "There is only one thing worse than fighting with allies, and that is fighting without them." Although he and Roosevelt admired each other, they disagreed about military strategy and the likely makeup of the postwar world. They often pursued the interests of their own coun-try at the expense of the military alliance; they occasionally deceived each other; in a few cases, they lied to each other. Roosevelt worried about Churchill's excessive drinking, and Churchill worried about Roosevelt's "naive" understanding of Soviet behavior and his innocent faith in Stalin's integrity.

Initially, at least, such differences of opinion and outlook were masked by the need to make basic decisions related to the conduct of the war. The meetings in Washington in 1942 produced several major and numerous minor decisions, including the one to name a supreme commander in each major theater of war. Each commander would be subject to orders from the British-American Combined Chiefs of Staff. Other joint boards allotted munitions, raw materials, and shipping.

American and British war plans thereafter proceeded in close con-cert, and often launched joint operations, especially against Germany. No such coordinated effort was ever effected with Russia, which fought its own war on the eastern front, separate except for the coordinated timing of some major offensives. In Washington on January 1, 1942, rep-resentatives of twenty-six governments then at war with the Axis signed the Declaration of the United Nations, affirming the principles of the Atlantic Charter, pledging their full resources to the war, and promising not to make separate peace with the common enemies. Finally, in the course of their talks, the British and American leaders reaffirmed the priority of war against Germany.

Agreement on war aims, however, did not bring agreement on strat-egy. Roosevelt and Churchill, meeting at the White House again in

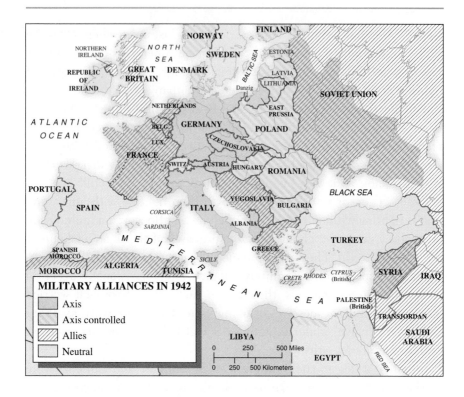

MILITARY ALLIANCES IN 1942

- Axis
- Axis controlled
- Allies
- Neutral

June 1942, could not agree on where to hit first. American military planners wanted to strike directly across the English Channel before the end of 1942, secure a beachhead, and move against Germany in 1943. The British preferred to keep the Germans off balance with hit-and-run raids and air attacks while continuing to build up their forces. With vivid memories of the last war, the British feared a mass bloodletting in trench warfare if they struck prematurely. The Russians, bearing the brunt of the German attack in the east, insisted that the Western Allies must do something to relieve the pressure. Finally, the Americans accepted Churchill's proposal to invade French North Africa.

THE NORTH AFRICA CAMPAIGN   On November 8, 1942, Anglo-American forces under the command of American general Dwight D. Eisenhower landed at Casablanca in Morocco and at Oran and Algiers in Algeria. Completely surprised, French forces under the Vichy government (which collaborated with the Germans) had little will to resist. Hitler therefore occupied the whole of France and sent German forces into French Tunisia. By chance Admiral Jean-François Darlan, second to Marshal Pétain in the collaborationist Vichy government, was visiting in Algiers and was persuaded by the Allies to order a cease-fire.

Farther east, General Bernard Montgomery's British forces were pushing the brilliant German tank commander General Erwin Rommel back across Libya, but green American forces confronted seasoned Nazis pouring into Tunisia. Before spring, however, Montgomery had taken Libya, and the Germans were caught in a gigantic pincers. Hammered from all sides, unable to retreat across the Mediterranean, an army of 275,000 surrendered on May 13, 1943, leaving all of North Africa in Allied hands.

While the battle of Tunisia unfolded, in January 1943 Roosevelt and Churchill and the Combined Chiefs of Staff met at Casablanca. Stalin declined to leave Russia for the meeting but continued to press for a second front in western Europe. For the time, however, they decided to postpone the cross-Channel invasion and to carry out Churchill's scheme to attack what he called the "soft underbelly of the Axis" by invading Sicily. Admiral Chester Nimitz and General Douglas MacArthur were authorized meanwhile to start an offensive to dislodge the Japanese from the Pacific islands. Top priority, however, went to an antisubmarine campaign in the Atlantic.

Before leaving Casablanca, Roosevelt announced, with Churchill's endorsement, that the war would end only with the "unconditional surrender" of all enemies. This was designed to reassure Stalin and to quiet suspicions that the Western Allies might negotiate separately with the enemy. The announcement owed a good bit also to the determination that, as Roosevelt put it, "every person in Germany should realize that this time Germany is a defeated nation." This dictum was later criticized for having stiffened enemy resistance, but it probably had little effect; in fact neither the Italian nor the Japanese surrender would be totally unconditional. But the decision did have one unexpected result: it opened an avenue for eventual Soviet control of eastern Europe because it required Russian armies to pursue Hitler's forces all the way to Germany. And as they liberated the countries of eastern Europe, the Soviets created new governments in their own image.

THE BATTLE OF THE ATLANTIC While fighting raged in North Africa, the more crucial Battle of the Atlantic reached its climax on the

American soldiers catching a last smoke before combat.

high seas. Several factors brought success to the Allied effort. Patrols by land-based planes covered much of the Atlantic from airfields in Britain and the Western Hemisphere, and in 1943 Portugal permitted American planes to operate from the Azores, thereby closing the last gap in coverage in the North Atlantic. Scientists perfected a variety of new detection devices: radar, which the British had already used to advantage in the Battle of Britain, bounced radio waves off objects above the surface and registered their positions on a screen; sonar gear detected sound waves from submerged U-boats, and sonobuoys, dropped from planes, radioed back their findings; advanced magnetic equipment enabled aircraft to detect objects under water. New escort carriers ("baby flat-tops") and improvements in depth charges added to the effectiveness of convoys.

By early 1943 there were in the western half of the North Atlantic at any one time an average of 31 convoys with 145 escorts and 673 merchant ships, and a number of heavily escorted troopships. None of the troopships going to Britain or the Mediterranean was lost, although submarines sank three en route to Greenland and Iceland. The U-boats kept up the Battle of the Atlantic until the war's end; when Germany finally collapsed, at least forty-nine were still at sea. But their commander later admitted that the Battle of the Atlantic was lost by the end of May 1943. He credited the difference largely to radar. What he did not know then was that the Allies had a secret weapon. By early 1943 their cryptanalysts were routinely decoding secret messages and telling their sub-hunters where to look for German U-boats.

SICILY AND ITALY   The North African campaign won, the Allies prepared to attack Sicily. On July 10, 1943, about 250,000 British and American troops landed on Sicily, the largest single amphibious action in the war to that time, scoring a complete surprise. The entire island was in Allied hands by August 17, although some 40,000 Germans escaped to the mainland. Allied success in Sicily ended Mussolini's twenty years of fascist rule. Italians never had had much heart for the war into which he had dragged them. On July 25, 1943, Italy's King Victor Emmanuel III notified the dictator of his dismissal as premier. A new regime startled the Allies when it offered not only to surrender but

Major-General George S. Patton, **commander of American invasion forces on Sicily.**

NORWAY

NORTH
SEA

SWE

NORTHERN
IRELAND

GREAT
BRITAIN

DENMARK

REPUBLIC
OF
IRELAND

★ *Sinking of
the Bismarck*

Hamburg
Elbe
River
Berlin
Potsdam
Torgau

19

London
Dover *Dunkirk*
NETHERLANDS
Ruhr
Cologne

English
Channel

1944

ATLANTIC
OCEAN

Calais
St.Lô
Normandy
Compiègne

Antwerp
Brussels
BELG.
Aachen
1945
ARDENNES
LUX.
Paris
Reims
Metz
Strasbourg
Maginot Line

GERMANY
*Battle of
the Bulge*
Frankfurt
Rhine River
Stuttgart

Prague
C Z E

Loire River
Seine River

FRANCE

SWITZERLAND

Munich

Danube Riv

AUST

Vichy

Rhône River

Po River

Trieste

PORTUGAL

SPAIN

Marseilles
Toulon

1944

Nice

ITALY
Florence

Mor
Cass

Lisbon

CORSICA
(French)

Rome
Anzio

Naples
Salerno

SARDINIA

MEDITER

Palermo

Gilbraltar (British)

1942

Tangier

SPANISH
MOROCCO
Casablanca

Oran

Algiers

Bizerte

1943

R

SICILY
S

A

MOROCCO

ALGERIA

TUNISIA

Tunis

N
E
A

WAR IN EUROPE AND AFRICA, 1942-1945

Axis Powers at outbreak of war

Maximum extent of Axis military power

◄— Allied offensives

◄- - Heaviest Allied aerial bombing

·········· Inside limit of German U-boat operations

LIBY

0   250   500 Mi

0   250   500 Kilometers

FINLAND

Leningrad

ESTONIA

LATVIA

1944

LITHUANIA

zig

EAST
PRUSSIA

Vistula R.

Warsaw

45

POLAND

VAKIA

Budapest

NGARY

ROMANIA

1944

elgrade

OSLAVIA

*Danube
River*

BULGARIA

Sofia

BANIA

GREECE

Athens

Dnieper River

S O V I E T   U N I O N

Moscow

Volga River

1943

1942

⋆ *Stalingrad*

CASPIAN
SEA

Sevastopol • • Yalta

B L A C K   S E A

Bucharest •

• Ankara

T U R K E Y

CRETE   *RHODES*   *CYPRUS
(British)*

SYRIA

IRAQ

S E A

Tobruk

Alexandria

El Alamein,
1942

1943

PALESTINE
(British)

TRANS-
JORDAN

*Suez
Canal*

SAUDI
ARABIA

E G Y P T

RED SEA

to switch sides in the war. Unfortunately, mutual suspicions prolonged talks until September 3, while the Germans poured reinforcements into Italy and seized key points. In the confusion the Italian army disintegrated, although most of the navy escaped to Allied ports. A few army units later joined the Allied effort, and many of the soldiers joined bands of partisans who fought behind the German lines. Mussolini, plucked from imprisonment by a daring German airborne raid, became head of a shadowy puppet government in northern Italy.

Allied landings on the mainland therefore did not turn into a walkover. The main landing at Salerno encountered heavy resistance, but American and British troops nevertheless secured beachheads within a week and soon captured Naples. The Germans had reduced much of the city to rubble, but the bay and port facilities were soon cleared and back in operation.

Rome was the next objective, but fighting stalled in the Appenine Mountains, where the Germans held the Allies through the winter of 1943–1944 in some of the most miserable, mud-soaked, and frostbitten fighting of the war. Finally, on June 4, 1944, the U.S. Fifth Army entered Rome. The capture of Rome provided only a brief moment of glory, however, for the long-awaited cross-Channel landing in France came

"Joe, yestiddy ya saved my life an' I swore I'd pay ya back. Here's my last pair of dry socks." *From Bill Mauldin's "Willie and Joe," a cartoon strip that appeared in the GI newspaper* Yank, *about two infantrymen slogging their way through the Italian campaign.*

two days later. Italy, always a secondary front, faded from the limelight of world attention.

STRATEGIC BOMBING OF EUROPE   Behind the long-postponed landings on the Normandy beaches lay months of preparation. While waiting, the United States Army Air Force (AAF) and the British Royal Air Force (RAF) carried the battle into the German-controlled areas of Europe. Early in 1943 Americans launched their first raid on Germany itself. Thereafter, American strategic bombers were full-fledged partners of the RAF in the effort to pound Germany into submission. The RAF, to cut losses during the hard days after the fall of France, had confined itself mostly to night raids, and continued now to specialize in nocturnal attacks. The Americans believed that they could be more effective with high-level daylight "precision" bombing. Between them the AAF and RAF kept German defenders on watch day and night.

Yet despite the widespread damage it caused, the strategic air offensive failed to cut severely into German production or, some contend, was not able to break civilian morale. German production in fact increased until the last few weeks of the war. Heavy Allied losses persisted through 1943. By the end of that year, however, jettisonable gas tanks permitted escort fighters to go as far as Berlin and back. In the "Big Week" of February 20–25, 1944, almost 4,000 American heavy bombers attacked aircraft plants in Germany. Badly damaged, the German aircraft industry continued to turn out planes to the end, but heavy losses of both planes and pilots forced the German Luftwaffe to conserve its strength and cease challenging every Allied mission.

Berlin, the air strategists assumed, was one target the German fighters would have to protect. But in March the capital became the object of repeated Allied raids, and the resultant losses left German fighters even more reluctant to rise to the bait. The horror at enemy attacks on civilians earlier in the war proved no barrier to a response in kind. Germany, Churchill said, was reaping the whirlwind it had started. With air supremacy assured, the Allies were free to concentrate on their primary urban and industrial targets, and when the time came, to provide cover for the Normandy landings. On April 14, 1944, General Eisenhower assumed control of the Strategic Air Forces for use in the Normandy landings, less than two months away. On D-Day he told the troops: "If you see fighting aircraft over you, they will be ours."

THE TEHERAN MEETING   By the summer of 1943, the growing American presence in Britain, combined with successes in the Battle of the Atlantic and the strategic bombing, brought Churchill around on the idea of a cross-Channel invasion. Late in the fall he and Roosevelt finally had their first joint meeting with Joseph Stalin, in Teheran, Iran. Prior to the conference, when England and America gave assurance that a cross-Channel invasion was coming, the Soviets promised to enter the war against Japan after Germany's defeat.

On the way to the Teheran meeting with Stalin, Churchill and Roosevelt met in Cairo with China's General Chiang Kai-shek from November 22 to 26. The resultant Declaration of Cairo (December 1, 1943) affirmed that war against Japan would continue until Japan's unconditional surrender, that all Chinese territories taken by Japan would be restored to China, that Japan would lose the Pacific islands acquired after 1941, and that "in due course Korea shall become free and independent."

From November 28 to December 1, the Big Three leaders conferred in Teheran. Their chief subject was the planned invasion of France and a Russian offensive timed to coincide with it. Stalin repeated his promise to enter the war against Japan, and the three leaders agreed to create an international organization to maintain peace after the war. At further discussions in Cairo (December 4–6) Roosevelt and Churchill decided to put General Eisenhower in command of the cross-Channel invasion.

D-DAY AND AFTER   In early 1944 General Dwight D. Eisenhower arrived in London to take command at Supreme Headquarters, Allied Expeditionary Forces (SHAEF). Already battle-tested in North Africa and the Mediterranean, he now faced the supreme test of planning and conducting Operation "Overlord," the cross-Channel assault on Hitler's "Atlantic Wall." Over a million American soldiers were already training along England's southern coast for the cross-Channel invasion. Of course, Hitler had been preparing for such an assault as well. German forces using captive Europeans for laborers had created what seemed to be an impregnable series of fortifications along the French coastline. Huge concrete blockhouses protected their artillery, and trenches and camouflage shielded their machine-gun nests. The Germans also used forced laborers to sow the beaches with 4 million mines interlaced with barbed wire and antitank obstacles.

General Dwight D. Eisenhower instructing paratroopers just before they board their airplanes to launch the D-Day assault.

The prospect of an amphibious assault against such defenses in a single huge battle unnerved some of the Allied planners. Churchill worried about "Channel tides running red with Allied blood." As D-Day approached, Eisenhower's chief of staff predicted only a 50-50 chance of success. Eisenhower had his doubts as well. He kept in his wallet a message for the press in case the invasion failed. It read: "My decision to attack at this time and place was based upon the best information available. If any blame or fault attaches to the attempt, it is mine alone."

Yet Operation Overlord succeeded. It did so largely because Eisenhower and the Allies surprised the Germans. They fooled Hitler's generals into believing that the invasion would come at Pas de Calais, on the French-Belgian border, where the English Channel was narrowest. Instead, the landings occurred in Normandy, almost 200 miles south. In April and May 1944, while the vast invasion forces made final preparations, the Allied air forces disrupted the transportation network of northern France, smashing railroads, bridges, and rolling stock. By early June all was ready, and D-Day fell on June 6, 1944.

On the evening of June 5, Eisenhower visited some of the 16,000 American paratroopers preparing to land behind the German lines to create chaos and disrupt communications. The men noticed his look of grave concern and tried to lift his spirits. "Now quit worrying, General," one of them said, "we'll take care of this thing for you." After the planes took off, Eisenhower returned to his car with tears in his eyes. "Well," he said quietly to his driver, "it's on." He knew that many of his troops would die within a few hours. The day before, Eisenhower's German counterpart, General Erwin Rommel, left his headquarters along the French coast to go to Berlin to see his family and meet with Hitler. As he departed, he confidently asserted that "there's not going to *be* an invasion. And if there is, then they won't even get off the beaches." When the American public learned that the invasion had been launched, routine activities gave way to anxious listening over the radio for reports from the front. Stores closed, baseball games and horse races were canceled, and church bells tolled across the country.

Airborne forces dropped behind the beaches during the night while planes and battleships pounded the coastal defenses. At dawn the invasion fleet of some 4,000 ships and 150,000 men (57,000 Americans)

The array of Allied forces at Normandy, June 1944.

filled the horizon off the Normandy coast. Overhead, thousands of Allied planes supported the invasion force. Sleepy German soldiers awoke to see the vast armada arrayed before them. Lieutenant Hans Heinze, a twenty-one-year-old veteran of the Russian front, could not believe his eyes. Wiping off his binoculars, he peered through the lifting fog and shouted to his messenger: *"Sie kommen!"* [They are coming!] He then scribbled a note for his headquarters and handed it to his messenger, thinking "They'll never believe it." Nearby, another German lookout peered through his binoculars and muttered, "That's not possible! That's not possible!" His aide retreated into their bunker to pray. For several hours, the local German commanders refused to believe that this was the real invasion. They interpreted the Normandy landings as merely a diversion for the "real" attack at Pas de Calais. When Hitler learned of the Allied landings, he boasted that "the news couldn't be better. As long as they were in Britain, we couldn't get at them. Now we have them where we can destroy them."

Despite Eisenhower's meticulous planning and the imposing array of Allied troops and firepower, the D-Day invasion almost failed. Cloud cover and German antiaircraft fire caused many of the paratroopers and glider pilots to miss their landing zones. Oceangoing landing craft delivered their troops to the wrong locations. Low clouds also led the Allied planes assigned to soften up the seaside defenses to drop their bombs too far inland. The naval bombardment was equally ineffective. Rough seas caused many of the soldiers to become seasick and capsized dozens of landing craft. Over a thousand men drowned. On Utah Beach the American invaders made it in against relatively light opposition, but farther east, on a four-mile segment designated Omaha Beach, bombardment had failed to take out German defenders, and the Americans were caught in heavily mined water. They then had to make it across a fifty-yard beach exposed to crossfire from concrete pillboxes before they could huddle under a seawall and begin to root out the defenders. In one rifle company 197 out of 205 men were killed or wounded within ten minutes.

A private remembered that he and his buddies at Omaha Beach were pinned down on the beach by relentless German gunfire. Finally, his colonel stood up and yelled, "There are only two kinds of people on this beach. Those who are dead and those who will die. Move in!" Such bold leadership worked. The private recalled that the colonel's words "had a

The landing at Normandy, D-Day, June 6, 1944.

galvanizing effect on me. I started to repeat them to the men around me. We pulled on our gear. We followed a path around the mines that had been inadvertently laid out for us by the wounded. It took five or six hours to reach the crest of the hill. I had seen a lot of terrible things by the time I got to the top." Still farther east, British forces had less difficulty on Gold, Juno, and Sword Beaches, but found themselves subjected to bitter counterattack by German forces. By nightfall there were some 5,000 killed or wounded Allied soldiers strewn across the sand and surf of Normandy.

German losses were even more incredible. Entire units were decimated or captured. Operation Overlord was the greatest military invasion in the annals of warfare, and the climactic battle of World War II. With the beachhead secured, the Allied leaders knew that victory was now in their grasp. "What a plan!" Churchill exclaimed to the British parliament. Stalin, who had been clamoring for the cross-Channel invasion for years, applauded the Normandy operation and heaped praise on the Allies. He declared that the "history of warfare knows no other like undertaking from the point of view of its scale, its vast conception and its orderly execution."

Within two weeks the Allies had landed a million troops, 556,000 tons of supplies, and 170,000 vehicles. They had seized a beachhead sixty miles wide and five to fifteen miles deep. They continued to pour men and supplies onto the beaches and to edge inland through the Norman marshes and hedgerows. On July 19, 1944, General Omar Bradley's troops took St. Lô, a transportation hub for roads and railroads into the heart of France. The German commanders advised withdrawal to defenses behind the Seine River, but a stubborn Hitler issued disastrous orders to contest every inch of land. General Erwin Rommel, convinced that all was lost, began to intrigue for a separate peace. Other like-minded officers, convinced that the war was hopeless, tried to kill Hitler at his headquarters on July 20, 1944, but the Führer survived the bomb blast, and hundreds of conspirators and suspects were tortured to death. Rommel was granted the option of suicide, which he took.

Meanwhile, the Führer's tactics brought calamity to the German forces in western France. On July 25 American units broke out westward into Brittany and eastward toward Paris. On August 15 a joint American-French invasion force landed on the French Mediterranean coast and raced up the Rhône Valley. German resistance in France collapsed. A Free French division, aided by American forces, had the honor of liberating Paris on August 25. Nazi forces retired pell-mell toward the German border, and by mid-September most of France and Belgium were cleared of enemy troops. By this time, the Americans were in Aachen, the old seat of Charlemagne's empire, the first German town to fall.

SLOWING MOMENTUM   Events had moved so much faster than expected, in fact, that the Allies were running out of gas. Neither their plans nor their supply system could keep up with the rapid movement of tanks and men. British and Canadian forces under General Bernard Montgomery had moved forward into Belgium, where they took Antwerp on September 4. From there, Montgomery argued, a quick fatal thrust toward Berlin could end things. On the right flank, General George Patton was just as sure he could take the American Third Army all the way to Berlin. Eisenhower reasoned, however, that a swift, narrow thrust into Germany would be cut off, counterattacked, and defeated. Instead he advocated advancing along a broad front. Prudence demanded getting his supply lines in order first, which required clearing out stubborn German forces and opening a supply channel to Antwerp—a long, hard battle that lasted until the end of November.

LEAPFROGGING TO TOKYO

Even in the Pacific, relegated to lower priority, Allied forces had brought the war within reach of the enemy homeland by the end of 1944. The war's first American offensive in fact had been in the southwest Pacific. There the Japanese, stopped at the Coral Sea and Midway, had thrust into the southern Solomons, and were building an airstrip on Guadalcanal from which they could attack transportation routes to Australia. On August 7, 1942, two months before the North Africa landings, the First Marine Division landed on Guadalcanal and seized the airstrip.

These quick victories, however, triggered a savage Japanese response. Reinforcements poured in via the "Tokyo Express" down the central channel, the Solomons "Slot," and the opposing navies challenged each other in a confusing series of battles that battered both so badly the sailors named the Savo Island Sound "Iron Bottom Bay." But while the Americans had lost heavily, they delivered such punishment to Japanese carrier groups, already battered at Midway, that the Japanese navy remained on the defensive for the rest of the war. The marines, helped by reinforcements, finally cleared Guadalcanal's steaming jungles of Japanese soldiers.

MACARTHUR IN NEW GUINEA   Meanwhile, American and Australian forces under General MacArthur had begun to push the Japanese out of their positions on the northern coast of New Guinea. These battles, fought through some of the hottest, most humid and mosquito-infested swamps in the world, bought advances at a heavy cost, but by the end of January 1943 the eastern tip of New Guinea was secured.

At this stage, American strategists made a critical decision. MacArthur proposed to move westward along the northern coast of New Guinea toward the Philippines and ultimately to Tokyo. Admiral Nimitz, with headquarters at Pearl Harbor, argued for a sweep through the islands of the central Pacific ultimately toward Formosa and China.

American medics assist a comrade on an island in the Admiralty group, March 1944.

In March 1943 the Combined Chiefs of Staff, meeting in Washington, agreed to MacArthur's plan and allotted resources for the purpose. Soon afterward they agreed that Nimitz should undertake his sweep too, for the central Pacific island complex would expose MacArthur's northern flank to a constant threat if it were left in Japanese hands. Another consideration in this decision was pitifully political: to keep both men satisfied, as well as the services they represented.

A new tactic expedited the movement. During the air Battle of the Bismarck Sea (March 2–3, 1943), American bombers sank eight Japanese troopships and ten warships bringing reinforcements. Thereafter the Japanese dared not risk sending transports to points under siege, making it possible to use the tactic of neutralizing Japanese strongholds with air and sea power, and moving on, leaving them to die on the vine. Some called it "leapfrogging," and Japanese leaders later acknowledged the strategy as a major cause of Allied victory. Meanwhile, in mid-April, before the offensive got under way, American fighter planes shot down a plane that code-breakers knew was carrying Admiral Yamamoto, Japan's naval commander and the planner of the Pearl Harbor attack. His death shattered Japanese morale.

SOVIET UNION

SEA
OF
OKHOTSK

Russians, 1944–1945

MONGOLIA

MANCHURIA

SAKHALIN

Peking

SEA OF
JAPAN

KOREA

JAPAN

C H I N A

YELLOW
SEA

Hiroshima

Tokyo

Nanking

Nagasaki

Shanghai

EAST
CHINA
SEA

BONIN
ISLANDS

HIMALAYAS

Chungking

Stilwell
Road

Ledo

1943

Burma
Road

OKINAWA

Iwo Jima

1945

INDIA

Kunming

FORMOSA

MARI
ISLA

Lashio
BURMA

HONG
KONG

PHILIPPINE

1945

Rangoon

THAILAND

Luzon

SEA

Corregidor
1942

Manila

Sa

FRENCH
INDOCHINA

BATAAN PENINSULA

SOUTH
CHINA
SEA

PHILIPPINES

Gu

Leyte

Mindanao

PALAU

CAROLI

BRITISH
NORTH
BORNEO

BRITISH
MALAYA

BRUNEI

1944–1945

ADMIR
ISLAN

SARAWAK

Singapore

BORNEO

1943

BISM
S

Equator

SUMATRA

CELEBES

MOLUCCAS

DUTCH EAST INDIES

Java Sea

NEW GUINEA

JAVA

TIMOR

Por
Mo

INDIAN

OCEAN

AUSTRALIA

| 0 | 400 | 800 | 1,200 Miles |
| 0 | 400 | 800 | 1,200 Kilometers |

BERING
SEA

ALASKA
(U.S.)

ALEUTIAN ISLANDS
KISKA

ATTU
1943

**THE WAR IN THE PACIFIC,
1942–1945**

Areas controlled by Japan, 1942
Major Allied offensives
Major Allied air offensives
Japanese advances
Limit of Japanese control
★ Major battle

PACIFIC

OCEAN

★ MIDWAY

HAWAIIAN

ISLANDS

WAKE
ISLAND

OAHU
Pearl Harbor ★

1944   Eniwetok

★ Truk
Kwajalein ★

MARSHALL
ISLANDS

LANDS

Makin ★
Tarawa ★

GILBERT
ISLANDS

1943

Equator

aul   BOUGAINVILLE
N   ● Arawa
TAIN

SOLOMON
ISLANDS   ★

1942

Guadalcanal

NEW
HEBRIDES

★

FIJI
ISLANDS

CORAL

SEA

NEW
CALEDONIA

The first strong point left stranded by the leapfrog strategy was Rabaul, New Britain. An amphibious force landed on an undefended coast in the northern Solomons and carved out a beachhead from which fighters and bombers brought Rabaul under daily attack. A Japanese fleet that moved to challenge the operation was decisively beaten in the Battle of Empress Augusta Bay on November 2, 1943.

In New Guinea, MacArthur's forces moved into command of the coast opposite Cape Gloucester, New Britain. Occupation of Arawe and Cape Gloucester in December secured the passageway to the north coast of New Guinea and the western Pacific. When the Admiralty Islands were taken in March 1944, the isolation of Rabaul was complete and nearly 100,000 Japanese were stranded.

NIMITZ IN THE CENTRAL PACIFIC   Admiral Nimitz's parallel advance through the central Pacific had as its first target two tiny atolls in the Gilberts: Makin and Tarawa. After advance bombing raids, a fleet of 200 ships delivered infantry and marines ashore at dawn on November 20, 1943. Makin, where the Japanese had only a small force, was soon cleared; after three days an American general radioed the terse message, "Makin taken." Tarawa, with its concrete bunkers behind a long coral reef and beach obstructions of wire and logs, was one of the most heavily protected islands in the Pacific. There nearly 1,000 American soldiers, sailors, and marines lost their lives rooting out a determined resistance by 4,000 Japanese who refused to surrender. The Gilberts provided costly lessons in amphibious operations, one of which was to confirm the value of bypassing strong points.

Invasion of the Marshall Islands, the next step "up the ladder" to Tokyo, began on January 31, 1944, at Kwajalein and Eniwetok, both of which were soon taken. During these operations, a carrier raid wrought heavy destruction on enemy ships and aircraft at Truk, the Japanese "Pearl Harbor" in the Carolines. Then the Americans bypassed Truk. They took Saipan in the Marianas on June 15, which brought the new American B-29 bombers within striking distance of Japan itself. The Japanese navy therefore had to resist with all it had, which was not enough, despite its crash program to build new carriers.

In the Battle of the Philippine Sea, fought mostly in the air on June 19 and 20, 1944, the Japanese lost three more carriers, two submarines, and over 300 planes, at the cost of only 17 American planes. The battle secured the Marianas, and soon B-29s were winging their way to the first systematic bombings of the Japanese homeland. Defeat in the Marianas finally brought home to General Tojo the realization that the war was lost. On July 18, 1944, he and his entire cabinet resigned, and General Kuniaki Koiso became the new premier.

THE BATTLE OF LEYTE GULF   With New Guinea and the Marianas all but conquered, President Roosevelt met with General MacArthur and Admiral Nimitz in Honolulu on July 27–28, 1944, to decide the next major step. Previous plans had marked China as the essential springboard for invading Japan, but a Japanese offensive in April 1944 had taken most of the south China airfields from which American air power had operated. This strengthened MacArthur's standing opinion that the Philippines would provide a safer staging area than Formosa. Sentimental and political considerations, as well as military, tipped the decision his way. MacArthur made his move into the Philippines on October 20, landing first on the island of Leyte. Wading ashore behind the first landings, he issued an announcement: "People of the Philippines: I have returned. . . . Rally to me. . . . Let no heart be faint."

General Douglas MacArthur (center) *staging his triumphant return to the Philippines, October 1944.*

The Japanese, knowing that loss of the Philippines would cut them off from the oil and other essential resources of the East Indies, brought in fleets from three directions. The three encounters that resulted on October 25, 1944, came to be known collectively as the Battle of Leyte Gulf. It proved to be the largest naval engagement in history. The Japanese lost most of their remaining sea power and the ability to defend the Philippines. The battle also brought the first of the suicide attacks by Japanese pilots who crash-dived into American carriers, sinking one and seriously damaging others. The "Kamikaze" units, named for the "Divine Wind" that centuries ago had saved Japan from Mongol invasion, inflicted severe damage on the American navy.

A New Age Is Born

ROOSEVELT'S FOURTH TERM   In 1944, war or no war, the calendar dictated another presidential election. This time the Republicans turned to the former crime-fighter and New York governor, Thomas E. Dewey, as their candidate. Once again no Democratic challenger rose high enough to contest Roosevelt, but a fight did develop over the second spot on the ticket. Vice-President Henry Wallace had earned the enmity of both southern conservative and northern city bosses who feared his ties with labor. Roosevelt finally fastened on the compromise choice of Missouri senator Harry S. Truman.

Dewey ran under the same handicap as Landon and Willkie before him. He did not propose to dismantle Roosevelt's programs, but argued that it was time for younger men to replace the tired old leaders of the New Deal. Roosevelt betrayed decided signs of illness and exhaustion, but nevertheless carried the battle to the enemy. On November 7, 1944, Roosevelt was once again elected, this time by a popular vote margin of 25.6 million to 22 million and an electoral vote of 432 to 99.

CONVERGING FRONTS   After their quick sweep across France, the Allies lost momentum in the fall of 1944 and settled down to slugging at the frontiers of Germany. Along this line the armies fought it out all winter. The Germans sprang a surprise in the rugged Ardennes Forest, where the Allied line was thinnest. Hitting on December 16, 1944, under clouds that prevented air reconnaissance, the Germans advanced

An American infantry regiment marching through the ruins of Bensheim, Germany, March 1945.

along a fifty-mile bulge in Belgium and Luxembourg—hence the Battle of the Bulge. In ten days they penetrated nearly to the Meuse River on their way to Antwerp, but they stalled at Bastogne. Reinforced by the Allies just before it was surrounded, Bastogne held for six days against all the Germans could bring against it. On December 22 American general "Tony" McAuliffe gave his memorable answer to the demand for surrender: "Nuts." When a German major asked what the term meant, an American officer said, "It's the same as 'Go to Hell.' And I will tell you something else—if you continue to attack, we will kill every goddamn German that tries to break into this city." The American situation remained desperate until the next day when the clouds lifted, allowing Allied airpower to hit the Germans and drop in supplies. On December 26, American forces broke through to the relief of Bastogne, but it would be mid-January 1945 before the previous lines were restored.

Germany's sudden thrust upset Eisenhower's timetable, but the outcome shook Nazi power and morale. Their effort had weakened the eastern front, and in January 1945 the Russians began their final offensive. The destruction of Hitler's last reserve units at the Battle of the Bulge had also left open the door to Germany's heartland from the west.

By early March, the Allies had reached the banks of the Rhine nearly all the way from Holland to Switzerland. On March 6 they took Cologne, and the next day, by remarkable luck, the Allies seized the bridge at Remagen before the Germans could blow it up. Troops poured across the Rhine there and soon afterward at other points.

The Allies then encircled the Ruhr Valley, center of Germany's heavy industry. In quick sweeps the army closed the pincers on some 400,000 German soldiers in the region and pounded them into submission. By mid-April resistance there was over. Meanwhile the Soviet offensive had also reached Germany itself, after taking Warsaw on January 17 and Vienna on April 13.

With the British and American armies racing across western Germany and the Soviets moving in from the east, the attention of the war planners turned to Berlin. Churchill had grown suspicious of the Soviets and worried that if they arrived in Berlin first, they would gain dangerous leverage in deciding the postwar map of Europe. He told Eisenhower of his concerns and urged him to get to Berlin first. Eisenhower, however, refused to mix politics with military strategy. Berlin, he said, no longer was of military significance. His purpose remained the destruction of the enemy's ground forces. Churchill disagreed and appealed to Roosevelt, but the American leader, now seriously ill, left the decision to the Supreme Commander. Eisenhower then asked his trusted lieutenant, General Omar Bradley, to estimate what it would take to liberate Berlin before the Soviets. Bradley estimated that it would cost 100,000 Allied casualties, which he described as a "pretty stiff price to pay for a prestige objective." Eisenhower agreed, and they left Berlin for the Soviets to conquer.

YALTA AND THE POSTWAR WORLD   As the final offensives got under way, the Yalta Conference (February 4–11, 1945) brought the Big Three leaders together again in a czar's palace at the Crimean resort. While the focus at Teheran in 1943 had been on wartime strategy, it was now on the shape of the postwar world. Two aims loomed large in Roosevelt's thinking. One was the need to ensure that the Soviet Union join the war against Japan. The other was based on the lessons he drew from the previous world war. Just as the Neutrality Acts of the 1930s were designed with lessons from the previous war in mind, thoughts about the future were now influenced by memories of the interwar years. Chief among the mistakes to be remedied this time were the fail-

The Yalta Conference, *February 1945. Stalin* (right), *FDR* (center), *and Churchill* (left) *confer on the shape of the postwar world.*

ure of the United States to join the League of Nations and the failure of the Allies to maintain a united front against the German aggressors.

The Yalta meeting began by calling for a conference on world organization to be held in the United States, beginning on April 25, 1945. The Yalta conferees decided also that substantive decisions in the Security Council would require the acquiescence of its five permanent members: the United States, Britain, the Soviet Union, France, and China.

GERMANY AND EASTERN EUROPE   With Hitler's "Thousand-Year Reich" stumbling to its doom, arrangements for the postwar governance of Germany had to be made. The war map dictated the basic pattern of occupation zones: the Soviets would control the east and the Western Allies would control the rich industrial areas of the west. Berlin, isolated within the Soviet zone, would be subject to joint occupation. At the behest of Churchill and Roosevelt, liberated France received an occupation zone along its border with Germany and also in Berlin. Similar arrangements were made for Austria, with Vienna like Berlin under joint occupation within the Soviet zone. Soviet demands for reparations of $20 billion, half of which would go to the Soviet Union, were referred to a Reparations Commission in Moscow. The commission never reached agreement, although the Soviets appropriated untold amounts of machinery and equipment from their occupation zone.

With respect to eastern Europe, where Soviet forces were advancing on a broad front, there was little the Western Allies could do to influence events. Roosevelt was inhibited by his wish to win Soviet cooperation in the fight against Japan and in the effort to build the proposed United Nations organization. Poland became the main focus of Western concern. Britain and France had gone to war in 1939 to defend Poland and now, six years later, the course of the war had left Poland's fate in the hands of the Soviets.

Events had long foreshadowed the outcome. Controversy over the Katyn Forest massacre of 1940, in which the Soviets had gunned down over 14,000 captured Polish officers, led the Soviets in 1943 to break relations with the Polish government-in-exile in London. When Soviet forces reentered Poland in 1944, they placed civil administration under a Committee of National Liberation in Lublin, a puppet regime representing few Poles. As Soviet troops reached the gates of Warsaw, the underground resistance in the city rose against the Nazi occupiers. The Polish underground, however, supported the Polish government-in-exile in London. The Soviets then stopped their offensive for two months while the Nazis wiped out thousands of Poles, potential rivals to their Lublin puppet government.

That optimism about postwar cooperation could survive such events was a triumph of hope over experience. The attitude was remotely reminiscent of 1919, when Wilson made concessions to win approval of the League of Nations in the hope that the League could later remedy any injustices that had crept into the peace settlement. But in any case the Western Allies at Yalta could do no more than acquiesce or stall. On the Soviet proposal to expand the Lublin Committee into a provisional government together with representatives of the London Poles, they acquiesced. On the issue of Poland's boundaries, they stalled. The Soviets proposed to keep eastern Poland, offering land taken from Germany as compensation. Roosevelt and Churchill accepted the proposal, but considered the western boundary at the Oder–Western Neisse Rivers only provisional. But the peace conference at which the western boundary of Poland was to be settled never took place because of later disagreements. The presence of the London Poles in the provisional government only lent a tone of legitimacy to a regime dominated by the Communists, who soon ousted their rivals.

At Yalta the Big Three promised to sponsor free elections, democratic governments, and constitutional safeguards of freedom throughout the rest of Europe. The Yalta Declaration of Liberated Europe reaffirmed faith in the principles of the Atlantic Charter and the United Nations, but in the end it made little difference. It may have postponed take-overs in eastern Europe for a few years, but before long Communist members of coalition governments had their hands on the levers of power and ousted the opposition. Aside from Czechoslovakia, though, the countries of eastern Europe lacked strong democratic traditions in any case. And Russia, twice invaded by Germany in the twentieth century, had reason for wanting buffer states between it and the Germans.

YALTA'S LEGACY   The Yalta agreements were later attacked for giving eastern Europe over to Soviet domination. But the course of the war shaped the actions at Yalta. By suppressing opposition in the occupied territories, moreover, the Soviets were not acting under the Yalta accords, but in violation of them.

Perhaps the most bitterly criticized of the Yalta understandings was a secret agreement on the Far East, not made public until after the war. As the Big Three met, fighting still raged in the Philippines and Burma. The Combined Chiefs of Staff still estimated that Japan could hold out for eighteen months after the defeat of Germany. Costly campaigns lay ahead, and the atomic bomb was still an expensive gamble on the unknown. Roosevelt therefore accepted Stalin's demands on postwar arrangements in the Far East, subject technically to later agreement by Chiang Kai-shek. Stalin wanted continued Soviet control of Outer Mongolia through its puppet People's Republic there, acquisition of the Kurile Islands from Japan, and recovery of rights and territory lost after the Russo-Japanese War of 1905. Stalin in return promised to enter the war against Japan two or three months after the German defeat, to recognize Chinese sovereignty over Manchuria, and to conclude a treaty of friendship and alliance with the Chinese Nationalists. Later Roosevelt's concessions would appear in a different light, but given their geographical advantages in Asia as in eastern Europe, the Soviets were in a position to get what they wanted in any case.

THE THIRD REICH COLLAPSES   The collapse of Nazi resistance was imminent, but President Roosevelt did not live to join the celebrations. All through 1944 his health had been declining, and photographs from early 1945 reveal a very sick man. In the spring of 1945 he went to his second home in Warm Springs, Georgia, to rest up for the Charter Conference of the United Nations at San Francisco. On April 12, 1945, he suffered a cerebral hemorrhage, which brought sudden death.

The end of Hitler's Germany came less than a month later. The Allied armies rolled up almost unopposed to the Elbe River, where they met advance detachments of Soviets on April 25. Three days later Italian partisans caught and killed Mussolini and his mistress as they tried to flee. In Berlin, which was under siege by the Soviets, Hitler married his mistress, Eva Braun, in an underground bunker on the last day of April just before killing her and himself in a suicide pact. On May 2 Berlin fell to the Soviets. That same day German forces in Italy surrendered. Hitler's designated successor desperately tried to surrender to the Western Allies, but Eisenhower declined to act except in concert with the Soviets. Finally, on May 7, General Alfred Jodl, Chief of Staff of the German armed forces, signed an unconditional surrender in Allied headquarters at Reims, France. So ended the Thousand-Year Reich, little more than twelve years after its Führer came to power.

Massive celebrations of victory in Europe on V-E Day, May 8, 1945, were tempered by the tragedies that had engulfed the world: mourning

A Russian soldier raises the Soviet flag over the Reichstag after the conquest of Berlin, May 1945.

The celebration in New York's Times Square on V-E Day.

for the lost president and the death and mutilation of untold millions. Most shocking was the discovery of the Holocaust, scarcely believable until the Allied armies came upon the death camps in which the Nazis had sought to apply their "final solution" to the Jewish "problem": the wholesale extermination of some 6 million Jews along with more than 1 million others.

During the war, testimony from underground and neutral relief agencies had piled up growing evidence of the Nazis' systematic genocide against the Jews of Europe. Reports appeared in major American newspapers as early as 1942, but were nearly always buried on inside pages. The falsehoods of World War I propaganda had conditioned too many people to doubt all atrocity stories, and rumors of such horror seemed beyond belief.

American government officials, even some Jewish leaders, dragged their feet for fear that relief for Jewish refugees might stir up latent anti-Semitism at home. Under pressure, Roosevelt set up a War Refugee Board early in 1944, but with few resources at its disposal. It nevertheless managed to rescue about 200,000 European Jews and some 20,000 others. More might have been done by broadcasts warning people in Europe that Nazi "labor camps" were really death traps. The Allies rejected bombing the rail lines into the largest camp, Auschwitz in

U.S. troops encounter surviving inmates at the Nazi concentration camp at Wobbelin, May 1945.

Poland, although American planes hit industries five miles away. And few refugees were accepted into the United States. The record was hardly one to inspire pride.

A GRINDING WAR   The sobering thought that the defeat of Japan remained to be accomplished cast a further pall over the victory celebrations in Europe. American forces continued to penetrate and disrupt the Japanese Empire in the early months of 1945, but at heavy cost. While fighting went on in the Philippines, on February 19, 1945, marine assault forces invaded Iwo Jima, a speck of volcanic rock 750 miles from Tokyo. It was needed to provide fighter escort for bombers over Japan and a landing strip for disabled B-29s. Nearly six weeks were required to secure an island five miles square from defenders hiding in an underground labyrinth. The cost was more than 20,000 American casualties, including nearly 7,000 dead.

The fight for Okinawa, beginning on Easter Sunday, April 1, was even bloodier. The largest island in the Ryukyu chain, Okinawa was large enough to afford a staging area for an invasion of Japan. It was the largest amphibious operation of the Pacific war, involving some 300,000 troops. From a beachhead on the northern coast the invaders fought their way south through rugged terrain. Desperate Japanese counterattacks inflicted heavy losses on land, by air, and by sea. Kamikaze planes attacked by the hundreds. Finally, the battleship *Yamato,* a survivor of Leyte Gulf, left Kyushu with nine other ships—the remnant of a once-great navy—with fuel only for a one-way trip, all that was available. American seaplanes intercepted the pathetic armada, sank the *Yamato* and two other warships, and badly damaged the rest. It was the end of the Japanese navy, but the fight for Okinawa raged until late June, when the bloody attrition destroyed any further Japanese ability to resist. The Japanese lost an estimated 140,000 dead. Casualties also included about 42,000 Okinawans.

When resistance on Okinawa collapsed, the Japanese emperor instructed his new premier to seek peace terms. Washington had picked this up by decoding Japanese messages, which suggested either an effort to avoid unconditional surrender or perhaps just a stall.

THE ATOMIC BOMB   By this time, however, a new force had changed all strategic calculations: during the summer of 1945 President Truman learned of the first successful test explosion of an atomic bomb, the result of several years of intensive work. The strands of scientific development that led to the bomb ironically ran back to Germany. Except for the Nazi bigotry that drove scientists into exile, Germany might well have developed the atomic bomb first. Early in 1939 a scientific journal revealed that the uranium atom had been split in Berlin; experiments in Denmark and the United States soon confirmed the finding. On October 11, 1939, President Roosevelt learned of the matter when an emissary delivered a letter from Albert Einstein and a memorandum explaining the potential of nuclear fission and warning that the Germans might develop a bomb first. Roosevelt quickly set up a committee to coordinate information in the field, and in 1940 some army and navy funds were diverted into research that grew ultimately into the $2 billion top-secret Manhattan Project.

On December 2, 1942, Dr. Enrico Fermi and other scientists achieved the first atomic chain reaction in a squash-court-turned-laboratory at the University of Chicago, removing any remaining doubts of the bomb's feasibility. Gigantic plants sprang up at Oak Ridge, Tennessee, and

Hanford, Washington, to provide materials for atomic bombs, while a group of physicists under Dr. J. Robert Oppenheimer worked out the scientific and technical problems of bomb construction in a laboratory at Los Alamos, New Mexico. On July 16, 1945, the first atomic fireball rose from the desert. Oppenheimer said later that in the observation bunker "A few people laughed, a few people cried, most people were silent." Colleagues crowded forward with their congratulations: "Oppie," said one, "now we're all sons of bitches."

The question of how to use this awful new weapon had already come before a committee of military and political officials and scientists. Some of the scientists, awed at the ghastly prospect, favored a demonstration in a remote area, but the decision went for military use because only two bombs were available, and even those might misfire. More consideration was given to the choice of targets. Four Japanese cities had been reserved from conventional bombing as potential targets. After Secretary of War Stimson eliminated Kyoto, Japan's ancient capital and center of many national and religious treasures, and Kokura, priority went to Hiroshima, a port city of 400,000 people in southern Japan, which was a major assembly point for Japanese naval convoys and a center of war industries, headquarters of the Second General Army, and command center for the homeland's defenses. This met Truman's guidelines. He had written that only military personnel and installations rather than "women and children" should be targeted. Of course, he had no idea that the bomb would destroy virtually an entire city.

On July 25, 1945, President Truman, then at the Big Three Conference in Potsdam, Germany, ordered the bomb dropped if Japan did not surrender before August 3. Although an intense scholarly debate has emerged over the decision to drop the atomic bomb, Truman never considered not using it at the earliest opportunity. He later stressed: "Let there be no mistake about it. I regarded the bomb as a military weapon and never had any doubt that it should be used." He was convinced that using the atomic bomb would in the end save lives by avoiding an American invasion against defenders who would fight like "savages, ruthless, merciless, and fanatic."

The ferocious Japanese defense of Okinawa had convinced American military planners that an amphibious invasion of Japan itself, scheduled to begin on November 1, 1945, could cost as many as 250,000 Allied casualties and even more Japanese losses. Moreover, some 100,000 Allied prisoners of war being held in Japan were to be executed whenever an invasion began. It is important to remember as well that the bombing of cities and the consequent killing of civilians had become accepted military practice during 1945. Once the Japanese navy was destroyed, American ships were able to roam the Japanese coastline, shelling targets on shore. American planes bombed at will and mined the waters of the Inland Sea. Tokyo, Nagoya, and other major cities were devastated by firestorms created by incendiary bombs. The prevalence of wooden structures in earthquake-prone Japan made the incendiary raids even more deadly. The firebomb raids on Tokyo on a single night in March 1945 killed over 100,000 civilians and left over a million people homeless. By July more than sixty of Japan's largest cities had been firebombed, resulting in 500,000 deaths and 13 million civilians left homeless. The use of atomic bombs on Japanese cities was thus seen as a logical next step in an effort to end the war without an invasion of Japan. As it turned out, American scientists greatly underestimated the physical effects of the atomic bomb. They predicted that 20,000 people would be killed.

On July 26 the heads of the American, British, and Russian governments issued the Potsdam Declaration demanding that Japan surrender or face "prompt and utter destruction." The deadline passed, and on August 6, 1945, a B-29 named the *Enola Gay,* with a crew commanded by Colonel Paul W. Tibbetts, took off at 2 A.M. from the island of Tinian and headed for Hiroshima. At 8:15 in the morning, flying at 31,600 feet, the *Enola Gay* released the five-ton uranium bomb nicknamed "Little Boy." Forty-three seconds later, as the *Enola Gay* turned sharply to avoid the blast, the bomb tumbled to an altitude of 1,900 feet, where it exploded as planned with the force of 15,000 tons of TNT. A blinding flash of light was followed by a fireball towering to 40,000 feet. The tail gunner on the *Enola Gay* described the scene: "It's like bubbling molasses down there . . . the mushroom is spreading out . . . fires are springing up everywhere . . . it's like a peep into hell."

The shock wave, firestorm, cyclonic winds, and radioactive rain killed some 80,000 people, including thousands of Japanese soldiers assigned to the Second General Army headquarters and 23 American prisoners of war housed in the city. Dazed survivors wandered the streets, so painfully burned that their skin began to peel in large strips. By the end of the year, the death toll had reached 140,000 as the effects

A charred watch marks the moment of nuclear conflagration in Hiroshima, August 6, 1945.

of radiation burns and infection took their toll. In addition, 70,000 buildings were destroyed, and four square miles of the city turned to rubble.

In the United States, Americans greeted the first news with elation: it promised a quick end to the long nightmare of war. "No tears of sympathy will be shed in America for the Japanese people," the *Omaha World Herald* predicted. "Had they possessed a comparable weapon at Pearl Harbor, would they have hesitated to use it?" Others were more circumspect. "Yesterday," journalist Hanson Baldwin wrote in the *New York Times*, "we clinched victory in the Pacific, but we sowed the whirlwind." Only later would people realize that it marked the start of a more enduring nightmare, the atomic age.

Two days after the Hiroshima bombing, an opportunistic Russia, eager to share in the spoils of victory, hastened to enter the war. On August 9, the second atomic bomb exploded over the port city of Nagasaki, a shipbuilding and torpedo-factory center, killing 36,000 people. That night the emperor urged his cabinet to accept the inevitable and surrender on the sole condition that he remain as sovereign. The next day the United States government, to facilitate surrender and an orderly transition, announced its willingness to let him keep the throne, but under the authority of an Allied Supreme Commander. Frantic exchanges ended with Japanese acceptance on August 14, 1945, when the emperor himself broke precedent to record a radio message announcing the surrender to his people. Even then a last-ditch palace revolt had to be squashed.

On September 2, 1945, General MacArthur and other Allied representatives accepted Japan's formal surrender on board the battleship *Missouri*. MacArthur then settled in at his headquarters across from the Imperial Palace.

THE FINAL LEDGER

Thus ended the most deadly conflict in human history. No effort to tabulate a ledger of death and destruction can ever take the full measure of the war's suffering, or hope to be more than an informed guess as to the numbers involved. One estimate has it that 70 million in all fought in the war, at a cost in human lives of 25 million military dead and more than 24 million civilian dead. Material costs were also enormous, perhaps $1 trillion in military expenditures and twice that in property losses. The Soviet Union suffered the greatest losses of all, over 13 million military deaths, over 7 million civilians dead, and at least 25 million left homeless. World War II was more costly for the United States than any other of the country's foreign wars: 292,000 battle deaths and 114,000 other deaths. But in proportion to population, the United States suffered a far smaller loss than any of the major Allies or enemies, and American territory escaped the devastation visited on so many other parts of the world.

World War II had profound effects on American life and society. Mobilization for war stimulated a phenomenal increase in American productivity and brought full employment, thus ending the Great Depression and laying the foundation for a new era of unprecedented prosperity. New technologies and products developed for military purposes—radar, computers, electronics, plastics and synthetics, jet engines, rockets, atomic energy—soon began to transform the private sector as well. And new opportunities for women as well as for blacks and other minorities set in motion changes that would culminate in the civil rights movement of the 1960s and the feminist movement of the 1970s.

The Democratic party benefited from the war effort by solidifying its control of both the White House and Congress. The dramatic expansion of the federal government occasioned by the war continued after 1945. Presidential authority and prestige increased enormously at the expense of congressional and state power. The isolationist sentiment in foreign relations that had been so powerful in the 1920s and 1930s fell into disrepute as the United States emerged from the war with global responsibilities and interests.

The war's end opened a new era for the United States in the world arena. It accelerated the growth of American power while devastating all other world powers, leaving the United States economically and militarily the strongest nation on earth. But the Soviet Union, despite its human and material losses, emerged from the war with much new territory and enhanced influence, making it the greatest power on the whole Eurasian landmass. Just a little over a century after Frenchman Alexis de Tocqueville had predicted that western Europe would come to be overshadowed by the power of the United States and Russia, his prophecy had come to pass.

MAKING CONNECTIONS

- Compare the impact of World War II on the home front to that of World War I, especially the effects of war on race and gender relations.

- The growing domestic conservatism of the war years continued into the 1950s, a topic discussed in the next chapter.

- Dwight D. Eisenhower's success as American general and Allied leader led to his nomination and election as president in 1952. Compare Eisenhower's experience to that of General Grant in and after the Civil War, and to the political experiences of other American military leaders.

Further Reading

John Keegan's *The Second World War* (1990) surveys the European conflict in its entirety, while Charles B. MacDonald's *The Mighty Endeavor: The American War in Europe* (rev. ed., 1992) concentrates on American involvement. Roosevelt's wartime leadership is analyzed in Eric Larrabee's *Commander in Chief: Franklin Delano Roosevelt, His Lieutenants and Their War* (1987).

Books on specific campaigns in Europe include Stephen E. Ambrose's *D Day, June 6, 1944: The Climactic Battle of World War II* (1994) and Charles B. MacDonald's *A Time for Trumpets: The Untold Story of the Battle of the Bulge* (rev. ed., 1997).

For the war in the Far East, see John Costello's *The Pacific War, 1941–1945* (1983), Ronald H. Spector's *Eagle against the Sun: The American War with Japan* (1984), John Dower's award-winning *War Without Mercy: Race and Power in the Pacific War* (1986), and Dan van der Vat's *The Pacific Campaign: The U.S.–Japanese Naval War, 1941–1945* (1992).

An excellent overview of the war's effects on the home front is Michael C. C. Adams's *The Best War Ever: America and World War II* (1993). The government's effort to use movies to influence public opinion is described in Clayton R. Koppes and Gregory D. Black's *Hollywood Goes to War: How Politics, Profits and Propaganda Shaped World War II Movies* (1987).

Susan M. Hartmann's *The Home Front and Beyond: American Women in the 1940s* (1982) and Karen Anderson's *Wartime Women: Sex Roles, Family Relations, and the Status of Women during World War II* (1981) treat the new working environment for women. Neil Wynn looks at the participation of blacks in *The Afro-American and the Second World War* (rev. ed., 1993). The story of the oppression of Japanese Americans is told in Peter Irons's *Justice at War* (1983) and David J. O'Brien and Stephen S. Fugita's *The Japanese American Experience* (1993).

A sound introduction to American diplomacy during the conflict can be found in Gaddis Smith's *American Diplomacy during the Second World War, 1941–1945* (2nd ed., 1985). To understand the role that Roosevelt played in policy-making, consult Warren F. Kimball's *The Juggler: Franklin Roosevelt as Wartime Statesman* (1991). Diane Shaver Clemens is critical of Roosevelt in *Yalta* (1970).

The issues and events that led to the deployment of atomic weapons are addressed in Gregg Herken's *The Winning Weapon: The Atomic Bomb in the Cold War, 1945–1950* (1980) and Martin J. Sherwin's *A World Destroyed: The Atomic Bomb and the Grand Alliance* (1975). Gar Alperovitz's *Atomic Diplomacy: Hiroshima and Potsdam* (2nd ed., 1995) details how the bomb helped shape American postwar policy.

PART SEVEN

THE AMERICAN AGE

Amid the joyous celebrations of the Allied victory in the Second World War, one commentator announced that the "American era was at hand." Such a declaration was filled with chauvinism, yet it contained a kernel of truth. The United States emerged from World War II the preeminent military and economic power in the world. At the end of the war, the United States enjoyed a commanding position in international trade and was the only nation in possession of the atomic bomb. While much of Europe and Asia struggled to recover from the horrific physical devastation of the war, the United States emerged virtually unscathed, its economic infrastructure intact and operating at peak efficiency. Jobs that were scarce in the 1930s were now available for the taking. By 1955 the United States, with only 6 percent of the world's population, was producing half of the world's goods. American capitalism not only demonstrated its economic strength, it became a dominant cultural force as well. In Europe, Japan, and elsewhere, American products and forms of entertainment and fashion attracted excited attention.

Yet the specter of the "cold war" cast a pall over the buoyant revival of the American economy after World War II. The ideological contest with the Soviet Union and Communist China produced numerous foreign crises and sparked a domestic witch-hunt for Communists that far surpassed earlier episodes of political and social repression in the nation's history.

There was widespread acceptance in both major political parties of the geopolitical assumptions embedded in the ideological cold war with international communism. Both Republican and Democratic presidents affirmed the need to "contain" the spread of Communist influence around the world. This bedrock assumption eventually embroiled the United States in a tragic war in Southeast Asia that destroyed Lyndon Johnson's presidency and revived neo-isolationist sentiments. The Vietnam War also was the catalyst for a countercultural movement in which young idealists of the "baby-boom" generation sought alternatives to a government and a society that in their eyes had become oppressive and corrupt. The youth revolt provided energy for many overdue social reforms, including the civil rights and environmental movements, but it also contributed to an array of social ills, from street riots to drug abuse to sexual license. The social upheavals of the 1960s and early 1970s provoked a conservative backlash that overreached itself as well. In their efforts to restore "law and order," mayors failed to protect civil liberties in their cities. Richard Nixon's paranoid reaction to his critics led to the destruction of his presidency as a result of the Watergate investigations.

Through all of this turmoil, however, the basic premises of welfare state capitalism that Franklin Roosevelt had instituted with his New Deal programs remained essentially intact. With only a few exceptions, both Republicans and Democrats after 1945 came to accept the notion that the federal government must assume greater responsibility for the welfare of individuals than had heretofore been the case. Even Ronald Reagan, a sharp critic of liberal social-welfare programs, recognized the need for the federal government to provide a "safety net" for those who could not help themselves.

Yet this fragile consensus about public policy began to disintegrate in the late 1980s amid stunning international developments and less visible domestic developments. The internal collapse of the Soviet Union and the disintegration of European communism surprised observers and sent policy makers scurrying to respond to a post–cold war world in which the United States remained the only legitimate superpower. After forty-five years, American foreign policy was no longer keyed to a single adversary, and world politics lost its bipolar quality. During the early 1990s, the European Community finally coalesced, the two Germanies reunited, apartheid in South Africa finally ended, and Israel and the Palestinians signed a heretofore unimaginable peace treaty.

At the same time, American foreign policy began to focus less on military power and more on economic competition and technological development. In those arenas, Japan and a reunited Germany challenged the United States for preeminence. By reducing the public's fear of nuclear annihilation, the ending of the cold war also reduced public interest in foreign affairs. The presidential election of 1992 was the first since 1936 in which foreign policy issues played virtually no role. This was an unfortunate development, for post–cold war world affairs remained volatile and dangerous. The implosion of Soviet communism unleashed a series of ethnic, nationalist, and separatist conflicts. In the face of inertia among other governments and pleas for assistance, the United States found itself being drawn into crises in faraway lands such as Bosnia, Rwanda, Somalia, and Chechnya.

As the new multipolar world careened toward the end of a century and the start of a new millennium, fault lines began to appear in the American social and economic landscape. A gargantuan federal debt and rising *annual deficits threatened to bankrupt a nation that was becoming top-heavy with retirees. Without fully realizing it, much less appreciating its cascading consequences, the American population was becoming disproportionately old. Those aged ninety-five to ninety-nine doubled between 1980 and 1990, and the number of centenarians increased 77 percent. The proportion of the population aged sixty-five and older rose steadily during the 1990s. By the year 2000, half of the elderly population would be over the age of seventy-five. This demographic fact harbored profound social and political implications. It exerted increasing stress on health care costs, nursing home facilities, and the very survival of the Social Security system.*

At the same time that the gap between young and old was increasing, so, too, was the disparity between rich and poor. This trend threatened to stratify a society already experiencing rising levels of racial and ethnic tension. Between 1960 and 1990, the gap between the richest 20 percent of the population and the poorest 20 percent doubled. Over 20 percent of all American children in 1990 lived in poverty, and the infant mortality rate rose. The infant death rate in Japan was less than half that in the United States. Despite the much-ballyhooed "war on poverty" programs initiated by Lyndon Johnson and continued in one form or another by all of his successors, the chronically poor in 1996 were more numerous and more bereft of hope than in 1964. Yet by the end of the century, a prolonged period of economic growth and a runaway stock market revived the myth of perennial prosperity.

31 ~ THE FAIR DEAL
AND CONTAINMENT

CHAPTER ORGANIZER

This chapter focuses on:

- the economic, social, and political aftermath of World War II and the origins and early development of the cold war.

- Truman's Fair Deal program.

- U.S. involvement in the Korean War.

- the sources of McCarthyism.

*N*o sooner did the Second World War end than a cold war began. The uneasy wartime alliance between the United States and the Soviet Union collapsed completely by the fall of 1945. The two strongest nations to emerge from the carnage of World War II could not bridge their ideological differences over such basic issues as essential human rights, individual liberties, and religious beliefs. Mutual suspicion and a race to gain influence and control over the so-called Third World countries further polarized the two nations. The defeat of Japan and Germany created power vacuums that sucked the Soviet Union and America into an unrelenting war of words fed by clashing strategic interests. At the same time, the destruction of western Europe and the exhaustion of its peoples led to anticolonial uprisings in Asia and Africa that threatened to strip Britain and France of their once-great empires. The postwar world was thus an unstable one in which international tensions shaped the contours of domestic politics and culture as well as foreign adventures.

DEMOBILIZATION UNDER TRUMAN

TRUMAN'S UNEASY START "Who the hell is Harry Truman?" Roosevelt's chief of staff asked the president in the summer of 1944. The question was on more lips when, after less than twelve weeks as vice-president, Harry Truman took the presidential oath on April 12, 1945. Clearly he was not Franklin Roosevelt, and that was one of the burdens he would bear. "With Roosevelt you'd have known he was President even if you hadn't been told," a journalist wrote years later. "He looked imperial, and he acted that way, and he talked that way. Harry Truman, for God's sake, looked and acted and talked like—well, like a failed haberdasher"—which he was.

Roosevelt and Truman came from quite different backgrounds. For Truman there had been no inherited wealth, no early contact with the great and near-great, no European travel, no Groton, no Harvard—indeed, no college at all. Born in 1884 in western Missouri, Truman grew up in Independence, once the staging area for the Oregon and Santa Fe Trails, but by the time of his youth an unglamorous town near Kansas City. Too nearsighted to join in the activities of other boys, Truman became bookish and withdrawn. But after high school he moved to his grandmother's farm, spent a few years working in Kansas City banks, and grew into an outgoing young man.

During World War I, Truman served in France as captain of an artillery battery. Afterward he and a partner went into the clothing business, but it failed in the recession of 1922, and Truman then became a professional politician under the tutelage of Kansas City's Democratic machine. Elected county judge in 1922, he was defeated in 1924 and elected once again in 1926. In 1934 Missouri sent him to the United States Senate, where he remained fairly obscure until he became chairman of the committee to investigate war mobilization.

Something about Harry Truman evoked the spirit of Andrew Jackson: his decisiveness, his feisty character, his family loyalty. But that was a side of the man that the American people came to know only as he settled into the presidency. On his first full day as president, he remained awestruck. "Boys, if you ever pray, pray for me now," he told a group of reporters. "I don't know whether you fellows ever had a load of hay fall on you, but when they told me yesterday what had happened, I felt like the moon, the stars and all the planets had fallen on me."

Truman favored much of the New Deal and was even prepared to extend its scope, but at the same time was uneasy with many New Dealers. "He was not of their clan and kidney," one newsman put it. Within ninety days he had replaced much of the Roosevelt cabinet with his own choices. On the whole they were more conservative in outlook and included several mediocrities. Truman suffered the further handicap of seeming to be a caretaker for the remainder of Roosevelt's term. Few, including Truman himself at first, expected him to run in 1948.

Truman gave one significant clue to his domestic policies on September 6, 1945, when he sent Congress a comprehensive peacetime program that in effect proposed to continue and enlarge the New Deal. Its twenty-one points included expansion of unemployment insurance, a higher minimum wage, a permanent Fair Employment Practices Commission, slum clearance and low-rent housing programs, regional development of the nation's river valleys, and a public-works program. "Not even President Roosevelt asked for so much at one sitting," said the House Republican leader. "It's just a plain case of out-dealing the New Deal." Beset by other problems, Truman soon saw his new domestic proposals mired in disputes over the transition to a peacetime economy.

CONVERTING TO PEACE The raucous celebrations that greeted Japan's surrender signaled the habitual American response to victory: a rapid demobilization and a return to more congenial pursuits. The public demanded that the president and Congress bring the boys home. By 1947 the total armed forces were down from 12 million to 1.5 million. In his memoirs Truman termed this "the most remarkable demobilization in the history of the world, or 'disintegration' if you want to call it that." It was in fact the same pattern that had prevailed since the days of the colonial wars, and it went on for several years, despite mounting

The Eldridge General Store, Fayette County, Illinois. *Postwar America quickly demobilized, turning its attention from rationing to the pursuit of abundance.*

international tensions. By early 1950 the army had fallen to 600,000 men.

The veterans eagerly returned to schools, new jobs, wives, and babies. Population growth, which had dropped off sharply in the depression decade, now soared: the population increase of 9 million during the 1930s exploded to a growth of 19 million in the 1940s. Americans born during this postwar period composed what came to be known as the "baby-boom" generation, and that generation became a dominant force in the nation's social and cultural life.

The end of the war, with its sudden demobilization and reconversion to a peacetime economy, brought sharp dislocations but not the postwar depression that many feared. Several shock absorbers cushioned the economic impact of demobilization: unemployment pay and other Social Security benefits; the Servicemen's Readjustment Act of 1944, known as the "GI Bill of Rights," under which $13 billion was spent for veterans on education, vocational training, medical treatment, unemployment insurance, and loans for building houses or going into business; and, most important, the pent-up demand for consumer goods that was fueled by wartime deprivation. Instead of sinking into depression, businesses seized upon options to buy up properties from the Defense Plant Corporation and began a spurt of private investment in new plants and equipment. The gross national product first exceeded the 1929 level in 1940, when it reached $101 billion, but by annual increases (except in 1946) it had grown to $347 billion by 1952, Truman's last full year in office.

CONTROLLING INFLATION   The most acute economic problem Truman faced was not depression but inflation. Released from wartime restraints, the demands of business owners and workers alike combined to frustrate efforts at controlling rising prices. Truman endorsed wage increases to sustain purchasing power. He felt that there was "room in the existing price structure" for business to grant such pay increases, a point management refused to concede. Within six weeks of war's end, corporations confronted a wave of union demands.

A series of strikes followed. The United Automobile Workers walked out on General Motors, with Walter Reuther, head of the union's General Motors division, arguing that the company could afford a 30 percent pay hike without raising car prices. (The company denied this claim.) A strike in the steel industry finally gave rise to a formula for settling most of the disputes. President Truman suggested a pay raise of 18½¢ per hour, which the Steel Workers accepted but management refused. To break the logjam, the administration in 1946 agreed to let the company increase its prices. That pattern then became the basis for settlements in other industries, and also set a dangerous precedent of price-wage spirals that would plague consumers in the postwar world.

Major disputes soon developed in the coal and railroad industries. John L. Lewis of the United Mine Workers wanted more than the 18½¢-per-hour wage increase. He also demanded improved safety regulations and a union health and welfare fund financed by a royalty on coal. Mine owners refused the demands, and a strike followed. The government used its wartime powers to seize the mines; Truman's interior secretary then accepted nearly all the union's demands.

In the rail dispute, the unions and management reached an agreement, but two brotherhoods, the trainmen and locomotive engineers, held out for rule changes as well as higher wages. Truman seized the railroads and won a five-day postponement of a strike. But when the union leaders refused to budge further, the president went before Congress in a burst of fury against their "obstinate arrogance" and demanded authority to draft strikers into the armed forces. In the midst of the speech, he learned that the strike had been settled, but after telling a jubilant Congress, he went on with his message. The House passed a bill including the president's demands, but with the strike settled, it died in the Senate.

Into 1946 the wartime Office of Price Administration (OPA) managed to maintain some restraint on price increases while gradually ending the rationing of most goods, and Truman asked for a one-year renewal of its powers. But during the late winter and spring of 1946, business leaders mounted a massive campaign against price controls and other restraints. Just a week before controls were to expire at the end of June, Congress passed a bill to continue the OPA, but with such cumbersome new procedures as to cripple the agency. Truman vetoed the bill, allowing controls to end. Congress finally extended controls in late July, but by then the cost of living had already gone up by 6 percent. When the OPA restored controls on meat prices, farmers responded by withholding beef from the market until they succeeded in forcing a reversal in October. After the congressional elections of 1946, Truman gave up the battle, ending all price controls except on rents, sugar, and rice.

PARTISAN COOPERATION AND CONFLICT   The legislative history of 1946 was not all deadlock and frustration. Amid the turmoil Congress and the administration worked out two new departures, the Employment Act of 1946 and the Atomic Energy Commission. A program of "full employment" had been a Democratic promise in the campaign of 1944, a pledge reaffirmed by Truman in 1945. The administration backed an employment bill proposing that the government make an annual estimate of the investment and production necessary to ensure full employment, and key its spending to that estimate in order to raise production to full-employment levels. Conservatives objected to what they denounced as carte blanche for deficit spending, and proposed a nonpartisan commission to advise the president on the economy. Compromise resulted in the Employment Act of 1946, which dropped the commitment to full employment and set up a three-member Council of

Economic Advisers to make appraisals of the economy and advise the president in an annual economic report. A new congressional Joint Committee on the Economic Report would propose legislation.

With regard to the new force that atomic scientists had released upon the world, there was little question that the public welfare required the control of atomic energy through a governmental monopoly. Disagreements over military versus civilian control were resolved when Congress, in 1946, created the civilian Atomic Energy Commission. The president alone was given power to order the use of atomic weapons in warfare. Subject to "the paramount objective of assuring the common defense and security," the act declared a policy of peaceful development "so far as practicable . . . toward improving the public welfare, increasing the standard of living, strengthening free competition in private enterprise, and promoting world peace." Technical problems and high costs, however, would delay for two decades the construction of nuclear power plants.

As congressional elections approached in the fall of 1946, public discontent ran high, most of it against the administration. Truman caught the blame for labor problems from both sides. A speaker at the CIO national convention tagged Truman "the No. 1 strikebreaker," while much of the public, angry at striking unions, also blamed the strikes on the White House. In 1946 Truman fired Henry A. Wallace as secretary of commerce in a disagreement over foreign policy, thus offending the Democratic left. At the same time, Republicans charged that Communists had infiltrated the government. Republicans had a field day coining slogans. "To err is Truman" was credited to Martha Taft, wife of Senator Robert Taft. But most effective was the simple question, "Had enough?" attributed to a Boston ad agency: their message was that the Democrats had simply been in control too long. In the elections Republicans won majorities in both houses of Congress for the first time since 1928.

Given the head of steam built up against organized labor, the new Republican Congress sought to curb the power of unions. The result was the Taft-Hartley Act of 1947, which banned the closed shop (in which nonunion workers could not be hired) but permitted a union shop (in which workers newly hired were required to join the union), unless banned by state law. It included provisions against "unfair" union practices such as secondary boycotts, jurisdictional strikes (by one union to exclude another from a given company or field), "featherbedding" (pay for work not done), refusal to bargain in good faith, and contributing to political campaigns. Unions' political action committees were allowed to function, but on a voluntary basis only, and union leaders had to take oaths that they were not members of the Communist party. Employers were permitted to sue unions for breaking contracts, to petition the National Labor Relations Board (NLRB) for votes for or against the use of specific unions as collective-bargaining agents, and to speak freely during union campaigns. The act forbade strikes by federal employees, and imposed a "cooling-off" period of eighty days on any strike that the president found to be dangerous to the national health or safety.

Truman's veto of the Taft-Hartley bill, which unions called the "slave-labor act," restored his credit with labor, and many unionists who had gone over to the Republicans in 1946 returned to the Democrats. But the bill passed over Truman's veto. Its most severe impact probably was on the CIO's "Operation Dixie," a drive to win for unions a more secure foothold in the South. By 1954 fifteen states, mainly in the South, had used the Taft-Hartley Act's authority to enact "right-to-work" laws forbidding the union shop and other union security devices.

Truman clashed with the Republicans on other domestic issues, including tax reduction. Congress passed a tax cut but it was vetoed by

"To the Rescue!" Organized labor is being pulled under by the Taft-Hartley Act as Congress, which passed the bill over Truman's veto, makes sure there is no rescue.

The CIO's Operation Dixie aimed to organize workers such as these in a North Carolina lumberyard.

Truman on the principle that in times of high production and employment the federal debt should be reduced. In 1948, however, Congress finally managed to override his veto of a $5 billion tax cut at a time when government debt still ran high. The controversy over the tax cut highlighted a soft point in Keynesian economics. In times of depression, people supported increasing governmental expenditures, but in prosperous times people resisted the taxes needed to reduce the deficits. Truman paid a political price for this weakness in economic theory.

The conflicts between Truman and Congress, so visible in the 1948 campaign, obscured the high degree of bipartisan cooperation marking matters of governmental reorganization and foreign policy. In 1947 Congress passed the National Security Act. It created a National Military Establishment, headed by a secretary of defense with subcabinet departments of army, navy, and air force, and a new National Security Council (NSC), which included the president, heads of the defense departments, and the secretary of state, among others. The act made permanent the Joint Chiefs of Staff, which had been a wartime innovation, and established the Central Intelligence Agency (CIA), descended from the wartime Office of Strategic Service (OSS), to coordinate intelligence-gathering activities.

THE COLD WAR

BUILDING THE U.N. The hope that the wartime alliance of the United Nations would carry over into the postwar world proved but another great illusion. The pragmatic Roosevelt shared no such hope. To the contrary, he expected that the Great Powers in the postwar world would have spheres of influence, but felt he had to support an organization "which would satisfy widespread demand in the United States for new idealistic or universalist arrangements for assuring the peace."

In the 1941 Atlantic Charter, Roosevelt and Churchill had looked forward to a "permanent system of general security." In the autumn of 1943 both houses of Congress passed a resolution favoring "international machinery with power adequate to establish and to maintain a just and lasting peace." That same autumn the foreign ministers of the "Big Four" (the United States, the Soviet Union, Britain, and China) issued the Moscow Declaration on General Security, which called for an international organization, and in the 1944 elections the platforms of both major parties endorsed the principle.

On April 25, 1945, two weeks after Roosevelt's death and two weeks before the German surrender, delegates from fifty nations at war with the Axis met in San Francisco's Opera House to draw up the Charter of the United Nations (U.N.). Additional members could be admitted by a two-thirds vote of the General Assembly. This body, one of the two major agencies set up by the charter, included delegates from all member nations and was to meet annually in regular session to approve the budget, receive annual reports from U.N. agencies, and choose members of the Security Council and other bodies. The Security Council, the other major charter agency, would remain in permanent session and would have "primary responsibility for the maintenance of international peace and security." Its eleven (after 1965, fifteen) members included six (later ten) members elected for two-year terms and five permanent members: the United States, the Soviet Union, Britain, France, and China. Each permanent member had a veto on any question of substance. The Security Council might investigate any dispute, recommend settlement or reference to an International Court at The Hague, in the Netherlands, and take measures, including a resort to military force.

The Senate ratified the U.N. charter by a vote of 89 to 2 after only six days of discussion. The organization held its first meeting in London in 1946, and the next year moved to temporary quarters at Lake Success, New York, pending completion of its permanent home in New York City.

TRYING WAR CRIMINALS   There was also a consensus that those responsible for the atrocities of World War II should face trial and punishment. Both German and Japanese officials went on trial for crimes against peace, against humanity, and against the established rules of war. At Nuremberg, site of the annual Nazi party rallies, twenty-one major German offenders faced an International Military Tribunal. After a ten-month trial filled with massive documentation of Nazi atrocities, the court acquitted three and sentenced eleven to death, three to life imprisonment, and four to shorter terms. In Tokyo, a similar tribunal put twenty-five Japanese leaders on trial in 1946, and pronounced

Nazi leaders Hermann Goering (standing) *and Rudolf Hess* (seated, arms folded) *at Nuremberg, where they are on trial for war crimes.*

death sentences on seven, life imprisonment on sixteen, and committed two for lesser prison terms. Other international tribunals tried thousands of others, while many accused war criminals were remanded to the courts of the countries in which they had committed their crimes. Well over 2,000 war-crimes trials are estimated to have taken place, not counting those in the Soviet Union and the East-bloc countries.

Critics argued that the trials set an unfortunate precedent of victors' taking revenge on the defeated. They argued as well that the convictions were condemnations *ex post facto,* for crimes against which no law existed at the time they were committed. Supporters responded by pointing to the Pact of Paris outlawing war, to the Geneva Convention for care of the sick and wounded prisoners, to the Hague declarations on the rules of war, and to the fact that crimes against humanity such as murder, rape, and pillage were already crimes under the laws of the countries where they occurred.

DIFFERENCES WITH THE SOVIETS   Since the end of World War II, historians have debated which side was more responsible for the onset of the cold war. The conventional or "orthodox" view declares that the Soviets, led by a paranoid dictator, tried to dominate the globe, and the United States had no choice but to stand firm in defense of democratic capitalist values. By contrast, those scholars known as "revisionists" argue that Truman and American economic imperialists were the culprits. Instead of maintaining Roosevelt's efforts to collaborate with Stalin and ensure the survival of the alliance after the war, these scholars assert, Truman adopted an unnecessarily belligerent stance and activist foreign policy that sought to create American spheres of influence around the world. He and his military advisers exaggerated the Soviet threat, in part to justify an American military buildup. Their provocative policies thus crystallized the tensions between the two countries. Yet such an interpretation fails to recognize that Truman inherited a deteriorating relationship with the Soviets. Events of 1945 made compromise and conciliation more and more difficult, whether for Roosevelt or Truman.

There were signs of trouble in the Grand Alliance as early as the spring of 1945, as the Soviet Union moved to set up compliant governments in eastern Europe, violating the Yalta promises of democratic elections. On February 1 the Polish Committee of National Liberation, a puppet group already claiming the status of provisional government, moved from Lublin to Warsaw. In March the Soviets installed a puppet premier in Romania. Protests against such actions led to Soviet counterprotests that the British and Americans were negotiating German surrender in Italy "behind the back of the Soviet Union" and that German forces were being concentrated against the Soviet Union. A few days before his death, Roosevelt responded to Stalin: "I cannot avoid a feeling of resentment toward your informers . . . for such vile misrepresentations."

Such was the atmosphere when Truman entered the White House. A few days before the San Francisco conference to organize the United Nations, Truman gave Soviet foreign minister Vyacheslav M. Molotov a dressing-down in Washington on the Polish situation. "I have never been talked to like that in my life," Molotov said. "Carry out your agreements," Truman snapped, "and you won't get talked to like that." On May 12, 1945, four days after victory in Europe, Winston Churchill sent a telegram to Truman: "What is to happen about Europe? An iron curtain is drawn down upon [the Russian] front. We do not know what is going on behind [it]. . . . Surely it is vital now to come to an understanding with Russia, or see where we are with her, before we weaken our armies mortally. . . ." Nevertheless, as a gesture of goodwill, and over Churchill's protest, the American forces withdrew from the German occupation zone assigned to the Soviet Union at Yalta. Americans still hoped that the Yalta agreements would be carried out, at least after a fashion, and that the Soviet Union would help against Japan.

Although the Soviets admitted British and American observers to their sectors of eastern Europe, there was little the Western powers could do to prevent Soviet control of the region, even if they had not let their military forces dwindle. The presence of Soviet armed forces frustrated the efforts of non-Communists to gain political influence. Coalition governments appeared temporarily as an immediate postwar expedient, but the Communists followed a long-range strategy of ensconcing themselves in the interior ministries in order to control the police. Opposition political leaders found themselves under accusation, "confessions" were extorted, and the leaders of the opposition were either exiled, silenced, executed, or consigned to prison.

Secretary of State James F. Byrnes struggled on through 1946 with the problems of postwar settlements. As early as September 1945, the first meeting of the Council of Foreign Ministers broke up because of

Byrnes's demand that the governments of Romania and Bulgaria be broadened. A series of almost interminable meetings of the Council of Foreign Ministers wrangled over border lines and reparations from Hitler's satellites, finally producing treaties for Italy, Hungary, Romania, Bulgaria, and Finland. The treaties, signed on February 10, 1947, in effect confirmed Soviet control over eastern Europe, which in Russian eyes seemed but a parallel to American control in Japan and Western control over most of Germany and all of Italy. The Yalta guarantees of democracy in eastern Europe had turned out much like the Open Door Policy in China, little more than pious cant that was subordinate to the pressures of raw power and national interests. Byrnes's impulse to pressure Soviet diplomats by brandishing the atomic bomb only added to the irritations, intimidating no one.

The United States, together with Britain and Canada (partners in developing the atomic bomb), had exclusive possession of atomic weapons at the time, but in 1946 proposed to internationalize the control of atomic energy through a plan presented to the U.N. Atomic Energy Commission. Under the plan an International Atomic Development Authority would have a monopoly of atomic explosives and atomic energy. The Soviets, fearing Western domination of the agency, proposed instead simply to outlaw the manufacture and use of atomic bombs, with enforcement vested in the Security Council and thus subject to a veto. Later they conceded the right of international inspection, but still refused to give up the veto, and the American government rejected the arrangement, which it considered a compromise of international control.

CONTAINMENT   By the beginning of 1947, relations with the Soviet Union had become even more troubled. A year before, Stalin had already pronounced international peace impossible "under the present capitalist development of the world economy." His statement impelled George F. Kennan, counselor of the American embassy in Moscow, to send the secretary of state an 8,000-word dispatch in which he sketched the roots of Soviet policy and warned that the Soviet Union was "committed fanatically to the belief that . . . it is desirable and necessary that the internal harmony of our society be disrupted, our traditional way of life be destroyed, the international authority of our state be broken, if Soviet power is to be secure."

George F. Kennan, whose 1947 For-eign Affairs *article spelled out the doctrine of containment.*

More than a year later, Kennan, now back at the State Department in Washington, spelled out his ideas for a proper response to the Soviets in a 1947 article published anonymously in *Foreign Affairs.* Kennan signed himself "X" so that readers would not mistake the article for an official State Department position. He did not offer a cohesive strategy or an operational plan but instead provided a psychological analysis of Soviet insecurity and intentions. He predicted that the Soviets would try to fill "every nook and cranny available . . . in the basin of world power." Yet their insecurity also meant that, in general, they would act cautiously and seek to reduce their risks. Therefore, he insisted, "the main element of any United States policy toward the Soviet Union must be that of a long-term, patient but firm and vigilant *containment* of Russian expansive tendencies. . . . Such a policy has nothing to do with outward histrionics: with threats or blustering or superfluous gestures of outward 'toughness.'" Americans, he argued, could hope for a long-term moderation of expansionist Soviet ideology and policy, so that in time tensions with the West would lessen. There was a strong possibility "that Soviet power, like the capitalist world of its conception, bears within it the seeds of its own decay, and that the sprouting of those seeds is well advanced."

Kennan's containment concept explained the new departure in foreign policy that America's political leaders had already decided to take. Behind this shift lay a growing fear that Soviet aims reached beyond eastern Europe, posing dangers in the eastern Mediterranean, the Middle East, and western Europe itself. The first major postwar crisis occurred in Iran, which borders the Soviet Union on the south and provided important trade routes to the U.S.S.R. Soviet troops had been stationed in northern Iran while British-American troops were in the south, and all were supposed to pull out six months after the war. But the Soviets remained beyond the deadline. The crisis finally blew over with a Soviet withdrawal.

Meanwhile the Soviet Union sought a breakthrough into the Mediterranean, long important to Russia for purposes of trade and defense. After the war the Soviet Union began to press Turkey for territorial concessions and the right to build naval bases on the Bosporus, an important gateway between the Black Sea and the Mediterranean. In 1946 civil war broke out in Greece between a government backed by the British and a Communist-led faction that held the northern part of Greece and drew supplies from Yugoslavia, Bulgaria, and Albania. In 1947 the British ambassador informed the American government that the British could no longer bear the economic and military burden of aiding Greece. When Truman conferred with congressional leaders on the situation, the chairman of the Senate Foreign Relations Committee recommended a strong appeal to the American people.

THE TRUMAN DOCTRINE AND THE MARSHALL PLAN   On March 12, 1947, President Truman appeared before Congress to request $400 million for economic aid to both Greece and Turkey and for the authority to send American personnel to train their soldiers. In his speech Truman enunciated what quickly came to be known as the Truman Doctrine. It justified aid to Greece and Turkey in terms more provocative than Kennan's idea of containment and more general than this specific case warranted. "I believe," Truman declared, "that it must be the policy of the United States to support free peoples who are resisting attempted subjugation by armed minorities or by outside pressures."

In 1947 Congress passed the Greek-Turkish aid bill, and by 1950 had spent $659 million on the program. Turkey achieved economic stability, and Greece defeated the Communist insurrection in 1949, partly because President Tito of Yugoslavia had broken with the Soviets in the summer of 1948 and ceased to aid the Greek Communists. But the principles embedded in the Truman Doctrine committed the United States to intervene throughout the world in order to "contain" the

George C. Marshall at the Harvard University commencement where he proposed the "Marshall Plan" for the reconstruction of postwar Europe.

spread of communism, and this global commitment would produce tragic consequences as well as successes in the years to come.

The Truman Doctrine marked the beginning, or at least the open acknowledgment, of a contest that Bernard Baruch named in a 1947 speech to the legislature of his native South Carolina: "Let us not be deceived—today we are in the midst of a cold war." Greece and Turkey were but the front lines of an ideological struggle that would involve western Europe as well. There wartime damage and dislocation had devastated factory production, and severe drought in 1947, followed by a harsh winter, had destroyed crops. Coal shortages in London left only enough fuel to heat and light homes for a few hours each day. In Berlin, people were freezing or starving to death. The transportation system in Europe was in shambles. Bridges were out, canals clogged, and rail networks destroyed. Amid the chaos the Communist parties of France and Italy were flourishing. Aid from the United Nations had staved off starvation, but had provided little basis for economic recovery.

In the spring of 1947, George C. Marshall, who had replaced Byrnes as secretary of state, called for a program of massive aid to rescue western Europe from disaster. The retired chairman of the Joint Chiefs of Staff who orchestrated the Allied victories over Germany and Japan, Marshall had been the highest-ranking army general during World War II. "He is the great one of the age," said Truman. Marshall used the occasion of the Harvard graduation ceremonies in 1947 to outline his plan for the reconstruction of Europe. "Our policy," he said, "is directed not against country or doctrine, but against hunger, poverty, desperation, and chaos." Marshall offered aid to all European countries, including the Soviet Union, and called upon them to take the lead in judging their own needs. On June 27 the foreign ministers of France, Britain, and the Soviet Union met in London to discuss Marshall's overture. Soviet foreign minister Vyacheslav Molotov arrived with eighty advisers, but during the talks he got word from Moscow to withdraw from this "imperialist" scheme. Two weeks later a meeting of delegates from western Europe formed a Committee of European Economic Cooperation (CEEC), which had a plan ready by September.

In December Truman submitted his proposal for the European Recovery Program to Congress. Two months later, a Communist coup d'état in Czechoslovakia ended the last remaining coalition government in eastern Europe. Coming less than ten years after Munich, the seizure of power in Prague assured congressional passage of the Marshall Plan. From 1948 until 1951 the Economic Cooperation Administration (ECA), which managed the Marshall Plan, poured $13 billion into European recovery through the CEEC.

DIVIDING GERMANY   The breakdown of the wartime alliance left the problem of postwar Germany unsettled. The German economy had stagnated, requiring the American army to support a staggering burden of relief. Slowly, zones of occupation evolved into functioning governments. In 1948 the British, French, and Americans united their zones. The West Germans then organized state governments and elected delegates to a federal constitutional convention.

Soviet leaders resented the Marshall Plan and the unification of West Germany. In April 1948 the Soviets began to restrict the flow of traffic into West Berlin; on June 23 they stopped all traffic. The Soviets hoped the blockade would force the Allies to give up either Berlin or the plan to unify West Germany. But the American commander in Germany proposed to stand firm. "When Berlin falls, Western Germany will be next," he told the Pentagon. "If we mean . . . to hold Europe against communism, we must not budge."

Truman agreed and, after considering the use of armed convoys to supply West Berlin, opted for a massive airlift. At the time this seemed

OCCUPATION OF GERMANY AND AUSTRIA

French zone	U.S. zone
British zone	Soviet zone

an enormous and perhaps impossible task, requiring, according to one estimate, 4,500 tons of food and coal a day. But by quick work the Allied air forces brought in planes from around the world, and by October 1948 were flying in nearly 5,000 tons of food and equipment a day. Altogether, from June 1948 to mid-May 1949, the Berlin Airlift provided more than 1.5 million tons of supplies, or well over a half ton for each of the 2.2 million West Berliners.

Finally, on May 12, 1949, after extended talks, the Soviets lifted the blockade in return for a meeting of the Council of Foreign Ministers in Paris. This was purely a face-saving gesture, and the meeting resulted in no important decision on Germany. Before the end of the year the German Federal Republic had a government functioning under Chancellor Konrad Adenauer of the Christian Democratic party. At the end of May 1949, a German "Democratic" Republic arose in the eastern zone, for-

The Berlin Airlift. *An American airplane arrives in West Berlin with much-needed supplies, 1948.*

malizing the division of Germany. West Germany gradually acquired more authority, until the Western powers recognized its full sovereignty in 1955.

BUILDING NATO   As relations between the Soviets and western Europe chilled, transatlantic unity ripened into an outright military alliance. On April 4, 1949, the North Atlantic Treaty was signed at Washington by representatives of twelve nations: the United States, Britain, France, Belgium, the Netherlands, Luxembourg, Canada, Denmark, Iceland, Italy, Norway, and Portugal. Greece and Turkey joined the alliance in 1952, Germany in 1955, Spain in 1982. Senate ratification of the North Atlantic Treaty by a vote of 82 to 13 suggested that the isolationism of the prewar period no longer exerted a hold on the American people.

The treaty pledged that an attack against any one of the signers would be considered an attack against all, and provided for a council of the North Atlantic Treaty Organization (NATO), which could establish other necessary agencies. In 1950 the council decided to create an integrated defense force for western Europe and later named General

NATO, a symbol of renewed strength for a battered Europe.

Dwight Eisenhower to head the Supreme Headquarters of the Allied Powers in Europe (SHAPE). In 1955 the Warsaw Treaty Organization appeared as the eastern European counterpart to NATO.

The eventful year 1948 produced one other foreign policy decision with long-term consequences. Palestine, as the biblical Holy Land had come to be known, was under Turkish rule until the League of Nations made it a British mandate after World War I. Over the early years of the twentieth century, many Zionists, who advocated a Jewish state in the region, had migrated there. More came after the British entered, and a greatly increased number arrived during the Nazi persecution in 1933 and after. Offered a promise by the British of a national homeland, the Jewish inhabitants demanded their own state.

Late in 1947, the U.N. General Assembly voted to partition Palestine into Jewish and Arab states, but this met fierce Arab opposition. Finally, the British mandate expired on May 14, 1948, and Jewish leaders proclaimed the independence of the state of Israel. President Truman, who had been in close touch with Jewish leaders, ordered recognition of the new state within minutes—the United States became the first nation to act. The neighboring Arab states thereupon went to war against Israel, which, however, held its own. U.N. mediators gradually worked out truce agreements with Israel's Arab neighbors, and an uneasy peace was restored by May 11, 1949, when Israel was admitted as a member of the United Nations. But the hard feelings and intermittent warfare between Israel and the Arab states have festered ever since, complicating American foreign policy, which has tried to maintain friendship with both sides.

HARRY GIVES 'EM HELL

CIVIL RIGHTS DURING THE 1940S   The social tremors triggered by World War II and the onset of the cold war transformed America's racial landscape. The vicious racism of the German Nazis, Italian fascists, and Japanese imperialists focused attention on the need for the United States to improve its own race relations and to provide for equal rights under the law. As a *New York Times* editorial explained in early 1946, "This is a particularly good time to campaign against the evils of bigotry, prejudice, and race hatred because we have witnessed the defeat of enemies who tried to found a mastery of the world upon such cruel and fallacious policy." The postwar confrontation with the Soviet Union also gave Americans an added incentive to improve race relations in the United States. In the ideological contest for influence in Africa, American diplomats were at a disadvantage as long as racial segregation continued in the United States. The Soviets often compared segregation in the American South to the Nazis' treatment of Jews.

For most of his political career, Harry Truman had shown little concern about the plight of African Americans. He had grown up in western Missouri assuming that both blacks and whites preferred to be segregated from one another. As president, however, he began to reassess his convictions. A recent biographer of Truman concludes that he "was magnificently right on what may have been the two most important issues of his time: civil rights and the Soviet challenge."

In the fall of 1946 Truman hosted a delegation of civil rights activists from the National Emergency Committee Against Mob Violence. They urged the president to issue a public statement condemning the resurgence of the Ku Klux Klan and the lynching of blacks. The delegation graphically described incidents of torture and intimidation against blacks in the South. Truman was aghast. "My God," he exclaimed. "I had no idea it was as terrible as that. We've got to do something." Two months later, he appointed a Committee on Civil Rights to investigate violence against African Americans and to recommend preventive measures.

The committee recommended the renewal of the Fair Employment Practices Committee (FEPC) and the creation of a permanent civil rights commission to investigate abuses. It also argued that federal aid be denied to any state that mandated segregated schools and public facilities.

On July 26, 1948, Truman banned racial discrimination in the hiring of federal employees. Four days later, he issued an Executive Order ending racial segregation in the armed forces. The air force and navy quickly complied, but the army dragged its feet until the early 1950s. By 1960 the armed forces were the most racially integrated of all American organizations. Desegregating the military was, Truman claimed, "the greatest thing that ever happened to America."

Meanwhile, racial segregation was being confronted in a much more public field of endeavor—professional baseball. In April 1947, as the baseball season opened, the National League's Brooklyn Dodgers included on their roster the first black player to cross the color line in major league baseball: Jackie Robinson. "This in a way is another Emancipation Day for the Negro race," wrote the sportswriter for the *Montreal Daily Star,* "a day that Abraham Lincoln would like." Another newspaper declared: "Jim Crow Dies at Second Base."

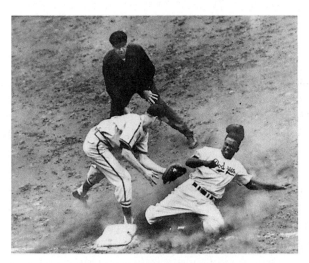

Jackie Robinson, 1949. *Racial discrimination remained widespread through the postwar period. In 1947 Jackie Robinson of the Brooklyn Dodgers became the first black to play major league baseball.*

Born in Georgia but raised in California, Robinson was an army veteran and baseball player in the Negro leagues. He earlier had been a football, basketball, baseball, and track star at UCLA. Branch Rickey, the courageous president of the Dodgers and the son of a Methodist minister, selected Robinson to integrate professional baseball, not only for his athletic potential but because of his willingness to control his temper in the face of virulent racism. Rickey knew that the first black player in the major leagues would face a storm of abuse. Many skeptics, including most of the other team owners, predicted that opposition from players and fans would force Rickey to drop Robinson from the roster. Teammates and opposing players viciously baited Robinson, pitchers threw at him, base runners spiked him, and spectators booed and taunted him in every city. Hotels refused him rooms, and restaurants denied him service. Hate mail arrived by the bucket load. On the other hand, black spectators were electrified by Robinson's courageous example. They turned out in droves to see him play.

What Branch Rickey called his noble experiment provided a public forum for people to confront the charged issue of segregation. The headline in the *Boston Chronicle* trumpeted: "Triumph of Whole Race Seen in Jackie's Debut in Major League Ball." Huge crowds flocked to see Robinson play, and he played well, doing everything necessary to help the Dodgers win games—bunt, sacrifice, draw walks, steal bases, hit for average and for power. His success earned him the Rookie of the Year Award in 1947. Leo Durocher, manager of the Dodgers, declared that Robinson "didn't just come to play. He come to beat ya."

As time passed, Robinson won over many fans and opposing players through his quiet courage, self-deprecating wit, and determined performance. Soon, other teams began to sign black players. In July 1947 the Cleveland Indians added Larry Doby to their roster, thus breaking the color barrier in the American League. That same month the St. Louis Browns signed three players from the Negro leagues. Baseball's path-breaking efforts stimulated other professional sports such as football and basketball to integrate their rosters. Jackie Robinson vividly demonstrated that racism, not inferiority, impeded African-American advancement in the postwar era and that segregation need not be a permanent condition of American life. "When Jackie took the field," the Reverend Jesse Jackson recalled, "something reminded us of our birthright to be free."

Truman's support of civil rights for African Americans had its political costs, as this 1948 cartoon suggests.

SHAPING THE FAIR DEAL   The determination Truman projected in foreign affairs did not alter his weak image on the domestic front. By early 1948, after three years in the White House, Truman had yet to shake the impression that he was not up to the job. Rather than go with a loser, New Deal stalwarts and party regulars tried to draft General Eisenhower for the 1948 presidential nomination, but in vain. The Democratic party seemed about to fragment: southern conservatives resented Truman's outspoken support of civil rights, while the left had flared up in 1946 over his firing of Secretary of Commerce Henry Wallace after a speech critical of the administration's policy. "Getting tough [with the Soviet Union]," Wallace had argued, "never brought anything real and lasting—whether for schoolyard bullies or world powers. The tougher we get, the tougher the Russians will get." The left itself was splitting between the Progressive Citizens of America (PCA), formed in 1946, which supported Wallace, and the Americans for Democratic Action (ADA), formed in 1947, which also criticized Truman but took a firm anti-Communist stance.

Truman made an aggressive effort to shore up the New Deal coalition. He needed the midwestern and western farm belts, and had fairly strong support among farmers. In metropolitan areas, he needed to carry the labor and black vote, which he wooed by working closely with unions and liberals, and pressing the cause of civil rights.

Like other presidents, Truman used his State of the Union message in 1948 to set the agenda for an election year. The speech offered something to nearly every group the Democrats hoped to attract. The first goal, Truman said, was "to secure fully the essential human rights of our citizens," and he promised a special message later on civil rights. "To protect human resources," he proposed federal aid to education, increased and extended unemployment and retirement benefits, a comprehensive system of health insurance, more federal support for housing, and extension of rent controls. He continued to pile on the demands: for reclamation projects, more rural electrification, a higher minimum wage, laws to admit thousands of displaced persons to the United States, money for the Marshall Plan, and a "cost-of-living" tax credit.

THE 1948 ELECTION   The Republican Congress for the most part spurned the Truman program, an action it would later regret. At the party convention, New York governor Thomas E. Dewey won the nomination on the third ballot. The platform endorsed most of the New Deal reforms as accomplished fact and approved the administration's bipartisan foreign policy, but as Landon had in 1936 and Willkie had in 1940, Dewey promised to run things more efficiently.

In July a glum Democratic convention gathered in Philadelphia, expecting to do little more than go through the motions, only to find itself doubly surprised: first by the battle over the civil rights plank, and then by Truman's acceptance speech. To keep from stirring southern hostility, the administration sought a platform plank that opposed racial discrimination only in general terms. Liberal Democrats, however, sponsored a plank that called on Congress for specific action and commended Truman "for his courageous stand on the issue of civil rights." Speaking last in favor of the change, Minneapolis mayor Hubert H. Humphrey electrified the delegates and set off a ten-minute demonstration: "The time has arrived for the Democratic party to get out of the shadow of states' rights and walk forthrightly into the bright sunshine of human rights." Segregationist delegates from Alabama and Mississippi walked, instead, out of the convention.

After the convention had nominated Truman, the president showed a new fighting style in his speeches. He pledged to "win this election and make the Republicans like it," he said, "don't you forget it!" He also

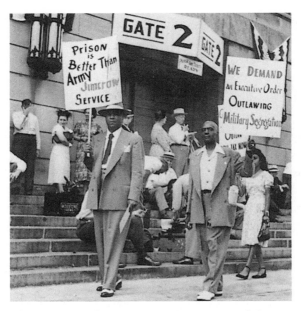

The opening of the 1948 Democratic National Convention is marked by demonstrations against racial segregation, led by A. Philip Randolph (left).

vowed to call Congress back into session "to get the laws the people need," many of which the Republican platform had endorsed.

On July 17 a group of rebellious southern Democrats met in Birmingham and nominated South Carolina governor J. Strom Thurmond on a States' Rights Democratic ticket, quickly dubbed the "Dixiecrat" ticket. The Dixiecrats hoped to draw enough electoral votes to preclude a majority for either major party, throwing the election into the House, where they might strike a sectional bargain. A few days later, on July 23, the left wing of the Democratic party gathered in Philadelphia to name Henry A. Wallace on a Progressive party ticket. These splits in the Democratic ranks seemed to spell the final blow to Truman. The special session of Congress petered out in futility.

But Truman, undaunted, set out on a 31,000-mile "whistle-stop" train tour during which he castigated the "do-nothing" Eightieth Congress to the accompaniment of cries from his audiences: "Pour it on, Harry!" and "Give 'em hell, Harry." Truman responded: "I don't give 'em

The "Dixiecrats" nominate South Carolina governor J. Strom Thurmond (center) *to lead their ticket in the 1948 election.*

hell. I just tell the truth and they think it's hell." Dewey, in contrast, ran a restrained campaign, designed to avoid rocking the boat. By so doing he may have snatched defeat from the jaws of victory.

To the end the polls and the pundits predicted a sure win for Dewey, and most speculation centered on his cabinet choices. But on election day Truman chalked up the biggest upset in American history, taking 24.2 million votes (49.5 percent) to Dewey's 22 million (45.1 percent) and winning a thumping 303 to 189 vote margin in the electoral college. Thurmond and Wallace each got more than a million votes, but the revolt of right and left worked to Truman's advantage. The Dixiecrat rebellion reassured black voters who had questioned the Democrats' commitment to civil rights, while the Progressive movement made it hard to tag Truman as "soft on communism." Thurmond carried four Deep South states (South Carolina, Mississippi, Alabama, and Louisiana) with 39 electoral votes, including one electoral vote from a Tennessee elector who repudiated his state's decision for Truman. Thurmond's success started a momentous disruption of the Democratic Solid South. But Truman's victory also carried Democratic majorities into Congress, where the new group of senators included Hubert

Humphrey and, by eighty-seven disputed votes, "Landslide Lyndon" B. Johnson of Texas.

Truman viewed the outcome as a vindication for the New Deal and a mandate for liberalism. "We have rejected the discredited theory that the fortunes of the nation should be in the hands of a privileged few," he said. His State of the Union message repeated the agenda he had set forth a year previously. "Every segment of our population and every individual," he declared, "has a right to expect from his government a fair deal." Whether deliberately or not he had invented a tag, the "Fair Deal," to set off his program from the New Deal.

Congress passed some of Truman's Fair Deal proposals, but they were mainly extensions or enlargements of New Deal programs already in place: a higher minimum wage, bringing more people under Social Security, extension of rent controls, farm price supports at 90 percent of parity, a sizable slum-clearance and public housing program, and more money for the Reclamation Bureau, the TVA, rural electrification, and farm housing. Despite Democratic majorities, however, the conservative coalition thwarted any drastic new departures in domestic policy. Congress rejected civil rights bills, national health insurance, federal

The Man Who "Done His Damndest." Truman's victory in 1948 was a huge upset.

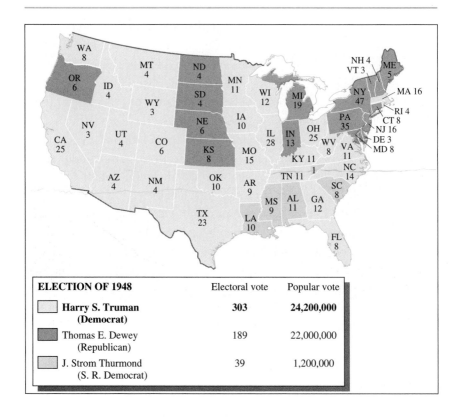

ELECTION OF 1948	Electoral vote	Popular vote
Harry S. Truman (Democrat)	**303**	**24,200,000**
Thomas E. Dewey (Republican)	189	22,000,000
J. Strom Thurmond (S. R. Democrat)	39	1,200,000

aid to education, and a plan to provide subsidies that would hold up farm incomes rather than farm prices. Congress also turned down Truman's demand for repeal of the Taft-Hartley Act.

THE COLD WAR HEATS UP

Global concerns, never far from center stage in the postwar world, plagued Truman's second term, as they had his first. People began to live in real fear that the Communists were infiltrating American society and were intent upon world domination. In his inaugural address Truman called for a vigilant anti-Communist foreign policy to rest on four pillars: the United Nations, the Marshall Plan, NATO, and a "bold new plan" for technical assistance to underdeveloped parts of the world, a sort of global Marshall Plan that came to be known simply as "Point Four." This program to aid the postwar world, never accomplished its

Mao Tse-tung on the march with Red Army troops in northern China, 1947.

goals, in part because other international problems soon diverted Truman's attention.

"LOSING" CHINA AND THE BOMB   One of the most intractable problems, the China tangle, was fast coming unraveled in 1949. The Chinese Nationalists (Kuomintang) of Chiang Kai-shek had at first accepted the help of Communists, but expelled them from the ranks in 1927. When a new leader, Mao Tse-tung,* began to rebuild the Communist party by organizing the peasants instead of urban workers, the Nationalists drove him out of his stronghold in the south. After an arduous trek, which the Communists later celebrated as the "Long March" of 1934–1935, they entrenched themselves in northern China at Yenan. The outbreak of war with Japan in 1937 relieved them of pressure from the Nationalists, and at the same time enabled them to assume a patriotic stance by fighting the Japanese. During the war, Roosevelt and Stalin believed that the Nationalists would organize China after the war.

---

*The traditional (Wade-Giles) spelling is used here. In 1958 the Chinese government adopted the "pinyin" transliterations that became more widely used after Mao's death in 1976, so that, for example, Mao Tse-tung became Mao Zedong, and Peking became Beijing.

But the commanders of American forces in China during World War II concluded that Chiang's government was hopelessly corrupt, tyrannical, and inefficient. After the war, American forces nevertheless ferried Nationalist armies back into the eastern and northern provinces as the Japanese withdrew. U.S. policy during and immediately after the war promoted peace between the factions in China, but sporadic civil war broke out late in 1945.

It soon became a losing fight for the Nationalists, as the Communists radicalized the land-hungry peasantry. By early 1949 Mao's forces were in Peking and headed southward. By the end of the year they had taken Canton, and the Nationalist government had fled to the island of Formosa, which it renamed Taiwan.

From 1945 through 1949 the United States had funneled some $2 billion in aid to the Nationalists, to no avail. Administration critics now asked bitterly: "Who lost China?" A State Department study blamed Chiang for his failure to hold the support of the Chinese people. In fact it is hard to imagine how the United States government could have prevented the outcome short of massive military intervention, which would have been very risky and unpopular. The United States continued to recognize the Nationalist government on Taiwan as the rightful government of China, delaying formal relations with Red China for thirty years. Seeking to shore up friendly regimes in Asia, in 1950 the United States recognized the French-supported regime of Emperor Bao Dai in Vietnam and shortly afterward extended aid to the French in their battle against Ho Chi Minh's guerrillas there.

As the Communists gained control of China, American intelligence in 1949 found an unusual level of radioactivity in the air, evidence that the Soviets had set off an atomic device. The American nuclear monopoly had lasted just four years, but under the umbrella of security that it seemed to offer, the wartime military establishment had been allowed to dwindle. If a crisis had occurred, it would have left American leaders with the choice of doing nothing or cremating millions of people. The discovery of the Soviet bomb provoked an intense reappraisal of the strategic balance in the world, causing Truman in 1950 to end a dispute among his scientific advisers by ordering the construction of a hydrogen bomb, a weapon far more frightful than those dropped on Japan, lest the Soviets make one first. The discovery also led the National Security Council to produce a top-secret document, known as NSC-68, that called for rebuilding conventional military forces to provide options other than nuclear war. This represented a major departure from America's time-honored aversion to keeping large standing armies in peacetime, and was an expensive proposition. But the American public was growing more receptive to the nation's role as world leader, and an invasion of South Korea by Communist forces from the north clinched the issue for most.

WAR IN KOREA The division of Korea at the end of World War II, like the division of Germany, began as a temporary expedient and ended as a permanent fact. In the hectic days of August 1945, a State-War-Navy Coordinating Committee adopted a hasty proposal to divide Korea at the 38th parallel. The Soviets accepted, to the surprise of American officials involved. Since they bordered on Korea, the Soviets could quickly have occupied the whole country. With the onset of the cold war, it became clear that agreement on unification was no more likely in Korea than in Germany, and by the end of 1948 separate regimes had appeared in the two sectors and occupation forces had withdrawn. The weakened state of the American military contributed to the impression that South Korea was vulnerable. A growing body of evidence later gleaned from Soviet archives reveals that Stalin encouraged the North Koreans to use force to unify their country and oust the Americans from the peninsula. The Soviets helped design and ultimately approved a war plan that called for North Korean forces to seize Seoul within three days and all of South Korea within a week.

North Korean forces crossed the boundary on June 25, 1950, and swept down the peninsula. President Truman responded decisively. He and his advisers assumed that the North Korean attack was directed by Moscow and was a brazen indication of the aggressive designs of monolithic communism. "The attack upon Korea makes it plain beyond all doubt," Truman told Congress, "that communism has passed beyond the use of subversion to conquer independent nations and will now use armed invasion and war."

An emergency meeting of the U.N. Security Council quickly censured the North Korean "breach of peace." The Soviet delegate, who held a veto power, was at the time boycotting the council because it would not seat Red China in place of Nationalist China. On June 27, its first resolution having been ignored, the Security Council called on U.N. members to "furnish such assistance to the Republic of Korea as may be necessary to repel the armed attack and to restore international peace and security in the area." Truman ordered American air, naval, and ground forces into action. In all, some fourteen other U.N. members sent military units, the largest from Britain and Turkey, and five sent medical units. Later, when the U.N. voted a unified command, General Douglas MacArthur was designated to take charge. The defense of South Korea remained chiefly an American affair, and one that set a precedent of profound consequence: war by order of the president rather than by vote of Congress. Yet, it had the sanction of the U.N. Security Council, and could technically be considered a "police action," not a war. To be sure, other presidents had ordered American troops into action without a declaration of war, but never on such a scale.

Truman's conviction that the invasion of South Korea was actually orchestrated by Stalin in Moscow led to two other decisions that had far-reaching consequences. Believing that the Korean action was actually a diversion for a Soviet advance into western Europe, Truman began a major expansion of American forces in NATO. By 1952 there were 261,000 American troops stationed in Europe, three times the number in 1950 and slightly more than the total number of American soldiers in Korea. While dispatching American forces to Korea and Europe, Truman also increased his assistance to the French in Indochina, creating the Military Assistance Advisory Group for Indochina. This was the start of America's deepening involvement in Vietnam.

For three months the fighting in Korea went badly for the Republic of Korea (ROK) and U.N. forces. Soviet pilots battled American planes over South Korea. To mask their identity, the Soviets wore Chinese uniforms and used Chinese phrases over the radio. By September the ROK and U.N. forces were barely hanging on to the Pusan perimeter in the southeast corner of Korea. Then, in a brilliant ploy, on September 15, 1950, MacArthur landed a new force to the North Korean rear at Inchon, the port city for Seoul. Synchronized with a breakout from Pusan, the sudden blow stampeded the enemy back across the border. At this point, MacArthur convinced Truman to allow him to push on and seek to reunify Korea. By now, the Soviet delegate was back in the Security Council, wielding his veto. So on October 7 the United States won approval for this course from the U.N. General Assembly, where the veto did not apply. United States forces had already crossed the boundary by October 1, and now continued northward against minimal resistance.

President Truman, concerned about broad hints of intervention by Red China, flew to Wake Island for a conference with General MacArthur on October 15. There the general discounted chances that the Red Chinese Army would act, but if it did, he predicted "there would be the greatest slaughter."

That same day Peking announced that China "cannot stand idly by." On October 20 U.N. forces had entered Pyongyang, the North Korean capital, and on October 26 advance units had reached Chosan on the Yalu River border with China. MacArthur predicted total victory by Christmas. But on the night of November 25 Chinese "volunteers" counterattacked, and massive "human wave" attacks, with the support of tanks and planes, turned the tables on the U.N. forces, sending them into a desperate retreat just at the onset of winter. It had become "an entirely new war," MacArthur said. He began to claim that the fault for the war's continuance lay with the administration for requiring that he conduct a limited war. He proposed air raids on China's "privileged

U.N. forces recapture Seoul from the North Koreans, September 1950.

sanctuary" in Manchuria, a naval blockade of China, and an invasion of the Chinese mainland by the Taiwan Nationalists. MacArthur seemed to have forgotten altogether his onetime reluctance to bog down the country in a major war on the Asian mainland.

Truman stood against leading the United States into the "gigantic booby trap" of war with China, and the U.N. forces soon rallied. By January 1951 U.N. troops under General Matthew B. Ridgway finally secured their lines below Seoul, and then launched a counterattack that in some places carried them back across the 38th parallel in March. When Truman seized the chance and offered negotiations to restore the prewar boundary, MacArthur undermined the move by issuing an ultimatum for China to make peace or be attacked. Truman decided then that MacArthur would have to go. On April 5, on the floor of the House, the Republican minority leader read a letter in which MacArthur criticized the president and said that "there is no substitute for victory." Such an act of open insubordination left the commander-in-chief no choice but to accept MacArthur's policy or fire him. Civilian control of the military was at stake, Truman later said, and he did not let it remain at stake very long. The Joint Chiefs of Staff all backed the decision, and on April 11, 1951, the president removed MacArthur from all his commands and replaced him with Ridgway.

Truman's action ignited an immediate uproar in the country, and a tumultuous reception greeted MacArthur upon his return home for the first time since 1937. MacArthur's speech to a joint session of Congress provided the climactic event. "Once war is forced upon us," he asserted, "there is no alternative than to apply every available means to bring it to a swift end." MacArthur ended the speech in memorable fashion. He recalled a barracks ballad of his youth "which proclaimed most proudly that old soldiers never die, they just fade away." And like the old soldiers of that ballad, he said, "I now close my military career and just fade away, an old soldier who tried to do his duty as God gave him the light to see that duty." A Senate investigation brought out the administration's arguments, best summarized by General Omar Bradley, chairman of the Joint Chiefs of Staff. "Taking on Red China," he explained, would lead only "to a larger deadlock at greater expense." The MacArthur strategy "would involve us in the wrong war at the wrong place at the wrong time and with the wrong enemy." Americans, nurtured on classic Western showdowns in which good always triumphed over evil, found the logic of limited war hard to take, but also found General Bradley's logic persuasive.

On June 24, 1951, the Soviet representative at the United Nations proposed a cease-fire and armistice along the 38th parallel; Secretary of State Dean Acheson accepted in principle a few days later with the consent of the United Nations. China and North Korea responded favorably—at the time General Ridgway's "meat-grinder" offensive was inflicting severe losses—and truce talks started on July 10, 1951, at Panmunjom, only to drag out for another two years while the fighting continued. The chief snags were prisoner exchanges and the insistence of the South Korean president on unification. By the time a truce was finally reached on July 27, 1953, Truman had relinquished the White House to Dwight D. Eisenhower. The truce line followed the front at that time, mostly a little north of the 38th parallel, with a demilitarized zone of two and a half miles separating the forces; repatriation of prisoners would be voluntary, supervised by a neutral commission. No final peace conference ever took place, and Korea, like Germany, remained divided. The war had cost the United States more than 33,000 battle deaths and 103,000 wounded and missing. South Korean casualties, all told, were about 1 million, and North Korean and Chinese casualties an estimated 1.5 million.

ANOTHER RED SCARE In calculating the costs of the Korean War one must add in the far-reaching consequences of the Second Red Scare, which had grown since 1945 as the domestic counterpart to the cold war abroad and reached a crescendo during the Korean conflict. Since 1938, the House Un-American Activities Committee (HUAC) had kept up a drumbeat of accusations about subversives in government. In 1945 government agents found that secret American documents had turned up in the offices of a Communist-sponsored magazine, and more dramatic revelations came from a Canadian royal commission that uncovered several spy rings in the Canadian bureaucracy. On March 21, 1947, just nine days after he announced the Truman Doctrine, Truman signed an executive order setting up procedures for an employee loyalty program in the federal government. Every person entering civil employ would be subject to a background investigation. By early 1951 the Civil Service Commission had cleared over 3 million people, while over 2,000 had resigned and 212 had been dismissed for doubtful loyalty, but no espionage ring was ever uncovered.

The loyalty program was designed partly if not mainly to protect the president's political flank, but it failed that purpose, mainly because of disclosures of earlier Communist penetrations into government that were few in number but sensational in character. The loyalty review program may in fact have heightened the politically explosive hysteria over Communist infiltration.

Perhaps the single case most damaging to the administration involved Alger Hiss, president of the Carnegie Endowment for International Peace, who had served in several government departments, and while in the State Department, had been secretary-general of the United Nations charter conference. Whittaker Chambers, a former Soviet agent and later an editor of *Time* magazine, told the House Un-American Activities Committee in 1948 that Hiss had given him secret documents ten years earlier, when Chambers worked for the Soviets. Hiss sued for libel, and Chambers produced microfilms of the State Department documents he said Hiss had passed on to him. Hiss denied the accusation, whereupon he was indicted for perjury and, after one mistrial, convicted in 1950. The charge was perjury, but he was convicted of lying about espionage—for which he could not be tried because the statute of limitations on the crime had expired.

Most damaging to the administration was that President Truman, taking at face value the many testimonials to Hiss's integrity, called the charges against him a "red herring." Secretary of State Acheson compounded the damage when, meaning to express compassion, he pledged not "to turn my back on Alger Hiss." The Hiss affair had another political consequence: it raised to national prominence a young California congressman, Richard M. Nixon, who doggedly insisted on pursuing the case and then exploited an anti-Communist stance to win election to the Senate in 1950.

More cases surfaced. In 1949 eleven top Communist party leaders were convicted under the Smith Act of 1940, which outlawed any conspiracy to advocate the overthrow of the government. The Supreme Court upheld the law under the doctrine of a "clear and present danger," which overrode the right to free speech. What was more, in 1950 the government unearthed the existence of a British-American spy network that had fed information about the development of the atomic bomb to the Soviet Union. These disclosures led to the arrest of, among

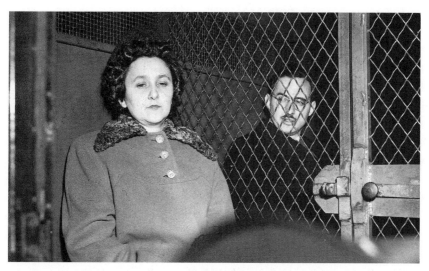

Ethel and Julius Rosenberg were convicted of passing along American secrets about the atom bomb to the Soviets. They were the only Americans to be executed for espionage during the 1950s Red Scare.

others, Klaus Fuchs in Britain and Julius and Ethel Rosenberg in the United States. The Rosenbergs, convicted of espionage, were executed in 1953.

MCCARTHY'S WITCH-HUNT Such revelations encouraged politicians to exploit public fears. If a man of such respectability as Hiss was guilty, many wondered, who then could be trusted? The United States, which bestrode the world like a colossus in 1945, had since "lost" eastern Europe and Asia, and "lost" its atomic secrets to Russia. Early in 1950 the hitherto obscure Republican senator Joseph R. McCarthy of Wisconsin suddenly surfaced as the shrewdest and most ruthless exploiter of such anxieties. He took up the cause, or at least the pose, of anti-communism. He began with a speech at Wheeling, West Virginia, on February 9, 1950, in which he said that the State Department was infested with Communists and that he held in his hand a list of their names. Later there was confusion as to whether he had said 205, 81, 57, or "a lot" of names, and even whether the sheet of paper carried a list. But such confusion always pursued McCarthy's charges.

Challenged to provide names, McCarthy finally pointed to Owen Lattimore of the Johns Hopkins University, an Asia expert, as head of "the espionage ring in the State Department." A special committee under Maryland senator Millard Tydings looked into the matter and pronounced McCarthy's charges "a fraud and a hoax." McCarthy then turned, in what became his common tactic, to other charges, other names. Whenever his charges were refuted, he loosed a scattershot of new charges. By his hit-and-run tactics, McCarthy planted suspicions without proof and grew ever more impudent. "He lied with wild abandon," one commentator wrote; "he lied without evident fear; . . . he lied vividly and with bold imagination; he lied, often, with very little pretense of telling the truth."

Despite his outlandish claims, McCarthy never uncovered a single Communist agent in government. But with the United States at war with Korean Communists in mid-1950, it was easy for him to mobilize true believers. In the elections of 1950 he intervened in Maryland and helped defeat the conservative Tydings with trumped-up charges that Tydings was pro-Communist. Republicans encouraged him to keep up the game. By 1951 he was riding so high as to list General George C. Marshall among the disloyal. His smear campaign went unchallenged until the end of the Korean War.

Senator Joseph McCarthy (left) *and his aide Roy Cohn* (right) *exchange comments during testimony.*

The anti-Communist hysteria led the Congress in 1950 to pass the McCarran Internal Security Act over President Truman's veto. The act made it unlawful "to combine, conspire, or agree with any other person to perform any act which would substantially contribute to . . . the establishment of a totalitarian dictatorship." Communist and Communist-front organizations had to register with the attorney-general. Aliens who had belonged to totalitarian parties were barred from admission to the United States, a provision that discouraged any temptation for Communists to defect to the United States. The McCarran Act, Truman said in his veto message, would "put the Government into the business of thought control." He might in fact have said as much about the Smith Act of 1940, or even his own program of loyalty investigations.

ASSESSING THE COLD WAR   In retrospect, the onset of the cold war takes on an appearance of terrible inevitability. American and Soviet misunderstanding of each other's motives was virtually unavoidable. America's preference for international principles, such as self-determination and democracy, conflicted with Stalin's preference for international spheres of influence. Russia, after all, had been invaded by Germany twice in the first half of the twentieth century, and Soviet leaders wanted tame buffer states on their borders for protection. The people of eastern Europe, as usual, were caught in the middle. But the Communists themselves held to a universal principle: world revolution. And since the time of President Monroe, Americans had bristled at the thought of foreign intervention in their own sphere of influence, the Western Hemisphere. Thus, to create a defensive shield against the spread of communism, the United States signed mutual defense treaties. Under the Treaty of Rio de Janeiro, the nations of the Western Hemisphere agreed to aid any country in the region that was attacked. In 1951, the United States and Japan signed a treaty that permitted the United States to maintain military forces in Japan. That same year, American negotiators signed other mutual defense treaties with the Philippines, Australia, and New Zealand.

If international conditions set the stage for the cold war, the actions of political leaders and thinkers set events in motion. President Truman may have erred in seeming to include all the world in his 1947 doctrine of Communist containment. The loyalty program, following on the heels of the Truman Doctrine, may have spurred on the anti-Communist hysteria of the times. Containment itself proved hard to contain, its author (George Kennan) later confessed, in part because he failed at the outset to spell out its limits explicitly.

The years after World War II were unlike any other postwar period in American history. Having taken on global burdens, the nation had become, if not a "garrison state," at least a country committed to a major and permanent National Military Establishment, along with the attendant National Security Council, Central Intelligence Agency, and by presidential directive in 1952, the enormous National Security Agency, entrusted with monitoring media and communications for foreign intelligence. The policy initiatives of the Truman years had led the country to abandon its long-standing aversion to peacetime alliances not only in the NATO pact but in the agreements with Japan, the Philippines, and the other American nations. It was a far cry from the world of 1796, when George Washington in his farewell address warned his countrymen against "those overgrown military establishments which . . . are inauspicious to liberty" and advised his country "to steer clear of permanent alliances with any portion of the foreign world." But, then, Washington had warned only against participation in the "ordinary" combinations and collusions of Europe, and surely the postwar years had seen extraordinary events.

MAKING CONNECTIONS

- The cold war had a major impact on American society: among other things, it helped create the "conforming culture" described in the next chapter.

- The New Frontier and Great Society programs of Presidents Kennedy and Johnson accomplished much of what Truman tried to do through his Fair Deal policies. See Chapter 34.

- The world seemed a dangerous place at the height of the cold war, but when seen from the perspective of the post–cold war world of the 1990s (see Chapters 36 and 37), it had a certain stability that discouraged political violence.

FURTHER READING

The cold war remains a hotly debated topic. The traditional interpretation is best reflected in John L. Gaddis's *The United States and the Origins of the Cold War, 1941–1947* (1972). Both superpowers, Gaddis argues, were responsible for causing the cold war, but the Soviet Union was more culpable. The revisionist perspective is represented by Gar Alperovitz's *Atomic Diplomacy* (rev. ed., 1994). He places primary responsibility for the conflict on the United States. Also see H. W. Brands's *The Devil We Knew: Americans and the Cold War* (1993), Michael J. Hogan's *The End of the Cold War: Its Meaning and Implications* (1992), Melvyn P. Leffler's *A Preponderance of Power: National Security, the Truman Administration, and the Cold War* (1992), John Lewis Gaddis's *The Long Peace: Inquiries into the History of the Cold War* (rev. ed., 1993), and Wilson D. Miscamble's *George F. Kennan and the Making of American Foreign Policy, 1947–1950* (1992).

Other scholars concentrate on more specific events in the buildup of international tensions. Lynn Etheridge Davis's *The Cold War Begins:*

Soviet-American Conflict over Eastern Europe (1974) and Bruce Kuklick's *American Policy and the Division of Germany* (1972) deal with initial tensions at the close of the war. For the Truman administration's reliance on the atomic bomb monopoly, see Michael Mandelbaum's *The Nuclear Question: The United States and Nuclear Weapons, 1946–1976* (1979) and Daniel Yergin's *Shattered Peace: The Origins of the Cold War and the National Security State* (1977).

For a positive assessment of Truman's leadership, see Alonzo Hamby's *Beyond the New Deal: Harry S. Truman and American Liberalism* (1973). The domestic policies of the Fair Deal are treated in William C. Berman's *The Politics of Civil Rights in the Truman Administration* (1970), Richard M. Dalfiumes's *Desegregation of the United States Armed Forces* (1969), and Maeva Marcus's *Truman and the Steel Seizure Case: The Limits of Presidential Power* (rev. ed, 1994). The most comprehensive biography of Truman is David McCullough's *Truman* (1992).

For an introduction to the tensions in Asia, see Akira Iriye's *The Cold War in Asia* (1974). For the Korean conflict, see Callum A. MacDonald's *Korea: The War before Vietnam* (1986) and Max Hasting's *The Korean War* (rev. ed., 1993). The high-command perspective is revealed in Michael Schaller's *Douglas MacArthur: The Far Eastern General* (1989).

The anti-Communist syndrome is surveyed in David Caute's *The Great Fear: The Anti-Communist Purge under Truman and Eisenhower* (1978). Thomas C. Reeves's *The Life and Times of Joe McCarthy* (1982) covers McCarthy himself. For a well-documented account of how the cold war was sustained by superpatriotism, intolerance, and suspicion, see Stephen J. Whitfield's *The Culture of the Cold War* (1990). See also Richard Fried's *Nightmare in Red: The McCarthy Era in Perspective* (1990).

32 THROUGH THE PICTURE WINDOW: SOCIETY AND CULTURE, 1945–1960

CHAPTER ORGANIZER

This chapter focuses on:

- the economic prosperity of America in the postwar period.

- the culture of the 1950s, with its strains of conformity and innovation.

- America's burgeoning consumer culture.

Americans emerged from World War II elated, justifiably proud of their military strength and industrial might. As the editors of *Fortune* magazine proclaimed in 1946, "This is a dream era, this is what everyone was waiting through the blackouts for. The Great American Boom is on." So it was, from babies to Buicks to Admiral television sets. An American public that had known mostly deprivation and sacrifice for the last decade and a half began to enjoy unprecedented prosperity. The postwar era witnessed tremendous economic growth and rising social contentment. Divorce and homicide rates fell, the birthrate soared, and the prevailing mood seemed aggressively upbeat.

Yet in the midst of such rising affluence and comfortable domesticity, many social critics, writers, and artists expressed a growing sense of unease. Was postwar American society becoming too complacent, too conformist, too materialistic? Such questions reflected the perennial tension in American life between idealism and materialism, a tension that arrived with the first settlers and remains with us today. Americans have always struggled to accumulate goods and cultivate goodness. During the postwar era, the nation again tried to do both. For a while, at least, it appeared to succeed.

PEOPLE OF PLENTY

THE POSTWAR ECONOMY   The dominant feature of post–World War II American society was its remarkable prosperity. After a surprisingly brief postwar recession, the economy soared to record heights. The gross national product (GNP) nearly doubled between 1945 and 1960, and the 1960s witnessed an even more spectacular expansion of the economy. By 1970 the gap between living standards in the United States and the rest of the world had become a chasm: with 6 percent of the world's population, America produced and consumed two-thirds of the world's goods.

During the 1950s, government officials assured the citizenry that they should not fear another economic collapse. "Never again shall we allow a depression in the United States," President Eisenhower promised. The leading economists of the postwar era agreed that the New Deal safeguards built into the economy would prevent another dramatic downturn. They and others led the public to believe that perpetual economic growth was possible, desirable, and, in fact, essential. The expectation of unending plenty became the reigning assumption of social thought in the postwar era.

Several factors contributed to this prolonged economic surge. The massive federal expenditures for military needs during World War II had catapulted the economy out of the Great Depression. High government spending was sustained in the postwar era, thanks to the tensions generated by the cold war and, in the early 1950s, the increase in defense spending provoked by the Korean conflict. The military budget after 1945 represented the single most important stimulant to the postwar economic boom. Defense research also helped spawn the new glamour industries of the postwar era: chemicals, electronics, and aviation.

Most of the other major industrial nations of the world—England, France, Germany, Japan, the Soviet Union—had been physically devastated during the war, which meant that American manufacturers enjoyed a virtual monopoly over international trade. In addition, technological innovations contributed to the "automation" of the workplace and thereby created spectacular increases in productivity. The widespread use of new and more efficient machinery and computers led to a 35 percent jump in worker productivity between 1945 and 1955. In 1945 it took 310 hours to make a car; in 1960, only 150.

The major catalyst in promoting economic expansion after 1945 was the unleashing of pent-up consumer demand. During the war, Americans had postponed purchases of such major items as cars and houses and in the process had saved over $150 billion. Now they were eager to buy. The United States after World War II thus experienced a purchasing frenzy.

THE GI BILL OF RIGHTS   Part of the purchasing frenzy was financed by the federal government. Fears that a sharp drop in military spending and the sudden influx of veterans as new workers would send the economy into a downward spiral and produce widespread unemployment led Congress to pass by a unanimous vote the Servicemen's Readjustment Act of 1944. Popularly known as the GI Bill of Rights (GI stood for the phrase "government issue" stamped on military uniforms and was slang for a serviceman), it led to the creation of a new government agency, the Veterans Administration, and it included provisions for mustering out pay, unemployment pay for veterans for one year, preference for civil service jobs, loans for home construction, access to government hospitals, and generous subsidies for college or professional training.

Almost 8 million veterans took advantage of $14.5 billion in GI Bill subsidies to attend college or job training programs. Some 5 million used additional monies from the GI Bill to buy new homes. These two programs combined to produce a social revolution. The infusion of funds into the economy provided by the GI Bill helped fuel the postwar prosperity. And the educational benefits encouraged people to consider pursuing higher education. Before World War II, approximately 160,000 Americans graduated from college each year. By 1950 the figure had risen to 500,000. In 1949 veterans accounted for 40 percent of all college enrollments, and the United States could boast the world's best-educated workforce.

The GI Bill democratized higher education. It provided a generation of working-class Americans with an opportunity to earn a college degree for the first time. In turn, a college education served as a lever into the middle class and economic security. But while the GI Bill helped erode class barriers, it was less successful in dismantling racial barriers. Many black veterans could not take equal advantage of the education benefits. Most colleges and universities after the war remained racially segregated, either by regulation or by practice. Of the 9,000 students enrolled at the University of Pennsylvania in 1946, for example, only 46 were African Americans. Those blacks who did manage to gain admission to white colleges or universities were barred from playing on athletic teams, attending dances and other social events, and joining fraternities or sororities.

The historically black colleges, most of which were in the South, could not expand quickly enough to meet the demand. In 1940 black colleges enrolled 43,000 students; in 1950 the number had soared to 77,000. Yet over 20,000 were denied admission because of overcrowded facilities. As a result, most black veterans did not get into a college. In 1946 only one-fifth of the 100,000 who had applied for educational benefits had enrolled. In other cases, black veterans were inadequately prepared for college-level work. As late as 1950, some 70 percent of black adults in the southern states had only a seventh-grade education or below.

The return of some 12 million veterans to private life also helped generate a postwar "baby boom," which peaked in 1957. Many young married couples who had delayed having children were intent on making up for lost time. Between 1945 and 1960, total population grew by some 40 million, an increase of almost 30 percent. Much of America's social history since the 1940s has been the story of the unusually large baby-boom generation and its progress through the stages of life. Initially, the postwar baby boom created a massive demand for diapers, baby food, toys, medicines, schools, books, teachers, furniture, and housing.

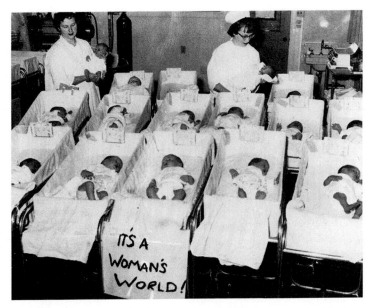

The Baby Boom. *Much of America's social history since the 1940s has been the story of the "baby-boom" generation.*

AN EXPANDING CONSUMER CULTURE   Postwar America soon became a hive of construction activity. The proportion of homeowners in the population increased by 50 percent between 1945 and 1960. And those new homes filled up with the latest appliances—refrigerators, washing machines, sewing machines, vacuum cleaners, freezers, electric mixers, carving knives, shoe polishers.

By far the most popular new household product was the television set. In 1946 there were only 7,000 primitive black-and-white TV sets in the country; by 1960 there were 50 million high-quality sets. Nine out of ten homes had one, and by 1970, 38 percent owned one of the new color sets. *TV Guide* was the fastest-growing new periodical of the 1950s. In 1953 *Business Week* noted that city engineers across the country discovered erratic surges in water consumption during the evening hours, only to discover that Americans, it turned out, were using their bathrooms at the end of television shows and during commercials.

The ubiquitous ownership of television sets not only created a multibillion-dollar industry, it also helped transform the patterns of American social and cultural life. Watching television became an essential daily

I Love Lucy, *starring Lucille Ball* (right), *was one of the most popular television series in the 1950s.*

activity for millions of people. Time previously devoted to reading, visiting, playing, listening to the radio, or movie-going was now spent in front of the "electronic hearth." With the development of "TV dinners" and "TV trays," families no longer had to assemble around a common dinner table; they could eat in silence while watching favorite shows.

What differentiated the affluence of the post–World War II era from earlier periods of prosperity was its ever-widening dispersion. Although rural and urban poverty persisted in every state, and were destined to explode in the 1960s, few commentators noticed such exceptions to the prevailing affluence during the 1950s. Weekly visits to beauty parlors and shopping centers became routine activities for many working-class housewives, and families with two cars were not uncommon. Many boasted a boat or camper as well. When George Meany was sworn in as head of the AFL-CIO in 1955, he proclaimed that "American labor never had it so good."

On the surface many blacks were also beneficiaries of the wave of prosperity that swept over postwar American society. By 1950, African Americans were earning on average more than four times their 1940 wages. One black journalist declared in 1951 that "the progressive improvement of race relations and the economic rise of the Negro in the United States is a flattering example of democracy in action." But while gains had been made, blacks and other minority groups lagged behind whites in their rate of improvement. Indeed, the gap between the average yearly income of whites and blacks widened during the decade of the 1950s. Yet such trends were rarely noticed amid the boosterism of the day. The need to present a united front against communism led commentators to ignore or gloss over issues of racial and economic injustice. Such corrosive neglect would fester and explode during the 1960s, but for now the emphasis was on consensus, conformity, and economic growth.

To perpetuate the postwar prosperity, marketing specialists accelerated their efforts to promote rising expectations and self-gratification. Planned obsolescence became a guiding principle for many manufacturers. Advertising was an even more crucial component of the consumer culture, and during the postwar era advertisers proved adept at exciting consumer desires and social envy. An advertisement for Ford automobiles assured customers that "you'll bask in the envious glances which Ford's Thunderbird styling draws." It then added, "Why not own two?" TV advertising expenditures increased 1,000 percent during the

Mink Coat for Father. *An advertisement for a Ford Thunderbird claims that "What a mink coat does to perk up a lady, a Thunderbird does for a male."*

1950s. Such startling results led the president of the National Broadcasting Company (NBC) to claim in 1956 that the primary reason for the postwar prosperity was that "advertising has created an American frame of mind that makes people want more things, better things, and newer things."

Paying for such "things" was no problem; the age of the credit card had arrived. Between 1945 and 1957, consumer credit soared 800 percent. Where families in other industrialized nations were typically saving 10 to 20 percent of their income, American families by the 1960s were saving only 5 percent. "Never before have so many owed so much to so many," *Newsweek* announced in 1953. "Time has swept away the Puritan conception of immorality in debt and godliness in thrift."

This consumer revolution had far-reaching cultural effects. Shopping became a major recreational activity. In 1945 there were only 8 shopping centers in the entire country; by 1960 there were 3,840. Much as life in a medieval town revolved around the cathedral, life in postwar America seemed to center on the new giant shopping centers and indoor malls.

YOUTH CULTURE   Young people occupied a distinctive place in postwar American life. The children of the postwar baby boom were becoming adolescents during the 1950s, and in the process, a distinctive "teen" subculture began to emerge. Living amid such a prosperous era, teenagers had more money and free time than any previous generation.

Shopping became increasingly important for young Americans. The disproportionate number of adolescents in the population generated a vast new market for goods ranging from transistor radios, Hula-Hoops, and "rock 'n' roll" records to cameras, surfboards, *Seventeen* magazine, and Pat Boone movies. "Today," explained a corporate executive in 1957, "the teenager's income runs to $10 to $15 a week as opposed to $1 to $2 fifteen years ago. It is getting to the point where nearly every teenager has a radio or phonograph, and, in many cases, more than one." Teenagers in the postwar era knew nothing of economic depressions or wartime rationing; immersed in abundance from an early age, the children of prospering parents took the notion of carefree consumption for granted. As a fifteen-year-old Los Angeles girl described her use of a $65 monthly allowance, "I have to save $10, but the rest is mine to do what I want with. I spend about $40 on clothes and the rest on

Hula-Hoop Derby, Brookside Swim Club, New Jersey. *The Hula-Hoop craze was one of many fads of the youth culture.*

records and jewelry. All the teenagers are on that swing. We just find it neat to spend money."

Parents also tended to be more permissive. One commentator described the American family in 1957 as a "child-centered anarchy." To be sure, most young people during the 1950s embraced the values of their parents and the capitalist system. It was "the reassuring truth," reported *Collier's* magazine in 1951, "that the average young American is probably more conservative than you or your neighbor." One critic labeled the college students of the postwar era "the silent generation," content to cavort at fraternity parties and "sock hops" before landing a job with a large corporation, marrying, and settling down into the routine of middle-class suburban life.

Yet such general descriptions masked a great deal of turbulence. During the 1950s, a wave of juvenile delinquency swept across middle-class society. One sociologist went so far as to declare that "no social problem has wrought deeper concern in the United States." By 1956, over a million teens a year were being arrested. Car theft was the leading offense, but larceny, rape, beatings, even murder, were not uncommon. A Boston judge announced that the entire city was being "terrorized" by juvenile gangs.

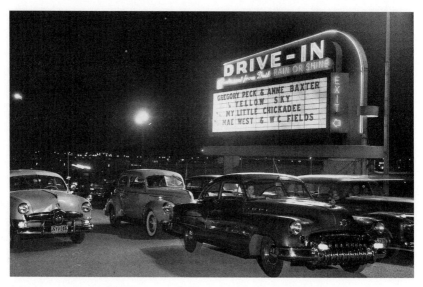

A Drive-in Movie, *1951. Accessibility to cars gave teenagers in the 1950s mobility and freedom from adult supervision—something that eluded previous generations of adolescents.*

What was causing such delinquency? J. Edgar Hoover, the head of the FBI, insisted that the root of the problem was a lack of religious training in more and more households. Others pointed to the growing number of urban slums. Such "bad" and "brutish" environments almost ensured that children would become criminals. The problem with such explanations was they failed to explain why so many middle-class kids from God-fearing families were becoming delinquents. One contributing factor may have been the unprecedented mobility of young people. Access to automobiles enabled teens to escape parental control, and in the words of a journalist, cars provided "a private lounge for drinking and for petting or sex episodes."

ROCK 'N' ROLL   Many concerned observers blamed the delinquency problem on a new form of music that emerged during the postwar era— rock 'n' roll. Indeed, when the film *The Blackboard Jungle* appeared in 1955, people drew a direct connection between the behavior of the film's juvenile gang members and the rock 'n' roll songs by Bill Haley and the Comets featured in the soundtrack. Rock music combined a strong beat with off-beat accents and repeated harmonic patterns to produce its distinctive sound, and the electric guitar provided the basic instrument. By the mid-1950s it had captured the imagination of young Americans. In 1955 *Life* magazine published a long article about a mysterious new "frenzied teenage music craze," that was creating "a big fuss."

Alan Freed, a Cleveland disc jockey, had coined the term "rock 'n' roll" in 1951. While visiting a record store, he had noticed an interesting new musical trend: white teenagers were buying rhythm and blues (R & B) records that had heretofore been purchased only by African Americans and Chicanos. Freed wanted to take advantage of the new trend, but he realized that few white households would listen to a radio program featuring what was then called "race music." So he began playing R & B records but labeled the music rock 'n' roll (a phrase used in black communities to refer to dancing and sex) to surmount the racial barrier.

Freed's radio program was an immediate success, and its popularity helped bridge the gap between "white" and "black" music. African-American singers such as Chuck Berry, Little Richard, and Ray Charles, and Chicano performers such as Ritchie Valens (Richard Valenzuela) suddenly were the rage among young, white middle-class audiences eager to claim their own cultural style and message. Berry, for example, was distinctive for his biting guitar riffs, inventive vocals, and athletic showmanship. He sang about dating and school life, about alienated teens riding around in cars "with no particular place to go." Valens, whose meteoric career was cut short by his death at age seventeen in a plane crash in 1959 (Buddy Holly was killed in the same accident), wrote a hit song entitled "Donna" about a failed romance with an Anglo classmate whose father ordered her to stop dating "that Mexican" boy. At the same time, Elvis Presley, a young white truck driver and aspiring singer born in Tupelo, Mississippi, and raised in Memphis, Tennessee, began experimenting with "rockabilly" music, his own unique blend of gospel, country-and-western, and R & B rhythms and lyrics.

In 1956 the twenty-one-year-old Presley released his smash hit "Heartbreak Hotel," and over the next two years the sensual baritone garnered fourteen gold records and emerged as the most popular musical entertainer in American history. Presley appeared on numerous television variety shows, starred in movies, and by the end of the decade had captured the attention of the world. His long hair and sideburns,

Elvis Presley, 1956. *The teenage children of middle-class America made rock 'n' roll a thriving industry in the 1950s and Elvis its first star.*

his knowing grins and disobedient sneers, his leather jacket and tight blue jeans—all shouted defiance against adult conventions. His sexually suggestive stage performances featuring twisting hips and a gyrating pelvis drove teenagers wild. Girls attending his performances went into a frenzy, often fainting or throwing themselves at Presley's feet.

Such hysterics prompted cultural conservatives to urge parents to confiscate and destroy Presley's records because they promoted "a pagan concept of life." A Catholic cardinal denounced Presley as a vile symptom of a new teen "creed of dishonesty, violence, lust and degeneration." Patriotic groups claimed that rock music was a tool of Communist insurgents designed to corrupt American youth. One anti-Communist book denounced rock 'n' roll disc jockeys as "Reds, left wingers, or hecklers of social convention." A Buffalo disc jockey was fired for playing Presley's records. And a congressional report concluded that "the gangster of tomorrow is the Elvis Presley type of today." But rock 'n' roll not only survived such assaults, it flourished as an exciting new musical idiom directed at young people experiencing the turbulence of puberty. It gave adolescents a self-conscious sense of being a unique social group with distinctive characteristics. And it represented an unprecedented intermingling of racial, ethnic, and class identities. As such, rock music would become one of the major vehicles of the youth revolt of the 1960s.

THE CRABGRASS FRONTIER The postwar era witnessed a mass migration to a new frontier—the suburbs. The burgeoning population created new communities and required an array of new services. Almost the entire population increase of the 1950s and 1960s (97 percent) was an urban or suburban phenomenon. Dramatic new technological advances in agricultural production reduced the need for manual laborers and thereby led 20 million Americans to leave the land for the city between 1940 and 1970.

Much of the urban population growth occurred in the South, the Southwest, and the West, in an arc that stretched from the Carolinas down through Texas and into California, diverse states that by the 1970s were being lumped together into the "Sunbelt." Air conditioning, developed by Willis Haviland Carrier in the first decade of the century, became a common household fixture in the 1950s and enhanced the appeal of warm climates. But the Northeast remained the most densely populated area; by the early 1960s, 20 percent of the national population lived in the corridor that stretched from Boston to Norfolk, Virginia.

While more concentrated in cities, post–World War II Americans were simultaneously spreading out within metropolitan areas. In 1950 the Census Bureau redefined the term "urban" to include suburbs as well as central cities. During the 1950s, suburbs grew six times faster than cities. By 1970, more Americans lived in suburbs (76 million) than in central cities (64 million). "Suburbia," proclaimed the *Christian Century* in 1955, "is now a dominant social group in American life." During the 1950s, some 3,000 acres of grassland and forests were bulldozed each day to make room for new suburban housing developments.

William Levitt, a brassy New York developer, led the suburban revolution. Levitt and his brother made a fortune during the depression by building houses. But the Levitts really struck it rich after the war, when the demand for new housing skyrocketed, and they developed an efficient system of mass production. In 1947, on 1,200 acres of Long Island farmland, they built 10,600 houses that were immediately sold and inhabited by more than 40,000 people—mostly young adults under thirty-five and their children. "Everyone is so young," one Levittowner

Levittown. *Identical and affordable housing was built in Levittown, Long Island, to provide homes for veterans and families in the suburbs.*

noted, "that sometimes it's hard to remember how to get along with older people."

Within a few years there were similar Levittowns in Pennsylvania and New Jersey, and other developers soon followed suit in places such as Lakewood, near Long Beach, California, and Park Forest, thirty miles south of Chicago. This suburban revolution benefited greatly from federal government assistance. "If it weren't for the government," one San Francisco developer explained, "the boom would end overnight." By insuring loans for up to 95 percent of the value of a house, the Federal Housing Administration made it easy for a builder to construct low-cost homes. Veterans got added benefits. A veteran could buy a Levitt house with no down payment and monthly mortgage installments of $56.

Expanded automobile production and highway construction also facilitated the rush to the suburbs, as more and more people were able to commute longer distances to work. Car production soared from 2 million in 1946 to 8 million in 1955, and a "car culture" soon transformed social behavior. As one commentator observed, the proliferation of automobiles "changed our dress, manners, social customs, vacation habits, the shape of our cities, consumer purchasing patterns, [and] common tastes." Widespread car ownership also necessitated an improved road network. Local and state governments built many new roads, but the guiding force was the federal government. In 1947 Congress authorized the construction of 37,000 miles of highways, and nine years later it funded over 42,000 additional miles in a new national system of inter-state expressways.

Cars and roads provided access to the suburbs, and Americans— mostly middle-class white Americans—rushed to take advantage of the new living spaces. The motives for moving to the suburbs were numer-ous. The availability of more spacious homes as well as greater security and better educational opportunities for children all played a role. Racial considerations were also a factor. After World War II, African Americans migrated to the cities of the North and Midwest. As they moved in, many white residents moved out. Those engaged in "white flight" were usually eager to maintain residential segregation in their new suburban communities. Contracts for houses in Levittown, Long Island, for example, specifically excluded "members of other than the Caucasian race." Such discrimination, whether explicit or implicit, was widespread; the nation's suburban population in 1970 was 95 percent white.

THE GREAT BLACK MIGRATION   World War II, like World War I, helped spur a mass migration of rural southern blacks to the urban North and Midwest. This second migratory stream was much larger in scope than the first, and its social consequences were much more dra-matic. After 1945 more than 5 million southern blacks, mostly farm folk, left their native region in search of better jobs, higher wages, decent housing, and greater social equality. During the 1950s, for example, the black population of Chicago more than doubled. As many as 3,000 mi-grants a week arrived at the Illinois Central train station. The South Side of Chicago soon became known as the capital of black America. It re-mains the largest concentration of African Americans in the country. In its scope and effects, this internal migration of blacks from South to North was as significant as the early settlement of the West.

Most of these southern blacks were sharecroppers and farm laborers from the Mississippi Delta, the richest cotton-producing land in the world. For over a century the Delta cotton culture had been dependent on black workers, first as slaves and then as sharecroppers and wage laborers. But a mechanical cotton picker invented in 1944 changed all that. The new machine could do the work of fifty people, thus making many farm workers superfluous. Displaced southern blacks, many of them illiterate and provincial, streamed northward in search of a new promised land, only to see many of their dreams dashed. The great writer Richard Wright, himself a migrant from the Delta to Chicago, observed that "never in history has a more utterly unprepared folk wanted to go to the city." In northern cities such as Chicago, Philadelphia, Newark, Detroit, New York, Boston, and Washington, D.C., rural blacks from the South confronted harsh new realities. Slumlords often gouged them for rent, many employers refused to hire them, and union bosses denied them membership. Soon the promised land had become for many an ugly nightmare of slum housing, joblessness, illiteracy, dysfunctional families, welfare dependency, street gangs, pervasive crime, and racism.

The unexpected tidal wave of black migrants severely taxed the resources of urban governments and the patience of white racists. For several nights during 1951, a white mob in a Chicago suburb assaulted a building into which a black family had moved. The National Guard had to quell the disturbance and disperse the crowd. Like other northern cities, Chicago sought to deal with the migrants and alleviate racial stress by constructing massive, all-black public housing projects to accommodate the newcomers. But these overcrowded racial enclaves were essentially segregated prisons. To be sure, many black migrants and their children did manage through extraordinary determination and ingenuity to "clear," that is, to climb out of the teeming ghettos and into the middle class. But most did not. As a consequence, the great black migration produced a web of complex social problems that in the 1960s would burgeon into a crisis.

A CONFORMING CULTURE

In the 1950s, American social commentators mostly ignored people and cultures outside the middle-class mainstream. As evidenced in many of the new look-alike suburbs sprouting up across the land, much of middle-class social life during the two decades after the end of World War II exhibited an increasingly homogenized character. Fears gener-

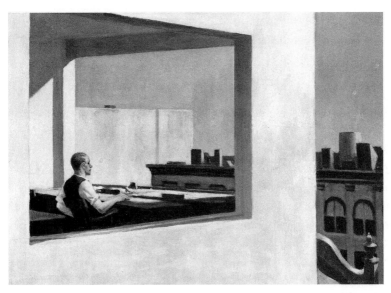

Office in a Small City. *Edward Hopper's 1953 painting suggests the alienation associated with white-collar work and a new corporate atmosphere in the 1950s.*

ated by the cold war initially played a key role in encouraging orthodoxy. But McCarthyism was simply the most visible symbol of the many political and social forces promoting common standards of behavior. Suburban life itself encouraged uniformity. In new communities of strangers, people felt a need for companionship and a sense of belonging. "Nobody wants people around who criticize and sit off by themselves and don't take part," observed one resident. Changes in corporate life as well as the influence of the consumer culture also played an important socializing role. "Conformity," predicted an editor in 1954, "may very well become the central social problem of this age."

CORPORATE LIFE The composition of the American workforce and the very nature of work itself were dramatically changing during the postwar era. More time became available for leisure, as the standard workweek shrank from five and a half days to five days. Fewer people were self-employed, and manual labor was rapidly giving way to mental labor. By the mid-1950s, white-collar (salaried) workers outnumbered blue-collar (hourly-wage) workers for the first time in American history.

Some 60 percent of the population enjoyed a "middle-class" standard of living (defined as annual family incomes of $3,000 to $10,000 in constant dollars). In 1929, before the stock market crash, only 31 percent were so designated. Managers, teachers, professors, researchers, salespeople, government employees, and office workers now constituted the bulk of the workforce, and they tended to work in larger and larger organizations.

This change happened because during World War II big business grew bigger. The government relaxed antitrust activity, and huge defense contracts tended to promote corporate concentration and consolidation. In 1940, for example, 100 companies were responsible for 30 percent of all manufacturing output; three years later, they were providing 70 percent. After the war, a wave of mergers occurred, and dominant corporate giants appeared in every major industry, providing the primary source of new jobs. By 1960, 38 percent of the workforce was employed by organizations with more than 500 employees. In such huge companies, as well as similarly large government agencies and universities, the working atmosphere began to take on a distinctive new cast. The traditional notion of the hardworking, strong-minded individual advancing by dint of competitive ability and creative initiative gave way to the concept of a new managerial personality and an ethic of corporate cooperation and achievement.

WOMEN'S PLACE Increasing conformity in the middle-class workplace was mirrored in the middle-class home. A special issue of *Life* magazine in 1956 featured the "ideal" middle-class woman, a thirty-two-year-old "pretty and popular" suburban housewife, mother of four, who had married at age sixteen. She was described as an excellent wife, mother, volunteer, and "home manager" who made her own clothes, hosted dozens of dinner parties each year, sang in the church choir, worked with the school PTA and Campfire Girls, and was devoted to her husband. "In her daily round," *Life* reported, "she attends club or charity meetings, drives the children to school, does the weekly grocery shopping, makes ceramics, and is planning to study French." She also exercised on a trampoline in order "to keep her size 12 figure."

Life's description of the middle-class woman was symptomatic of a cult of feminine domesticity that witnessed a dramatic revival in the postwar era. The soaring birthrate reinforced the deeply embedded no-

The Ideal Woman. *A 1956* Life *magazine cover story pronounced the ideal woman a "pretty and popular" suburban housewife who "attends club or charity meetings, drives the children to school, does the weekly grocery shopping, makes ceramics, and is planning to study French."*

tion that a woman's place was in the home as tender of the hearth and guardian of the children. "Of all the accomplishments of the American woman," the *Life* cover story proclaimed, "the one she brings off with the most spectacular success is having babies."

Even though millions of women had responded to wartime appeals and joined the traditionally male workforce, afterward they were encouraged—and even forced—to turn their jobs over to the returning male veterans and resume their full-time commitment to home and family. A 1945 article in *House Beautiful* lectured women on their postwar responsibilities. The returning veteran, it said, was "head man again. . . . Your part in the remaking of this man is to fit his home to him, understanding why he wants it this way, forgetting your own preferences." Women were also to forget wartime-generated thoughts of their own career in the workplace. "Back to the kitchen," was the repeated refrain. "Women must boldly announce," a Barnard College trustee asserted in 1950, "that no job is more exacting, more necessary, or more rewarding than that of housewife and mother." She then pleaded:

"God protect us all from the efficient, go-getter businesswoman whose feminine instincts have been completely sterilized."

Throughout the postwar era, educators, politicians, ministers, advertisers, and other commentators exalted the cult of domesticity and castigated the few feminists who were encouraging women to broaden their horizons beyond crib and kitchen. Two social psychologists, Marynia Farnham and Ferdinand Lundberg, published a best-selling book in 1947 entitled *Modern Woman: The Lost Sex,* in which they invoked the authority of science to reinforce the view that women could achieve fulfillment *only* by accepting their natural functions as wives and mothers. Such notions sound farfetched today, but they were widely embraced in the postwar era. Even such a liberal politician and self-styled progressive intellectual as Adlai Stevenson preached a similar doctrine. He reminded Smith College graduates in 1955 that their heroic purpose in life was to "influence man and boy" in the "humble role of housewife."

SEARCH FOR COMMUNITY   Another illustration of the conformist tendencies of middle-class life during the Eisenhower years was the growth of membership in social organizations. Americans were on the move after World War II. Not only were they moving from the central cities to the suburbs, they were moving from suburb to suburb, farm to city, state to state. Some 20 percent of the population changed their place of residence each year. In Levittown an average of 3,000 homes

Moving Day, 1953. *A new subdivision opens its doors.*

Sewing Club, Fort Hays, Kansas, 1950. *Club membership provided quick friends and a sense of community for those who frequently moved from place to place.*

per year turned over. A major cause of such mobility was the standard policy of the largest corporations to relocate their sales and managerial employees. IBM executives told friends that the company initials actually stood for "I've Been Moved." Such flux led people to search for a sense of community and rootedness. Hence middle-class Americans, even more than usual, tended to be joiners; they joined civic clubs, garden clubs, bridge clubs, carpools, and babysitting groups.

They also joined churches and synagogues in record numbers. "One comes early to get a seat in suburban churches," a writer observed in 1956; "they overflow, and new ones are being built every day." The postwar era witnessed a massive renewal of religious participation. "Since Communists are anti-God," FBI director J. Edgar Hoover urged, "encourage your child to be active in the church." Many American parents heeded his warning. In 1940 less than half the adult population belonged to churches; by 1960 over 65 percent were official communicants. Sales of Bibles soared during the postwar era, and books, movies, and songs with religious themes were pervasive.

President Eisenhower repeatedly promoted a patriotic crusade to bring Americans back to God. "Recognition of the Supreme Being," he declared, "is the first, the most basic, expression of Americanism. Without God, there could be no American form of government, nor an American way of life." The president had himself first joined a church only in 1953, but he characterized himself as the "most intensely religious man I know." Not to be outdone, Congress in 1954 added the phrase "one nation under God" to the Pledge of Allegiance, and the following year made the statement "In God We Trust" mandatory on all American currency.

Another reason for the increase in popular piety and church membership was that religious groups adopted the same marketing techniques successfully employed by American manufacturers. Billboards across the country urged viewers to "bring the whole family to church," and television commercials declared that the "family that prays together stays together." Catholic bishop Fulton J. Sheen's weekly television show, *Life Is Worth Living,* was a prime-time hit. At another point on the denominational spectrum, Baptist evangelical Billy Graham used both radio and television in promoting his huge crusades. Religious leaders even catered to the new car culture by performing services at drive-in movie theaters.

The prevailing tone of the popular religious revival during the 1950s was upbeat and soothing. Many ministers assumed that people were not interested in "fire-and-brimstone" harangues from the pulpit; they did not want their consciences overly burdened with a sense of personal sin or social guilt over such issues as racial segregation or inner-city poverty. Instead they wanted to be reassured that their own comfortable way of life was indeed God's will. As the Protestant Council of New York City explained to its corps of radio and television speakers, their addresses "should project love, joy, courage, hope, faith, trust in God, goodwill. Generally avoid condemnation, criticism, controversy. In a very real sense we are 'selling' religion, the good news of the Gospel."

By far the best salesman of this gospel of reassuring "good news" was the Reverend Norman Vincent Peale. Drawing on a long tradition of "positive thinking" in American social and religious thought, Peale perfected feel-good theology. No speaker was more in demand during the 1950s, and no writer was more widely read. Peale's book *The Power of Positive Thinking* (1952) was a phenomenal best-seller throughout the decade—and for good reason. It offered a simple "how-to" course in personal happiness. "Flush out all depressing, negative, and tired

Billy Graham Preaches to Thousands, *1955. Encouraged by the president and Congress, radio, television, and billboard advertising, droves of Americans joined churches and synagogues and attended revival meetings.*

thoughts," Peale advised. "Start thinking faith, enthusiasm, and joy." By following this simple formula for success, he pledged, the reader could become "a more popular, esteemed, and well-liked individual."

Peale's message of psychological security and material success was powerfully reassuring, and the psychological needs he addressed were indeed real. By 1957 tranquilizers were the fastest-growing new medication in the country, suggesting that considerable anxiety accompanied America's much-trumpeted affluence. Many people, living uneasily amid the moral and social dilemmas of the postwar period, were profoundly anxious about the meaning of life in general and their lives in particular. Peale offered them peace of mind and soul, assuring them that everything was fine and for the best as long as they believed in God, the American Way, and themselves.

NEO-ORTHODOXY "Stop worrying and start living" was Peale's simple credo. But was it too simplistic? The "peace of mind" and "positive thinking" psychology promoted by Peale and other feel-good ministers struck some members of the religious community as shallow and misleading. In *Protestant–Catholic–Jew* (1955), Will Herberg, professor of Judaic Studies at Drew University, described the popular spiritual revival as representing "religiousness without religion, a religiousness with almost any kind of content or none, a way of sociability or 'belonging,' rather than a way of reorienting life toward God." Such consoling religiosity, he felt, lacked genuine conviction and depth of commitment. Herberg and other theologians steadfastly resisted the dilution of traditional Judeo-Christian beliefs. These advocates of "neo-orthodoxy" especially criticized those who identified the United States as the only truly providential society and who used faith as a sanction for the social status quo.

The most significant spokesman for such "neo-orthodoxy" was Reinhold Niebuhr. A brilliant, penetrating, ironic, and erratic preacher-professor at New York's Union Theological Seminary, Niebuhr lambasted the "undue complacency and conformity" that had settled over American life in the postwar era. Like Herberg, he found the popular religion of self-assurance and psychology of material success woefully inadequate prescriptions for the ills of modern society. "They can not be taken seriously by responsible religious or secular people," he admonished in 1955, "because they do not come to terms with the basic collective problems of our atomic age, and because the peace which they seek to inculcate is rather too simple and neat." True peace, Niebuhr insisted, involves not the cheap comfort and sedating reassurance offered by Peale and other popular evangelists but the reality of pain, a pain "caused by love and responsibility" for the well-being of the entire human race, rather than concern only with one's tortured self. Self-love, he reminded smug Americans, was the very basis of sin.

CRACKS IN THE PICTURE WINDOW

Niebuhr was one of many impassioned disturbers of the peace who challenged the moral complacency and social conformity that he and others felt had come to characterize American social life during the 1950s and early 1960s. The widely publicized evidence of middle-class prosperity masked festering poverty in rural areas and urban ghettos. Moreover, one of the most striking aspects of postwar American life was the sharp contrast between the buoyant public mood and the increasingly bitter criticism of American life coming from intellectuals, theologians, novelists, playwrights, poets, and artists. As the philosopher and editor Joseph Wood Krutch recognized in 1960, "the gap between those who find the spirit of the age congenial and those who do not seems to have grown wider and wider."

THE LONELY CROWD   The criticism of postwar American life and values began in the early 1950s and quickly gathered momentum. Scores of books and articles swollen with mournful righteousness and unsettling truths decried virtually every area of the nation's social life. A common fear unified such fulminations: America in the age of Eisenhower was becalmed in a sea of conformity, content to succumb to the soul-denying demands of the corporate "rat race," and eager to wallow in the consumer culture. In *The Affluent Society* (1958), for example, the economist John Kenneth Galbraith attacked the prevailing notion that sustained economic growth would solve America's chronic social problems. The public sector was starved for funds, Galbraith argued, and public enterprises were everywhere deteriorating. He reminded readers that for all of America's vaunted postwar prosperity, the nation had yet to eradicate poverty.

Commuters on the 5:57, Park Forest, Illinois. *Postwar social critics commented on the overwhelming conformity of middle-class corporate and suburban life.*

Another frequent target of postwar cultural criticism was the supposed serenity of middle-class corporate and suburban life. John Keats, in *The Crack in the Picture Window* (1956), launched the most savage assault on life in the huge new suburban developments. He ridiculed Levittown and other such mass-produced communities as having been "conceived in error, nurtured in greed, corroding everything they touch." In these rows of "identical boxes spreading like gangrene," commuter fathers were always at work and "mothers were always delivering children, obstetrically once and by car forever after." Locked into a monotonous routine, hounded by financial insecurity, and engulfed by mass mediocrity, suburbanites, he concluded, were living in a "homogeneous, postwar Hell."

Mass-produced suburban developments did exhibit a startling sameness. Levittown, for example, encouraged and even enforced uniformity. The houses all sold for the same price—$7,990—and featured the same floor plan and accessories. Each had a picture window, a living room, bath, kitchen, and two bedrooms. Kitchens were equipped with a refrigerator, stove, and Bendix washer, and the living room featured a built-in Admiral television set. A tree was planted every twenty-eight feet. Homeowners were required to cut their grass once a week, fences were prohibited, and laundry could not be hung out on weekends. However, Levittown was in many ways distinctive rather than representative. There were thousands of suburbs by the mid-1950s, and few were as regimented or as unvarying as Keats and other critics implied. Keats also failed to recognize the benefits that the suburbs offered those who would have otherwise remained in crowded urban apartments.

Still, there was more than a grain of truth to the charge that postwar American life was becoming oppressively regimented, and the huge modern corporation was repeatedly cited by social critics as the primary villain. The most comprehensive and provocative analysis of the docile new corporate character was David Riesman's *The Lonely Crowd* (1950). Riesman and his research associates detected a fundamental shift in the dominant American personality from what they called the "inner-directed" to the "other-directed" type. Inner-directed people possessed a deeply internalized set of basic values implanted by strong-minded parents or other elders. This core set of fixed principles, analogous to the traditional Protestant ethic of piety, diligence, and thrift, acted, in Riesman's words, like an internal gyroscope. Once set in mo-

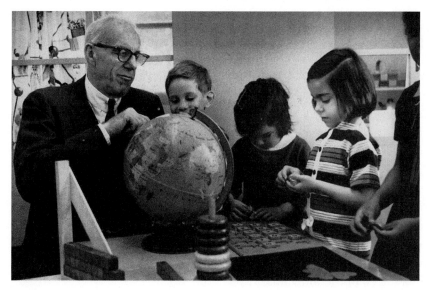

Dr. Benjamin Spock's The Common Sense Book of Baby and Child Care *was enormously influential with the parents of baby boomers.*

tion by parents and other authority figures, inner-directed people had a built-in stabilizer of fixed values that kept them on course.

Such an assured, self-reliant personality, Riesman argued, had been dominant in American life throughout the nineteenth century. But during the mid–twentieth century, an other-directed personality had displaced it. As the emphasis of industrial capitalism shifted from manipulating machines to manipulating workers, the new corporate culture demanded employees who could win friends and influence people rather than rugged individualists indifferent to personal popularity. Other-directed people were more concerned with being well liked than being independent. In the workplace they were always smiling, always glad-handing, always trying to please the boss.

Riesman amassed considerable evidence to show that the other-directed personality was not just an aspect of the business world; its premises were widely dispersed throughout middle-class life. Dr. Benjamin Spock's advice on raising children, Riesman pointed out, had become immensely influential. Spock's popular manual, *The Common Sense Book of Baby and Child Care,* sold an average of 1 million copies a year between its first appearance in 1946 and 1960. Spock said that parents should foster in their children qualities and skills that would enhance their chances in what Riesman called the "popularity market."

By the mid-1950s, social commentators were growing increasingly concerned that such a managerial personality had come to dominate American life. In his influential study, *White Collar Society* (1956), the sociologist C. Wright Mills attacked the attributes and influence of modern corporate life. "When white-collar people get jobs," Mills explained, "they sell not only their time and energy, but their personalities as well. They sell by the week or month their smiles and their kindly gestures, and they must practice the prompt repression of resentment and aggression." William A. Whyte, Jr., the editor of *Fortune,* presented a similar critique in his widely discussed book *The Organization Man* (1956). The new corporate culture, he charged, stressed "a belief in the group as the source of creativity; a belief in 'belongingness' as the ultimate need of the individual."

ALIENATION AND LIBERATION

THE STAGE Many of the best dramatic plays of the postwar period reinforced Riesman's image of modern American society as a "lonely crowd" of individuals without internal values, hollow at the core, groping for a sense of belonging and affection. Arthur Miller's play *Death of a Salesman* (1949), for example, was a powerful exploration of the theme. Willy Loman, an aging, confused salesman in decline, has centered his life and that of his family on the notion that material success is secured through personal popularity, only to be abruptly told by his boss that he is in fact a failure. Loman insists that it is "not what you say, it's how you say it—because personality always wins the day." He had tried to raise his sons, Biff and Happy, in his own image, encouraging them to be athletic, outgoing, popular, and ambitious. As he instructs them: "Be liked and you will never want." Happy followed his father's advice but was anything but happy: "Sometimes I sit in my apartment—all alone. And I think of the rent I'm paying. And it's crazy. But then, it's what I always wanted. My own apartment, a car, and plenty of women. And still, goddammit, I'm lonely." Such vacant loneliness is the play's recurring theme. Willy, for all his puffery about being well liked, admits in a fit of candor that he is "terribly lonely." He has no real

In Arthur Miller's Death of a Salesman, *Willy Loman (center, played by Lee J. Cobb) destroys his life and family with the credo "Be liked and you will never want."*

friends; even his relations with his family are neither honest nor intimate. "He never knew who he was," Biff sighs. When Willy finally realizes that he has been leading a counterfeit existence, he is so dumbfounded that he decides he can endow his life with meaning only by ending it.

Death of a Salesman and many other postwar plays written by Arthur Miller, Edward Albee, and Tennessee Williams portray a central concern of American literature and art during the postwar era: the sense of alienation experienced by sensitive individuals in the midst of an oppressive mass culture. As the novelist Philip Roth, author of *Goodbye Columbus* (1959), observed in 1961: "The American writer in the middle of the twentieth century has his hands full in trying to understand, and then describe, and then make credible much of American reality. It stupefies, it sickens, it infuriates, and finally it is even a kind of embarrassment to one's own meager imagination." Such a gloomy assessment illustrated the revulsion felt by other writers and artists, and many of them were determined to lay bare the conceits and illusions of their times.

THE NOVEL   The most enduring novels of the postwar period display a shared preoccupation with the individual's struggle for survival amid the smothering and disorienting forces of mass society. While the millions were reading heartwarming religious epics such as *The Cardinal*

(1950), *The Robe* (1953), and *Exodus* (1959), critics were praising the more disturbing writings of James Baldwin, Saul Bellow, John Cheever, Ralph Ellison, Joseph Heller, James Jones, Norman Mailer, Joyce Carol Oates, J. D. Salinger, William Styron, John Updike, and Eudora Welty. Their works had few happy endings—and even fewer celebrations of contemporary American life.

A brooding sense of resigned alienation animated the best literature in the two decades after 1945. J. D. Salinger's *The Catcher in the Rye* (1951) was an unsettling exploration of a young man's search for meaning and self in a stifling society. Holden Caulfield finally decides that rebellion against conformity is useless. "If you want to stay alive," he concludes, "you have to say that stuff like 'Glad to meet you' to people you are not at all glad to meet." The characters in novels such as Jones's *From Here to Eternity,* Ellison's *Invisible Man,* Bellow's *Dangling Man* and *Seize the Day,* Styron's *Lie Down in Darkness,* and Updike's *Rabbit, Run,* among many others, tended to be like Willy Loman—restless, tormented, and often socially impotent individuals who can find neither contentment nor respect in an overpowering or uninterested world.

In *From Here to Eternity* (1951) the hero, Private Prewitt, can neither "stomach nor understand nor explain nor change" the world around him. African-American writer Ralph Ellison also explored the theme of

Ralph Ellison, author of Invisible Man.

the lonely individual imprisoned in privacy in his kaleidoscopic novel *Invisible Man* (1952). By using a black narrator struggling to find and liberate himself in the midst of an oppressive white society, Ellison forcefully accentuated the problem of alienation. The narrator opens by confessing: "All my life I had been looking for something, and everywhere I turned someone tried to tell me what it was. I accepted their answers too, though they were often in contradiction and even self-contradictory. I was naive. I was looking for myself and asking everyone except myself questions which I, and only I, could answer."

PAINTING   The artist Edward Hopper also explored the theme of desolate loneliness in urban-industrial American life. His concern grew more acute in the postwar era. Virtually all of his paintings of the period depict isolated individuals, melancholy, anonymous, motionless. A woman undressing for bed, a diner seated at a table in an all-night restaurant, a housewife in a doorway, a businessman at his desk, a lone passerby in the street—these are the characters of Hopper's world. The silence of his scenes is deafening, the monotony striking, the alienation absorbing.

A younger group of painters in New York City decided that postwar society was so chaotic that it precluded any attempt at literal representation. As Jackson Pollock maintained, "the modern painter cannot express this age—the airplane, the atomic bomb, the radio—in the old form of the Renaissance or of any past culture. Each age finds its own technique." The technique Pollock adopted came to be called abstract expressionism, and during the late 1940s and 1950s it dominated not only the American art scene but the international field as well. In addition to Pollock, its adherents included Robert Motherwell, Willem de Kooning, Arshile Gorky, Franz Kline, Clyfford Still, and Mark Rothko. "Abstract art," Motherwell explained, "is an effort to close the void that modern men feel."

In practice this meant that the *act* of painting was as important as the final result. If artists could not bridge the gap between themselves and their contemporary society, they could find meaning through the spontaneous expression of their subjective selves. To do so they adopted a technique called "action painting." Pollock, for example, would place his huge canvases flat on the floor, then walk around each side, pouring and dripping his paints, all in an effort to "literally be *in* the painting." As an approving art critic recognized, a Pollock "canvas was not a pic-

Jackson Pollock at Work. *Pollock poured paint from a can and then dripped and splattered it across the canvas with a stick to create his "action paintings."*

ture but an event. . . . It is the artist's existence . . . he is living on the canvas." Such action paintings were vibrant, frenzied, meditative, disorienting, provocative. Needless to say, the general public found them simply provoking. As one wit observed: "I suspect any picture I think I could have made myself."

THE BEATS   In Saul Bellow's novel *Dangling Man* (1946), a character concludes that the dynamic of life is the "desire for pure freedom." The desire to liberate self-expression, to surmount organizational constraints and discard traditional conventions, was an abiding goal of the abstract expressionists. It was also the central concern of a small but highly visible and controversial group of young writers, poets, painters, and musicians known as the Beats. These angry young men—Jack Kerouac, Allen Ginsberg, Gary Snyder, William Burroughs, and Gregory Corso, among others—rebelled against the regimented horrors of war and the mundane horrors of middle-class life. *Time* called the Beats "a pack of oddballs who celebrate booze, dope, sex, and despair." The Beats, however, were not lost in despair; they strenuously embraced life. But it was life on their own terms, and those terms were shocking to most observers.

The Beats grew out of the bohemian underground in New York's Greenwich Village. They were all unique personalities. Kerouac was a handsome, athletic, working-class kid from Lowell, Massachusetts, who went to Columbia University on a football scholarship. In 1943 he quit school to join the navy. But he soon tired of military discipline, and one day he simply lay down his gun at drill and went to the library. He was arrested and confined in the psychiatric ward, and later was discharged for "indifferent character."

Ginsberg, a skinny New Jersey boy with horn-rimmed glasses, an unstable mother, and an intense love for poetry and ideas, had declared at age fourteen that "I'll be a genius of some kind or another, probably in literature. Either I'm a genius, I'm eccentric, or I'm slightly schizophrenic. Probably the first two." Probably all three, some thought. Ginsberg also studied at Columbia, where he became friends with Kerouac and where a dean directed him to undergo psychotherapy. Ginsberg chose Burroughs as his therapist.

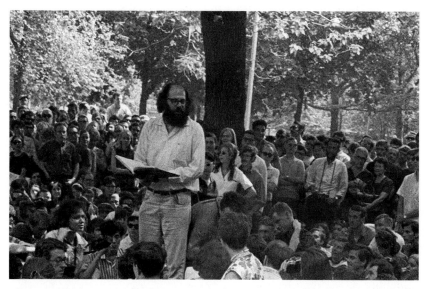

Allen Ginsberg, considered the poet laureate of the Beat generation, reading his uncensored poetry to a crowd in Washington Square Park in New York City.

It was an interesting choice, for Burroughs was the most eccentric of the trio. A graduate of Harvard in 1936, he had studied medicine in Vienna, then worked as an advertising copywriter, detective, bartender, and pest exterminator. He had also cut off one of his fingers during a "Van Gogh kick." Later he would become a heroin addict, kill his wife while trying to shoot an apple off her head, and write the influential experimental novel *Naked Lunch* (1959).

This fervent threesome soon added a fourth member: Neal Cassady, a twenty-year-old ex-convict who arrived in New York from Denver, hoping to enroll at Columbia. Cassady was pure physical and sensual energy. He could throw a football seventy yards and run a hundred yards in less than ten seconds. He claimed he had stolen over 500 cars and had had sex with almost as many people. Ginsberg, Kerouac, and Burroughs were enthralled by Cassady's frenzied sexuality and vital force. They viewed him as a mythic cowboy turned "cool" hipster, free and rootless because he defied both maturity and reason. Soon others joined this quartet in quest of *real* life, and the Beat culture was born. Ginsberg explained that the glue binding them together was their sense of estrangement from a hostile culture and their ability to confess to one another their innermost feelings.

In New York the self-described "Beats" began their quest for a visionary sensibility and spontaneous way of life. Essentially apolitical throughout the 1950s, they were more interested in transforming themselves than in reforming the world. They sought personal rather than social solutions to their anxieties. Kerouac defined the Beat generation as "basically a religious generation. Beat means beatitude, not beat up. You *feel* this. You feel it in a beat, in jazz—real cool jazz or a good gutty rock number." As Kerouac insisted, his friends were not beat in the sense of beaten; they were "mad to live, mad to talk, mad to be saved." Their road to salvation lay in hallucinogenic drugs and alcohol, sex, a penchant for jazz and the street life of urban ghettos, an affinity for Buddhism, and a restless, vagabond spirit that took them speeding back and forth across the country between San Francisco and New York during the 1950s.

This existential mania for intense experience and frantic motion provided the subject matter for the Beats' writings. Ginsberg's long prose-poem *Howl,* published in 1956, featured an explicit sensuality as well as an impressionistic attempt to catch the color, movement, and dynamism of modern life. Ginsberg howled at the "Robot apartments! invincible suburbs! skeleton treasuries! blind capitals! demonic industries!" Kerouac issued his autobiographical novel *On the Road* a year later. In frenzied prose and plotless ramblings, it portrayed the Beats' life of "bursting ecstasies" and maniacal traveling. At one point Dean Moriarty (Neal Cassady) has the following exchange with Sal Paradise (Kerouac): "We gotta go and never stop going till we get there." "Where we going, man?" "I don't know, but we gotta go."

Howl and *On the Road* provoked sarcasm and anger from many reviewers, but the books enjoyed a brisk sale, especially among young people. *On the Road* made the best-seller list, and soon the term "Beat generation" or "beatnik" referred to almost any young rebel who openly dissented from the comfortable ethos of middle-class life. Defiant, unruly actors such as James Dean and Marlon Brando were added to the pantheon of Beat "anti-heroes." In *The Wild One* (1954) a waitress asks Brando what he is rebelling against. He replies: "Whattaya got?" Acid-tongued comedians Mort Sahl and Lenny Bruce displayed affinities with the Beats, and a young folksinger from Minnesota named Bob Dylan was directly inspired by *Howl* and *On the Road*. In this sense, the anarchic gaiety of the Beats played an important role in preparing the way for the more widespread youth revolt of the 1960s.

A PARADOXICAL ERA

For all their color and vitality, the Beats had little impact on the larger patterns of postwar social and cultural life. Nor did most of the other critics who attacked the smug conformity and excessive materialism they saw pervading society. The tone of the nation's social life exuded a sense of tranquil fulfillment and bouncy optimism. By the mid-1960s, however, tensions between innovation and convention would erupt into open conflict. The children of the postwar boom times would become the leaders of the 1960s rebellion against the corporate and consumer cultures. Ironically, the person who would warn Americans of the 1960s about the mounting dangers of the burgeoning "military-industrial complex" was the president who had long symbolized its growth—Dwight D. Eisenhower.

MAKING CONNECTIONS

- The culture of the 1950s laid the groundwork for the counterculture of the 1960s. See Chapters 34 and 35.

- There are fruitful comparisons between American culture in the 1950s and the earlier postwar period, the 1920s. See Chapter 26.

- The women's movement of the 1970s, discussed in Chapter 35, was led by women who rejected the cult of domesticity described in this chapter.

- The baby boom of the postwar period would have continuing economic, social, political, and cultural significance as this generation moved through the life cycle. Follow along in coming chapters.

FURTHER READINGS

Two excellent overviews of social and cultural trends in the postwar era are William H. Chafe's *The Unfinished Journey: America Since World War II* (rev. ed., 1995) and William E. Leuchtenburg's *A Troubled Feast: America Since 1945* (rev. ed., 1983). For fascinating insights into the cultural life of the 1950s, see Douglas T. Miller and Marion Nowak's *The Fifties: The Way We Really Were* (1977), Jeffrey Hart's *When the Going Was Good: American Life in the Fifties* (1982), and David Halberstam's *The Fifties* (1993).

The baby-boom generation and its impact are vividly described in Paul C. Light's *Baby Boomers* (1988). Readers interested in economic trends should consult David P. Calleo's *The Imperious Economy* (1981). A comprehensive history of the advertising industry and its cultural implications can be found in Jackson Lears's *Fables of Abundance: A Cul-*

tural History of Advertising in America (1994). The emergence and impact of the television industry are discussed in Erik Barnouw's *Tube of Plenty: The Evolution of American Television* (1982) and Ella Taylor's *Prime-Time Families: Television Culture in Postwar America* (1989).

A comprehensive account of the process of suburban development is Kenneth Jackson's award-winning study *Crabgrass Frontier: The Suburbanization of the United States* (1985). Michael Danielson examines racial discrimination in the suburbs in *The Politics of Exclusion* (1976). For an analysis of the development of western cities in this century, see Carl Abbott's *The Metropolitan Frontier: Cities in the Modern American West* (1993).

The middle-class ideal of family life in the 1950s is examined in Elaine Tyler May's *Homeward Bound: American Families in the Cold War Era* (1988). Thorough accounts of women's issues in the twentieth century are found in William Chafe's *The American Woman: Her Changing Social, Economic, and Political Roles: 1920–1970* (rev. ed., 1988) and Wini Breines Young's *Young, White and Miserable: Growing Up Female in the 1950s* (1992).

For an overview of the resurgence of religion in the 1950s, see George Marsden's *Religion and American Culture* (1990). For treatments of the two leading religious leaders, see Carol V. R. George's *God's Salesman: Norman Vincent Peale and the Power of Positive Thinking* (1992) and William Martin's *A Prophet with Honor: The Billy Graham Story* (1992).

A lively discussion of movies of the 1950s can be found in Peter Biskind's *Seeing Is Believing: How Hollywood Taught Us to Stop Worrying and Love the Fifties* (1983). The origins and growth of rock 'n' roll music are surveyed in Carl Belz's *The Story of Rock* (1972). Thoughtful interpretive surveys of postwar American literature include Josephine Hendin's *Vulnerable People: A View of American Fiction Since 1945* (1978) and Malcolm Bradbury's *The Modern American Novel* (1984). The colorful Beats are brought to life in Steven Watson's *The Birth of the Beat Generation: Visionaries, Rebels, and Hipsters, 1944–1960* (rev. ed., 1998).

33. CONFLICT AND DEADLOCK: THE EISENHOWER YEARS

CHAPTER ORGANIZER

This chapter focuses on:

- Eisenhower's "dynamic conservatism."

- American foreign policy in the 1950s.

- the civil rights movement in the 1950s.

- the background to the Vietnam War.

The New Deal coalition established by Franklin Roosevelt and sustained by Harry Truman posed a formidable challenge to Republicans after World War II. To counter the unlikely but potent combination of "Solid South" white Democrats, blacks and ethnics, and organized labor, the Grand Old Party turned to General Dwight David Eisenhower, a military hero capable of attracting independent voters as well as tenuous Democrats. His commitment to a "moderate Republicanism" promised to slow the rate of federal government expansion while at the same time retaining many of the coveted social programs established by Roosevelt and Truman. His two terms as president are often characterized as representing a lull between two eras of Democratic activism. But Eisenhower wanted to restore the authority of state and local governments and restrain the executive branch from political and social "engineering." In the process, he sought to revivify traditional virtues and inspire people with a vision of a brighter future.

"TIME FOR A CHANGE"

By 1952 the Truman administration had piled up a heavy burden of political liabilities. Its bold stand in Korea had brought a bloody stalemate abroad, renewed wage and price controls at home, reckless charges of Communist subversion and disloyalty, and the exposure of corrupt lobbyists and influence peddlers who rigged favors in Washington. The disclosure of corruption led Truman to fire nearly 250 employees of the Bureau of Internal Revenue and, among others, an assistant attorney-general in charge of the Justice Department's Tax Division. But doubts lingered that Truman would ever finish the housecleaning.

EISENHOWER'S POLITICAL RISE It was, Republicans claimed, "time for a change." The Republican field quickly narrowed to two men, Ohio senator Robert A. Taft and General Dwight D. Eisenhower. Taft had become the foremost spokesman for domestic conservatism and for a foreign policy that his enemies branded as isolationist. His conservatism left room for federal aid to education and public housing, and his foreign policy, a "unilateralist" one, favored an active American role in opposing communism but opposed "entangling alliances" such as NATO. In Korea, he felt, the time had come to go all out for victory or to withdraw completely.

But Taft inspired little enthusiasm beyond the party regulars. He projected a lackluster image, and as a leader used to taking controversial stands, he had made enemies. The eastern, internationalist wing of the party turned instinctively to Eisenhower, then the NATO commander. As a war hero he had the glamour that Taft lacked, and his captivating, unpretentious manner inspired confidence. His leadership had been tested in the fires of war, but as a professional soldier he had escaped the scars of political combat. He stood, therefore, outside and above the crass arena of public life, although his political instincts and skills were sharpened during his successful army career.

In 1952 the general affirmed that he was a Republican and permitted his name to be entered in party primaries. He left his NATO post and joined the battle in person. An outpouring of public enthusiasm began to overwhelm Republican party regulars. Bumper stickers across the land announced simply, "I like Ike." Eisenhower won the nomination on the first ballot. He balanced the ticket with a youthful Californian, the thirty-nine-year-old Senator Richard M. Nixon, who had built a career on opposition to left-wing "subversives" and gained his greatest notoriety as the member of the House Un-American Activities Committee most eager in the pursuit of Alger Hiss.

THE 1952 ELECTION The Twenty-second Amendment, ratified in 1951, forbade any president to seek a third term. The amendment exempted the incumbent, but weary of the war in Korea, harassed by charges of subversion and corruption in government, his popularity declining, Truman chose to withdraw and threw his support to Governor Adlai E. Stevenson of Illinois, who aroused the Democratic delegates with an eloquent speech welcoming them to Chicago.

The campaign matched two of the most magnetic personalities ever pitted against each other in a presidential contest. Both men attracted new followings among people previously apathetic about politics, but the race was uneven from the start. Eisenhower, though a political novice, was a world hero who had been in the public eye for a decade.

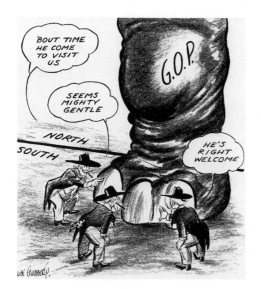

Good First Impression. *In the 1952 election the Republican party won significant support in the South for the first time.*

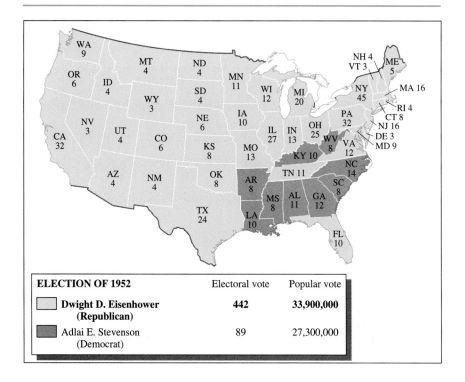

ELECTION OF 1952	Electoral vote	Popular vote
Dwight D. Eisenhower (Republican)	442	33,900,000
Adlai E. Stevenson (Democrat)	89	27,300,000

Stevenson, the politician, was hardly known outside of Illinois and was never able to escape the burden of Truman's liabilities. The genial general, who had led the crusade against Hitler, now opened a domestic crusade to clean up "the mess in Washington." To this he added a promise, late in the campaign, that as president-elect he would go to Korea to secure "an early and honorable" peace. Stevenson possessed a lofty eloquence spiced with a quick wit, but his resolve to "talk sense" and "tell the truth to the American people" came across as just a bit too aloof, a shade too intellectual. The Republicans labeled him an "egghead," an indecisive, latter-day Hamlet, in contrast to Eisenhower, the man of the people, the general of decisive action.

The war hero triumphed in a landslide of 33.9 million votes to Stevenson's 27.3 million, and 442 electoral votes to Stevenson's 89. The election marked a turning point in Republican fortunes in the South: for the first time since the 1850s the South was moving toward a two-party system. Stevenson carried only eight southern states plus West Virginia. Eisenhower picked up five states on the periphery of the Deep South: Florida, Oklahoma, Tennessee, Texas, and Virginia. In the former Confederacy the Republican ticket garnered 49 percent of the votes. The "nonpolitical" Eisenhower had made it respectable, even fashionable, to vote Republican in the South. Elsewhere, too, the former general made inroads in the New Deal coalition, attracting supporters among the ethnic and religious minorities in the major cities.

The voters, it turned out, liked Ike better than they liked his party. Democrats retained most of the governorships, lost control of the House by only eight votes, and broke even in the Senate, where only the vote of the vice-president ensured Republican control. The congressional elections two years later would weaken the Republican grip on Congress, and Eisenhower would have to work with a Democratic Congress until he left office.

Eisenhower's Hidden-Hand Presidency

IKE   Born in Denison, Texas, on October 14, 1890, Dwight David Eisenhower grew up in Abilene, Kansas. After finishing West Point, he spent nearly his entire adult life in the military service. After the attack on Pearl Harbor, General George C. Marshall made Brigadier-General Eisenhower his chief of operations. Later, as a major-general, Eisenhower took command of American forces in the European theater and directed the invasion of North Africa in 1942. Two years later he assumed the post of supreme commander of Allied forces in preparation for the invasion of the continent. After the war, by then a five-star general of the army, he became chief-of-staff and supreme commander of NATO forces, with a brief interlude as president of Columbia University.

Eisenhower's inauguration brought a change in style to the White House. The contrast in character between the feisty Truman and the genial Ike was reinforced by a contrast in philosophy and approach to the presidency. Eisenhower's military experience developed in him an instinct for methodical staff work. He met with the cabinet and the National Security Council nearly every week, and he relied heavily on them as consultative bodies.

Far from being a "do-nothing" president, as some have charged, Eisenhower was in fact an effective leader. The art of leadership, he once explained, did not require "hitting people over the head. Any damn fool can do that. . . . It's persuasion—and conciliation—and education—and patience. That's the only kind of leadership I know—or believe in—or will practice."

The public image of Ike was that of a man who rose above partisan politics. He was unpretentious, an ardent golfer, a common man with a winning smile who read little but Western novels, was uninformed about trends in intellectual and artistic life, and was prone to giving folksy advice: "Everybody ought to be happy every day. Play hard, have fun doing it, and despise wickedness." A diplomat labeled him "the nation's number one Boy Scout." But those who were closer to Ike have presented another side to the man. When provoked, he could release a fiery temper and scalding profanity. While Ike talked with genuine feeling about such traditional virtues as duty, honesty, and thrift, he was not above a calculated dissimulation. One student of Eisenhower's techniques has spoken of a "hidden-hand presidency" in which Ike deliberately cultivated a public image of passivity to hide his active involvement in policy decisions.

"DYNAMIC CONSERVATISM" AT HOME   Like Ulysses Grant, Eisenhower betrayed a weakness for hobnobbing with rich men. His cabinet, a columnist in the *New Republic* quipped, consisted of "eight millionaires and a plumber." The plumber, Secretary of Labor Martin Durkin, resigned after eight months, charging that the administration had reneged on a promise to change the Taft-Hartley Act. The president of General Motors became secretary of defense, and two auto distributors became secretary of the interior and postmaster-general, respectively. The New Dealers, Adlai Stevenson wryly remarked, "have all left Washington to make way for the car dealers."

Unaccustomed to the glare of Washington publicity, several cabinet members succumbed to foot-in-mouth disease. It was perhaps innocent enough for the former GM president to say at his confirmation hearings, "I thought what was good for our country was good for General Motors, and vice versa," except that it was readily translated into: "What is good for General Motors is good for the country." The interior secretary put it more baldly: "We're here in the saddle as an Administration representing business and industry."

Eisenhower called his domestic program "dynamic conservatism," which meant being "conservative when it comes to money and liberal when it comes to human beings." In response, Adlai Stevenson conjectured: "I assume what it means is that you will strongly recommend the building of a great many schools to accommodate the needs of our children, but not provide the money." Budget cutting was a high priority for the new administration, which set out to slash both domestic programs and national defense spending. Eisenhower warned repeatedly against the dangers of "creeping socialism," "huge bureaucracies," and budget deficits.

Eisenhower abolished the Reconstruction Finance Corporation, ended wage and price controls, and reduced farm price subsidies. He also moved the government away from the Roosevelt-Truman commitment to public electric power. In fact, had Ike had his way the government would have sold the Tennessee Valley Authority.

In 1954 the administration formulated tax reductions that resembled Republican programs of the 1920s in providing benefits mainly to corporations and individuals in the upper brackets. The new budget slashed expenditures by $6.5 billion, nearly 10 percent, and the Federal Reserve Board reinforced administration policy by tightening credit and raising interest rates to avert inflation. But a business slump followed, which reduced government revenues, making it harder to balance the budget. After that experience, Eisenhower's fiscal and monetary policies became less doctrinaire and more flexible. The government accepted easier credit and deficits as necessary "countercyclical" methods. The Keynesian Age, if not yet acknowledged, endured.

Although Eisenhower chipped away at several New Deal programs, his presidency in the end served rather to legitimate the New Deal by keeping its basic structure and premises intact during an era of prosperity. In a letter to his brother in 1954, Eisenhower observed: "Should any political party attempt to abolish Social Security and eliminate labor laws and farm programs, you would not hear of that party again in our political history." In some ways, the administration not only maintained the New Deal but extended its reach, especially after 1954 when it had the help of Democratic Congresses. Amendments to the Social Security Act in 1954 and 1956 brought coverage to millions in categories formerly excluded: professional people, domestic and clerical workers, farm workers, and members of the armed forces. In 1959 the program's benefits went up 7 percent. The federal minimum wage rose in 1955 from 75¢ to $1 an hour. Federal expenditures for public health rose steadily in the Eisenhower years, and the president went so far as to endorse federal participation in health insurance, but Congress twice refused to act. Low-income housing continued to be built with federal funds, although on a much reduced scale.

Some farm-related aid programs were expanded during the Eisenhower years. The Rural Electrification Administration would announce on its twenty-fifth birthday in 1960 that 97 percent of American farms had electricity. In 1954 the government undertook on a large scale to finance the export of surplus farm products in exchange for foreign currencies. Surpluses were also exported as gifts to needy nations and to provide milk for schoolchildren. In 1959 surpluses became available to Americans by issuing food stamps redeemable at grocery stores.

Despite Eisenhower's general disapproval of public power programs, he continued to support public works for which he saw a legitimate need. Indeed, two such programs left major monuments to his presidency: the St. Lawrence Seaway and the interstate highways. The plan for the St. Lawrence Seaway, designed to open the Great Lakes to oceangoing ships by means of locks and dredging, had languished in Congress since the time of President Hoover because of opposition by eastern business and railroad interests afraid of the competition. In 1954 Eisenhower finally broke the opposition, citing Canadian determination to go ahead anyway and the growing need of American steel producers for Canadian ore as domestic deposits gave out. Congress then approved joint participation with the Canadians, and five years later the seaway opened. In 1956 a new federal highway construction act authorized the federal government to put up 90 percent of the cost of building 42,500 miles of limited-access interstate highways to serve the needs of commerce and defense, as well as private convenience. The states put up the remaining 10 percent. It was only afterward that people realized that the huge national commitment to the automobile might have come at the expense of America's railroad system, already in a state of advanced decay.

CONCLUDING AN ARMISTICE America's new global responsibilities in the postwar world, however, continued to absorb Eisenhower's attention. The most pressing problem when he entered office was the continuing, painful deadlock in the Korean peace talks. Many prisoners from North Korea wished to remain in South Korea. United Nations negotiators refused to agree to return prisoners of war who did not want to go back to the North. North Korean and Red Chinese negotiators insisted that all prisoners be returned regardless of their wishes. To break the deadlock, Eisenhower resolved upon a bold stand. In mid-May 1953 he stepped up aerial bombardment of North Korea, then had Secretary of State John Foster Dulles make a secret threat to Peking to remove all limits on weapons and targets. It was a thinly veiled warning of atomic warfare. Whether for that reason or others, negotiations then moved quickly toward an armistice along the established border just above the 38th parallel, and toward a complicated arrangement for prisoner exchange that allowed captives to accept or refuse repatriation.

On July 26, 1953, President Eisenhower announced the end of fighting in Korea. Whether Eisenhower had pulled a masterful bluff in getting the armistice has never become clear; no one knows if he would have used atomic weapons. Perhaps the more decisive factors in bringing about a settlement were rising Chinese Communist losses, which they increasingly found unacceptable, and the new spirit of uncertainty and caution felt by Russian Communists after the death of Joseph Stalin on March 5, 1953—six weeks after Ike's inauguration.

CONCLUDING A WITCH-HUNT   The Korean armistice helped to end another dismal episode: the meteoric career of Senator Joseph R. McCarthy, which had flourished amid the anxieties of wartime. Convinced that the government was infested with Communists and spies, the Wisconsin senator launched a one-man crusade to root them out. In the process, he and his aides lied, falsified evidence, and bullied or blackmailed witnesses. During the summer of 1953, he sent two assistants on a junket to Europe to purge American government libraries of "subversive works" such as the writings of Ralph Waldo Emerson and Henry David Thoreau, Theodore Dreiser and John Steinbeck. Eventually McCarthy's unscrupulous tactics led to his self-destruction, but not before he had left still more careers and reputations in ruins. The Republicans thought their victory in 1952 would curb his recklessness, but McCarthy actually grew more outlandish in his charges and his investigative methods. And many Americans caught up in the anti-Communist hysteria viewed him as a heroic knight doing battle against the forces of darkness.

McCarthy finally overreached himself when he made the absurd charge that the United States Army itself was "soft" on communism. From April 22 to June 17, 1954, the Army-McCarthy hearings displayed McCarthy to a large television audience at his capricious worst,

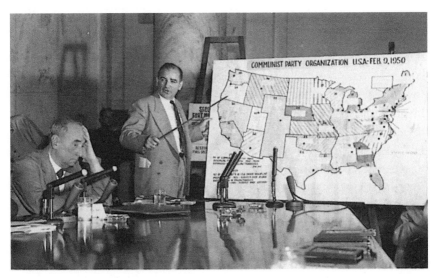

The Army-McCarthy Hearings, June 1954. *Joseph Welch* (hand on head) *listens incredulously after McCarthy's attempt to smear one of Welch's associates.*

bullying witnesses, dragging out lengthy irrelevancies, repeatedly calling "point of order." He became the perfect foil for the army's gentle but unflappable counsel, Joseph Welch of Boston, whose rapier wit repeatedly drew blood. When a witness used the word "pixie," McCarthy demanded a definition and Welch sweetly explained that a pixie was "a kind of fairy." But when McCarthy tried to smear one of Welch's young associates, the counsel went into a cold rage: "Until this moment, Senator, I think I never really gauged your cruelty or your recklessness. . . . Have you no sense of decency, sir, at long last?" When the audience burst into applause, the confused, skulking senator was reduced to whispering, "What did I do?"

McCarthy descended into new depths of scurrility, now directed at his own colleagues, calling one senator "senile" and another "a living miracle . . . the only man who has lived so long with neither brains nor guts." On December 2, 1954, the Senate voted 67 to 22 to "condemn" McCarthy for contempt of the Senate. McCarthy was finished, and increasingly took to alcohol. Three years later, at the age of forty-eight, he was dead.

McCarthyism, Ike joked, had become McCarthywasm, though not for those whose reputations and careers had been wrecked. To the end, Eisenhower kept his resolve not to "get down in the gutter with that guy" and sully the dignity of the presidency, but he did work resolutely against McCarthy behind the scenes. Eisenhower shared, nevertheless, the deeply held conviction of many citizens that espionage posed a real danger to national security. He denied clemency to Julius and Ethel Rosenberg, convicted of transmitting atomic secrets to the Russians, on the grounds that they "may have condemned to death tens of millions of innocent people." The Rosenbergs went to the electric chair on June 19, 1953.

INTERNAL SECURITY   The anti-Communist crusade survived the downfall of McCarthy. Eisenhower stiffened the government security program that Truman had set up six years before. In 1953 an executive order broadened the basis for firing government workers by replacing Truman's criterion of "disloyalty" with the new category of "security risk." Under the new edict, federal workers could lose their jobs because of dubious associations or personal habits that might make them careless or vulnerable to blackmail. In 1953 the Atomic Energy Commission removed the security clearance of the physicist J. Robert Oppenheimer, the "father of the atomic bomb," on the grounds that he had expressed qualms about the hydrogen bomb in 1949–1950 and had associated with Communists or former Communists in the past. Lacking evidence of any disloyalty or betrayal, the AEC nevertheless branded him a "security risk" because of "fundamental defects in his character."

The Supreme Court, however, modified some of the more extreme expressions of the Red Scare. In 1953 Eisenhower appointed former governor Earl Warren of California as chief justice, a decision the president later pronounced the "biggest damnfool mistake I ever made." Warren, who had seemed safely conservative while active in politics, proved to have a social conscience and a streak of libertarianism that another Eisenhower appointee, William J. Brennan, Jr., shared. The Warren Court (1953–1969), under the chief justice's influence, became an important agency of social and political change on through the 1960s.

In connection with security programs and loyalty requirements, the Court veered back in the direction of traditional individual rights. A 1957 opinion narrowly construed the Smith Act of 1940, aimed at conspirators against the government, to apply only to those advocating "revolutionary" action. Merely teaching revolutionary doctrine in the abstract could not be construed as a crime under the act. This, plus other decisions setting rigid standards for evidence, rendered the Smith Act a dead letter.

FOREIGN INTERVENTION

DULLES AND FOREIGN POLICY   The Eisenhower administration promised new departures in foreign policy under the direction of Secretary of State John Foster Dulles. Grandson of one former secretary of state and nephew of another, Dulles had pursued a lifetime career as an international lawyer and sometime diplomat. In 1919 he had assisted the American delegates at the Versailles Conference. As counselor to the Truman State Department he had, among other things, negotiated the Japanese peace treaty. Son of a minister and himself an active Presbyterian layman, Dulles, in the words of the British ambassador, resembled those old zealots of the wars of religion who "saw the world as an arena in which the forces of good and evil were continuously at war." Tall, spare, and stooped, he gave the appearance of dour sternness and Calvinist righteousness. But he was also a man of immense energy, intelligence, and experience. As Eisenhower once said of Dulles, "There's only one man I know who has seen *more* of the world, and talked with more people and *knows* more than he does—and that's me."

The foreign policy planks of the 1952 Republican platform, which Dulles wrote, showed both the moralist and the tactician at work. The

Secretary of State John Foster Dulles.

Democratic policy of containment was needlessly defensive, Dulles thought. Containment implied contentment with the status quo. He saw no need for the United States to accept the Soviet presence in eastern Europe. Americans should instead work toward the "liberation" of eastern Europe from Soviet domination. The 1952 Republican platform promised to end "the negative, futile and immoral policy of 'containment' which abandons countless human beings to a despotism and godless terrorism." A new policy of liberation, the platform promised, "will inevitably set up strains and stresses within the captive world which will make the rulers impotent to continue in their monstrous ways and mark the beginning of the end."

The policy came perilously close to proclaiming a holy war, but Dulles took care to explain that he did not intend forcible liberation of Communist-bloc countries. Soon it became apparent that it was less a policy than a web of rhetoric to catch ethnic voters whose homelands had fallen captive to Soviet control. That Dulles's liberation rhetoric rang false became more evident in 1953 when workers in East Germany rebelled against working conditions and food shortages. When Russian tanks rolled over the demonstrators, the administration did nothing except to deplore the situation. For three years more Dulles maintained that his rhetoric was undermining the Communist hold on eastern Europe—until suppression of the 1956 uprising in Hungary underscored the danger of stirring futile hopes among captive peoples.

COVERT ACTIONS Insofar as American interventions occurred abroad, they were covert operations by the Central Intelligence Agency (CIA) in countries outside the Soviet sphere. Under Eisenhower, Allen Dulles, brother of the secretary of state, rose from second in command to chief of the CIA. A veteran of the wartime Office of Strategic Services, he enhanced the CIA's capacity for cloak-and-dagger operations. In two cases early in the Eisenhower years, the CIA actually helped overthrow governments believed hostile to American interests: in Iran (1953) and in Guatemala (1954).

In Iran, Premier Mohammed Mossadegh, a seventy-year-old nationalist, whipped up popular feeling against British control of Iranian oil production and then took over the foreign properties. In challenging Western interests, he had the support of the Tudeh, Iran's Communist party, and left the impression that he either had joined their side or would become their dupe. Under these circumstances, Allen Dulles sent a crack CIA agent along with an adviser to help the shah of Iran organize his secret police. Armed chiefly with about a million dollars, they stirred up street demonstrations against Mossadegh that, reinforced by soldiers loyal to the shah, toppled the premier, sent him to jail, and brought the young shah back from exile in Rome.

In Guatemala, Jacobo Arbenz Guzman had become president in an election in which he had Communist backing. While the administration lacked evidence that Arbenz was a Communist, the American ambassador said "he talked like a Communist, he thought like a Communist, and he acted like a Communist, and if he is not one, he will do until one comes along." Critics of the intervention contended that Arbenz's chief sin was that he had expropriated 225,000 acres of United Fruit Company land. With Eisenhower's consent, the CIA chose a Guatemalan colonel to stage a coup from a base in Honduras.

BRINKSMANSHIP   For all his bold talk of liberation, Dulles made no significant departure from the strategy of containment created under Acheson and Truman. Instead he institutionalized containment in the rigid mold of his cold war rhetoric and extended it into the military strategy of deterrence. He betrayed a fatal affinity for colorful phrases that left him, according to one observer, "perpetually poised between a cliché and an indiscretion." To his lexicon of "liberation" and "roll back," Dulles added two major new contributions while in office: "massive retaliation" and "going to the brink."

"Massive retaliation" was actually a shorthand version of Dulles's phrase "massive retaliatory power," an effort to get, in the slogan soon current, "more bang for the buck" or "more rubble for the ruble." Budgetary considerations lay at the root of military plans, for Eisenhower and his cabinet feared that in the effort to build a superior war power the country could spend itself into bankruptcy. During 1953 members of the Joint Chiefs of Staff began planning a new military posture. The heart of their so-called New Look was the assumption that nuclear weapons could be used in limited-war situations, allowing reductions in conventional forces and thus budgetary savings. Dulles, who announced the policy in early 1954, explained that savings would come "by placing more reliance on deterrent power, and less dependence on local defensive power." No longer could an enemy "pick his time and place and method of warfare." American responses would be "by means and at places of our choosing." No longer would "the Communists nib-

"Don't Be Afraid—I Can Always Pull You Back." *Secretary of State Dulles pushes a reluctant America to the brink of war.*

ble us to death all over the world in little wars," Vice-President Nixon explained.

By this time both the United States and the Soviet Union had exploded hydrogen bombs. With the new policy of deterrence, what Winston Churchill called a "balance of terror" had replaced the old "balance of power." The threat of nuclear holocaust was terrifying, but the notion that the United States would risk such a disaster in response to local wars had little credibility.

Dulles's policy of "brinksmanship" depended for its strategic effect on those very fears of nuclear disaster. Dulles argued in 1956 that in following a tough policy of confrontation with communism, a nation sometimes had to "go to the brink" of war. Such a firm stand had halted further aggression in Korea in 1953 when America threatened to break the stalemate by removing restraints from the armed forces. Dulles had also employed brinksmanship in 1954 in Indochina when the United States sent aircraft carriers into the South China Sea "both to deter any Red Chinese attack against Indochina and to provide weapons for instant retaliation."

INDOCHINA: THE BACKGROUND TO WAR   Dulles's use of brinksmanship in Indochina neglected the complexity of the situation there, which presented a special if not unique case of the nationalism that swept the old colonial world of Asia and Africa after World War II, damaging both the power and prestige of the colonial powers. By the early

1950s, most of British Asia was independent or on the way: India, Pakistan, Ceylon (later Sri Lanka), Burma (later Myanmar), and the Malay States (later the Federation of Malaysia). The Dutch and French, however, were less ready than the British to give up their colonies, which created a dilemma for American policy makers. Americans sympathized with colonial nationalists who sometimes invoked the example of 1776, but Americans also wanted Dutch and French help against communism. The Truman administration felt obliged to answer their pleas for aid. Both the Dutch and the French had to reconquer areas that had passed from Japanese occupation into the hands of local patriots.

In the Dutch East Indies the Japanese had created a puppet Indonesian Republic, which emerged from World War II virtually independent. The Dutch effort to regain control met resistance that exploded into open warfare. Eventually, American pressure persuaded the Dutch to accept self-government under a Dutch-Indonesian Union in 1949, but that lasted only until 1954, when the Republic of Indonesia became independent. In 1955 the Bandung Conference in Indonesia, attended by delegates from twenty-nine independent countries of Asia and Africa, signaled the emergence of a "Third World" of underdeveloped countries, unaligned with either the United States or the Soviet bloc. Among other actions, the conference denounced "colonialism in all its manifestations," a statement that implicitly condemned both the Soviet Union and the West.

French Indochina, created in the nineteenth century out of the old kingdoms of Cambodia, Laos, and Vietnam, offered a variation on Third World nationalism. During World War II, when the Japanese controlled the area, they had supported pro-Vichy French civil servants and had opposed the local nationalists. Chief among the latter were members of the Viet Minh (Vietnamese League for Independence), which fell under the influence of Communists led by Ho Chi Minh. At the end of the war, this group controlled part of northern Vietnam, and on September 2, 1945, Ho Chi Minh proclaimed a Democratic Republic of Vietnam, with its capital in Hanoi.

Ho's declaration of Vietnamese independence borrowed from Thomas Jefferson, opening with the words "We hold these truths to be self-evident. That all men are created equal." American officers were on the reviewing stand in Hanoi and American planes flew over the celebration. Ho had received secret American help against the Japanese during the war, but bids for further aid after the war went unanswered. Viet-

Ho Chi Minh.

nam took low priority in American diplomatic concerns at the time, and Truman could not stomach aiding a professed Communist.

In 1946 the French government, preoccupied with domestic politics, recognized Ho's new government as a "free state" within the French union. Before the year was out, however, Ho's forces challenged French efforts to establish another regime in the southern provinces, and this clash soon expanded into the First Indochina War. In 1949, having set up puppet rulers in Laos and Cambodia, the French reinstated former emperor Bao Dai as head of state in Vietnam. The victory of the Chinese Communists later in 1949 was followed by Red China's diplomatic recognition of the Viet Minh government in Hanoi, and then the recognition of Bao Dai by the United States and Britain.

The Viet Minh movement thereafter became more completely dominated by Ho Chi Minh and his Communist associates, and more dependent on the Soviet Union and Red China for help. In 1950, with the outbreak of fighting in Korea, the struggle in Vietnam became a battleground in the cold war. When the Korean War ended, American aid to the French in Vietnam, begun by the Truman administration, continued. By the end of 1953, the Eisenhower administration was paying about two-thirds of the cost of the French effort, or about $1 billion annually. By 1954 the United States found itself at the edge of the "brink" to which Dulles later referred. A major French force had been sent to Dien Bien Phu, near the Laos border, in the hope of luring Viet Minh guerrillas into a set battle and grinding them up with superior firepower. The French instead found themselves trapped by a Viet Minh force that threatened to overrun their stronghold.

In March 1954 the French government requested an American air strike to relieve the pressure on Dien Bien Phu. As noted earlier, Dulles had U.S. aircraft carriers move into the South China Sea in anticipation of such an air strike. Eisenhower himself seemed to endorse forceful action, but when congressional leaders expressed reservations, he opposed American intervention unless the British lent support. When they refused, he backed away from unilateral action in Vietnam.

On May 7, 1954, the massive attacks loosed by Viet Minh general Vo Nguyen Giap finally overwhelmed the last French resistance at Dien Bien Phu. It was the very eve of the day that an international conference at Geneva took up the question of Indochina. Six weeks later, as French forces continued to suffer defeats in Vietnam, a new French government promised to get an early settlement. On July 20 representatives of France, Britain, the Soviet Union, the People's Republic of China, and the Viet Minh reached agreement on the Geneva Accords. They proposed to neutralize Laos and Cambodia and divided Vietnam at the 17th parallel. The Viet Minh would take power in the north, and the French would remain south of the line until elections in 1956 would reunify Vietnam. American and South Vietnamese representatives refused to join in the accord. This led the Soviet Union and China to back away from their earlier hints that they would guarantee the settlement.

Dulles responded to the growing Communist influence in Vietnam by organizing mutual defense arrangements for Southeast Asia. On September 8, 1954, at a meeting in Manila, the United States joined seven other countries in the Southeast Asia Treaty Organization (SEATO). The impression that it paralleled NATO was false, for SEATO was neither a common defense organization like NATO nor was it primarily Asian. The signers agreed that in case of attack on one, the others would act according to their "constitutional practices," and in case of threats or subversion they would "consult immediately." The members included only three Asian countries—the Philippines, Thailand, and Pakistan—together with Britain, France, Australia, New Zealand, and the United States. India and Indonesia, the two most populous countries in the region, refused to join. A special protocol added to the treaty extended coverage to Indochina. The treaty reflected what

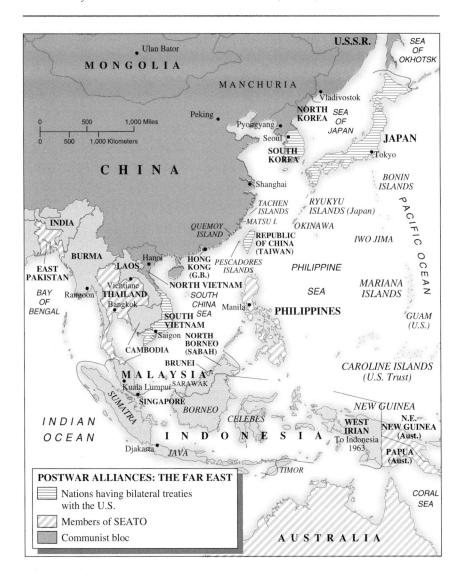

Dulles's critics called "pactomania," which by the end of the Eisenhower administration contracted the United States to defend forty-three other countries.

Eisenhower announced that though the United States "had not itself been party to or bound by the decision taken at the [Geneva] Conference," any renewal of Communist aggression "would be viewed by us as a matter of grave concern." (He failed to note that the United States had agreed at Geneva to "refrain from the threat or use of force to disturb" the agreements.) In Vietnam, when Ho Chi Minh took over the north, those who wished to leave for South Vietnam, mostly Catholics, did so with American aid. Power in the south gravitated to a new premier imposed on Emperor Bao Dai by the French at American urging: Ngo Dinh Diem, who had opposed both the French and the Viet Minh. Diem took office during the Geneva talks. Before that he had been in exile at a Catholic seminary in New Jersey. In 1954 Eisenhower offered to assist Diem "in developing and maintaining a strong, viable state, capable of resisting attempted subversion or aggression through military means." In return, the United States expected "needed reforms." American aid took the form of CIA and military cadres charged with training Diem's armed forces and police.

Instead of instituting political and economic reforms, however, Diem tightened his grip on the country, suppressing opposition on both right and left, offering little or no land distribution, and permitting widespread corruption. In 1956 he refused to join in the elections to reunify Vietnam. After French withdrawal from the country, he ousted Bao Dai and installed himself as president. His efforts to eliminate all opposition played into the hands of the Communists, who found recruits and fellow travelers among the discontented. By 1957 guerrilla forces known as the Viet Cong had begun attacks on the Diem government, and in 1960 the resistance coalesced as the National Liberation Front. As guerrilla warfare gradually disrupted South Vietnam, the Eisenhower administration was helpless to do anything but "sink or swim with Ngo Dinh Diem."

PROTECTING TAIWAN   Just before the Manila Conference in 1954, Red Chinese artillery began shelling the South China Sea islands of Quemoy and Matsu, held by Chiang Kai-shek's Nationalists. On his way back from Manila, Dulles stopped in Taipei and worked out a mutual defense treaty that bound the United States to defend Taiwan and the nearby Pescadores Islands, and that bound Taiwan to undertake offensive action only with American consent. The treaty omitted mention of the offshore islands, and the mainland Chinese continued their pressure, occupying one of the Tachens. In 1955 the president secured in Congress a resolution giving him full power to go to the defense of Taiwan and the Pescadores, and also authorizing him to secure and protect "related positions of that area now in friendly hands" in order to defend Taiwan. Congress's endorsement was overwhelming—the resolution drew only three negative votes in each house—for so sweeping a grant of power.

The Red Chinese kept up their provocative activity nonetheless, and under pressure from the American government the Nationalists evacuated the Tachens as indefensible. But Quemoy and Matsu became symbols of the American will to protect Taiwan, and were perhaps strategically useful too. In any case, the American chief of naval operations "leaked" word to journalists that the administration was considering a plan "to destroy Red China's military potential and thus end its expansionist tendencies." Soon afterward the Chinese backed away from the brink. At the Bandung Conference in April, with diplomatic encouragement from other Asian nations, Premier Chou En-lai said Red China was ready to discuss the Formosa Strait issue directly with the United States. In 1955 representatives of the two governments began meetings in Geneva, and the guns fell silent.

REELECTION AND FOREIGN CRISES

As the United States continued to forge postwar alliances and to bring pressure to bear on foreign governments by practicing brinksmanship, a new presidential campaign unfolded. Despite having suffered a coronary seizure in the fall of 1955 and an operation for ileitis (an intestinal inflammation) in early 1956, Eisenhower decided to run for reelection. He retained the support and confidence of the public, although the Democrats controlled Congress. Meanwhile, new crises in foreign and domestic affairs required him to take decisive action.

A LANDSLIDE FOR IKE   In 1956 the Republican convention renominated Eisenhower by acclamation and again named Nixon as the vice-presidential candidate. The party platform endorsed Eisenhower's "modern Republicanism." The Democrats turned again to Stevenson. The platform revived old Democratic issues: less "favoritism" to big business, repeal of the Taft-Hartley Act, parity for farmers, tax relief for those in low-income brackets.

Neither candidate generated much excitement during the campaign. The Democrats centered their fire on the heir apparent, Richard Nixon, a "man of many masks." Stevenson aroused little enthusiasm for two controversial proposals: to drop conscription and rely on an all-volunteer army, and to ban H-bomb tests by international agreement. Both involved military questions that put Stevenson at a disadvantage by pitting his judgment against that of a successful general.

During the last week of the campaign, fighting erupted along the Suez Canal in Egypt and in the streets of Budapest, Hungary. These twin crises were unrelated, but they occurred almost as if placed in malicious juxtaposition by some evil force. The attack on Egypt by Britain, France, and Israel disrupted the Western alliance and damaged any claim to moral outrage at Soviet actions in Hungary. For the Soviets, the Suez War afforded both a smokescreen for the subjugation of Hungary and a chance to enlarge their influence in the Middle East, an increasingly important source of oil.

The two crises led Stevenson to declare the administration's foreign policy "bankrupt." Most voters, however, reasoned that the crises spelled a poor time to switch horses, and they handed Eisenhower a landslide victory. He lost one border state, Missouri, but in carrying Louisiana became the first Republican to win a Deep South state since Reconstruction; nationally, he carried all but seven states. The decision was unmistakably clear: he won more than 35 million popular votes to a little over 26 million for Stevenson, 457 electoral votes to the Democrat's 73.

In the euphoria of his landslide victory on November 6, Eisenhower declared on election night "that modern Republicanism has now proved itself. And America has approved of modern Republicanism." He later defined this as "the political philosophy that recognizes clearly the responsibility of the Federal Government to take the lead in making certain that the productivity of our great economic machine is distributed so that no one will suffer disaster, privation, through no fault of his own." Eisenhower Republicans, it seemed clear, had assimilated the New Deal as an accomplished fact. But Eisenhower's decisive win failed to swing a congressional majority for his own party in either house, the first time this had happened since the election of Zachary Taylor in 1848.

CRISIS IN THE MIDDLE EAST   After 1953 the Eisenhower-Dulles policy in the Middle East had departed from the Truman-Acheson focus on Israel and distanced itself from British-French economic interests in order to cultivate Arab friendship. To forestall Soviet penetration, Dulles in 1955 had completed his line of alliances across the

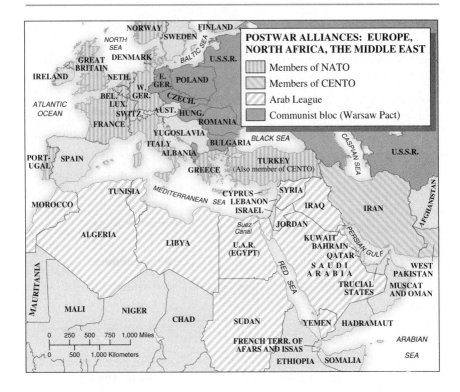

"northern tier" of the Middle East. Under American sponsorship, Britain had joined the Muslim states of Turkey, Iraq, Iran, and Pakistan in the Middle East Treaty Organization (METO), or Baghdad Pact, as the treaty was commonly called. By linking the easternmost NATO state (Turkey) to the westernmost SEATO state (Pakistan), METO had a certain superficial logic, but after Iraq, the only Arab member, withdrew in 1959, it became clear that the whole thing had been bound to fail from the start. Below the northern tier, moreover, the Arab states remained aloof from the organization. These were the states of the Arab League (Egypt, Jordan, Syria, Lebanon, and Saudi Arabia), which had warred on Israel in 1948–1949 and remained committed to its destruction.

The most fateful developments in the region turned on the rise of Egyptian general Gamal Abdel Nasser after the overthrow of King Farouk in 1952. The bone of contention was the Suez Canal, which had opened in 1869 as a joint French-Egyptian venture. But in 1875 the British government had acquired the largest block of stock, and from 1882 on British forces were posted there to protect the British Empire's "lifeline" to India and other colonies. When Nasser's new nationalist

General Moshe Dayan (center), *commander of Israeli forces during the Sinai campaign, 1956.*

regime pressed for the withdrawal of British forces from the canal zone, Eisenhower and Dulles supported its demand, and in 1954 an Anglo-Egyptian treaty provided for British withdrawal within twenty months. Nasser, like other leaders of the Third World, remained unaligned in the cold war and sought to play both sides off against each other. The United States, meanwhile, courted Egyptian support by offering a loan to build a great hydroelectric plant at Aswan on the Nile River.

From the outset, the administration's proposal was opposed by Jewish constituencies concerned with Egyptian threats to Israel, and by southern congressmen who feared the competition from Egyptian cotton. When Nasser then increased trade with the Soviet bloc and recognized Red China, Dulles abruptly canceled the loan offer in 1956. The outcome was far from a triumph of American diplomacy. The chief victims, it turned out, were Anglo-French interests in the Suez. Unable to retaliate against the United States, Nasser nationalized the Suez Canal Company and earmarked its revenues for the Aswan Dam project, thereby enhancing his prestige in the Arab world. The British and French, faced with loss of control of the crucial Suez Canal, reacted strongly. Fruitless negotiations dragged out through the summer, and finally, on October 29, 1956, Israeli forces invaded the Gaza Strip and the Sinai peninsula. The Israelis invaded ostensibly to root out Arab guerrillas, but actually to synchronize with the British and French, who began bombing Egyptian air bases and occupied Port Said. Their actions, the British and French claimed, were meant to protect the canal against the opposing belligerents.

The Suez War put the United States in a quandary. Either the administration could support its Western allies and see the troublesome Nasser crushed, or it could stand on the United Nations charter and champion Arab nationalism against imperialistic aggression. Eisenhower opted for the latter course, with the unusual result that the Soviet Union sided with the United States. Once the threat of American embargoes had forced Anglo-French-Israeli capitulation, the Soviets capitalized on the situation by threatening to use missiles against the Western aggressors. This belated bravado won for the Soviet Union some of the credit in the Arab world for what the United States had actually accomplished.

REPRESSION IN HUNGARY   In the Soviet Union, Nikita Khrushchev had come out on top in the post-Stalinist power struggles. In 1955, the Soviets had agreed to end the four-power occupation of Austria and to restore its independence as a neutral but Western-oriented state. Khrushchev had delivered a "secret speech" on the crimes of the Stalin era in 1956 before the Communist Party Congress and hinted at relaxed policies and suggestions that different countries might take "different roads to socialism." This new policy of "de-Stalinization" put Stalinist leaders in the satellite countries of eastern Europe on the defensive and emboldened the more independent leaders to take action. Riots in the Polish city of Poznan led to the rise of Wladyslaw Gomulka, a Polish nationalist, to leadership of the Polish Communist party. Gomulka managed to win a greater degree of independence by avoiding an open break with the Soviets.

In Hungary, however, a similar movement got out of hand. On October 23, 1956, fighting broke out in Budapest, followed by the installation of Imre Nagy, a moderate Communist, as head of the government. Again the Soviets seemed content to let "de-Stalinization" follow its course, and on October 28 they withdrew their forces from Budapest. But Nagy's announcement three days later that Hungary would withdraw from the Warsaw Pact brought Soviet tanks back into Budapest. Although Khrushchev was willing to relax relations with the eastern European satellites, he refused to allow them to break with the Soviet

Union or abandon their mutual defense obligations. The Soviets installed a more compliant leader, Janos Kadar, and hauled Nagy off to Moscow, where a firing squad executed him in 1958. It was a tragic ending to a movement that, at the outset, promised the sort of moderation that might have vindicated Kennan's policy of "containment," if not Dulles's notion of "liberation."

DOMESTIC PROBLEMS

THE BUDGET BATTLE   Domestic problems in Eisenhower's second term were first evident in the "great budget battle" of 1957. The president sent up to Capitol Hill the biggest peacetime budget ever. The size of the budget, which increased foreign aid, military spending, and allocations for atomic energy, housing, public works, and education, alarmed even the president, who had little time to cut it back. Eisenhower sent the bill to Congress, still hopeful that continued prosperity and high revenues would supply a surplus.

On the day the budget went to Congress the secretary of the treasury told reporters "there are a lot of places in this budget that can be cut," and suggested that if government could not reduce the "terrific" tax burden "you will have a depression that will curl your hair." Eisenhower claimed to share this desire to reduce the budget, but the spectacle of a treasury secretary's challenging the budget on the day it went to Congress conveyed an impression of divided purpose and conflict in the administration. Both Democrats and Old Guard Republicans declared an open season on the administration's budget request. In the end they hacked out about $4 billion, including heavy cuts in foreign aid, the United States Information Agency, and the Defense Department. By the time the battle was over in August, an economic slump had set in and tax revenues had dropped. In spite of the cuts, the administration projected a $500 million deficit.

U.S. REACTIONS TO SPUTNIK   On October 4, 1957, the Soviets launched the first satellite, called *Sputnik,* an acronym for the Russian phrase "fellow traveler of earth." Sputnik I weighed 194 pounds, but less than a month later the Soviets launched Sputnik II, and it carried a dog wired up for monitoring. Americans, until then complacent about their technical primacy, suddenly discovered an apparent "missile gap."

By the Rocket's Red Glare. *The Soviet success in space shocked Americans.*

If the Soviets were so advanced in rocketry, then perhaps they could hit American cities. *Life* magazine published a cover story entitled "The Case for Being Panicky." A Democratic senator demanded that Eisenhower call a special session of Congress to address the Sputnik crisis. The president refused, not wanting to heighten American anxiety.

All along Eisenhower knew that the "missile gap" was more illusory than real, but he could not reveal that high-altitude American U-2 spy planes were gathering this information. Even so, American missile development was in a state of disarray, with a tangle of agencies and committees engaged in waste and duplication. The launching of Explorer I, the first American satellite, on January 31, 1958, did not quiet the outcry.

The Soviet Union's success with Sputnik led to efforts in America to enlarge defense spending, to offer NATO allies intermediate-range ballistic missiles (IRBMs) pending development of long-range intercontinental ballistic missiles (ICBMs), to set up a new agency to coordinate space efforts, and to establish a crash program in science education. The "Sputnik syndrome," compounded by a sharp recession through the winter of 1957–1958, loosened the purse strings of frugal legislators, who added to the new budget more than Eisenhower wanted for both defense and domestic programs. During 1958, Britain, Italy, and Turkey accepted American missiles on their territory. In 1958 Congress created the National Aeronautics and Space Administration (NASA) to coordinate research and development in the field. Before the end of the year, NASA had a program to put a manned craft in orbit, but the first manned flight, by Commander Alan B. Shepard, Jr., did not take place until May 5, 1961. Finally, in 1958 Congress enacted the National Defense Education Act, which authorized federal grants especially for training in mathematics, science, and modern languages, as well as for student loans and fellowships.

CORRUPT PRACTICES During the first two years of Eisenhower's second term, public confidence in his performance, as registered by opinion polls, dropped sharply from 79 percent to 49 percent. Emotional issues such as civil rights and defense policy had compounded his troubles. The president's image was further tarnished when congressional investigations revealed that the administration, which had promised to clean up "the mess in Washington," was itself soiled by scandals, one of which involved Sherman Adams, the White House "chief-of-staff." Adams, it seemed, had done little more than open some doors at the Securities and Exchange Commission and the Federal Trade Commission with introductions for a Boston industrialist, but he had taken in return gifts of a fur coat and an Oriental rug. In 1958 the president reluctantly accepted Adams's resignation. Republicans also faced the growing opposition of farmers, angry over cuts in price supports, and of labor, angry because many Republicans had made "right-to-work" (or open-shop) laws a campaign issue in 1958. The Democrats came out of the midterm elections with nearly two-to-one majorities in Congress: 282 to 154 in the House, 64 to 34 in the Senate.

Eisenhower would be the first president to face three successive Congresses controlled by the opposition party, and this meant that he could manage few new initiatives in domestic policy. The most important legislation of the last two years in the Eisenhower presidency were the Landrum-Griffin Labor-Management Act of 1959, the Civil Rights Act of 1960, and the admission of the first states not contiguous to the continental forty-eight. Alaska became the forty-ninth state on January 3, 1959, and Hawaii the fiftieth on August 21, 1959.

The Landrum-Griffin Act, aimed at controlling union corruption, was actually a compromise between the views of its House sponsors and the somewhat less stringent views of Senator John F. Kennedy and some of his colleagues. It reflected, nevertheless, popular feeling against racketeering and monopolistic practices in unions, especially those of the Teamsters, which had been revealed by an extensive Senate probe. The act safeguarded democratic procedures, penalized the misuse of union funds and coercion of members, and excluded from office persons convicted of certain crimes. The act also strengthened restrictions on secondary boycotts and blackmail picketing. Most of its provisions were directed against unfair union practices, but the act also monitored employer payments to union officers or labor-management consultants.

FESTERING PROBLEMS ABROAD

Once the Suez and Hungary crises faded from the front pages, Eisenhower enjoyed eighteen months of smooth sailing in foreign affairs. Nonetheless, a brief flurry occurred in 1958 over hostile demonstrations in Peru and Venezuela against Vice-President Nixon, who was on a goodwill tour of eight Latin American countries.

CRISIS IN THE MIDDLE EAST   In 1958 the Middle East flared up again. By this time the president had secured from Congress authority for what came to be called the Eisenhower Doctrine, which promised to extend economic and military aid to Middle East nations, and to use armed forces if necessary to assist any such nation against armed aggression from any Communist country.

President Nasser of Egypt meanwhile had emerged from the Suez crisis with heightened prestige, and in 1958 he created the United Arab Republic (UAR) by merger (a short-lived one) with Syria. Then on July 14 a leftist coup in Iraq, supposedly inspired by Nasser and the Soviets, threw out the pro-Western government and killed the king, the crown prince, and the premier. In Lebanon, already unsettled by internal conflict, the government appealed to the United States for support against a similar fate. Eisenhower immediately ordered 5,000 marines into Lebanon. British forces meanwhile went into Jordan at the request of King Hussein. Once the situation stabilized, and the Lebanese factions reached a compromise, American forces (up to 15,000 at one point) withdrew in October.

CRISIS IN EAST ASIA   East Asia heated up again when, on August 23, 1958, Red China renewed its shelling of the Nationalists on Quemoy and Matsu. In September the American Seventh Fleet began to escort Nationalist convoys, but stopped short of entering Chinese territorial waters. To abandon the islands, President Eisenhower said, would amount to a "Western Pacific 'Munich.'" But on October 1 he suggested that a cease-fire would provide "an opportunity to negotiate in good faith." Red China ordered such a cease-fire on October 6, and on October 25, which happened to be the day the last American forces left Lebanon, said that it would reserve the right to bombard the islands on alternate days. With that strange stipulation the worst of the crisis passed, but the problem continued to fester.

CRISIS IN BERLIN The problem of Berlin festered too: Premier Khrushchev called it a "bone in his throat." West Berlin provided a "showplace" of Western democracy and prosperity, a listening post for Western intelligence, and a funnel through which news and propaganda from the West penetrated what Winston Churchill had called "the iron curtain." Although East Germany had sealed its western frontiers, refugees could still pass from East to West Berlin. On November 10, 1958, at a Soviet-Polish friendship rally in Moscow, Khrushchev threatened to give East Germany control of East Berlin and the air lanes into West Berlin. After the deadline he set, May 27, 1959, Western occupation authorities would have to deal with the East German government, in effect recognizing it, or face the possibility of another blockade.

But Eisenhower refused to budge from his position on Berlin. At the same time, he refused to engage in saber-rattling or even to cancel existing plans to reduce the size of the army. Khrushchev, it turned out, was no more eager for confrontation than Eisenhower. In talks with British prime minister Harold Macmillan, he suggested that the main thing was to begin discussions of the Berlin issue, and not the May 27 deadline. Macmillan in turn won Eisenhower's consent to a meeting of the Big Four foreign ministers.

There was little hope of resolving different views on Berlin and German reunification, but the talks distracted attention from Khrushchev's deadline of May 27: it passed almost unnoticed. In September, after the Big Four talks had adjourned, Premier Khrushchev visited the United States, going to New York, Washington, Los Angeles, San Francisco, and Iowa, and dropping in on Eisenhower at Camp David. In talks there Khrushchev endorsed "peaceful coexistence," and Eisenhower

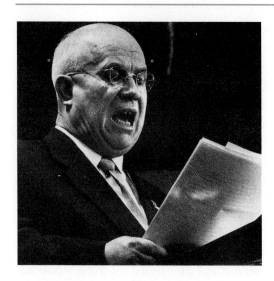

Soviet premier Nikita Khrushchev speaking on the problem of Berlin, 1959.

admitted that the Berlin situation was "abnormal." They agreed that the time was ripe for a summit meeting in the spring.

THE U-2 SUMMIT   The summit meeting blew up in Eisenhower's face. On May 1, 1960, a Soviet rocket brought down an American U-2 spy plane. Such planes had been flying missions over the Soviet Union for three and a half years. Khrushchev set out to entrap Eisenhower and succeeded, by announcing first only that the plane had been shot down. When the State Department insisted that there had been no attempt to violate Soviet airspace, Khrushchev disclosed that the Soviets had pilot Francis Gary Powers, "alive and kicking," and had his pictures of Soviet military installations. On May 11 Eisenhower abandoned his efforts to cover up the incident and finally took personal responsibility—an unprecedented action for a head of state—and justified the action on grounds of national security. "No one wants another Pearl Harbor," he said. In Paris, five days later, Khrushchev withdrew an invitation for Eisenhower to visit the Soviet Union and called on the president to repudiate the U-2 flights and "pass severe judgment on those responsible." When Eisenhower refused, Khrushchev left the meeting. (Later, in 1962, Powers was exchanged for a Soviet spy.)

CASTRO'S CUBA   The greatest thorn in Eisenhower's side was the Cuban regime of Fidel Castro, which came to power on January 1,

1959, after three years of guerrilla warfare against the dictator Fulgencio Batista. In their struggle against Batista, Castro's forces had the support of many Americans who hoped for a new day of democratic government in Cuba. When American television covered trials and executions conducted by the victorious Castro, however, such hopes were dashed. Staged before crowds of howling spectators, the trials vented anger against Batista's corrupt officials and police, but offered little in the way of legal procedure or proof. Castro, moreover, planned a social and agrarian revolution and opposed the widespread foreign control of the Cuban economy. When he began programs of land redistribution and nationalization of foreign-owned property, relations worsened. Some observers believed, however, that by rejecting Castro's requests for loans and other help, the American government lost a chance to influence the direction of the revolution, and by acting on the assumption that Communists already had the upper hand in his movement, the administration may have ensured that fact.

Fidel Castro (center) *became Cuba's first Communist premier in 1959 after three years of guerrilla warfare against the Batista regime.*

Castro, on the other hand, showed little reluctance to accept the Communist embrace. In 1960 he entered a trade agreement to swap Cuban sugar for Soviet oil and machinery. Then, after Cuba had seized three British-American oil refineries that refused to process Soviet oil, Eisenhower cut sharply the quota for Cuban sugar imports. Premier Khrushchev in response warned that any military intervention in Cuba would encounter Soviet rockets. The United States next suspended imports of Cuban sugar and embargoed most shipments to Cuba. One of Eisenhower's last acts as president was to suspend diplomatic relations with Cuba on January 3, 1961. In the hope of creating "some kind of nondictatorial 'third force,' neither Castroite nor Batistiano," as Eisenhower put it, the president authorized the CIA to begin training a force of Cuban refugees (some of them former Castro stalwarts) for a new revolution. But the final decision on its use would rest with the next president, John F. Kennedy.

THE EARLY CIVIL RIGHTS MOVEMENT

While the cold war produced an uneasy stalement by the mid-1950s, race relations in the United States threatened to explode the domestic tranquility masking years of injustice. Eisenhower entered office committed to civil rights in principle, and he pushed the issue in areas of federal authority. During his first three years, public services in Washington, D.C., were desegregated, as were navy yards and veterans' hospitals. Beyond that, however, two aspects of the president's philosophy inhibited vigorous action in enforcing the principle of civil rights: his preference for state or local action over federal involvement, and his doubt that laws could change racial attitudes. "I don't believe you can change the hearts of men with laws or decisions," he said. For the time, then, leadership in the civil rights field came from the judiciary more than from the executive or legislative branch of the government.

In the 1930s, the National Association for the Advancement of Colored People (NAACP) had resolved to test the "separate but equal" doctrine that had upheld racial segregation since the *Plessy* decision in 1896. Charles H. Houston, dean of the Howard University Law School, laid the plans, and his former student, Thurgood Marshall, served as chief NAACP lawyer. They decided to begin with the expensive field of postgraduate study. In *Sweatt* v. *Painter* (1950) the Supreme Court

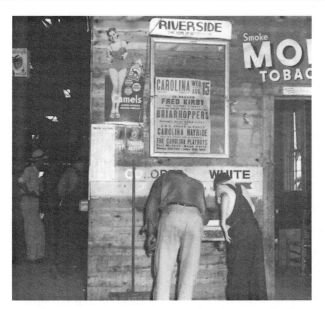

Racial segregation began to be tested in the courts by the NAACP in the late 1930s.

ruled that a separate black law school in Texas failed to measure up be-cause of intangible factors, such as its isolation from most of the future lawyers with whom its graduates would interact.

THE *BROWN* DECISION   By that time, challenges to state laws man-dating segregation in the public schools were rising through the appel-late courts. Five such cases, from Kansas, Delaware, South Carolina, Virginia, and the District of Columbia—usually cited by reference to the first, *Brown v. Board of Education of Topeka, Kansas*—came to the Supreme Court for joint argument by NAACP attorneys in 1952. Chief Justice Earl Warren wrote the opinion, handed down on May 17, 1954, in which a unanimous Court declared that "in the field of public educa-tion the doctrine of 'separate but equal' has no place." In support of its opinion, the Court cited current sociological and psychological find-ings—demonstrating that even if separate facilities were equal in qual-ity, the mere fact of separating people by race engendered feelings of inferiority. A year later, after further argument, the Court directed "a prompt and reasonable start toward full compliance," ordering that the process should move "with all deliberate speed."

Eisenhower refused to take any part in leading white southerners toward compliance. Privately he maintained "that the Supreme Court decision *set back* progress in the South *at least fifteen years*. The fellow who tries to tell me you can do these things by *force* is just plain *nuts*." While token integration began as early as 1954 in the border states, hostility mounted in the Deep South and Virginia, led by the newly formed Citizens' Councils. The Citizens' Councils were middle- and upper-class versions of the Ku Klux Klan that spread quickly across the region and eventually enrolled 250,000 members. Instead of physical violence and intimidation, the Councils used economic coercion to discipline blacks who crossed racial boundaries. African Americans who defied white supremacy would lose their jobs, have their insurance policies canceled, or be denied personal loans or home mortgages. The Citizens' Councils grew so powerful that membership in them became almost a prerequisite for an aspiring white politician.

Before the end of 1955, moderate sentiment in the South gave way to surly reaction against desegregation of the schools. Virginia senator Harry F. Byrd supplied a rallying cry: "Massive Resistance." State legislatures sought futilely to interpose their power between the courts and the schools. In 1956, 101 southern members of Congress signed a "Southern Manifesto," which denounced the Court's decision in the *Brown* case as "a clear abuse of judicial power." At the end of 1956, in six southern states, not a single black child attended school with whites. In several others, the degree of desegregation was minuscule.

THE MONTGOMERY BUS BOYCOTT   The essential role played by the NAACP and the courts in providing a legal lever for the civil rights movement often overshadows the courageous contributions of individual African Americans who took great personal risks to challenge segregation. For example, in Montgomery, Alabama, on December 1, 1955, Mrs. Rosa Parks, a black seamstress tired after a day's work, was arrested for refusing to give up her seat on a city bus to a white man. "I'm going to have you arrested," the driver said. "You may do that," Parks replied. As was the case in many southern communities, Montgomery had a local ordinance that required blacks to give up their bus or train seat to a white when asked. The next night black community leaders met in the Dexter Avenue Baptist Church to organize a massive bus boycott under the aegis of the the Montgomery Improvement Association.

In Dexter Avenue's twenty-six-year-old pastor, Martin Luther King, Jr., the movement found a charismatic leader. Born in Atlanta, the grandson of a slave and the son of a minister, King was endowed with intelligence, courage, and eloquence. After attending Morehouse College in Atlanta and then receiving a seminary degree, he earned a Ph.D. in philosophy from Boston University before accepting a call to preach in Montgomery. He brought the movement a message of nonviolent disobedience based on the Gospels, the writings of Henry David Thoreau, and the example of Mahatma Gandhi in India. "We must use the weapon of love," he told his people. "We must realize so many people are taught to hate us that they are not totally responsible for their hate." To his antagonists he said: "We will soon wear you down by our capacity to suffer, and in winning our freedom we will so appeal to your heart and conscience that we will win you in the process."

The bus boycott achieved a remarkable solidarity. For months blacks in Montgomery formed carpools, hitchhiked, or simply walked. But the white town fathers held out against the boycott and against the pleas of a bus company tired of losing money. The boycotters finally won a fed-

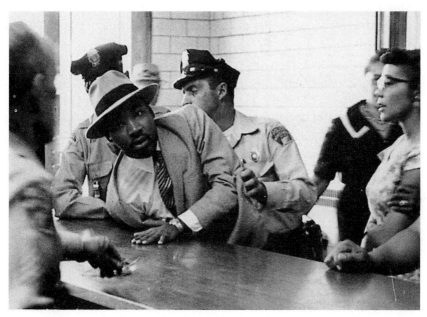

Martin Luther King, Jr., here facing arrest for leading a civil rights march, advocated nonviolent resistance to racial segregation.

eral case they had initiated against bus segregation, and in 1956 the Supreme Court let stand without review an opinion of a lower court that "the separate but equal doctrine can no longer be safely followed as a correct statement of the law." The next day King and other blacks boarded the buses, but they still had a long way to travel before segregation ended.

Trying to keep alive the spirit of the bus boycott, King and a group of associates in 1957 organized the Southern Christian Leadership Conference (SCLC). Several days later, King found an unexploded dynamite bomb on his front porch. Two hours later, he addressed his congregation: "I'm not afraid of anybody this morning. Tell Montgomery they can keep shooting and I'm going to stand up to them; tell Montgomery they can keep bombing and I'm going to stand up to them. If I had to die tomorrow morning I would die happy because I've been to the mountain top and I've seen the promised land and it's going to be here in Montgomery."

Despite Eisenhower's reluctance to take the lead in desegregating schools, he supported the right of blacks to vote. In 1956, hoping to exploit divisions between northern and southern Democrats and to reclaim some of the black vote for Republicans, Eisenhower proposed legislation that became the Civil Rights Act of 1957. The first civil rights law passed since Reconstruction, it finally got through the Senate, after a year's delay, with the help of Majority Leader Lyndon B. Johnson, who won southern acceptance by watering down the act. Republican Clifford Case of New Jersey dismissed the final bill as a "pitiful remnant" of the original measure, while Georgia Democrat Richard Russell trumpeted it as the "sweetest victory in my twenty-five years as a Senator." The act established for a period of two years the Civil Rights Commission, which was later extended indefinitely, and a new Civil Rights Division in the Justice Department, which could seek injunctions to prevent interference with the right to vote. Yet, by 1959 the Civil Rights Act had not added a single southern black to the voting rolls. Neither did the Civil Rights Act of 1960, which provided for federal court referees to register blacks where a court found a "pattern and practice" of discrimination, and also made it a federal crime to interfere with any court order or to cross state lines to destroy any building. This bill, too, lacked any real teeth and depended upon vigorous presidential enforcement.

DESEGREGATION IN LITTLE ROCK   There had been sporadic violence in resistance to civil rights efforts, but a few weeks after the Civil
Rights Act of 1957 passed, Arkansas governor Orval Faubus called out
the National Guard to prevent nine black students from entering Little
Rock's Central High School under federal court order. A conference between the president and the governor proved fruitless, but on court order Faubus withdrew the National Guard. When the students tried to
enter the school, an hysterical white mob forced their removal for their
own safety. At that point Eisenhower, who had said two months before
that he could not "imagine any set of circumstances that would ever induce me to send federal troops," ordered a thousand paratroopers to
Little Rock to protect the students, and placed the National Guard on
federal service. The soldiers stayed through the school year.

The following year Faubus closed the high schools of Little Rock
rather than allow integration, and court proceedings dragged on into
1959 before the schools could be reopened. In that year, massive resistance to integration in Virginia collapsed when both state and federal
courts struck down state laws that had cut off funds from integrated
schools. Thereafter, massive resistance for the most part was confined
to the Deep South where five states, from South Carolina west through
Louisiana, still opposed even token integration.

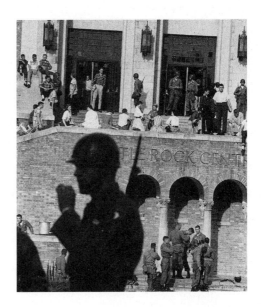

*National Guardsmen were sent
to Little Rock, Arkansas, to
protect newly enrolled black
students who faced violent resistance from those opposed to
integration.*

ASSESSING THE EISENHOWER YEARS

Until recent years, the Eisenhower administration has not drawn much acclaim from journalists and historians. One journalist called the Eisenhower years "the time of the great postponement," during which the president "lived off the accumulated wisdom, the accumulated prestige, and the accumulated military strength of his predecessors" and left domestic and foreign policies "about where he found them in 1953." Yet even these critics granted that Eisenhower had succeeded in ending the war in Korea and settling the dust raised by McCarthy. But if he had failed to end the cold war and in fact had institutionalized it as a global confrontation, he sensed the limits of American power and kept its application to low-risk situations. If he took few initiatives in addressing the racial and social problems that would erupt in the 1960s, he left the major innovations of the New Deal in place and thereby legitimized them. If he tolerated unemployment of as much as 7 percent at times, inflation remained at a very low rate of 1.6 percent during his terms. His farewell address to the American people, delivered on radio and television three days before he left office, showed his remarkable foresight in his own area of special expertise, the military.

Like Washington, Eisenhower couched his wisdom largely in the form of warnings: that America's "leadership and prestige depend, not merely upon our unmatched material strength, but on how we use our power in the interests of world peace and human betterment"; that the temptation to find easy answers should take into account "the need to maintain balance in and among national problems"; and above all that Americans "must avoid the impulse to live only for today, plundering, for our own ease and convenience, the precious resources of tomorrow."

Eisenhower highlighted the dangers of a military establishment in a time of peace. "This conjunction of an immense military establishment and a large arms industry is new in the American experience," he noted. "In the councils of government we must guard against the acquisition of unwarranted influence, whether sought or unsought, by the military-industrial complex. The potential for the disastrous rise of misplaced power exists and will persist."

Eisenhower confessed great disappointment at his inability to affirm "that a lasting peace is in sight," only that "war has been avoided." But he prayed "that, in the goodness of time, all peoples will come to live together in a peace guaranteed by the binding force of mutual respect and love."

MAKING CONNECTIONS

- The civil rights movement of the 1950s aimed to achieve the racial integration of public services and equal access to political rights. This struggle would continue into the 1960s and then move in several new directions. See Chapter 34.

- American involvement in Vietnam grew in the 1950s, but remained limited to an advisory role. Escalation to an active fighting role came under Lyndon Johnson in 1965, a topic covered in Chapter 34.

- Eisenhower's "hands-off" approach to the presidency was reminiscent of the Gilded-Age presidencies and those of the 1920s. See Chapters 18, 22, and 27.

FURTHER READING

Scholarship on the Eisenhower years is extensive. A carefully balanced overview of the period is Chester Pach, Jr., and Elmo Richardson's *The Presidency of Dwight D. Eisenhower* (1991). For the manner in which Eisenhower conducted foreign policy, see Robert A. Divine's *Eisenhower and the Cold War* (1981).

The conservatism of the 1950s is documented in George H. Nash's *The Conservative Intellectual Movement in America: Since 1945* (1976) and Richard M. Fried's *Nightmare in Red: The McCarthy Era in Perspective* (1990). On the relationship between business and government, see Louis Galambos and Joseph Pratt's *The Rise of the Corporate Commonwealth: United States Business and Public Policy in the Twentieth Century* (1988).

Several specialized studies are illuminating. See Robert A. Divine's *The Sputnik Challenge: Eisenhower's Response to the Soviet Satellite* (1993) and Tom Lewis's *Divided Highways: Building the Interstate Highways, Transforming American Life* (1997).

For the buildup of American involvement in Indochina, consult Lloyd C. Gardner's *Approaching Vietnam: From World War II through Dien Bien Phu, 1941–1954* (1988), and David L. Anderson's *Trapped by Success: The Eisenhower Administration and Vietnam, 1953–1961* (1991). How the Eisenhower Doctrine came to be implemented is traced in Stephen Ambrose and Douglas Brinkley's *Rise to Globalism: American Foreign Policy Since 1938* (rev. ed., 1997). For studies of two important foreign policy topics, see James A. Bill's *The Eagle and the Lion: The Tragedy of American-Iranian Relations* (1988) and Stephen G. Rabe's *Eisenhower and Latin America: The Foreign Policy of Anticommunism* (1988).

Two introductions to the impact wrought by the Warren Supreme Court during the 1950s are Alexander Bickel's *The Supreme Court and the Idea of Progress* (1970) and Paul Murphy's *The Constitution in Crisis Times, 1918–1969* (1972). Also helpful is Archibald Cox's *The Warren Court: Constitutional Decision as an Instrument of Reform* (1968). A masterful study of the important Warren Court decision on school desegregation is Richard Kluger's *Simple Justice: The History of Brown v. Board of Education and Black America's Struggle for Equality* (1975).

For the story of the early civil rights movement, see Taylor Branch's *Parting the Waters: America in the King Years, 1954–1963* (1988), and Robert Weisbrot's *Freedom Bound: A History of America's Civil Rights Movement* (1990).

34 ∾ NEW FRONTIERS: POLITICS AND SOCIAL CHANGE IN THE 1960S

CHAPTER ORGANIZER

This chapter focuses on:

- Kennedy's New Frontier and Johnson's Great Society.

- the achievements of the civil rights movement and ensuing splinter movements.

- America's growing involvement in Vietnam and the rising opposition to it.

- Kennedy's efforts to combat communism in Cuba.

or those who considered the social and political climate of the 1950s dull, the following decade would provide a striking contrast. The 1960s were years of extraordinary social turbulence and innovation in public affairs—as well as sudden tragedy and trauma. Many social ills that had been festering for decades suddenly forced their way onto the national agenda. At the same time, the deeply entrenched assumptions of cold war ideology led the country into the longest, most controversial, and least successful war in the nation's history.

THE NEW FRONTIER

KENNEDY VS. NIXON   In 1960, few sensed such dramatic change on the horizon. The presidential election of that year pitted two candidates—Richard M. Nixon and John F. Kennedy—who seemed to symbolize the unadventurous politics of the 1950s. Though better known than Kennedy because of his eight years as Eisenhower's vice-president, Nixon had also developed the reputation of a cunning chameleon, the "Tricky Dick" who concealed his duplicity behind a series of masks. "Nixon doesn't know who he is," Kennedy told an aide, "and so each time he makes a speech he has to decide which Nixon he is, and that will be very exhausting."

But Nixon could not be so easily dismissed. He possessed a shrewd intelligence and a compulsive love for politics, the more combative the better. His worst flaw was a callous disregard for the rules of political combat, a trait he displayed from his first campaign to his last. Born in suburban Los Angeles in 1913, he grew up amid a working-class Quaker family struggling to make ends meet. In 1946, having completed law school and a wartime stint in the navy, Richard Nixon jumped into the political arena as a Republican, and, with the help of a powerful group of conservative southern California businessmen, he unseated a popular congressman.

Nixon arrived in Washington eager to reverse the tide of New Deal liberalism. "I was elected to smash the labor bosses," he explained. Four years later he won election to the Senate. In his campaigns, Nixon unleashed scurrilous personal attacks on his opponents, employing half-truths, lies, and rumors, and he shrewdly manipulated and fed the growing anti-Communist hysteria. Yet Nixon became both a respected and effective member of Congress, and by 1950 he was the most requested Republican speaker in the country. The reward for his rapid rise to political stardom was the vice-presidential nomination in 1952, which led to successive terms as the partner of the popular Eisenhower.

In comparison to his Republican opponent, Kennedy was inexperienced. Despite an abundance of assets, including a record of heroism in World War II, a glamorous young wife, a bright, agile mind and Harvard education, a rich, powerful family, a handsome face, movie-star charisma, and robust outlook, the forty-three-year-old Kennedy had not distinguished himself in the House or Senate. Indeed, his political rise owed not so much to his abilities or accomplishments as to the effective public relations campaign engineered by his ambitious father, Joseph Kennedy, who was a self-made tycoon. The older Kennedy had made millions on Wall Street in the twenties, gained control of much of the Hollywood film industry in the thirties, and finessed from President Franklin Roosevelt an appointment as ambassador to Great Britain. Ambassador Joseph Kennedy soon developed a consuming ambition to see one of his sons elected president. When the eldest boy, Joseph Jr., was killed in the war, the mantle of paternal expectation fell on John's shoulders.

John F. Kennedy subsequently suffered from criticism that there was more image to him than substance. And there was some truth to the charge. Although he won a Pulitzer Prize for *Profiles in Courage* (1956), a book (ghostwritten by an aide) about past political leaders who had "made the tough decisions," Kennedy, claimed Washington critics, had shown more profile than courage during the McCarthy era of the early 1950s, and he had a weak record on civil rights. Eleanor Roosevelt declined to endorse Kennedy in 1960, noting that presidential authority should not be vested in "someone who understands what courage is and admires it, but has not quite the independence to have it."

During his campaign for the Democratic nomination, Kennedy had shown that he had the energy to match his grace and ambition, even though he suffered from serious spinal problems, Addison's disease (a debilitating disorder of the adrenal glands), recurrent blood disorders, venereal disease, and fierce fevers. He took medicine daily, sometimes hourly. But like Franklin Roosevelt, he and his aides and family members successfully masked such physical ailments from the public.

By the time of the convention in 1960, Kennedy had traveled over 65,000 miles, visited twenty-five states, and made over 350 speeches. In his acceptance speech, he found the stirring, muscular rhetoric that would stamp the rest of his campaign and his presidency: "We stand today on the edge of a New Frontier—the frontier of unknown opportunities and perils—a frontier of unfulfilled hopes and threats." Kennedy and his staff quite consciously fastened upon the frontier metaphor as the label for their domestic program. As an avid student of American history himself, Kennedy knew that the frontier image possessed a special resonance for the American people. Americans had always been ad-

John F. Kennedy's poise and precision in the debates with Richard Nixon impressed viewers and voters.

venturers, eager to conquer and exploit new frontiers, and Kennedy promised to use his administration to continue the process.

Three events shaped the campaign that fall. First, as the only Catholic to run for the presidency since Al Smith, Kennedy strove to dispel the impression that his religion was a major political liability. In a speech before the Houston Ministerial Association in 1960, he directly confronted the political implications of his Catholicism. In America, he told the Protestant clergy, "the separation of church and state is absolute," and "no Catholic prelate would tell the President—should he be a Catholic—how to act and no Protestant minister should tell his parishioners for whom to vote." The religious question thereafter drew little public attention; Kennedy's candor had neutralized it.

Second, Nixon violated one of the cardinal rules of politics when he agreed to debate his less prominent opponent on television. During the first of four debates, few significant policy differences surfaced, allowing viewers to shape their opinions more on matters of style. Some 70 million people watched this first-ever television debate, and they saw an obviously uncomfortable Nixon, still weak from a recent illness, perspiring heavily and sporting his perpetual five-o'clock shadow. He looked haggard, uneasy, and even sinister before the camera. Kennedy, on the other hand, projected a cool poise and offered crisp answers that made him seem equal, if not superior, in his fitness for the office. Kennedy's popularity immediately shot up in the polls. In the words of a bemused southern senator, Kennedy combined "the best qualities of Elvis Presley and Franklin D. Roosevelt."

Still, the momentum created by the first debate was not enough to ensure a Kennedy victory. The third key event in the campaign involved the civil rights issue. Democratic strategists knew that in order to offset the loss of southern conservatives suspicious of Kennedy's Catholicism and strong civil rights positions, they had to woo black voters. To do so they set up a special committee to increase minority voter registration and to attract the black vote.

Perhaps the most crucial incident of the campaign occurred when Martin Luther King, Jr., and some fifty demonstrators were arrested in Atlanta for "trespassing" in an all-white restaurant. Although the other demonstrators were soon released, King was sentenced to four months in prison, ostensibly because of an earlier traffic violation. Robert Kennedy, the candidate's younger brother and campaign manager, called the judge handling King's case, who also happened to be a close friend of the Georgia governor, alerting him "that if he was a decent American, he would let King out of jail by sundown." King was soon released on bail, and the Kennedy campaign seized full advantage of the outcome, distributing some 2 million pamphlets in black neighborhoods extolling Kennedy's efforts on behalf of Dr. King.

When the votes were counted, Kennedy and his running mate, Lyndon B. Johnson of Texas, had won the closest presidential election since 1888. The winning margin was only 118,574 votes out of 68 million cast. Kennedy's wide lead in the electoral vote, 303 to 219, belied the paper-thin margin in several key states, especially Illinois, where Chicago mayor Richard Daley's Democratic machine appeared to have lived up to its legendary campaign motto: "In Chicago we tell our people to vote early and to vote often." Nixon had in fact carried more states than Kennedy, sweeping most of the West, and holding four of the six southern states Eisenhower had carried in 1956. Kennedy's majority was built out of victories in southern New England, the populous Middle Atlantic states, and key states in the South where black voters provided the critical margin of victory. Yet ominous rumblings of discontent ap-

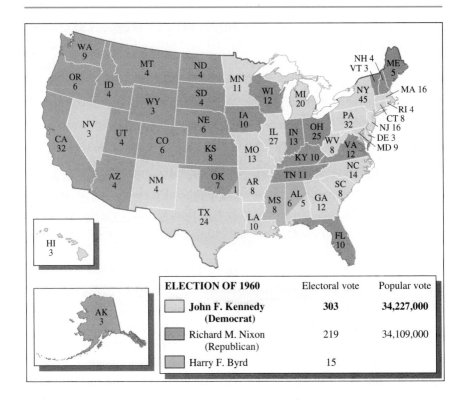

ELECTION OF 1960	Electoral vote	Popular vote
John F. Kennedy (Democrat)	303	34,227,000
Richard M. Nixon (Republican)	219	34,109,000
Harry F. Byrd	15	

peared in the once-solid Democratic South, as all eight of Mississippi's electors and six of Alabama's eleven (as well as one elector from Oklahoma) defied the national ticket and voted for Virginia senator Harry Byrd, the arch-segregationist.

THE NEW ADMINISTRATION   Kennedy was the youngest person ever elected president, and his cabinet appointments put an accent on youth and "Eastern Establishment" figures. As a self-described "idealist without illusions," he was determined to attract the "best and the brightest" minds available, individuals who would inject a tough, pragmatic, and vigorous outlook into governmental affairs. Adlai Stevenson was favored by liberal Democrats for secretary of state, but Kennedy chose Dean Rusk, a career diplomat who then headed the Rockefeller Foundation. Stevenson received the relatively minor post of ambassador to the United Nations. Robert S. McNamara, one of the "whiz kids" who had reorganized the Ford Motor Company with his "systems-

Kennedy and his wife, Jacqueline, at the inauguration, January 20, 1961.

analysis" techniques, was asked to bring his managerial magic to bear on the Department of Defense. C. Douglas Dillon, a Republican banker, was made secretary of the treasury in an effort to reassure conservative business owners. When critics attacked the appointment of Kennedy's thirty-five-year-old brother, Robert, as attorney-general, the president quipped, "I don't see what's wrong with giving Bobby a little experience before he goes into law practice." McGeorge Bundy, whom Kennedy called "the second smartest man I know," was made special assistant for national security affairs, lending additional credence to the impression that foreign policy would remain under tight White House control.

The inaugural ceremonies set the tone of elegance and youthful vigor that would come to be called the "Kennedy style." The glittering atmosphere of snow-clad Washington seemed to symbolize fresh promise. After poet Robert Frost paid tribute to the administration in verse, Kennedy dazzled listeners with uplifting rhetoric. "Let the word go forth from this time and place," he proclaimed. "Let every nation know, whether it wishes us well or ill, that we shall pay any price, bear any burden, meet any hardship, support any friend, oppose any foe, to assure the survival and success of liberty. And so, my fellow Americans: ask not what your country can do for you—ask what you can do for your country." Spines tingled at the time; Kennedy, one journalist wrote, was the first president to be a Prince Charming.

THE KENNEDY RECORD   But for all of his idealistic rhetoric, Kennedy had a difficult time launching his New Frontier domestic program. Elected by a razor-thin margin, he did not enjoy a popular mandate. Nor did he show much skill in shepherding legislation through a Congress in the grip of a conservative southern coalition that blocked his efforts to increase federal aid to education, provide health insurance for the aged, and create a new Department of Urban Affairs. The Senate killed his initiatives on behalf of unemployed youth, migrant workers, and mass transit. When Kennedy finally came around to the advice of his Keynesian advisers in 1963 and submitted a drastic tax cut, Congress blocked that as well.

Administration proposals, nevertheless, did win some notable victories in Congress. Those involving defense and foreign policy generally won favor; indeed, defense appropriations exceeded administration requests. On foreign aid there were some cuts, but Congress readily approved broad "Alliance for Progress" programs to help Latin America, and the celebrated Peace Corps, created in 1961 to supply volunteers to provide educational and technical services abroad. Kennedy's greatest legislative accomplishment, however, may have been the Trade Expansion Act of 1962, which eventually led to tariff cuts averaging 35 percent between the United States and the European Common Market.

In the field of domestic social legislation, the administration did score a few victories. They included a new Housing Act, which earmarked nearly $5 billion for urban renewal over four years, a raise in the minimum wage from $1 to $1.25 and its extension to more than 3 million additional workers, the Area Redevelopment Act of 1961, which provided nearly $400 million in loans and grants to "distressed areas," an increase in Social Security benefits, and additional funds for sewage treatment plants. Kennedy also won support for an accelerated space program with the goal of landing on the moon before the end of the decade.

THE WARREN COURT   Under Chief Justice Earl Warren, the Supreme Court continued to be a decisive influence on American domestic life during the 1960s. The Court's decisions on civil liberties proved as controversial as its earlier decisions on civil rights. In 1962 the Court ruled that a school prayer adopted by the New York State Board of Regents violated the constitutional prohibition against an established religion. In *Gideon* v. *Wainwright* (1963) the Court required that every felony defendant be provided a lawyer regardless of the defendant's ability to pay. In 1964 the Court ruled in *Escobedo* v. *Illinois* that a person accused of a crime must also be allowed to consult a lawyer before being interrogated by police. Two years later, in *Miranda* v. *Arizona,* the Court issued perhaps its most bitterly criticized ruling when it ordered that an accused person in police custody must be informed of certain basic rights: the right to remain silent; the right to know that anything said can be used against the individual in court; and the right to have a defense attorney present during interrogation. In addition, the Court established rules for police to follow in informing suspects of their legal rights before questioning could begin.

EXPANSION OF THE CIVIL RIGHTS MOVEMENT

The most important development in American domestic life during the 1960s occurred in civil rights. Kennedy entered the White House reluctant to challenge conservative southern Democrats on the race issue. He was never as personally committed to the cause of civil rights as his brother Robert. Despite a few dramatic gestures of support toward black leaders, John Kennedy only belatedly grasped the moral and emotional significance of the most widespread reform movement of the decade. Eventually, however, his conscience was pricked by the grassroots civil rights movement led by Martin Luther King, Jr.

SIT-INS AND FREEDOM RIDERS   After the Montgomery bus boycott of 1955–1956, King's philosophy of "militant nonviolence" inspired others to challenge the deeply entrenched patterns of racial segregation in the South. At the same time, lawsuits to desegregate the schools got thousands of parents and young people involved. The momentum generated the first genuine mass movement in African-American history when four black college students sat down and demanded service at a "whites-only" Woolworth lunch counter in Greensboro, North Carolina, on February 1, 1960. Within a week, the "sit-in" movement had spread to six more towns in the state, and within two months, demonstrations had occurred in fifty-four cities in nine states.

Sit-in at the Woolworth's Lunch Counter in Greensboro, North Carolina, *February 1, 1960. The four protesters, students at North Carolina A & T College, were* (from left) *Joseph McNeil, Franklin McCain, Billy Smith, and Clarence Henderson.*

In 1960 the student participants, black and white, formed the Student Nonviolent Coordinating Committee (SNCC), which worked with King's Southern Christian Leadership Conference (SCLC) to broaden the movement. The sit-ins at restaurants became "kneel-ins" at churches and "wade-ins" at segregated public pools. Music provided a common source of inspiration and solace to the demonstrators. Drawing upon the tradition of slave spirituals, they developed freedom songs such as "Ain't Gonna Let That Sheriff Turn Me Around" and "We Shall Overcome." A participant in an organizational meeting at a church recalled that after the last speaker concluded, "tears filled the eyes of hard, grown men who had seen with their own eyes merciless atrocities committed. . . . Bertha told of spending Thanksgiving in jail . . . and when we rose to sing 'We Shall Overcome,' nobody could imagine what kept the church on four corners. . . . I threw my head back and closed my eyes as I sang with my whole body."

Everywhere they demonstrated, the protesters refused to retaliate, even when struck with clubs or poked with cattle prods. The conservative white editor of the *Richmond News Leader* conceded his admiration for their courage:

> Here were the colored students, in coats, white shirts, ties, and one of them was reading Goethe, and one was taking notes from a biology text. And here, on the sidewalk, was a gang of white boys come to heckle, a ragtail rabble, slack-jawed, black-jacketed, grinning fit to kill, and some of them, God save the mark, were waving the proud and honored flag of the Southern States in the last war fought by gentlemen.

Words cannot do justice to the suffering, sacrifice, courage, and commitment of the young protesters. During the year after the Greensboro sit-ins, over 3,600 black and white activists spent some time in jail. In many communities they were pelted with rocks, burned with cigarettes, and subjected to unending verbal abuse. In Orangeburg, South Carolina, officers used fire hoses against the demonstrators amid subfreezing temperatures.

In 1961 the Congress of Racial Equality (CORE) sent a group of black and white "freedom riders" on buses to test a federal court ruling that had banned segregation on buses and trains and in terminals. In Alabama mobs attacked the travelers with fists and pipes, burned one of the buses, and assaulted Justice Department observers, but the demonstrators persisted and drew national attention, generating new respect and support for their cause.

FEDERAL INTERVENTION In 1962 Governor Ross Barnett of Mississippi, who believed that God made the Negro "different to punish him," defied a court order and refused to allow James H. Meredith, a black student, to enroll at the University of Mississippi. Attorney-General Robert Kennedy thereupon dispatched federal marshals to enforce the law. When the marshals were assaulted by a white mob, federal troops had to intervene, but only after two deaths and many injuries. Meredith was finally registered at "Ole Miss" a few days later.

Eugene "Bull" Connor's police unleash attack dogs on civil rights demonstrators in Birmingham, Alabama, May 1963.

Everywhere it seemed black activists and white supporters were challenging deeply entrenched patterns of segregation and prejudice. In 1963 Martin Luther King launched a series of nonviolent demonstrations in Birmingham, Alabama, where Police Commissioner Eugene "Bull" Connor served as the perfect foil for King's tactic of nonviolent civil disobedience. Connor used attack dogs, tear gas, electric cattle prods, and fire hoses on the protesters while millions of outraged Americans watched the confrontations on television.

King, who was arrested and jailed during the demonstrations, took the opportunity to write his "Letter from Birmingham City Jail," a stirring defense of the nonviolent strategy that became a classic of the civil rights movement. "One who breaks an unjust law," he stressed, "must do so openly, lovingly, and with a willingness to accept the penalty." He also signaled a shift in his strategy for social change. Heretofore, King had emphasized the need to educate southern whites about the injustice of segregation and other patterns of discrimination. Now he fo-

cused more on gaining federal enforcement and new legislation by provoking racists to display their violent hatreds in public. As King admitted in his "Letter," he sought through organized nonviolent protest to
"create such a crisis and foster such a tension that a community which
has constantly refused to negotiate is forced to confront the issue." This
concept of civil disobedience did not set well with J. Edgar Hoover, the
powerful head of the FBI, who labeled King "the most dangerous Negro
of the future in this nation." He ordered agents to follow King and authorized the use of wiretaps on his telephones and in his motel rooms.

The sublime courage and resolve that King and many other protesters
displayed in carrying out their program of nonviolent coercion helped
mobilize national support for their integrationist objectives. (Indeed, in
1964 King would be awarded the Nobel Peace Prize.) Nudged by his
brother Robert, a man of passion, compassion, and vision, President
Kennedy finally decided that enforcement of existing statutes was not
enough; new legislation was needed to deal with the race question. In

Martin Luther King, Jr. (second from left), *and other civil rights leaders
at the head of the March on Washington for Jobs and Freedom, August 28,
1963.*

1963 he told the nation that racial discrimination "has no place in American life or law." He then endorsed an ambitious civil rights bill intended to end discrimination in public facilities, desegregate the public schools, and protect black voters. But the bill was quickly blocked in Congress by southern conservatives.

Throughout the Deep South, traditionalists remained steadfast. In the fall of 1963, Governor George Wallace dramatically stood in the doorway of a building at the University of Alabama to block the enrollment of several black students, but he stepped aside in the face of insistent federal marshals. That night President Kennedy spoke eloquently of the moral issue facing the nation: "If an American, because his skin is black, cannot enjoy the full and free life which all of us want, then who among us would be content to have the color of his skin changed and stand in his place? Who among us would be content with the counsels of patience and delay?" Later the same night, NAACP official Medgar Evers was shot to death as he returned to his home in Jackson, Mississippi.

The high point of the integrationist phase of the civil rights movement occurred on August 28, 1963, when over 200,000 blacks and whites marched down the Mall in Washington, D.C., toward the Lincoln Memorial singing "We Shall Overcome." The March on Washington was the largest civil rights demonstration in American history. Standing in front of Lincoln's statue, King delivered one of the memorable public speeches of the century:

> I say to you today, my friends, that in spite of the difficulties and frustrations of the moment I still have a dream. It is a dream deeply rooted in the American dream.
>
> I have a dream that one day this nation will rise up and live out the true meaning of its creed: "We hold these truths to be self-evident; that all men are created equal."
>
> -- I have a dream that one day . . . the sons of former slaves and the sons of former slaveowners will be able to sit together at the table of brotherhood.

That such racial harmony had not yet arrived, however, became clear two weeks later when a bomb exploded in a Birmingham church, killing four black girls who had arrived early for Sunday school. Yet King's dream—shared and promoted by thousands of other activists—survived. The intransigence and violence that civil rights workers encountered won converts to their cause all across the country.

FOREIGN FRONTIERS

EARLY SETBACKS   Kennedy's record in foreign relations, like that in domestic affairs, was mixed, but more spectacularly so. Although he had made the existence of a "missile gap" a major part of his campaign, he learned upon taking office that there was no "missile gap"—the United States remained far ahead of the Soviets in nuclear weaponry. Kennedy also discovered that there was in the works a CIA operation training 1,500 anti-Castro Cubans for an invasion of their homeland. The Joint Chiefs of Staff assured Kennedy that the plan was feasible in theory; analysts predicted that the invasion would inspire Cubans on the island to rebel against Castro.

In retrospect, it is clear that the scheme, poorly planned and poorly executed, had little chance of succeeding. When the invasion force landed at the Bay of Pigs in Cuba on April 17, 1961, it was brutally subdued in two days and more than 1,100 men were captured. A *New York Times* columnist lamented that the United States "looked like fools to our friends, rascals to our enemies, and incompetents to the rest." It was hardly an auspicious way for the new president to demonstrate his mastery of foreign policy.

Two months after the Bay of Pigs debacle, Kennedy met Soviet premier Khrushchev in Vienna, Austria. It was a tense confrontation during which Khrushchev browbeat the inexperienced Kennedy and threatened to limit Western access to Berlin, the divided city located deep within Communist East Germany. Kennedy was shaken by the aggressive Soviet stand. Upon his return home, he demonstrated American resolve by calling up Army Reserve and National Guard units. The Soviets responded by erecting the Berlin Wall, which cut off movement between East and West Berlin. Although no shooting incident triggered an accidental war, the Berlin Wall plugged the most accessible escape hatch for East Germans, showed Soviet willingness to challenge American resolve in Europe, and became another intractable barrier to the opening of new diplomatic frontiers.

A West Berlin couple climbs up and looks over the newly constructed Berlin Wall to communicate with the woman's mother on the other side. The Berlin Wall both physically divided the city itself and served as a wedge between the United States and the Soviet Union.

THE CUBAN MISSILE CRISIS   A year later Khrushchev posed another challenge, this time ninety miles off the coast of Florida. Kennedy's unwillingness to commit the forces necessary to overthrow Castro and his acquiescence to the erection of the Berlin Wall seemed to signify a failure of will, and the Soviets apparently reasoned that they could install their missiles in Cuba with relative impunity. Their motives were to protect Cuba from another American-backed invasion, which Castro believed to be imminent, and to redress the strategic imbalance caused by the presence of American missiles in Turkey aimed at the Soviet Union.

American officials feared that Soviet missiles in Cuba would be placed in areas not covered by radar systems and, if launched, would arrive too quickly for warning. More important to Kennedy was the psychological effect of American acquiescence to a Soviet presence on its doorstep. This might weaken the credibility of the American nuclear deterrent for Europeans and demoralize anti-Castro elements in Latin

America. At the same time, the installation of Soviet missiles served Khrushchev's purpose of demonstrating his toughness to both Chinese and Soviet critics of his earlier advocacy of peaceful coexistence. But he misjudged the American response.

On October 14, 1962, American intelligence experts discovered based on photographs made from high-altitude U-2 flights that Soviet missile sites were under construction in Cuba. From the beginning, the administration decided that they had to be removed; the only question was how. In a series of secret meetings, the Executive Committee of the National Security Council narrowed the options to a choice between a "surgical" air strike and a naval blockade of Cuba. They opted for a blockade, which was carefully disguised by the euphemism "quarantine," since a blockade was technically an act of war. It offered the advantage of forcing the Soviets to shoot first, if it came to that, and left open the further options of stronger action. Monday, October 22, began one of the most anxious weeks in world history. On that day, the president announced to members of Congress and then to the public the discovery of the missile sites in Cuba; he also announced the naval quarantine.

On October 14, 1962, a U2 surveillance plane revealed both missile launchers and shelters in San Cristóbal, Cuba.

Tensions grew as Khrushchev blustered that Kennedy had pushed humankind "to the abyss of a world missile-nuclear war." Soviet ships, he declared, would ignore the quarantine. But on Wednesday, October 24, five Soviet ships, presumably with missiles aboard, stopped short of the quarantine line. Two days later an agent of the Soviet embassy privately approached an American television reporter with a proposal for an agreement: the Soviet Union would withdraw the missiles in return for a public pledge by the United States not to invade Cuba. The reporter was asked to relay the idea to the White House. Secretary of State Dean Rusk replied that the administration was interested, but told the newscaster: "Remember, when you report this, that eyeball to eyeball, they blinked first."

That same evening Kennedy received two messages from Khrushchev, the first repeating the original offer and the second demanding in addition the removal of American missiles from Turkey. The two messages probably reflected divided counsels in the Kremlin. Ironically, Kennedy had already ordered removal of the outmoded missiles in Turkey, but he refused now to act under the gun. Instead he followed Robert Kennedy's suggestion that he respond favorably to the first letter and ignore the second. On Sunday, October 28, Khrushchev agreed to remove the missiles.

In the aftermath of the crisis, tension between the United States and the Soviet Union quickly subsided. Several symbolic steps helped to relax tensions: an agreement to sell the Soviet Union surplus wheat, the installation of a "hot line" telephone between Washington and Moscow to provide instant contact between the heads of government, and the removal of obsolete American missiles from Turkey, Italy, and Britain. On June 10, 1963, the president announced that direct discussions with the Soviets would soon begin, and he called upon the nation to reexamine its attitude toward peace, the Soviet Union, and the cold war. Those discussions resulted in a treaty with the Soviet Union and Britain to stop nuclear testing in the atmosphere. The treaty, ratified in September 1963, did not provide for on-site inspection, nor did it ban underground testing, which continued, but it promised to end the dangerous pollution of the atmosphere with radioactivity. The treaty was an important symbolic and substantive move toward détente. As Kennedy put it: "A journey of a thousand miles begins with one step."

KENNEDY AND VIETNAM   In Southeast Asia events were moving toward what would become within a decade the greatest American foreign policy calamity of the century. During John Kennedy's "thousand days" in office, the turmoil of Indochina never preoccupied public attention for any extended period, but it dominated international diplomatic debates from the time the administration entered office.

The landlocked kingdom of Laos, along with neighboring Cambodia, had been declared neutral in the Geneva Accords of 1954, but had fallen into a complex struggle for power between the Communist Pathet Lao insurgents and the Royal Laotian Army. There matters stood when Eisenhower left office and told Kennedy: "You might have to go in there and fight it out." The chairman of the Joint Chiefs of Staff argued in favor of a stand against the Pathet Lao, even if it meant direct intervention. After a lengthy consideration of alternatives, Kennedy decided to favor a neutralist coalition government including Pathet Lao representatives that would preclude American military involvement in Laos, yet prevent a Pathet Lao victory. The Soviets, who were extending aid to the Pathet Lao, indicated a readiness to negotiate, and in 1961 talks began in Geneva. After more than a year of tangled negotiations, the three factions in Laos agreed to a neutral coalition. American and Soviet aid to the opposing parties was supposed to end, but both countries in fact continued covert operations, while North Vietnam kept open the Ho Chi Minh Trail through eastern Laos, over which it supplied its Viet Cong allies in South Vietnam.

There the situation worsened under the leadership of the Catholic premier Ngo Dinh Diem, despite encouraging reports from the commander of American military "advisers" in South Vietnam. At the time the problem was less the scattered Communist guerrilla attacks than Diem's failure to deliver social and economic reforms and his inability to rally popular support. His repressive tactics, directed not only against Communists but also against the Buddhist majority and other critics, played into the hands of his enemies. In 1961 White House Assistant Walt Rostow and General Maxwell Taylor became the first in a long train of presidential emissaries to South Vietnam's capital, Saigon. Focusing on the military situation, they proposed a major increase in the American military presence. Kennedy refused, but continued to dispatch more military "advisers" in the hope of stabilizing the situation:

South Vietnamese troops in combat with Viet Cong guerrillas in the Mekong River Delta, 1961.

when he took office there had been 2,000; by the end of 1963 there were 16,000, none of whom had been officially committed to battle.

By 1963 sharply divergent reports were coming in from the South Vietnamese countryside. American military advisers, their eyes on the inflated "kill ratios" reported by the Army of the Republic of Vietnam (ARVN), drew optimistic conclusions. On-site political reporters, watching the reactions of the Vietnamese people, foresaw continued deterioration without the promised political and economic reforms. By mid-year, growing Buddhist demonstrations made the discontent in South Vietnam more plainly visible. The spectacle of Buddhist monks setting themselves on fire in protest against government tyranny stunned Americans. By the fall of 1963, the Kennedy administration had decided that the autocratic Diem was a lost cause. When dissident generals proposed a coup d'état, U.S. ambassador Henry Cabot Lodge assured them that Washington would not stand in the way. On November 1 they seized the government and murdered Diem, though without explicit American approval. But the generals provided no more stability than earlier regimes, as successive coups set the country spinning from one military leader to another.

KENNEDY'S ASSASSINATION   By the fall of 1963, Kennedy seemed to be facing up to the intractability of the situation in Vietnam. In September he declared of the South Vietnamese: "In the final analysis it's their war. They're the ones who have to win it or lose it. We can help them as advisers but they have to win it." The following month he announced the administration's intention to withdraw United States forces from South Vietnam by the end of 1965. What Kennedy would have done thereafter has remained a matter of endless controversy among historians, endless because it is unanswerable and unanswerable because on November 22, 1963, while visiting Dallas, he was shot in the neck and head by Lee Harvey Oswald.

Oswald's motives remain unknown. Although a blue-ribbon federal commission appointed by President Johnson and headed by Chief Justice Earl Warren concluded that Oswald acted alone, debate still swirls around various conspiracy theories. Kennedy's death and then the murder of Oswald by Jack Ruby, a Dallas nightclub owner, were shown over and over again on television, the medium that had so helped Kennedy's rise to the presidency and that now captured his death and the moving funeral at Arlington Cemetery.

Kennedy's vice-president, Lyndon B. Johnson, takes the presidential oath as Air Force One *returns from Dallas with Jacqueline Kennedy* (right), *the presidential party, and the body of the assassinated president.*

Shortly after the funeral, Jacqueline Kennedy reminisced for a reporter about their family life. At night they would play records, and the song John Kennedy loved most came from a current Broadway hit, *Camelot,* based on the legends of King Arthur: " 'Don't let it be forgot, that once there was a spot, for one brief shining moment, that was known as Camelot'—and it will never be that way again." This "Camelot mystique" soon enshrouded the fallen president, magnifying his accomplishments and creating an aura of glamour and poignancy around his legacy. A Gallup poll in 1976 showed that a majority of Americans regarded Kennedy as the greatest of all presidents, a judgment that time has since eroded.

Lyndon Johnson and the Great Society

Texan Lyndon Johnson took the oath as president of the United States on board the plane that took John Kennedy's body back to Washington from Dallas. At age fifty-five he had spent twenty-six years on the Washington scene and had served nearly a decade as Democratic leader in the Senate, where he had displayed the greatest gift for compromise since Henry Clay. Johnson brought to the White House a marked change of style from Kennedy. A self-made man who through gritty determination and shrewd manipulation had worked his way out of a hardscrabble rural Texas background to become one of Washington's most powerful figures, Johnson had none of the Kennedy elegance or charisma. He was a rough-hewn, gregarious, and domineering man who craved both political power and public affection. The first southern president since Woodrow Wilson, he harbored, like another southern president, Andrew Johnson, a sense of being the perpetual "outsider" despite his long experience with legislative power. And indeed he was so regarded by Kennedy "insiders."

Those who viewed Johnson as a stereotypical southern conservative failed to appreciate his long-standing admiration for Franklin Roosevelt, the depth of his concern for poor people, and his commitment to the cause of civil rights. "By political background, by temperament, by personal preference," wrote one journalist, Johnson was "the riverboat man. He was brawny and rough and skilled beyond measure in the full use of tricky tides and currents, in his knowledge of the hidden shoals. He was a swashbuckling master of the political midstreams—but only in the crowded, well-traveled and familiar inland waterways of domestic politics." In foreign affairs, however, he was, like Woodrow Wilson, a novice.

THE JOHNSON MYSTIQUE   Lyndon Johnson was a paradox. He was neither southern nor western but that unique blend of the two regions, a Texan capable of altering himself to fit any occasion. On the one hand, he was a compulsive worker and achiever, animated by greed, ambition, and an all-consuming lust for power, an overbearing man capable of ruthlessness and deceit. On the other hand, he could be warm, caring, and gracious. He made friends easily and displayed genuine concern for the welfare of the disadvantaged.

After a stint in the navy during World War II, which Johnson, like Kennedy, later exaggerated to appear more heroic than it was, he ran for the Senate in 1948. His lieutenants bribed local political bosses to "stuff" ballot boxes in their precincts, and at the last minute Johnson won by eighty-seven votes. Johnson tried to deflect criticism by jokingly referring to himself as "Landslide Lyndon," but a cloud of suspicion hung over him as he assumed his Senate seat. During the early 1950s, Johnson kept his seat by engaging in the required "Red-baiting," catering to the oil and natural gas interests in Texas, and opposing civil rights legislation. In 1951, at age forty-four, he became the youngest Senate minority leader in Democratic party history.

After reelection in 1954, Johnson was elected Senate majority leader when the Democrats recaptured the upper house of Congress. During the next six years he displayed a remarkable ability for manipulating others to get legislation passed, resorting to horse-trading and backroom deals in order to shepherd some 1,300 bills through the Senate. He engineered the censure of Joseph McCarthy and the passage of the Civil Rights Act of 1957. His accomplishments made him a natural contender for the presidency in 1960, but he was unable to project himself as anything more than a regional candidate. Having done all he could as a legislative leader, he eagerly accepted Kennedy's invitation to join the ticket. The invitation resulted not from affection or admiration. Kennedy simply needed Johnson to help carry the South for him.

POLITICS AND POVERTY   Quite naturally, domestic politics became Johnson's first priority as president. Amid the national grief after the assassination, he declared that Kennedy's cabinet and advisers would stay on and that his legislative program, stymied in several congressional committees, would be passed. Johnson loved the kind of political infighting and legislative detail that Kennedy had loathed. Recalcitrant congressmen and senators were brought to the White House for what became famous as "the Johnson Treatment." A journalist described the technique: "He moved in close, his face a scant millimeter from his target, his eyes widening and narrowing, his eyebrows rising and falling. From his pockets poured clippings, memos, statistics. Mimicry, humor, and the genius of analogy made the Treatment an almost hypnotic experience and rendered the target stunned and helpless." The logjam in the Congress that had blocked Kennedy's program broke under Johnson's forceful leadership, and a torrent of legislation poured through.

Before the year 1963 was out Congress had approved the pending foreign aid bill and a plan to sell wheat to the Soviet Union. But Amer-

The Johnson Treatment. *Johnson used powerful body language and facial expressions to intimidate and manipulate anyone who dared to disagree with him.*

ica's commitment to foreign aid pointed up its own people's needs. In 1964 the Council of Economic Advisers reported that 9.3 million American families, about 20 percent of the population, were below the "poverty line" of $3,000 per year for a family of four. "Unfortunately, many Americans live on the outskirts of hope," Johnson told the Congress in his first State of the Union message, "some because of their poverty and some because of their color, and all too many because of both." At the top of his agenda he put the stalled measures for tax reduction and civil rights, then added to his "must" list a bold new idea that bore the LBJ brand: "This Administration today, here and now, declares unconditional war on poverty in America." The particulars of this "war on poverty" were to come later, the product of a task force already at work before Johnson took office.

Americans had suddenly rediscovered poverty in the early 1960s when the social critic Michael Harrington published a powerful exposé titled *The Other America* (1962). Harrington argued that while most Americans had been celebrating their rising affluence during the postwar era, more than 40 million people were mired in a "culture of poverty," hidden from view and passed on from one generation to the next. Unlike the upwardly mobile immigrant poor at the turn of the century, these modern poor were impervious to hope. "To be impoverished," he asserted, "is to be an internal alien, to grow up in a culture that is radically different from the one that dominates the society." Television only exacerbated the problem by accentuating the relative deprivation of the poor. They saw how different they were from middle-class Americans, leaving many fatalistic about their condition.

President Kennedy read *The Other America* in 1963 and asked his advisers to investigate the problem and suggest a plan of attack. Upon taking office, Johnson announced that he wanted an antipoverty package that was "big and bold, that would hit the nation with real impact." When his advisers told him that their research was still incomplete, he declared his determination to act anyway. Money for the program would come from the tax revenues generated by corporate profits that had resulted from the surge in capital investment and increased individual purchasing power made possible by the tax reduction of 1964, which had led to one of the longest sustained economic booms in American history.

The administration's "war on poverty" was embodied in an Economic Opportunity Bill that incorporated a wide range of programs: a Job

Corps for inner-city youths aged sixteen to twenty-one, a Head Start program for disadvantaged preschoolers, work-study jobs for college students, grants to farmers and rural businesses, loans to those willing to hire the chronically unemployed, the Volunteers in Service to America (VISTA, a "domestic Peace Corps"), and the Community Action Program, which would provide "maximum feasible participation" of the poor in directing neighborhood programs designed for their benefit. Speaking at Ann Arbor, Michigan, in 1964, Johnson called for a "Great Society" resting on "abundance and liberty for all. The Great Society demands an end to poverty and racial injustice, to which we are fully committed in our time."

THE 1964 ELECTION   Johnson's liberal social program provoked a Republican counterattack. For years party regulars had come to fear that the party had fallen into the hands of an "Eastern Establishment" that had given in to the same internationalism and big-government policies as liberal Democrats. Ever since 1940, so the theory went, the party had nominated "me-too" candidates who merely promised to run more efficiently the programs that Democrats designed. Offer the voters "a choice, not an echo," they reasoned, and a conservative majority would assert itself. The Republican right thus began to drift toward varieties of dogmatic conservatism, ranging from a kind of "aristocratic" intellectual "new conservatism," which found voice in the *National Review,* edited by William F. Buckley, Jr., to the John Birch Society, founded by Robert Welch, a New England candy manufacturer given to accusing such distinguished citizens as Eisenhower, Dulles, and Chief Justice Earl Warren of supporting a Communist conspiracy.

By 1960 Arizona senator Barry Goldwater, a millionaire department-store magnate, had emerged as the leader of the Republican right. In his book *The Conscience of a Conservative* (1960), Goldwater proposed abolition of the income tax, sale of the TVA, and a drastic overhaul of Social Security. Almost from the time of Kennedy's victory in 1960 a movement to draft Goldwater began, mobilizing right-wing activists to capture party caucuses and contest primaries. In 1964 they took an early lead, and after sweeping the all-important California primary, Goldwater's forces controlled the Republican convention when it gathered in Los Angeles. "I would remind you," Goldwater told the delegates, "that extremism in the defense of liberty is no vice."

Many voters feared that the Republican candidate for president in 1964, Arizona senator Barry Goldwater, was trigger-happy. In this cartoon he wields his book, The Conscience of a Conservative, *in one hand and a hydrogen bomb in the other.*

By the end of the 1964 campaign, Goldwater had achieved a position of splendid isolation on the far right of the political spectrum. He had a gift for frightening voters. Accusing the administration of waging a "no-win" war in Vietnam, he urged wholesale bombing of North Vietnam and left the impression of being trigger-happy. He savaged Johnson's war on poverty and the entire New Deal tradition. At times he was fool-ishly candid. In Tennessee he proposed the sale of the Tennessee Valley Authority; in St. Petersburg, Florida, a major retirement community, he questioned the value of Social Security. He was on record as opposing both the nuclear test ban and the Civil Rights Act. To Republican cam-paign buttons that claimed "In your heart, you know he's right," Demo-crats responded, "In your guts you know he's nuts."

Johnson, on the other hand, moved to the center. He appealed to the great consensus that spanned most of the political spectrum. Having the Democratic nomination from the start, he chose as his running mate Hubert Humphrey from Minnesota, a prominent liberal senator who had long promoted the cause of civil rights. In contrast to Goldwater's bellicose rhetoric on Vietnam, Johnson pledged: "We are not about to send American boys nine or ten thousand miles from home to do what Asian boys ought to be doing for themselves"—a statement reminiscent of the assurance that Johnson's idol, Franklin Roosevelt, had voiced regarding the European war in 1940.

The result was a landslide. Johnson polled 61 percent of the total votes; Goldwater carried only Arizona and five states in the Deep South, where race remained the salient issue. Vermont went Democratic for the first time ever in a presidential election. Johnson won the electoral vote by a whopping 486 to 52. In the Senate the Democrats increased their majority by two (68 to 32) and in the House by thirty-seven (295 to 140). But LBJ was aware that a mandate such as he had received could quickly erode. He shrewdly told aides, "every day I'm in office, I'm going to lose votes. I'm going to alienate somebody. . . . We've got to get this legislation fast. You've got to get it during my honeymoon."

LANDMARK LEGISLATION   Johnson flooded the new Congress with Great Society legislation that, he promised, would end poverty, revitalize the decaying central cities, provide every young American with the chance to attend college, protect the health of the elderly, enhance cultural life, clean up the air and water, and make the highways safer and prettier. The scope of Johnson's legislation was unparalleled since Franklin Roosevelt's Hundred Days.

Priority went to health insurance and aid to education, proposals that had languished since President Truman advanced them in 1945. For twenty years the proposal for a comprehensive plan of medical insurance had been stalled by the steadfast opposition of the American Medical Association (AMA). But now that Johnson had the votes, the AMA joined Republicans in boarding the bandwagon for a bill serving those over age sixty-five. The AMA proposed, in addition to hospital insurance, a program for payment of doctor bills and drug costs, with the government footing half the premium. The act that finally emerged went well beyond the original program. It not only incorporated the new proposal into the Medicare program for the aged, but added another program, dubbed Medicaid, for federal grants to states that would help cover medical payments for the indigent. President Johnson signed the bill on July 30, 1965, in Independence, Missouri, with eighty-one-year-old Harry Truman looking on.

Five days after he submitted his Medicare program, Johnson sent to Congress his proposal for $1.5 billion in federal aid to elementary and secondary education. Such proposals had been ignored since the 1940s, blocked alternately by issues of segregation or separation of church and state. The first issue had been laid to rest, legally at least, by the Civil Rights Act of 1964. Now the Congress devised a means of extending aid to "poverty-impacted" school districts, regardless of their public or parochial character.

The momentum generated by the progress of these measures had already begun to carry others along, and the momentum continued through the following year. Before the Eighty-ninth Congress adjourned, it had established a record in the passage of landmark legislation unequaled since the time of the New Deal. Altogether the tide of Great Society legislation had carried 435 bills through the Congress. Among them was the Appalachian Regional Development Act of 1966, which provided $1 billion for programs in remote mountain coves. The Housing and Urban Development Act of 1965 provided aid for construction of 240,000 housing units and $3 billion for urban renewal. Funds for rent supplements for low-income families followed in 1966, and in that year a new Department of Housing and Urban Development appeared, headed by Robert C. Weaver, the first black cabinet member. Johnson had, in the words of one Washington reporter, "brought to harvest a generation's backlog of ideas and social legislation."

Little noticed in the stream of legislation flowing from the Congress was a major new immigration bill that had originated in the Kennedy White House. Johnson used his 1964 State of the Union address to endorse immigration reform in general and the Kennedy bill in particular. A modified version finally passed the Congress in the fall of 1965.

President Johnson signed the Immigration Act of 1965 in a ceremony held on Liberty Island in New York Harbor, with Ellis Island in the background. In his speech, he stressed that the new law would redress the wrong done to those "from southern and eastern Europe" and the "developing continents" of Asia, Africa, and Latin America. It did so by abolishing the discriminatory quotas based on national origins that had governed immigration policy since the 1920s. The new law, whose provisions were to take full effect in 1968, treated all nationalities and races equally. In place of national quotas it created hemispheric ceilings on visas issued: 170,000 for persons from outside the Western Hemisphere, 120,000 for persons from within. It also stipulated that no more than 20,000 people could come from any one country each year. The new act allowed the entry of immediate family members of American residents without limit. Most of the annual visas were to be given on a first-come-first-served basis to "other relatives" of American residents, and only a small proportion (about 10 percent) were allocated to those with special talents or job skills.

During the prosperous sixties, few western Europeans sought to emigrate to the United States; those living in Communist-controlled eastern Europe could not leave. But Asians and Latin Americans flocked to American consulates in search of visas. And within a few years the new arrivals in turn used the family-preference system to bring their family members as well. This so-called chain immigration quickly filled the annual quotas for nations such as the Philippines, Mexico, Korea, and the Dominican Republic, and Hispanics and Asians became the largest contingent of new Americans.

The Great Society programs included several genuine success stories. The Highway Safety Act and the Traffic Safety Act (1966) established safety standards for automobile manufacturers and highway design, and the scholarships provided for college students under the Higher Education Act (1965) were quite popular. Many Great Society initiatives aimed at improving the health, nutrition, and education of poor Americans, young and old, made some headway against these problems. So, too, did federal efforts to clean up air and water pollution. But several ambitious programs were hastily designed and ill conceived, others were vastly underfunded, and many were mismanaged. Medicare, for example, removed any incentives for hospitals to control costs, and medical bills skyrocketed. Often funds appropriated for various programs never made it through the tangled bureaucracy to the needy. Widely publicized cases of welfare fraud became a powerful weapon in the hands of those who were opposed to liberal social programs. By 1966 middle-class resentment over the cost and waste of the Great Society programs helped to generate a conservative backlash.

FROM CIVIL RIGHTS TO BLACK POWER

CIVIL RIGHTS LEGISLATION   Among the successes of the Great Society were several landmark pieces of civil rights legislation. After Kennedy's death, President Johnson, who had maneuvered through the Senate the Civil Rights Acts of 1957 and 1960, called for passage of a new civil rights bill as a memorial to the fallen leader. With bipartisan support, he finally broke the Senate filibuster mounted by southern segregationists. On July 2 Johnson signed the Civil Rights Act of 1964, the most far-reaching civil rights measure ever enacted by the Congress. The act outlawed discrimination in hotels, restaurants, and other public accommodations. It required that literacy tests for voting be administered in writing, and defined as literate anybody who had finished the sixth grade. The attorney-general could now bring suits for school desegregation, relieving parents of a painful necessity. Federally assisted programs and private employers alike were required to eliminate discrimination. An Equal Employment Opportunity Commission (the old Fair Employment Practices Commission reborn) administered a ban on job discrimination by race, religion, national origin, or sex.

Early in 1965, Martin Luther King, Jr., announced a drive to enroll the 3 million blacks in the South who had not registered to vote. In Selma, Alabama, civil rights protesters began a march to Montgomery, about 50 miles away, only to be violently dispersed by state troopers and a mounted posse. A federal judge agreed to allow the march, and President Johnson provided protection with National Guardsmen and army military police. By March 25, when the demonstrators reached Montgomery, some 35,000 people were with them, and King delivered a rousing address from the steps of the state capitol.

Several days before the march, President Johnson went before Congress with a moving plea that reached its climax when he slowly intoned the words of the movement's hymn: "And we shall overcome." The resulting Voting Rights Act of 1965 was passed to ensure all citizens the right to vote, and authorized the attorney-general to dispatch federal examiners to register voters. In states or counties where fewer than half the adults had voted in 1964, the act suspended literacy tests and other devices commonly used to defraud citizens of the vote. By the end of the year some 250,000 blacks were newly registered.

"BLACK POWER"   In the midst of this success, the civil rights movement began to fragment. On August 11, 1965, less than a week after the passage of the Voting Rights Act, Watts, a predominantly black and poor community in Los Angeles, exploded in a frenzy of riots and looting. When the uprising ended, there were thirty-four dead, almost 4,000 rioters in jail, and property damage exceeding $35 million. Liberal commentators were stunned, as the riots occurred in the wake of the greatest legislative victories for black Americans since Reconstruction.

But events did not stand still to await white liberal comprehension. Chicago and Cleveland, along with forty other American cities, experienced racial riots in the summer of 1966. The following summer Newark and Detroit burst into flames. Detroit provided the most graphic example of urban violence, as tanks rolled through the streets and soldiers used machine guns to deal with snipers in the tenements. Firemen who tried to put out the flames in several of the urban riots were showered by bricks and bottles thrown by the very people whose houses were burning.

In retrospect, it was predictable that the civil rights movement would

During the 1965 riots in Watts, Los Angeles, more than 800 armed guards were stationed on area streets to quell looting and violence.

focus on the plight of urban blacks. By the middle 1960s, about 70 percent of America's black population lived in metropolitan areas, most of them in central-city ghettos that had been bypassed by the postwar prosperity. And again it seemed clear, in retrospect, that the nonviolent tactics that had worked in the rural South would not work in the northern cities. In the North the problems were *de facto* segregation resulting from residential patterns, not *de jure* segregation amenable to changes in law. Moreover, northern white ethnic groups did not have the cultural heritage that southern whites shared with blacks. "It may be," wrote a contributor to *Esquire,* "that looting, rioting and burning . . . are really nothing more than radical forms of urban renewal, a response not only to the frustrations of the ghetto but the collapse of all ordinary modes of change, as if a body despairing of the indifference of doctors sought to rip a cancer out of itself." A special Commission on Civil Disorders noted that, unlike earlier race riots, the urban upheavals of the middle 1960s were initiated by blacks themselves; earlier riots had been started by whites, which had then provoked black counterattacks. Now blacks visited violence and destruction on themselves in an effort to destroy what they could not stomach and what civil rights legislation seemed unable to change.

By 1966 "black power" had become the new rallying cry. Radical members of the SNCC had become estranged from Martin Luther King's theories of militant nonviolence. As King became the center of attention from the white media, SNCC members began to refer to him cynically as "de Lawd." When Stokely Carmichael, a twenty-five-year-old graduate of Howard University, became head of the SNCC in 1966, he made the separatist philosophy of black power the official objective of the organization and ousted whites from the organization. "We reject an American dream defined by white people and must work to construct an American reality defined by Afro-Americans," said the author of a SNCC position paper. H. Rap Brown, who succeeded Carmichael as head of the SNCC in 1967, urged blacks to "get you some guns" and "kill the honkies." Meanwhile Carmichael had moved on to the Black Panther party, a self-professed group of urban revolutionaries founded in Oakland, California, in 1966. Headed by Huey P. Newton and Eldridge Cleaver, the Black Panthers terrified the public by wearing bandoleras and carrying rifles, but eventually fragmented in spasms of violence.

Malcolm X, influential spokesman for the Black Muslim movement.

The most articulate spokesman for black power was Malcolm X (formerly Malcolm Little, with the "X" denoting his lost African surname). Malcolm had risen from a ghetto childhood of narcotics and crime to become the chief disciple of Elijah Muhammad, the Black Muslim leader in the United States. "Yes, I'm an extremist," Malcolm acknowledged in 1964. "The black race in the United States is in extremely bad shape. You show me a black man who isn't an extremist and I'll show you one who needs psychiatric attention." By 1964 Malcolm had broken with Elijah Muhammad and founded his own organization committed to the establishment of alliances between African Americans and the nonwhite peoples of the world. But just after the publication of his *Autobiography* in 1965, Malcolm was gunned down in Harlem by assassins representing a rival faction of Black Muslims. With him went the most effective voice for urban black militancy since Marcus Garvey. What made the assassination of Malcolm X especially tragic was that he had just months before begun to abandon his strident antiwhite rhetoric and to preach a biracial message of social change.

Although widely publicized and highly visible, the black power movement never attracted more than a small minority of African Americans. Only about 15 percent of blacks labeled themselves separatists. The preponderant majority continued to identify with the philosophy of nonviolent integration promoted by Martin Luther King, Jr., and organizations such as the NAACP. King dismissed black separatism and the promotion of violent social change as a "nihilistic philosophy." He reminded his followers that "we can't win violently. We have neither the instruments nor the techniques at our disposal, and it would be totally absurd for us to believe we could do it."

Yet the black power philosophy, despite its hyperbole, violence, and the small number of its adherents, had two positive effects upon the civil rights movement. First, it helped African Americans take pride in their racial heritage. As Malcolm X often pointed out, prolonged slavery and institutionalized racism had eroded the self-esteem of many blacks in the United States. "The worst crime the white man has committed," he declared, "has been to teach us to hate ourselves." He and others helped blacks appreciate their African roots and their American accomplishments. In fact, it was Malcolm X who insisted that blacks call themselves African Americans as a symbol of pride in their roots and as a spur to learn more about their history as a people. As the popular singer James Brown urged, "Say it loud—I'm black and I'm proud."

Second, the black power phenomenon forced King and other mainstream black leaders and organizations to launch a new stage in the civil rights movement that would focus attention on the plight of poor inner-city blacks. Legal access to restaurants, schools, and other public accommodations, King pointed out, meant little to people mired in a culture of urban poverty. They needed jobs and decent housing as much as they needed legal rights. To this end, King began to emphasize the economic plight of the black urban underclass. The time had come for radical measures "to provide jobs and income for the poor." Yet as King and others sought to escalate the war on poverty at home, the war in Vietnam was commandeering more and more of America's resources and energies.

THE TRAGEDY OF VIETNAM

As racial violence erupted in America's cities, the war in Vietnam reached new levels of intensity and destruction. In November 1963, when John Kennedy was assassinated, there were 16,000 American military "advisers" in South Vietnam. Lyndon Johnson inherited an American commitment to prevent a Communist takeover there as well as a reluctance on the part of American presidents to assume primary responsibility for fighting the Viet Cong (Communist-led guerrillas in South Vietnam) and their North Vietnamese allies. Beginning with Truman, one president after another had done just enough to avoid being charged with having "lost" Vietnam to communism. Johnson initially sought to do the same, fearing that any other course of action would undermine his political influence and jeopardize his Great Society programs in Congress. But this path took him and the United States inexorably deeper into an expanding military commitment in Southeast Asia.

During the presidential campaign of 1964, Johnson had opposed the use of American combat troops and had privately described Vietnam as "a raggedy-ass fourth-rate country" not worthy of American blood and money. Nevertheless, by the end of 1965, there were 184,000 American troops in Vietnam; in 1966 the troop level reached 385,000; and by 1969, the height of the American presence, 542,000. By the time the last American troops left in March 1973, some 58,000 Americans had died and another 300,000 had been wounded. The war had cost the American taxpayers $150 billion, generated economic dislocations that destroyed many Great Society programs, produced 570,000 draft offenders and 563,000 less-than-honorable discharges from the service, toppled Johnson's administration, and divided the country as no event in American history had since the Civil War.

ESCALATION The official sanction for "escalation"—a Defense Department term coined in the Vietnam era—was the Tonkin Gulf Resolution, voted by Congress on August 7, 1964. Johnson told a national television audience that two American destroyers, the U.S.S. *Maddox* and the *C. Turner Joy,* had been attacked by North Vietnamese vessels on August 2 and 4 in the Gulf of Tonkin off the coast of North Vietnam. Although Johnson described the attack as unprovoked, in truth the destroyers had been monitoring South Vietnamese attacks against two North Vietnamese islands—attacks planned by American advisers. Even though there was no tangible evidence of the attack on the American ships, the Tonkin Gulf Resolution authorized the president to "take all necessary measures to repel any armed attack against the forces of the United States and to prevent further aggression." Only

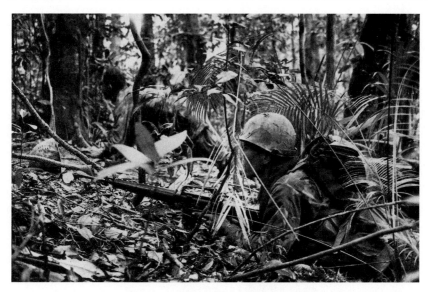

U.S. troops faced a difficult and unfamiliar environment during the Vietnam War. Here two U.S. soldiers take cover in the jungle southwest of Da Nang.

Senator Wayne Morse of Oregon and Senator Ernest Gruening of Alaska voted against the resolution, which Johnson thereafter interpreted as equivalent to a congressional declaration of war.

Soon after his landslide victory over Goldwater in 1964, Johnson made the crucial decisions that shaped American policy in Vietnam for the next four years. On February 5, 1965, the Viet Cong killed 8 and wounded 126 Americans at Pleiku. Further attacks on Americans later that week led Johnson to order operation "Rolling Thunder," the first sustained bombings of North Vietnam, which were intended to stop the flow of soldiers and supplies into the south. Six months later, a task force conducted an extensive study of the bombing's effects on the supplies pouring down the Ho Chi Minh Trail from North Vietnam through Laos. It concluded that there was "no way" to stop the traffic.

In March 1965 the new American army commander in Vietnam, General William C. Westmoreland, received the first installment of combat troops. By the summer, American forces were engaged in "search-and-destroy" operations throughout South Vietnam. As combat operations increased, so did the mounting list of American casualties, announced each week on the nightly news along with the "body count" of alleged Viet Cong dead. "Westy's War," although fought with helicopter gunships, chemical defoliants, and napalm, became like the trench warfare of World War I—a war of attrition.

THE CONTEXT FOR POLICY   Johnson's decision to "Americanize" the Vietnam War, so ill-starred in retrospect, was consistent with the foreign policy principles pursued by all American presidents after World War II. The version of the containment theory articulated in the Truman Doctrine, endorsed by Eisenhower and Dulles throughout the 1950s, and reaffirmed by Kennedy, pledged United States opposition to the advance of communism anywhere in the world. "Why are we in

"How deep do you figure we'll get involved, sir!" Although American soldiers were first sent to Vietnam as noncombatant advisers, they soon found themselves involved in actual fighting.

Vietnam?" Johnson asked rhetorically at Johns Hopkins University in 1965. "We are there because we have a promise to keep. . . . To leave Vietnam to its fate would shake the confidence of all these people in the value of American commitment." Secretary of State Dean Rusk repeated this rationale before countless congressional committees, warning that Thailand, Burma, and the rest of Southeast Asia would fall like dominoes to communism if American forces withdrew. Military intervention in Vietnam was thus a logical culmination of the assumptions that were widely shared by the foreign policy establishment and the leaders of both political parties since the early days of the cold war.

It was clear to Johnson and his advisers from the start that American military involvement must not reach levels that would provoke the Chinese or Soviets into direct intervention. And this meant, in effect, that a complete military victory was never possible. "It was startling to me to find out," said the new secretary of defense, Clark Clifford, in 1968, "that we have no military plan to end the war." The goal of the United States was not to win the war in any traditional sense, but to prevent the North Vietnamese and Viet Cong from winning. This meant that America would have to maintain a military presence as long as the enemy retained the will to fight.

As it turned out, American support for the war eroded faster than the will of the North Vietnamese leaders to tolerate devastating casualties. Systematic opposition to the war on college campuses began in 1965 with "teach-ins" at the University of Michigan. The following year, Senator J. William Fulbright of Arkansas, chairman of the Senate Foreign Relations Committee, began congressional investigations into American policy. George Kennan, the founding father of the containment doctrine, told Fulbright's committee that the doctrine was appropriate for Europe, but not for Southeast Asia. And a respected general testified that Westmoreland's military strategy had no chance of achieving victory. By 1967 antiwar demonstrations in New York and at the Pentagon attracted massive support. Nightly television accounts of the fighting—Vietnam was the first war to receive extended television coverage, and hence has been dubbed "the living room war"—made the official optimism appear fatuous. By May 1967 even Secretary of Defense McNamara was wavering: "The picture of the world's greatest superpower killing or injuring 1,000 noncombatants a week, while trying to pound a tiny backward nation into submission on an issue whose merits are hotly disputed, is not a pretty one."

In a war of political will, North Vietnam had the advantage. Johnson and his advisers grievously underestimated the tenacity of the North Vietnamese commitment to unify Vietnam and expel the United States. Ho Chi Minh had warned the French in the 1940s that "You can kill ten of my men for every one I kill of yours, but even at those odds, you will lose and I will win." He predicted that the Vietnamese Communists would win a war of attrition, for they were willing to sacrifice all for their cause. While the United States fought a limited war for limited objectives, the Vietnamese Communists fought an all-out war for their very survival. Indeed, just as General Westmoreland was assuring Johnson and the American public that the American war effort in early 1968 was on the verge of gaining the upper hand, the Communists again displayed their cunning and tenacity.

THE TURNING POINT   On January 31, 1968, the first day of the Vietnamese New Year (Tet), the Viet Cong defied a holiday truce to launch assaults on American and South Vietnamese forces throughout South Vietnam. The old capital city of Hué fell to the Communists, and

During the 1968 Tet offensive, Viet Cong units temporarily infiltrated the American embassy in Saigon. Here, American military police lead a captured Viet Cong guerrilla away from the embassy.

Viet Cong units temporarily occupied the grounds of the American embassy in Saigon. General Westmoreland proclaimed the Tet offensive a major defeat for the Viet Cong, and most students of military strategy later agreed with him. But while Viet Cong casualties were enormous, the impact of the events on the American public was more telling. *Time* and *Newsweek* soon ran antiwar editorials urging American withdrawal. Walter Cronkite, the dean of American television journalists, confided to his viewers that he no longer believed the war was winnable. "If I've lost Walter," Johnson was reported to say, "then it's over. I've lost Mr. Average Citizen." Polls showed that Johnson's popularity had declined to 35 percent, lower than any president since Truman's darkest days. Civil rights leaders and social activists felt betrayed as they saw federal funds earmarked for the war on poverty siphoned off by the expanding war. In 1968 the United States was spending $322,000 on every Communist killed in Vietnam; the poverty programs at home received only $53 per person.

During 1968 Johnson grew increasingly embittered and isolated. It had become painfully evident that the Vietnam War was a never-ending stalemate. Secretary of Defense Clark Clifford reported to Johnson that a task force of prominent soldiers and civilians saw no prospect for a military victory. Robert Kennedy was reportedly considering a run for the presidency in order to challenge Johnson's Vietnam policy. And Senator Eugene McCarthy of Minnesota had already decided to oppose Johnson in the Democratic primaries. With antiwar students rallying to his candidacy, McCarthy polled 42 percent of the vote to Johnson's 48 percent in New Hampshire's March primary. It was a remarkable showing for a little-known senator. Each presidential primary now promised to become a referendum on Johnson's Vietnam policy. In Wisconsin, scene of the next primary, the president's political advisers forecast a humiliating defeat.

On March 31 Johnson appeared on national television to announce a limited halt to the bombing of North Vietnam and fresh initiatives for a negotiated cease-fire. Then he added a dramatic postscript: "I have concluded that I should not permit the Presidency to become involved in the partisan divisions that are developing in this political year. Accordingly, I shall not seek, and I will not accept the nomination of my party for another term as your President." Although American troops would

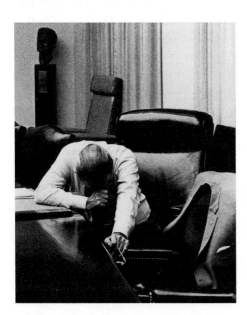

The Vietnam War sapped the spirit of Lyndon Johnson, who decided not to run for reelection in 1968.

remain in Vietnam for five more years and the casualties would continue, the quest for military victory had ended. Now the question was how the most powerful nation in the world could extricate itself from Vietnam with a minimum of damage to its prestige.

Sixties Crescendo

A TRAUMATIC YEAR History moved at a fearful pace throughout the 1960s, but 1968 was a year of extreme turbulence even for that tumultuous decade. On April 4, only four days after Johnson's announced withdrawal, Martin Luther King, Jr., was gunned down while standing on the balcony of his motel in Memphis, Tennessee. The assassin, James Earl Ray, had expressed hostility toward blacks, but debate still continues over whether he was a pawn in an organized conspiracy. King's death set off an outpouring of grief among whites and blacks. It also ignited riots in over sixty American cities, with the most serious occurring in Chicago and Washington, D.C.

Two months later, on June 6, Robert Kennedy was shot in the head by a young Palestinian, Sirhan Sirhan, who resented Kennedy's strong support of Israel. Kennedy's death occurred at the end of the day on which he had convincingly defeated Eugene McCarthy in the California Democratic primary, thereby assuming leadership of the antiwar forces in the race for the nomination for president. Political reporter David Halberstam of the *New York Times* thought back to the assassinations of John Kennedy and Malcolm X, then the violent end of King, the most influential black leader of the twentieth century, and then Robert Kennedy, the heir to leadership of the Kennedy clan. "We could make a calendar of the decade," Halberstam wrote, "by marking where we were at the hours of those violent deaths."

CHICAGO AND MIAMI In August 1968 Democratic delegates gathered inside the convention hall at Chicago to nominate Hubert Humphrey, while 24,000 police and National Guardsmen and a small army of television reporters stood watch over an eclectic gathering of protesters herded together miles away in a public park. Chicago mayor Richard Daley, who had given "shoot-to-kill" orders to police during the April riots protesting the King assassination, warned that he would not tolerate disruptions. Nonetheless, riots broke out in front of the Hilton Hotel and were televised nationwide. As police tear gas and billy clubs struck demonstrators, others chanted, "The whole world is watching."

The liberal tradition represented by the Democratic party was clearly in disarray, a fact that gave heart to the Republicans who gathered in Miami to nominate Richard Nixon. Only six years earlier, after he had lost the California gubernatorial race, Nixon had told reporters, "You won't have Nixon to kick around anymore, because, gentlemen, this is my last press conference." But by 1968 he had become a spokesman for all the values of "Middle America." Nixon and the Republicans offered a vision of stability and order that a majority of Americans—soon to be called "the silent majority"—wanted desperately.

George Wallace, the Democratic governor of Alabama who had made his reputation as a defender of segregation, ran as a third candidate in the campaign on the American Independent party ticket. Wallace moderated his position on the race issue, but appealed even more candidly than Nixon to the fears generated by protesters, the welfare system, and the growth of the federal government. Wallace's reactionary candidacy generated considerable appeal outside his native South, especially among white working-class communities, where resentment flourished against Johnson's Great Society liberalism. Although never a possible

Richard Nixon (right) *and Spiro Agnew* (left), *victors in the 1968 election.*

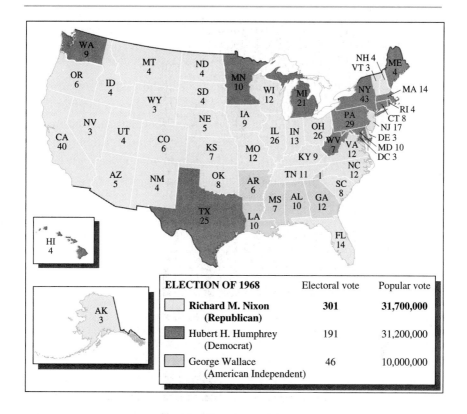

ELECTION OF 1968	Electoral vote	Popular vote
Richard M. Nixon (Republican)	**301**	**31,700,000**
Hubert H. Humphrey (Democrat)	191	31,200,000
George Wallace (American Independent)	46	10,000,000

winner, Wallace did pose the possibility of denying Humphrey or Nixon an electoral majority and thereby throwing the choice into the House of Representatives, which would have provided an appropriate climax to a chaotic year.

NIXON AGAIN   It did not happen that way. Nixon enjoyed an enormous lead in the polls, which narrowed as the election approached. Wallace's campaign was hurt by his outspoken running mate, retired air force general Curtis LeMay, who favored expanding the war in Vietnam and using nuclear weapons. In October 1968 Humphrey announced that he would stop bombing North Vietnam "as an acceptable risk for peace."

Nixon and Governor Spiro Agnew of Maryland, his running mate, eked out a narrow victory by about 500,000 votes, a margin of about 1 percentage point. The electoral vote was more decisive, 301 to 191. Wallace received 10 million votes, 13.5 percent of the total, for the best showing by a third-party candidate since Robert La Follette in 1924. All but one of Wallace's 46 electoral votes were from the Deep South. Nixon swept all but four of the states west of the Mississippi. Humphrey's support came almost exclusively from the Northeast.

And so at the end of a turbulent year near the end of a traumatic decade, power passed peacefully to a president who was associated with the complacency of the 1950s. A nation that had seemed on the verge of consuming itself in spasms of violence looked to Richard Nixon to provide what he had promised in the campaign: "peace with honor" in Vietnam and a middle ground on which a majority of Americans, silent or otherwise, could come together.

MAKING CONNECTIONS

- The reform movements of the 1960s galvanized the baby-boom generation into a new youth movement, described in the next chapter, that continued through the early 1970s.

- The conflict in Vietnam, America's longest war, would come to a bitter end for American forces, but the divisions it spawned would echo through the rest of the century.

- The Immigration Act of 1965 would have profound and unexpected consequences on American society: see Chapter 37.

- The success of the civil rights movement in the 1960s led to similar movements for women, gays, Native Americans, and Hispanics, as we will see in the next chapter.

FURTHER READING

Herbert Parmet traces the influence of John F. Kennedy in two volumes, *Jack: The Struggle of John Fitzgerald Kennedy* (1980) and *JFK: The Presidency of John Fitzgerald Kennedy* (1983). Critical assessments can be found in Thomas C. Reeves's *A Question of Character: The Life of John F. Kennedy* (rev. ed., 1998) and Bruce Miroff's *Pragmatic Illusions: The Presidential Politics of John F. Kennedy* (1976). The best study of the Kennedy administration's domestic policies is Irving Bernstein's *Promises Kept: John F. Kennedy's New Frontier* (1991). For details on the assassination, see David W. Belin's *Final Disclosure: The Full Truth about the Assassination of President Kennedy* (1988). A more recent critique of the conspiracy theories is Gerald L. Posner's *Case Closed: Lee Harvey Oswald and the Assassination of John F. Kennedy* (1993).

The most comprehensive biography of LBJ is Robert Dallek's two-volume work, *Lone Star Rising: Lyndon Johnson and His Times, 1908–1960* (1991) and *Flawed Giant: Lyndon B. Johnson, 1960–1973* (1998). An intriguing analysis of the tense relationship between Johnson and Robert Kennedy is Jeff Shesol's *Mutual Contempt: Lyndon Johnson, Robert Kennedy, and the Feud That Defined a Decade* (1997).

Among the works that interpret liberal social policy during the 1960s, John Schwarz's *America's Hidden Success: A Reassessment of Twenty Years of Public Policy* (1983) offers a glowing endorsement of Democratic programs. For a contrasting perspective, see Charles Murray's *Losing Ground: American Social Policy, 1950–1980* (rev. ed., 1995).

On foreign policy, see *Kennedy's Quest for Victory: American Foreign Policy, 1961–1963* (1989), edited by Thomas G. Paterson. To learn more about Kennedy's problems in Cuba, see Mark White's *Missiles in Cuba: Kennedy, Krushchev, Castro and the 1962 Crisis* (1997). For an understanding of the Alliance for Progress, see Jerome Levinson and Juan de Onis's *The Alliance That Lost Its Way* (1970). On the Peace Corps, see Elizabeth Hoffman's *All You Need Is Love: The Peace Corps and the Spirit of the 1960s* (1998).

American involvement in Vietnam has received voluminous treatment from all political perspectives. For an overview, see Larry Berman's *Planning a Tragedy: The Americanization of the War in Vietnam* (1982) and *Lyndon Johnson's War: The Road to Stalemate in Vietnam* (1989), as well as Stanley Karnow's *Vietnam: A History* (rev. ed., 1991). Tensions between the secretary of defense and the military leadership are detailed in H. R. McMaster's *Dereliction of Duty: Johnson, McNamara, the Joint Chiefs of Staff and the Lies That Led to Vietnam* (1997). Works that portray American policy in a favorable light include Norman Podhoretz's *Why We Were in Vietnam* (1982), Guenter Lewy's *America in Vietnam: Illusion, Myth and Reality* (1978), and Leslie Gelb and Richard Bett's *The Irony of Vietnam: The System Worked* (1979). An excellent analysis of policy making concerning the Vietnam War is David M. Barrett's *Uncertain Warriors: Lyndon Johnson and His Vietnam Advisors* (1994). Former secretary of defense Robert McNamara confesses his mistakes in *In Retrospect: The Tragedy and Lessons of Vietnam* (1995).

Many scholars have dealt with various aspects of the civil rights movement and race relations of the 1960s. See especially Carl Brauer's *John F. Kennedy and the Second Reconstruction* (1977), David Garrow's *Bearing the Cross: Martin Luther King, Jr., and the Southern Christian Leadership Conference* (1986), Adam Fairclough's *To Redeem the Soul of America: The Southern Christian Leadership Conference and Martin Luther King, Jr.* (1987), and David Lewis's *King: A Biography* (2nd. ed., 1978). For the legal turns the civil rights movement took during the 1960s, see J. Harvey Wilkinson's *From Brown to Bakke: The Supreme Court and School Integration, 1954–1978* (1978). William Chafe's *From Civilities to Civil Rights: Greensboro, North Carolina and the Black Struggle for Freedom* (1980) details the original sit-ins. An award-winning study of racial and economic inequality in a representative American city is Thomas J. Sugrue's *The Origins of the Urban Crisis: Race and Inequality in Postwar Detroit* (1996).

35 REBELLION AND REACTION IN THE 1960S AND 1970S

As Richard Nixon entered the White House, he faced a nation whose social fabric was in tatters. Everywhere, it seemed, traditional institutions and notions of authority had come under attack. The turbulent events of 1968 revealed how deeply divided American society had become and how difficult a task Nixon faced in carrying out his pledge to restore social harmony. Yet the stability he promised proved to be elusive. His policies and his combative temperament served to heighten rather than reduce the tensions wracking the nation. Those tensions had been long in developing and reflected profound fissures in the postwar consensus promoted by

Eisenhower and inherited by Kennedy and Johnson. What had caused such a seismic breakdown in social harmony? Ironically, many of the same forces that had promoted the flush times of the Eisenhower years helped generate the social upheavals of the 1960s and 1970s.

THE ROOTS OF REBELLION

YOUTH REVOLT   By the 1960s the "baby-boomers" were maturing. Now young adults, they differed from their elders in that they had experienced neither economic depression nor a major war. They also had grown up amid the homogenizing effects of a flourishing consumer culture and television. Moreover, they viewed the cold war primarily as a battle of words and gestures without immediate consequences for them. Record numbers of these young people were attending American colleges and universities during the 1960s: college enrollment quadrupled between 1945 and 1970. At the same time, many universities had become gigantic institutions dependent on research contracts from huge corporations and the federal government. As these "multiversities" grew more bureaucratic and hierarchical, they unknowingly invited resistance from a generation of students wary of involvement in what Eisenhower had labeled the "military-industrial complex."

The success of the Greensboro sit-ins in 1960 not only precipitated a decade of civil rights activism, it also signaled an end to the supposed apathy that had enveloped college campuses and social life during the 1950s. Although most immediately concerned with the rights and status of African Americans, the sit-ins, marches, protests, principles, and sacrifices associated with the civil rights movement provided the model and inspiration for other groups that demanded justice, freedom, and equality as well.

During 1960–1961 a small but significant number of white students joined African Americans in the sit-in movement. They and many others were also inspired by President Kennedy's direct appeals to their youthful idealism. Thousands enrolled in the Peace Corps and VISTA (Volunteers in Service to America, the domestic version of the Peace Corps), and others continued to participate in civil rights demonstrations. But as it became clear that politics was mixed with principle in the president's position on civil rights, and later, as criticism of escalating American involvement in Vietnam mounted, more and more young people grew disillusioned with the government and other institutional bastions of the status quo.

Folksinger Bob Dylan translated the ferment of rebellion into these lyrics in 1963:

> Come mothers and fathers,
> Throughout the land
> And don't criticize
> What you can't understand
> Your sons and your daughters
> Are beyond your command
> There's a battle
> Outside and it's ragin'
> It'll soon shake your windows
> And rattle your walls
> For the times they are a-changin'.

There was a growing feeling among young people that something was fundamentally wrong, not just with the political system but with the entire structure of American life and values. By the mid-1960s, a full-fledged youth revolt had broken out on campuses across the country. Rebellious students began to flow into two distinct, yet frequently overlapping, movements: the New Left and the counterculture.

THE NEW LEFT   The explicitly political strain of the youth revolt had its official origin when Tom Hayden and Al Haber, two University of Michigan students, formed the Students for a Democratic Society (SDS) in 1960. As an ardent critic of American capitalism, Hayden was both charismatic and convincing. A Marxist radical who heard him speak in 1962 rushed home and told his wife, "I've just seen the next Lenin."

In 1962 Hayden and Haber convened a meeting of sixty activists at Port Huron, Michigan. After four days of intense discussion and a final all-night session, Hayden drafted what became known as the Port Huron Statement: "We are the people of this generation, bred in at least moderate comfort, housed in universities, looking uncomfortably to the world we inherit." Hayden's earnest manifesto focused on the absence of individual freedom in modern American life. The country, he insisted, was dominated by huge organizational structures—governments, corporations, unions, universities—all of which conspired to oppress and alienate the individual. Inspired by the example of black activism in the South, Hayden declared that students had the power to restore "participatory democracy" to American life by wresting "control of the educational process from the administrative bureaucracy" and then forging links with other dissident movements. He and others adopted the term "New Left" to distinguish their efforts at grassroots democracy from the Old Left of the 1930s that had espoused an orthodox Marxism and had embraced Stalinism.

In the fall of 1964 students at the University of California at Berkeley took Hayden's program to heart. Many of them had returned to the campus after spending the summer working with hundreds of other students in the SNCC voter registration project in Mississippi. Three volunteers had been killed, dozens shot, and nearly a thousand arrested. The Berkeley student activists returned to school with mixed emotions—exhilarated, frustrated, and embittered. When University Chancellor Clark Kerr announced that political demonstrations would no longer be allowed at the Telegraph Avenue street corner traditionally used for such activity, several hundred students staged a sit-in at the scene. Soon thereafter over 2,000 more joined in. After a tense thirty-two-hour standoff the administration relented. Student groups then formed the Free Speech Movement (FSM).

Led by Mario Savio, a philosophy major and compelling public speaker, the FSM initially protested on behalf of student rights. But it quickly escalated into a more general criticism of the modern university and what Savio called the "depersonalized, unresponsive bureaucracy" infecting American life. In 1964 Savio led hundreds of students into the administration building and organized a sit-in. In the early-morning hours 600 policemen, dispatched by the governor, arrested the protesters. Jerry Rubin, one of the young demonstrators, later observed: "The war against Amerika [*sic*] in the schools and the streets by white middle-class kids thus commenced."

The program and tactics of the FSM and SDS soon spread to colleges throughout the country. Issues large and small became the subject of student protest: unpopular faculty tenure decisions, mandatory ROTC programs, dress codes, curfews, dormitory regulations, appearances by

Johnson administration officials. Michigan students rallied against higher movie prices; at Fairleigh Dickinson in New Jersey students marched for no particular reason but as "an expression of general student discontent."

Escalating American involvement in Vietnam soon changed the student agenda. With the dramatic expansion of the draft after 1965, millions of young American men faced the grim prospect of being drafted to fight in an increasingly unpopular Asian war. In fact, however, the Vietnam conflict, like virtually every other American war, was primarily a poor man's fight. Deferments enabled college students to postpone military service until they received their degree or reached the age of twenty-four; in 1965–1966 they made up only 2 percent of all military inductees. In 1966, however, the Selective Service System modified the provisions so even undergraduates were eligible for the draft.

As the war dragged on and opposition mounted, students and others developed sophisticated ways to evade or resist the draft. Some 200,000 young men simply refused to obey their draft notices, and some 4,000 of those served prison sentences. Those on college campuses or in urban areas took advantage of newly established draft counseling centers that provided legal advice, and hundreds of young men instituted court challenges to the draft. One result was a much broader interpretation of the term "conscientious objector" so as to allow exemptions for those with moral and ethical objections to war rooted in secular rather than religious principles. Some 56,000 men qualified for conscientious-objector status during the Vietnam War, compared with 7,600 during the Korean conflict. Still others left the country altogether—several thousand fled to Canada or Sweden—to avoid military service. The most popular way to avoid the draft was to flunk the physical examination. Many gorged themselves so as to exceed the weight limit; others raised their blood pressure by drinking excessive amounts of coffee; some pretended to be drug addicts or alcoholics; a few feigned homosexuality. Whatever the preferred method, many students succeeded in avoiding military service. Of the 1,200 men in the Harvard class of 1970, only fifty-six served in the military, and just two of those went to Vietnam.

In the spring of 1967, 500,000 war protesters of all ages converged on Manhattan's Central Park, chanting "Hey, hey, LBJ, how many kids did you kill today?" Dozens ceremoniously burned their draft cards, and the so-called resistance phase of the antiwar movement was born. Thereafter a coalition of draft-resistance groups around the country sponsored draft-card-burning rallies and sit-ins that led to numerous arrests. Meanwhile, some SDS leaders were growing even more militant. Inspired by the rhetoric and revolutionary violence of black power spokesmen such as Stokely Carmichael, Rap Brown, and Huey Newton, Tom Hayden abandoned his earlier commitment to participatory democracy and passive civil disobedience. "If necessary," he now could "shoot to kill." Rap Brown told the white radicals to remember the heritage of John Brown: "Take up a gun and go shoot the enemy." As the SDS became more militant, it grew more centralized and authoritarian. Capitalist imperialism replaced university bureaucracy as the primary foe.

Throughout 1967 and 1968, the antiwar movement grew more volatile at the same time that inner-city ghettos were seething with tension and exploding into flames. "There was a sense everywhere, in 1968," the journalist Garry Wills wrote, "that things were giving way. That man had not only lost control of his history, but might never regain it." At the end of March, Lyndon Johnson announced that he would not run for reelection, and in early April Martin Luther King, Jr., was murdered.

During that eventful spring, campus unrest spread across the country. Over 200 major demonstrations took place. The turmoil reached a climax with the disruption of Columbia University. There Mark Rudd, leader of the SDS chapter, who had earlier thrown pies at the faces of Selective Service officials and disrupted speeches at the campus memorial service for King, led a small cadre of radicals in occupying the president's office and classroom buildings. They also kidnapped a dean—all in protest of the university's insensitive decision to displace neighboring black housing in order to build a new gymnasium. During the next week, more buildings were occupied, faculty and administrative offices were ransacked, and classes were canceled. University officials finally called in the New York City police. In the process of arresting the protesters, the police injured a number of innocent bystanders. Their excessive force aroused the anger of many unaligned students, and they staged a strike that shut down the university for the remainder of the semester.

The events at Columbia buoyed the militants. Tom Hayden an-

Mark Rudd, leader of the SDS at Columbia University, talking to the media during student protests over various university policies, April 1968.

nounced: "We are moving toward power." Similar clashes between students, administrators, and police occurred at Harvard, Cornell, and San Francisco State. In response to unrest at Berkeley, Governor Ronald Reagan dispatched a small army of police to evict 5,000 students and activists who had turned a vacant lot into a "people's park." In the melee one student was killed and another blinded.

At the 1968 Democratic convention in Chicago, the polarization of American society reached a tragic and bizarre climax. Inside the tightly guarded convention hall, Democrats nominated Lyndon Johnson's faithful vice-president, Hubert Humphrey. Meanwhile, outside on Chicago's streets, the whole spectrum of antiwar dissenters was gathered, from the earnest supporters of Eugene McCarthy, through the Resistance and SDS to the nihilistic Yippies, members of the new Youth International party. The Yippies were determined to provoke anarchy in the streets of Chicago. Abbie Hoffman, one of their leaders, explained that they were "revolutionary artists. Our conception of revolution is that it's fun." The Yippies distributed a leaflet at the convention calling for the immediate legalization of marijuana and all psychedelic drugs, the abolition of money, student-run schools, and free sex.

*The violence at the 1968
Democratic National Convention in Chicago seared the
nation.*

The outlandish behavior of the Yippies and the other demonstrators
did not justify the unrestrained response of Mayor Richard M. Daley
and his army of 12,000 police. As a horrified television audience
watched, many of the police went berserk, clubbing and gassing demonstrators as well as bystanders caught up in the chaotic scene. The
spectacle lasted three days and seriously damaged Humphrey's candidacy. The Chicago riots also generated a wave of anger among many
middle-class Americans, anger that Richard Nixon and the Republicans
shrewdly exploited at their convention in Miami. At the same time, the
riots helped to fragment the antiwar movement. Those groups committed to nonviolent protest, while castigating the reactionary policies of
Mayor Daley and the police, also felt betrayed by the actions of the Yippies and other anarchistic militants.

In 1968 SDS began to break up into rival factions, the most extreme
of which was the Weathermen, a term derived from one of Bob Dylan's
lyrics: "You don't need a weatherman to know which way the wind
blows." These hardened young activists embarked on a campaign of violence and disruption, firebombing university buildings and killing innocent people—as well as several of themselves. Government forces responded in kind, arresting most of the Weathermen and sending the
rest underground. By 1971 the New Left was dead as a political move-

ment. In large measure it had committed suicide by abandoning the democratic and pacifist principles that had originally inspired participants and given the movement moral legitimacy. The larger antiwar movement also began to fade. There would be a wave of student protests against the Nixon administration in 1970, but thereafter, campus unrest virtually disappeared.

If the social mood was changing during the Nixon years, still a large segment of the public continued the quest for personal fulfillment and social justice. The burgeoning environmental and consumer movements attested to the continuity of sixties idealism. A *New York Times* survey of college campuses in 1969 revealed that many students were transferring their attention from the antiwar movement to the environment. This ecological conscience would blossom in the 1970s into one of the most compelling items on the nation's social agenda.

THE COUNTERCULTURE   The numbing events of 1968 led other disaffected activists away from radical politics altogether and toward another manifestation of the sixties youth revolt: the "counterculture." Long hair, jeans, tie-dyed shirts, sandals, mind-altering drugs, rock music, and cooperative living arrangements were more important than revolutionary ideology to the "hippies," the direct descendants of the Beats of the 1950s. These advocates of the counterculture were, like their New Left peers, primarily affluent, well-educated young whites alienated by the Vietnam War, racism, political and parental demands, runaway technology, and a crass corporate mentality that equated the good life with material goods. In their view, a bland materialism and smug complacency had settled over urban and suburban life. But they were uninterested in or disillusioned with organized political action. Instead they eagerly embraced the tantalizing credo outlined by the zany Harvard professor Timothy Leary: "Tune in, turn on, drop out."

For some the counterculture entailed the study and practice of Oriental mysticism. For many it meant the daily use of hallucinogenic drugs. Collective living in urban enclaves such as San Francisco's Haight-Ashbury district, New York's East Village, or Atlanta's Fourteenth Street was the rage for a time among hippies, until conditions grew so crowded, violent, and depressing that residents migrated elsewhere. Rural communes also attracted many of the bourgeois rebels. During the 1960s and early 1970s, thousands of young and inexperi-

This dinner scene with the members of Hog Farm epitomizes the camaraderie of collective living. But communes were rarely able to last as money and food quickly ran out.

enced romantics flocked to the countryside, eager to be liberated from parental and institutional restraints, to live in harmony with nature, and to coexist in an atmosphere of love and openness.

But only a handful of these utopian homesteads survived more than a few months. Rooted in the pleasure principle, rustic hippies often produced more babies than bread. One such "flower child" confessed that "we are so stupid, so unable to cope with anything practical. Push forward, smoke dope. But maintain? Never. We don't know how." Initially intent upon rejecting conventional society, many found themselves utterly dependent on it, and they were soon panhandling on street corners or lined up at government offices, collecting welfare, unemployment compensation, and food stamps to help them survive the rigors of natural living. A participant at Paper Farm in northern California said of its residents: "They had no commitment to the land—a big problem. All would take food from the land, but few would tend it. . . . We were entirely open. We did not say no. We felt this would make for a more dynamic group. But we got a lot of sick people."

Huge outdoor rock music concerts were also a popular source of community for hippies. The largest of these was the Woodstock Music Festival. In August 1969 some 500,000 young people converged on a 600-acre farm near the tiny rural town of Bethel, New York. The musi-

The Woodstock Festival drew nearly a half million people to a farm in Bethel, New York. The concert was billed as three days of "peace, music, . . . and love."

cians—including Joan Baez; Jimi Hendrix; Crosby, Stills, Nash, and Young; Santana; and Richie Havens—were a powerful attraction. So too was the easy availability of drugs. For three days the assembled flower children reveled in good music, cheap marijuana, and free love. "Everyone swam nude in the lake," a journalist reported. He added that the country had never "seen a society so free of repression."

But the Woodstock karma was short-lived. When other promoters tried to repeat the scene four months later, this time at Altamont, California, the counterculture encountered the criminal culture. The Rolling Stones hired Hell's Angels motorcycle gang members to provide the "security" for their show. In the midst of Mick Jagger's performance of "Sympathy for the Devil," the drunken white motorcyclists beat to death a black man wielding a knife in front of the stage. Three other spectators were accidentally killed that night; much of the vitality and innocence of the counterculture died with them.

After 1969 the hippie phenomenon began to wane. "It was good for a time," drug guru Timothy Leary lamented; "then we went so far that we lost it." The counterculture had become counterproductive and had developed both faddish and fashionable overtones. Entrepreneurs were quick to see profits in protest. Retailers developed a banner business in faded blue jeans, surplus army jackets, beads, incense, and sandals.

Health-food stores and "head" shops appeared in shopping malls along-side Nieman Marcus and Sears. Rock music groups, for all their lyrical protests against the capitalist "system," made millions from it. As one wit recognized, the "difference between a rock king and a robber baron [was] about six inches of hair." Many of the flower children themselves grew tired of their riches-to-rags existence and returned to school to become lawyers, doctors, politicians, or accountants. The search on the part of alienated youth for a better society and a good life was strewn with both comic and tragic aspects, and it reflected the deep social ills that had been allowed to fester throughout the post–World War II period.

FEMINISM   The logic of liberation spawned during the sixties helped accelerate a powerful women's rights crusade that aggressively challenged the cult of domesticity. Like the New Left, the new feminism drew much of its inspiration and tactics from the civil rights movement.

The mainstream of the women's movement was led by Betty Friedan. Her immensely influential book, *The Feminine Mystique* (1963), launched the new phase of female protest on a national level. Friedan, a Smith College graduate, had married in 1947. During the 1950s, she raised three children in a New York suburb. Politically active but socially domestic, she mothered her children, pampered her husband, "read *Vogue* under the hair dryer," and occasionally did some freelance

Betty Friedan, author of The Feminine Mystique.

writing. In 1957 she conducted a poll of her fellow Smith alumnae and discovered that, despite all the rhetoric about the happy suburban housewife during the fifties, many—too many—were in fact miserable. This revelation led to more research, which culminated in the publication of *The Feminine Mystique*.

Women, Friedan wrote, had actually lost ground during the years after World War II, when many left wartime assembly lines and settled down in suburbia. A propaganda campaign engineered by advertisers and women's magazines encouraged them to do so by creating the "feminine mystique" of blissful domesticity. This notion that women were "gaily content in a world of bedroom, kitchen, sex, babies, and home" thus served to imprison women. In Friedan's view, the American middle-class home had become "a comfortable concentration camp" where women suffocated in an atmosphere of mindless materialism, daytime television, and neighborhood gossip.

Friedan's book, an immediate best-seller, raised the consciousness of many women who had long suffered from a feeling of being trapped in a rut with no way out. Moreover, Friedan came to realize that there were far more women working outside the home than the pervasive "feminine mystique" suggested. Many of these working women were frustrated by the demands of holding "two full-time jobs instead of just one—underpaid clerical worker and unpaid housekeeper."

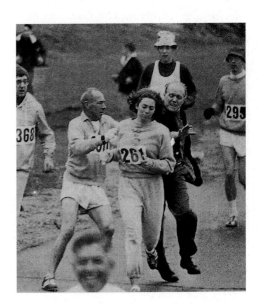

In 1967 Syracuse University student Kathy Switzer challenged the Boston Marathon's men-only tradition. Officials tried to pull her from the course, but with the aid of fellow runners she completed the race. Women became official entrants in 1971.

"Well, girls, at least the only way we can go is up."
*Despite support by Congress, the Equal Rights
Amendment failed to muster enough popular support to gain ratification. Equality of rights, regardless
of gender, remained out of reach.*

In 1966 Friedan and a small group of other spirited activists founded
the National Organization for Women (NOW). Soon regarded as the
NAACP of the women's movement, NOW grew rapidly. It initially
sought to end discrimination in the workplace on the basis of sex, and
went on to spearhead efforts to legalize abortion, and to obtain federal
and state support for child-care centers.

In the early 1970s, Congress and the Supreme Court advanced the
cause of sexual equality. Under Title IX of the Educational Amendments Act of 1972, colleges were required to institute "affirmative action" programs to ensure equal opportunity for women. In the same
year Congress overwhelmingly approved the Equal Rights Amendment,

which had been bottled up in a House committee for almost half a century. In 1973 the Supreme Court, in *Roe* v. *Wade,* struck down state laws forbidding abortions during the first three months of pregnancy. Meanwhile the educational bastions of male segregation, including Yale and Princeton, led a new movement for coeducation that swept the country. "If the 1960s belonged to blacks," said one feminist, "the next ten years are ours."

By the end of the 1970s, however, continuing divisions between moderate and radical feminists, as well as the movement's failure to broaden its appeal much beyond the confines of the middle class, caused reform efforts to stagnate. The Equal Rights Amendment, which had once seemed a straightforward assertion of equal opportunity ("Equality of rights under the law shall not be denied or abridged by the United States or by any State on account of sex") and assured of ratification, was stymied in several state legislatures. Despite a congressional extension of the normal time allowed for ratification, by 1982 it died, several states short of passage. And the very success of NOW's efforts to liberalize local and state abortion laws generated a powerful backlash, especially among Catholics and fundamentalist Protestants, who mounted a potent "right-to-life" crusade.

But the success of the women's movement endured long after the militant rhetoric had evaporated. Their growing presence in the labor force assured women of a greater share of economic and political influence. By 1976, over half the married women in America and nine of ten women college graduates were employed outside the home, a development that one economist called "the single most outstanding phenomenon of this century." Yet, many career women did not regard themselves as "feminists"; they took jobs because they and their families needed the money to survive or to achieve higher levels of material comfort. Whatever their motives, traditional sex roles and childbearing practices were being changed to accommodate the two-career family.

HISPANIC RIGHTS   The activism that animated the student revolt, the civil rights movement, and the crusade for women's rights soon spread to various ethnic minority groups. The labor shortages during World War II led defense industries to offer Hispanic Americans their first significant access to industrial and skilled-labor jobs in the cities.

And as was the case with African Americans, service in the military during the war years helped to heighten an American identity among Hispanic Americans and to excite their desire for equal rights and opportunities.

But equality was elusive. After World War II, Hispanic Americans still faced widespread discrimination in hiring, housing, and education. Poverty was widespread. In 1960, for example, the median income of a Mexican-American family was only 62 percent of the median income of a family in the general population. Hispanic-American activists during the 1950s and 1960s mirrored the efforts of black civil rights leaders such as Martin Luther King, Jr. They too denounced segregation, promoted efforts to improve the quality of public education, and struggled to increase Hispanic-American political influence and economic opportunities. Like their black peers, Hispanic college students during the 1960s seized upon ways to heighten their sense of ethnic pride and distinctiveness and to bolster their solidarity.

One of the most popular initiatives was the use of the term *Chicano* as an inclusive label for all Mexican immigrants, Spanish Americans in New Mexico, as well as old *Californios* (descendants of the inhabitants of California before it was seized by the United States, most of whom were Indians or of mixed ancestry), and *Tejanos* (descendants of the inhabitants of Texas before it became independent). The word *Chicano* was originally a Mexican slang term for a clumsy person. Over the years, Anglo Americans had fastened upon the term as a pejorative reference. Now *Chicano* took on a positive connotation. In southern California, students formed Young Chicanos for Community Action, a social service group designed to promote greater self-reliance and local involvement within Chicano neighborhoods. Wearing brown berets, the members protested the disproportionate number of Hispanics being killed in the Vietnam War and demanded improvements in their neighborhood schools. Others promoted Hispanic Studies as a new academic discipline at colleges. In 1968 nearly 10,000 Chicano students walked out of five Los Angeles high schools as a protest against inadequate facilities, racist teachers, and a high dropout rate. Their actions prompted students in other states to stage similar demonstrations.

Unlike their black counterparts, however, Chicano leaders faced an awkward dilemma: what should they do about the continuing stream of

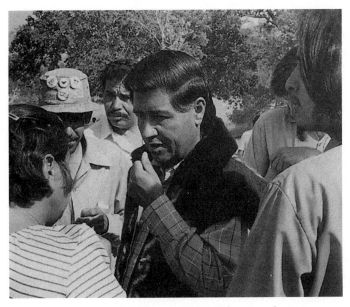

César Chavez (center) *with organizers of the grape boycott.*

illegal Mexican aliens flowing across the border? Many Mexican Americans argued that their own hopes for economic advancement and social equality were put at risk by the influx of Mexican laborers willing to accept low-paying jobs. Mexican-American leaders thus helped to end the *bracero* program (which trucked in *braceros,* Mexican contract day laborers, at harvest time) in 1964 and to form the United Farm Workers (UFW) in 1962 (originally the National Farm Workers Association) to represent Mexican-American migrant workers.

The founder of the UFW was César Chavez. Born in Yuma, Arizona, in 1927 to Mexican immigrant parents, Chavez moved with his parents and four siblings to California in 1939. There they joined thousands of other migrant farm workers traversing the state, moving from job to job, living in tents, cars, or ramshackle cabins. In 1944, at age seventeen, Chavez joined the navy and served for two years in the Pacific. After the war he married and found work, first as a sharecropper raising strawberries and then as a migrant laborer in apricot orchards. In 1952 Chavez joined the Community Service Organization (CSO), a social service group that sought to educate and organize the migrant poor so that they could become more self-reliant. He founded new CSO chapters and was named general director in 1958.

Chavez left the organization in 1962 when it refused to back his proposal to establish a union for farm workers. Other CSO leaders believed that it was impossible to organize migrant workers into an effective union. They thought they were too mobile, too poor, too illiterate, too ethnically diverse, and too easily replaced by *braceros.* Moreover, farm workers did not enjoy protected status under the National Labor Relations Act of 1935 (the Wagner Act). Unlike industrial laborers, they were not guaranteed the right to organize or to receive a minimum wage. Nor did federal regulations govern the safety of their workplaces.

Despite such obstacles, Chavez resolved to organize the migrant farm workers. His fledgling Farm Workers Association gained national attention in 1965 when it joined a strike by Filipino farm workers against the corporate grape farmers in California's San Joaquin Valley. Chavez's personal charisma and Catholic piety, his insistence on nonviolent tactics and his reliance upon college student volunteers, his skillful alliance with organized labor and religious groups, all combined to attract media interest and popular support. Soon the UFW began organizing migrant workers in the lettuce fields of the Salinas Valley.

Still, the grape strike itself brought no tangible gains. So Chavez organized a nationwide consumer boycott of grapes. Contrary to Chavez's own principles and orders, some of the striking workers used violence to express their frustration at the recalcitrant growers. In an effort to break the impasse and defuse the tension among his followers, Chavez began a personal fast in 1968. He explained that "the truest act of courage, the strongest act of manliness, is to sacrifice ourselves for others in a totally nonviolent struggle for justice." After fasting for three weeks, he had lost thirty-five pounds, and doctors began to fear for his life. A week later he ended his fast by taking communion and breaking bread with Senator Robert F. Kennedy.

Two years later, in 1970, the grape strike and consumer boycott finally succeeded in bringing twenty-six grape growers to the bargaining table. They signed formal contracts recognizing the UFW, and soon migrant workers throughout the West were benefiting from Chavez's strenuous efforts on their behalf. Wages increased and working conditions improved. In 1975 the California state legislature passed a bill that required growers to bargain collectively with the elected representatives of the farm workers. As Robert Kennedy had observed, César Chavez was "one of the heroic figures of our time."

But the chief strength of the Hispanic movement lay less in the duplication of civil rights strategies than in the rapid growth of the Hispanic population. In 1960 Hispanics had numbered slightly more than 3 million; by 1970 they had increased to 9 million, and by 1990 they numbered 22.4 million, making them the largest minority in America after African Americans. The most numerous among them were Mexican Americans, who were concentrated in California and the Southwest. Next came the Puerto Rican population, most of whom lived in New York City and the Connecticut Valley. Third largest were the Cubans, many of them refugees from Castro's regime, who were concentrated in southern Florida.

By 1980, aspiring presidential candidates were openly courting the Hispanic vote, promising support for urban renewal projects in New York and amnesty programs for illegal immigrants in Texas, and delivering rousing anti-Castro speeches in Miami. The voting power of Hispanics and their concentration in states with key electoral votes helped give the Hispanic point of view political clout. During the 1960s, four Mexican Americans—Senator Joseph Montoya of New Mexico and Representatives Elizio ("Kika") de la Garza of Texas, Henry B. Gonzalez of Texas, and Edward R. Roybal of California—were elected to Congress. In 1974 two Chicanos were elected governor—Jerry Apodaca in New Mexico and Raul Castro in Arizona. In 1981 Henry Cisneros of San Antonio became the first Mexican-American mayor of a large city. He later served as the secretary of housing and urban development and then as secretary of energy in the Clinton administration.

NATIVE AMERICANS   American Indians—many of whom now called themselves Native Americans—also emerged as a new political force in the late 1960s. Two conditions combined to make Indian rights a priority: first, white Americans felt a deep and persistent sense of guilt for the destructive policies of their ancestors toward a people who had, after all, been here first; second, the plight of the Native American minority was more desperate than that of any other group in the country. Indian unemployment was ten times the national rate, life expectancy was twenty years lower than the national average, and the suicide rate was a whopping one hundred times higher than the rate for whites.

Although President Lyndon Johnson recognized the poverty of the Native Americans and attempted to target federal antipoverty program funds into the reservations, militants within the Indian community became impatient with the slow pace of change and organized protests and demonstrations against local, state, and federal agencies. At first the Indian activists copied the tactics of civil rights and black power activists. In 1968 two Chippewas living in Minneapolis, George Mitchell and Dennis Banks, founded the American Indian Movement (AIM) to promote "red power." The leaders of AIM occupied Alcatraz Island in San Francisco Bay in 1969, claiming the site "by right of discovery." And in 1972, a sit-in at the Department of the Interior's Bureau of Indian Affairs (BIA) in Washington attracted national attention to their cause. The BIA, then and since, has been widely viewed as the worst-managed federal agency. Instead of finding creative ways to promote tribal auton-

Foot soldiers of AIM marched on Wounded Knee, South Dakota, to bring attention to dependence on welfare, poor living conditions, and rampant alcoholism that plagued Indians on reservations nationwide.

omy and economic self-sufficiency, the BIA was a classic example of government inefficiency and paternalism gone awry.

In 1973 AIM led two hundred Sioux in occupying the tiny village of Wounded Knee, South Dakota, the site where the U.S. 7th Cavalry had massacred a Sioux village in 1890. Provoked by the light sentences given a group of local whites who had killed a Sioux in 1972, the organizers also sought to draw attention to the plight of the Indians living on the reservation there. Half of the families were dependent on government welfare checks, alcoholism was rampant, and over 80 percent of the children had dropped out of school. After the Indian militants took eleven hostages, federal marshals and FBI agents surrounded the encampment. For ten weeks, the two sides engaged in a tense standoff. When AIM leaders tried to bring in food and supplies, a shoot-out resulted, and one Indian was killed and another wounded. Soon thereafter, the tense confrontation ended with a government promise to reexamine Indian treaty rights.

Thereafter, Indian protesters discovered a more effective tactic than direct action and sit-ins. They went into federal courts armed with copies of old treaties and demanded that these become the basis for restitution. In Alaska, Maine, South Carolina, and Massachusetts they won significant settlements that provided legal recognition of their tribal rights and financial compensation at levels that upgraded the standard of living on several reservations.

GAY RIGHTS   The liberationist impulses of the sixties also encouraged homosexuals to organize and assert their own right to equal treatment and basic dignity. On June 17, 1969, New York City police raided the Stonewall Inn, a male gay bar in the heart of Greenwich Village. Efforts to close down homosexual gathering places were then commonplace around the country. But this time the patrons fought back and the struggle spilled into the streets. Hundreds of other gays and their supporters joined the fracas against the police. Rioting lasted throughout the weekend. When it ended, gays had forged a new sense of solidarity and a new organization called the Gay Liberation Front (GLF). "Gay is good for all of us," proclaimed one member of the GLF. "The artificial categories 'heterosexual' and 'homosexual' have been laid on us by a sexist society. As gays we demand an end to the gender programming which starts when we are born."

As news of the Stonewall riots spread across the country, the gay rights movement assumed national proportions. One of its main tactics was to encourage people to "come out" and make public their homosexuality. This was by no means an easy decision, for professing gays faced social ostracism, physical assaults, exclusion from the military and civil service, and discrimination in the workplace. Yet despite the risks, thousands of homosexuals did "come out." By 1973 almost 800 gay and lesbian organizations had been formed across the country, and every major city had a visible gay community and cultural life.

But as was the case with the civil rights crusade and the women's movement, the campaign for gay rights soon suffered from internal divisions and a conservative backlash. Gay activists engaged in fractious disputes over tactics and objectives, and conservative moralists and Christian fundamentalists launched a nationwide counterattack against the gay community. In Miami, St. Paul, and Wichita, conservatives managed to repeal new laws banning discrimination against homosexuals. By the end of the 1970s, the gay movement had lost its initial momentum and was struggling to salvage many of its hard-won gains.

NIXON AND VIETNAM

The numerous liberation movements of the 1960s fundamentally changed the tone and texture of American social life. But by the early 1970s, the pendulum of national mood was swinging back. The election of Richard Nixon and Spiro Agnew in 1968 and the rise of George Wallace as a serious political force reflected the emergence of the "silent majority"—those predominantly white working-class and middle-class citizens who were determined to regain control of a society they felt had become awash in permissiveness, anarchy, and tyranny by the minority. Large as the gap was between the silent majority and the forces of dissent, both sides agreed that the Vietnam War remained the dominant event of the time. Until the war was ended and all American troops had returned home, the nation would find it difficult to achieve the equilibrium that the new president had promised.

GRADUAL WITHDRAWAL   During the campaign of 1968, Nixon had claimed to have a secret plan that would bring "peace with honor" in

Vietnam. Peace, however, was long in coming and not very honorable. Although Henry Kissinger, the professor of international relations at Harvard who became Nixon's special assistant for national security affairs, insisted that the war in Indochina was a mere "sideshow" of considerably less significance than American interests in Europe and the Middle East, American withdrawal from Vietnam was agonizingly slow nonetheless. By the time a settlement was finally reached in 1973, another 20,000 Americans had died, the morale of the American army had been shattered, millions of additional Asians were killed or wounded, and fighting continued in Southeast Asia. In the end, Nixon's policy gained nothing he could not have accomplished in 1969.

The new Vietnam policy of the Nixon administration moved along three separate fronts. First, American negotiators in Paris demanded the withdrawal of Communist forces from South Vietnam and the preservation of the American-supported regime of President Nguyen Van Thieu. The North Vietnamese and Viet Cong negotiators insisted on the retention of a military presence in the south and the reunification of the Vietnamese people under a government dominated by the Communists. There was no common ground on which to come together. It required months before the parties could even agree on the shape of the table around which they would meet.

Second, Nixon tried to quell domestic unrest over the war. He reduced the number of American troops in Vietnam, justifying the reduction as the natural result of "Vietnamization"—the equipping and training of the South Vietnamese to assume the burden of ground combat in place of Americans. From a peak of 540,000 in 1969, American combat troops were withdrawn at a gradual and steady pace that matched almost precisely the pace of the American buildup from 1965 to 1969. By 1973 only 50,000 American troops remained in Vietnam. In 1969 Nixon also established a draft lottery system that eliminated many inequities and clarified the likelihood of being drafted—only those nineteen-year-olds with low lottery numbers would have to go—and in 1973 he did away with the draft altogether by creating an all-volunteer military. Nixon was more successful in achieving the goal of reducing antiwar activity than at forcing concessions from the North Vietnamese in Paris.

Third, while reducing the number of American combat troops, Nixon and Kissinger expanded the air war in an effort to persuade the enemy

Even as the Nixon administration began a phased withdrawal of American troops from Vietnam, the war took a heavy toll on Vietnamese and Americans alike.

to come to terms. In March 1969, American planes began a fourteen-month-long bombing campaign aimed at Communist sanctuaries in Cambodia. Congress did not learn of these secret raids until 1970, although the total tonnage of bombs dropped was four times that dropped on Japan during World War II. Then on April 30, 1970, Nixon announced what he called an "incursion" into "neutral" Cambodia by United States troops to "clean out" North Vietnamese staging areas. The head of Cambodia's government for two decades, Prince Norodom Sihanouk, had previously objected to such American raids into his country, but Sihanouk had been replaced in a coup by General Lon Nol earlier in the spring, clearing the way for the American invasion.

DIVISIONS AT HOME   America's slow withdrawal from Vietnam had a devastating effect on the morale and reputation of the military. "No one wants to be the last grunt to die in this lousy war," said one soldier. Between 1969 and 1971, there were 730 reported "fragging" incidents, efforts by American troops to kill or injure their own officers, usually with fragmentation grenades. Drug abuse became a major problem. In 1971 four times as many American troops were hospitalized for drug abuse as for combat-related wounds.

Back on the home front, the public learned of previously suppressed events in Vietnam that caused even the staunchest supporters of the war to wince. Late in 1969 the story of the My Lai massacre broke in the press and plunged the country into two years of exposure to the gruesome tale of Lieutenant William Calley, who ordered the murder of over 200 civilians in My Lai village in 1968. Twenty-five army officers were charged with complicity in the massacre and subsequent cover-up, but only Calley was convicted; Nixon soon granted him parole.

Perhaps the loudest public outcry against Nixon's Indochina policy occurred in the wake of the Cambodian "incursion." Campuses across the country exploded in what the president of Columbia University called "the most disastrous month of May in the history of American higher education." Student protests led to the closing of hundreds of colleges and universities. At Kent State University, the Ohio National Guard was called in to quell rioting in which the campus Reserve Officer Training Corps (ROTC) building was burned down by antiwar protesters. The poorly trained Guardsmen panicked and opened fire on the demonstrators, killing four student bystanders. Eleven days later, on May 15, Mississippi highway patrolmen riddled a dormitory at Jackson State College with bullets, killing two black students. Although an offi-

National Guardsmen shot and killed four student bystanders during antiwar demonstrations on the campus of Kent State University.

"Son . . . !" "Dad . . . !" The Vietnam War caused vehement divisions between "hawks" and "doves," old and young, even parents and children.

cial investigation of the Kent State episode condemned the "casual and indiscriminate shooting," polls indicated that the American public supported the National Guard; students had "got what they were asking for." In New York City, antiwar demonstrators who gathered to protest the deaths at Kent State and the invasion of Cambodia were attacked by "hard-hat" construction workers, who forced the student protesters to disperse and then marched on City Hall to raise the flag that had been lowered to half staff in mourning for the Kent State victims.

The following year, in June 1971, the *New York Times* began publishing excerpts from *The History of the U.S. Decision Making Process in Vietnam,* a secret Defense Department study commissioned by Robert McNamara before his resignation as secretary of defense in 1968. The so-called Pentagon Papers, leaked to the press by a former Defense Department official, Daniel Ellsberg, confirmed what many critics of the war had long suspected: Congress and the public had not received the full story on the Gulf of Tonkin incident of 1964, and contingency plans for American entry into the war were being drawn up while Johnson was promising the American people that combat troops would never be sent to Vietnam. Moreover, there was no plan for bringing the war to an end so long as the North Vietnamese persisted. Although the Pentagon Papers dealt with events only up to 1965, the Nixon administration attempted to block their publication, arguing that they endangered national security and that their publication would prolong the war. By a vote of 6 to 3, the Supreme Court ruled against the government. Newspapers throughout the country began publication the next day.

WAR WITHOUT END   The mounting social divisions at home and the approach of the 1972 presidential election combined to produce a shift in the American negotiating position in Paris. In the summer of 1972 Henry Kissinger again began meeting privately with Le Duc Tho, the North Vietnamese negotiator, and he now dropped his insistence on the removal of all North Vietnamese troops from the south before the withdrawal of American troops. On October 26, only a week before the American presidential election, Kissinger announced: "Peace is at hand." But this was a cynical ploy to win votes. Several days earlier the Thieu regime in South Vietnam had rejected the Kissinger plan for a cease-fire, fearful that the presence of North Vietnamese troops in the south virtually guaranteed an eventual Communist victory. The talks broke off on December 16, and two days later the president ordered the saturation bombing of Hanoi and Haiphong, the two largest cities in North Vietnam. These so-called Christmas bombings, and the simultaneous mining of North Vietnamese harbors, aroused worldwide protest.

But the bombings also made the North Vietnamese more flexible at the negotiating table. The "Christmas bombings" stopped on December 29, and the resumption of talks in Paris soon followed. On January 27, 1973, the United States, North and South Vietnam, and the Viet Cong signed an "agreement on ending the war and restoring peace in Vietnam." While Nixon and Kissinger both claimed that the bombing had brought North Vietnam to its senses, in truth the North Vietnamese never altered their basic stance; they kept troops in the south and remained committed to the reunification of Vietnam under one government. What had changed since the previous fall was the willingness of the South Vietnamese to accept these terms, albeit reluctantly, on the basis of Nixon's promise that the United States would respond "with full force" to any violation of the agreement.

On March 29, 1973, the last American combat troops left Vietnam. And on that same day, the last of several hundred American prisoners of war, most of them downed pilots, were released from Hanoi. Within a period of months, however, the cease-fire in Vietnam ended, the war between north and south resumed, and the military superiority of the Communist forces soon became evident. In Cambodia (renamed Kampuchea after it fell to the Communists) and Laos, where fighting had been more sporadic, Communist victory also seemed inevitable. In 1975 the North Vietnamese launched a full-scale armored invasion against the south, and South Vietnamese president Thieu appealed to

The scramble to board evacuation helicopters on the roof of the American Embassy, Saigon, April 30, 1975.

Washington for assistance. Congress refused. The much-mentioned "peace with honor" had proved to be, in the words of one CIA official, only a "decent interval"—enough time for the United States to extricate itself from Vietnam before the collapse of the South Vietnamese government. On April 30, 1975, Americans watched on television as North Vietnamese tanks rolled into Saigon, soon to be renamed Ho Chi Minh City, and helicopters lifted the officials in the American embassy to ships waiting offshore. In those last desperate moments, terrified South Vietnamese fought to get on the helicopters as they took off.

The longest war in American history was finally over, leaving in its wake a bitter legacy. During the period of American involvement in the fighting, almost 2 million combatants and civilians were killed on both sides. North Vietnam absorbed incredible losses—some 600,000 soldiers and countless civilians killed. More than 58,000 Americans died in Vietnam, 300,000 were wounded, 2,500 were declared missing, almost 100,000 returned missing one or more limbs, and over 150,000 combat veterans suffered drug or alcohol addiction or severe psychological disorders. To be sure, most of the Vietnam veterans readjusted well to civilian life, but even they carried for years the stigma of a "lost war."

The "loss" of the war and revelations of American atrocities such as My Lai eroded respect for the military so thoroughly that many young Americans came to regard military service as corrupting and ignoble. The war, described as a noble crusade on behalf of democratic ideals, instead suggested that democracy was not easily transferable to Third World regions that lacked any historical experience with liberal values and representative government. The war fought to show the world that the United States would be steadfast in containing the spread of communism instead sapped the national will and fragmented the national consensus that had governed foreign affairs since 1947. It also changed the balance of power in domestic politics. Not only did the war cause the downfall of Lyndon Johnson's presidency; it also created enduring fissures in the Democratic party. Said antiwar senator and 1972 Democratic presidential candidate George McGovern: "The Vietnam tragedy is at the root of the confusion and division of the Democratic party. It tore up our souls."

Little wonder that most people at war's end wanted to "put Vietnam behind us" and forget. Although subsequent debates over American foreign policy in the Middle East, Africa, and Latin America frequently referred to "the lessons of Vietnam," the phrase was used by different factions for diametrically opposed purposes, ranging from refusal to commit any American troops and resources in El Salvador and Nicaragua to an insistence on massive military commitments unfettered by any diplomatic restrictions that might preclude outright victory. "In the end, then," one journalist wrote concerning the Vietnam era, "there was no end at all."

NIXON AND MIDDLE AMERICA

Richard Nixon had been elected in 1968 as the representative of "Middle America," those middle-class citizens fed up with the liberal politics and promises of the 1960s. The Nixon cabinet and White House staff reflected their values. The chief figures were John Mitchell, the gruff attorney-general who had made his fortune as a municipal bond lawyer in Nixon's old firm; H. R. Haldeman and John Ehrlichman, advisers on domestic policy whose major experience before their association with the Nixon campaign had been in advertising; William Rogers, the secretary of state, an old-time Nixon friend whose control over foreign policy was quickly preempted by Henry Kissinger; and Melvin Laird, the secretary of defense, who also found his influence undercut by Kissinger's access to the White House. The cabinet was all white, all male, all Republican. "There are no blooded patricians in the lot," said *Time* magazine, "just strivers who have acted out the middle-class dream."

DOMESTIC AFFAIRS   Nixon was the first president since Eisenhower in 1957 to confront a Congress in which both houses were under the control of the opposition party. It followed that he focused his energies on foreign policy, where presidential initiatives were less encumbered and where he, in tandem with Kissinger, achieved several stunning breakthroughs. He also continued to support the American space program and the efforts to beat the Soviets to the moon. In July 1969 American astronaut Neil Armstrong became the first man to walk on the moon. Back on earth, however, Nixon sought to stop social-welfare programs in their tracks. Yet, like Eisenhower before him, he found it difficult to dismantle liberal programs.

In July 1969, a program begun by President Kennedy reached its goal: putting a man on the moon.

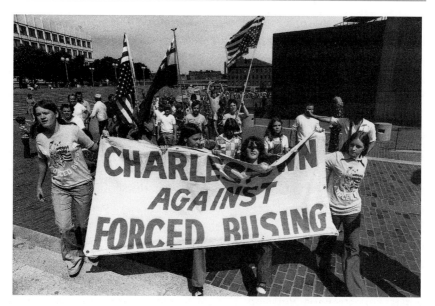

White teenagers march on City Hall Plaza, Boston, 1975, to protest the busing of students to racially integrate their school system.

Despite the efforts of the Nixon administration, the civil rights legislation enacted during the Johnson years continued to take effect. "There are those who want instant integration and those who want segregation forever," said Nixon in 1969. "I believe we need to have a middle course between these extremes." In practice this "middle course" took the shape of a concerted effort in 1970 to block congressional renewal of the Voting Rights Act of 1965 and to delay implementation of court orders requiring the desegregation of school districts in Mississippi. "For the first time since Woodrow Wilson," said the head of the NAACP, "we have a national administration that can be rightly characterized as anti-Negro." Sixty-five lawyers in the Justice Department signed a letter of protest against the administration's stance. Congress then extended the Voting Rights Act over Nixon's veto. The Supreme Court, in the first decision made under the new chief justice, Warren Burger—a Nixon appointee—ordered the integration of the Mississippi public schools. In *Alexander* v. *Holmes County Board of Education* (1969), a unanimous Court ordered a quick end to segregation. During Nixon's first term and despite his wishes, more schools were desegregated than in all the Kennedy-Johnson years combined.

Nixon's attempts to block desegregation efforts in urban areas also failed. The Burger Court ruled unanimously in *Swann* v. *Charlotte-Mecklenburg Board of Education* (1971) that school systems must bus students out of their neighborhoods if necessary to achieve integration. Protest over desegregation now began to manifest itself more in the North than in the South, as white families in Boston, Denver, and other cities denounced the destruction of "the neighborhood school," and angry parents in Pontiac, Michigan, firebombed school buses.

Nixon asked Congress to impose a moratorium on all busing orders by the federal courts. The House of Representatives, equally attuned to voter outrage at busing to achieve racial integration, went along. But a Senate filibuster blocked the president's antibusing bill. Busing opponents won a limited victory when the Supreme Court ruled, in *Milliken* v. *Bradley* (1974), that desegregation plans in Detroit requiring the transfer of students from the inner city to the suburbs were unconstitutional. This landmark decision, along with the *Bakke v. Board of Regents of California* (1978) decision, which restricted the use of quotas to achieve racial balance, marked the transition of desegregation from an issue of simple justice to a more tangled thicket of conflicting group and individual rights.

Fate and the aging of the justices on the Warren Court gave Nixon the chance to make four new appointments. His first, Warren Burger, caused no dissent. But Nixon's next two nominations generated opposition in the Senate. Clement F. Haynsworth, a federal appeals court judge from South Carolina, had the support of the American Bar Association but drew fire from civil rights groups and labor unions for his conservative record. There was no question of Haynsworth's integrity, but the Senate rejected him when it learned that he had heard a case involving a subsidiary of a corporation in which he owned a small amount of stock.

The nomination of G. Harrold Carswell, a judge of the Florida appeals court, created far more trouble. Carswell had not only been an out-and-out defender of white supremacy, but he was acknowledged by all parties to be singularly lacking in distinction. By a vote of 51 to 45, the Senate rejected Carswell. Nixon condemned the Senate rejection as "an act of regional discrimination." But he took care thereafter to nominate jurists of stature for the Supreme Court: Harry Blackmun, a compatriot of Burger from Minnesota; Lewis F. Powell, Jr., a respected conservative judge from Virginia; and William Rehnquist, an articulate, conservative lawyer in the Justice Department. None encountered serious opposition in the Senate. And none, save perhaps Rehnquist, would consistently support Nixon's interpretation of the Constitution.

Nixon invented several names for his domestic program. At one point it was called the "New Federalism," which would "start resources and power flowing back from Washington to the States and to the people." To that end, in 1972 he pushed through Congress a five-year revenue-sharing plan that would distribute $30 billion of federal revenues to the states for use as they saw fit. At another point Nixon called for a "New American Revolution" to revive traditional values. These catchphrases never caught on, as had the "New Frontier" or the "Great Society," because Nixon's domestic program was mostly defensive and negative.

Meanwhile, the Democratic Congress moved forward with new legislation: the right of eighteen-year-olds to vote in national elections (1970), and in all elections under the Twenty-sixth Amendment (1971); increases in Social Security benefits indexed to the inflation rate and a rise in food-stamp funding; the Occupational Safety and Health Act (1970); the Clean Air Act (1970); new bills to control water pollution (1970 and 1972); and the Federal Election Campaign Act (1972), which modified the rules of campaign finance. These measures accounted for a more rapid rise in spending on social programs than Johnson's Great Society programs had.

ECONOMIC MALAISE The economy continued to prove troublesome. Overheated by the expense of the Vietnam War, the annual inflation rate began to rise in 1967, when it was 3 percent. By 1973 it was at 9 percent; a year later it was at 12 percent, and it remained in double digits for most of the 1970s. The Dow Jones average of major industrial stocks fell by 36 percent between 1968 and 1970, its steepest decline in more than thirty years. Meanwhile unemployment, at a low of 3.3 percent when Nixon took office, climbed to 6 percent by the end of 1970 and threatened to keep rising. Somehow the American economy was undergoing a recession and inflation at the same time. Economists coined the term "stagflation" to describe the syndrome that defied the orthodox laws of economics.

The economic malaise had at least three deep-rooted causes. First, the Johnson administration had attempted to pay for both the Great Society social-welfare programs and the war in Vietnam without a major tax increase, generating larger federal deficits, a major expansion of the money supply, and price inflation. Second, and more important, by the late 1960s, American goods faced stiff competition in international markets from West Germany, Japan, and other emerging industrial powers. No longer was American technological superiority unquestioned. Third, the American economy had depended heavily on cheap sources of energy; no nation was more dependent on the automobile and the automobile industry, and no nation was more careless in its use of fossil fuels in factories and homes.

Just as domestic petroleum reserves began to dwindle and dependence on foreign sources increased, the Organization of Petroleum Exporting Countries (OPEC) combined to use their oil as a political and economic weapon. In 1973, when the United States sent massive aid to Israel after a devastating Syrian-Egyptian attack during Yom Kippur, the holiest day in the Jewish calendar, OPEC announced that it would not sell oil to nations supporting Israel and that it was raising its prices by 400 percent. Motorists thereafter faced long lines at gas stations and factories cut production.

Another condition leading to stagflation was the flood of new workers—mainly baby-boomers and women—entering the labor market. From 1965 to 1980 the workforce grew by 40 percent, almost 30 million workers, a number greater than the total labor force of France or West Germany. The number of new jobs could not keep up, leaving many unemployed. At the same time, worker productivity declined, pushing up inflation in the face of rising demand.

Stagflation posed a new set of economic problems, but Nixon responded erratically and ineffectively, trying old remedies for a new problem. First, he tried to reduce the federal deficit by raising taxes and cutting the budget. When the Democratic Congress refused to cooperate with this approach, he encouraged the Federal Reserve Board to reduce the money supply by raising interest rates. The stock market immediately collapsed, and the economy plunged into the "Nixon recession."

In 1969, when asked about government restrictions on wages and prices, Nixon had been unequivocal: "Controls. Oh, my God, no! . . . We'll never go to controls." But in 1971, he reversed himself. He froze all wages and prices for ninety days and announced that the United

States would no longer convert dollars into gold for foreign banks. The dollar, its link to gold cut, now drifted lower on world currency exchanges. After ninety days, Nixon established mandatory guidelines for subsequent wage and price increases under the supervision of a federal agency. Still the economy floundered. By 1973 the wage and price guidelines were made voluntary, and therefore almost entirely ineffective.

ENVIRONMENTAL PROTECTION   The widespread recognition that America faced limits to economic growth fueled broad support for environmental protection in the early 1970s. The realization that cities and industrial development were damaging the physical environment and altering the earth's ecology was not new: Rachel Carson's book *Silent Spring* (1962) had sounded the warning years earlier. But in Nixon's first term the Democratic-controlled Congress took concerted action, passing several acts to protect and clean up the environment. The administration also created by executive order the Environmental Protection Agency, a consolidation of existing agencies, to oversee federal guidelines for controlling air pollution, toxic wastes, and water quality.

The Arab oil boycott and the OPEC price increase led to an energy crisis in the United States. People began to realize that natural resources were not infinitely expendable. "Although it's positively un-American to think so," said one sociologist, "the environmental move-

An Earth Day demonstration dramatizing the dangers of air pollution, April 1972.

ment and energy shortage have forced us all to accept a sense of our limits, to lower our expectations, to seek prosperity through conservation rather than growth."

Although the environmental movement cut across class, racial, and ethnic lines by appealing to the collective interests of all Americans in clean air and water, it simultaneously aggravated the competition between regional vested interests. In Texas, where the oil lobby resented controls on gas prices and speed limits, bumper stickers read: "Drive fast, freeze a Yankee." In Tennessee, where a federal dam project was halted because it threatened the snail darter—a species of fish—with extinction, local developers took out ads asking residents to "tell the government that the size of your wallet is more important than some two-inch-long minnow."

As stagflation persisted into the middle and late 1970s, corporate criticism that environmental regulations were cutting into jobs and profit margins began to sound more persuasive, especially when the staggering cost of cleaning up accumulated toxic wastes became known. "Why worry about the long run," said one unemployed steelworker in 1976, "when you're out of work right now." Polls showed that protection of the environment remained a high priority among a majority of Americans, but that few were willing to suffer a cutback in their standard of living to achieve that goal. "It was," bemoaned one journalist, "as if passengers knew they were boarding the *Titanic,* but preferred to jostle with one another for first class accommodations so they might enjoy as much of the voyage as possible."

Nixon Triumphant

CHINA If the ailments of the economy proved more than Nixon could remedy, in foreign policy his administration managed to diagnose and improve American relations with the major powers of the Communist world—China and the Soviet Union—and to shift fundamentally the pattern of the cold war. In 1971 Nixon's diplomatic adviser Henry Kissinger made a secret trip to Beijing (Peking) to explore the possibility of American recognition of China. Since 1949, when Mao Tse-tung's revolutionary movement established control in China, the United States had refused to recognize Communist China, preferring to regard Chiang Kai-shek's exiled regime on Taiwan as the legitimate govern-

With President Richard Nixon's visit to China in 1972, the United States formally recognized China's Communist government. In this photo, Nixon and Chinese premier Chou En-lai drink a toast.

ment of China. In one simple but stunning stroke, Nixon and Kissinger ended two decades of diplomatic isolation for the People's Republic of China and drove a wedge between the two chief bastions of communism in the world.

In 1972 Americans watched on television as their president visited famous Chinese landmarks, which had been invisible to Americans for over two decades, and drank toasts with Premier Chou En-lai and Mao Tse-tung. The United States and China agreed to scientific and cultural exchanges, steps toward the resumption of trade, and the eventual reunification of Taiwan with the mainland. A year after the Nixon visit, "liaison offices" were established in Washington and Beijing (Peking) that served as unofficial embassies, and in 1979 diplomatic recognition was formalized. Richard Nixon, the former anti-Communist crusader who had condemned the State Department for "losing" China in 1949, had accomplished a diplomatic feat that his Democratic predecessors could not.

DÉTENTE   In truth, China welcomed the breakthrough in relations with the United States because its rivalry with the Soviet Union, with which it shared a long border, had become more bitter than its rivalry with the West. The Soviet leaders, troubled by the Sino-American agreements, were also anxious for an easing of tensions with the United

States now that they had, as the result of a huge arms buildup following the Cuban missile crisis, achieved virtual parity with the United States in nuclear weapons. Once again the president surprised the world, by announcing that he would visit Moscow in 1972 for discussions with Leonid Brezhnev, the Soviet premier. The high theater of the China visit was repeated in Moscow, with toasts and elegant dinners between world leaders who had previously regarded each other as incarnations of evil.

What became known as "détente" with the Soviets offered the promise of a more orderly and restrained competition between the two superpowers. Nixon and Brezhnev signed agreements reached at the Strategic Arms Limitation Talks (SALT), which negotiators had been working on since 1969. The SALT agreement did not end the arms race, but it did limit both the number of intercontinental ballistic missiles (ICBMs) and the construction of antiballistic missile systems (ABMSs). In effect, the Soviets were allowed to retain a greater number of missiles with greater destructive power, while the United States retained a lead in the total number of warheads. No limitations were placed on new weapons systems, though each side agreed to work toward a permanent freeze on all nuclear weapons. The Moscow summit also produced new trade agreements, including an arrangement whereby the United States sold almost one-quarter of its wheat crop to the Soviets at a favorable price. American farmers rejoiced, since the wheat deal assured them a high price for their crop, but domestic critics grumbled that the deal would raise food prices in the United States and rescue the Soviets from troublesome economic problems.

SHUTTLE DIPLOMACY   The Nixon-Kissinger initiatives in the Middle East were less dramatic and less conclusive than the agreements with China and the Soviet Union, but they did show that America recognized Arab power in the region and its own dependence on the oil from Islamic states fundamentally opposed to Israel. After the Six-Day War of 1967, in which Israeli forces routed the armies of Egypt, Syria, and Jordan, Israel seized territory from all three Arab nations. Moreover, the number of Palestinian refugees, many of them homeless since the creation of Israel in 1948, increased after the Israeli victory in 1967. When Israel recovered from the initial shock of the surprise Yom Kippur War of 1973, Kissinger negotiated a cease-fire and exerted pressure to prevent Israel from taking additional Arab territory. American reliance on Arab oil led to closer ties with Egypt and its president, Anwar el-Sadat, and more restrained support for Israel. Though Kissinger's "shuttle diplomacy" among the capitals of the Middle East won acclaim from all sides, he failed to find a comprehensive formula for peace in the troubled region and ignored altogether the Palestinian problem. But he did lay groundwork for the subsequent accord between Israel and Egypt in 1977.

THE 1972 ELECTION   Nixon's foreign policy achievements allowed him to stage the campaign of 1972 as a triumphal procession. The main threat to his reelection came from Alabama governor George Wallace, who had the potential as a third-party candidate to deprive the Republicans of conservative votes and thereby throw the election to the Democrats or the Democratic-controlled Congress. But on May 15, 1972, Wallace was shot and left paralyzed below the waist by a white midwesterner anxious to achieve a grisly brand of notoriety. Wallace was forced to withdraw from the campaign.

Meanwhile, the Democrats were further ensuring Nixon's victory by nominating Senator George S. McGovern of South Dakota, a crusading liberal who embodied antiwar and social-welfare values associated with the turbulence of the 1960s. At the Democratic convention in Miami Beach, McGovern benefited from party reforms that increased the representation of women, blacks, and minorities. But such changes alienated party regulars. Mayor Richard Daley of Chicago was actually ousted from the convention, and the AFL-CIO refused to endorse the liberal Democratic candidate. McGovern also suffered from his handling of the crisis that developed when it was revealed that his running mate, Senator Thomas Eagleton of Missouri, had undergone shock treatments for depression. McGovern first announced complete support for Eagleton, then bowed to critics and dropped him, leaving an impression of vacillation and indecisiveness.

The campaign was an exercise in futility for McGovern, while Nixon made only a few formal political trips and cast himself in the role of "global peacekeeper." Nixon won the greatest victory of any Republican presidential candidate in history, capturing 520 electoral votes to only 17 for McGovern. The popular vote was equally decisive: 46 million to 28 million, a proportion of the total vote (60.8 percent) that was second only to Johnson's victory over Goldwater in 1964.

During the course of the campaign McGovern complained about the "dirty tricks" of the Nixon administration, most especially the curious incident in which a group of burglars was caught breaking into the Democratic National Committee headquarters in the Watergate apartment complex in Washington, D.C. McGovern's accusations seemed shrill and biased at the time, the lamentations of an obvious loser. Nixon and his staff made plans for "four more years" as the investigation of the fateful Watergate break-in proceeded apace.

WATERGATE

During the trial of the accused Watergate burglars, the relentless prodding of Judge John J. Sirica led one of the accused to tell the full story of the Nixon administration's complicity in the Watergate episode. James W. McCord, a former CIA agent and security chief for the Committee to Re-elect the President (CREEP), was the first in a long line of informers and penitents in a melodrama that unfolded over the next two years. It ended in the first resignation of a president in American history, the conviction and imprisonment of twenty-five officials of the Nixon administration, including four cabinet members, and the most serious constitutional crisis since the impeachment trial of President Andrew Johnson.

UNCOVERING THE COVER-UP   The trail of evidence pursued first by Judge Sirica, then by a grand jury, and then by a Senate investigation committee headed by Senator Samuel J. Ervin, Jr., of North Carolina, led directly to the White House. Republican senator Howard Baker of Tennessee, a member of the Ervin Committee, put the crucial questions succinctly: "What did the President know and when did he know it?" There was never any evidence that Nixon ordered the break-in or that he was aware of plans to burglarize the Democratic National Committee. But from the start, Nixon was personally involved in the cover-up of the incident. He used his presidential powers to discredit and block the investigation. And, most alarming, the Watergate burglary was merely one small part of a larger pattern of corruption and criminality sanctioned by the Nixon White House.

The White House had become committed to illegal tactics in 1970 when the *New York Times* disclosed that the secret American bombings in Cambodia had been going on for years. Nixon had ordered illegal telephone taps on several journalists and government employees suspected of leaking the story. The covert activity against the press and critics of Nixon's Vietnam policies increased in 1971 during the crisis generated by the publication of the Pentagon Papers, when a team of burglars under the direction of White House adviser John Ehrlichman had broken into Daniel Ellsberg's psychiatrist's office in an effort to obtain damaging information on Ellsberg, the man who had given the Pentagon Papers to the press. By the spring of 1972, Ehrlichman commanded a team of "dirty tricksters" who performed various acts of sabotage against prospective Democratic candidates for the presidency, including falsely accusing Hubert Humphrey and Senator Henry Jackson of sexual improprieties, forging press releases, setting off stink bombs at Democratic rallies, and associating the opposition candidates with racist remarks. By the time of the Watergate break-in, the money to finance such "pranks" was being illegally collected through the Committee to

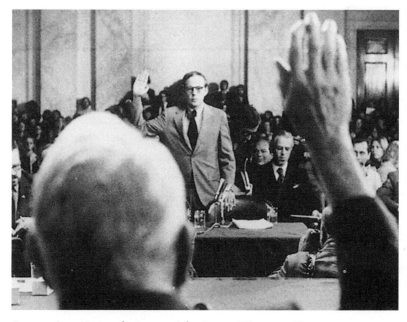

Senator Sam Ervin, chairman of the Senate Watergate Committee, swears in the ex–White House counsel John Dean, whose testimony linked President Nixon to the cover-up.

Re-elect the President and placed under the control of the White House staff.

The cover-up began to unravel as various people, including John Dean, legal counsel to the president, began to believe they were being set up as fall guys, and began to cooperate with prosecutors. It unraveled further in 1973 when L. Patrick Gray, acting director of the FBI, resigned after confessing that he had confiscated and destroyed several incriminating documents. On April 30 Ehrlichman and Haldeman resigned, together with Attorney-General Richard Kleindienst. A few days later the president nervously assured the public in a television address, "I am not a crook." But then John Dean, whom Nixon had dismissed because of his cooperation with prosecutors, testified to the Ervin Committee that there had been a cover-up and that Nixon had approved it. In another "bombshell" disclosure, a White House aide told the committee that Nixon had installed a taping system in the White House and that many of the conversations about Watergate had been recorded.

A year-long battle for the "Nixon tapes" began. Harvard law professor Archibald Cox, who had been appointed as special prosecutor to handle the Watergate case, took the president to court in October 1973 in order to obtain the tapes. Nixon, pleading "executive privilege," refused to release the tapes and ordered Cox fired. In what became known as the "Saturday Night Massacre," Attorney-General Elliot Richardson and Deputy Attorney-General William Ruckelshaus resigned rather than execute the order. Solicitor-General Robert Bork finally fired Cox. Cox's replacement as special prosecutor, Leon Jaworski, proved no more pliable than Cox, and he also took the president to court. In March 1974 the Watergate grand jury indicted Ehrlichman, Haldeman, and Mitchell for obstruction of justice, and it named Nixon as an "unindicted co-conspirator."

On July 24, 1974, the Supreme Court ruled unanimously that the president must surrender the tapes. No sooner were the tapes handed over than investigators learned that sections of certain recordings were missing, including eighteen minutes of a key conversation during which Nixon first mentioned the Watergate burglary. The president's loyal secretary tried to accept blame for the erasure, claiming she accidentally pushed the wrong button. But experts later concluded that the missing segments had been intentionally deleted.

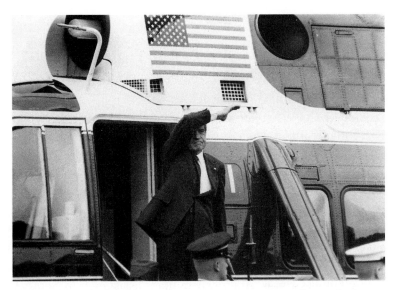

Having resigned his office, Richard Nixon waves farewell outside the White House, August 9, 1974.

A few days later the House Judiciary Committee dramatically voted to recommend three articles of impeachment: obstruction of justice through the payment of "hush money" to witnesses and the withholding of evidence; abuse of power through using federal agencies to deprive citizens of their constitutional rights; and defiance of Congress by withholding the tapes. But before the House of Representatives could meet to vote on impeachment, Nixon handed over the complete set of White House tapes. On August 9, 1974, fully aware that the evidence on the tapes implicated him in the cover-up, Richard Nixon resigned from office, the only president ever to do so.

EFFECTS OF WATERGATE   Spiro Agnew did not succeed Nixon because he himself had been forced to resign in October 1973 when it became known that he had accepted bribes from contractors before and during his term as vice-president. In a plea bargain with prosecutors he agreed to resign and to a single charge of tax evasion. The vice-president at the time of Nixon's resignation was Gerald Ford, the former House minority leader from Michigan whom Nixon had appointed, with the approval of Congress, under provisions of the Twenty-fifth Amendment. Ratified in 1967, the amendment provided for the appointment of a vice-president when the office became vacant. Ford insisted that he had no intention of pardoning Nixon, who was still liable for criminal prosecution. "I do not think the public would stand for it," said Ford. But a month after Nixon's resignation, the new president did issue the pardon, explaining that it was necessary to end the national obsession with the Watergate scandals. Many suspected that Nixon and Ford had made a deal, though there was no evidence to confirm the speculation. President Ford testified personally to a congressional committee: "There was no deal, period."

If there was a silver lining in the dark cloud of Watergate, it was the vigor and resiliency of the institutions that had brought a president down—the press, Congress, the courts, and an aroused public opinion. Congress responded to the Watergate revelations with several pieces of legislation designed to curb executive power. Already nervous about possible efforts to renew American military assistance to South Vietnam, the Democratic-led Congress passed the War Powers Act (1973), which required the president to inform Congress within forty-eight hours if U.S. troops were being deployed in combat abroad and to withdraw troops after sixty days unless Congress specifically approved their stay. In an effort to correct abuses of campaign funds, Congress enacted legislation in 1974 that set new ceilings on political contributions and expenditures. And in reaction to the Nixon claim of "executive privilege" as a means of withholding evidence, Congress strengthened the 1966 Freedom of Information Act to require prompt responses to requests for information from government files and to place on government agencies the burden of proof for classifying information as secret.

With Nixon's resignation, the nation had weathered a profound constitutional crisis, but the aftershock of the Watergate episode produced a deep sense of disillusionment with the so-called imperial presidency. Apart from Nixon's illegal actions, the scurrilous language used in the White House and made public on the tapes stripped away the veils of mystery surrounding national leaders and left even the die-hard defenders of presidential authority shocked at the crudity and duplicity of Nixon and his subordinates. Coming on the heels of the erosion of public confidence generated by the Vietnam War, the Watergate affair renewed public cynicism toward a government that had systematically lied to the people and violated their civil liberties. Said one bumper sticker of the day: "Don't vote. It only encourages them."

Nixon's resignation pleased his critics but also initiated a prolonged crisis of confidence. A poll taken in 1974 asked people how much faith they had in the executive branch of government. Only 14 percent answered "a great deal"; 43 percent said "hardly any." Restoring credibility and respect thus became the primary challenge facing Nixon's successors. Unfortunately a new array of economic and foreign crises would make that task doubly difficult.

An Unelected President

During Richard Nixon's last year in office the Watergate crisis so dominated the Washington scene that major domestic and foreign problems received little executive attention. The perplexing combination of inflation and recession worsened, as did the oil crisis. At the same time, Henry Kissinger, who assumed control over the management of foreign policy, watched helplessly as the South Vietnamese forces began to crumble before North Vietnamese attacks, attempted with limited success to establish a framework for peace in the Middle East, and supported a CIA role in overthrowing Salvador Allende, the popularly elected Marxist president of Chile. Allende was subsequently murdered and replaced by General Augusto Pinochet, a military dictator supposedly friendly to the United States.

THE FORD YEARS   Gerald Ford inherited these simmering problems when he assumed office after Nixon's resignation. An amiable, honest man, Ford candidly admitted upon becoming vice-president, "I am a Ford, not a Lincoln." He enjoyed widespread popular support for only a short time. His pardon of Nixon on September 8, 1974, generated a storm of criticism. The *New York Times* called it "an unconscionable act."

As president, Ford soon adopted the posture he had developed as a conservative minority leader in the House: nay-saying leader of the opposition who believed that the federal government exercised too much power over domestic affairs. In his fifteen months as president, Ford vetoed thirty-nine bills, thereby outstripping Herbert Hoover's veto record in less than half the time. By resisting congressional pressure to reduce taxes and increase federal spending, he succeeded in plummeting the economy into the deepest recession since the Great Depression. Unemployment jumped to 9 percent in 1975, and the federal deficit hit a record the next year. When New York City announced that it was near bankruptcy, unable to meet its payrolls and bond payments, Ford vowed "to veto any bill that has as its purpose a federal bailout." The headline in the *New York Daily News* was: "Ford to New York: Drop Dead." But the president relented after the Senate and House banking committees voted to guarantee a loan; New York was saved from insolvency. Ford rejected wage and price controls to curb inflation, preferring voluntary restraints that he tried to bolster by passing out "WIN" buttons, symbolizing his campaign to "Whip Inflation Now." The WIN buttons instead became a national joke and a popular symbol of Ford's ineffectiveness in the fight against stagflation.

In foreign policy, Ford retained Henry Kissinger as secretary of state and attempted to pursue Nixon's goals of stability in the Middle East, rapprochement with China, and détente with the Soviet Union. Late in 1974, Ford met with Soviet leader Leonid Brezhnev at Vladivostok in Siberia and accepted the framework for another arms-control accord that was to serve as the basis for SALT II. Meanwhile Kissinger's tireless shuttling between Cairo and Tel Aviv produced an agreement: Israel promised to return to Egypt most of the Sinai territory captured in the 1967 war, and the two nations agreed to rely on negotiations rather than force to settle future disagreements. These limited but significant achievements should have enhanced Ford's image, but they were drowned in the sea of criticism and carping that followed the collapse of South Vietnam to Communists in May 1975.

Not only had a decade of American effort in Vietnam proved futile, but the Khmer Rouge, the Cambodian Communist movement, had also won a resounding victory, plunging that country into a bloodbath. Meanwhile, the OPEC oil cartel was threatening another worldwide boycott while other Third World nations denounced the United States as a depraved and declining imperialistic power. Ford lost his patience when he sent in the marines to rescue the crew of the American merchant ship *Mayaguez,* which had been captured by the Cambodian Communists. This vigorous move won popular acclaim until it was disclosed that the Cambodians had already agreed to release the captured Americans: the forty-one Americans killed in the operation had died for no purpose.

THE 1976 ELECTION   In the midst of such turmoil, the Democrats could hardly wait for the 1976 election. At the Republican convention Ford managed to fend off a powerful challenge for the nomination from the former California governor and Hollywood actor, Ronald Reagan, whose robust appearance belied his sixty-five years. Because even the Republicans were divided over Ford's leadership, and because Ford's failure to solve the economic and energy problems was beyond dispute, the Democratic nominee seemed a shoo-in for the presidency. "We could run an aardvark this year and win," predicted one Democratic leader.

The Democrats chose an obscure former naval officer and engineer turned peanut farmer who had served one term as governor of Georgia. Jimmy Carter campaigned harder than any of the other Democratic hopefuls; he capitalized on the post-Watergate cynicism by promising "I will never tell a lie to the American people" and by citing his inexperience in the byways of Washington politics as an asset. Carter promised to revive the moral presidency of Woodrow Wilson. In the midst of the continuing revulsion against the political corruption unearthed by the Watergate inquiries, he preached the need for national repentance and personal self-sacrifice. Facing the prospect of the first president from the Deep South since 1849, and the first ever born and bred in that particular briar patch, reporters marveled at a Baptist candidate who claimed to be "born again," and began to speculate that Carter's native region harbored some forgotten virtues after all.

To the surprise of many pundits, Carter revived the New Deal coalition of southern whites, blacks, urban labor, and ethnic groups to win 41 million votes to Ford's 39 million, and a narrow electoral vote majority of 297 to 241. A heavy turnout of blacks in the South enabled Carter to sweep every state in the region except Virginia. Carter also benefited from the appeal of Walter F. Mondale, his liberal running mate and a favorite among blue-collar workers and the urban poor. Carter lost most of the trans-Mississippi West, but no other Democratic candidate had made much headway there since Harry Truman in 1948. The big story of the election was the low voter turnout. "Neither Ford nor Carter won as many votes as Mr. Nobody," said one reporter, commenting on the fact that almost half the eligible voters, apparently alienated by Watergate and the lackluster candidates, chose to sit out the election.

THE CARTER INTERREGNUM

POLICY STALEMATE   Once in office, Carter suffered the fate of all American presidents since Kennedy: after an initial honeymoon, during which Carter displayed folksy charm by walking down Pennsylvania Avenue after his inauguration rather than riding in a limousine, and wearing cardigan sweaters during televised "fireside chats," his popularity and political effectiveness waned. Soon *Newsweek* was referring to the "corn bread-and-cardigan atmospherics." The truth was that, like Ford before him, Carter faced an almost insurmountable set of domestic and international problems. He was expected to cure the economic recession and inflation at a time when all industrial economies were shaken by a shortage of energy and confidence. He was expected to reassert America's global power at a time of waning respect for America's international authority. And he was expected to do this, as well as buoy the national spirit, through a set of political institutions in which many Americans had lost faith.

Yet, during the first two years of his term, Carter enjoyed several successes, most reflecting the values of moderate liberalism. His administration included more blacks and women than ever before; his appoint-

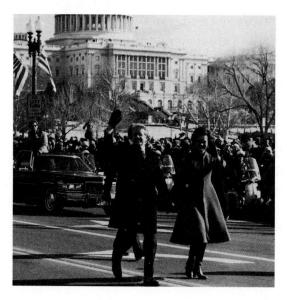

President Jimmy Carter and wife, Rosalynn, forgo the traditional limousine and walk down Pennsylvania Avenue after the inauguration, January 20, 1977.

ment of Andrew Young, a former protégé of Martin Luther King, as ambassador to the United Nations attracted the most attention. Carter created a federal task force to study the problem of Vietnam-era draft evaders and eventually offered amnesty to the thousands of young Americans who had fled the country rather than serve in Vietnam. He reformed the civil service to provide rewards for merit, and he created new cabinet-level Departments of Energy and Education. He also pushed several significant environmental initiatives through Congress, including a bill to establish controls over strip mining, a "superfund" of $1.6 billion to clean up chemical waste sites, and a proposal to protect over 100 million acres of Alaskan land from development.

But success was short-lived. Carter's political predicament surfaced in the protracted debate over energy policy. Carter, like Hoover, served at a time of diminishing resources, and like that other engineer-businessman, he had a distaste for stroking legislators or wheeling and dealing to get legislation through. The energy bill passed in 1978 was a gutted version of the original proposed by the administration, reflecting the power of both conservative and liberal special-interest lobbies. One Carter aide said that the energy bill looked like it had been "nibbled to death by ducks." The clumsy political maneuvers that plagued Carter and his inexperienced aides repeatedly frustrated efforts to remedy the energy crisis. Moreover, with party discipline in the Congress a shambles and each special-interest group clamoring for its own program, the White House was repeatedly forced to create what one Carter aide described as a "roll-your-own majority" for each presidential proposal.

In the summer of 1979, when renewed violence in the Middle East produced a second fuel shortage in the United States, motorists were again forced to wait in long lines for limited supplies of gas that they regarded as excessively expensive. Opinion polls showed Carter with an approval rating of only 26 percent, lower than Nixon during the worst moments of the Watergate crisis. During July Carter called his advisers to an extraordinary retreat at Camp David, Maryland, and emerged ten days later proclaiming a need for "a rebirth of the American spirit." He also called for a "new and positive energy program." But Congress only partially funded the major feature of his new plan—a federal agency to encourage development of synthetic fuels.

Several of Carter's early foreign policy initiatives also got caught in political crossfires. Soon after his inauguration, Carter vowed that "the soul of our foreign policy" should be the defense of human rights abroad. This human rights campaign, however, provoked attack from two sides: those who feared it sacrificed a detached appraisal of national interest for high-level moralizing, and those who believed that human rights were important but that the administration was applying the standard inconsistently.

Similarly, Carter's successful negotiation of treaties to turn over control of the Panama Canal to the government of Panama generated intense criticism. Republican Ronald Reagan claimed that the Canal Zone was sovereign American soil purchased "fair and square" in Theodore Roosevelt's administration. (In the congressional debate one senator quipped, "We stole it fair and square, so why can't we keep it?") Carter argued that the limitations on American influence in Latin America, and the deep resentment toward American colonialism in Panama left the United States with no other choice. The Canal Zone would revert in stages to Panama by 1999. The Senate ratified the treaties by a paper-thin margin (68 to 32, two votes more than the required two-thirds), but conservatives lambasted Carter for surrendering American authority in a strategically critical part of the world.

THE CAMP DAVID ACCORDS Carter's crowning foreign policy achievement, which even his most bitter critics applauded, was the arrangement of a peace agreement between Israel and Egypt. In 1977 Egyptian president Anwar el-Sadat flew to Tel Aviv at the invitation of Israeli prime minister Menachem Begin. Sadat's bold act, and his accompanying announcement that Egypt was now willing to recognize the legitimacy of the Israeli state, opened up diplomatic opportunities that Carter and Secretary of State Cyrus Vance quickly pursued.

In 1978 Carter invited Sadat and Begin to the presidential retreat at Camp David for two weeks of difficult negotiations. The first part of the eventual agreement called for Israel to return all land in the Sinai in exchange for Egyptian recognition of Israel's sovereignty. This agreement was successfully implemented in 1982 when the last Israeli settler vacated the Sinai. But the second part of the agreement, calling for Israel to negotiate with Sadat to resolve the Palestinian refugee dilemma, began to unravel soon after the Camp David summit.

By March 26, 1979, when Begin and Sadat returned to Washington to sign the formal treaty, Begin had already made clear his refusal to

Egyptian president Anwar Sadat (left), *Jimmy Carter* (center), *and Israeli prime minister Menachem Begin* (right) *at the announcement of the Camp David accords, September 1978.*

block new Israeli settlements on the West Bank of the Jordan River, which Sadat had regarded as a prospective homeland for the Palestinians. In the wake of the Camp David accords, most of the Arab nations condemned Sadat as a traitor to their Islamic cause. Still, Carter and Vance were responsible for a dramatic display of high-level diplomacy that, whatever its limitations, made an all-out war between Israel and the Arab world less likely in the foreseeable future.

MOUNTING TROUBLES   Carter's crowning failure, which even his most avid supporters acknowledged, was his management of the economy. In effect he inherited a bad situation and left it worse. Carter employed the same economic policies as Nixon and Ford to fight stagflation, but he reversed the order of the federal "cure," preferring first to fight unemployment with a tax cut and increased public spending. Unemployment declined slightly, from 8 to 7 percent in 1977, but inflation soared; at 5 percent when he took office, it reached 10 percent in 1978 and kept going. During one month in 1980 it measured at an annual rate of no less than 18 percent. Like previous presidents, Carter then reversed himself to fight the other side of the economic malaise.

By midterm he was delaying tax reductions and vetoing government spending programs that he had proposed in his first year. The result, however, was the worst of both possible worlds: a deepened recession with unemployment at 7.5 percent in 1980, mortgage rates at 15 percent, interest rates at an all-time high of 20 percent, and a runaway inflation averaging between 12 and 13 percent.

The signing of a controversial new Strategic Arms Limitation Treaty (SALT II) with the Soviets put Carter's leadership to the test just as the mounting economic problems made him the subject of biting editorial cartoons nationwide. Like SALT I, the new agreement did not do much to slow down the nuclear arms race. It placed a ceiling of 2,250 bombers and missiles on each side and set limits on the number of warheads and new weapons systems. To pacify his conservative critics, who charged that SALT II would give the Soviets a decided advantage in the number and destructive power of land-based missiles, Carter announced that the United States would build a new missile system, called the MX, that would be housed in a vast maze of underground tunnels connected by railroad, creating a sort of "nuclear shell game" that would prevent Soviet planners from knowing where to strike. Liberal critics called the MX plan "a combination of Disney World and Armageddon" and criticized the SALT II agreement as "a step sideways rather than backwards in the arms race." Conservatives questioned the whole idea of détente, arguing that the Soviets would never have signed the agreement if it did not guarantee them nuclear superiority. Whether SALT II would pass the Senate became an open question.

The question became moot in 1979 when the Soviet army invaded Afghanistan to rescue the faltering Communist government there, which was being challenged by Muslim rebels. Carter immediately shelved SALT II, suspended grain shipments to the Soviet Union, and began a campaign for an international boycott of the 1980 Olympics, which were to be held that summer in Moscow.

IRAN   Then came the Iranian crisis, a year-long cascade of unwelcome events that epitomized the inability of the United States to control world affairs. The crisis began with the fall of the shah of Iran in 1979. The revolutionaries who toppled the shah rallied around Ayatollah Ruhollah Khomeini, a Muslim religious leader who symbolized the Islamic values the shah had tried to replace with Western ways. Khomeini's hatred of the United States dated back to the CIA-sponsored overthrow of Iran's Mossadegh government in 1953. Nor did it help the American image that the CIA had trained SAVAK, the shah's ruthless secret police force. Late in 1979 the exiled shah was allowed to enter the United States in order to undergo treatment for cancer. A few days later, a frenzied mob stormed the American embassy in Teheran and seized the diplomats and staff inside. Khomeini endorsed the mob action and demanded the return of the shah along with all his wealth in exchange for the release of the fifty-three American hostages. In the meantime, the Iranian militants staged daily demonstrations for the benefit of worldwide news and television coverage in which the American flag and effigies of the American president were burned and otherwise desecrated.

Indignant Americans demanded a military response to such outrages, but Carter's range of options was limited. He appealed to the United Nations, protesting what was a clear violation of diplomatic immunity and international law. Khomeini scoffed at U.N. requests for the release of hostages. Carter then froze all Iranian assets in the United States and appealed to American allies for a trade embargo of Iran. The trade restrictions were only partially effective—even America's most

Iranian militants stormed the U.S. Embassy in Teheran in 1979, taking 53 Americans hostage for over a year. Here one of the hostages (face covered) is paraded before a camera.

loyal European allies did not want to lose their access to Iranian oil—so a frustrated and besieged Carter authorized a risky rescue attempt by American commandos in 1980. Secretary of State Vance resigned in protest against the rescue attempt, and against Carter's sharp turn toward a more hawkish foreign policy. The commando raid was aborted because of helicopter failures, and ended with eight fatalities when another helicopter collided with a transport plane in the desert.

Nightly television coverage of the taunting Iranian rebels generated widespread popular craving for action and a near obsession with the falling fortunes of the United States and the fate of the hostages. The end came after 444 days of captivity when Carter released several billion dollars of Iranian assets to ransom the kidnapped hostages. A plane carrying them left Teheran for Algiers, and Carter then flew to Wiesbaden, West Germany, to greet the released hostages at an American base. Few noted the irony that Algiers was one of the Barbary states that had extorted tribute from the early republic by holding American prisoners until 1815.

MAKING CONNECTIONS

- Foreign affairs in the 1970s show the changing patterns of the cold war. The next chapter details the end of both the cold war and the Soviet Union.

- Presidents Nixon and Ford tried, with limited success, to decrease the power of the federal government over domestic affairs. President Reagan was much more successful at advancing the conservative agenda, a topic covered in the next chapter.

- The rebellion and turbulence of the 1960s and 1970s became less apparent in the following decade; as Chapter 37 shows, however, that turbulence reappeared, in a somewhat different form, in the 1990s.

FURTHER READING

Engaging overviews of the cultural trends of the 1960s include William L. O'Neill's *Coming Apart: An Informal History of America in the 1960s* (1972) and Godfrey Hodgson's *America in Our Time* (1976). The scholarly literature on the New Left includes Irwin Unger's *The Movement: A History of the American New Left 1959–1972* (1974). On the Students for a Democratic Society, see Kirkpatrick Sale's *SDS* (1973) and Allen J. Matusow's *The Unraveling of America: A History of Liberalism in the 1960s* (1984). Also useful is Todd Gitlin's *The Sixties: Years of Hope, Days of Rage* (rev. ed., 1993).

Two influential assessments of the counterculture by sympathetic commentators are Theodore Roszak's *The Making of a Counterculture: Reflections on the Technocratic Society and Its Youthful Opposition* (1969) and Charles Reich's *The Greening of America* (1970). A good scholarly analysis of the hippies that takes them seriously is Timothy Miller's *The Hippies and American Values* (1991). On the communal movement, see Keith Melville's *Communes in the Counter Culture* (1972).

There is a wealth of good books dealing with the women's liberation movement. Among the most powerful accounts are those by participants. See Shulamith Firestone's *The Dialectic of Sex* (1972), Betty Friedan's *It Changed My Life: Writings on the Women's Movement* (1976), Kate Millett's *Sexual Politics* (1971), and *Sisterhood Is Powerful* (1970), edited by Robin Morgan. Sara Evans explains the ambivalent relationship of feminism with the civil rights movement in *Personal Politics: The Roots of Women's Liberation in the Civil Rights Movement and the New Left* (1980).

The organizing efforts of César Chavez are detailed in Ronald Taylor's *Chavez and the Farm Workers* (1975). The struggles of Native Americans for recognition and power are sympathetically described in Stan Steiner's *The New Indians* (1968). On the shifting cultural mood of the 1970s, see Christopher Lasch's influential critique, *The Culture of Narcissism* (1978). Peter Clecak convincingly questions the stereotypic notion of the seventies as an age of apathy and narcissism in *America's Quest for the Ideal Self* (1983).

On Nixon, see Stephen Ambrose's *Nixon: The Triumph of a Politician, 1962–1972* (1989) and *Nixon: Ruin and Recovery, 1973–1990* (1991). Equally valuable is Herbert S. Parmet's *Richard Nixon and His America* (1990). For a solid overview of the Watergate scandal, see

Stanley Kutler's *The Wars of Watergate: The Last Crisis of Richard Nixon* (1990).

For the way the Republicans handled affairs, consult Tad Szulc's *The Illusion of Peace: Foreign Policy in the Nixon Years* (1978). Secretary of State Henry Kissinger recounts his role in policy formation in *The White House Years* (1978). A less favorable report of the Kissinger role appears in Seymour M. Hersh's *The Price of Power: Kissinger in the Nixon White House* (1983).

The loss of Vietnam and the end of American involvement are traced in Allan E. Goodman's *The Lost Peace: America's Search for a Negotiated Settlement of the Vietnam War* (1978), Frank Snepp's *Decent Interval: An Insider's Account of Saigon's Indecent End Told by the CIA's Chief Strategy Analyst in Vietnam* (1977), and Gareth Porter's *A Peace Denied: The United States, Vietnam and the Paris Agreement* (1975). William Shawcross's *Sideshow: Kissinger, Nixon, and the Destruction of Cambodia* (1978) deals with the broadening of the war, while Larry Berman's *Planning a Tragedy: The Americanization of the War in Vietnam* (1982) assesses the final impact of American involvement. The most comprehensive treatment of the antiwar movement in the United States is Tom Wells's *The War Within: America's Battle over Vietnam* (1994). A recent effort to reflect upon the lingering impact of the Vietnam War is Arnold R. Isaacs's *Vietnam Shadows: The War, Its Ghosts, and Its Legacy* (1997).

To examine the rise of Jimmy Carter, consult Betty Glad's *Jimmy Carter: In Search of the Great White House* (1980). The best overview of the Carter administration is Burton I. Kaufman's *The Presidency of James Earl Carter, Jr.* (1993). A work more sympathetic to the Carter administration is John Dumbrell's *The Carter Presidency: A Re-Evaluation* (1993). Also useful is Kenneth E. Morris's *Jimmy Carter: American Moralist* (1997). Gaddis Smith's *Morality, Reason, and Power* (1986) provides an overview of American diplomacy in the Carter years. Zbigniew Brzezinski's *Power and Principle: Memories of the National Security Advisor, 1977–1981* (1983) and Cyrus Vance's *Hard Choices: Critical Years in America's Foreign Policy* (1983) lend insight into the Carter approach to foreign policy. Background on how the Middle East came to dominate much of American policy is found in William B. Quandt's *Decade of Decisions: American Policy toward the Arab-Israeli Conflict, 1967–1976* (1977).

36 ✂A CONSERVATIVE
INSURGENCY

CHAPTER ORGANIZER

This chapter focuses on:

* the demographic, social, and economic reasons for the rise of Ronald Reagan and Republican conservatism.

* changing relations with the Soviet Union, including the end of the cold war.

* the economic and social aspects of the 1980s.

* the cause and aftermath of the Gulf War.

*P*resident Jimmy Carter and his embattled Democratic administration hobbled through 1979. The economy remained sluggish, double-digit inflation continued unabated, and failed efforts to free the American hostages in Iran made the administration appear indecisive. Carter's inability to mobilize the nation behind his ill-fated energy program revealed mortal flaws in his reading of the public mood and his understanding of legislative politics. In July 1979, a much ballyhooed presidential address to the nation aroused more criticism than support. Carter's claim that a "crisis of confidence" was paralyzing the nation and his insistence that the days of dramatic economic growth were over fell on deaf or indignant ears. As a Phoenix newspaper editorial declared, the nation did not want "sermons" from the president; it wanted "action."

While the lackluster Carter administration was foundering, Republican conservatives were forging a plan to win the White House in 1980 and to assault the "New Deal welfare state" mentality in Washington. Those plans centered on the popularity and charisma of Ronald Reagan, the Hollywood actor turned California governor and prominent political commentator. Reagan was not a deep thinker, but he was a superb analyst of the public mood, an unabashed patriot, and a committed advocate of conservative principles. He was also charming and cheerful, a likable politician renowned for his relentless anecdotes. Where the dour Carter denounced the evils of free enterprise capitalism and tried to scold Americans into reviving long-forgotten virtues of frugality, a sunny Reagan promised a "revolution of ideas" designed to unleash the capitalist spirit, restore national pride, and regain international respect.

During the late 1970s, Reagan's simple message promoting a grassroots political revolution and a restoration of American pride and prosperity offered an uplifting alternative to Carter's strident moralism. More specifically, Reagan wanted to increase military spending, dismantle the "bloated" federal bureaucracy, reduce taxes and regulations, and in general, undo the welfare state. He also wanted to affirm old-time morality by ending abortions and reinstituting school prayer. Reagan's appeal derived from his remarkable skills as a public speaker and his dogmatic commitment to a few overarching ideas and simple themes. As a true believer and an able compromiser, he combined the fervor of a revolutionary with the pragmatism of a diplomat.

Such attributes won Reagan two presidential terms in 1980 and 1984 and ensured the election of his successor, George Bush, in 1988. Just how revolutionary the Reagan era was remains a subject of intense partisan debate. What cannot be denied, however, is that Reagan's actions and beliefs set the tone for the decade and continue to affect American political and economic life.

The Reagan Revolution

THE MAKING OF A PRESIDENT   Ronald Reagan seemed at first a more remote presidential possibility than Carter, if longer in the public

President Ronald Reagan, "the Great Communicator."

eye as a screen and television personality. A small-town boy from Dixon, Illinois, Reagan became a radio sports announcer in Iowa after graduation in 1932 from Eureka College. In 1937 he went west and wangled a screen test, the start of a movie career. As president of the Screen Actors Guild, Reagan was at first a liberal and a New Dealer. But he bounced to the far right on the political spectrum during the 1950s. Repelled by Communist infiltrators in liberal groups, he said, "I was beginning to see the seamy side of liberalism." He campaigned for both Eisenhower (1952, 1956) and Nixon (1960), switched his registration to Republican in 1962, then achieved political stardom in 1964 when he delivered a rousing speech on national television on behalf of Barry Goldwater.

The Republican right had a new idol whose appeal survived the Goldwater debacle. Those who discounted Reagan as a minor actor and a mental midget underrated his many virtues, including the importance of his years in front of the camera. Politics had always been a performing art, the more so in an age of television, and few, if any, others in public life had Reagan's stage presence. He had, moreover, a contagious zest for life and a genuine instinct for the witty one-liner. Drawn by wealthy admirers into the campaign for governor of California in 1966, Reagan moderated his rawest rhetoric, and won the governorship by a landslide.

Reagan appealed especially to middle-class and lower-middle-class voters resentful of "high" taxes, welfare programs for the dependent, the "neurotic vulgarities" of university students running wild, crime in the streets, and challenges to traditional values in general. In the forefront of the counterculture, California was in the forefront of reaction against it as well.

From the start of his gubernatorial term, Reagan had his eye on the presidency, but in the mid-1970s his rhetoric still seemed too extreme for the mainstream, and his "back-to-basics" speeches provoked barbed jokes from journalists: "Ronald Reagan wants to take us back to the fifties," wrote one reporter, "back to the 1950s in foreign policy and back to the 1850s in economic and domestic policy."

By the eve of the 1980 election, however, Reagan had become the beneficiary of a development that made his conservative vision of America more than a harmless flirtation with nostalgia. The 1980 census revealed that the elderly proportion of the nation's population was increasing and moving to the "Sunbelt" states of the South and West. This dual development—an increase in the numbers of senior citizens and the steady transfer of population to regions of the country where hostility to "big government" was endemic—meant that demographics were carrying the United States toward Reagan's political philosophy.

THE MORAL MAJORITY Reagan's presidential aspirations also benefited from a major revival of evangelical religion, not unlike the Great Awakenings of the eighteenth and nineteenth centuries. No longer a local or provincial phenomenon that could be easily dismissed, Christian evangelicals now owned their own television and radio stations and operated their own schools and universities. A survey in 1977 revealed that more than 70 million Americans described themselves as born-again Christians who had a personal relationship with Jesus.

During the previous two decades, widely publicized Supreme Court decisions had stirred fundamentalist indignation and thus unwittingly helped arouse a political backlash. Among these were rulings for abortion, against prayer in public schools, for the right to teach Darwinism, and for narrower definitions of pornography.

The Reverend Jerry Falwell's "Moral Majority" (later the Liberty Lobby) expressed the sentiments of the religious right wing: the economy should operate without "interference" by the government, which should be reduced in size; the Supreme Court decision in *Roe* v. *Wade* (1973) legalizing abortion should be reversed; Darwinian evolution should be replaced in schoolbooks by the biblical story of creation; and Soviet expansion should be opposed as a form of pagan totalitarianism. "Our task is not to Christianize America," said Falwell, "but to bring about a moral and conservative revolution." By not focusing on divisive theological questions, he and others sought to use "traditional morality" to create an interdenominational political force drawing upon millions of evangelical Christians. The moralistic zeal and financial resources of the religious right made them formidable opponents of liberal political candidates and programs. By 1980 Falwell's Moral Majority organization claimed over 4 million members, including 72,000 ministers, priests, and rabbis. Its base of support was in the South and was strongest among Baptists, but its appeal extended across the country.

A curiosity of the 1980 campaign was that the religious right opposed Jimmy Carter, a self-professed born-again Christian, and supported Ronald Reagan, a man who was neither conspicuously pious nor even often in church. His divorce and remarriage, once an almost automatic disqualification for the presidency, got little mention. Nor did the fact that as governor he had signed one of the most permissive abortion laws in the country. That Ronald Reagan became the Messiah of the Religious Right, God's man for the hour, was a tribute both to the force of social issues and the candidate's political skills.

THE 1980 ELECTION   Reagan, who had lost a last-minute try for the Republican nomination in 1968 and had failed to wrest it from Gerald Ford in 1976, easily won the nomination in 1980. Reagan was an adept campaigner who presented a consistent message to the voters: Carter and the Democrats, he insisted, believed that the United States had entered an era of permanent limits on economic growth and personal initiative. On the contrary, he asserted, the Republicans believed that America's greatest economic accomplishments were just around the corner. Reagan pledged that his recovery plans would restore prosperity and public confidence. He used folksy maxims and jokes to punctuate his themes. For instance, at one campaign stop he quipped: "A recession is when your neighbor loses his job. A depression is when you lose yours. A recovery is when Jimmy Carter loses his."

On November 4, before the polls had closed on the West Coast, Carter conceded the election. Reagan won a bare majority (50.7 per-

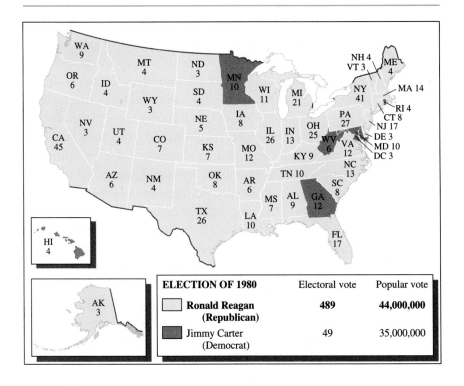

ELECTION OF 1980	Electoral vote	Popular vote
Ronald Reagan (Republican)	489	44,000,000
Jimmy Carter (Democrat)	49	35,000,000

cent) of the popular vote, but that was well ahead of Carter's 41 percent. John Anderson, a liberal Republican congressman running as an independent, got most of the rest. In the electoral college, Reagan's victory was overwhelming—489 to 49. Carter carried only six states and the District of Columbia.

More than a victory for the conservative policies Reagan championed, the election may have reflected the triumph of what one political scientist called the "largest mass movement of our time"—nonvoting. Almost as striking as Reagan's one-sided victory was the fact that his vote total represented only 28 percent of the potential electorate. Only 53 percent of eligible voters cast ballots in the 1980 election; in western European countries such as France and Germany, voter participation hovered at 85 percent in national elections during the 1970s.

Where had all the voters gone? Political analysts noted that most of the nonvoters were working-class Democrats in the major urban centers. Voter turnout was lowest in poor inner-city neighborhoods such as New York's Bedford-Stuyvesant district, which had a 19 percent voter participation rate. Turnout was highest, by contrast, in the affluent suburbs of large cities, areas where the Republican party was experiencing a dramatic surge in popularity. Such trends meant that American office-holders were being selected during the 1970s by an electorate increasingly dominated by middle- and upper-class voters.

Explanations for the high levels of voter apathy among working-class Americans vary. Some argue that they reflected the continuing sense of disillusionment with government itself, growing out of the Watergate affair. Another widespread perception influencing voting behavior was that the Democratic party had turned its back on its traditional blocs of support among common folk. Democratic leaders no longer spoke eloquently on behalf of those at the bottom of America's social scale. By embracing a fiscal conservatism indistinguishable from that of the Republicans, as Carter had done, Democrats lost their appeal among blue-collar workers and ghetto dwellers. And so the largest group of nonvoters in the 1980 election were former Democrats who had decided that neither party served their interests. When viewed in this light, Ronald Reagan's victory represented less a resounding victory for conservative Republicans than a self-inflicted defeat by a fractured Democratic party. But for the moment, at least, such results were masked by the Republicans' euphoric victory celebrations. Flush with a sense of power and destiny, Ronald Reagan headed toward Washington with a blueprint for dismantling the welfare state.

REAGAN'S FIRST TERM

REAGANOMICS Reagan's inaugural address prescribed full-strength conservative medicine for the decade-long stagflation. "Government is not the solution to our problem," Reagan insisted; "government is the problem." Reagan credited Calvin Coolidge and his treasury secretary, Andrew Mellon, with demonstrating that by reducing taxes and easing government regulation of business, the elixir of free-market capitalism would revive the economy. Like his Republican predecessors of the 1920s, he wanted to unleash entrepreneurial energy as never before. By cutting taxes and domestic federal spending, he claimed, a surging economy would produce *more* government revenues that would help reduce the budget deficit. This "supply-side" economic program, soon dubbed "Reaganomics," derived from a group of economists who challenged the Keynesian doctrine that the problems of the economy were mainly on the demand side. Supply-siders contended, to the contrary, that these problems resulted from governmental intrusions into the marketplace and from excessive taxes that reduced incentives to work, save, and invest.

One of Reagan's first steps was to abandon price controls on oil; another was to call off the embargo on wheat exports to the Soviet Union. But the administration's energies focused on the tax reform plan advanced during the election campaign. Reagan had become entranced by the idea of the "Laffer curve," named for economist Arthur Laffer of the University of Southern California. Derived from the truism that neither a tax of 0 nor a tax of 100 percent would produce revenue, the theory held that somewhere in between these two extremes tax rates reached a point beyond which they began to reduce a person's incentive to seek more income.

For a while, during his first two months in office, Reagan's popularity declined in the polls and doubts arose that he could get his economic program through a Democratic House. Then on March 30, 1981, a tragic event, an attempted assassination, fortuitously boosted support of Reagan's program. The troubled young assailant, obsessed by the hope of impressing a movie actress, fired several shots as Reagan's party emerged from a speech in a Washington hotel. A bullet hit Reagan in the chest, another inflicted permanent brain damage on his press secretary, and other bullets wounded a policeman and a Secret Service agent. While recovering from his wound, Reagan aroused universal admiration for his courage and wit.

Reagan's economic program gained ground along with his physical recovery. Enough Democrats—sympathetic southern "boll weevils" or centrists and liberals frightened by his popularity—went along to pass it by overwhelming majorities. On August 4, 1981, Reagan signed the Economic Recovery Tax Act, which cut personal income taxes 25 percent across the board over thirty-three months, lowered the maximum rate from 70 to 50 percent for 1982, cut the capital gains tax from a 28 percent maximum to 20 percent, and offered a broad array of other tax concessions.

Reaganomics departed from the Coolidge record mainly in the mounting deficits of the 1980s and in their major cause—growing expenditures for the armed forces. While Republican administrations of the 1920s had steadily reduced the national debt by holding the line on government expenditures, the Republican administration of the 1980s built ever-larger deficits, debts larger than those under all its predecessors put together. To be sure, the congressional Democrats were even more reluctant to cut domestic spending. Most items other than defense were deemed politically inviolable. The biggest category in the projected $700 billion budget involved payments to individuals: Social Security checks, pension checks, reimbursements for Medicare and Medicaid services, veterans' checks, and welfare checks. About 48 cents of every dollar the government spent thus went to well-organized social groups capable of capturing attention in Congress.

BUDGET CUTS   Reagan staffers discovered that there was not enough waste and fraud to make the substantial budget cuts that had been so easily promised in the campaign. Along with the 1981 tax cuts went budget cuts of $35 billion, while defense spending in 1982 went up $12 billion. Despite Democratic opposition, budget cuts were aimed at educational programs, along with health, housing, urban aid, food stamps, school meals, the National Endowments for the Arts and Humanities, and the Corporation for Public Broadcasting. Synthetic fuel projects were completely canceled as oil imports continued to rise.

Amid his budget cutting, Reagan clarified his assault on the welfare state. He wanted to eliminate aid to those who could presumably help themselves through their own efforts. He promised to retain a "safety net" for the "truly needy" and not to eliminate all federal aid programs. This new approach targeted for aid only those who could not work because of disability or child care. This, in fact, had been the original purpose of New Deal welfare, but during the 1930s the government had provided WPA jobs for those able to work.

In 1981 the administration declared that support from the Aid for Dependent Children (AFDC) program should last only four months after one joined the working poor, and that every dollar earned should reduce one's welfare payments by that amount. As a consequence, more than 400,000 people lost AFDC coverage, many of whom also lost the benefits of Medicaid. The administration argued that the working poor would keep working despite the loss of AFDC-Medicaid, and studies confirmed this in many cases. Still, a determination to work proved costly. Many working mothers, however eager to be self-reliant, refused to penalize their children and returned to welfare full time.

While publicly proclaiming a great accomplishment in making such cuts in domestic spending, Reagan and his advisers knew privately that the figures were not adding up to those they had pledged. David Stockman, the whiz-kid head of the Office of Management and Budget, realized that the cuts in domestic spending were far short of what would be needed to balance the budget in four years as Reagan had promised. He pleaded with Reagan to cut back on new defense spending and to slow the proposed tax cuts. But the president refused. The result was a soaring budget deficit and the worst economic recession since the 1930s.

Wall Street, perversely fearful that a rising public debt would send interest rates up, responded to the most pro-business president in years with sagging bond and stock markets. A business slump and rising unemployment carried through most of 1982. Government economic policy was strangely out of sync, a combination of fiscal stimulus (tax cuts) and monetary restraint (interest rates kept high by an independent Federal Reserve to control inflation).

Aides persuaded the president that to reassure the public about deficits and the threat of inflation the government needed "revenue enhancements," a fine euphemism for tax increases. With Reagan lending support, Congress and the administration cobbled together the Tax Equity and Fiscal Responsibility Bill of 1982, which would raise an estimated $98 billion. Nonetheless, the economic slump persevered through November, with unemployment standing at 10.4 percent, and the Republicans experienced moderate losses in the midterm elections.

NEW PRIORITIES Like Coolidge and Harding in the 1920s, Reagan named to government posts people who were less than sympathetic to the regulatory functions for which they were responsible. The most visible early example was Interior Secretary James Watt, who had a gift for provocative denunciations of environmentalists. A Colorado champion of the "Sagebrush Rebellion," which proposed to turn federal lands over to the states, he breezily proposed to encourage commercial development of public resources. He was finally forced out of office by the uproar over an offensive remark about affirmative action appointments.

From the start, the Reagan administration failed to comprehend potential conflicts of interest in offices of public trust and showed a dangerous insensitivity to borderline ethics and outright scandals that one pundit soon labeled the "sleaze factor." Yet the president himself remained so totally untouched by hints of impropriety that Reagan was tagged the "Teflon president," since the buck never stopped because the blame never stuck.

As in the 1920s, organized labor encountered severe setbacks during the Reagan years. Nearly half of all union members, entranced by Reagan's personality and showmanship, had voted for him against the advice of their leaders. Reagan's smashing electoral victories in 1980 and 1984 broke the political power of the AFL-CIO, a longtime pillar of support for the Democratic party. Reagan himself made much of being the only president to have headed a national union (the Screen Actors Guild), but his appointees to the National Labor Relations Board tended to favor management. In 1981, early in his term, Reagan fired members of the Professional Air Traffic Controllers who organized an illegal strike. Reagan's public criticism of unions reflected a general trend in public opinion. Although a record number of new jobs were created during the 1980s, union membership steadily dropped. In 1979 unions represented 24 percent of the workforce. By 1987 union membership was down to 17 percent, and in 1995 it reached 15.5 percent.

Reagan also went on the offensive against feminism. He cut welfare programs, which especially affected impoverished women and their children, and opposed the Equal Rights Amendment and abortion on demand, as well as the idea of requiring equal pay for jobs of comparable worth. Women critics were little mollified by his naming the first female justice to the Supreme Court, Sandra Day O'Connor. Polls consistently reported a "gender gap" in opinion on Reagan, who had less support among women than among men.

Blacks and other minorities shared with women aggravation at the administration's limited support for affirmative action programs in employment. In the administration itself the Civil Rights Commission reported in 1982 that only 8 percent of its appointments had gone to females and 8 percent to minorities, in contrast to 12 and 17 percent, respectively, under Carter. Because of the commission's criticisms, the president in 1983 fired three of its members and tried to fire two more.

Funds for civil rights enforcement were among those targeted for reduction, and the Equal Employment Opportunity Commission's staff was sharply reduced. The administration supported in the courts the action of its Internal Revenue Service in granting tax exemptions to fundamentalist schools that practiced racial segregation. On that it was overruled by the Supreme Court, 8 to 1.

THE DEFENSE BUILDUP   Reagan's conduct of foreign policy reflected his belief that world troubles stemmed mainly from Moscow. He also feared that Americans had overlearned the lessons of Vietnam and forgotten the lessons of Munich in 1938. At times, he insisted, the United States must use military force to protect its interests around the globe. As a consequence of these assumptions, he promoted a major buildup of nuclear and conventional weapons, to close the gap that he claimed had developed between Soviet and American forces.

In 1983 Reagan escalated the nuclear arms race by authorizing the Defense Department to develop a Strategic Defense Initiative (SDI). It involved a complex anti-missile defense system using super-secret laser and high-energy particles weapons to destroy enemy missiles in outer space well before they reached their targets. To Reagan its great appeal was the ability to destroy weapons rather than people, thereby freeing defense strategy from the concept of mutually assured destruction that had long governed Soviet and American attitudes toward nuclear war. Journalists quickly dubbed the program "Star Wars" in reference to the popular science fiction film. Despite skepticism among the media and many scientists that such a "foolproof" celestial defense system could be built, it forced the Soviets to launch an expensive research and development program of their own to keep pace. As a West German defense analyst commented, "I have never seen Soviets so emotional as they are over Star Wars."

Reagan borrowed the rhetoric of John Foster Dulles and the Kennedy inaugural to express American resolve in the face of "Communist aggression anywhere in the world." At his first news conference, he pronounced the Soviet rulers men who "reserved unto themselves the right to commit any crime, to lie, to cheat." Someday, however, the West would "transcend Communism," leaving it "a sad, bizarre chapter in human history whose last pages are even now being written." Few at the time realized how accurate his prediction would become.

THE AMERICAS   Reagan's foremost international concern was in Central America. In 1981 an endemic guerrilla war in El Salvador intensified. Reagan's State Department believed it was a textbook case of indirect Soviet aggression. Many of the weapons reaching the Salvadoran rebels were American arms earlier seized in Vietnam and Ethiopia. The administration abandoned Jimmy Carter's efforts to promote a

"Shhhh. It's top secret." *A comment on Reagan administration covert operations in Nicaragua.*

compromise and sent in more arms and advisers to help the government of President José Napoleón Duarte defeat the rebels. The fighting persisted on through the 1980s, but after elections in 1982 showed heavy turnouts in support of moderate candidates, Duarte's government gained a tenuous stability, but one still threatened from both the left and right.

Reagan also confronted trouble in Nicaragua. Carter had believed that a rebel victory over the corrupt regime of dictator Anastasio Somoza in Nicaragua was inevitable, even though Cuban-sponsored "Sandinistas" were part of the rebel National Liberation Front (FSLN). He argued that America should help democratic elements in the Front. Nonetheless, when the Somoza government fell, it was the Sandinistas who gradually emerged as the dominant power in the new government.

The Reagan State Department claimed that the Sandinista government in Nicaragua was funneling Soviet and Cuban arms to Salvadoran rebels. In response, the administration set the CIA and the American ambassador in Honduras to mobilizing guerrilla bands of disgruntled Nicaraguans, soon tagged "Contras." The administration's hidden agenda, it soon became clear, was not only to prevent arms from reaching the rebels in El Salvador but to overthrow the Sandinistas, to make them "cry uncle," in Reagan's words.

Fearing a military tinderbox in Central America, neighboring countries pressed for a negotiated settlement. Representatives of Mexico, Panama, Colombia, and Venezuela began the Contadora Process (after the Panamanian island where they first met). By late 1983, the Contadora countries had advanced the first of many proposals for a compromise peace, the withdrawal of foreign advisers, and an end to imports of foreign arms. Drawn into the talks, the Reagan administration raised so many technical objections as to suggest that it would settle for nothing less than an overthrow of the Sandinistas.

THE MIDDLE EAST In the Middle East, no peaceable end seemed possible for the prolonged, bloody Iran-Iraq war, entangled as it was with the passions of Islamic fundamentalism. In 1984 both sides began to attack tankers in the Persian Gulf, a major source of the world's oil. (The main international response was the sale of arms to both sides.) Nor was any settlement in sight for Afghanistan, where the Soviets had bogged down as badly as the Americans had in Vietnam.

American governments continued to see Israel as the strongest and most reliable ally in the region, all the while seeking to encourage moderate Arab groups. But the forces of moderation were dealt a blow during the mid-1970s when Lebanon, long an enclave of peace despite its ethnic complexity, collapsed into an anarchy of warring groups. The capital, Beirut, became a battleground for Sunni and Shi'ite Muslims, the Druze, the Palestine Liberation Organization (PLO), Arab Christians, Syrian invaders cast as peacekeepers, and Israelis responding to PLO attacks across the border.

In 1982 Israeli forces pushed the PLO out of southern Lebanon all the way north to Beirut and then the Israelis began heavy shelling of PLO strongholds in Beirut. The United States neither endorsed nor condemned the invasion, but sent a special ambassador to negotiate a settlement. Israeli troops moved into Beirut and looked the other way when Christian militiamen slaughtered Muslim women and children in Palestinian refugee camps. French, Italian, and American forces then moved into Lebanon as "peacekeepers," but in such small numbers as to become only targets. Angry Muslims kept them under constant harassment. American warships and planes responded by shelling and bombing Muslim positions in the highlands behind Beirut, which only increased Muslim resentment. On October 23, 1983, an Islamic suicide bomber drove a truck laden with explosives into the U.S. Marine headquarters at Beirut airport; the explosion left 241 Americans dead. Reagan declared that a continued American presence was "central to our credibility," but soon began preparations to pull out. In early 1984, he announced that the marines would be "redeployed" to warships offshore. The Israelis pulled back to southern Lebanon, while the Syrians remained in eastern Lebanon. And bloody anarchy remained a way of life in a formerly peaceful country.

GRENADA   Fortune, as it happened, presented Reagan the chance for an easy triumph closer to home, a "rescue mission" that eclipsed news of the debacle in Lebanon. On the tiny island of Grenada, the smallest independent country in the Western Hemisphere, a leftist government had admitted Cuban workers to build a new airfield and signed military agreements with Communist countries. In 1983 an even more radical military council seized power.

Appeals from the governments of neighboring islands led Reagan to order 1,900 marines to invade the island, depose the new government, and evacuate a small group of American students at Grenada's medical school. The U.N. General Assembly condemned the action, and many Latin Americans saw it as a revival of gunboat diplomacy, but it was popular among Grenadans and their neighbors, and immensely popular in the United States. Although a lopsided affair, the action made Reagan look decisive, and served notice on Latin American revolutionaries to beware of American force.

REAGAN'S SECOND TERM

By 1983, prosperity had returned, and the Reagan economic program seemed to be working as touted. Contradictory policies of fiscal stimulus (tax cuts and heavy expenditures for defense) and monetary restraint (high interest rates) brought at least in the short run an economic recovery without inflation. The gradual unraveling of the OPEC cartel and resultant decline in oil prices was the greatest stroke of luck for Reagan and the economy.

THE ELECTION OF 1984   Republican strategy for the presidential election worked on the old principle that if you have a good thing, you should stick with it. By contrast, the nominee of the Democrats, former vice-president Walter Mondale, never quite got his act together. Endorsed by the AFL-CIO, the National Organization for Women, and many blacks despite a serious challenge from Jesse Jackson, Mondale was tagged the candidate of the "special interests." He set a precedent by choosing as his running mate New York representative Geraldine Ferraro. Unhappily for the Democratic campaign, she was quickly placed on the defensive by the need to explain her spouse's complicated finances, something no male candidate had been called upon to do. One politician observed that "the pioneers take all the arrows."

A fit of frankness in his acceptance speech further complicated Mondale's campaign. "Mr. Reagan will raise taxes, and so will I," he told the convention. "He won't tell you. I just did." Remembered as a political blunder, it was a brilliant opportunity missed. Mondale seemed unaware that just the previous day, while attention was focused on the Democratic convention, Reagan had quietly signed a bill that raised taxes $50 billion, the Deficit Reduction Act of 1984. Nor did he mention that Reagan had signed tax increases in each of the two previous years. Reagan responded by vowing never to approve a tax increase, and by chiding Mondale for his candid stand. Mondale never caught up. In the end, Reagan took 59 percent of the popular vote and lost only Minnesota and the District of Columbia. His coattails were not as strong, however. Republicans had a net gain of only fifteen seats in the House, and lost two in the Senate. Entering his second term, Reagan faced several political time bombs ticking away. They were planted around the world from Nicaragua to Afghanistan.

DOMESTIC CHALLENGES   Although Reagan had won an overwhelming victory, domestic problems that he had tried to ignore demanded his attention and shook his complacency. Episodes of borderline ethics and outright scandals that had emerged during his first term could not be ignored forever. Strains seemed bound to arise as well in a political coalition of the indulgent rich and the ultra-righteous.

Still, for a while, the Reagan luck held out. OPEC continued to lower oil prices, sending inflation down and the stock market up. In his State of the Union message, Reagan called for "a Second American

Revolution of hope and opportunity." He dared Congress to raise taxes. His veto pen was ready: "Go ahead and make my day," he said in echo of a movie line.

Through much of 1985 the president drummed up support for a tax simplification plan to eliminate loopholes and set only two or three brackets. It was a retreat from the principle of a progressive tax, which levied higher rates on high incomes, but that principle had long since been eroded by a variety of complex tax dodges within the reach mainly of the rich.

After vigorous debate that ran nearly two years, Congress passed, and in 1986 the president finally signed, a comprehensive Tax Reform Act. The new measure would reduce the number of tax brackets from fourteen to two and reduce rates from the maximum of 50 percent to 15 and 28 percent—the lowest since Coolidge. Tax shelters were also sharply limited. Economists were cautious about predicting the effects of the tax "simplification." One pundit noted that the "simplified" tax law remained a good bit longer than the Constitution and a good bit harder to understand.

ARMS CONTROL   Meanwhile Reagan, for all his bluff talk about the Soviet Union being an "evil empire," seemed unwilling to be the first president since World War II to arrive at no agreement on arms with the Soviets. In 1985, for the first time in six years, an American president met with the leader of the Soviet Union. After much preliminary maneuvering, Reagan and Mikhail Gorbachev, the recently elected Soviet president, met in Geneva on November 19 for a series of talks. They soon signed six agreements on cultural and scientific exchanges and other matters. They also issued statements, but reached no agreements, on arms limitations.

Nearly a year later, on sudden notice and with limited preparation, Gorbachev and Reagan met in Reykjavik, Iceland, for two days. Reagan subsequently said that the United States put forward the "most sweeping and generous arms-control proposal in history," but the talks collapsed over disagreement about Reagan's SDI.

THE IRAN-CONTRA AFFAIR   The year 1986 opened with a terrible tragedy when the space shuttle *Challenger* exploded minutes after liftoff, killing its seven crew members, including a teacher. Then came

Soviet premier Mikhail Gorbachev (left) *and U.S. president Ronald Reagan* (right) *during a light moment at the Geneva summit, November 1985.*

a double blow to Reagan's agenda on November 4, 1986. In the midterm elections the Senate went from a Republican majority of 53 to 47 to Democratic control by 55 to 45. Senators elected in 1980 on Reagan's coattails lacked that advantage this time. All seven Senate races in the South went to Democrats. Farm problems in the Midwest damaged Republicans there. The Democrats picked up only six seats in the House, but they increased their already comfortable margin there to 259 to 176. For his last two years as president Reagan would face an opposition Congress.

What was worse, on election day one of the administration's political time bombs went off. Reports arrived from an obscure publication in Beirut that the United States had been secretly selling arms to Iran in hopes of securing the release of American hostages held in Lebanon by extremist groups sympathetic to Iran. Such actions contradicted Reagan's repeated public insistence that his administration would never negotiate with terrorists. The disclosures angered America's allies as well as many Americans who vividly remembered the 1979 Iranian takeover of their country's embassy in Teheran.

There was even more to the sordid story. Over the next several months, a series of revelations reminiscent of the Watergate affair disclosed a more complicated and even more incredible series of covert activities carried out by administration officials. At the center of the Iran-Contra affair was the much-decorated Marine lieutenant-colonel Oliver North. A swashbuckling aide to the National Security Council who specialized in counterterrorism, North had been running secret operations from the basement of the White House involving many governmental, private, and foreign individuals. His most farfetched scheme sought to use the profits gained from the secret sale of military hardware to Iran to subsidize the Contra rebels fighting in Nicaragua, at a time when Congress had voted to ban such aid.

North's activities, it turned out, had been approved by National Security Adviser Robert McFarlane, his successor Admiral John Poindexter, and CIA Director William Casey. Secretary of State George Shultz and Secretary of Defense Caspar Weinberger both criticized the arms sale to Iran, but their objections were ignored, and they were thereafter kept in the dark about what was going on. Later, on three occasions, Shultz threatened to resign over the continuing operation of the "pathetic" scheme. As information about the secret (and illegal) dealings surfaced in the press, McFarlane attempted suicide, Poindexter resigned, North was fired, and Casey, who denied any connection, left the CIA for health reasons. Casey died shortly thereafter from a brain tumor.

The White House, meanwhile, assumed a siege mentality as the president's popularity plummeted. Worse was yet to come. During the spring and summer of 1987, a joint House-Senate investigating committee began holding televised hearings into the Iran-Contra affair. The sessions dominated public attention for months and revealed a tangled web of inept financial and diplomatic transactions, the shredding of incriminating government documents, crass profiteering, and misguided patriotism.

The investigations of the independent counsel led to six indictments in 1988. A Washington jury found Oliver North guilty of three relatively minor charges but innocent of nine more serious counts, apparently reflecting the jury's reasoning that he acted as an agent of higher-ups. His conviction was later overturned on appeal. Of those involved in the affair, only John Poindexter got a jail sentence—six months for his conviction on five felony counts of obstructing justice and lying to Congress.

CENTRAL AMERICA   The Iran-Contra affair showed the lengths to which members of the Reagan administration would go to support the rebels fighting the ruling Sandinistas in Nicaragua. Fearing heightened Soviet and American involvement in Central America, neighboring countries pressed during the mid-1980s for a negotiated settlement to the unrest in Nicaragua. In 1988 Daniel Ortega, the Nicaraguan president, pledged to negotiate directly with the Contra rebels. In the spring of 1988 these negotiations produced a cease-fire agreement, ending nearly seven years of fighting in Nicaragua. Secretary of State George Shultz called the pact an "important step forward," but the settlement surprised and disappointed hardliners within the Reagan administration who saw in it a Contra surrender. The Contra leaders themselves, aware of the eroding support for their cause in the United States Congress, saw the truce as their only chance for tangible concessions such as amnesty for political prisoners, the return of the Contras from exile, and "unrestricted freedom of expression."

Meanwhile, in neighboring El Salvador, the Reagan administration's attempt to shore up the centrist government of José Napoleón Duarte through economic and military aid suffered a body blow when the far-right ARENA party scored an upset victory at the polls during the spring of 1988.

LEVERAGED BUYOUTS AND S&L'S   Throughout the 1980s, social commentators repeatedly bemoaned the virus of greed and self-absorbed materialism that seemed to infect the nation. One prominent symptom was the largest outbreak of corporate mergers and acquisitions ever. Hijacking corporations was nothing new, but by the mid-1980s an innovative technique had come into play: using the value of the company itself as a means of taking it over. The corporate "raiders" would buy out the target company's public stockholders with borrowed money, to be repaid from the future earnings of the company. They then used its value to underwrite voluminous "junk bonds"—speculative issues that drew investors into risky investments with the promise of very high returns. Given this magic act, no company was out of reach now, no matter how big.

The charm of the device was that the takeover targets got stuck with the debts, while stockholders could bail out at handsome prices driven up by the acquisition. Commonly, the company was then broken up and sold piece by piece on the principle that components could be sold off separately for more than the whole. A character in a popular movie of 1990 likened the process to stealing cars and selling the parts.

These shenanigans were not unusual during the 1980s. Other financial buccaneers pursued quick profits within the "thrift institutions"— the savings and loan banks (S&L's) designed at first to serve aspiring homeowners. In 1982 Congress permitted S&L's to invest up to 40 percent of their assets in nonresidential real estate. High-rise office buildings began to clutter the landscape. California, not to be outdone, then permitted state-chartered S&L's to invest 100 percent of their assets in any venture, and other states followed suit. From a conservative industry designed to encourage homeowning, many of the S&L's became major customers for junk bonds, among other risky ventures.

The opportunities for outrageous profits, with regulators and Congress reducing capital reserve requirements and looking the other way, brought hustlers flocking into the business, often with borrowed capital. Vernon Savings and Loan, which served a town of 12,000 in Texas, at one time kept a fleet of six jets; company funds also bought expensive homes for its head and provided $5.5 million to decorate the walls.

DEBT AND THE PLUNGE IN THE STOCK MARKET The getting and spending of more money seemed to become the pervasive concern throughout the 1980s. Debt, all kinds of debt—personal, corporate, and governmental—increased dramatically during the decade. Whereas in the 1960s Americans on average saved 10 percent of their income, in 1987 the figure was less than 4 percent. The Reagan budget deficits also reached record levels as legislators reluctant to offend constituents by raising taxes or cutting popular programs engaged in talk and symbolic action with a president ideologically resistant to taxes. The federal debt more than tripled from $908 billion in 1980 to $2.9 trillion at the end of the 1989 fiscal year.

Then, on October 19, 1987, the bill collector suddenly arrived at the nation's doorstep. On that "Black Monday," the stock market, already buffeted by sharp declines the previous week, experienced a tidal wave of selling reminiscent of the 1929 crash. The Dow Jones industrial average plummeted 508 points, or an astounding 22.6 percent. The market plunge nearly doubled the record 12.8 percent fall on October 28, 1929. Almost $560 billion in paper value disappeared, an amount larger than the gross national product of France. With cyclonic suddenness, the nation's financial mood went from boom to gloom during the fall of 1987. Wall Street's selling frenzy reverberated throughout the capitalist world, sending stock prices plummeting in Tokyo, London, Paris, and Toronto.

What caused the goring of the bull market? Some analysts argued that the runaway market of the 1980s had become artifically high, driven by excessive greed and hope rather than by the economy's actual performance. Others blamed new computerized trading programs that distorted market activity. But most agreed that the fundamental problem was the nation's spiraling indebtedness and chronically high trade deficits. Americans were consuming more than they were producing, importing the difference, and paying for imported goods with borrowed money and dollars whose value had sharply declined. Foreign investors had lost confidence in Reaganomics and were no longer willing to finance America's spending binge.

In the aftermath of the calamitous selling spree on Black Monday, President Reagan insisted that the "underlying economy remains sound," an unsettling echo of Herbert Hoover's equally sunny assurances in 1929. Few observers actually feared a depression of the magnitude of the 1930s; there were too many safeguards built into the system to allow that. But there was real concern of an impending recession, and this led business leaders and economists to attack the president for glossing over such a profound warning signal. Within a few weeks, Reagan agreed to work with Congress in developing a deficit reduction package, and for the first time indicated that he was willing to include increased taxes in such a package. But the eventual compromise plan was so modest that it did little to restore investor confidence. As one Republican senator lamented, "There is a total lack of courage among those of us in the Congress to do what we all know has to be done."

THE POOR, THE HOMELESS, AND AIDS VICTIMS   Against the picture that the president's supporters envisioned of roaring prosperity,

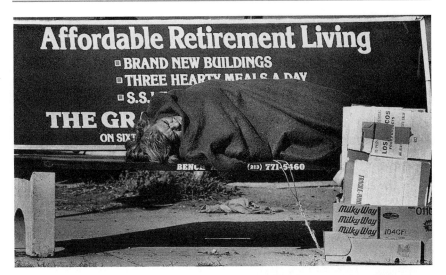

Despite the nation's prosperity and some efforts to build low-cost housing, the number of homeless people continued to increase during the 1980s.

burgeoning new technology, and 19 million new jobs in the Reagan years could be set the picture of uncounted beggars in the streets and homeless people sleeping in doorways, in cardboard boxes, and on heat grates—street scenes once associated with Calcutta. A variety of causes could be adduced for the shortage of low-cost housing: government had given up on building public housing; with the best of intentions, urban renewal had demolished blighted areas but provided no housing for the displaced; and owners had abandoned unprofitable buildings in poor neighborhoods or converted them into expensive condominiums. The last was called "gentrification." Other causes of homelessness included family disorganization, and the deinstitutionalization of the mentally ill thanks to new medications for treatment and based on the promise of community mental health services that failed to materialize—a program started under President Kennedy but never adequately funded. By the summer of 1988, the *New York Times* estimated, more than 45 percent of the city's adult residents constituted an underclass totally outside the labor force for lack of skills, lack of motivation, drug use, and other problems.

Still another group cast aside were those suffering from a strange new malady known as AIDS (acquired immune deficiency syndrome). At the beginning of the decade, public health officials had begun to re-

A quilt commemorating the deaths of many thousands of Americans from AIDS, is stretched out and displayed before the White House in October 1988, so that friends and family can walk amidst the entire quilt and view the various sections up close.

port that gay men and intravenous drug users were especially at risk for this syndrome. Those infected with AIDS showed signs of fatigue, developed a strange combination of infections, and eventually died. Researchers struggled to discern the origins of the new malady. Eventually they linked it to a virus (HIV) originating in Africa and spread from there to Europe and America. People contracted it by coming into contact with the blood or body fluids of an infected person. One reason the Reagan administration showed little interest in AIDS was that it initially was viewed as a "gay" disease. Patrick Buchanan, the conservative spokesman who served as White House director of communications, said that homosexuals had "declared war on nature, and now nature is extracting an awful retribution."

By 1998, however, AIDS had claimed over 270,000 American lives and was spreading among the larger population. Nearly a million Americans were estimated to be carrying the deadly HIV virus, and it had become the leading cause of death among men aged twenty-five to forty-four. The potential for exponential spread of HIV, owing to the very long incubation period before the onset of symptoms, provoked the surgeon general to launch a controversial public education program that included encouraging "safe sex" through the use of condoms. With no prospect for an early cure and with skyrocketing treatment costs,

AIDS emerged as one of the nation's most horrifying and intractable problems.

A HISTORIC TREATY   In the midst of a weak, unpredictable economic situation, the main prospect for positive achievement before the end of Reagan's second term seemed to lie in arms-reduction agreements with the Soviet government. Under Mikhail Gorbachev, the Soviets pursued renewed détente in order to free their energies and financial resources to address pressing domestic problems. The logjam that had impeded arms negotiations since the summit at Reykjavik suddenly broke in 1987, when Gorbachev announced that he was willing to deal separately on a medium-range missile treaty. After nine more months of strenuous, highly technical negotiations, Reagan and Gorbachev met amid much fanfare in Washington on December 9, 1987, and signed a treaty to eliminate intermediate-range (300–3,000 miles) nuclear forces (INF).

It was an epochal event, not only because it marked the first time that the two nations had agreed to destroy a whole class of weapons systems, but because it represented a key first step toward the eventual end of the arms race altogether. Under the terms of the treaty, the United States would destroy 859 missiles, and the Soviets would eliminate 1,752. On-site inspections by each side would verify compliance. Still, this winnowing would represent only 4 percent of the total nuclear missile count on both sides. Arms-control advocates thus looked toward a second and more comprehensive treaty dealing with long-range strategic missiles.

Gorbachev's successful efforts to liberalize Soviet domestic life and improve East-West foreign relations cheered Americans. The Soviets suddenly began stressing cooperation with the West in dealing with "hot spots" around the world. They urged the Palestine Liberation Organization to recognize Israel's right to exist and advocated a greater role for the U.N. in the volatile Persian Gulf. Perhaps the most dramatic symbol of a thawing cold war was the phased withdrawal of 115,000 Soviet troops from Afghanistan, which began in 1988.

THE REAGAN LEGACY   Historians are just beginning to assess the legacy of the nation's fortieth president. Although Reagan had declared in 1981 his intention to "curb the size and influence of the federal establishment," the New Deal welfare state remained intact when Reagan left office. Neither the Social Security system nor Medicare nor other major welfare programs were dismantled or overhauled. And the federal agencies that Reagan threatened to abolish, such as the Department of Education, not only remained in place in 1989, their budgets grew. The federal budget as a percentage of the gross domestic product (GDP) was actually higher when Reagan left office than when he had entered. Moreover, he did not try to push through Congress the incendiary social issues championed by the religious right such as school prayer and a ban on abortions.

Yet Ronald Reagan nonetheless succeeded in redefining the national political agenda and accelerated the conservative insurgency that had been developing for over twenty years. His greatest successes were in renewing America's soaring sense of possibilities, bringing inflation under control and stimulating the longest sustained period of peacetime prosperity in history, and negotiating the nuclear disarmament treaty and helping to light the fuse of democratic freedom in eastern Europe. By redirecting the thrust of both domestic and foreign policy, he put the Democratic party on the defensive and forced conventional New Deal "liberalism" into a panicked retreat. The fact that Reagan's tax policies widened the gap between the rich and poor and created huge budget deficits for future presidents to confront did not diminish the popularity of the "Great Communicator."

THE 1988 ELECTION In 1988 a gaggle of eight Democratic presidential candidates entered a wild scramble for their party's nomination. As the primary season progressed, however, it soon became a two-man race between Massachusetts governor Michael Dukakis and Jesse Jackson, the charismatic black civil rights activist who had been one of Martin Luther King, Jr.'s chief lieutenants. Dukakis eventually won out and managed a difficult reconciliation with the Jackson forces that left the Democrats unified and confident as the fall campaign began.

The Republicans nominated Reagan's two-term vice-president, George Bush, who after a bumpy start had easily cast aside his rivals in the primaries. As Reagan's handpicked heir, Bush claimed credit for the administration's successes, but like all dutiful vice-presidents, he also faced the challenge of asserting his own political identity. Although a veteran government official, having served as a Texas congressman, en-

George Bush (right) *at the 1988 Republican National Convention with his newly chosen running mate, Dan Quayle, a former senator from Indiana.*

voy to China, ambassador to the U.N., and head of the CIA, Bush projected none of Reagan's charisma or rhetorical skills. Cartoonists caricatured the patrician vice-president, the son of a rich Connecticut senator, schooled at Andover and Yale, as a well-heeled "wimp," and one Democrat described him as a man born "with a silver foot in his mouth." Early polls showed Dukakis with a surprisingly wide lead.

Yet Bush, a genuinely decent and honorable man with a distinguished record of heroism in World War II, delivered a surprisingly forceful convention address that sharply enhanced his stature. Although pledging to continue the Reagan agenda, he also recognized that "things aren't perfect" in America, an admission his boss rarely acknowledged. Bush promised to use the White House to fight bigotry, illiteracy, and homelessness. Humane sympathies, he insisted, would guide his conservatism. "I want a kinder, gentler nation," Bush said softly in his acceptance speech. But the most memorable line was a defiant statement on taxes: "Congress will push me to raise taxes, and I'll say no, and they'll push, and I'll say no, and they'll push again. And all I can say to them is, read my lips: *no new taxes.*"

In a campaign given over to mudslinging, Bush and his aides fastened on an effective strategy: they attacked Dukakis as a camouflaged liberal in the mold of McGovern, Carter, and Mondale. The Republican on-

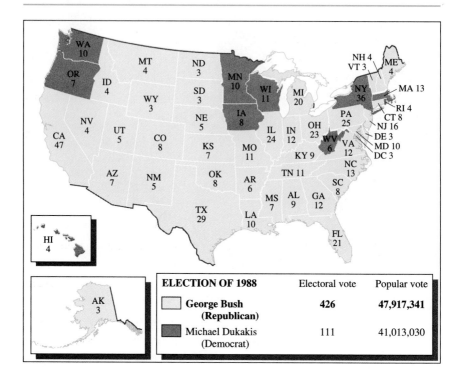

ELECTION OF 1988

	Electoral vote	Popular vote
George Bush (Republican)	426	47,917,341
Michael Dukakis (Democrat)	111	41,013,030

slaught took its toll against the less organized, less focused Dukakis campaign. In the end, Dukakis took only ten states plus the District of Columbia, with clusters in the Northeast, Midwest, and Northwest. Bush carried the rest, with a margin of about 54 percent to 46 percent in the popular vote and 426 to 111 in the electoral college.

Generally speaking, the more affluent and better-educated voters preferred the Republican ticket. While Dukakis won the inner-city vote, garnering 86 percent of the black vote, Bush scored big in the suburbs and in rural areas, especially in the once-Democratic South, where his margins of white voters ranged from a low of 63 percent in Florida to a high of 80 percent in Mississippi. More significant was Bush's success among blue-collar workers. He captured 46 percent of these typically Democratic voters.

Hidden among the election returns was a long-term trend that did not bode well for the American political system: voter turnout continued to decline. In the 1988 election, only 50 percent of the voting-age population cast ballots, the lowest in any presidential election since

Calvin Coolidge defeated Democrat John W. Davis in 1924. The most important third party emerging in national politics were those so disengaged from the process that they did not vote at all. Voting was highest among affluent whites (52 percent), while 46 percent of eligible blacks and only 23 percent of eligible Hispanics turned out. But the most alarming statistic was that two-fifths of all the nonvoters were under thirty years of age. Apparently, many young adults no longer viewed the political process as significant enough to participate in.

THE BUSH YEARS

George Bush viewed himself as a guardian president rather than an activist. Lacking Reagan's visionary outlook and his skill as a speaker, Bush was a prudent patrician, a pragmatist caretaker eager to avoid "stupid mistakes" and to find a way to get along with the Democratic majority in Congress. "We don't need to remake society," he announced. As a consequence, Bush sought to consolidate and nurture the programs that Reagan had put in place rather than launch his own array of new programs and policies.

DOMESTIC INITIATIVES   The Reagan administration left some issues that demanded immediate attention from the Bush White House. In 1989 Bush tackled the most pressing of these, the savings and loan crisis, with a rescue plan to close or sell ailing thrifts and bail out the depositors. Congress consolidated the insurance fund for savings and loan deposits with the fund covering banks, the Federal Deposit Insurance Corporation (FDIC). A new agency, the Resolution Trust Corporation (RTC), was created to sell off failed thrifts—or at least their assets. At the time, the cost to taxpayers of the bailout was put at $300 billion over thirty years, although in 1990 the General Accounting Office estimated the cost at $500 billion.

The biggest hangover from the binge years of the 1980s was the national debt, which stood at $2.6 trillion by the time Bush was elected, nearly three times its 1980 level. Bush's taboo on tax increases (meaning, mainly, income taxes) and his insistence upon lowering capital gains taxes—on profits from the sales of stocks and other property—made it more difficult to reduce the annual deficit or trim the long-term debt. By 1990 the country faced "a fiscal mess." Bipartisan budget talks between administration and congressional leaders spawned "rancorous partisanship [and] deep divisions within the two parties." Eventually, Bush decided "that both the size of the deficit problem and the need for a package that can be enacted" required a number of measures, including "tax revenue increases." Then he claimed that the Democrats had forced him to accept such language, a message that did not convey strong leadership. These elaborate partisan dances continued through the summer, until a budget plan was announced in September 1990. Through a combination of tax hikes and spending cuts, the measure promised to reduce the budget deficit by $43 billion in 1991 and by $331 billion in 1991–1995.

Another domestic initiative was Bush's war on drugs. During the 1980s, cocaine addiction spread through sizable segments of American society, luring those with money to spend and—in its smokable form, known as crack—those with little money to spare. Bush vowed to make drug abuse his number-one domestic priority, and appointed William J. Bennett, former education secretary, as "drug czar," or head of a new Office of National Drug Control Policy, with cabinet status but no department. Total outlays in the war on drugs would amount to $8 billion in fiscal 1990, although only $716 million represented new spending. The message, on this and on education, housing, and other social problems, was that more of the burden should fall on state and local authorities.

THE DEMOCRACY MOVEMENT ABROAD Bush entered the White House with more foreign policy experience than most presidents, and he found the spotlight of the world stage more congenial than wrestling with the intractable problems of the inner cities, drug abuse, or the deficit. Within two years of his inauguration, George Bush would lead the United States into two wars, a record unequaled by any of his predecessors. Throughout most of 1989, however, he merely had to sit back and observe the dissolution of one totalitarian or authoritarian regime after another. For the first time in years, democracy was suddenly on the march in a sequence of mostly bloodless revolutions that surprised most of the world.

Although a suddenly risen democracy movement in China came to a tragic end in 1989 when government forces mounted a deadly assault on demonstrators in Beijing's (Peking's) Tiananmen Square, eastern Europe had an entirely different experience. With a rigid economic system failing to deliver the goods to the Soviet peoples, Mikhail Gorbachev responded with policies of "perestroika" (restructuring) and "glasnost" (openness), a loosening of central economic planning and censorship. His foreign policy sought rapprochement and trade with the West, and to relieve the Soviet economy of burdensome military costs.

Gorbachev also backed off from Soviet imperial ambitions. Early in 1989, Soviet troops left Afghanistan, after nine years of being bogged down in civil war there. Gorbachev then repudiated the "Brezhnev doctrine," which had asserted the right of the Soviet Union to intervene in the internal affairs of Communist countries. The days when Soviet tanks rolled through Warsaw and Prague were over, and hardline leaders in the East-bloc countries found themselves beset by demands for reform from their own peoples. With opposition strength building, the old regimes fell in rapid order, and with surprisingly little bloodshed. Communist party rule ended first in Poland and Hungary, then in hardline Czechoslovakia and in Bulgaria. In Romania, the year of peaceful revolution ended in a bloodbath when the Romanian people joined the army in a bloody uprising against the brutal dictator Nicolae Ceausescu. He and his wife were captured, tried, and then executed on Christmas Day. But lacking experienced opposition leaders, as did all the eastern European countries, the new government fell under the control of members of the old Communist establishment.

The most spectacular event in the collapse of the Soviet empire in eastern Europe came on November 9, when the chief symbol of the cold war—the Berlin Wall—was torn down by Germans using small tools and even their hands. With the borders to the West now fully open, the Communist government of East Germany collapsed, a freely elected government came to power, and on October 3, 1990, the five states of East Germany were united with those of West Germany. The unified German nation remained in NATO, and the Warsaw Pact alliance was dissolved.

The democratic movement also reached other parts of the world. During 1990, the Communist party of Mongolia—strategically located on the borders of the Soviet Union and China—voted to give up its monopoly on power, and in Nicaragua, where the ruling Sandinista party avowed Marxism, President Daniel Ortega was defeated in a presidential

West Germans hacking away at the Berlin Wall on November 11, 1989, two days after all crossings between East and West Germany were opened.

election in February. Even in isolated Albania, the ruling party yielded to demands for an election in 1991.

Democratic change overtook authoritarian regimes of a different stripe as well. In Chile, Augusto Pinochet, who had become military dictator in a bloody coup in 1973, yielded to a popular vote in 1988 against his remaining in office, and was defeated in presidential elections the following year. And in South Africa, to which the U.S. Congress had applied trade sanctions in protest of its apartheid (racial segregation) policies since 1986, a new prime minister, Frederik W. DeKlerk, came to office in 1989, released black nationalist Nelson Mandela from twenty-seven years in prison, and announced plans to abandon apartheid gradually.

The reform impulse that Gorbachev helped unleash in the East-bloc countries began to careen out of control within the Soviet Union itself. Gorbachev proved unusually adept at political restructuring, yielding the Communist monopoly of government but building a new presidential system that gave him, if anything, increased powers. His skills in the Byzantine politics of the Kremlin, though, did not extend to an antiquated economy that resisted change. The revival of old ethnic allegiances added to the instability. Although Russia proper included slightly over half the Soviet Union's population, it was only one of fifteen constituent republics, most of which began to seek autonomy, if not independence. Along the fringes of the Russian republic, to the west and south, lay a jigsaw puzzle of about a hundred nationalities and languages.

Gorbachev's popularity shrank in the Soviet Union as it grew abroad. It especially eroded among the Communist hardliners, who saw in his reforms the unraveling of their bureaucratic and political empire. Once the genie of freedom was released from the Communist lamp, however, it took on a momentum of its own. On August 18, 1991, a cabal of political and military leaders suddenly tried to seize the reins of power. They accosted Gorbachev at his vacation retreat in the Crimea and demanded that he sign a decree proclaiming a state of emergency and transferring his powers to them. He replied: "Go to hell," whereupon he was placed under house arrest.

The coup, however, was doomed from the start. Poorly planned and clumsily implemented, it lacked effective coordination. The plotters failed to arrest popular leaders such as Boris Yeltsin, the populist president of the Russian republic, they neglected to close the airports or cut off telephone and television communications, and they were opposed by key elements of the military and KGB (secret police). But most important, the plotters failed to recognize the strength of the democratic idealism unleashed by Gorbachev's reforms. Upon learning of the attempted overthrow, tens of thousands of Muscovites poured into the streets outside Yeltsin's headquarters to act as human shields against efforts to arrest him. Three were killed in the process. Yeltsin himself clambered atop a menacing tank and publicly defied the conspirators, calling them a "gang of bandits."

As the drama unfolded in the Soviet Union, a crescendo of indignation welled up from foreign leaders around the world. On August 20 President Bush, after a day of indecision, responded favorably to Yeltsin's request for support and convinced world leaders to join him in refusing to recognize the legitimacy of the new Soviet government. Siberian coal miners went on strike to oppose the coup. The next day word began to seep out that the plotters had given up and were fleeing. Several committed suicide, and a newly released Gorbachev ordered the others arrested. Yet, things did not go back to the way they had

As a final act against the Communist regime, people toppled the statues that had been erected to honor their former leaders.

been. Although Gorbachev reclaimed the title of president, he was forced to resign as head of the Communist party and admit that he had made a grave mistake in appointing the men who had turned against him. Yeltsin emerged as the most popular political figure in the country.

What began as a reactionary coup turned into a powerful accelerant for stunning new changes in the Soviet Union, or the "Soviet Disunion," as one wag termed it. No sooner had the plotters been arrested than most of the fifteen republics proclaimed their independence, with the Baltic republics of Latvia, Lithuania, and Estonia regaining the status of independent nations. The Communist party apparatus was dismantled, prompting celebrating crowds to topple statues of Lenin and other mythic Communist heroes.

A chastened Gorbachev could only acquiesce in the breakup of the Soviet empire. The man who had put reform into motion was now buffeted by the whirlwind of change. In the midst of the political turmoil, the systemic problems burdening the Soviet Union before the coup remained intractable. The economy was stagnant, languishing between the promise of free-market principles and the gridlock of state collectivism. Food and coal shortages loomed on the horizon, and consumer goods remained scarce. It would take decades before the economies of the fifteen republics would approach Western standards of production and efficiency. The reformers had won, but they had yet to establish deep roots in a country with no democratic tradition. Leaping into the unknown, they faced years of hardship and uncertainty ahead.

The aborted coup also accelerated Soviet and American efforts to reduce the stockpiles of nuclear weapons. In late 1991 President Bush stunned the world by announcing that the United States would destroy all its tactical nuclear weapons on land and at sea in Europe and Asia, take its long-range bombers off twenty-four-hour alert status, and initiate discussions with the Soviet Union for the purpose of instituting sharp cuts in ICBMs with multiple warheads. Bush explained that the prospect of a Soviet invasion of western Europe was "no longer a realistic threat," and this presented an unprecedented opportunity for reducing the threat of nuclear holocaust. President Gorbachev responded by announcing reciprocal Soviet cutbacks.

PANAMA   The end of the cold war did not spell the end of international tensions and conflict, however. Indeed, before the end of 1989, American troops were engaged in battle in Panama, where a petty tyrant provoked the first of America's military engagements under George Bush. In 1983 General Manuel Noriega had maneuvered himself into the leadership of the Panamanian Defense Forces—which made him head of government in fact if not in title. Earlier, as chief of intelligence, Noriega had developed a profitable business of supplying information on the region to the CIA, including during the period when Bush headed the agency. At the same time, he was developing avenues in the region for drug smuggling and gunrunning, laundering the money through Panamanian banks. For a time, American intelligence analysts looked the other way, regarding him as too useful a contact, but eventually he became too great an embarrassment. In 1987 a rejected associate published charges of Noriega's drug activities and accused him further of rigged elections and political assassination.

In 1988 federal grand juries in Miami and Tampa indicted Noriega and fifteen others on drug charges. The Panamanian president tried to fire Noriega, but the National Assembly ousted the president instead and named Noriega "maximum leader." It then proclaimed that Panama "is declared to be in a state of war" with the United States. The next day, December 16, 1989, four off-duty American servicemen were stopped at a roadblock, and as they tried to proceed, one marine was shot and killed. President Bush thereupon ordered an invasion of Panama with the purpose of capturing Noriega for trial on the American indictments and installing a government headed by President Guillermo Endara.

The 12,000 American military personnel in Panama were quickly joined by 12,000 more, and in the early morning of December 20, five military task forces struck at strategic targets in the country. Noriega surrendered to American forces. Twenty-three American servicemen were killed in the action, and estimates of Panamanian casualties ranged up to 4,000, including many civilians caught in the crossfire. In April 1992 Noriega was convicted in the United States on eight counts of racketeering and drug distribution.

THE GULF WAR   Months after Panama had moved to the background of public attention, Saddam Hussein, dictator of Iraq, focused attention on the Middle East when his army suddenly fell upon his tiny, wealthy neighbor Kuwait on August 2, 1990. Kuwait had raised its production of oil, contrary to agreements with the Organization of Petroleum Exporting Countries (OPEC). The resultant drop in oil prices offended Saddam, deep in debt and heavily dependent on oil revenues. Complaining of "economic aggression" against Iraq, he demanded that Kuwait reduce its oil production and, with Saudi Arabia, cancel Iraqi debts of $30 million.

Saddam did not expect the sudden storm his invasion of Kuwait provoked. The U.N. Security Council quickly voted 14–0 to condemn the invasion and demand withdrawal. American secretary of state James Baker and Soviet foreign minister Eduard Shevardnadze issued a joint statement of condemnation. On August 6, the Security Council endorsed Resolution 661, an embargo on trade with Iraq, by a vote of 13–0, with Cuba and Yemen abstaining. Such unanimity, of course, would have been unlikely during the cold war era.

On August 2, Bush condemned Iraq's "naked aggression" and said he was not ruling any options out. He vowed to reporters: "This aggression will not stand." Asked how it would be undone, he replied: "Just wait, watch, and learn." On August 6–7, the United States responded to Saddam's threats against Saudi Arabia by dispatching planes and troops to Saudi Arabia on a "wholly defensive" mission—to protect Saudi Arabia. British forces soon joined in, as did Arab troops from Egypt, Morocco,

Syria, Oman, the United Arab Emirates, and Qatar. On August 22, Bush began to order the mobilization of American reserve forces for the operation now dubbed "Desert Shield." Later in September, after meeting with Gorbachev in Helsinki, Bush told Congress that dictators could no longer find comfort in East-West divisions, and proclaimed a "New World Order," which he described as "A world where the strong respect the rights of the weak."

On November 8, Bush announced that he was doubling American forces in the Middle East from about 200,000 to 400,000, to build up "an adequate offensive military capability." Bush asserted that he already had authority to take such action under the Security Council resolutions. Congress erupted in debate, with many arguing that the embargo should have a chance to work, and that it would be ill advised to go to war without formal congressional support. Bush's position was strengthened on November 29 by U.N. Resolution 678, which authorized the use of force to dislodge Iraq from Kuwait, and set a deadline for Iraqi withdrawal of January 15, 1991.

A flurry of peace efforts sent diplomats scurrying all over, but without result. Saddam refused to yield. On January 10, Congress began to debate a resolution authorizing the use of U.S. armed forces. Senate Majority Leader George Mitchell warned, "A grave decision for war is being made prematurely. There has been no clear rationale, no convincing explanation for shifting American policy from one of sanctions to one of war." Others insisted on the need to present a united front behind the president. The outcome was uncertain to the end, but on January 12 the resolution for the use of force passed the House by 250–183, and the Senate by 52–47.

By January 1991, a twenty-eight-nation allied force was committed to Operation Desert Shield. Some nations sent only planes, ships, or support forces, but sixteen committed ground combat forces, ten of these Islamic countries. Desert Shield became Operation Desert Storm when the first missiles and planes began to hit Iraq at about 2:30 A.M., January 17, Baghdad time, or about 6:30 P.M., January 16, Washington time.

With the allies in control of the air from the beginning, Saddam's only recourse was to fire off lumbering Soviet-made SCUD missiles, which he aimed from the first day into Israel with the hope of provoking Israeli retaliation and undermining the Arab coalition against him. But the resulting damage and casualties were light, and the Israelis showed remarkable restraint in the face of the continuing attacks. The Iraqis responded also with desperation moves, which did more damage to the environment than to enemy forces: releasing oil into the Persian Gulf from tankers and loading platforms in Kuwait and setting fire to Kuwaiti oil wells.

Saddam's key strategy of digging in and prolonging the war into a costly land struggle, as he did in his war with Iran, never had a chance. Saddam concentrated his forces in Kuwait and expected an allied attack northward into Kuwait and a landing on the coast. But the Iraqis were outflanked when 200,000 allied troops, largely American, British, and French, vanished with much of their heavy armor and turned up on the undefended border with Saudi Arabia 100–200 miles to the west. The allied ground assault began on February 24 and lasted only four days. Iraqi soldiers surrendered in wholesale lots.

On February 28, six weeks after the fighting began, President Bush called for a cease-fire, the Iraqis accepted, and the shooting ended. American fatalities were 137. The lowest estimates of Iraqi fatalities, civilian and military, were around 100,000. The coalition forces occu-

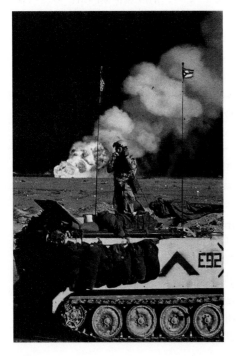

An American soldier watches a burning Kuwaiti oil well, which was set on fire by desperate Iraqi troops.

pied about one-fifth of Iraq. In late March, after a quick survey, a U.N. official reported: "Bombing had wrought near apocalyptic results upon the infrastructure of what had been, until January 1991, a rather highly urbanized and mechanized society." The Persian Gulf War, the "mother of all battles" in Saddam Hussein's words, had been intense and deadly and had left consequences to be played out far into the future. Despite all the destruction, Saddam Hussein remained in power.

The Middle East, as it had for centuries, still resisted any quick fix. There was an understanding—details to be worked out—that the United States would maintain a military presence in the Persian Gulf. It was, ironically, an American missionary who said to one of the British planners carving up the former Ottoman territory after World War I: "You are flying in the face of four millenniums of history." The words retain their haunting quality.

THE COMPUTER REVOLUTION

Among the most important factors promoting the surge in productivity and prosperity during the 1980s was a dramatic revolution in information technology. Cellular phones, laser printers, VCRs, fax machines, and personal computers became commonplace at work and in homes. The computer age had arrived.

The idea of a programmable machine that would rapidly perform mental tasks had been around since the eighteenth century, but it took the crisis atmosphere of World War II to bring to bear the intellectual and financial resources needed to create such a "computer." The Allies needed machines to decipher the complex German and Japanese military codes and to calculate the ballistics for new artillery systems. They also needed sophisticated mathematical tools to aid in the development of the atomic bomb.

Funding for such priorities enabled a team of engineers at the University of Pennsylvania to create ENIAC (Electronic Numerical Integrator and Computer), the first all-purpose, all-electronic digital computer. Unveiled in 1944, it could perform 5,000 operations per second. ENIAC, however, was so large that it was almost impractical. It took up 3,000 cubic feet of space and included 18,000 vacuum tubes (glass canisters designed to amplify electrical current), 70,000 resistors, 10,000

The Electronic Numerical Integrator and Computer (ENIAC), *1946. Developed for the army, the ENIAC was cumbersome but could perform complex calculations in minutes.*

capacitors, and 6,000 switches. John Von Neumann, a Hungarian-born American mathematician at the Institute for Advanced Study at Princeton, where he was a colleague of Albert Einstein, volunteered his services to help solve some of ENIAC's weaknesses—too little memory storage, too many tubes, and too lengthy programming. His insights led to a new machine, EDVAC (Electronic Discrete Variable Automatic Computer), unveiled in 1949, which became the model for the worldwide computer industry.

During the 1950s and 1960s, corporations (such as International Business Machines—IBM) and government agencies transformed computers from being mathematical calculators to electronic data-processing machines. The key development in facilitating such a transformation occurred in 1947 when three physicists at Bell Laboratories in central New Jersey invented the transistor (so named because it *trans*fers electric current across a re*sistor,* which is a conductor used to control voltage in an electrical circuit). Transistors were a dramatic breakthrough because they took the place of the much larger and more fragile, glass vacuum tubes. Like the vacuum tube, the transistor could amplify an electric signal. Unlike the vacuum tube, however, transistors were cheap, durable, required less power and, as future research would demonstrate, they could be made almost infinitely tiny. The availability of transistors led to the development of hearing aids and portable radios.

They also led to faster and more reliable, smaller and less expensive, mainframe computers. These "second-generation" computers were ten times as fast as EDVAC, but programming remained slow, requiring the use of punch cards fed into the machines. The next major breakthrough was the invention in 1971 of the microprocessor—literally a computer on a silicon chip—by Ted Hoff of Intel Corporation. The functions that had once been performed by computers taking up an entire room could now be performed by a microchip circuit the size of a postage stamp. Microchips were incorporated into television sets, wristwatches, automobiles, kitchen appliances, and the spacecraft being developed by NASA.

The use of such microchips enabled computers not only to be smaller but also cheaper. These "third-generation" computers were so much faster that a new word had to be created to measure their processing speeds: *nanoseconds* (billionths of a second). High-performance computers heightened efficiency throughout the American economy and helped fuel an information revolution that affected virtually every aspect of life.

The invention of the microchip made possible the idea of a personal computer. In 1975 Ed Roberts, an engineer, made the first prototype of a "personal computer." The Altair 8800, which cost $397, was imperfect and cumbersome, with no display, no keyboard, and not enough memory to do anything useful. But its potential excited a young Harvard sophomore named Bill Gates. He was a self-described "computer nerd," a student lacking in social skills and addicted to computing, willing to skip his classes in order to work night and day on programming projects.

Gates offered his software programming services for the Altair 8800 and formed a new company called Microsoft. Against the objections of his parents, Gates dropped out of Harvard to devote all his time to the new venture. "We realized that the revolution had started," Gates recalled, "and there was no question of where life would focus." By 1977 he and others had helped to transform the personal computer from a hobby machine to a mass consumer product. In 1986 Gates became a billionaire at the age of thirty-one.

Hundreds of new firms sprang up to produce the hardware and software for the burgeoning new industry. The infant personal computer industry soared into the 1980s, offering word processing, games, and perhaps most important, the capacity to calculate financial spreadsheets. This last feature convinced the corporate community that personal computers could indeed become a mass-production commodity. By the end of the decade, there were 60 million personal computers in the United States, and people began to talk about an "information superhighway," a worldwide network of linked computers and databases connected by fiber-optic lines that facilitated high-speed transmission. "We're all connected," declared a telephone company commercial.

During the 1990s, the development of the Internet and electronic mail enabled anyone with a personal computer and modem the opportunity to travel on the information superhighway. Such advances had the effect of shrinking the globe and facilitating almost instantaneous communication across the continents. Yet those too poor to gain easy access to the information revolution faced a bleak future. To the extent

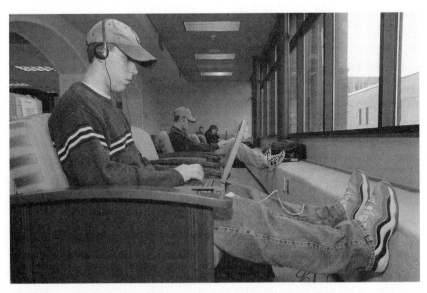

Students at Mansfield University in Pennsylvania work on laptop computers in the school libary. Rapid developments in technology have made computers, e-mail, and the Internet readily accessible and affordable.

that computers become essential tools for educational and economic success, they threaten to widen the gap between rich and poor. As always, it seems, technological progress provides uneven benefits.

MAKING CONNECTIONS

- Much of what happened in the 1980s, from economic and social policy to presidential leadership style, was reminiscent of the late nineteenth century as well as the 1920s and 1950s.

- Another parallel between the late nineteenth century and the 1980s was a rise in immigration and a change in immigration patterns. This is discussed in the next chapter.

- Chapter 37 shows how the economic and political conservatism of the 1980s became much more ideological in the early 1990s.

FURTHER READING

It is too early for a definitive scholarly analysis of the Reagan administration, but two brief accounts are David Mervin's *Ronald Reagan and the American Presidency* (1990) and Michael Schaller's *Reckoning with Reagan: America and Its President in the 1980s* (1992).

On Reaganomics, see David Stockman's *The Triumph of Politics: How the Reagan Revolution Failed* (1986) and Robert Lekachman's *Greed Is Not Enough: Reaganomics* (1982). On the issue of arms control, see Strobe Talbott's *Deadly Gambits: The Reagan Administration and the Stalemate in Nuclear Arms Control* (1984).

For Reagan's foreign policy in Central America, see James Chace's *Endless War: How We Got Involved in Central America and What Can Be Done* (1984) and Walter LaFeber's *Inevitable Revolutions: The United States in Central America* (2nd ed., 1993). Insider views of Reagan's foreign policy are offered in Alexander M. Haig, Jr.'s *Caveat: Realism, Reagan, and Foreign Policy* (1984) and Caspar W. Weinberger's *Fighting for Peace: Seven Critical Years in the Pentagon* (1990).

On Reagan's second term, see Jane Mayer and Doyle McManus's *Landslide: The Unmaking of the President, 1984–1988* (1988). For a masterful work on the Iran-Contra affair, see Theodore Draper's *A Very Thin Line: The Iran Contra Affair* (1991). Several collections of essays include varying assessments of the Reagan years. Among these are *The Reagan Revolution* (1988), edited by B. B. Kymlicka and Jean V. Matthews; *The Reagan Presidency: An Incomplete Revolution* (1990), edited by Dilys M. Hill, et al.; and *Looking Back on the Reagan Presidency* (1990), edited by Larry Berman.

On the 1988 campaign see Jack Germond and Jules Witcover's *Whose Broad Stripes and Bright Stars? The Trivial Pursuit of the Presidency, 1988* (1989) and Sidney Blumenthal's *Pledging Allegiance: The Last Campaign of the Cold War* (1990). Major issues in economic and social policy are addressed in Robert Reich's *The Work of Nations: Preparing Ourselves for Twenty-first Century Capitalism* (1991) and William Julius Wilson's *The Truly Disadvantaged: The Inner City, the Underclass, and Public Policy* (1987).

37   CULTURAL POLITICS

CHAPTER ORGANIZER

This chapter focuses on:

- demographic patterns from the 1990 census and the "new immigrants" of the 1980s and 1990s.

- the Democratic resurgence of the early 1990s; the Republican landslide of 1994; and the Contract with America.

- the remarkable performance of the economy and stock market during the 1990s.

- the revelations of scandal that recall earlier sexual escapades during the Harding administration.

*D*uring the 1980s and 1990s, various cultural and political developments combined to transform American society and institutions. The makeup of the population shifted as the baby-boomers entered middle age. Immigrants to America were now primarily from Asia and Latin America rather than from Europe. In the 1980s and 1990s, the political landscape also began to be transformed, as many conservative politicians won election to local, state, and federal government offices, and many conservative judges were appointed or elected to the courts. In an effort to become more productive and competitive, American businesses engaged in "reengineering" efforts that often brought widespread job cuts. As corporations began to downsize, people began to lose faith in company loyalty and job security. At the same time, a backlash against racial preferences created new social tensions. Whites in large numbers began to argue that affirmative action would limit their access to the nation's colleges and business contracts. They supported a balanced budget, feared for their jobs, and yearned for an end to corruption in government and a revival of "traditional" moral values.

AMERICA'S CHANGING FACE

DEMOGRAPHIC SHIFTS   During the 1980s, the nation's population grew by 10 percent, or some 23 million people, boosting the total to almost 250 million. The median age of the quarter-billion Americans rose from thirty to thirty-three, and the much-discussed baby-boom generation—the 43 million people born between 1946 and 1964—entered middle age. Because of its disproportionate size, the baby-boom generation magnifies changes in American society as it moves through the life cycle. As one demographer noted, it resembles a "pig in a python." Political analysts suggested that this generation's maturation and preoccupation with practical concerns such as raising families, paying for college, and buying houses helped explain the surge of political conservatism during the 1980s. Surveys revealed that baby-boomers wanted stronger family and religious ties and promoted a greater respect for authority. Yet having come to maturity during the turbulent sixties and early seventies, the baby-boomers also displayed more tolerance of social and cultural diversity than their parents.

The "Sunbelt" states of the South and West continued to lure residents from the Midwest and Northeast. Fully 90 percent of the nation's total population growth during the 1980s occurred in southern or western states. California gained more people than any other state during the eighties, boosting its total to 30 million, 5 million more than in 1980. Texas and Florida each added more than 3 million new residents, while West Virginia, Iowa, and the District of Columbia experienced a net loss of residents. The Northeast became the nation's least populous region. These population shifts forced a massive redistricting of the House of Representatives, with Florida and California gaining three more seats each and Texas two, while states such as New York lost seats.

Americans in the 1980s tended to settle in large communities. Almost 90 percent of the decade's population growth occurred in large metropolitan areas. The number of cities with 100,000 people or more increased by 29 to a total of 195, with 18 of the new metropolises in California alone. In 1990 some 78 percent of the population lived in a metropolitan area, and for the first time, a majority of Americans lived in cities of a million or more people. This move to the cities largely reflected trends in the job market, as the "postindustrial" economy continued to shift from manufacturing to professional service industries, particularly those specializing in telecommunications and information processing. By 1990 fewer than 5 million people out of a total population of 250 million—or 2 percent—lived on farms.

Women continued to enter the workforce in large numbers. Indeed, one of the most significant sociological developments in American life since 1970 was the accelerated entry of women into the world of work outside the home. In 1970, 38 percent of the workforce was female; in 1990 the figure was almost 50 percent. Women workers accounted for 60 percent of labor force growth since 1980, and fully 58 percent of all adult women were gainfully employed. A third of the new medical doctors during the eighties were women (4 percent in 1970); 40 percent of new lawyers were female (8.4 percent in 1970); and 23 percent of new dentists were women (less than 1 percent in 1970).

The decline of the traditional family unit—two parents with children—continued during the 1980s. The proportion of the nation's households in that category dropped from 31 percent in 1980 to 26 percent in 1990. And more people were living alone than ever before, largely as a result of high divorce rates or a growing practice of delaying marriage until well into the twenties. One out of every four households in 1990 was made up of a person living alone, a 26 percent increase over 1980. The number of single mothers increased 35 percent during the decade. The rate was much higher for African Americans: in 1990 less than 38 percent of black children lived with both parents, down from 67 percent in 1960.

Young blacks burdened by the absence of one or both parents faced shrinking economic opportunities in the 1980s. The 1990 census documented a slight rise in the proportion of Americans living in poverty but a substantially heightened inequality in the distribution of income. By 1992, roughly 14.5 percent of the American people were living at or below the official poverty level, pegged at $14,335 in annual income for a family of four. The urban poor were particularly victimized by a developing underclass culture, with young black males suffering the most. In 1990 the leading cause of death among black males between the ages of fifteen and twenty-four was homicide. Twenty-five percent of black males aged twenty to twenty-nine were in prison, on parole, or on probation, while only 4 percent were enrolled in college. Forty percent of black adult males were functionally illiterate.

THE NEW IMMIGRANTS   The racial and ethnic composition of the country also changed rapidly during the 1980s, with nearly one in every four Americans claiming African, Asian, Hispanic, or American Indian ancestry. Among an overall population of 250 million, blacks represented 12 percent of the total, Hispanics 9 percent, Asians about 3 percent, and American Indians almost 1 percent. The rate of increase

Increased numbers of Chinese risked their money and their lives trying to gain entry into the United States. These illegal immigrants from China are trying to keep warm after being captured when the freighter carrying them to the United States ran aground in Rockaway, New York City.

among those four groups was twice as fast as it had been during the 1970s.

The primary cause of this dramatic change in the nation's ethnic mix was a surge of immigration. During the 1980s, legal immigration into the United States totaled over 7 million people, 30 percent higher than the previous decade and more than in any other decade except 1901–1910. These figures do not include the hundreds of thousands of illegal aliens, mostly Mexicans and Haitians. In 1990 the United States welcomed more than twice as many immigrants as all other countries in the world put together.

Even more significant than the overall number of newcomers were their places of origin. For the first time in the nation's history, the majority of immigrants came not from Europe but from other parts of the world. The percentage of European immigrants to the United States declined from 53 percent of the total in the 1950s to 12 percent in the 1980s and 1990s. Asian Americans were the fastest-growing segment of the population in the eighties, with their numbers increasing by 80 percent, a rate seven times as great as the general population. Among the legal immigrants during the decade, Mexicans made up the largest share, averaging about 60,000 a year. The second-highest number came from the Philippines (46,000), while immigrants from mainland China, Taiwan, and Hong Kong totaled 45,000 annually. The next largest groups were Vietnamese and Koreans, followed by Dominicans, Asian Indians, Jamaicans, Iranians, Cubans, Cambodians, and Laotians.

Heightening the social impact of these new immigrants was their tendency to cluster in a handful of states and cities. Most of them gravitated to New York, Illinois, and New Jersey, as well as Florida, Texas, Hawaii, California, and other Sunbelt states. By 1990, California had 64 percent of the Asian Americans in the country and 34 percent of the Hispanics. The population of Miami, Florida, was 64 percent Hispanic, and San Antonio, Texas, boasted 55 percent. Los Angeles contained 2 million Mexican Americans.

The wave of new immigration brought rising conflict between old and new ethnicities. African-American leaders worried that the newcomers were gaining an economic foothold at the expense of poor blacks. And many native whites resented the influx of newcomers into their communities.

Such reactions recall earlier chapters in American immigrant history, a story marked from the start by ambivalence about the nation's tradi-

RESIDENT POPULATION DISTRIBUTION FOR THE UNITED STATES BY RACE AND ETHNIC ORIGIN: 1980 AND 1990

	1980		1990		
	Number	%	Number	%	Change
Total population	**226,545,805**	**100.0**	**248,709,873**	**100.0**	**9.8**
White	188,371,622	83.1	199,686,070	80.3	6.0
Black	26,495,025	11.7	29,986,060	12.1	13.2
American Indian, Eskimo, or Aleut	1,420,400	0.6	1,959,234	0.8	37.9
Asian or Pacific Islander	3,500,439	1.5	7,273,662	2.9	107.8
Other race	6,758,319	3.0	9,804,847	3.9	45.1
Hispanic origin	14,608,673	6.4	22,354,059	9.0	53.0

Source: U.S. Bureau of the Census, 1991.

tion of inclusiveness. With rhetoric reminiscent of the nativist movement a century earlier, critics of the new tide of immigration charged that America was being "overrun" with foreigners; they questioned whether Hispanics and Asians could be "assimilated" into American culture. In 1994 a large majority of California voters approved Proposition 187, a controversial initiative that denied the state's estimated 4 million illegal immigrants access to public schools, nonemergency health care, and other social services. It also required teachers, doctors, and government officials to report anyone suspected of being an undocumented immigrant. Proponents of the new measure claimed it would save taxpayers billions of dollars. Critics labeled Proposition 187 racist in motive and effect. In 1998 California voters passed a referendum ending bilingual education.

The bitter irony of this new nativism was that it targeted recent immigrants for bringing with them to the United States virtues long prized by Americans—hope, energy, persistence, and an aggressive work ethic. Like most of their predecessors who braved tremendous hardships to make their way to America, they toiled long and hard for a slice of the American dream, and most economic studies concluded that their presence was beneficial to the nation. They created more wealth than they consumed, and many of them compiled an astonishing record of achievement. The median household income of Asian Americans, for example, exceeded every other group, including native whites, and

IMMIGRANTS ADMITTED BY
TOP 15 COUNTRIES OF BIRTH
IN FISCAL YEAR 1990

Country of Birth	1990
Total	**656,111**
Mexico	56,549
Philippines	54,907
Vietnam	48,662
Dominican Republic	32,064
Korea	29,548
China (mainland)	28,746
India	28,679
Soviet Union	25,350
Jamaica	18,828
Iran	18,031
Taiwan	13,839
United Kingdom	13,730
Canada	13,717
Poland	13,334
Haiti	11,862
Other	248,265

Source: U.S. Immigration and Naturalization Service, 1991.

Asian Americans were disproportionately represented in the nation's most prestigious colleges and universities. Although constituting only 1.6 percent of the total population in 1985, Asian Americans made up over 11 percent of Harvard's freshman class and almost 20 percent at Berkeley and the California Institute of Technology. Yet the very success of the new immigrants contributed to the resentment they encountered from other groups.

CULTURAL CONSERVATISM

Cultural conservatives helped elect Reagan and Bush in the 1980s, but they were disappointed in the results. Once in office, neither president had, in their eyes, adequately addressed their moral agenda, including a complete ban on abortions and the restoration of prayer in public schools. By the 1990s, a new generation of young conservative activists, mostly political independents or Republicans, began to emerge as a force to be reckoned with in national affairs. They were more ideological, more libertarian, more partisan, and more impatient than their predecessors.

ATTACKS ON THE LIBERAL AGENDA   The new breed of cultural conservatives abhorred the excesses of cultural and political liberalism. They lamented the disappearance of basic forms of decency and propriety, and believed that fundamental liberties were at risk. They attacked affirmative action programs designed to redress historic injustices against women and minorities. During the 1990s, powerful groups inside and outside the Republican party mobilized to roll back government programs giving preferences to specified social groups. Prominent black conservatives supported such efforts, arguing that racially based preferences were demeaning and condescending remedies. They argued that preferential government treatment of African Americans raised doubts in the minds of both blacks and whites about the inherent worth of any black achievement.

THE RELIGIOUS RIGHT   Although quite diverse, cultural conservatives tended to be evangelical Christians or orthodox Catholics who joined together to exert increasing pressure on the political process. In 1989 the television evangelist Pat Robertson organized the Christian Coalition to replace Jerry Falwell's Moral Majority as the flagship organization of the resurgent religious right. The Christian Coalition encouraged religious conservatives to vote, run for public office, and support only those candidates who shared the organization's views.

With a well-organized grassroots movement in every state, the Christian Coalition chose the Republican party as the best vehicle for transforming its pro-family campaign into new public policies. It encouraged its supporters to withhold political support from any candidate who did not provide an ironclad promise to support the Coalition's school prayer, anti-abortion, anti–gay rights positions. In addition to promoting "traditional family values," it urged politicians to "radically downsize and delimit government."

As a centrist professional politician, George Bush initially tried to keep the cultural conservatives at arm's length, only to find himself the target—and victim—of their in-your-face attacks and take-no-prisoners tenacity. His Democratic successor, Bill Clinton, also underestimated the growing strength of organized groups such as the Christian Coalition. In the 1994 congressional elections, religious conservatives went to the polls in record numbers, and 70 percent of them voted Republican tickets. A third of the voters identified themselves as "white, evangelical, born-again Christians." In many respects, they took control of the political and social agendas in the nineties. As one journalist acknowledged in 1995, "the religious right is moving toward center stage in American secular life."

BUSH TO CLINTON

For months after the Gulf War, George Bush seemed unbeatable. In the polls his approval rating rose to 91 percent. But the aftermath of Desert Storm was mixed, with Saddam Hussein's grip on Iraq still intact. Despite his image of strength abroad, the president began to look weak even on foreign policy. The Soviet Union meanwhile stumbled on to its surprising end. On December 25, 1991, the Soviet flag over the Kremlin was replaced by the flag of the Russian Federation. The cold war had ended with not just the collapse but the dismemberment of the Soviet Union into its fifteen constituent republics. As a result, the United States was now the world's only superpower.

"Containment" of the Soviet Union, the bedrock of American foreign policy for more than four decades, had lost its reason for being. Bush, the ultimate cold war careerist—ambassador to the U.N., envoy to China, head of the CIA, vice-president under Reagan—struggled to interpret the fluid new international scene. He spoke of a "New World Order" but never defined it. By his own admission he had trouble with the "vision thing." The situation, in fact, did not lend itself to a simple vision—unless the answer was to drift into isolation, a great temptation, with foreign dangers seemingly lessened. By the end of 1991, Bush faced a primary challenge from the Republican commentator and former White House aide Patrick Buchanan, who adopted the slogan "America First" and called on Bush to "bring home the boys." As the Gulf War victory euphoria wore off, a popular bumper sticker reflected the growing public frustration with the Bush administration: "Saddam Hussein still has his job. What about you?"

RECESSION AND DOWNSIZING   In November 1988, a few days after George Bush was elected president, a journalist observed that the most important issue to be addressed by the new administration was the nation's deepening financial debt. "It is the issue that probably will determine the fate of the President. Indeed, it could also be his ultimate undoing." It was an accurate prediction. For the Bush administration and for the nation, the most devastating development in the early nineties was a prolonged economic recession that began in 1990. The first economic setback in more than eight years, it grew into the longest, if not the deepest, since the Great Depression. By early 1992, over 2 million jobs had dried up. During 1991, 25 million workers—about 20 percent of the labor force—were unemployed at some time.

What made this recession unusual was that its victims included large numbers of white-collar workers. In 1991, for instance, General Motors, Xerox, and IBM cut 100,000 salaried employees from their payrolls. In the corporate world, terms such as "restructuring" and "downsizing" ruled the day. Companies began reducing personnel, switching employees to part-time status to reduce benefits, and finding other ways to cut labor costs.

Prosperity gave way to firings, growing unemployment, declining sales and profits, the continuing imbalance in foreign trade, and the lack of a plan for the demobilization of the military-industrial complex after the cold war. With soaring expenditures on defense and social entitlement programs, a $150 billion annual deficit had become a $450 billion shortfall during 1991.

A Senate committee analysis of the stagnant economy confirmed a chilling fact. Under the Bush administration "the average standard of living has actually declined." Some critics with a historical bent compared Bush to Hoover: both presidents and their aides initially denied that there was a problem with the economy and then assured the nation that the recession would be short and self-correcting. The euphoria over the Allied victory in the Gulf War quickly gave way to anxiety and resentment generated by the depressed economy. At the end of 1991, *Time* magazine declared that "no one, not even George Bush" could deny "that the economy was sputtering."

Whatever the reasons for recession, the cure remained elusive. Although the Federal Reserve Board began cutting interest rates, the economy remained in the doldrums through 1992. The Democratic Congress and the Republican president squabbled over legislation to promote economic recovery but little was done to prod new growth or to reduce the hemorrhaging deficits. With his domestic policies in disarray and his foreign policy abandoned, George Bush tried a clumsy balancing act in addressing the recession, on the one hand acknowledging that "people are hurting" while on the other urging Americans that "this is a good time to buy a car."

THE COURT VEERS RIGHT   Other developments affected the president's popularity, among them the retirement in 1991 of the first black Supreme Court justice, Thurgood Marshall, after twenty-four years on the bench. To succeed him Bush named Clarence Thomas, a black federal judge who had been raised in poverty in the segregated South and educated in Catholic schools. After graduating from Yale Law School, Thomas had worked as an aide to a Republican senator before serving as chairman of the Equal Employment Opportunity Commission (EEOC) from 1982 to 1990. Then, after sixteen months on the U.S. Court of Appeals, he was tapped for the Supreme Court.

Despite Thomas's limited time in the judiciary, his views delighted conservative senators. He had questioned the wisdom of the minimum wage, school busing for desegregation, and affirmative action hiring programs, and he had preached "black self-help," once declaring that all civil rights leaders ever did was "bitch, bitch, bitch, moan, and whine."

Such opinions promised trouble in the Democratic Senate, but the real explosion occurred when Anita Hill, a soft-spoken law professor at the University of Oklahoma, charged that Thomas had sexually harassed her when she worked for him at the EEOC. Pro-Thomas senators orchestrated an often savage and sometimes absurd cross-examination of Hill. Some accused her of mental instability. An indignant Thomas denied her charges and called the hearings a "high-tech lynching for uppity blacks." He implied that Hill had fabricated the charges at the behest of civil rights groups determined to thwart his confirmation.

The televised hearings revealed that either Hill or Thomas had lied, and the committee's tie vote reflected the doubt: seven to recommend confirmation and seven against. The full Senate then narrowly confirmed Thomas by a 52–48 margin.

The hearings marked a new surge in the women's movement. Before the galvanizing effects of Anita Hill's rough treatment at the hands of male senators, feminism as an organized political movement had been in disarray. As early as 1975 Betty Friedan had broken away from the National Organization for Women (NOW), the organization she had started less than a decade before, claiming that its radical leaders had abandoned the core constituency of working women. By 1992 many claimed that NOW had reached a dead end. Columnist Sally Quinn charged that "many women have come to see the feminist movement as anti-male, anti-child, anti-family, anti-feminine. And therefore it has nothing to do with us."

In the ambiguous aftermath of the Thomas hearings, many women grew incensed at the treatment of Hill, and an unprecedented number of women ran for national and local offices in 1992. The Thomas confirmation struggle thus widened the gender gap for a Republican party already less popular with women than with men. As one political commentator put it: "The war with Anita Hill was not a war Bush needed."

REPUBLICAN TURMOIL   The president had already set a political trap for himself when he declared in his 1988 convention address: "Read my lips. No new taxes!" Fourteen months into his term, he had decided that the deficit was a greater risk than violating his "no tax" pledge. After intense negotiations with congressional Democrats, Bush had announced that reducing the federal deficit required "tax revenue increases." He had not exactly said "new taxes," but as one House Democrat put it, "the charade is over." Bush's backsliding set off a revolt among House Republicans, but a bipartisan majority (most Republicans opposing) finally approved a tax measure raising the top personal rate from 28 to 31 percent, disallowing certain deductions to the upper brackets, and raising various excises. Conservative Republicans would not let George Bush forget his abandoned pledge.

Social issues had been one of the adhesives in the Reagan coalition, keeping the focus away from divisive economic issues, but as hardships crowded in on the attention of blue-collar workers, the economy surged to the fore. Moreover, social issues strengthened the force of the new "Christian Right" and grated on traditional Republicans. Reagan had been adept at exploiting moral issues, especially abortion, while doing little or nothing about them in practice. Bush's efforts to talk up such issues eventually ran out of control when right-wing militants seized the podium and the attention of the TV cameras at the 1992 convention. Patrick Buchanan, who had won about a third of the votes in the Republican primaries, used the occasion for a defense of "family values." Pat Robertson, the television evangelist, insisted that the proposed

Equal Rights Amendment represented "a socialist, anti-family, political movement that encourages women to leave their husbands, kill their children, practice witchcraft, destroy capitalism and become lesbians."

DEMOCRATIC RESURGENCE   In contrast to such strident rhetoric, the Democrats presented an image of centrist forces in control. For several years the Democratic Leadership Council (DLC), in which Arkansas governor William Jefferson Clinton figured prominently, had pushed the party to the center. Clinton strove to move the Democrats closer to the mainstream of political opinion. A graduate of Georgetown University, he had won a Rhodes scholarship to Oxford, and then earned a law degree from Yale, where he met and married Hillary Rodham. By 1979, at age thirty-two, he was back in his native Arkansas as the youngest governor in the country. He served three more terms as governor and in the process emerged as a dynamic young leader within the national Democratic party committed to winning back the middle-class white voters who had voted Republican during the eighties. Democrats had grown so liberal, he argued, that they had alienated their key constituencies.

A self-described moderate, Clinton promised to cut the defense budget, provide tax relief for the middle class, and create a massive economic aid package for the former republics of the Soviet Union. He was less precise about how such initiatives would be funded. Handsome, witty, intelligent, and a compelling speaker, Clinton reminded many political observers of John F. Kennedy. But underneath the veneer of Clinton's charisma were several flaws. He often seemed so determined to become president that he was willing to sacrifice consistency and principle. He made extensive use of polls to shape his stance on issues, pandered to special-interest groups, and flip-flopped on controversial issues, leading critics to label him "Slick Willie." Said one former opponent in Arkansas, "He'll be what people want him to be. He'll do or say what it will take to get elected." Even more enticing to the media and more embarrassing to Clinton were unending reports that he was a chronic adulterer and that he had manipulated the ROTC program during the Vietnam War to avoid the draft. Clinton's denials of both allegations could not dispel a lingering distrust of his personal character.

After a series of bruising party primaries, Clinton emerged as the front-runner by the time of the nominating convention in the summer of 1992. The Clinton forces dominated the convention, where Clinton chose Albert Gore, Jr., of Tennessee as his running mate. So the candidates were two southern Baptists from adjoining states.

Flushed with their convention victory, sporting a ten-point lead in the polls, the Clinton-Gore team stressed economic issues to win over working-class white and black voters. This strategy worked. Exit polls showed that the most important issue had been the economy. Clinton won with 370 electoral votes and about 43 percent of the vote; Bush had 168 electoral votes and 39 percent of the vote; and off-and-on independent candidate H. Ross Perot of Texas garnered 18 percent of the popular vote but no electoral votes. A feisty billionaire, Perot found a big audience for his simplified explanations of public problems and his offers to just "get under the hood and fix them." Yet during the Democratic convention, Perot withdrew, explaining that the Democratic party had "revitalized itself." Later he got back in the race as a third-party candidate and stayed for a surprisingly strong finish, one that suggested a widespread disillusionment with politics-as-usual.

DOMESTIC POLICY IN CLINTON'S FIRST TERM

Once inaugurated and faced with the realities of governing, Clinton alienated many who had voted for him when he reneged on several of his campaign promises. His infant presidency lurched from one cliffhanger to another. He abandoned his promised middle-class tax cut in order to keep down the federal deficit. When his attempt to allow professed homosexuals in the military provoked strong opposition among military commanders and in Congress, he backed down nine days into office and later announced an ambiguous new policy concerning gays in the military that came to be summed up in the words "Don't ask, don't tell." These inconsistent actions at the start of his administration had a negative effect on public impressions of the president, whom opponents accused on the one hand of putting a leftist agenda first and on the other hand of being too quick to cave in to criticism. In Clinton's first two weeks in office, his approval ratings dropped 20 percent.

Clinton had no traditional honeymoon of bipartisan support as he assumed office, partly because he seemed to live life as a perpetual campaign, partly because his critics permitted no letup. He therefore failed to enlarge substantially the narrow margin of support he had won during the election. He also failed to receive deserved credit for his achievements, such as the Family and Medical Leave Act, which enabled government workers and workers in companies with more than fifty employees to take off twelve weeks (unpaid leave) each year to deal with birth or adoption or an illness in the family. During the campaign, Clinton had promised to submit to Congress within 100 days a comprehensive economic program and a health care reform plan. In both cases, he failed to muster the necessary support of Congress and the public.

THE ECONOMY   Clinton entered office determined to reduce the federal deficit without damaging the economy. To this end, on February 17, he laid out a program of tax hikes and spending cuts. He proposed higher taxes for corporations and for individuals in higher tax brackets and called for an economic stimulus package for "investment" in public works (transportation, utilities, and the like) and in "human capital" (education, skills, health, and welfare). The Republican minority in the Senate used a filibuster to block the stimulus package, which they described as a "budget buster" that would fail to pep up the economy. The Democrats were unable to muster enough votes to cut off debate, and the stimulus package lay dead in the water. In response to Clinton's deficit reduction package of spending cuts and tax hikes on upper incomes, both Republicans and conservative Democrats who favored even deeper spending cuts opposed the package. The hotly contested bill finally passed by 218–216 in the House and 51–50 in the Senate, with Vice-President Gore breaking the tie.

The major scuffle of the fall also concerned the economy and was over approval of the North American Free Trade Agreement (NAFTA), which the Bush administration had negotiated with Canada and Mexico. The debate revived old arguments on the tariff, pro and con. Clinton stuck with his party's tradition of low tariffs and urged approval of NAFTA, which would make North America the largest free trade area in the world. He and his supporters argued that tariff reductions would open up foreign markets to American industries. Opponents of the bill like wealthy gadfly Ross Perot and organized labor favored barriers against cheaper foreign products and believed that with NAFTA the country would hear a "giant sucking sound" of American jobs being drawn to Mexico. Yet Clinton prevailed with solid Republican support while losing a sizable minority of Democrats, mostly from the South.

The final vote in the House was 234–200, with 102 Democrats and 132 Republicans making up the majority. The Senate approved NAFTA on November 21, 1993.

HEALTH CARE REFORM   Clinton's major public policy initiative was a new health care plan. Government-subsidized health insurance was not a new idea. Other industrial countries had long since started national health insurance programs, Germany as early as 1883, Britain in 1911. Off and on the idea had been a subject of political discussion in the United States throughout the twentieth century. Medicare, initiated in 1965, provided insurance for people sixty-five and older, and Medicaid supported state medical assistance for the indigent. These programs had grown enormously in the years since, as had business spending on private health insurance.

Sentiment for health care reform spread as annual medical costs approached the trillion-dollar mark, and some 39 million Americans went without insurance either by choice or out of necessity. The administration argued that universal medical insurance would reduce the overall costs of health care. Medicare covered older people, the most vulnerable to medical expenses, and the costs were soaring. Many of the working poor could not afford insurance, and many younger, healthier people took a chance on doing without. When they got in trouble, they reported to emergency rooms, which were reluctant to reject desperate people. As a result, those who could pay covered the others' costs in higher fees.

Universal medical coverage as proposed by Clinton would entitle every American and legal immigrant to health insurance. Government would subsidize all or part of the payments for small businesses and the poor, the latter from funds that formerly went to Medicaid, and would collect a "sin tax" on tobacco and perhaps on alcoholic beverages to pay for the program. Hillary Clinton chaired the health care plan task force and became the administration's lead witness on the plan before congressional committees. In January 1994, in his first State of the Union address, Clinton promised to veto any health care bill that "does not guarantee every American private health insurance that can never be taken away." For the remainder of 1994, a comprehensive health insurance plan remained the centerpiece of the Clinton agenda.

Hillary Clinton testifying before a congressional committee on the administration's health care legislation, September 1993.

But the bill aroused opposition from vested interests, especially the pharmaceutical and insurance industries. Drug companies insisted that they needed large profits to support expensive research. Insurance interests funded TV advertisements that questioned the bill's benefits. Small-business groups attacked the requirements that employers share the cost of medical insurance, already a common practice in old-age, unemployment, and health insurance, even though government would provide subsidies to small business. By midsummer 1994, the health insurance plan was pretty well doomed. Republican senators began a filibuster to prevent a vote on the bill. Lacking the votes to stop the filibuster, the Democrats acknowledged defeat and gave up the fight for universal medical coverage.

HANDGUNS AND THE CRIME BILL   During Clinton's first year in office, fear of violent crime prompted legislators to limit the availability of unregistered guns. In 1993, Congress passed the Brady Bill, which required a five-day wait to buy a handgun. Clinton called for passage of a crime bill in his State of the Union message. The bill had been passed in both houses in 1993, but when a conference committee reported back a compromise bill, a coalition of unlikely bedfellows—black Democrats who objected to expanding use of the death penalty, pro-gun Democrats who objected to a ban on assault weapons, and Republicans who dismissed crime-prevention programs as "pork" and who sought to embarrass the administration—joined together to oppose the legislation. After Congress voted 225–210 to postpone consideration of the bill, the Clinton administration pulled out all the stops to win its approval, and the new vote in the House in favor of the bill was 235–195. When the Senate passed the bill, people characterized it as one of Clinton's greatest victories. Ironically, however, it damaged the chances for health care legislation, as Clinton was preoccupied with the crime bill for ten days and used up much of his political leverage in the final moves to win its approval. This meant that there were fewer favors he could pull in to overcome the growing opposition to universal health care.

MISTRUST OF GOVERNMENT AND THE MILITIA MOVEMENT While Clinton sparred with Republicans in Washington, a burgeoning "militia" or "patriot" movement spread across the country in the 1990s. It represented the paranoid and populist strain in cultural politics. Convinced that the federal government was conspiring against individual liberties (especially the right to bear arms), thousands of mostly working-class folk joined well-armed militia organizations. Some militias harkened back to the origins of the Ku Klux Klan and fomented racial and ethnic hatred. Others aligned themselves with right-wing Christian groups, particularly the militant wing of the anti-abortion movement. In the Far West, several of the militias challenged the federal control of public lands, refused to pay taxes, and threatened to arrest and execute local government officials and judges.

Militia groups grew in numbers in reaction to dramatic government actions at Ruby Ridge, Idaho, and Waco, Texas. In Idaho in 1992, white supremacist Randy Weaver held off federal agents when they laid siege to his mountain cabin because he had failed to appear in federal court on weapons charges. Crossfire at the cabin killed Weaver's wife and son and convinced many people that the government intended to confiscate all weapons and to start a war against the radical right.

In Waco, Texas, another siege also resulted in catastrophic consequences. Responding to reports and rumors about the stockpiling of weapons, false imprisonment, child abuse, and the violation of immigration laws by the Branch Davidians, an apocalyptic sect headed by David Koresh, agents from the Treasury Department's Bureau of Alcohol, Tobacco, and Firearms (BATF) tried to serve a warrant on the sect on February 28, 1993. When the agents entered the sect's compound, they were met with gunfire. Four agents and two Branch Davidians were killed, and twenty or so people were injured. The next day, the FBI took over the siege of the compound. After fifty days of fruitless psychological warfare against the Branch Davidians, the FBI yielded to frustration and hints of child abuse, and on April 19, the fifty-first day of the siege, agents attacked the compound with armored vehicles and tear gas. Amid the commotion, the compound caught fire and quickly burned to the ground. The fire was so intense that no one could be certain of the number dead, but at least seventy-seven people died in the inferno.

On the second anniversary of the Waco incident, April 19, 1995, a massive truck bomb exploded in front of the federal office building in

The Murrah Federal Building in Oklahoma City after it was bombed, April 19, 1995.

Oklahoma City, Oklahoma. The entire front portion of the nine-story building collapsed, killing 168 people, 19 of them children in a day-care center that was in the building. Six hundred others were injured. Within days, the FBI arrested Timothy McVeigh and Terry Nichols and charged them with the bombing. A third man pleaded guilty to separate charges of conspiring to produce explosives. All three men were militia members who hated the federal government and who had been incensed by the way the BATF and FBI had dealt with the Branch Davidians at Waco.

The Oklahoma City bombing shocked and saddened the nation. It brought to public attention the rise of right-wing militia groups and also revealed the depth of anti-government sentiment among such fringe groups. A year later, in the spring of 1996, the FBI lay siege to a dozen members of the Freemen, a heavily armed militia group that kept federal authorities at bay outside a remote Montana homestead. The Freemen refused to pay taxes or be evicted from the property, which had been foreclosed upon eighteen months earlier. They declared their right to exercise governmental authority, posted bounties for the capture of local police and judges, and threatened to shoot their neighbors' livestock. Unlike the incident at Waco, this time federal officials resolved to wait out the fugitives. "The FBI," said Attorney-General Janet Reno, "has gone to great pains to ensure that there is no armed confrontation, no siege, no armed perimeter, and no use of military-assault-type tactics or equipment. The FBI is trying to negotiate a peaceful solution." The tactics succeeded, and eventually the Freemen were arrested.

Foreign Policy Challenges

Foreign policy under Clinton initially took a low priority. Yet, like Woodrow Wilson, Lyndon Johnson, and Jimmy Carter before him, Clinton was a Democratic president who came into office determined to focus on the nation's domestic problems, only to find himself mired down in foreign entanglements that had no easy resolution. In the search for a new rationale or paradigm of foreign policy, however, the Clinton administration faced a more complex situation than before.

Attention focused on the transition in eastern Europe from a politics of Communist party rule into one of ethnic loyalties and clashes. With the collapse of Communist power, old ethnic and religious enmities quickly resurfaced in eastern Europe and elsewhere, often leading to violent clashes that were difficult to resolve quickly. The Clinton administration struggled to find a consistent vision of its role in international affairs. In the meantime, it operated mostly on an ad hoc basis, often failing to win international backing for its initiatives. As one of Clinton's own ambassadorial appointees admitted, "We're always too ramshackle, we've never been smooth."

In 1993 Clinton aides defined the administration's foreign policy doctrine. National Security Adviser Anthony Lake announced that "the successor to a doctrine of containment must be a strategy of . . . enlargement of the world's free community of market democracies." That had a distinct echo of Woodrow Wilson's dictum: "The world must be made safe for democracy."

One place to expand democratic capitalism was in Russia itself. On this, as on other issues, Clinton continued the Bush administration policy of support for Russian president Boris Yeltsin, a position articulated in Secretary of State Warren Christopher's statement that "helping to consolidate democracy in Russia is not a matter of charity but a security concern of the highest order." Yet American assistance continued to be centered on the exchange of goods, expertise, and training instead of financial assistance. And for want of a better candidate, Clinton stuck with Yeltsin through his brutal invasion of Chechnya, a crime-ridden ethnic region on the Caucasus border with Georgia, to prevent its secession. The struggle dragged on until October 1996, when an agreement was reached to give Chechnya an autonomy that amounted to independence in all but name.

Clinton also continued the Bush policy of sponsoring patient negotiations between Arabs and Israelis. After the Gulf War, an Arab-Israeli Peace Initiative with American and Russian sponsorship led to an ongoing conference in Madrid attended by most Arab countries plus, in a new departure, the Palestine Liberation Organization (PLO), accepted by Israel as part of Jordan's delegation. The meetings were dogged by bloody incidents between Israelis and Palestinians, and interrupted when Israel expelled some 400 Palestinians. But none of the parties deemed it wise to abandon the talks.

On August 30, 1993, word leaked out that secret talks had been going on between Israeli and Palestinian representatives in Oslo, with the Norwegian foreign minister as intermediary. A draft agreement between

Israel and the PLO provided for the restoration of Palestinian self-rule in the occupied Gaza Strip and in Jericho on the West Bank, in an exchange of land for peace as provided in U.N. Security Council resolutions. A formal signing was quickly arranged at the White House where on September 13, with President Clinton presiding, Prime Minister Yitzhak Rabin and PLO leader Yasir Arafat exchanged handshakes and their foreign ministers signed the agreement.

In the aftermath of this dramatic agreement, talks continued by fits and starts, punctuated by violent incidents provoked by extremist Jewish settlers and Palestinian factions. But a movement toward peace seemed to be proceeding deliberately when on October 26, 1994, Israel and the kingdom of Jordan signed an agreement at ceremonies on their border, which were attended by President Clinton. The Middle East peace process suffered a terrible blow in early November 1995, however, when Israeli prime minister Yitzhak Rabin was assassinated at a peace rally in Tel Aviv. The gunman was an Israeli Jewish zealot who resented Rabin's efforts to negotiate with the Palestinians.

Some observers feared that the assassin had killed the peace process as well when seven months later conservative hardliner Benjamin Netanyahu narrowly defeated the U.S.-backed Shimon Peres in the election for a new prime minister. Netanyahu campaigned against the Rabin-Peres peace efforts, arguing that returning land to Arab control endangered Israeli security. In the face of a flurry of suicide bombings conducted by Islamic extremists against Israelis, he promised to slow the peace process, build new Jewish settlements along the West Bank, block the creation of a Palestinian state in the West Bank and Gaza, and retain control of the Golan Heights, captured from Syria in 1967.

Arab leaders responded to Netanyahu's election by threatening to reconsider the concessions they had made over the previous five years. Finally, in October 1998, Clinton brought together Arafat and Netanyahu at Wye Mills, Maryland, and with the ailing King Hussein of Jordan, brokered an agreement whereby Israel would surrender land in return for security guarantees by the Palestinians. As hardliners attempted to derail the tenuous peace, however, stability in the Middle East remained a dream rather than a reality.

Clinton continued the Bush administration's intervention in Somalia, on the northeastern horn of Africa, where collapse of the government early in 1991 had left the country in anarchy, prey to tribal marauders. The televised scenes of starvation horrified American viewers, many of whom demanded action. President Bush in December 1992 had gained U.N. sanction for a military force led by American troops to relieve hunger and restore peace. In January 1993, U.S. troop levels peaked and began to shrink with the arrival of international forces. Clinton inherited this situation. The Somalia operation proved successful at its primary mission, but never solved the political problems that lay at the root of the starvation.

Bush had gone into Somalia in part to counter criticism that he had failed to act decisively in the former Yugoslavia, now a volatile, fractious mixture of warring ethnic groups, chiefly Eastern Orthodox Serbs, Catholic Croats, and Bosnian Muslims. Many of them took pride in how well they got along, but when Yugoslavia imploded in 1991, fanatics and tyrants set out to stir ethnic conflict as four of its six republics seceded. Serb minorities, backed by Serbia itself, stirred up civil wars in Croatia and Bosnia. In Bosnia especially, the war involved "ethnic cleansing"—driving Muslims from their homes and towns—and mass rape of Muslim women. The options facing the United States were sobering: to ignore the butchery, to accept the refugees, to use American airpower, or to risk introducing ground troops.

Once in the White House, Clinton backed off from his hawkish campaign statements about using force in Yugoslavia. Western European countries dispatched "peacekeeping" forces and put an embargo on arms shipments—which favored Serbs who had fallen heir to the equipment of the Yugoslav army. Clinton started with the apparent purpose of acting vigorously, but confronted by European reluctance, he settled for dropping food and medical supplies to besieged Bosnians and sending planes to retaliate a few times for attacks on places designated "safe havens" by the United Nations. Serb forces soon learned that by alternating defiance and parleys, they could avoid any real deterrence except by Bosnian forces.

Despite a cease-fire agreement at the end of 1994, fighting continued in many parts of the faction-ridden country. In September 1995 American negotiators finally convinced the foreign ministers of Croatia, Bosnia, and Yugoslavia to agree to a comprehensive peace plan. Bosnia would remain a single nation but would be divided into two states: a Muslim-Croat federation controlling 51 percent of the territory and a Bosnian Serb republic controlling the remaining 49 percent. Basic human rights would be restored and free elections held to appoint a parliament and joint presidency. To enforce the agreement, 20,000 American troops would be dispatched to Bosnia as part of a 60,000-person NATO peacekeeping operation. A cease-fire went into effect in October, and a final agreement confirming these provisions was signed in Paris in December 1995. Yet in 1998, events seemed to replay yet again, this time in the Yugoslav province of Kosovo, where Serbian-led troops attacked ethnic Albanians and destroyed their villages. Faced with threats of air strikes by NATO, however, some Serbian forces withdrew from Kosovo.

The U.S. Congress had given only grudging support to the use of American forces in the Balkans. "I was opposed" to the Bosnian policy, explained Senator John McCain, an Arizona Republican and Vietnam veteran. "But if the president made a commitment and if we reversed it, it would be a terrible blow to the credibility of the United States."

The most successful new departure in foreign policy for the Clinton administration came in Haiti. The end of the cold war had removed any threat of Soviet infiltration in the Caribbean, and brought a new emphasis on Wilsonian themes of democracy. Haiti had emerged suddenly from a cycle of coups with a rebellion in the army rank and file and a democratic election in 1990, which brought to the top a popular priest, Jean-Bertrand Aristide. Old habits returned, however, when a Haitian army general ousted Aristide. The United States immediately announced its intention to bring back Aristide.

Another new element in the situation was the appearance of thousands of Haitian refugees desperate to reach Florida in leaky wooden boats. Coast Guard vessels began to pick them up and take them back to Haiti or to Guantanamo Bay in Cuba, denying that they were refugees. Public reaction to the flood of new immigrants put the Clinton administration under even greater pressure to resolve the situation.

With drawn-out negotiations leading nowhere, Clinton eventually moved in July 1994 to get a U.N. resolution authorizing force as a last resort. At this juncture, former president Jimmy Carter asked permission to negotiate. He went to Port-au-Prince and convinced the military leaders to quit by October 15. The first American forces were already in the air and landed September 19, without opposition and to a cordial welcome from the people.

Clinton had promised that the bulk of American forces would be quickly withdrawn and replaced by an international force of peacekeepers, and in November the American withdrawal began. Aristide returned to Haiti and on March 31, 1995, the occupation was turned over to a U.N. force commanded by an American general. Only about 2,400 American troops remained to retrain Haitian military and police in orderly procedures. They had a tough assignment, maybe an impossible one, but there was occasion for hope. Aside from Haiti, the status of American foreign policy remained in 1995 without drastic change from that of 1992.

REPUBLICAN INSURGENCY

During 1994, Clinton began to see his presidency unravel. Unable to get either health care reform or welfare reform bills through the Democratic Congress, and having failed to carry out his campaign pledge for middle-class tax relief, he and his party found themselves on the defensive. This opened up opportunities for the Republicans to capture control of Congress.

In the midterm elections of 1994, the Democrats suffered a humbling defeat. It was the first election since 1952 in which Republicans captured both houses of Congress at the same time. In both, the majority was solid: 52–48 in the Senate, a majority that soon increased when two Democrats switched parties, and 230–204 in the House. Not a single Republican incumbent was defeated. Republicans also won a net gain of eleven governorships and fifteen state legislatures. It was a thorough repudiation of the Democratic party, one that occurred in all regions.

There could be little question that the returns signaled a repudiation of Clinton and the Democratic Congress. Squabbling between the president and congressional Democrats did not help matters. Nor did Clinton's response to the Republican takeover of Congress in 1994 endear him to party loyalists. Initially, he and his aides decided to adopt a passive role, letting the Republicans initiate policies and programs and then hoping that they would be decimated by the affected interest groups. He offered no deficit reduction plan, no welfare reform proposal, no new health reform initiative.

Clinton's waffling on major issues began to convince many in his own party that he was a politician rather than a leader, someone who thrived as a campaigner but was bereft of genuine convictions. Said Democratic congressman David Obey: "I think most of us learned some time ago that if you don't like the president's position on a particular issue, you simply need to wait a few weeks." When Clinton joined the chorus of conservatives calling for a scaling back of affirmative action plans designed to remedy historic patterns of racial discrimination in hiring and the awarding of government contracts, liberals felt betrayed.

CONTRACT WITH AMERICA   A Georgian named Newton Leroy Gingrich led the Republican insurgency in Congress. In early 1995 he became the first Republican Speaker of the House in forty-two years. Most of the new Republicans in Congress credited "Newt" Gingrich for their election. In the late 1980s he had launched a series of attacks on the ethics of the Democratic leadership in the House, ultimately leading to the resignation of both Democratic Speaker Jim Wright and Democratic Whip Tony Coelho. Gingrich had also helped mobilize religious and social conservatives associated with the Christian Coalition.

In 1995 Gingrich assaulted the "welfare state" and sought to restore conservative values and principles. He was aided by the freshman Republicans, who came to Washington filled with ardor for Gingrich. More than half of all the House members and more than 60 percent of the Republicans had been first elected in the 1990s. Now the majority in the House, freshman Republicans promoted what Gingrich called the "Contract with America." The ten-point contract outlined an anti-big-government program with less regulation, less conservation, term limits for members of Congress, a line-item veto for the president, welfare reform, and a balanced-budget amendment. New members hailed their electoral victory as a mandate to enact the "Contract."

By April 13, exactly 100 days after taking office, the Republicans had passed twenty-six bills growing out of the Contract with America, and had failed to pass only two: a proposal for an anti-missile ("Star Wars") defense system and term limits for Congress. Nonetheless, twenty-two of these bills did not become law. The four bills that did become law were: a law mandating that all laws applicable to ordinary Americans should also apply to members of Congress; a law in which Congress agreed to stop imposing mandated programs on local and state governments without footing the bill; a large defense spending bill, which Clinton reluctantly accepted, lest Republicans rebel on foreign policy; and a new crime bill providing for stiff penalties for child abuse and pornography. The line-item veto would not pass until a year later.

Thereafter, the much ballyhooed GOP revolution and the "Contract with America" fizzled out. The revolution that Gingrich touted was far too ambitious to carry out in so limited a time, with so slim a majority, and with so little sense of crisis. What is more, many of the Republican freshmen were scornful of compromise and amateurs at the rules of order, and they limited the Speaker's room for maneuver. The Senate rejected many of the bills that had been passed in the House, as senators were less under Gingrich's spell and not party to the Contract with America anyway. And beyond them, a presidential veto stood in the path. Finally, President Clinton shrewdly moved to the political center and co-opted much of the Republican agenda. His distinctive strength—at least in the eyes of his supporters—resided in his agile responsiveness to changing public moods. To Clinton, the Republican victory in the 1994 congressional elections and in the passage of the Contract with America initiatives bore a simple message: he must recapture the political center by radically changing his agenda.

The Republicans' Contract with America succeeded in focusing public and presidential attention on basic questions of governmental philosophy. But Gingrich and other House Republican insurgents had overestimated the public's interest in dismantling the federal government and many of its social programs. To be sure, voters wanted to reduce the size and intrusiveness of the Washington bureaucracy, but they did not want to return to the laissez-faire approach of Calvin Coolidge and Herbert Hoover. By the end of 1995, it seemed clear that Clinton's fortunes were back on the rise as the Gingrich revolution petered out, leaving Gingrich with a bag of unfilled promises and with low ratings in the polls. If the American people had voted a mandate for anything, it may have been a mandate for the status quo. Said one contrite Republican freshman in 1996: "We scared too many people in the last year talking with such revolutionary fervor. I think we showed more guts than brains sometimes."

LEGISLATIVE BREAKTHROUGH   In the late summer of 1996, as lawmakers were preparing to adjourn and participate in the presidential nominating conventions, the 104th Congress broke through its partisan gridlock and passed a flurry of important legislation that President Clinton quickly signed.

Two of the bills increased the minimum wage and broadened access to health insurance. The $4.25 per hour minimum wage was increased by 90¢ over thirteen months. In exchange for their support of the wage increase, Republicans obtained $21 billion in tax cuts over ten years for small businesses. The health care measure, sponsored by Senator Nancy Kassebaum, a Kansas Republican, and Senator Edward Kennedy, a Massachusetts Democrat, allowed workers to keep their insurance coverage even if they changed jobs. The Kennedy-Kassebaum bill also made it harder for insurers to deny coverage to patients with a history of illness.

Even more significant was a comprehensive welfare reform measure that ended the federal government's open-ended guarantee of aid to the poor, a guarantee that had been in place since 1935. The Personal Responsibility and Work Opportunity Act turned over the major federal welfare programs to the states. In exchange, the states would receive federal grants to fund the programs. The bill also limited the amount of time a person could receive welfare benefits funded by federal money and required that at least half of a state's welfare recipients have jobs or be enrolled in job training programs by the year 2002. Those states failing to meet the deadline would have their federal funds cut.

The Republican-sponsored welfare reform legislation passed the Senate by a vote of 74–24. It had the effect of cutting $56 billion over six years from Aid to Families with Dependent Children, food stamps, and other programs, several of which dated back to Franklin Roosevelt's New Deal. In total budgets of about $1.5 trillion, that amounted to less than 1 percent. Senator Patrick Moynihan, the New York Democrat who had been a champion of federal social-welfare programs since the 1960s, predicted that over 3.5 million children would be thrown into poverty as a result of the bill. He and other liberals charged that Clinton was abdicating Democratic social principles in order to gain reelection amid the conservative climate of the times. Democratic senator Christopher Dodd of Connecticut called the president's action "unconscionable."

Clinton and his centrist advisers, however, dismissed such criticisms. With his reelection bid at stake, he was determined to live up to his 1992 campaign pledge to "end welfare as we know it." Clinton also knew that most voters in both parties were eager to see major cuts in federal entitlement programs.

THE 1996 CAMPAIGN   After clinching the Republican nomination in March 1996, Majority Leader Bob Dole resigned his Senate seat in order to devote his attention to defeating Bill Clinton. "I will seek the

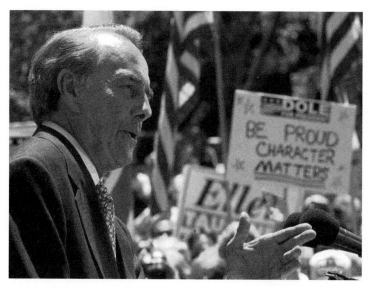

Former Republican Senate Majority Leader Bob Dole on the campaign trail.

presidency," he said, "with nothing to fall back on but the judgment of the people, and nowhere to go but the White House or home."

Born in Kansas in 1923, the product of a hardscrabble existence in a small prairie town, Dole enrolled in the University of Kansas in 1941, only to be drawn into military service during World War II. During a battle in Italy, a piece of shrapnel shattered his right shoulder and fractured his neck. It took thirty-nine months and seven separate operations before he could leave the hospital. His right arm and hand remained permanently paralyzed.

Driven by a gritty determination to succeed despite his physical setback, Dole graduated from college and law school and then entered local politics. By 1960 he was a member of the House of Representatives, and nine years later he gained election to the Senate. In 1976 Dole served as Gerald Ford's running mate, only to return to the Senate after the Carter-Mondale victory. Dole developed a reputation as a brilliant legislative tactician and a tough, smart, and honest leader known for his ability to build consensus and forge coalitions. An unsuccessful candidate for the presidential nomination in 1980 and 1988, Dole was officially nominated at the Republican convention in San Diego in mid-August 1996.

As the 1996 presidential campaign unfolded, Clinton maintained a large lead in the polls. With a generally healthy economy and with no major foreign policy crises to confront, cultural and personal issues surged into prominence. Concern about Dole's age (seventy-three) and his acerbic manner, as well as rifts in the Republican party between economic and social conservatives over issues such as abortion and gun control, hampered Dole's efforts to generate widespread support.

To jump-start his lagging campaign, Dole announced a surprise choice for his running mate: Jack Kemp, the former pro football star for the Buffalo Bills, a congressman, secretary of Housing and Urban Development under Bush, and presidential candidate himself. On economic issues, Kemp and Dole had been poles apart. Dole represented the Eisenhower wing of the Republican party in promoting deficit reduction and a balanced budget. Kemp was a Reaganite in his commitment to supply-side economic theory and large tax cuts. Yet Dole now embraced not only Kemp but his economics, proposing a 15 percent income tax cut across the board coupled with increased tax credits for dependent children and capital gains tax cuts and a balanced budget. This program assumed that people would spend the estimated $600 billion from tax cuts over the next six years and thereby generate record economic growth that in turn would raise tax revenues.

Clinton scorned Dole's tax cut and responded with smaller targeted tax reductions. Democrats claimed that Republicans wanted to "pay for" the tax cut with cuts in Medicare. Republicans had come to rely heavily on cultural issues, largely under the rubric of "family values," but Clinton had co-opted much of that with his Family and Medical Leave Act, student loans, and increase in the minimum wage.

Late in the campaign, Dole charged that the Democrats had raised unprecedented sums of money by dubious means. The role of people with foreign connections in the fund-raising even gave rise to suspicions that money from abroad had found its way into Democratic accounts. Yet while Clinton excited extreme animosity in his enemies, he was also like Reagan, the "Teflon president," to whom none of their charges stuck. The polls favored Clinton so heavily that a pall of depression seemed to fall over the Dole campaign.

On November 5 Clinton won again with an electoral vote of 379 to 159 and 49 percent of the popular vote. He lost Georgia, Colorado, and Montana, but added Arizona and Florida to his column. Dole received

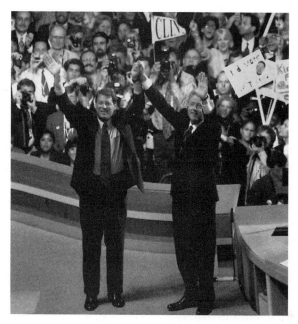

*President Bill Clinton and Vice-President Al Gore at
the 1996 Democratic National Convention in
Chicago.*

41 percent and Perot got 8 percent of the popular vote. Thus Clinton
would remain a minority president, and once again he would be denied
a Democratic majority in Congress. The Republicans lost eight seats in
the House, but suspicions of Democratic money scandals may have
helped them hold control of Congress. They held a 227–207 edge over
the Democrats in the House; in the Senate Republicans gained two
seats for a 55–45 majority. The resulting deadlock reflected the conservative mood of the times.

CLINTON'S SECOND TERM

After the election, Clinton reshuffled his cabinet and other posts.
Madeleine Albright, ambassador to the United Nations, became the
first woman to head the State Department, and Senator William Cohen, a Republican from Maine, took over at the Defense Department.
The overall direction of his changes was a move to the right.

THE "NEW ECONOMY" As the twentieth century comes to a close, the United States has benefited from a prolonged period of unprecedented prosperity. Buoyed by low inflation, high employment, declining federal budget deficits, dramatic improvements in productivity, the rapid "globalization" of economic life, and the firm and astute leadership of Federal Reserve Board Chairman Alan Greenspan, American business and industry have witnessed record profits.

The stock market soared during the late 1990s. In 1993 the Dow Jones industrial average hit 3,500. By 1996 it had topped 6,000. During 1998, it reached 9,000, defying the predictions of experts that the economy could not sustain such performance. In 1998 unemployment was only 4.3 percent, the lowest since 1970. Inflation was a measly 1.7 percent. "The current economic performance," observed Greenspan, ". . . is as impressive as any I have witnessed." He and others began to talk of a "new economy" that defied the boom-and-bust cycles of the previous hundred years. "It is possible," Greenspan suggested, "that we have moved 'beyond history.' "

By 1998 swelling tax revenues generated a federal budget surplus. Such sustained prosperity seemed to support the "monetarist" philosophy of the Nobel Prize–winning economist Professor Milton Friedman. Keynesian economics, which had emerged against the background of deflation and prolonged depression in the 1930s, had favored fiscal remedies (deficit spending) to stimulate economic growth. Monetarists such as Friedman believed that economic growth would best be promoted by a stable monetary supply (cash plus bank accounts), and they feared inflation more than unemployment. To them, the key to economic stability was the Federal Reserve's power to regulate interest rates.

Before President Clinton took office, he was persuaded to support Greenspan's monetarist policies and was convinced that a balanced budget was necessary to keep government borrowing from putting inflationary pressure on interest rates. Clinton chose to reduce deficits in part by spending cuts, in part by a tax hike on upper income brackets. At the same time, he abandoned promised tax cuts for middle income brackets. His supporters claimed, however, that he had put the country on the way to a balanced budget and financial stability.

In the past, invention and innovation had been basic to economic booms. Much of this had been in electronics, ever since the transistor replaced the vacuum tube in 1947 and created the television revolution at mid-century. Yet, in the 1990s, much of the surging economy resulted from "globalization." The "new" classical economics of Friedman and Greenspan favored free markets on a world scale—markets without tariffs and other barriers. More and more gigantic corporations such as International Business Machines or General Electric had become international in scope. This encouraged free trade agreements such as NAFTA or most-favored-nation treatment for China and other countries. American companies might then "outsource" much of their production to plants in countries with lower labor costs. This led to a decline of the labor union movement and to corporate moves toward "downsizing," which worked wonders with stock prices, whether or not it served business efficiency. Blue-collar labor lost ground to cheap labor in assembly plants or "sweatshops" elsewhere in the world. Part-time labor became popular because employers could avoid paying for expensive benefits—whether for flipping hamburgers or for teaching. At the same time, it became notorious for chief executives to win extravagant rewards for downsizing workers, even for sheer arrogance, it sometimes seemed, as in the case of Albert J. Dunlop, a.k.a. "Chain Saw Al," "the Shredder," "Rambo in Pinstripes."

RACE INITIATIVE   Since the triumphs of the civil rights movement in the 1960s, the momentum for minority advancement had run out—except for gains in college admissions and employment under the rubric of "affirmative action." The principle of affirmative action, as stated by President Lyndon Johnson in 1965, involved an effort to overcome the effects of past discrimination. "We seek not just equality as a right and theory," Johnson said, "but equality as a fact and equality as a result." Affirmative action covered a variety of devices, but mainly involved the inclusion of race among other criteria for jobs and admissions. Such measures were extended under Richard Nixon.

Despite moves by Reagan and Bush staff members to limit such measures, the outcry from minority leaders caused both administrations to back away from outright opposition to affirmative action. The Supreme Court, as well, accepted such measures, including voluntary programs of corporations and other institutions. Race could be a factor among others, but racial quotas were ruled out.

In the 1980s and 1990s, however, the outlook of the federal courts began to shift to the right. The conservative mood during the mid-

1990s also manifested itself in the Supreme Court. One consequence was a challenge to the legality of gerrymandering (redrawing) congressional and legislative districts to create black or Hispanic majorities. Minorities had favored gerrymandering to increase minority officeholding, and Republicans had favored it because such districts would draw minority votes from other districts. But in *Thaw* v. *Reno* (1993), the Court ruled that such districts in North Carolina violated equal protection of the law.

In 1995, a conservative Court again ruled against election districts redrawn to create black or Hispanic majorities, narrowed federal affirmative action programs, and limited the legal remedies for segregated public schools. All were decided by the same vote of 5–4 (Chief Justice Rehnquist, and Justices Kennedy, O'Connor, Scalia, and Thomas deciding against Justices Breyer, Ginsburg, Souter, and Stevens).

In one of the cases, *Adarand Constructors* v. *Peña* (1995), the Court assessed a program that gave some advantages to businesses owned by "disadvantaged" minorities. An Hispanic-owned firm had won a highway guard rail contract over a lower bid by a white-owned company. The white-owned company sued on the ground of "reverse discrimination." For the majority, Justice O'Connor said that such programs had to be "narrowly tailored" to serve a "compelling national interest." O'Connor did not define what the Court meant by a "compelling national interest," but the implication of her language was clear: the Court had come to embrace the growing public suspicion of the value and legality of such race-based programs.

Conservatives found a new battle cry in "racial preferences." In the area of college admissions, especially, this would mean falling back on such criteria as scores on the Scholastic Aptitude Test (SAT), high school grades, and special consideration for children of alumni or those talented at playing the oboe or basketball—none of which is above suspicion of racial bias one way or the other.

In 1996 two major new steps were taken against affirmative action in college admissions. In *Hopwood* v. *Texas* (1996), the Fifth Circuit Court ruled that considering race to achieve a diverse student body at the University of Texas was "not a compelling interest under the Fourteenth Amendment." In November, the state of California, while voting for Clinton, also passed Proposition 209, an initiative that ruled out race, sex, ethnicity, or national origin as criteria for preferring any group.

These rulings eviscerated affirmative action programs and drastically reduced black enrollments, something that caused second thoughts. In Texas, for instance, a new state law guaranteed admission to the state university for 10 percent of any high school class—some argued for high school grades as a better predictor of college performance than SAT scores—and in Houston voters rejected a proposition to abandon an affirmative action program adopted by the city.

Programs of affirmative action, which had gained widespread acceptance over a quarter of a century, remained under siege. And affirmative action still did not address intractable problems that lay beyond civil rights, that is, problems of dependency—illiteracy, poverty, unemployment, urban decay, and slums.

THE SCANDAL MACHINE   Since before his first election in 1992, Clinton had faced allegations of both sexual and financial scandal that grew into a relentless inquiry such as no previous president had ever before encountered. In the 1970s, the Watergate scandal had provoked the Ethics in Government Act of 1978, which created an office of "special prosecutor" (renamed "independent counsel" in 1988) to investigate allegations against high officials in the government. The law, renewed in 1982 and 1988, was allowed to lapse in 1992, but it was renewed early in 1994.

During his first term, Clinton was dogged by allegations of improper involvement in the Whitewater Development Company. In 1978, as governor of Arkansas, he had invested in a resort project on the White River in northern Arkansas. The project turned out to be a fraud and a failure, and the Clintons took a loss on their investment. James MacDougal, the promoter of the project, also took over a small savings and loan, Madison Guaranty, and turned it into one of the go-go ventures of the flush years of wildcat banking in the 1980s. It collapsed in 1989, but in the fall of 1993, reports surfaced that Madison money had gone into the foundering Whitewater project and that Madison Guaranty had misused funds in the Clinton campaign. Robert Fiske was named as independent counsel to investigate the allegations of improper Clinton involvement in Whitewater. While revealing that Hillary Clinton had handled some legal work for the Whitewater Development Company, Fiske did not uncover evidence that the Clintons were involved in the fraud.

The ongoing Whitewater investigation threatened to derail important initiatives as it occupied the attention of the president and Congress.

In 1994, Fiske was replaced with another Republican independent counsel, Kenneth Starr, who continued to investigate the Whitewater case. Although Starr had a reputation for fairness, many believed that his unwillingness to end the investigation and his former subcabinet position in the Bush administration suggested a taint of partisanship. After nearly four years of expensive investigation, Starr found no criminal involvement by the Clintons, although a number of their close associates had been caught in the web and convicted of various charges, some related to Whitewater and some not.

The office of independent counsel, created to insure investigations free from conflict of interest, instead contributed to a political culture of scandal. Every president after Nixon saw at least one of his subordinates, if not himself, under criminal investigation. By early 1998, some $50 million had been spent investigating Clinton and his administration. Besides Whitewater, these investigators looked into Paula Jones's allegations that Clinton had sexually harassed her while he was governor and she was a state employee in Arkansas. Clinton's lawyers sought postponement of the Paula Jones case until 2001 on the principle that such spiteful actions against a sitting president could foster enough lawsuits to disable the presidency. But in May 1997 the Supreme Court unanimously dismissed that claim. Clinton's lawyers then sought to invoke executive privilege to prevent the questioning of aides and secret service personnel, but that too was rejected by the Court.

In the course of the investigation, it surfaced that the president may have had a sexual affair with a former White House intern, Monica Lewinsky, and may have pressed her to lie about it under oath. The public was titillated by the initial allegations of the alleged affair as expressed by Lewinsky in phone conversations that a coworker had taped without her knowledge. By the spring of 1998, some Republicans in Congress were even discussing the possibility of impeachment proceedings. Meanwhile, the Paula Jones case was dismissed by a judge in Arkansas on the ground that, even if everything charged against the president were true, Paula Jones still did not have a legal claim to sexual harassment under the law, which required that the claimant must have suffered discrimination in her employment. At the same time, polls suggested that a majority did not care whether Clinton had had an affair with Lewinsky. This seemed to imply the public's contentment with the way things were going, especially the soaring economy—and perhaps a wish that the scandal would simply go away and not become a constitutional crisis.

But the tawdry scandal would not disappear. In August 1998, in the face of a possible subpoena from the independent counsel, President Clinton agreed to testify before the grand jury investigating the allegations about him. He was the first president in history to do so. On August 17, with the nation anxiously awaiting the results, the federal grand jury watched on closed-circuit television while Clinton testified using a video hookup from the White House. During his six hours of closed-door testimony, the president recanted his earlier denials and acknowledged having had "inappropriate intimate physical contact" with White House intern Monica Lewinsky.

That evening Clinton delivered a four-minute televised address to the nation in which he admitted that he did, in fact, have an inappropriate and "wrong" relationship with Lewinsky, but insisted he had done nothing illegal. "I know that my public comments and my silence about this matter gave a false impression. I misled people, including even my wife," Clinton said. "I deeply regret that."

Clinton's admission was a stunning reversal from his insistent public denials over the previous seven months. His dishonesty, he explained, was motivated by a desire to protect his family and "myself from the embarrassment of my own conduct." Had Clinton stopped there, he might have avoided much of the angry criticism that greeted his disclosure. But he went on to attack the "politically inspired" investigation.

Public reaction to Clinton's remarkable about-face was mixed. A majority of Americans expressed sympathy for the president because of his public humiliation and wanted the entire matter dropped. But polls also showed that Clinton's credibility had suffered a serious blow.

Meanwhile, Starr continued his tenacious investigation, trying to determine if Clinton had obstructed the investigation and had encouraged Lewinsky to lie about their affair. On September 9, 1998, Starr submitted to Congress his 445-page report and eighteen boxes of supporting evidence. The report found "substantial and credible" evidence of wrongdoing by the president. The Republican-controlled House Judiciary Committee voted to recommend a full impeachment inquiry into perjury and obstruction of justice allegations against Clinton, and on October 8, the House of Representatives voted 258–176 to begin the inquiry. Yet, with a surprisingly strong Democratic showing in the November elections, the Republicans found their majority in Congress eroded, perhaps as a result of public disgust with the continuing investigation. Republican dismay at their losses prompted Speaker of the House Newt Gingrich to resign. He announced that he could no longer effectively lead congressional Republicans. As House Judiciary Committee hearings got underway in the late fall, the fate of the Clinton presidency still hung in the balance.

Fin-de-Siècle America

The approach of the year 2000 has prompted contradictory reflections upon American life at the end of a millennium and the start of the twenty-first century. As at the close of the last century, referred to as the *fin-de-siècle* (a French term for "end of the century"), many people are celebrating the unprecedented prosperity and amazing technological breakthroughs of the times. But, as in 1900, other observers are more gloomy. Skeptical of material notions of perpetual progress and worried about the cohesion of an increasingly diverse population, they have expressed an anxious foreboding about societal dissolution and decay.

As the twentieth century draws to a close, the United States seems to be experiencing the best and worst of times. The economy remains on the crest of a wave of record-setting productivity and profits, inflation is dormant, and the federal government is enjoying balanced budgets for the first time in over a generation. The cold war is over, the nuclear arms race has ended, and the digital revolution is in full swing. Americans are enjoying their personal freedoms, their cornucopia of consumer goods, and their sophisticated technologies. They are also living longer than ever.

Yet a *Times Mirror* survey portrays a prosperous nation awash in anxiety and self-doubt, with some 73 percent of Americans expressing dissatisfaction with "the way things are going." Soaring rates of teenage drug use, violence, and suicide provide conspicuous evidence of social problems. Moreover, people express growing concern about job security and job-related stress, rising health care costs, the adequacy of savings for college and retirement, and turmoil in the world economy—especially Asia and South America—and the resulting tremors in the American stock market, which threaten the stability of the U.S. economy. New technologies are improving productivity and efficiency, but many people are working harder and longer than ever before to keep up with the "wired" workplace and a culture of rising expectations.

The most acute concern is the ability of our multicultural society to get along in the midst of our seductive freedoms. Seemingly intractable issues threaten to unravel the social fabric. Religious, racial, and ethnic-related tensions are growing, and the gap between rich and poor is widening. Our obsession with individual rights is eroding our ability to behave socially. In-your-face confrontation, narrow group loyalties, and bipartisan moral arrogance have displaced respectful dialogue and civic virtue. As the perceptive cartoonist Walt Kelly once observed in his Pogo comic strip, "We have met the enemy and he is us."

Some cultural analysts worry that the ferocious, take-no-prisoners nature of public discourse and political campaigns is undermining the consensus needed for democracy to work. Divisive issues such as abortion, gun control, doctor-assisted suicide, affirmative action, prayer in schools, political correctness, and gay rights, to name a few, have fostered a special-interest sectarianism that has disrupted and divided communities, political parties, and churches.

In 1995 Harvard political scientist Robert Putnam addressed such issues in a provocative essay entitled "Bowling Alone: The Decline of Social Capital" in which he declared that the "social fabric is becoming visibly thinner, our connections among each other are becoming visibly thinner. We don't trust one another as much, and we don't know one another as much. And, of course, this is behind the deterioration of the political dialogue, the deterioration of public debate." Putnam highlighted plummeting membership in organizations such as the PTA, Red Cross, Boy Scouts, and the League of Women Voters, as well as civic clubs and labor unions. He blamed such declining civic involvement on many aspects of popular culture—television, VCRs, and personal computers—for distracting people from their social responsibilities. Technological change, Putnam noted, is privatizing leisure time by promoting solitary forms of entertainment.

But Putnam's influential thesis overlooks contrary evidence of civic energy and social interaction. Today Americans engage with each other in many different forms of association. Voluntarism is soaring, as are other group activities. Youth soccer leagues and spectator sports, fitness centers and social clubs, for instance, are examples of popular culture activities that generate a shared discourse and bring people together.

Yet more needs to be done to strengthen the social fabric. "Our greatest responsibility," said President Clinton in his second inaugural address, "is to embrace a new spirit of community for a new century." It is an old ideal. In 1630 Governor John Winthrop told the Puritan colonists settling near Boston that "We must delight in each other, make others' conditions our own, rejoice together, mourn together, labor and suffer together, having always before our eyes our community as members of the same body." *E pluribus unum*—one out of many. At the start of a new century, it remains the best definition of what the unique American experiment in self-government means. It also remains America's greatest hope—and its greatest challenge.

FURTHER READING

On the Bush presidency, see Ryan J. Barilleaux and Mary E. Stuckey's *Leadership and the Bush Presidency: Prudence or Drift in an Era of Change* (1992), Charles Tiefer's *The Semi-Sovereign Presidency: The Bush Administration's Strategy for Governing without Congress* (1994). Among the journalistic accounts of the presidential election of 1992, the best narrative is Jack Germond and Jules Witcover's *Mad as Hell: Revolt at the Ballot Box, 1992* (1993). The best scholarly study is Theodore J. Lowi and Benjamin Ginsberg's *Democrats Return to Power: Politics and Policy in the Clinton Era* (1994).

On Bill Clinton, up to his presidency, the best treatment is David Maraniss's *First in His Class: A Biography of Bill Clinton* (1995). The early months of the Clinton presidency are most thoroughly covered in Elizabeth Drew's *On the Edge: The Clinton Presidency* (1994). Bob Woodward's *The Agenda: Inside the Clinton White House* (1994) focuses on financial policies and the economy. For a psychoanalytic assessment of Clinton, see Stanley A. Renshon's *High Hopes: The Clinton Presidency and the Politics of Ambition* (1996). Recent analysis of the Clinton years can be found in *The Clinton Presidency: First Appraisals* (1995), edited by Colin Campbell and Bert A. Rockman, and *Back to Gridlock?: Governance in the Clinton Years* (1996), edited by James L. Sundquist. For a Republican perspective, see Haley Barbour's *Agenda for America: A Republican Direction for the Future* (1996).

On social and cultural problems and issues of the times, a good account is Haynes Johnson's *Divided We Fall: Gambling with History in the Nineties* (1994), based on street interviews around the country during 1992. Collections of magazine and newspaper articles are in John Leo's *Two Steps Ahead of the Thought Police* (1994), Molly Ivins's *Nothin' But Good Times Ahead* (1993), and George F. Will's *The Leveling Wind: Politics, the Culture, and Other News, 1990–1994* (1994). The onset and growth of the AIDS epidemic are traced in *And the Band Played On: Politics, People, and the AIDS Epidemic* (1987) by Randy Shilts, a journalist who reported much of the story, and in essays edited by historians Elizabeth Fee and Daniel M. Fox, *AIDS: The Burdens of History* (1988) and *AIDS: The Making of a Chronic Disease* (1992).

Aspects of fundamentalist and apocalyptic movements are the subject of Paul L. Boyer's *When Time Shall Be No More: Prophecy and Belief in Modern American Culture* (1992), George M. Marsden's *Understanding Fundamentalism and Evangelicalism* (1991), and Ralph Reed's *Politically Incorrect: The Emerging Faith Factor in American Politics* (1994).

Aspects of recent cultural debates can be found in *Culture Wars: Documents from the Recent Controversies in the Arts* (1992), edited by Richard Bolton; Gerald Graff's *Beyond the Culture Wars: How Teaching* the *Conflicts Can Revitalize American Education* (1992); and *The Politics of Liberal Education* (1992), edited by Darryl Gless and Barbara Herrnstein Smith.

On the banking and other scandals, see L. William Seidman's *Full Faith and Credit: The Great S & L Debacle and Other Washington Sagas* (1993). Aspects of corporate restructuring and downsizing are the subject of Bennett Harrison's *Lean and Mean: The Changing Landscape of Corporate Power in the Age of Flexibility* (1994). The story of the Whitewater affair is the subject of Martin L. Gross's *The Great Whitewater Fiasco: An American Tale of Money, Power, and Politics* (1994).

For further treatment of the end of the cold war, see Michael R. Beschloss's *At the Highest Levels: The Inside Story of the End of the Cold War* (1993), Thomas J. McCormick's *America's Half Century: United States Foreign Policy in the Cold War and After* (2nd ed., 1995), Richard Crockatt's *The Fifty Years War: The United States and the Soviet Union in World Politics, 1941–1991* (1995), and Zbigniew Brzezinski's *Out of Control: Global Turmoil on the Eve of the Twenty-first Century* (1994). On the Panama and Persion Gulf conflicts, see Edward W. Flanagan's *Battle for Panama: Inside Operation Just Cause* (1993), Bruce W. Jentleson's *With Friends Like These: Reagan, Bush, and Saddam, 1982–1990* (1994), and Lester H. Brune's *America and the Iraqi Crisis, 1990–1992: Origins and Aftermath* (1993).

APPENDIX

THE DECLARATION
OF INDEPENDENCE

WHEN IN THE COURSE OF HUMAN EVENTS, it becomes necessary for one people to dissolve the political bands which have connected them with another, and to assume the Powers of the earth, the separate and equal station to which the Laws of Nature and of Nature's God entitle them, a decent respect to the opinions of mankind requires that they should declare the causes which impel them to the separation.

We hold these truths to be self-evident, that all men are created equal, that they are endowed by their Creator with certain unalienable rights, that among these are Life, Liberty, and the pursuit of Happiness. That to secure these rights, Governments are instituted among Men, deriving their just powers from the consent of the governed. That whenever any Form of Government becomes destructive of these ends, it is the Right of the People to alter or to abolish it, and to institute new Government, laying its foundation on such principles and organizing its powers in such form, as to them shall seem most likely to effect their Safety and Happiness. Prudence, indeed, will dictate that Governments long established should not be changed for light and transient causes; and accordingly all experience hath shown, that mankind are more disposed to suffer, while evils are sufferable, than to right themselves by abolishing the forms to which they are accustomed. But when a long train of abuses and usurpations, pursuing invariably the same Object evinces a design to reduce them under absolute Despotism, it is their right, it is their duty, to throw off such Government, and to provide new Guards for their future security.— Such has been the patient sufferance of these Colonies; and such is now the necessity which constrains them to alter their former Systems of Government. The history of the present King of Great Britain is a history of repeated injuries and usurpations, all having in direct object the establishment of an absolute Tyranny over these States. To prove this, let Facts be submitted to a candid world.

He has refused his Assent to Laws, the most wholesome and necessary for the public good.

He has forbidden his Governors to pass Laws of immediate and pressing importance, unless suspended in their operation till his Assent should be obtained; and when so suspended, he has utterly neglected to attend to them.

He has refused to pass other Laws for the accommodation of large districts of people, unless those people would relinquish the right of Representation in the Legislature, a right inestimable to them and formidable to tyrants only.

He has called together legislative bodies at places unusual, uncomfortable, and distant from the depository of their public Records, for the sole purpose of fatiguing them into compliance with his measures.

He has dissolved Representative Houses repeatedly, for opposing with manly firmness his invasions on the rights of the people.

He has refused for a long time, after such dissolutions, to cause others to be elected; whereby the Legislative powers, incapable of Annihilation, have returned to the People at large for their exercise; the State remaining in the mean time exposed to all dangers of invasion from without, and convulsions within.

He has endeavoured to prevent the population of these States; for that purpose obstructing the Laws of Naturalization of Foreigners; refusing to pass others to encourage their migrations hither, and raising the conditions of new Appropriations of Lands.

He has obstructed the Administration of Justice, by refusing his Assent to Laws for establishing Judiciary powers.

He has made Judges dependent on his Will alone, for the tenure of their offices, and the amount and payment of their salaries.

He has erected a multitude of New Offices, and sent hither swarms of Officers to harass our People, and eat out their substance.

He has kept among us, in times of peace, Standing Armies without the Consent of our legislatures.

He has affected to render the Military independent of and superior to the Civil Power.

He has combined with others to subject us to a jurisdiction foreign to our constitution, and unacknowledged by our laws; giving his Assent to their Acts of pretended Legislation:

For quartering large bodies of armed troops among us:

For protecting them, by a mock Trial, from Punishment for any Murders which they should commit on the Inhabitants of these States:

For cutting off our Trade with all parts of the world:

For imposing taxes on us without our Consent:

For depriving us in many cases, of the benefits of Trial by jury:

For transporting us beyond Seas to be tried for pretended offences:

For abolishing the free System of English Laws in a neighbouring Province, establishing therein an Arbitrary government, and enlarging its Boundaries so as to render it at once an example and fit instrument for introducing the same absolute rule into these Colonies:

For taking away our Charters, abolishing our most valuable Laws, and altering fundamentally the Forms of our Governments:

For suspending our own Legislatures, and declaring themselves in vested with Power to legislate for us in all cases whatsoever.

He has abdicated Government here, by declaring us out of his Protection and waging War against us.

He has plundered our seas, ravaged our Coasts, burnt our towns, and destroyed the lives of our people.

He is at this time transporting large armies of foreign mercenaries to compleat the works of death, desolation, and tyranny, already begun with circumstances of Cruelty & perfidy scarcely paralleled in the most barbarous ages, and totally unworthy the Head of a civilized nation.

He has constrained our fellow Citizens taken Captive on the high Seas to bear Arms against their Country, to become the executioners of their friends and Brethren, or to fall themselves by their Hands.

He has excited domestic insurrections amongst us, and has endeavoured to bring on the inhabitants of our frontiers, the merciless Indian Savages, whose known rule of warfare, is an undistinguished destruction of all ages, sexes, and conditions.

In every stage of these Oppressions We have Petitioned for Redress in the most humble terms: Our repeated Petitions have been answered only by repeated injury. A Prince, whose character is thus marked by every act which may define a Tyrant, is unfit to be the ruler of a free people.

Nor have We been wanting in attention to our British brethren. We have warned them from time to time of attempts by their legislature to extend an unwarrantable jurisdiction over us. We have reminded them of the circumstances of our emigration and settlement here. We have appealed to their native justice and magnanimity, and we have conjured them by the ties of our common kindred to disavow these usurpations, which, would inevitably interrupt our connections and correspondence. They too must have been deaf to the voice of justice and of consanguinity. We must, therefore, acquiesce in the necessity, which denounces our Separation, and hold them, as we hold the rest of mankind, Enemies in War, in Peace Friends.

WE, THEREFORE, the Representatives of the UNITED STATES OF AMERICA, in General Congress, Assembled, appealing to the Supreme Judge of the world for the rectitude of our intentions, do, in the Name, and by Authority of the good People of these Colonies, solemnly publish and declare, That these United Colonies are, and of Right ought to be FREE AND INDEPENDENT STATES; that they are Absolved from all Allegiance to the British

Crown, and that all political connection between them and the State of Great Britain, is and ought to be totally dissolved; and that as Free and Independent States, they have full Power to levy War, conclude Peace, contract Alliances, establish Commerce, and to do all other Acts and Things which Independent States may of right do. And for the support of this Declaration, with a firm reliance on the Protection of Divine Providence, we mutually pledge to each other our Lives, our Fortunes, and our sacred Honor.

The foregoing Declaration was, by order of Congress, engrossed, and signed by the following members:

John Hancock

NEW HAMPSHIRE
Josiah Bartlett
William Whipple
Matthew Thornton

MASSACHUSETTS BAY
Samuel Adams
John Adams
Robert Treat Paine
Elbridge Gerry

RHODE ISLAND
Stephen Hopkins
William Ellery

CONNECTICUT
Roger Sherman
Samuel Huntington
William Williams
Oliver Wolcott

NEW YORK
William Floyd
Philip Livingston
Francis Lewis
Lewis Morris

NEW JERSEY
Richard Stockton
John Witherspoon
Francis Hopkinson
John Hart
Abraham Clark

PENNSYLVANIA
Robert Morris
Benjamin Rush
Benjamin Franklin
John Morton
George Clymer
James Smith
George Taylor
James Wilson
George Ross

DELAWARE
Caesar Rodney
George Read
Thomas M'Kean

MARYLAND
Samuel Chase
William Paca
Thomas Stone
*Charles Carroll, of
  Carrollton*

VIRGINIA
George Wythe
Richard Henry Lee
Thomas Jefferson
Benjamin Harrison
Thomas Nelson, Jr.
Francis Lightfoot Lee
Carter Braxton

NORTH CAROLINA
William Hooper
Joseph Hewes
John Penn

SOUTH CAROLINA
Edward Rutledge
Thomas Heyward, Jr.
Thomas Lynch, Jr.
Arthur Middleton

GEORGIA
Button Gwinnett
Lyman Hall
George Walton

Resolved, That copies of the Declaration be sent to the several assemblies, conventions, and committees, or councils of safety, and to the several commanding officers of the continental troops; that it be proclaimed in each of the United States, at the head of the army.

ARTICLES OF
CONFEDERATION

To all to whom these Presents shall come, we the undersigned Delegates of the States affixed to our Names send greeting.

Whereas the Delegates of the United States of America in Congress assembled did on the fifteenth day of November in the Year of our Lord One Thousand Seven Hundred and Seventy-seven, and in the Second Year of the Independence of America agree to certain articles of Confederation and perpetual Union between the States of Newhampshire, Massachusetts-bay, Rhodeisland and Providence Plantations, Connecticut, New York, New Jersey, Pennsylvania, Delaware, Maryland, Virginia, North-Carolina, South-Carolina and Georgia in the Words following, viz.

Articles of Confederation and perpetual Union between the States of Newhampshire, Massachusetts-bay, Rhodeisland and Providence Plantations, Connecticut, New-York, New-Jersey, Pennsylvania, Delaware, Maryland, Virginia, North-Carolina, South-Carolina and Georgia.

Article I. The stile of this confederacy shall be "The United States of America."

Article II. Each State retains its sovereignty, freedom and independence, and every power, jurisdiction and right, which is not by this confederation expressly delegated to the United States, in Congress assembled.

Article III. The said States hereby severally enter into a firm league of friendship with each other, for their common defence, the security of their liberties, and their mutual and general welfare, binding themselves to assist each other, against all force offered to, or attacks made upon them, or any of them, on account of religion, sovereignty, trade or any other pretence whatever.

ARTICLE IV. The better to secure and perpetuate mutual friendship and intercourse among the people of the different States in this Union, the free inhabitants of each of these States, paupers, vagabonds and fugitives from justice excepted, shall be entitled to all privileges and immunities of free citizens in the several States; and the people of each State shall have free ingress and regress to and from any other State, and shall enjoy therein all the privileges of trade and commerce, subject to the same duties, impositions and restrictions as the inhabitants thereof respectively, provided that such restrictions shall not extend so far as to prevent the removal of property imported into any State, to any other State of which the owner is an inhabitant; provided also that no imposition, duties or restriction shall be laid by any State, on the property of the United States, or either of them.

If any person guilty of, or charged with treason, felony, or other high misdemeanor in any State, shall flee from justice, and be found in any of the United States, he shall upon demand of the Governor or Executive power, of the State from which he fled, be delivered up and removed to the State having jurisdiction of his offence.

Full faith and credit shall be given in each of these States to the records, acts and judicial proceedings of the courts and magistrates of every other State.

ARTICLE V. For the more convenient management of the general interests of the United States, delegates shall be annually appointed in such manner as the legislature of each State shall direct, to meet in Congress on the first Monday in November, in every year, with a power reserved to each State, to recall its delegates, or any of them, at any time within the year, and to send others in their stead, for the remainder of the year.

No State shall be represented in Congress by less than two, nor by more than seven members; and no person shall be capable of being a delegate for more than three years in any term of six years; nor shall any person, being a delegate, be capable of holding any office under the United States, for which he, or another for his benefit receives any salary, fees or emolument of any kind.

Each State shall maintain its own delegates in a meeting of the States, and while they act as members of the committee of the States.

In determining questions in the United States, in Congress assembled, each State shall have one vote.

Freedom of speech and debate in Congress shall not be impeached or questioned in any court, or place out of Congress, and the members of Congress shall be protected in their persons from arrests and imprisonments, during the time of their going to and from, and attendance on Congress, except for treason, felony, or breach of the peace.

ARTICLE VI. No State without the consent of the United States in Congress assembled, shall send any embassy to, or receive any embassy from, or enter into any conference, agreement, alliance or treaty with any king, prince or state; nor shall any person holding any office of profit or trust under the United States, or any of them, accept of any present, emolument, office or title of any kind whatever from any king, prince or foreign state; nor shall the United States in Congress assembled, or any of them, grant any title of nobility.

No two or more States shall enter into any treaty, confederation or alliance whatever between them, without the consent of the United States in Congress assembled, specifying accurately the purposes for which the same is to be entered into, and how long it shall continue.

No State shall lay any imposts or duties, which may interfere with any stipulations in treaties, entered into by the United States in Congress assembled, with any king, prince or state, in pursuance of any treaties already proposed by Congress, to the courts of France and Spain.

No vessels of war shall be kept up in time of peace by any State, except such number only, as shall be deemed necessary by the United States in Congress assembled, for the defence of such State, or its trade; nor shall any body of forces be kept up by any State, in time of peace, except such number only, as in the judgment of the United States, in Congress assembled, shall be deemed requisite to garrison the forts necessary for the defence of such State; but every State shall always keep up a well regulated and disciplined militia, sufficiently armed and accoutred, and shall provide and constantly have ready for use, in public stores, a due number of field pieces and tents, and a proper quantity of arms, ammunition and camp equipage.

No State shall engage in any war without the consent of the United States in Congress assembled, unless such State be actually invaded by enemies, or shall have received certain advice of a resolution being formed by some nation of Indians to invade such State, and the danger is so imminent as not to admit of a delay, till the United States in Congress assembled can be consulted: nor shall any State grant commissions to any ships or vessels of war, nor letters of marque or reprisal, except it be after a declaration of war by the United States in Congress assembled, and then only against the kingdom or state and the subjects thereof, against which war has been so declared, and under such regulations as shall be established by the United States in Congress assembled, unless such State be infested by pirates, in which case vessels of war may be fitted out for that occasion, and kept so long as the danger shall continue, or until the United States in Congress assembled shall determine otherwise.

ARTICLE VII. When land-forces are raised by any State of the common defence, all officers of or under the rank of colonel, shall be appointed by the

Legislature of each State respectively by whom such forces shall be raised, or in such manner as such State shall direct, and all vacancies shall be filled up by the State which first made the appointment.

ARTICLE VIII. All charges of war, and all other expenses that shall be incurred for the common defence or general welfare, and allowed by the United States in Congress assembled, shall be defrayed out of a common treasury, which shall be supplied by the several States, in proportion to the value of all land within each State, granted to or surveyed for any person, as such land and the buildings and improvements thereon shall be estimated according to such mode as the United States in Congress assembled, shall from time to time direct and appoint.

The taxes for paying that proportion shall be laid and levied by the authority and direction of the Legislatures of the several States within the time agreed upon by the United States in Congress assembled.

ARTICLE IX. The United States in Congress assembled, shall have the sole and exclusive right and power of determining on peace and war, except in the cases mentioned in the sixth article—of sending and receiving ambassadors—entering into treaties and alliances, provided that no treaty of commerce shall be made whereby the legislative power of the respective States shall be restrained from imposing such imposts and duties on foreigners, as their own people are subjected to, or from prohibiting the exportation or importation of and species of goods or commodities whatsoever—of establishing rules for deciding in all cases, what captures on land or water shall be legal, and in what manner prizes taken by land or naval forces in the service of the United States shall be divided or appropriated—of granting letters of marque and reprisal in times of peace—appointing courts for the trial of piracies and felonies committed on the high seas and establishing courts for receiving and determining finally appeals in all cases of captures, provided that no member of Congress shall be appointed a judge of any of the said courts.

The United States in Congress assembled shall also be the last resort on appeal in all disputes and differences now subsisting or that hereafter may arise between two or more States concerning boundary, jurisdiction or any other cause whatever; which authority shall always be exercised in the manner following. Whenever the legislative or executive authority or lawful agent of any State in controversy with another shall present a petition to Congress, stating the matter in question and praying for a hearing, notice thereof shall be given by order of Congress to the legislative or executive authority of the other State in controversy, and a day assigned for the appearance of the parties by their lawful agents, who shall then be directed to appoint by joint consent, commissioners or judges to constitute a court for hearing and determining the matter in question: but if they cannot agree, Congress shall name three persons out of each of the United States, and from the list of such persons each party shall alternately strike out one, the petitioners beginning, until the number shall be reduced to thirteen; and from that number not less than seven, nor more than nine names as Congress shall direct, shall in the presence of Congress be drawn out by lot, and the persons whose names shall be so drawn or any five of them, shall be commissioners or judges, to hear and finally determine the controversy, so always as a major part of the judges who shall hear the cause shall agree in the determination: and if either party shall neglect to attend at the day appointed, without reasons, which Congress shall judge sufficient, or being present shall refuse to strike, the Congress shall proceed to nominate three persons out of each State, and the Secretary of Congress shall strike in behalf of such party absent or refusing; and the judgment and sentence of the court to be appointed, in the manner before prescribed, shall be final and conclusive; and if any of the parties shall refuse to submit to the authority of such court, or to appear or defend their claim or cause, the court shall nevertheless proceed to pronounce sentence, or judgment, which shall in like manner be final and decisive, the judgment or sentence and other proceedings being in either case transmitted to Congress, and lodged among the acts of Congress for the security of the parties concerned: provided that every commissioner, before he sits in judgment, shall take an oath to be administered by one of the judges of the supreme or superior court of the State where the case shall be tried, "well and truly to hear and determine the matter in question, according to the best of his judgment, without favour, affection or hope of reward:" provided also that no State shall be deprived of territory for the benefit of the United States.

All controversies concerning the private right of soil claimed under different grants of two or more States, whose jurisdiction as they may respect such lands, and the states which passed such grants are adjusted, the said grants or either of them being at the same time claimed to have originated antecedent to such settlement of jurisdiction, shall on the petition of either party to the Congress of the United States, be finally determined as near as may be in the same manner as is before prescribed for deciding disputes respecting territorial jurisdiction between different States.

The United States in Congress assembled shall also have the sole and exclusive right and power of regulating the alloy and value of coin struck by their own authority, or by that of the respective States—fixing the standard of weights and measures throughout the United States—regulating the trade and managing all affairs with the Indians, not members of any of the States, provided that the legislative right of any State within its own limits be not infringed or violated—establishing and regulating post-offices from one State to another, throughout all of the United States, and exacting such postage on the papers passing thro' the same as may be requisite to defray the expenses of the said office—appointing all officers of the land forces, in the service of the United States, excepting regimental officers—appointing all the officers of the naval forces, and commissioning all officers whatever in the service of the United States—making rules for the government and regulation of the said land and naval forces, and directing their operations.

The United States in Congress assembled shall have authority to appoint a committee, to sit in the recess of Congress, to be denominated "a Committee of the States," and to consist of one delegate from each State; and to appoint such other committees and civil officers as may be necessary for managing the general affairs of the United States under their direction—to appoint one of their number to preside, provided that no person be allowed to serve in the office of president more than one year in any term of three years; to ascertain the necessary sums of money to be raised for the service of the United States, and to appropriate and apply the same for defraying the public expenses—to borrow money, or emit bills on the credit of the United States, transmitting every half year to the respective States an account of the sums of money so borrowed or emitted,—to build and equip a navy—to agree upon the number of land forces, and to make requisitions from each State for its quota, in proportion to the number of white inhabitants in such State; which requisition shall be binding, and thereupon the Legislature of each State shall appoint the regimental officers, raise the men and cloath, arm and equip them in a soldier like manner, at the expense of the United States; and the officers and men so cloathed, armed and equipped shall march to the place appointed, and within the time agreed on by the United States in Congress assembled: but if the United States in Congress assembled shall, on consideration of circumstances judge proper that any State should not raise men, or should raise a smaller number of men than the quota thereof, such extra number shall be raised, officered, cloathed, armed and equipped in the same manner as the quota of such State, unless the legislature of such State shall judge that such extra number cannot be safely spared out of the same, in which case they shall raise officer, cloath, arm and equip as many of such extra number as they judge can be safely spared. And the officers and men so cloathed, armed and equipped, shall march to the place appointed, and within the time agreed on by the United States in Congress assembled.

The United States in Congress assembled shall never engage in a war, nor grant letters of marque and reprisal in time of peace, nor enter into any treaties or alliances, nor coin money, nor regulate the value thereof, nor ascertain the sums and expenses necessary for the defence and welfare of the United States, or any of them, nor emit bills, nor borrow money on the credit of the United

States, nor appropriate money, nor agree upon the number of vessels to be built or purchased, or the number of land or sea forces to be raised, nor appoint a commander in chief of the army or navy, unless nine States assent to the same: nor shall a question on any other point, except for adjourning from day to day be determined, unless by the votes of a majority of the United States in Congress assembled.

The Congress of the United States shall have power to adjourn to any time within the year, and to any place within the United States, so that no period of adjournment be for a longer duration than the space of six months, and shall publish the journal of their proceedings monthly, except such parts thereof relating to treaties, alliances or military operations, as in their judgment require secresy; and the yeas and nays of the delegates of each State on any question shall be entered on the Journal, when it is desired by any delegate; and the delegates of a State, or any of them, at his or their request shall be furnished with a transcript of the said journal, except such parts as are above excepted, to lay before the Legislatures of the several States.

ARTICLE X. The committee of the States, or any nine of them, shall be authorized to execute, in the recess of Congress, such of the powers of Congress as the United States in Congress assembled, by the consent of nine States, shall from time to time think expedient to vest them with; provided that no power be delegated to the said committee, for the exercise of which, by the articles of confederation, the voice of nine States in the Congress of the United States assembled is requisite.

ARTICLE XI. Canada acceding to this confederation, and joining in the measures of the United States, shall be admitted into, and entitled to all the advantages of this Union: but no other colony shall be admitted into the same, unless such admission be agreed to by nine States.

ARTICLE XII. All bills of credit emitted, monies borrowed and debts contracted by, or under the authority of Congress, before the assembling of the United States, in pursuance of the present confederation, shall be deemed and considered as a charge against the United States, for payment and satisfaction whereof the said United States, and the public faith are hereby solemnly pledged.

ARTICLE XIII. Every State shall abide by the determinations of the United States in Congress assembled, on all questions which by this confederation are submitted to them. And the articles of this confederation shall be inviolably observed by every State, and the Union shall be perpetual; nor shall any alteration at any time hereafter be made in any of them; unless such alteration be agreed to in a Congress of the United States, and be afterwards confirmed by the Legislatures of every State.

And whereas it has pleased the Great Governor of the world to incline the hearts of the Legislatures we respectively represent in Congress, to approve of, and to authorize us to ratify the said articles of confederation and perpetual union. Know ye that we the undersigned delegates, by virtue of the power and authority to us given for that purpose, do by these presents, in the name and in behalf of our respective constituents, fully and entirely ratify and confirm each and every of the said articles of confederation and perpetual union, and all and singular the matters and things therein contained: and we do further solemnly plight and engage the faith of our respective constituents, that they shall abide by the determinations of the United States in Congress assembled, on all questions, which by the said confederation are submitted to them. And that the articles thereof shall be inviolably observed by the States we respectively represent, and that the Union shall be perpetual.

In witness thereof we have hereunto set our hands in Congress. Done at Philadelphia in the State of Pennsylvania the ninth day of July in the year of our Lord one thousand seven hundred and seventy-eight, and in the third year of the independence of America.

THE CONSTITUTION OF
THE UNITED STATES

WE THE PEOPLE OF THE UNITED STATES, in order to form a more perfect Union, establish Justice, insure domestic Tranquility, provide for the common defence, promote the general Welfare, and secure the Blessings of Liberty to ourselves and our Posterity, do ordain and establish this Constitution for the United States of America.

ARTICLE. I.

Section. 1. All legislative Powers herein granted shall be vested in a Congress of the United States, which shall consist of a Senate and House of Representatives.

Section. 2. The House of Representatives shall be composed of Members chosen every second Year by the People of the several States, and the Electors in each State shall have the Qualifications requisite for Electors of the most numerous Branch of the State Legislature.

No Person shall be a Representative who shall not have attained to the Age of twenty five Years, and been seven Years a Citizen of the United States, and who shall not, when elected, be an Inhabitant of that State in which he shall be chosen.

Representatives and direct Taxes shall be apportioned among the several States which may be included within this Union, according to their respective Numbers, which shall be determined by adding to the whole Number of free Persons, including those bound to Service for a Term of Years, and excluding Indians not taxed, three fifths of all other Persons. The actual Enumeration shall be made within three Years after the first Meeting of the Congress of the United States, and within every subsequent Term of ten Years, in such Manner as they shall by Law direct. The Number of Representatives shall not exceed one for every thirty Thousand, but each State shall have at Least one Representative; and until such enumeration shall be made, the State of New Hampshire shall be entitled to chuse three, Massachusetts eight, Rhode-Island and

Providence Plantations one, Connecticut five, New-York six, New Jersey four, Pennsylvania eight, Delaware one, Maryland six, Virginia ten, North Carolina five, South Carolina five, and Georgia three.

When vacancies happen in the Representation from any state, the Executive Authority thereof shall issue Writs of Election to fill such Vacancies.

The House of Representatives shall chuse their Speaker and other Officers; and shall have the sole Power of Impeachment.

Section. 3. The Senate of the United States shall be composed of two Senators from each State, chosen by the legislature thereof, for six Years; and each Senator shall have one Vote.

Immediately after they shall be assembled in Consequence of the first Election, they shall be divided as equally as may be into three Classes. The Seats of the Senators of the first Class shall be vacated at the Expiration of the second Year, of the second Class at the Expiration of the fourth Year, and of the third Class at the Expiration of the sixth Year, so that one third may be chosen every second Year; and if Vacancies happen by Resignation, or otherwise, during the Recess of the Legislature of any State, the Executive thereof may make temporary Appointments until the next Meeting of the Legislature, which shall then fill such Vacancies.

No Person shall be a Senator who shall not have attained to the Age of thirty Years, and been nine Years a Citizen of the United States, and who shall not, when elected, be an Inhabitant of that State for which he shall be chosen.

The Vice President of the United States shall be President of the Senate, but shall have no Vote, unless they be equally divided.

The Senate shall chuse their other Officers, and also a President pro tempore, in the Absence of the Vice President, or when he shall exercise the Office of President of the United States.

The Senate shall have the sole Power to try all Impeachments. When sitting for that Purpose, they shall be on Oath or Affirmation. When the President of the United States is tried, the Chief Justice shall preside: And no Person shall be convicted without the Concurrence of two thirds of the Members present.

Judgment in Cases of Impeachment shall not extend further than to removal from Office, and disqualification to hold and enjoy any Office of honor, Trust or Profit under the United States: but the Party convicted shall nevertheless be liable and subject to Indictment, Trial, Judgment and Punishment, according to Law.

Section. 4. The Times, Places and Manner of holding Elections for Senators and Representatives, shall be prescribed in each State by the Legislature thereof; but the Congress may at any time by Law make or alter such Regulations, except as to the Places of chusing Senators.

The Congress shall assemble at least once in every Year, and such Meeting shall be on the first Monday in December, unless they shall by Law appoint a different Day.

Section. 5. Each House shall be the Judge of the Elections, Returns and Qualifications of its own Members, and a Majority of each shall constitute a Quorum to do Business; but a smaller Number may adjourn from day to day, and may be authorized to compel the Attendance of absent Members, in such Manner, and under such Penalties as each House may provide.

Each House may determine the Rules of its Proceedings, punish its Members for disorderly Behaviour, and, with the Concurrence of two thirds, expel a Member.

Each House shall keep a Journal of its Proceedings, and from time to time publish the same, excepting such Parts as may in their Judgment require Secrecy; and the Yeas and Nays of the Members of either House on any question shall, at the Desire of one fifth of those Present, be entered on the Journal.

Neither House, during the Session of Congress, shall, without the Consent of the other, adjourn for more than three days, not to any other Place than that in which the two Houses shall be sitting.

Section. 6. The Senators and Representatives shall receive a Compensation for their Services, to be ascertained by Law, and paid out of the Treasury of the United States. They shall in all Cases, except Treason, Felony and Breach of the Peace, be privileged from Arrest during their Attendance at the Session of their respective Houses, and in going to and returning from the same; and for any Speech or Debate in either House, they shall not be questioned in any other Place.

No Senator or Representative shall, during the Time for which he was elected, be appointed to any civil Office under the Authority of the United States, which shall have been created, or the Emoluments whereof shall have been encreased during such time; and no Person holding any Office under the United States, shall be a Member of either House during his Continuance in Office.

Section. 7. All Bills for raising Revenue shall originate in the House of Representatives; but the Senate may propose or concur with Amendments as on other Bills.

Every Bill which shall have passed the House of Representatives and the Senate shall, before it become a Law, be presented to the President of the United States; If he approve he shall sign it, but if not he shall return it, with his Objections to that House in which it shall have originated, who shall enter the Objections at large on their Journal, and proceed to reconsider it. If after such Reconsideration two thirds of that House shall agree to pass the Bill, it shall be sent, together with the Objections, to the other House, by which it shall likewise be reconsidered, and if approved by two thirds of that House, it shall become a Law. But in all such Cases the Votes of both Houses shall be determined by yeas and Nays, and the Names of the Persons voting for and against the Bill shall be entered on the Journal of each House respectively. If any Bill shall not be returned by the President within ten Days (Sundays excepted) after it shall have been presented to him, the Same shall be a Law, in like Manner as if he had signed it, unless the Congress by their Adjournment prevent its Return, in which Case it shall not be a Law.

Every Order, Resolution, or Vote to which the Concurrence of the Senate and House of Representatives may be necessary (except on a question of Adjournment) shall be presented to the President of the United States; and before the Same shall take Effect, shall be approved by him, or being disapproved by him, shall be repassed by two thirds of the Senate and House of Representatives, according to the Rules and Limitations prescribed in the Case of a Bill.

Section. 8. The Congress shall have Power To lay and collect Taxes, Duties, Imposts and Excises, to pay the Debts and provide for the common Defence and general Welfare of the United States; but all Duties, Imposts and Excises shall be uniform throughout the United States;

To borrow Money on the credit of the United States;

To regulate Commerce with foreign Nations, and among the several States, and with the Indian Tribes;

To establish an uniform Rule of Naturalization, and uniform Laws on the subject of Bankruptcies throughout the United States;

To coin Money, regulate the Value thereof, and of foreign Coin, and fix the Standard of Weights and Measures;

To provide for the Punishment of counterfeiting the Securities and current Coin of the United States;

To establish Post Offices and Post Roads;

To promote the Progress of Science and useful Arts, by securing for limited Times to Authors and Inventors the exclusive Right to their respective Writings and Discoveries;

To constitute Tribunals inferior to the supreme Court;

To define and punish Piracies and Felonies committed on the high Seas, and Offences against the Law of Nations;

To declare War, grant Letters of Marque and Reprisal, and make Rules concerning Captures on Land and Water;

To raise and support Armies, but no Appropriation of Money to that Use shall be for a longer Term than two Years;

To provide and maintain a Navy;

To make Rules for the Government and Regulation of the land and naval Forces;

To provide for calling forth the Militia to execute the Laws of the Union, suppress Insurrections and repel Invasions;

To provide for organizing, arming, and disciplining, the Militia, and for governing such Part of them as may be employed in the Service of the United States, reserving to the States respectively, the Appointment of the Officers, and the Authority of training the Militia according to the discipline prescribed by Congress.

To exercise exclusive Legislation in all Cases whatsoever, over such District (not exceeding ten Miles square) as may, by Cession of Particular States, and the Acceptance of Congress, become the Seat of the Government of the United States, and to exercise like Authority over all Places purchased by the Consent of the Legislature of the State in which the Same shall be, for the Erection of Forts, Magazines, Arsenals, dock-Yards, and other needful Buildings;—And

To make all Laws which shall be necessary and proper for carrying into Execution the foregoing Powers, and all other Powers vested by this Constitution in the Government of the United States, or in any Department or Officer thereof.

Section. 9. The Migration or Importation of such Persons as any of the States now existing shall think proper to admit, shall not be prohibited by the Congress prior to the Year one thousand eight hundred and eight, but a Tax or duty may be imposed on such Importation, not exceeding ten dollars for each Person.

The Privilege of the Writ of Habeas Corpus shall not be suspended, unless when in Cases of Rebellion or Invasion the public Safety may require it.

No Bill of Attainder or ex post facto Law shall be passed.

No Capitation, or other direct, Tax shall be laid, unless in Proportion to the Census or Enumeration herein before directed to be taken.

No Tax or Duty shall be laid on Articles exported from any State.

No Preference shall be given by any Regulation of Commerce or Revenue to the Ports of one State over those of another: nor shall Vessels bound to, or from, one State, be obliged to enter, clear, or pay Duties in another.

No Money shall be drawn from the Treasury, but in Consequence of Appropriations made by Law; and a regular Statement and Account of the Receipts and Expenditures of all public Money shall be published from time to time.

No Title of Nobility shall be granted by the United States: And no Person holding any Office of Profit or Trust under them, shall, without the Consent of the Congress, accept of any present, Emolument, Office, or Title, of any kind whatever, from any King, Prince, or foreign State.

Section 10. No State shall enter into any Treaty, Alliance, or Confederation; grant Letters of Marque and Reprisal; coin Money; emit Bills of Credit; make any Thing but gold and silver Coin a Tender in Payment of Debts; pass any Bill of Attainder, ex post facto Law, or Law impairing the Obligation of Contracts, or grant any Title of Nobility.

No State shall, without the Consent of the Congress, lay any Imposts or Duties on Imports or Exports, except what may be absolutely necessary for executing its inspection Laws: and the net Produce of all Duties and Imposts, laid by any State on Imports or Exports, shall be for the Use of the Treasury of the United States; and all such Laws shall be subject to the Revision and Controul of the Congress.

No State shall, without the Consent of Congress, lay any Duty of Tonnage, keep Troops, or Ships of War. in time of Peace, enter into any Agreement or Compact with another State, or with a foreign Power, or engage in War, unless actually invaded, or in such imminent Danger as will not admit of delay.

ARTICLE. II.

Section. 1. The executive Power shall be vested in a President of the United States of America. He shall hold his Office during the term of four Years, and, together with the Vice President, chosen for the same Term, be elected, as follows:

Each State shall appoint, in such Manner as the Legislature thereof may direct, a Number of Electors, equal to the whole Number of Senators and Representatives to which the State may be entitled in the Congress: but no Senator or Representative, or Person holding an Office of Trust or Profit under the United States, shall be appointed an Elector.

The Electors shall meet in their respective States, and vote by Ballot for two Persons, of whom one at least shall not be an Inhabitant of the same State with themselves. And they shall make a List of all the Persons voted for, and of the Number of Votes for each; which List they shall sign and certify, and transmit sealed to the Seat of the Government of the United States, directed to the President of the Senate. The President of the Senate shall, in the Presence of the Senate and House of Representatives, open all the Certificates, and the Votes shall then be counted. The Person having the greatest Number of Votes shall be the President, if such Number be a Majority of the whole Number of Electors appointed; and if there be more than one who have such Majority, and have an equal Number of Votes, then the House of Representatives shall immediately chuse by Ballot one of them for President; and if no Person have a Majority, then from the five highest on the List the said House shall in like Manner chuse the President. But in chusing the President, the Votes shall be taken by States, the Representation from each State having one Vote; A quorum for this Purpose shall consist of a Member or Members from two thirds of the States, and a Majority of all the States shall be necessary to a Choice. In every Case, after the Choice of the President, the Person having the greatest Number of Votes of the Electors shall be the Vice President. But if there should remain two or more who have equal Votes, the Senate shall chuse from them by Ballot the Vice President.

The Congress may determine the Time of chusing the Electors, and the Day on which they shall give their Votes; which Day shall be the same throughout the United States.

No Person except a natural born Citizen, or a Citizen of the United States, at the time of the Adoption of this Constitution, shall be eligible to the Office of President; neither shall any Person be eligible to that Office who shall not have attained to the Age of thirty five Years, and been fourteen Years a Resident within the United States.

In Case of the Removal of the President from Office, or of his Death, Resignation, or Inability to discharge the Powers and Duties of the said Office, the Same shall devolve on the Vice President, and the Congress may by Law provide for the Case of Removal, Death, Resignation or Inability, both of the President and Vice President, declaring what Officer shall then act as President, and such Officer shall act accordingly, until the Disability be removed, or a President shall be elected.

The President shall, at stated Times, receive for his Services, a Compensation, which shall neither be encreased or diminished during the Period for which he shall have been elected, and he shall not receive within that Period any other Emolument from the United States, or any of them.

Before he enters on the Execution of his Office, he shall take the following Oath or Affirmation:—"I do solemnly swear (or affirm) that I will faithfully execute the Office of President of the United States, and will to the best of my Ability, preserve, protect and defend the Constitution of the United States."

Section. 2. The President shall be Commander in Chief of the Army and Navy of the United States, and of the Militia of the several States, when called into the actual Service of the United States; he may require the Opinion, in writing, of the principal Officer in each of the executive Departments, upon any Subject relating to the Duties of their respective Offices, and he shall have Power to grant Reprieves and Pardons for Offences against the United States, except in Cases of Impeachment.

He shall have Power, by and with the Advice and Consent of the Senate, to make Treaties, provided two thirds of the Senators present concur; and he shall nominate, and by and with the Advice and Consent of the Senate, shall appoint Ambassadors, other public Ministers and Consuls, Judges of the supreme Court, and all other Officers of the United States, whose Appointments are not herein otherwise provided for, and which shall be established by Law;

but the Congress may by Law vest the Appointment of such inferior Officers, as they think proper, in the President alone, in the Courts of Law, or in the Heads of Departments.

The President shall have Power to fill up all Vacancies that may happen during the Recess of the Senate, by granting Commissions which shall expire at the End of their next Session.

Section. 3. He shall from time to time give to the Congress Information of the State of the Union, and recommend to their Consideration such Measures as he shall judge necessary and expedient; he may, on extraordinary Occasions, convene both Houses, or either of them, and in Case of Disagreement between them, with Respect to the Time of Adjournment, he may adjourn them to such Time as he shall think proper; he shall receive Ambassadors and other public Ministers; he shall take Care that the Laws be faithfully executed, and shall Commission all the Officers of the United States.

Section. 4. The President, Vice President and all civil Officers of the United States, shall be removed from Office on Impeachment for, and Conviction of, Treason, Bribery, or other high Crimes and Misdemeanors.

Article. III.

Section. 1. The judicial Power of the United States, shall be vested in one supreme Court, and in such inferior Courts as the Congress may from time to time ordain and establish. The Judges, both of the supreme and inferior Courts, shall hold their Offices during good Behavior, and shall, at stated Times, receive for their Services, a Compensation, which shall not be diminished during their Continuance in Office.

Section. 2. The judicial Power shall extend to all Cases, in Law and Equity, arising under this Constitution, the Laws of the United States, and Treaties made, or which shall be made, under their Authority;—to all Cases affecting Ambassadors, other public Ministers and Consuls;—to all Cases of admiralty and maritime Jurisdiction;—the Controversies to which the United States shall be a Party;—to Controversies between two or more States;—between a State and Citizens of another State;—between Citizens of different States;—between Citizens of the same State claiming Lands under Grants of different States, and between a State, or the Citizens thereof, and foreign States, Citizens or Subjects.

In all cases affecting Ambassadors, other public Ministers and Consuls, and those in which a State shall be Party, the supreme Court shall have original Jurisdiction. In all the other Cases before mentioned, the supreme Court shall have appellate Jurisdiction, both as to Law and Fact, with such Exceptions, and under such Regulations as the Congress shall make.

The Trial of all Crimes, except in Cases of Impeachment, shall be by Jury; and such Trial shall be held in the State where the said Crimes shall have been committed; but when not committed within any State, the Trial shall be at such Place or Places as the Congress may by Law have directed.

Section. 3. Treason against the United States, shall consist only in levying War against them, or in adhering to their Enemies, giving them Aid and Comfort. No Person shall be convicted of Treason unless on the Testimony of two Witnesses to the same overt Act, or on Confession in open Court.

The Congress shall have Power to declare the Punishment of Treason, but no Attainder of Treason shall work Corruption of Blood, or Forfeiture except during the Life of the Person attainted.

Article. IV.

Section. 1. Full Faith and Credit shall be given in each State to the public Acts, Records, and judicial Proceedings of every other State. And the Congress may by general Laws prescribe the Manner in which such Acts, Records and Proceedings shall be proved, and the Effect thereof.

Section. 2. The Citizens of each State shall be entitled to all Privileges and Immunities of Citizens in the several States.

A Person charged in any State with Treason, Felony, or other Crime, who shall flee from Justice, and be found in another State, shall on Demand of the executive Authority of the State from which he fled, be delivered up, to be removed to the State having Jurisdiction of the Crime.

No Person held to Service or Labour in one State, under the Laws thereof, escaping into another, shall, in Consequence of any Law or Regulation therein, be discharged from such Service or Labour, but shall be delivered up on Claim of the Party to whom such Service or Labour may be due.

Section. 3. New States may be admitted by the Congress into this Union; but no new State shall be formed or erected within the Jurisdiction of any other State; nor any State be formed by the Junction of two or more States, or Parts of States, without the consent of the Legislatures of the States concerned as well as of the Congress.

The Congress shall have Power to dispose of and make all needful Rules and Regulations respecting the Territory or other Property belonging to the United States; and nothing in this Constitution shall be so construed as to Prejudice any Claims of the United States, or of any particular States.

Section. 4. The United States shall guarantee to every State in this Union a Republican Form of Government, and shall protect each of them against Invasion; and on Application of the Legislature, or of the Executive (when the Legislature cannot be convened) against domestic Violence.

ARTICLE. V.

The Congress, whenever two thirds of both Houses shall deem it necessary, shall propose Amendments to this Constitution, or, on the Application of the Legislatures of two thirds of the several States, shall call a Convention for proposing Amendments, which, in either Case, shall be valid to all Intents and Purposes, as Part of this Constitution, when ratified by the Legislatures of three fourths of the several States, or by Conventions in three fourths thereof, as the one or the other Mode of Ratification may be proposed by the Congress; Provided that no Amendment which may be made prior to the Year One thousand eight hundred and eight shall in any Manner affect the first and fourth Clauses in the Ninth Section of the first Article; and that no State, without its Consent, shall be deprived of its equal Suffrage in the Senate.

ARTICLE. VI.

All Debts contracted and Engagements entered into, before the Adoption of this Constitution, shall be as valid against the United States under this Constitution, as under the Confederation.

This Constitution, and the Laws of the United States which shall be made in Pursuance thereof; and all Treaties made, or which shall be made, under the Authority of the United States, shall be the supreme Law of the Land; and the Judges in every State shall be bound thereby, any Thing in the Constitution or Laws of any State to the Contrary notwithstanding.

The Senators and Representatives before mentioned, and the Members of the several State Legislatures, and all executive and judicial Officers, both of the United States and of the several States, shall be bound by Oath or Affirmation, to support this Constitution; but no religious Test shall ever be required as a Qualification to any Office or public Trust under the United States.

ARTICLE. VII.

The Ratification of the Conventions of nine States, shall be sufficient for the Establishment of this Constitution between the States so ratifying the Same.

Done in Convention by the Unanimous Consent of the States present the Seventeenth Day of September in the Year of our Lord one thousand seven hundred and Eighty seven and of the Independence of the United States of America the Twelfth. In witness thereof We have hereunto subscribed our Names,

G°. WASHINGTON—Presd^t.
and deputy from Virginia.

New Hampshire	{ John Langdon { Nicholas Gilman		Geo: Read
		Delaware	{ Gunning Bedford jun { John Dickinson { Richard Bassett
Massachusetts	{ Nathaniel Gorham { Rufus King		Jaco: Broom
Connecticut	{ Wm Saml Johnson { Roger Sherman	Maryland	{ James McHenry { Dan of St Thos Jenifer { Danl Carroll
New York: . . .	Alexander Hamilton		
		Virginia	{ John Blair— { James Madison Jr.
New Jersey	{ Wil: Livingston { David A. Brearley. { Wm Paterson. { Jona: Dayton		
		North Carolina	{ Wm Blount { Richd Dobbs Spaight. { Hu Williamson
Pennsylvania	{ B Franklin { Thomas Mifflin { Robt Morris { Geo. Clymer { Thos FitzSimons { Jared Ingersoll { James Wilson { Gouv Morris	South Carolina	{ J. Rutledge { Charles Cotesworth { Pinckney { Charles Pinckney { Pierce Butler.
		Georgia	{ William Few { Abr Baldwin

AMENDMENTS TO THE CONSTITUTION

ARTICLES IN ADDITION TO, and Amendment of the Constitution of the United States of America, proposed by Congress, and ratified by the Legislatures of the several States, pursuant to the fifth Article of the original Constitution.

AMENDMENT I.

Congress shall make no law respecting an establishment of religion, or prohibiting the free exercise thereof; or abridging the freedom of speech, or of the press; or the right of the people peaceably to assemble, and to petition the Government for a redress of grievances.

Amendment II.

A well regulated Militia, being necessary to the security of a free State, the right of the people to keep and bear Arms, shall not be infringed.

Amendment III.

No Soldier shall, in time of peace be quartered in any house, without the consent of the Owner, nor in time of war, but in a manner to be prescribed by law.

Amendment IV.

The right of the people to be secure in their persons, houses, papers, and effects, against unreasonable searches and seizures, shall not be violated, and no Warrants shall issue, but upon probable cause, supported by Oath or affirmation, and particularly describing the place to be searched, and the persons or things to be seized.

Amendment V.

No person shall be held to answer for a capital, or otherwise infamous crime, unless on a presentment or indictment of a Grand Jury, except in cases arising in the land or naval forces, or in the Militia, when in actual service in time of War or public danger; nor shall any person be subject for the same offence to be twice put in jeopardy of life or limb; nor shall be compelled in any criminal case to be a witness against himself, nor be deprived of life, liberty, or property, without due process of law; nor shall private property be taken for public use, without just compensation.

Amendment VI.

In all criminal prosecutions, the accused shall enjoy the right to a speedy and public trial, by an impartial jury of the State and district wherein the crime shall have been committed, which district shall have been previously ascertained by law, and to be informed of the nature and cause of the accusation; to be confronted with the witnesses against him; to have compulsory process for obtaining witnesses in his favor, and to have the Assistance of Counsel for his defence.

Amendment VII.

In Suits at common law, where the value in controversy shall exceed twenty dollars, the right of trial by jury shall be preserved, and no fact tried by a jury, shall be otherwise re-examined in any Court of the United States, than according to the rules of the common law.

Amendment VIII.

Excessive bail shall not be required, nor excessive fines imposed, nor cruel and unusual punishments inflicted.

Amendment IX.

The enumeration in the Constitution, of certain rights, shall not be construed to deny or disparage others retained by the people.

Amendment X.

The powers not delegated to the United States by the Constitution, nor prohibited by it to the States, are reserved to the States respectively, or to the people. [The first ten amendments went into effect December 15, 1791.]

Amendment XI.

The Judicial power of the United States shall not be construed to extend to any suit in law or equity, commenced or prosecuted against one of the United States by Citizens of another State, or by Citizens or Subjects of any Foreign State. [January 8, 1798.]

Amendment XII.

The Electors shall meet in their respective States, and vote by ballot for President and Vice-President, one of whom, at least, shall not be an inhabitant of the same state with themselves; they shall name in their ballots the person voted for as President, and in distinct ballots the person voted for as Vice-President, and they shall make distinct lists of all persons voted for as President, and of all persons voted for as Vice President, and of the number of votes for each, which lists they shall sign and certify, and transmit sealed to the seat of the government of the United States, directed to the President of the Senate;—The President of the Senate shall, in the presence of the Senate and House of Representatives, open all the certificates and the votes shall then be counted;—The person having the greatest number of votes for President, shall be the President, if such number be a majority of the whole number of Electors appointed; and if no person have such majority, then from the persons having the highest numbers not exceeding three on the list of those voted for as President, the House of Representatives shall choose immediately, by ballot, the President. But in choosing the President, the votes shall be taken by states, the representation from each state having one vote; a quorum for this purpose shall consist of a member or members from two-thirds of the states, and a majority of all the states shall be necessary to a choice. And if the House of Representatives shall not choose a President whenever the right of choice shall devolve upon them, before the fourth day of March next following, then the Vice-President shall act as President, as in the case of the death or other constitutional disability of the President.—The person having the greatest number of votes as Vice-President, shall be the Vice-President, if such number be a majority of the whole number of Electors appointed, and if no person have a majority, then from the two highest numbers on the list, the Senate shall choose the Vice-President; a quorum for the purpose shall consist of two-thirds of the whole number of Senators, and a majority of the whole number shall be necessary to a choice. But no person constitutionally ineligible to the office of President shall be eligible to that of Vice-President of the United States. [September 25, 1804.]

AMENDMENT XIII.

Section 1. Neither slavery nor involuntary servitude, except as a punishment for crime whereof the party shall have been duly convicted, shall exist within the United States, or any place subject to their jurisdiction.

Section 2. Congress shall have power to enforce this article by appropriate legislation. [December 18, 1865.]

AMENDMENT XIV.

Section 1. All persons born or naturalized in the United States, and subject to the jurisdiction thereof, are citizens of the United States and of the State wherein they reside. No State shall make or enforce any law which shall abridge the privileges or immunities of citizens of the United States; nor shall any State deprive any person of life, liberty, or property, without due process of law; nor deny to any person within its jurisdiction the equal protection of the laws.

Section 2. Representatives shall be apportioned among the several States according to their respective numbers, counting the whole number of persons in each State, excluding Indians not taxed. But when the right to vote at any election for the choice of electors for President and Vice President of the United States, Representatives in Congress, the Executive and Judicial officers of a State, or the members of the Legislature thereof, is denied to any of the male inhabitants of such State, being twenty-one years of age, and citizens of the United States, or in any way abridged, except for participation in rebellion, or other crime, the basis of representation therein shall be reduced in the proportion which the number of such male citizens shall bear to the whole number of male citizens twenty-one years of age in such State.

Section 3. No person shall be a Senator or Representative in Congress, or elector of President and Vice President, or hold any office, civil or military, under the United States, or under any State, who, having previously taken an oath, as a member of Congress, or as an officer of the United States, or as a member of any State legislature, or as an executive or judicial officer of any State, to support the Constitution of the United States, shall have engaged in insurrection or rebellion against the same, or given aid or comfort to the enemies thereof. But Congress may by a vote of two-thirds of each House, remove such disability.

Section 4. The validity of the public debt of the United States, authorized by law, including debts incurred for payment of pensions and bounties for services in suppressing insurrection or rebellion, shall not be questioned. But neither the United States nor any State shall assume or pay any debt or obligation incurred in aid of insurrection or rebellion against the United States, or any claim for the loss or emancipation of any slave; but all such debts, obligations and claims shall be held illegal and void.

Section 5. The Congress shall have power to enforce, by appropriate legislation, the provisions of this article. [July 28, 1868.]

Amendment XV.

Section 1. The right of citizens of the United States to vote shall not be denied or abridged by the United States or by any State on account of race, color, or previous condition of servitude—

Section 2. The Congress shall have power to enforce this article by appropriate legislation.—[March 30, 1870.]

Amendment XVI.

The Congress shall have power to lay and collect taxes on incomes, from whatever source derived, without apportionment among the several States, and without regard to any census or enumeration. [February 25, 1913.]

Amendment XVII.

The Senate of the United States shall be composed of two senators from each State, elected by the people thereof, for six years; and each Senator shall have one vote. The electors in each State shall have the qualifications requisite for electors of the most numerous branch of the State legislatures.

When vacancies happen in the representation of any State in the Senate, the executive authority of such State shall issue writs of election to fill such vacancies: *Provided,* That the legislature of any State may empower the executive thereof to make temporary appointments until the people fill the vacancies by election as the legislature may direct.

This amendment shall not be so construed as to affect the election or term of any senator chosen before it becomes valid as part of the Constitution. [May 31, 1913.]

Amendment XVIII.

After one year from the ratification of this article, the manufacture, sale, or transportation of intoxicating liquors within, the importation thereof into, or the exportation thereof from the United States and all territory subject to the jurisdiction thereof for beverage purposes is hereby prohibited.

The Congress and the several States shall have concurrent power to enforce this article by appropriate legislation.

This article shall be inoperative unless it shall have been ratified as an amendment to the Constitution by the legislatures of the several States, as provided in the Constitution, within seven years from the date of the submission thereof to the States by Congress. [January 29, 1919.]

AMENDMENT XIX.

The right of citizens of the United States to vote shall not be denied or abridged by the United States or by any State on account of sex.

The Congress shall have power by appropriate legislation to enforce the provisions of this article. [August 26, 1920.]

AMENDMENT XX.

Section 1. The terms of the President and Vice-President shall end at noon on the twentieth day of January, and the terms of Senators and Representatives at noon on the third day of January, of the years in which such terms would have ended if this article had not been ratified; and the terms of their successors shall then begin.

Section 2. The Congress shall assemble at least once in every year, and such meeting shall begin at noon on the third day of January, unless they shall by law appoint a different day.

Section 3. If, at the time fixed for the beginning of the term of the President, the President-elect shall have died, the Vice-President-elect shall become President. If a President shall not have been chosen before the time fixed for the beginning of his term, or if the President-elect shall have failed to qualify, then the Vice-President-elect shall act as President until a President shall have qualified; and the Congress may by law provide for the case wherein neither a President-elect nor a Vice-President-elect shall have qualified, declaring who shall then act as President, or the manner in which one who is to act shall be selected, and such person shall act accordingly until a President or Vice-President shall have qualified.

Section 4. The Congress may by law provide for the case of the death of any of the persons from whom the House of Representatives may choose a President whenever the right of choice shall have devolved upon them, and for the case of the death of any of the persons from whom the Senate may choose a Vice-President whenever the right of choice shall have devolved upon them.

Section 5. Sections 1 and 2 shall take effect on the 15th day of October following the ratification of this article.

Section 6. This article shall be inoperative unless it shall have been ratified as an amendment to the Constitution by the legislatures of three-fourths of the several States within seven years from the date of its submission. [February 6, 1933.]

AMENDMENT XXI.

Section 1. The eighteenth article of amendment to the Constitution of the United States is hereby repealed.

Section 2. The transportation or importation into any State, Territory or possession of the United States for delivery or use therein of intoxicating liquors, in violation of the laws thereof, is hereby prohibited.

Section 3. This article shall be inoperative unless it shall have been ratified as an amendment to the Constitution by convention in the several States, as provided in the Constitution, within seven years from the date of the submission thereof to the States by the Congress. [December 5, 1933.]

AMENDMENT XXII.

Section 1. No person shall be elected to the office of the President more than twice, and no person who has held the office of President, or acted as President, for more than two years of a term to which some other person was elected President shall be elected to the office of the President more than once. But this Article shall not apply to any person holding the office of President when this Article was proposed by the Congress, and shall not prevent any person who may be holding the office of President, or acting as President, during the term within which this Article becomes operative from holding the office of President or acting as President during the remainder of such term.

Section 2. This article shall be inoperative unless it shall have been ratified as an amendment to the Constitution by the legislatures of three-fourths of the several states within seven years from the date of its submission to the States by the Congress. [February 27, 1951.]

AMENDMENT XXIII.

Section 1. The District constituting the seat of government of the United States shall appoint in such manner as the Congress may direct:

A number of electors of President and Vice-President equal to the whole number of Senators and Representatives in Congress to which the District would be entitled if it were a State, but in no event more than the least populous State; they shall be in addition to those appointed by the States, but they shall be considered, for the purposes of the election of President and Vice-President, to be electors appointed by a State; and they shall meet in the District and perform such duties as provided by the twelfth article of amendment.

Section 2. The Congress shall have the power to enforce this article by appropriate legislation. [March 29, 1961.]

AMENDMENT XXIV.

Section 1. The right of citizens of the United States to vote in any primary or other election for President or Vice President, for electors for President or Vice President, or for Senator or Representative in Congress, shall not be denied or abridged by the United States or any State by reason of failure to pay any poll tax or other tax.

Section 2. The Congress shall have power to enforce this article by appropriate legislation. [January 23, 1964.]

AMENDMENT XXV.

Section 1. In case of the removal of the President from office or of his death or resignation, the Vice President shall become President.

Section 2. Whenever there is a vacancy in the office of Vice President, the President shall nominate a Vice President who shall take office upon confirmation by a majority vote of both Houses of Congress.

Section 3. Whenever the President transmits to the President pro tempore of the Senate and the Speaker of the House of Representatives his written declaration that he is unable to discharge the powers and duties of his office, and until he transmits to them a written declaration to the contrary, such powers and duties shall be discharged by the Vice President as Acting President.

Section 4. Whenever the Vice President and a majority of either the principal officers of the executive departments or of such other body as Congress may by law provide, transmit to the President pro tempore of the Senate and the Speaker of the House of Representatives their written declaration that the President is unable to discharge the powers and duties of his office, the Vice President shall immediately assume the powers and duties of the office as Acting President.

Thereafter, when the President transmits to the President pro tempore of the Senate and the Speaker of the House of Representatives his written declaration that no inability exists, he shall resume the powers and duties of his office unless the Vice President and a majority of either the principal officers of the executive departments or of such other body as Congress may by law provide, transmit within four days to the President pro tempore of the Senate and the Speaker of the House of Representatives their written declaration that the President is unable to discharge the powers and duties of his office. Thereupon Congress shall decide the issue, assembling within forty-eight hours for that purpose if not in session. If the Congress, within twenty-one days after receipt of the latter written declaration, or, if Congress is not in session, within twenty-one days after Congress is required to assemble, determines by two-thirds vote of both Houses that the President is unable to discharge the powers and duties of his office, the Vice President shall continue to discharge the same as Acting President; otherwise, the President shall resume the powers and duties of his office. [February 10, 1967.]

Amendment XXVI.

Section 1. The right of citizens of the United States, who are eighteen years of age or older, to vote shall not be denied or abridged by the United States or by any State on account of age.

Section 2. The Congress shall have power to enforce this article by appropriate legislation [June 30, 1971.]

Amendment XXVII.

No law, varying the compensation for the services of the Senators and Representatives shall take effect, until an election of Representatives shall have intervened. [May 8, 1992.]

PRESIDENTIAL ELECTIONS

Year	Number of States	Candidates	Parties	Popular Vote	% of Popular Vote	Electoral Vote	% Voter Participation
1789	11	**GEORGE WASHINGTON**	No party designations			69	
		John Adams				34	
		Other candidates				35	
1792	15	**GEORGE WASHINGTON**	No party designations			132	
		John Adams				77	
		George Clinton				50	
		Other candidates				5	
1796	16	**JOHN ADAMS**	Federalist			71	
		Thomas Jefferson	Democratic-Republican			68	
		Thomas Pinckney	Federalist			59	
		Aaron Burr	Democratic-Republican			30	
		Other candidates				48	
1800	16	**THOMAS JEFFERSON**	Democratic-Republican			73	
		Aaron Burr	Democratic-Republican			73	
		John Adams	Federalist			65	
		Charles C. Pinckney	Federalist			64	
		John Jay	Federalist			1	
1804	17	**THOMAS JEFFERSON**	Democratic-Republican			162	
		Charles C. Pinckney	Federalist			14	

Year	Number of States	Candidates	Parties	Popular Vote	% of Popular Vote	Electoral Vote	% Voter Participation
1808	17	**JAMES MADISON**	Democratic-Republican			122	
		Charles C. Pinckney	Federalist			47	
		George Clinton	Democratic-Republican			6	
1812	18	**JAMES MADISON**	Democratic-Republican			128	
		DeWitt Clinton	Federalist			89	
1816	19	**JAMES MONROE**	Democratic-Republican			183	
		Rufus King	Federalist			34	
1820	24	**JAMES MONROE**	Democratic-Republican			231	
		John Quincy Adams	Independent			1	
1824	24	**JOHN QUINCY ADAMS**	Democratic-Republican	108,740	30.5	84	26.9
		Andrew Jackson	Democratic-Republican	153,544	43.1	99	
		Henry Clay	Democratic-Republican	47,136	13.2	37	
		William H. Crawford	Democratic-Republican	46,618	13.1	41	
1828	24	**ANDREW JACKSON**	Democratic	647,286	56.0	178	57.6
		John Quincy Adams	National-Republican	508,064	44.0	83	

Year	Number of States	Candidates	Parties	Popular Vote	% of Popular Vote	Electoral Vote	% Voter Participation
1832	24	**ANDREW JACKSON**	Democratic	688,242	54.5	219	55.4
		Henry Clay	National-Republican	473,462	37.5	49	
		William Wirt	Anti-Masonic	101,051	8.0	7	
		John Floyd	Democratic			11	
1836	26	**MARTIN VAN BUREN**	Democratic	765,483	50.9	170	57.8
		William H. Harrison	Whig	739,795	49.1	73	
		Hugh L. White	Whig			26	
		Daniel Webster	Whig			14	
		W. P. Mangum	Whig			11	
1840	26	**WILLIAM H. HARRISON**	Whig	1,274,624	53.1	234	80.2
		Martin Van Buren	Democratic	1,127,781	46.9	60	
1844	26	**JAMES K. POLK**	Democratic	1,338,464	49.6	170	78.9
		Henry Clay	Whig	1,300,097	48.1	105	
		James G. Birney	Liberty	62,300	2.3		
1848	30	**ZACHARY TAYLOR**	Whig	1,360,967	47.4	163	72.7
		Lewis Cass	Democratic	1,222,342	42.5	127	
		Martin Van Buren	Free Soil	291,263	10.1		
1852	31	**FRANKLIN PIERCE**	Democratic	1,601,117	50.9	254	69.6
		Winfield Scott	Whig	1,385,453	44.1	42	
		John P. Hale	Free Soil	155,825	5.0		
1856	31	**JAMES BUCHANAN**	Democratic	1,832,955	45.3	174	78.9
		John C. Frémont	Republican	1,339,932	33.1	114	
		Millard Fillmore	American	871,731	21.6	8	

Year	Number of States	Candidates	Parties	Popular Vote	% of Popular Vote	Electoral Vote	% Voter Participation
1860	33	**ABRAHAM LINCOLN**	Republican	1,865,593	39.8	180	81.2
		Stephen A. Douglas	Democratic	1,382,713	29.5	12	
		John C. Breckinridge	Democratic	848,356	18.1	72	
		John Bell	Constitutional Union	592,906	12.6	39	
1864	36	**ABRAHAM LINCOLN**	Republican	2,206,938	55.0	212	73.8
		George B. McClellan	Democratic	1,803,787	45.0	21	
1868	37	**ULYSSES S. GRANT**	Republican	3,013,421	52.7	214	78.1
		Horatio Seymour	Democratic	2,706,829	47.3	80	
1872	37	**ULYSSES S. GRANT**	Republican	3,596,745	55.6	286	71.3
		Horace Greeley	Democratic	2,843,446	43.9	66	
1876	38	**RUTHERFORD B. HAYES**	Republican	4,036,572	48.0	185	81.8
		Samuel J. Tilden	Democratic	4,284,020	51.0	184	
1880	38	**JAMES A. GARFIELD**	Republican	4,453,295	48.5	214	79.4
		Winfield S. Hancock	Democratic	4,414,082	48.1	155	
		James B. Weaver	Greenback-Labor	308,578	3.4		
1884	38	**GROVER CLEVELAND**	Democratic	4,879,507	48.5	219	77.5
		James G. Blaine	Republican	4,850,293	48.2	182	
		Benjamin F. Butler	Greenback-Labor	175,370	1.8		
		John P. St. John	Prohibition	150,369	1.5		
1888	38	**BENJAMIN HARRISON**	Republican	5,477,129	47.9	233	79.3
		Grover Cleveland	Democratic	5,537,857	48.6	168	
		Clinton B. Fisk	Prohibition	249,506	2.2		
		Anson J. Streeter	Union Labor	146,935	1.3		

Year	Number of States	Candidates	Parties	Popular Vote	% of Popular Vote	Electoral Vote	% Voter Participation
1892	44	**GROVER CLEVELAND**	Democratic	5,555,426	46.1	277	74.7
		Benjamin Harrison	Republican	5,182,690	43.0	145	
		James B. Weaver	People's	1,029,846	8.5	22	
		John Bidwell	Prohibition	264,133	2.2		
1896	45	**WILLIAM McKINLEY**	Republican	7,102,246	51.1	271	79.3
		William J. Bryan	Democratic	6,492,559	47.7	176	
1900	45	**WILLIAM McKINLEY**	Republican	7,218,491	51.7	292	73.2
		William J. Bryan	Democratic; Populist	6,356,734	45.5	155	
		John C. Wooley	Prohibition	208,914	1.5		
1904	45	**THEODORE ROOSEVELT**	Republican	7,628,461	57.4	336	65.2
		Alton B. Parker	Democratic	5,084,223	37.6	140	
		Eugene V. Debs	Socialist	402,283	3.0		
		Silas C. Swallow	Prohibition	258,536	1.9		
1908	46	**WILLIAM H. TAFT**	Republican	7,675,320	51.6	321	65.4
		William J. Bryan	Democratic	6,412,294	43.1	162	
		Eugene V. Debs	Socialist	420,793	2.8		
		Eugene W. Chafin	Prohibition	253,840	1.7		
1912	48	**WOODROW WILSON**	Democratic	6,296,547	41.9	435	58.8
		Theodore Roosevelt	Progressive	4,118,571	27.4	88	
		William H. Taft	Republican	3,486,720	23.2	8	
		Eugene V. Debs	Socialist	900,672	6.0		
		Eugene W. Chafin	Prohibition	206,275	1.4		

Year	Number of States	Candidate	Party	Popular Vote	% of Popular Vote	Electoral Vote	% Voter Participation
1916	48	**WOODROW WILSON**	Democratic	9,127,695	49.4	277	61.6
		Charles E. Hughes	Republican	8,533,507	46.2	254	
		A. L. Benson	Socialist	585,113	3.2		
		J. Frank Hanly	Prohibition	220,506	1.2		
1920	48	**WARREN G. HARDING**	Republican	16,143,407	60.4	404	49.2
		James M. Cox	Democratic	9,130,328	34.2	127	
		Eugene V. Debs	Socialist	919,799	3.4		
		P. P. Christensen	Farmer-Labor	265,411	1.0		
1924	48	**CALVIN COOLIDGE**	Republican	15,718,211	54.0	382	48.9
		John W. Davis	Democratic	8,385,283	28.8	136	
		Robert M. La Follette	Progressive	4,831,289	16.6	13	
1928	48	**HERBERT C. HOOVER**	Republican	21,391,993	58.2	444	56.9
		Alfred E. Smith	Democratic	15,016,169	40.9	87	
1932	48	**FRANKLIN D. ROOSEVELT**	Democratic	22,809,638	57.4	472	56.9
		Herbert C. Hoover	Republican	15,758,901	39.7	59	
		Norman Thomas	Socialist	881,951	2.2		
1936	48	**FRANKLIN D. ROOSEVELT**	Democratic	27,752,869	60.8	523	61.0
		Alfred M. Landon	Republican	16,674,665	36.5	8	
		William Lemke	Union	882,479	1.9		
1940	48	**FRANKLIN D. ROOSEVELT**	Democratic	27,307,819	54.8	449	62.5
		Wendell L. Willkie	Republican	22,321,018	44.8	82	
1944	48	**FRANKLIN D. ROOSEVELT**	Democratic	25,606,585	53.5	432	55.9
		Thomas E. Dewey	Republican	22,014,745	46.0	99	

Year	Number of States	Candidates	Parties	Popular Vote	% of Popular Vote	Electoral Vote	% Voter Participation
1948	48	**HARRY S. TRUMAN**	Democratic	24,179,345	49.6	303	53.0
		Thomas E. Dewey	Republican	21,991,291	45.1	189	
		J. Strom Thurmond	States' Rights	1,176,125	2.4	39	
		Henry A. Wallace	Progressive	1,157,326	2.4		
1952	48	**DWIGHT D. EISENHOWER**	Republican	33,936,234	55.1	442	63.3
		Adlai E. Stevenson	Democratic	27,314,992	44.4	89	
1956	48	**DWIGHT D. EISENHOWER**	Republican	35,590,472	57.6	457	60.6
		Adlai E. Stevenson	Democratic	26,022,752	42.1	73	
1960	50	**JOHN F. KENNEDY**	Democratic	34,226,731	49.7	303	62.8
		Richard M. Nixon	Republican	34,108,157	49.5	219	
1964	50	**LYNDON B. JOHNSON**	Democratic	43,129,566	61.1	486	61.9
		Barry M. Goldwater	Republican	27,178,188	38.5	52	
1968	50	**RICHARD M. NIXON**	Republican	31,785,480	43.4	301	60.9
		Hubert H. Humphrey	Democratic	31,275,166	42.7	191	
		George C. Wallace	American Independent	9,906,473	13.5	46	
1972	50	**RICHARD M. NIXON**	Republican	47,169,911	60.7	520	55.2
		George S. McGovern	Democratic	29,170,383	37.5	17	
		John G. Schmitz	American	1,099,482	1.4		

Year		Candidate	Party	Popular Vote	% Popular Vote	Electoral Vote	% Voter Participation
1976	50	**JIMMY CARTER**	Democratic	40,830,763	50.1	297	53.5
		Gerald R. Ford	Republican	39,147,793	48.0	240	
1980	50	**RONALD REAGAN**	Republican	43,901,812	50.7	489	52.6
		Jimmy Carter	Democratic	35,483,820	41.0	49	
		John B. Anderson	Independent	5,719,437	6.6		
		Ed Clark	Libertarian	921,188	1.1		
1984	50	**RONALD REAGAN**	Republican	54,451,521	58.8	525	53.1
		Walter F. Mondale	Democratic	37,565,334	40.6	13	
1988	50	**GEORGE H. BUSH**	Republican	47,917,341	53.4	426	50.1
		Michael Dukakis	Democratic	41,013,030	45.6	111	
1992	50	**BILL CLINTON**	Democratic	44,908,254	43.0	370	55.0
		George H. Bush	Republican	39,102,343	37.4	168	
		H. Ross Perot	Independent	19,741,065	18.9	0	
1996	50	**BILL CLINTON**	Democratic	47,401,185	49.0	379	49.0
		Bob Dole	Republican	39,197,469	41.0	159	
		H. Ross Perot	Independent	8,085,295	8.0	0	

Candidates receiving less than 1 percent of the popular vote have been omitted. Thus the percentage of popular vote given for any election year may not total 100 percent.

Before the passage of the Twelfth Amendment in 1804, the Electoral College voted for two presidential candidates; the runner-up became vice-president.

ADMISSION OF STATES

Order of Admission	State	Date of Admission	Order of Admission	State	Date of Admission
1	Delaware	December 7, 1787	26	Michigan	January 26, 1837
2	Pennsylvania	December 12, 1787	27	Florida	March 3, 1845
3	New Jersey	December 18, 1787	28	Texas	December 29, 1845
4	Georgia	January 2, 1788	29	Iowa	December 28, 1846
5	Connecticut	January 9, 1788	30	Wisconsin	May 29, 1848
6	Massachusetts	February 7, 1788	31	California	September 9, 1850
7	Maryland	April 28, 1788	32	Minnesota	May 11, 1858
8	South Carolina	May 23, 1788	33	Oregon	February 14, 1859
9	New Hampshire	June 21, 1788	34	Kansas	January 29, 1861
10	Virginia	June 25, 1788	35	West Virginia	June 30, 1863
11	New York	July 26, 1788	36	Nevada	October 31, 1864
12	North Carolina	November 21, 1789	37	Nebraska	March 1, 1867
13	Rhode Island	May 29, 1790	38	Colorado	August 1, 1876
14	Vermont	March 4, 1791	39	North Dakota	November 2, 1889
15	Kentucky	June 1, 1792	40	South Dakota	November 2, 1889
16	Tennessee	June 1, 1796	41	Montana	November 8, 1889
17	Ohio	March 1, 1803	42	Washington	November 11, 1889
18	Louisiana	April 30, 1812	43	Idaho	July 3, 1890
19	Indiana	December 11, 1816	44	Wyoming	July 10, 1890
20	Mississippi	December 10, 1817	45	Utah	January 4, 1896
21	Illinois	December 3, 1818	46	Oklahoma	November 16, 1907
22	Alabama	December 14, 1819	47	New Mexico	January 6, 1912
23	Maine	March 15, 1820	48	Arizona	February 14, 1912
24	Missouri	August 10, 1821	49	Alaska	January 3, 1959
25	Arkansas	June 15, 1836	50	Hawaii	August 21, 1959

POPULATION OF THE UNITED STATES

Year	Number of States	Population	% Increase	Population per Square Mile
1790	13	3,929,214		4.5
1800	16	5,308,483	35.1	6.1
1810	17	7,239,881	36.4	4.3
1820	23	9,638,453	33.1	5.5
1830	24	12,866,020	33.5	7.4
1840	26	17,069,453	32.7	9.8
1850	31	23,191,876	35.9	7.9
1860	33	31,443,321	35.6	10.6
1870	37	39,818,449	26.6	13.4
1880	38	50,155,783	26.0	16.9
1890	44	62,947,714	25.5	21.1
1900	45	75,994,575	20.7	25.6
1910	46	91,972,266	21.0	31.0
1920	48	105,710,620	14.9	35.6
1930	48	122,775,046	16.1	41.2
1940	48	131,669,275	7.2	44.2
1950	48	150,697,361	14.5	50.7
1960	50	179,323,175	19.0	50.6
1970	50	203,235,298	13.3	57.5
1980	50	226,504,825	11.4	64.0
1985	50	237,839,000	5.0	67.2
1990	50	250,122,000	5.2	70.6
1995	50	263,411,707	5.3	74.4

IMMIGRATION TO THE UNITED STATES, FISCAL YEARS 1820–1990

Year	Number	Year	Number	Year	Number	Year	Number
1820–1989	55,457,531	1871–80	2,812,191	1921–30	4,107,209	1971–80	4,493,314
1820	8,385	1871	321,350	1921	805,228	1971	370,478
1821–30	143,439	1872	404,806	1922	309,556	1972	384,685
1821	9,127	1873	459,803	1923	522,919	1973	400,063
1822	6,911	1874	313,339	1924	706,896	1974	394,861
1823	6,354	1875	227,498	1925	294,314	1975	386,914
1824	7,912	1876	169,986	1926	304,488	1976	398,613
1825	10,199	1877	141,857	1927	335,175	1976	103,676
1826	10,837	1878	138,469	1928	307,255	1977	462,315
1827	18,875	1879	177,826	1929	279,678	1978	601,442
1828	27,382	1880	457,257	1930	241,700	1979	460,348
1829	22,520	1881–90	5,246,613	1931–40	528,431	1980	530,639
1830	23,322	1881	669,431	1931	97,139	1981–90	7,338,062
1831–40	599,125	1882	788,992	1932	35,576	1981	596,600
1831	22,633	1883	603,322	1933	23,068	1982	594,131
1832	60,482	1884	518,592	1934	29,470	1983	559,763
1833	58,640	1885	395,346	1935	34,956	1984	543,903
1834	65,365	1886	334,203	1936	36,329	1985	570,009
1835	45,374	1887	490,109	1937	50,244	1986	601,708
1836	76,242	1888	546,889	1938	67,895	1987	601,516
1837	79,340	1889	444,427	1939	82,998	1988	643,025
1838	38,914	1890	455,302	1940	70,756	1989	1,090,924
1839	68,069	1891–1900	3,687,564	1941–50	1,035,039	1990	1,536,483
1840	84,066	1891	560,319	1941	51,776		
1841–50	1,713,251	1892	579,663	1942	28,781		
1841	80,289	1893	439,730	1943	23,725		
1842	104,565	1894	285,631	1944	28,551		
		1895	258,536	1945	38,119		
		1896	343,267	1946	108,721		

Year	Number	Year	Number	Year	Number
1843	52,496	1897	230,832	1947	147,292
1844	78,615	1898	229,299	1948	170,570
1845	114,371	1899	311,715	1949	188,317
1846	154,416	1900	448,572	1950	249,187
1847	234,968	**1901–10**	**8,795,386**	**1951–60**	**2,515,479**
1848	226,527	1901	487,918	1951	205,717
1849	297,024	1902	648,743	1952	265,520
1850	369,980	1903	857,046	1953	170,434
1851–60	**2,598,214**	1904	812,870	1954	208,177
1851	379,466	1905	1,026,499	1955	237,790
1852	371,603	1906	1,100,735	1956	321,625
1853	368,645	1907	1,285,349	1957	326,867
1854	427,833	1908	782,870	1958	253,265
1855	200,877	1909	751,786	1959	260,686
1856	200,436	1910	1,041,570	1960	265,398
1857	251,306	**1911–20**	**5,735,811**	**1961–70**	**3,321,677**
1858	123,126	1911	878,587	1961	271,344
1859	121,282	1912	838,172	1962	283,763
1860	153,640	1913	1,197,892	1963	306,260
1861–70	**2,314,824**	1914	1,218,480	1964	292,248
1861	91,918	1915	326,700	1965	296,697
1862	91,985	1916	298,826	1966	323,040
1863	176,282	1917	295,403	1967	361,972
1864	193,418	1918	110,618	1968	454,448
1865	248,120	1919	141,132	1969	358,579
1866	318,568	1920	430,001	1970	373,326
1867	315,722				
1868	138,840				
1869	352,768				
1870	387,203				

Source: U.S. Immigration and Naturalization Service, 1991.

IMMIGRATION BY REGION AND SELECTED COUNTRY OF LAST RESIDENCE, FISCAL YEARS 1820–1989

Region and Country of Last Residence[1]	1820	1821–30	1831–40	1841–50	1851–60	1861–70	1871–80	1881–90
All countries	8,385	143,439	599,125	1,713,251	2,598,214	2,314,824	2,812,191	5,246,613
Europe	7,690	98,797	495,681	1,597,442	2,452,577	2,065,141	2,271,925	4,735,484
Austria-Hungary	—[2]	—[2]	—[2]	—[2]	—[2]	7,800	72,969	353,719
Austria	—[2]	—[2]	—[2]	—[2]	—[2]	484[3]	63,009	226,038
Hungary	—[2]	—[2]	—[2]	—[2]	—[2]	7,124[3]	9,960	127,681
Belgium	1	27	22	5,074	4,738	6,734	7,221	20,177
Czechoslovakia	—[4]	—[4]	—[4]	—[4]	—[4]	—[4]	—[4]	—[4]
Denmark	20	169	1,063	539	3,749	17,094	31,771	88,132
France	371	8,497	45,575	77,262	76,358	35,986	72,206	50,464
Germany	968	6,761	152,454	434,626	951,667	787,468	718,182	1,452,970
Greece	—	20	49	16	31	72	210	2,308
Ireland[5]	3,614	50,724	207,381	780,719	914,119	435,778	436,871	655,482
Italy	30	409	2,253	1,870	9,231	11,725	55,759	307,309
Netherlands	49	1,078	1,412	8,251	10,789	9,102	16,541	53,701
Norway-Sweden	3	91	1,201	13,903	20,931	109,298	211,245	568,362
Norway	—[6]	—[6]	—[6]	—[6]	—[6]	—[6]	95,323	176,586
Sweden	—[6]	—[6]	—[6]	—[6]	—[6]	—[6]	115,922	391,776
Poland	5	16	369	105	1,164	2,027	12,970	51,806
Portugal	35	145	829	550	1,055	2,658	14,082	16,978
Romania	—[7]	—[7]	—[7]	—[7]	—[7]	—[7]	11	6,348
Soviet Union	14	75	277	551	457	2,512	39,284	213,282
Spain	139	2,477	2,125	2,209	9,298	6,697	5,266	4,419
Switzerland	31	3,226	4,821	4,644	25,011	23,286	28,293	81,988
United Kingdom[5,8]	2,410	25,079	75,810	267,044	423,974	606,896	548,043	807,357
Yugoslavia	—[9]	—[9]	—[9]	—[9]	5	—[9]	—[9]	—[9]
Other Europe	—	3	40	79	5	8	1,001	682

Asia	6	30	55	141	41,538	64,759	124,160	69,942
China[10]	1	2	8	35	41,397	64,301	123,201	61,711
Hong Kong	—[11]	—[11]	—[11]	—[11]	—[11]	—[11]	—[11]	—[11]
India	1	8	39	36	43	69	163	269
Iran	—[12]	—[12]	—[12]	—[12]	—[12]	—[12]	—[12]	—[12]
Israel	—[13]	—[13]	—[13]	—[13]	—[13]	—[13]	—[13]	—[13]
Japan	—[14]	—[14]	—[14]	—[14]	—[14]	186	149	2,270
Korea	—[15]	—[15]	—[15]	—[15]	—[15]	—[15]	—[15]	—[15]
Philippines	—[16]	—[16]	—[16]	—[16]	—[16]	—[16]	—[16]	—[16]
Turkey	1	20	7	59	83	131	404	3,782
Vietnam	—[11]	—[11]	—[11]	—[11]	—[11]	—[11]	—[11]	—[11]
Other Asia	3	—	1	11	15	72	243	1,910
America	387	11,564	33,424	62,469	74,720	166,607	404,044	426,967
Canada & Newfoundland[17,18]	209	2,277	13,624	41,723	59,309	153,878	383,640	393,304
Mexico[18]	1	4,817	6,599	3,271	3,078	2,191	5,162	191,319
Caribbean	164	3,834	12,301	13,528	10,660	9,046	13,957	29,042
Cuba	—[12]	—[12]	—[12]	—[12]	—[12]	—[12]	—[12]	—[12]
Dominican Republic	—[20]	—[20]	—[20]	—[20]	—[20]	—[20]	—[20]	—[20]
Haiti	—[20]	—[20]	—[20]	—[20]	—[20]	—[20]	—[20]	—[20]
Jamaica	—[21]	—[21]	—[21]	—[21]	—[21]	—[21]	—[21]	—[21]
Other Caribbean	164	3,834	12,301	13,528	10,660	9,046	13,957	29,042
Central America	2	105	44	368	449	95	157	404
El Salvador	—[20]	—[20]	—[20]	—[20]	—[20]	—[20]	—[20]	—[20]
Other Central America	2	105	44	368	449	95	157	404
South America	11	531	856	3,579	1,224	1,397	1,128	2,304
Argentina	—[20]	—[20]	—[20]	—[20]	—[20]	—[20]	—[20]	—[20]
Colombia	—[20]	—[20]	—[20]	—[20]	—[20]	—[20]	—[20]	—[20]
Ecuador	—[20]	—[20]	—[20]	—[20]	—[20]	—[20]	—[20]	—[20]
Other South America	11	531	856	3,579	1,224	1,397	1,128	2,304
Other America	—[22]	—[22]	—[22]	—[22]	—[22]	—[22]	—[22]	—[22]
Africa	1	16	54	55	210	312	358	857
Oceania	1	2	9	29	158	214	10,914	12,574
Not specified[22]	300	33,030	69,902	53,115	29,011	17,791	790	789

Region and Country of Last Residence[1]	1891–1900	1901–10	1911–20	1921–30	1931–40	1941–50	1951–60	1961–70
All countries	3,687,564	8,795,386	5,735,811	4,107,209	528,431	1,035,039	2,515,479	3,321,677
Europe	3,555,352	8,056,040	4,321,887	2,463,194	347,566	621,147	1,325,727	1,123,492
Austria-Hungary	592,707[23]	2,145,266[23]	896,342[23]	63,548	11,424	28,329	103,743	26,022
Austria	234,081[3]	668,209[3]	453,649	32,868	3,563[24]	24,860[24]	67,106	20,621
Hungary	181,288[3]	808,511[3]	442,693	30,680	7,861	3,469	36,637	5,401
Belgium	18,167	41,635	33,746	15,846	4,817	12,189	18,575	9,192
Czechoslovakia	—[4]	—[4]	3,426[4]	102,194	14,393	8,347	918	3,273
Denmark	50,231	65,285	41,983	32,430	2,559	5,393	10,984	9,201
France	30,770	73,379	61,897	49,610	12,623	38,809	51,121	45,237
Germany	505,152[23]	341,498[23]	143,945[23]	412,202	114,058[24]	226,578[24]	477,765	190,796
Greece	15,979	167,519	184,201	51,084	9,119	8,973	47,608	85,969
Ireland[5]	388,416	339,065	146,181	211,234	10,973	19,789	48,362	32,966
Italy	651,893	2,045,877	1,109,524	455,315	68,028	57,661	185,491	214,111
Netherlands	26,758	48,262	43,718	26,948	7,150	14,860	52,277	30,606
Norway-Sweden	321,281	440,039	161,469	165,780	8,700	20,765	44,632	32,600
Norway	95,015	190,505	66,395	68,531	4,740	10,100	22,935	15,484
Sweden	226,266	249,534	95,074	97,249	3,960	10,665	21,697	17,116
Poland	96,720[23]	—[23]	4,813[23]	227,734	17,026	7,571	9,985	53,539
Portugal	27,508	69,149	89,732	29,994	3,329	7,423	19,588	76,065
Romania	12,750	53,008	13,311	67,646	3,871	1,076	1,039	2,531
Soviet Union	505,290[23]	1,597,306[23]	921,201[23]	61,742	1,370	571	671	2,465
Spain	8,731	27,935	68,611	28,958	3,258	2,898	7,894	44,659
Switzerland	31,179	34,922	23,091	29,676	5,512	10,547	17,675	18,453
United Kingdom[5,8]	271,538	525,950	341,408	339,570	31,572	139,306	202,824	213,822
Yugoslavia	—[9]	—[9]	1,888[9]	49,064	5,835	1,576	8,225	20,381
Other Europe	282	39,945	31,400	42,619	11,949	8,486	16,350	11,604

Asia	74,862	323,543	247,236	112,059	16,595	37,028	153,249	427,642
China[10]	14,799	20,605	21,278	29,907	4,928	16,709	9,657	34,764
Hong Kong	—[11]	—[11]	—[11]	—[11]	—[11]	15,541[11]	15,541[11]	75,007
India	68	4,713	2,082	1,886	496	1,761	1,973	27,189
Iran	—[12]	—[12]	—[12]	241[12]	195	1,380	3,388	10,339
Israel	—[13]	—[13]	—[13]	—[13]	—[13]	476[13]	25,476	29,602
Japan	25,942	129,797	83,837	33,462	1,948	1,555	46,250	39,988
Korea	—[15]	—[15]	—[15]	—[15]	—[15]	107[15]	6,231	34,526
Philippines	—[16]	—[16]	—[16]	—[16]	528[16]	4,691	19,307	98,376
Turkey	30,425	157,369	134,066	33,824	1,065	798	3,519	10,142
Vietnam	—[11]	—[11]	—[11]	—[11]	—[11]	—[11]	335[11]	4,340
Other Asia	3,628	11,059	5,973	12,739	7,435	9,551	21,572	63,369
America	38,972	361,888	1,143,671	1,516,716	160,037	354,804	996,944	1,716,374
Canada & Newfoundland[17,18]	3,311	179,226	742,185	924,515	108,527	171,718	377,952	413,310
Mexico[18]	971[19]	49,642	219,004	459,287	22,319	60,589	299,811	453,937
Caribbean	33,066	107,548	123,424	74,899	15,502	49,725	123,091	470,213
Cuba	—[12]	—[12]	—[12]	15,901[12]	9,571	26,313	78,948	208,536
Dominican Republic	—[20]	—[20]	—[20]	—[20]	1,150[20]	5,627	9,897	93,292
Haiti	—[20]	—[20]	—[20]	—[20]	191[20]	911	4,442	34,499
Jamaica	—[21]	—[21]	—[21]	—[21]	—[21]	—[21]	8,869[21]	74,906
Other Caribbean	33,066	107,548	123,424	58,998	4,590	16,874	20,935[21]	58,980
Central America	549	8,192	17,159	15,769	5,861	21,665	44,751	101,330
El Salvador	—[20]	—[20]	—[20]	—[20]	673[20]	5,132	5,895	14,992
Other Central America	549	8,192	17,159	15,769	5,188	16,533	38,856	86,338
South America	1,075	17,280	41,899	42,215	7,803	21,831	91,628	257,954
Argentina	—[20]	—[20]	—[20]	—[20]	1,349[20]	3,338	19,486	49,721
Colombia	—[20]	—[20]	—[20]	—[20]	1,223[20]	3,858	18,048	72,028
Ecuador	—[20]	—[20]	—[20]	—[20]	337[20]	2,417	9,841	36,780
Other South America	1,075	17,280	41,899	42,215	4,894	12,218	44,253	99,425
Other America	—[22]	—[22]	—[22]	31[22]	25	29,276	59,711	19,630
Africa	350	7,368	8,443	6,286	1,750	7,367	14,092	28,954
Oceania	3,965	13,024	13,427	8,726	2,483	14,551	12,976	25,122
Not specified[22]	14,063	33,523[25]	1,147	228	—	142	12,491	93

Region and Country of Last Residence[1]	1971–80	1981–89	1984	1985	1986	1987	1988	1989	Total 170 Years 1820–1989
All countries	4,493,314	5,801,579	543,903	570,009	601,708	601,516	643,025	1,090,924	55,457,531
Europe	800,368	637,524	69,879	69,526	69,224	67,967	71,854	94,338	36,977,034
Austria-Hungary	16,028	20,152	2,846	2,521	2,604	2,401	3,200	3,586	4,338,049
Austria	9,478	14,566	2,351	1,930	2,039	1,769	2,493	2,845	1,825,172[3]
Hungary	6,550	5,586	495	591	565	632	707	741	1,666,801[3]
Belgium	5,329	6,239	787	775	843	859	706	705	209,729
Czechoslovakia	6,023	6,649	693	684	588	715	744	526	145,223
Denmark	4,439	4,696	512	465	544	515	561	617	369,738
France	25,069	28,088	3,335	3,530	3,876	3,809	3,637	4,101	783,322
Germany	74,414	79,809	9,375	10,028	9,853	9,923	9,748	10,419	7,071,313
Greece	92,369	34,490	3,311	3,487	3,497	4,087	4,690	4,588	700,017
Ireland[5]	11,490	22,229	1,096	1,288	1,757	3,032	5,121	6,983	4,715,393
Italy	129,368	51,008	6,328	6,351	5,711	4,666	5,332	11,089	5,356,862
Netherlands	10,492	10,723	1,313	1,235	1,263	1,303	1,152	1,253	372,717
Norway-Sweden	10,472	13,252	1,455	1,557	1,564	1,540	1,669	1,809	2,144,024
Norway	3,941	3,612	403	386	367	372	446	556	800,672[6]
Sweden	6,531	9,640	1,052	1,171	1,197	1,168	1,223	1,253	1,283,097[6]
Poland	37,234	64,888	7,229	7,409	6,540	5,818	7,298	13,279	587,972
Portugal	101,710	36,365	3,800	3,811	3,804	4,009	3,290	3,861	497,195
Romania	12,393	27,361	2,956	3,764	3,809	2,741	2,915	3,535	201,345
Soviet Union	38,961	42,898	3,349	1,532	1,001	1,139	1,408	4,570	3,428,927
Spain	39,141	17,689	2,168	2,278	2,232	2,056	1,972	2,179	282,404
Switzerland	8,235	7,561	795	980	923	964	920	1,072	358,151
United Kingdom[5,8]	137,374	140,119	16,516	15,591	16,129	15,889	14,667	16,961	5,100,096
Yugoslavia	30,540	15,984	1,404	1,521	1,915	1,793	2,039	2,464	133,493
Other Europe	9,287	7,324	611	719	771	708	785	741	181,064

Asia	1,588,178	2,416,278	247,775	255,164	258,546	248,293	254,745	296,420	5,697,301
China[10]	124,326	306,108	29,109	33,095	32,389	32,669	34,300	39,284	873,737
Hong Kong	113,467	83,848	12,290	10,795	9,930	8,785	11,817	15,257	287,863[11]
India	164,134	221,977	23,617	24,536	24,808	26,394	25,312	28,599	426,907
Iran	45,136	101,267	11,131	12,327	12,031	10,323	9,846	13,027	161,946[12]
Israel	37,713	38,367	4,136	4,279	5,124	4,753	4,444	5,494	131,634[13]
Japan	49,775	40,654	4,517	4,552	4,444	4,711	5,085	5,454	455,813[14]
Korea	267,638	302,782	32,537	34,791	35,164	35,397	34,151	33,016	611,284[15]
Philippines	354,987	477,485	46,985	53,137	61,492	58,315	61,017	66,119	955,374[16]
Turkey	13,399	20,028	1,652	1,690	1,975	2,080	2,200	2,538	409,122
Vietnam	172,820	266,027	25,803	20,367	15,010	13,073	12,856	13,174	443,522[11]
Other Asia	244,783	557,735	55,998	55,595	56,179	51,793	53,717	74,458	940,099
America	1,982,735	2,564,698	208,111	225,519	254,078	265,026	294,906	672,639	12,017,021
Canada & Newfoundland[17,18]	169,939	132,296	15,659	16,354	16,060	16,741	15,821	18,294	4,270,943
Mexico[18]	640,294	975,657	57,820	61,290	66,753	72,511	95,170	405,660	3,208,543
Caribbean	741,126	759,416	68,368	79,374	98,527	100,615	110,949	87,597	2,590,542
Cuba	264,863	135,142	5,699	17,115	30,787	27,363	16,610	9,523	739,274[12]
Dominican Republic	148,135	209,899	23,207	23,861	26,216	24,947	27,195	26,744	468,000[20]
Haiti	56,335	118,510	9,554	9,872	12,356	14,643	34,858	13,341	214,888[20]
Jamaica	137,577	184,481	18,997	18,277	18,916	22,430	20,474	23,572	405,833[21]
Other Caribbean	134,216	111,384	10,911	10,249	10,252	11,232	11,812	14,417	762,547
Central America	134,640	321,845	27,626	28,447	30,086	30,366	31,311	101,273	673,385
El Salvador	34,436	133,938	8,753	10,093	10,881	10,627	12,043	57,628	195,066[20]
Other Central America	100,204	187,907	18,873	18,354	19,205	19,739	19,268	43,645	478,319
South America	295,741	375,026	38,636	40,052	42,650	44,782	41,646	59,812	1,163,482
Argentina	29,897	21,374	2,287	1,925	2,318	2,192	2,556	3,766	125,165[20]
Colombia	77,347	99,066	10,897	11,802	11,213	11,482	10,153	14,918	271,570[20]
Ecuador	50,077	43,841	4,244	4,601	4,518	4,656	4,736	7,587	143,293[20]
Other South America	138,420	210,745	21,208	21,724	24,601	26,452	24,201	33,541	623,454
Other America	995	458	2	2	2	11	9	3	110,126
Africa	80,779	144,096	13,594	15,236	15,500	15,730	17,124	22,485	301,348
Oceania	41,242	38,401	4,249	4,552	4,352	4,437	4,324	4,956	197,818
Not specified[22]	12	582	295	12	8	63	72	86	267,009

Source: U.S. Immigration and Naturalization Service, 1991.

[1]Data for years prior to 1906 relate to country whence alien came; data from 1906–79 and 1984–89 are for country of last permanent residence; and data for 1980–83 refer to country of birth. Because of changes in boundaries, changes in lists of countries, and lack of data for specified countries for various periods, data for certain countries, especially for the total period 1820–1989, are not comparable throughout. Data for specified countries are included with countries to which they belonged prior to World War I.

[2]Data for Austria and Hungary not reported until 1861.

[3]Data for Austria and Hungary not reported separately for all years during the period.

[4]No data available for Czechoslovakia until 1920.

[5]Prior to 1926, data for Northern Ireland included in Ireland.

[6]Data for Norway and Sweden not reported separately until 1871.

[7]No data available for Romania until 1880.

[8]Since 1925, data for United Kingdom refer to England, Scotland, Wales, and Northern Ireland.

[9]In 1920, a separate enumeration was made for the Kingdom of Serbs, Croats, and Slovenes. Since 1922, the Serb, Croat, and Slovene Kingdom recorded as Yugoslavia.

[10]Beginning in 1957, China includes Taiwan.

[11]Data not reported separately until 1952.

[12]Data not reported separately until 1925.

[13]Data not reported separately until 1949.

[14]No data available for Japan until 1861.

[15]Data not reported separately until 1948.

[16]Prior to 1934, Philippines recorded as insular travel.

[17]Prior to 1920, Canada and Newfoundland recorded as British North America. From 1820 to 1898, figures include all British North America possessions.

[18]Land arrivals not completely enumerated until 1908.

[19]No data available for Mexico from 1886 to 1893.

[20]Data not reported separately until 1932.

[21]Data for Jamaica not collected until 1953. In prior years, consolidated under British West Indies, which is included in "Other Caribbean."

[22]Included in countries "Not specified" until 1925.

[23]From 1899 to 1919, data for Poland included in Austria-Hungary, Germany, and the Soviet Union.

[24]From 1938 to 1945, data for Austria included in Germany.

[25]Includes 32,897 persons returning in 1906 to their homes in the United States.

—represents zero.

NOTE: From 1820 to 1867, figures represent alien passengers arrived at seaports; from 1868 to 1891 and 1895 to 1897, immigrant aliens arrived; from 1892 to 1894 and 1898 to 1989, immigrant aliens admitted for permanent residence. From 1892 to 1903, aliens entering by cabin class were not counted as immigrants. Land arrivals were not completely enumerated until 1908. For this table, fiscal year 1843 covers 9 months ending September 1843; fiscal years 1832 and 1850 cover 15 months ending December 31 of the respective years; and fiscal year 1868 covers 6 months ending June 30, 1868.

PRESIDENTS, VICE-PRESIDENTS, AND SECRETARIES OF STATE

	President	*Vice-President*	*Secretary of State*
1.	George Washington, Federalist 1789	John Adams, Federalist 1789	Thomas Jefferson 1789 Edmund Randolph 1794 Timothy Pickering 1795
2.	John Adams, Federalist 1797	Thomas Jefferson, Dem.-Rep. 1797	Timothy Pickering 1797 John Marshall 1800
3.	Thomas Jefferson, Dem.-Rep. 1801	Aaron Burr, Dem.-Rep. 1801 George Clinton, Dem.-Rep. 1805	James Madison 1801
4.	James Madison, Dem.-Rep. 1809	George Clinton, Dem.-Rep. 1809 Elbridge Gerry, Dem.-Rep. 1813	Robert Smith 1809 James Monroe 1811
5.	James Monroe, Dem.-Rep. 1817	Daniel D. Tompkins, Dem.-Rep. 1817	John Q. Adams 1817
6.	John Quincy Adams, Dem.-Rep. 1825	John C. Calhoun, Dem.-Rep. 1825	Henry Clay 1825
7.	Andrew Jackson, Democratic 1829	John C. Calhoun, Democratic 1829 Martin Van Buren, Democratic 1833	Martin Van Buren 1829 Edward Livingston 1831 Louis McLane 1833 John Forsyth 1834
8.	Martin Van Buren, Democratic 1837	Richard M. Johnson, Democratic 1837	John Forsyth 1837
9.	William H. Harrison, Whig 1841	John Tyler, Whig 1841	Daniel Webster 1841

President	Vice-President	Secretary of State
10. John Tyler, Whig and Democratic 1841	None	Daniel Webster 1841 Hugh S. Legaré 1843 Abel P. Upshur 1843 John C. Calhoun 1844
11. James K. Polk, Democratic 1845	George M. Dallas, Democratic 1845	James Buchanan 1845
12. Zachary Taylor, Whig 1849	Millard Fillmore, Whig 1849	John M. Clayton 1849
13. Millard Fillmore, Whig 1850	None	Daniel Webster 1850 Edward Everett 1852
14. Franklin Pierce, Democratic 1853	William R. King, Democratic 1853	William L. Marcy 1853
15. James Buchanan, Democratic 1857	John C. Breckinridge, Democratic 1857	Lewis Cass 1857 Jeremiah S. Black 1860
16. Abraham Lincoln, Republican 1861	Hannibal Hamlin, Republican 1861 Andrew Johnson, Unionist 1865	William H. Seward 1861
17. Andrew Johnson, Unionist 1865	None	William H. Seward 1865
18. Ulysses S. Grant, Republican 1869	Schuyler Colfax, Republican 1869 Henry Wilson, Republican 1873	Elihu B. Washburne 1869 Hamilton Fish 1869
19. Rutherford B. Hayes, Republican 1877	William A. Wheeler, Republican 1877	William M. Evarts 1877

	President	Vice-President	Secretary of State
20.	James A. Garfield, Republican 1881	Chester A. Arthur, Republican 1881	James G. Blaine 1881
21.	Chester A. Arthur, Republican 1881	None	Frederick T. Frelinghuysen 1881
22.	Grover Cleveland, Democratic 1885	Thomas A. Hendricks, Democratic 1885	Thomas F. Bayard 1885
23.	Benjamin Harrison, Republican 1889	Levi P. Morton, Republican 1889	James G. Blaine 1889 John W. Foster 1892
24.	Grover Cleveland, Democratic 1893	Adlai E. Stevenson, Democratic 1893	Walter Q. Gresham 1893 Richard Olney 1895
25.	William McKinley, Republican 1897	Garret A. Hobart, Republican 1897 Theodore Roosevelt, Republican 1901	John Sherman 1897 William R. Day 1898 John Hay 1898
26.	Theodore Roosevelt, Republican 1901	Charles Fairbanks, Republican 1905	John Hay 1901 Elihu Root 1905 Robert Bacon 1909
27.	William H. Taft, Republican 1909	James S. Sherman, Republican 1909	Philander C. Knox 1909
28.	Woodrow Wilson, Democratic 1913	Thomas R. Marshall, Democratic 1913	William J. Bryan 1913 Robert Lansing 1915 Bainbridge Colby 1920
29.	Warren G. Harding, Republican 1921	Calvin Coolidge, Republican 1921	Charles E. Hughes 1921
30.	Calvin Coolidge, Republican 1923	Charles G. Dawes, Republican 1925	Charles E. Hughes 1923 Frank B. Kellogg 1925

	President	Vice-President	Secretary of State
31.	Herbert Hoover, Republican 1929	Charles Curtis, Republican 1929	Henry L. Stimson 1929
32.	Franklin D. Roosevelt, Democratic 1933	John Nance Garner, Democratic 1933 Henry A. Wallace, Democratic 1941 Harry S. Truman, Democratic 1945	Cordell Hull 1933 Edward R. Stettinius, Jr. 1944
33.	Harry S. Truman, Democratic 1945	Alben W. Barkley, Democratic 1949	Edward R. Stettinius, Jr. 1945 James F. Byrnes 1945 George C. Marshall 1947 Dean G. Acheson 1949
34.	Dwight D. Eisenhower, Republican 1953	Richard M. Nixon, Republican 1953	John F. Dulles 1953 Christian A. Herter 1959
35.	John F. Kennedy, Democratic 1961	Lyndon B. Johnson, Democratic 1961	Dean Rusk 1961
36.	Lyndon B. Johnson, Democratic 1963	Hubert H. Humphrey, Democratic 1965	Dean Rusk 1963
37.	Richard M. Nixon, Republican 1969	Spiro T. Agnew, Republican 1969 Gerald R. Ford, Republican 1973	William P. Rogers 1969 Henry Kissinger 1973
38.	Gerald R. Ford, Republican 1974	Nelson Rockefeller, Republican 1974	Henry Kissinger 1974
39.	Jimmy Carter, Democratic 1977	Walter Mondale, Democratic 1977	Cyrus Vance 1977 Edmund Muskie 1980

	President	Vice-President	Secretary of State
40.	Ronald Reagan, Republican 1981	George Bush, Republican 1981	Alexander Haig 1981 George Schultz 1982
41.	George Bush, Republican 1989	J. Danforth Quayle, Republican 1989	James A. Baker 1989 Lawrence Eagleburger 1992
42.	William J. Clinton, Democrat 1993	Albert Gore, Jr., Democrat 1993	Warren Christopher 1993 Madeleine Albright 1997

CREDITS

CHAPTER 18: p. 790, Courtesy, Massachusetts Historical Society, Boston; **p. 792,** Library of Congress; **p. 794,** Library of Congress; **p. 795,** Library of Congress/Corbis; **p. 799,** Courtesy George Eastman House; **p. 800,** Library of Congress; **p. 803,** *Harper's Weekly;* **p. 804,** *(left)* Library of Congress, and *(right)* U. S. Signal Corps photo no. 111-B-1084 (Brady Collection) in the National Archives; **p. 807,** National Portrait Gallery, Smithsonian Institution/Art Resource, NY; **p. 811,** U. S. Signal Corps photo no. 111-B-4371 (Brady Collection) in the National Archives; **p. 815,** Corbis-Bettman; **p. 816,** National Archives; **p. 820,** Library of Congress; **p. 824,** National Portrait Gallery, Smithsonian Institution/Art Resource, NY; **p. 826,** Library of Congress; **p. 827,** Library of Congress; **p. 830,** Library of Congress.

CHAPTER 19: p. 842, *Harper's Weekly,* March 1883, photo courtesy of Davis Library, University of North Carolina Library at Chapel Hill; **p. 847,** The Granger Collection, New York; **p. 852,** The Warder Collection; **p. 854,** Library of Congress; **p. 855,** The Warder Collection; **p. 858,** Courtesy Denver Public Library, Western History Collection; **p. 859,** Library of Congress; **p. 861,** Idaho State Historical Society #349; **p. 865,** Courtesy Colorado Historical Society; **p. 869,** Princeton University Press; **p. 870,** The Smithsonian Institution; **p. 871,** Amon Carter Museum, Fort Worth, Texas; **p. 872,** National Archives; **p. 874,** National Archives; **p. 878,** National Archives; **p. 880,** Haynes Foundation Collection, Montana Historical Society, Helena; **p. 881,** Western History Collections, University of Oklahoma Libraries.

CHAPTER 20: p. 888, Amon Carter Museum, Fort Worth, Texas; **p. 891,** Union Pacific Museum Collection; **p. 893,** © Collection of the New-York Historical Society; **p. 894,** National Archives; **p. 895,** © Collection of the New-York Historical Society; **p. 897,** Courtesy, Gotham Book Mart, NY; **p. 899,** Courtesy of American Petroleum Institute Historical Photo Collection; **p. 900,** The Warder Collection; **p. 901,** Carnegie Library, Pittsburgh; **p. 903,** Keystone-Mast Collection (WX 13101), UCR/California Museum of Photography, University of California, Riverside; **p. 904,** The Pierpont Morgan Library; **p. 906,** Carnegie Library, Pittsburgh; **p. 907,** Courtesy of Sears, Roebuck and Co.; **p. 911,** Carnegie Library, Pittsburgh; **p. 914,** Chicago Historical Society; **p. 918,** Library of Congress; **p. 921,** Library of Congress; **p. 923,** Collection of The Archives of Labor and Urban Affairs, University Archives, Wayne State University; **p. 925,** Brown Brothers.

CHAPTER 21: p. 930, Library of Congress; **p. 934,** © Collection of the New-York Historical Society; **p. 935,** New York Transit Museum Archives, Brooklyn; **p. 938,** Museum of the City of New York; **p. 939,** The New York Public Library, Astor, Lenox and

Tilden Foundations; **p. 941,** The New York Public Library, Astor, Lenox and Tilden Foundations; **p. 942,** Museum of the City of New York; **p. 944,** Library of Congress; **p. 947,** Courtesy Denver Public Library, Western History Collection; **p. 949,** Library of Congress; **p. 950,** Texas A&M University Archives; **p. 951,** Mount Holyoke College Library; **p. 956,** Library of Congress; **p. 959,** Winslow Homer, American, 1869–1910, *Croquet Scene,* oil on canvas, 15 7/8 x 26 1/16 in, Friends of American Art Collection, 1942.35, photograph © 1998, The Art Institute of Chicago, All rights reserved; **p. 960,** Brown Brothers; **p. 961,** Old York Library; **p. 964,** Library of Congress; **p. 966,** Negative No. 326662, Courtesy Department of Library Services, American Museum of Natural History; **p. 967,** The Warder Collection; **p. 968** Courtesy of the John Carter Brown Library at Brown University; **p. 970,** (*left*) National Library of Medicine, and (*right*) The Warder Collection; **p. 973,** Mansell/TIME Inc.; **p. 974,** (*left*) Library of Congress, and (*right*) The Warder Collection; **p. 978,** The Salvation Army; **p. 981,** University of Illinois at Chicago, University Library, Jane Addams Memorial Collection; **p. 983,** Nebraska State Historical Society.

CHAPTER 22: p. 991, Library of Congress; **p. 995,** Rutherford B. Hayes Presidential Center; **p. 999,** The Warder Collection; **p. 1000,** The Warder Collection; **p. 1002,** The Warder Collection; **p. 1004,** United Press International Photo; **p. 1009,** The Warder Collection; **p. 1014,** Corbis-Bettman; **p. 1016,** Photo by John Wesley Rand, from the Collection of the Minnesota Historical Society; **p. 1018,** Wooten Studios; **p. 1020,** Kansas State Historical Society, Topeka, Kansas; **p. 1022,** University of North Carolina, Chapel Hill; **p. 1023,** Nebraska State Historical Society; **p. 1025,** Library of Congress; **p. 1027,** Kansas State Historical Society, Topeka, Kansas.

CHAPTER 23: p. 1038, Library of Congress; **p. 1040,** Hawaii State Archives; **p. 1043,** Brown Brothers; **p. 1045,** National Archives; **p. 1046,** Library of Congress; **p. 1050,** National Archives; **p. 1052,** Library of Congress; **p. 1055,** National Archives; **p. 1060,** National Archives; **p. 1062,** *The New York Times*; **p. 1066,** Library of Congress/Corbis-Bettman; **p. 1067,** Library of Congress.

CHAPTER 24: p. 1075, AP/Wide World Photos; **p. 1077,** Valdis Kupris; **p. 1079,** Library of Congress; **p. 1081,** Library of Congress; **p. 1082,** Underwood & Underwood/Corbis-Bettman; **p. 1083,** Kansas State Historical Society, Topeka, Kansas; **p. 1085,** Library of Congress; **p. 1088,** (*top*) © Collection of the New-York Historical Society; and (*bottom*) Library of Congress; **p. 1090,** Schlesinger Library, Radcliffe College; **p. 1092,** The Warder Collection; **p. 1094,** Library of Congress; **p. 1099,** Library of Congress; **p. 1102,** Library of Congress; **p. 1107,** Library of Congress; **p. 1108,** The Warder Collection; **p. 1109,** Historical Picture Service; **p. 1112,** Library of Congress.

CHAPTER 25: p. 1119, Library of Congress; **p. 1121,** Corbis-Bettman; **p. 1124,** The Warder Collection; **p. 1127,** *The New York Times*; **p. 1129,** Princeton University Libraries; **p. 1131,** UPI/Corbis-Bettman; **p. 1135,** National Archives; **p. 1137,** National Archives; **p. 1139,** National Archives; **p. 1143,** National Archives; **p. 1145,** National Archives; **p. 1147,** National Archives; **p. 1148,** The Warder Collection; **p. 1149,** National Archives; **p. 1154,** Ding Darling Foundation; **p. 1155,** Library of Congress; **p. 1157,** Corbis-Bettman; **p. 1159,** Chicago Historical Society.

CHAPTER 26: p. 1164, Shahn, Ben, *Bartolomeo Vanzetti and Nicola Sacco,* From the Sacco-Vanzetti series of twenty-three paintings, Tempera on paper over composition board, 10.5 x 14.5", Collection, The Museum of Modern Art, New York, Gift of Abby Aldrich Rockefeller; **p. 1167,** UPI/ Corbis-Bettman; **p. 1169,** Corbis-Bettman; **p. 1171,** Ben Shahn, *Speakeasy Scene, Interior,* Mural Project for Central Park Casino,

© Museum of the City of New York, L1226.3G; **p. 1172,** Chicago Historical Society; **p. 1174,** Ramsey Archive; **p. 1175,** Henry Rockwell; **p. 1177,** Photographs and Prints Division, Schomburg Center for Research in Black Culture, The New York Public Library, Astor, Lenox and Tilden Foundations; **p. 1178,** Library of Congress; **p. 1179,** Brown Brothers; **p. 1182,** University of Chicago Press; **p. 1183,** AP/Wide World Photos; **p. 1186,** The Warder Collection; **p. 1189,** Pablo Picasso, *Portrait of Gertrude Stein,* All rights reserved, The Metropolitan Museum of Art/© 1999 Estate of Pablo Picasso/Artists Rights Society (ARS), New York; **p. 1190,** Brown Brothers; **p. 1193,** Brown Brothers.

CHAPTER 27: **p. 1199,** Brown Brothers; **p. 1202,** Library of Congress; **p. 1205,** Library of Congress; **p. 1208,** Brown Brothers; **p. 1209,** The National Broadcasting Company; **p. 1210,** (*top*) National Archives, and (*bottom*) Library of Congress; **p. 1211,** From the Collections of the Henry Ford Museum & Greenfield Village; **p. 1216,** The Warder Collection; **p. 1219,** Herbert Hoover Presidential Library; **p. 1220,** Historical Association of Southern Florida; **p. 1222,** AP/Wide World Photos; **p. 1223,** Ohio Historical Society; **p. 1226,** Museum of the City of New York; **p. 1229,** *New York Daily News* Photo.

CHAPTER 28: **p. 1235,** AP/Wide World Photos; **p. 1237,** UPI/Corbis-Bettman; **p. 1239,** National Archives; **p. 1242,** UPI/Corbis-Bettman; **p. 1245,** National Archives; **p. 1247,** Library of Congress; **p. 1251,** Courtesy, Tennessee Valley Authority; **p. 1252,** Corbis-Bettman; **p. 1255,** Library of Congress; **p. 1257,** Moses Soyer, *Artists on WPA,* National Museum of American Art, Washington, DC/Art Resource, NY; **p. 1260,** Library of Congress; **p. 1266,** UPI/Corbis-Bettman; **p. 1269,** National Archives; **p. 1273,** Library of Congress; **p. 1279,** AP/Wide World Photos; **p. 1282,** Corbis-Bettman; **p. 1283,** Corbis-Bettman.

CHAPTER 29: **p. 1290,** AP/Wide World Photos; **p. 1293,** The Warder Collection; **p. 1295,** The Granger Collection, New York; **p. 1297,** National Archives; **p. 1299,** The Warder Collection; **p. 1301,** Library of Congress; **p. 1303,** Imperial War Museum, London; **p. 1306,** National Archives; **p. 1307,** British Information Services; **p. 1310,** UPI/Corbis-Bettman; **p. 1316,** National Archives; **p. 1317,** National Archives.

CHAPTER 30: **p. 1322,** The Warder Collection; **p. 1325,** The Granger Collection, New York; **p. 1330,** Library of Congress; **p. 1331,** Culver Pictures; **p. 1332,** AP/Wide World Photos; **p. 1335,** Library of Congress; **p. 1340,** National Archives; **p. 1341,** AP/Wide World Photos; **p. 1344,** Bill Mauldin and Wil-Jo Associates, Inc.; **p. 1347,** Army Photographic Agency; **p. 1348,** UPI/Corbis-Bettman; **p. 1350,** National Archives; **p. 1353,** The Warder Collection; **p. 1357,** National Archives; **p. 1359,** National Archives; **p. 1361,** National Archives; **p. 1364,** Globe Photos; **p. 1365,** National Archives; **p. 1366,** National Archives; **p. 1370,** Yuichiro Sasaki, UN Photo 149443.

CHAPTER 31: **p. 1382,** University of Louisville, Photographic Archives; **p. 1386,** The New York Public Library, Astor, Lenox and Tilden Foundations; **p. 1387,** The George Meany Memorial Archives; **p. 1389,** Library of Congress; **p. 1393,** © Herman Landshoff; **p. 1395,** AP/Wide World Photos; **p. 1398,** U.S. Information Agency; **p. 1399,** Courtesy *Hartford Courant;* **p. 1401,** Life Picture Service; **p. 1403,** C. K. Berryman, *The Washington Star;* **p. 1405,** Corbis-Bettman; **p. 1406,** AP/Wide World Photos; **p. 1407,** Harry S. Truman Library; **p. 1409,** Eastfoto; **p. 1414,** AP/Wide World Photos; **p. 1417,** UPI/Corbis-Bettman; **p. 1419,** Yale Joel/LIFE Magazine © TIME, Inc.

INDEX

Page numbers in *italics* refer to illustrations.

CANADA

Lake Manitoba

Olympic Peninsula
Puget Sound
Seattle
Olympia ★ Tacoma ● Spokane ●
Astoria
Vancouver ●
WASHINGTON
Portland
Salem ★
Eugene ●
OREGON

R O C K Y

Bitterroot Range

Missouri R.
Great Falls ●
Helena ★
MONTANA

G R E A T

NORTH DAKOTA

Bismark ●

Fargo ●

Columbia R.
Blue Mts.

Billings ●

Yellowstone R.

SOUTH DAKOTA

Pierre ★

Sioux Falls ●

Harney Basin

Boise ★
IDAHO

Snake R.
Pocatello ●

M O U N T A I N S

Teton Ra.
Wind River Ra.
Big Horn Mts.

Black Hills

WYOMING

Casper ●

N. Platte R.

Missouri R.

P L A I N S

NEBRASKA

Lincoln ●

CASCADE RANGE

Humboldt R.

Reno ●
Sacramento ●
Carson City ★
Oakland ●
San Francisco ●
NEVADA

Fresno ●

SIERRA NEVADA

Central Valley

Death Valley

Great Salt Lake Desert
Great Salt Lake
Salt Lake City ★
UTAH

Uinta Mts.

Grand Junction ●

Cheyenne ★

Denver ★
COLORADO

S. Platte R.
Platte R.

KANSAS

Arkansas R.

Wichita ●

Santa Barbara ●
Bakersfield ●
Mojave Desert
Los Angeles ●
Long Beach ●
San Diego ●

Las Vegas ●
Lake Mead

Colorado R.
San Juan Mts.
Sangre de Cristo Ra.

Grand Canyon
Painted Desert
Flagstaff ●
Colorado Plateau
San Bernardino ●
ARIZONA

Colorado R.
Gila R.
Phoenix ★

Yuma ●

Tucson ●

Santa Fe ★
Albuquerque ●
NEW MEXICO

Amarillo ●

OKLAHOMA

Oklahoma City ★

Llano Estacado (Staked Plains)

Pecos R.

Dallas ●
Fort Worth ●

Colorado R.
Brazos R.

PACIFIC OCEAN

El Paso ●

M E X I C O

Rio Grande

TEXAS

Austin ★

San Antonio ●

Nueces R.

Corpus Christi ●

Brownsville ●

HAWAII

0   200 miles
0   300 km

Kauai
Niihau   Oahu
Honolulu ★
Molokai
Lanai   Maui
Kahoolawe
Hilo ●

PACIFIC OCEAN   Hawaii

RUSSIA

Bering Strait

BROOKS RANGE

Yukon R.

Fairbanks ●

ALASKA

ALASKA RANGE

Kuskokwim R.

Anchorage ●

CANADA

Bering Sea

Juneau ★

0   200 miles
0   300 km

Kodiak Is.

Gulf of Alaska

Aleutian Islands

PACIFIC OCEAN

THE
UNITED STATES

THE WORLD

Map 1 — Asia, Indian Ocean, and Pacific (hemisphere projection)

30° E 45° E 60° E 75° E 90° E 105° E 120° E 135° E 150° E 165° E 180° 90° N (North Pole)

80° N

70° N

60° N

50° N

40° N

30° N

20° N

10° N

0°

10° S

20° S

30° S

40° S

50° S

60° S

70° S

80° S

90° S (South Pole)

TIC OCEAN

Arctic Circle

RUSSIA

Moscow

SWEDEN

FINLAND

OSE... LAN...

POLAND BELARUS

LITH.

KAZAKHSTAN

MONGOLIA

UZBEKI-STAN

KYRGYZ-STAN

TAJIKI-STAN

TURKMENI-STAN

Beijing

Tianjin

NORTH KOREA

SOUTH KOREA

Seoul

JAPAN

Tokyo

CHINA

Shanghai

East China Sea

NORTH PACIFIC OCEAN

Tropic of Cancer

GEORGIA

ARMENIA AZER-BAIJAN

A S I A

AFGHANI-STAN

PAKISTAN

BHUTAN

NEPAL

New Delhi

BANGLA-DESH

TAIWAN

Hong Kong

GREECE

TURKEY

CYPRUS

LEBANON

ISRAEL

SYRIA

IRAQ

IRAN

JORDAN

KUWAIT

BAHRAIN

Teheran

Karachi

Calcutta

INDIA

MYANMAR (BURMA)

LAOS

VIETNAM

South China Sea

PHILIPPINES

Manila

TRUST TERRITORY OF THE PACIFIC ISLANDS (U.S.)

WAKE ISLAND (U.S.)

MALTA

NISIA

LIBYA

EGYPT

Cairo

SAUDI ARABIA

QATAR

UNITED ARAB EMIRATES

OMAN

Bombay

Arabian Sea

THAILAND

Bangkok

Bay of Bengal

CAMBODIA

GUAM (U.S.)

CHAD

SUDAN

ERITREA

YEMEN

DJIBOUTI

SOMALILAND

SRI LANKA

FEDERATED STATES OF MICRONESIA

KIRIBATI

NAURU

RICA

RJA

CENTRAL AFRICAN REPUBLIC

ETHIOPIA

SOMALIA

MALDIVES

BRUNEI

MALAYSIA

ROON

CONGO REP.

RWANDA

BURUNDI

UGANDA

KENYA

SEYCHELLES

Equator

SINGAPORE

INDONESIA

Jakarta

PAPUA NEW GUINEA

SOLOMON ISLANDS

TUVALU

TANZANIA

COMOROS

ANGOLA

ZAMBIA

MALAWI

MOZAMBIQUE

MADAGASCAR

MAURITIUS

INDIAN OCEAN

VANUATU

FIJI

MIBIA

ZIMBABWE

BOTSWANA

SWAZILAND

Tropic of Capricorn

AUSTRALIA

AUSTRALIA

SOUTH PACIFIC OCEAN

SOUTH AFRICA

LESOTHO

NEW ZEALAND

Antarctic Circle

A N T A R C T I C A

0 1000 2000 3000 miles

Map 2 — Central Asia / Caspian region

UKRAINE

RUSSIA

Omsk

Novosibirsk

Black Sea

Ural

KAZAKHSTAN

Irtysh

GEORGIA

Tbilisi

TURKEY

ARMENIA

Yerevan

Caspian Sea

Aral Sea

Syr Darya

Lake Balkhash

SYRIA

AZERBAIJAN

Baku

UZBEKI-STAN

Amu Darya

Alma-Ata

IRAQ

TURKMENI-STAN

Tashkent

Bishkek

KYRGYZSTAN

CHINA

Ashkhabad

TAJIKISTAN

Dushanbe

TAKLAMAKAN DESERT

Teheran

IRAN

AFGHANISTAN

PAKISTAN

Kabul

KUWAIT

INDIA